# MANAGING EMPLOYEE PERFORMANCE AND REWARD

*Managing Employee Performance and Reward* is the first major text to explore employee performance and reward in a conceptually integrated way. It offers students, managers and general readers alike a detailed and cohesive coverage of these two pivotal and closely connected yet controversial and challenging facets of human resource management (HRM).

The book critically examines current theory and practice in each field and provides a conceptually informed yet practical framework for analysing and addressing the myriad performance and reward issues that confront today's managers and HRM professionals. In doing so, it draws on a wide range of up-to-date research evidence drawn from a wide range of academic disciplines – from organisational psychology and strategic management to critical management studies.

Chapters addressing performance and reward basics and key themes in employee psychology and human resource strategy are followed by multi-chapter parts dealing with options for performance management practice, for structuring and managing base pay and benefits, and for configuring performance-related rewards for individual employees, work groups and executives. Each part includes a major 'hands-on' case study exercise, complete with model solutions.

Written for a global readership, the book will have particular appeal to those studying and practising people management in the Asia–Pacific region.

JOHN SHIELDS is Associate Professor in the Faculty of Economics and Business at the University of Sydney, where he teaches human resource management. His principal areas of research and publication include reward management, executive remuneration and corporate governance, and business and labour history.

# MANAGING EMPLOYEE PERFORMANCE AND REWARD

## Concepts, Practices, Strategies

JOHN SHIELDS

CAMBRIDGE UNIVERSITY PRESS
Cambridge, New York, Melbourne, Madrid, Cape Town, Singapore, São Paulo

Cambridge University Press
477 Williamstown Road, Port Melbourne, Vic 3207, Australia

Published in the United States of America by Cambridge University Press, New York

www.cambridge.org
Information on this title: www.cambridge.org/9780521820462

First published 2007
Reprinted 2009

Printed in China by Printplus

*A catalogue record for this book is available from the British Library*

*National Library of Australia Cataloguing in Publication data*

   Shields, John.
Managing Employee Performance and Reward: Concepts, Practices, Strategies.
Bibliography.
Includes index.
ISBN-13  978-0-52182-046-2 paperback
ISBN-10  0-52182-046-4 paperback
1. Personnel management.   I. Title.
658.3

ISBN-13 978-0-52182-046-2
ISBN-10 0-52182-046-4

For Catherine, Erin and Julia.
They know why, only too well.

# CONTENTS

# FIGURES AND TABLES

## Figures

# Tables

# FOREWORD

The design and management of remuneration programs in organisations of varying scale and style have become extremely complex. The influences include prevailing economic conditions, the perceptions of society, competition for scarce skills and changing theories and fashions in the marketplace. The relationships between these often conflicting elements can be confusing and, for many organisations, threatening.

In this book, John Shields teases out the principal frameworks and objectives of remuneration policy, the challenges that organisations face in the context of contemporary theories of remuneration structuring and the alignment to performance. He identifies how they fit into the overall process and how changes at one level affect the process at other levels. This he does with careful and comprehensive referencing of the sources of his proposals and by offering guidance towards understanding the prevailing practices. Useful comparisons are drawn between Australian and overseas practice, particularly that of the United States.

Unlike much that is currently written in this area, this book treats remuneration of executives as part of the overall reward pattern of the whole organisation, addressing the motivational and organisational challenges in formulating pay structures that can apply to individual entities, business groups and teams within them. It provides valuable insights into the effect of different incentive plans when used in concert and how these effects can be used or guarded against depending on prevailing circumstances.

The book addresses the following essential information:

- a clear analysis of the scope of remuneration theory
- useful research findings on market practice in the area
- a structure for the design of remuneration programs in widely differing circumstances.

This book is therefore very helpful for students, as it offers a comprehensive theoretical structure thoroughly referenced to a very detailed and rapidly changing body of knowledge, while demonstrating the basic elements contrasted with the distractions supplied by the highly publicised changes of fad and fashion in remuneration structuring.

On the other hand, while the book is not intended to be a practitioner's primer, it provides management and professionals with a sound foundation for the analysis of existing policies and the basis for developing new proposals. It is refreshing that the author compares the prevailing theoretical approaches to remuneration management and provides helpful syntheses of theories that more readily reflect the decision-making dilemmas faced by many managers. It also offers useful sources of reference for more comprehensive consideration of these complex issues.

These insights are particularly useful in the current governance climate. Because of the intense media attention to the remuneration of CEOs and other executives, and the increasing disclosure requirements under legislation, scrutiny of remuneration is widespread. This can place managers, directors and their advisers in an awkward position. The book provides refreshing insights that offer a framework for developing a contemporary viewpoint.

For many decades, executives were proud to work for an agreed annual remuneration. They were expected to provide their best level of performance on the basis of that payment. Payment on the basis of performance was limited to sales staff and agents. Current discourse on remuneration no longer canvasses whether or not executives should have some remuneration at risk; that is taken for granted. This does not acknowledge that organisations may need a range of executive types – some intrepid risk-takers and some more cautious, who are charged with the conservation and protection of company assets.

John Shields' analysis of incentives and performance management provides the background for a clear-minded assessment of a whole range of employer challenges in addressing this vexed issue unencumbered by the influences of current fashion and market pressures. In a period of such fast change, this guidance should be most useful.

From time to time, in most specialities, it is necessary to record the current state of development in the elements being considered. This book is most timely in providing that service for the study of performance and reward management. With comprehensive and contemporary references and evidence supporting its propositions and conclusions, this book will provide the basis for a fruitful and ongoing dialogue between academe and management practitioners on performance and reward matters for many years to come.

John V. Egan

Principal, Egan Associates

Adjunct Professor, Faculty of Economics and Business,

University of Sydney

# ACKNOWLEDGEMENTS

Evidently, at his peak, Charles Dickens managed to knock out a book chapter a day, armed only with quill and ink, midnight oil, a marvellous eye for the human condition, and varying quantities of the demon drink. Even in the era of the word processor, authorial output of this quantity and quality is something to which we lesser mortals can only aspire. In one sense, perhaps novelists have an easier task, since they are unencumbered by the burden of facts, figures and footnotes and limited only by the power of their imagination. An academic monograph, however, entails an altogether different purpose and a quite different type of intellectual and emotional journey. In some ways, it is perhaps a more onerous and exacting challenge than that faced by novelists – at least, this has been my experience. Almost a decade has passed since this book was first mooted. In truth, it has been a long, demanding and constantly evolving task. The final product is very different from that first envisaged; and the writer is also a very different person from the one who began the journey all those years ago. However, its writing has also been an immensely rewarding experience – and my abiding hope is that readers will also find the book worthy of its set brief: an integrated examination of the theory and practice of employee performance and reward management.

Texts of this type necessarily have a long gestation; they are also a collective intellectual exercise – and my indebtedness to others is thus inestimable. But let me try to tally the debt nevertheless. My first thanks goes to those who, in their own utterly different ways, first awakened my interest in the matter of employee reward more than a decade ago: Edward Lawler, George Milkovich, Barry Gerhart, Michael Armstrong and Ian Kessler, and, closer to home, David Plowman, Braham Dabschek, Michael Quinlan, Chris Wright, Robin Kramar and John Egan, as well as the remarkable Australian worker–intellectual, the late Jack Hutson. Then there are those who encouraged me to take my neophyte interest further, and to sharpen my conceptual take on the strategic and behavioural dimensions of reward management, none more so than my Canadian friend and mentor, Rick Long. Along the way, my horizons were also broadened by practitioners with a wealth of knowledge in the field, including the doyen of Australian remuneration advisers, John Egan, and the practitioner members of the Australian Human Resources Institute.

This is also a text crafted in the cut and thrust of the classroom. The ideas, the arguments, the interpretations have all had to run the gauntlet of student scrutiny and, in a very real sense, the book is testimony to the dialogue and debate that I have been privileged to enjoy with the students in my human resource management units since the mid-1990s. Some, like my friend and sometime colleague Ben Jelden, have artfully turned the tables, becoming the teacher rather than the taught. Special thanks are also due to Alex Capezio, Vera Lim and my other doctoral students, past and present, for their critical but constructive contribution to my chapter drafts and for awaiting the return of their own chapter drafts with such patience and good humour.

Book-writing, of necessity, is also a most solitary activity and, as such, there is a further debt that I know I shall never be able to repay – that to my family. They have been my rock, even as the months rolled into years, and the magic and laughter of childhood yielded to the exhilaration and promise of youth. They have lost a year of Sundays to this cause – but, to my relief and delight, they have stayed the course.

My thanks, too, to the Australian staff of Cambridge University Press, past and present, for their forbearance and encouragement. To Glen Sheldon, in particular, I own a deep dept of gratitude for showing faith in the project – and in this most troublesome author. I am also eternally grateful for having had the benefit of Cathryn Game's exceptional editing skills. I am in awe of her powers of literary concentration and, more to the point, her ability to conjure up a silk purse from a sow's ear.

Finally, I must thank those organisations that have kindly granted me permission to reproduce their material in the text: the Hay Group Australia, CSi – the Remuneration Specialists Pty Ltd and Egan Associates.

# INTRODUCTION: SETTING THE SCENE

As the iconic Silicon Valley computer hardware firm Hewlett-Packard (H-P) discovered to its cost in the mid-1990s, the road to performance and reward hell is sometimes paved with good intentions. For years, H-P had prided itself on having an inclusive, high-trust work culture – known affectionately as the 'H-P way'. During the 1980s, H-P was lauded as an archetype of high-involvement people management. H-P's decision-making processes were inclusive and democratic, and its workers were rewarded generously via traditional 'merit'-based pay increases and egalitarian profitsharing and employee share ownership arrangements. The company also avoided the use of executive bonus payments, a further signifier of its egalitarian approach to reward management.

Then, in the early 1990s, under growing cost pressure from local and international competitors, and in a bid to lift plant productivity and performance, H-P rolled out a range of 'alternative' pay plans in more than a dozen of its American and European plants. Senior plant managers leapt at the chance to 're-engineer' their performance and reward management systems and proceeded to install a range of new pay practices, chiefly involving skill-based pay, team incentives, gain- or goalsharing and other group incentives, as well as some individual cash incentive plans. In several plants where teamworking was in place, peer evaluation was also introduced as a means of keeping team members on their toes. In large part, the new measures were intended to support the adoption of self-managed teams and a focus on team effort. *Prima facie*, the new plans also appeared to be compatible with the firm's celebrated high-commitment work culture and its focus on a high-skill, high-quality competitive strategy (Beer & Cannon 2004: 5–7).

Yet it was not to be. There were unintended consequences aplenty; the company was badly burned and continued to lose market share. Most of the plans impaired employee satisfaction and morale while failing to show a positive return on investment. In some plants, the competition for cash set team against team in a destructive cycle of talent hoarding, while peer evaluation caused a breakdown in intra-team relationships. Even those initiatives that appeared to have enhanced performance proved far more costly than anticipated. All but a few of the new pay plans were abandoned within a few short years. At H-P's San Diego site, employees even organised a party to celebrate the demise of management's experiment with skill pay and team incentives (Beer & Cannon 2004: 6–9).

So why did these seemingly laudable initiatives founder? Was it more a case of the wrong ideas full stop, the wrong ideas for the time and context, too much change too soon, naive optimism – faddism even – on the part of the management innovators, or just a case of good ideas badly applied? Some commentators (e.g. Kohn 1993a & b) argue that all incentive schemes – that is, reward plans that seek to elicit greater work contribution by promising higher rewards for higher contribution – are doomed to failure because they are based on supposedly invalid assumptions about the true wellsprings of employee motivation and effort. In essence, their argument is that once incentives come into play, employees are all too easily distracted from their real work responsibilities by the pursuit of rewards themselves. Others, like Beer and Cannon (2004), suggest that small-group financial incentive plans of the type applied at the H-P plants were incompatible with the company's once-prized high-commitment, high-trust culture, and that other means, such as expanded training and development programs, would have been a better choice for enhancing workforce capability and contribution. Still others contend that the problem lay not in the plans themselves but in the way they were conceived and applied. Heneman, Kochan and Locke (commentaries in Beer & Cannon 2004: 33–4, 35–7, 41–3) note that most of the plans were badly designed, were poorly communicated to line employees, team leaders and supervisors, were conceived and applied with minimal employee consultation, involvement and training, and were subject to arbitrary changes to team performance standards. Locke (in Beer & Cannon 2004: 41) is particularly critical of the attempt to combine performance incentives and skill-based pay, which, he suggests, sent conflicting signals to employees about what the firm valued most. Locke also contends that the devolution of responsibility for change management to the site managers also seems to have deprived the experiment of vital expertise and guidance that could have been provided by the corporate human resources department. So take your pick! – bad ideas *per se* or good ideas, badly applied?

Multinational firms are not the only organisations to have experienced the unintended consequences of experimentation with performance pay as a driver of organisational change. There are many examples of public sector experiments that have not gone according to plan. The Australian Public Service (APS) is a case in point.

The APS, the administrative apparatus of the Government of the Commonwealth of Australia, comprises about a hundred agencies, both departments of state and statutory bodies, with a total of around 120,000 employees. Since the mid-1990s, a new performance 'paradigm' emphasising individual performance appraisal and performance-contingent rewards has been applied throughout virtually the entire APS. The emergence of this new performance model is attributable to a combination of political and economic pressures that compelled the APS to search for improved efficiency and performance and a more results-oriented culture (Grant, O'Donnell & Shields 2003). The model represents a fundamental shift in management approach to employee motivation in the APS. It also signifies an attempt to radically reshape the image and outlook of the APS employees themselves: from the traditional concept of loyal 'public servant' to that of innovative 'strategic contributor'.

The motivational centrepiece of the APS performance management model is performance-related pay. The traditional system for rewarding APS employees for superior performance involved merit-based promotion through a classification system and regular increments to base pay based on time service and seniority. Under the newer system, superior individual performance may be recognised through accelerated progression through the new classification system or via performance bonus payments. Since 1997 there has been a pronounced move away from semi-automatic seniority-based salary increases to increases contingent on appraised or measured individual performance. Pay-for-performance measures are now widespread throughout the APS, and in many agencies this has also been accompanied by a substantial reconfiguration of existing performance assessment practices, including a stronger emphasis on corporate values and strategic awareness and contribution.

However, there is now a solid body of evidence that, for many employees in APS agencies, the experience of the new performance and reward management practices has been anything but uniformly positive (O'Donnell 1998; O'Donnell & Shields 2002b; Grant, O'Donnell & Shields 2003; APS Commission 2005).

Initial research on outcomes from the APS performance management model highlighted employees' belief that supervisors' assessments were influenced by factors unrelated to individual performance. Employees were also concerned that performance ratings were being used by management to target individuals for dismissal on the grounds of under-performance or to facilitate staff reductions. Preliminary performance ratings by supervisors were frequently moderated or 'normalised' by means of forced distribution, ostensibly to ensure consistency across the organisation. However, employees suspected that the initial ratings were 'moderated' downwards for budgetary reasons to limit the overall cost of the performance management scheme. In addition, employees pointed to the potential for performance pay to rupture relationships between supervisors and subordinates. Although many of the new performance management systems introduced in APS agencies in the late 1990s contained appeal mechanisms, staff reported either being unaware of the details of the appeal process or considered more senior managers unlikely to alter the rating decision of their supervisor. Employees also reported being reluctant to appeal performance rating scores because they feared that doing so might damage their prospects for career advancement. Other employees expressed concern that the revised performance criteria were frequently imprecise and ambiguous and allowed supervisors undue discretion to make idiosyncratic and arbitrary judgements regarding employee behaviour and work performance. Linking assessment scores to short-term pay outcomes also generated increased conflict between supervisors and staff, and often created tensions among employees themselves (Grant, O'Donnell & Shields 2003).

Moreover, from a management perspective, in many APS agencies, initial outcomes were less than stellar. In some agencies, schemes failed to differentiate adequately between 'effective' and 'superior' job performance, with most agencies falling back on automatic annual 'merit' increments to base pay for all employees achieving an 'effective' performance rating. Indeed, some agencies abandoned performance pay for non-executive employees altogether, citing either their failure to motivate or the corrosive impact of performance-contingent pay on the performance management process itself (O'Donnell & Shields 2002b; Grant, O'Donnell & Shields 2003).

Of course, it could be argued that these findings simply reflect the 'teething' problems that are typical of any change process. However, more recent evidence confirms that the problems with the APS performance management initiatives are widespread and deep-seated. An employee survey undertaken in 2005 by the Australian Public Service Commission, and based on more than 3,600 responses obtained by means of a stratified random sample of 6,160 APS employees, reveals that only 43 per cent of respondents agree that their last performance review helped them to perform well. In this regard, one respondent (APS Commission 2005: 160) remarked: 'I have never been satisfied with our performance feedback system. Supervisors tend to use it as a tick and flick exercise – there is no detailed assessment of my performance. Worse, supervisors do not give enough feedback between formal assessments. In the case of my current supervisor, if he does give me informal feedback, it tends to be of the negative variety.'

As before, however, the most negative employee attitudes are those concerning performance pay. Most significantly: only 39 per cent of respondents agree that their agency's performance pay system 'operates fairly and consistently'; only 36 per cent agree that it 'acts as an incentive to perform well'; and only 31 per cent agree that it 'contributes to a workplace which upholds the APS values'. Of still greater concern is the fact that only a fifth of respondents agree that their performance pay system 'accurately reflects differences in individuals' performance', 'provides appropriate rewards for top performers' and 'contributes to a workplace culture in which individuals work together effectively'. A comparison of survey results for previous years indicates that far from employees being won over to performance pay, in attitudinal terms the situation throughout the APS is actually deteriorating: 'This year's survey results add to the evidence presented in last year's report that the credibility of performance pay systems amongst employees is not high in most agencies and the gap is widening.' (APS Commission 2005: 161, 164.)

So, what is the underlying problem here? Is this also a case of a bad idea gone predictably wrong or, alternatively, of good ideas being poorly applied? Well-designed and administered performance appraisal has for decades been a vital element of merit-based promotion and pay progression in public service contexts. Yet there is evidence that performance-contingent pay may be a poor motivator in public sector contexts and may even have dysfunctional consequences (Marsden & Richardson 1994; Marsden 2004). It may also be that public service employees are motivated chiefly by a sense of public purpose and promotion-based status and achievement rather than by short-term pay outcomes (Gaertner & Gaertner 1985). Alternatively, it may be that the APS plans are a good idea badly applied. Could good system design and implementation have anticipated and forestalled many of the concerns raised by APS employees themselves?

Either way, as these two cases make abundantly clear, performance and reward management is fraught with peril. Despite their many differences, the H-P and APS experiences are instructive examples of how not to go about altering an organisation's performance recognition and reward practices. Perhaps more so than other facets of human resource management, the management of employee performance and rewards is an attitudinal, emotional and behavioural minefield. Ill-chosen, badly designed or poorly implemented performance management systems can communicate entirely the wrong messages as to what the organisation expects from its employees. An ill-conceived reward system may not only fail to elicit desired behaviour; it may also encourage behaviour that is dysfunctional, deceptive or even destructive; that is, it may give rise to endemic organisational misbehaviour.

The challenges and potential problems associated with performance and reward management are certainly not lost on human resource managers themselves. Survey data on Australian human resource managers' perceptions of the efficacy of performance management systems in their organisations indicates that while such systems have become more complex and strategically focused since the 1990s, only 49 per cent of human resource managers rate their current system as 'effective', while just 20 per cent believe that their system is 'highly effective'. The same study also suggests that manager satisfaction with system effectiveness has actually declined since the early 1990s (Nankervis & Compton 2006: 99).

Clearly, from both a management and an employee perspective, managing employee performance and reward is something that is difficult to do well – and very easy to do badly. Yet both the stakes and the potential are simply enormous. As we shall see in subsequent chapters, whether wittingly or unwittingly, performance and reward practices can play a powerful role in shaping and reshaping employee work attitudes and perceptions of trust and fairness, and especially in determining the state of that complex constellation of employee cognitions known as the 'psychological contract'. And this is one of the main reasons this book has been written: to offer readers a balanced coverage of both the potential and the possible pitfalls of performance and reward practice. The driving purpose of this book is to equip readers with the knowledge and critical insight necessary to make their own informed judgements and choices about these two pivotal human resource processes. Equally, the book aims to provide readers with the analytical tools required to avoid the all-too-common problems of performance and reward mismanagement.

While the book's central concerns are with performance and reward processes, attention is also paid throughout to recognising and analysing the interconnectedness of these and other human resource processes, including staffing (i.e. recruitment and selection) and employee training and development. As we shall see, misalignment between any of these four key functional areas can be very detrimental to both organisational effectiveness and employee well-being. Figure 0.1 (p. 8) illustrates the mutual interdependence of these four key human resource management functions. We shall return to these cross-functional synergies throughout the book.

## Conceptual approach

Over the years, my own students have frequently decried the absence of cohesion in many standard human resource teaching texts. Their complaints are not without foundation. It is not at all uncommon to encounter teaching tomes on human resource management that amount to little more than an assemblage of prolifically illustrated but poorly connected chapter-length treatments of specific human resource functions. Such books generally have no identifiable integrative argument or thesis to offer, and hapless readers are left largely to tie the pieces together for themselves. Mindful of this, what I have sought to offer throughout this book is an explicit and sustained line of *argument* regarding key performance and reward management concepts, principles and practices. As a reader, you may ultimately disagree with the argument and recommendations proffered, but you will at least know where I stand on the matters in dispute.

There is always a danger in authors nailing their conceptual colours to the metaphorical mast at the outset, but to do so is, arguably, a core requirement of intellectual honesty and transparency. In the United States, virtually all of the major mainstream texts on 'compensation' (i.e. remuneration) are authored either by labour economists or by organisational psychologists. While these disciplines are of pivotal importance to the matters we are about to explore, a range of equally useful insights from other fields of intellectual inquiry is now available. To this end, this book draws on

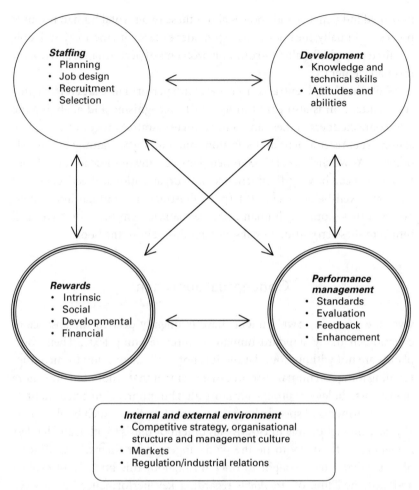

**Figure 0.1** The matrix of human resource processes

multidisciplinary insights not only from labour economics and organisational psychology but also from organisational studies, strategic management and human resource management studies, corporate governance, industrial and employment relations, business economics, business ethics, sociology, business and labour history, cultural studies and critical management studies.

But intellectual orientation is not simply a matter of the disciplinary terrain traversed; it also has to do with ontological and epistemological considerations. In all areas of humanities inquiry, whatever the subject under investigation, the questions of ontology (What is the nature of 'being'? What is 'real'?) and epistemology (How are 'being' and 'reality' best understood?) warrant close consideration (Crotty 1998: 8–17). Put simply, ontology and epistemology have to do with our approach to characterising and explaining any phenomenon under investigation. For instance, should we regard employee and organisational 'performance' as objectively 'real', or is it more meaningful to see these as being facets of a number of subjectively determined 'realities'? Our conceptual choices here will influence how we go about relating 'performance' to other categories or factors that we see as being part of the same 'reality'. The same questions apply equally to every one of the other ontological categories that we shall be considering in this book: from 'employee' and 'manager' to 'organisation' and 'market'; from 'strategy' to 'practice'; from 'competency' to 'commitment'; from 'satisfaction' to 'reward'.

Thankfully, we have a few useful pointers to guide us through these philosophical questions. As Legge (1995a: 1–9) and others have noted, there are various approaches to understanding 'human resource management' and its proposed constituent parts, including 'performance management' and 'reward management'. Of these alternative approaches, the three most significant, we suggest, are: (1) the prescriptive, (2) the descriptive and (3) the critical (structuralist and post-structuralist).

The prescriptive approach, which is commonplace in the practitioner literature, is based on the premise that there are human resource 'problems', which are both knowable and amenable to analysis and solution by rational means through 'good' management practice. The focus of this approach is on prescribing the ways in which employees, as the objects of people management, *should* be managed to achieve organisational ends. It also assumes that it is possible to achieve outcomes that are mutually beneficial to employers and employees, and without 'interference' from 'third parties', such as industrial tribunals or trade unions. In the mainstream industrial relations literature, such an approach is usually described as a 'managerialist' or 'unitarist' frame of reference. As such, its orientation is essentially value-based or 'normative' in nature, although generally with little conscious reflection on the norms involved. In the field of reward management, the publications of US 'compensation' writers Edward Lawler (2000) and Patricia Zingheim and Jay Schuster (2000a) are typical of the prescriptive genre. Of course, the prescriptions themselves may differ, but the approach remains the same.

The descriptive approach, which is typical of much of the mainstream academic literature on human resource management, is evidence-based in nature and grounded in a 'positivist' epistemology. On this basis, human resource management is a phenomenon worthy of empirical inquiry – for its own sake. So, a researcher might wish to discover why and how a certain management 'problem' arises; or she may wish to establish why certain reward practices are more effective in certain types of organisation than others, and perhaps to identify the main predictor variables and mediating variables of pay plan effectiveness. Descriptive research of this sort is one of the mainstays of academic journal publishing, and it also plays an important part in the generation of management theory and models and, to a lesser extent, in giving rise to new management practices. In general, and in contrast to the unitarism typical of most purely prescriptive orientations, a descriptive approach is apt to acknowledge the legitimacy of a multistakeholder or 'pluralist' perspective on organisational life and, in particular, to see employees as having interests that are distinct from, yet overlapping with, those of the organisation and its managers. As such, the descriptive view is also likely to be open-minded about the possibility of mutual gains arising from people management practices. Two exemplars of the descriptive–positivist approach are University of London academic David Guest (1997, 1999, 2001, 2002) and University of Wisconsin academic Barry Gerhart (Gerhart & Rynes 2003; Rynes & Gerhart 2000). While both Guest and Gerhart do express strong views about appropriate and inappropriate human resource practices, their prescriptions are grounded firmly in solid research evidence.

A critical approach, by contrast, is one that eschews any supportive association with management purpose; rather it focuses, first, on analysing and critiquing the intentions and impact of management actions on employees and their families and, second, on exploring how employees respond individually and collectively. The critical approach is also premised on the assumption that the relationship between employee and employer is inherently antagonistic and unequal.

Beyond this, however, we encounter a significant complication, since there are actually two distinct variants of the critical approach. One, the critical–structuralist (or critical–realist) approach, tends to focus on the role of 'material' (i.e. economic and institutional) factors in reproducing inequalities in the employment relationship, on the indeterminacy of the relationship itself, and on the ways in which employees accommodate themselves to or resist employer and management actions. For the most part, this approach dismisses prescriptive models of human resource management as little more than empty 'rhetoric' intended either to keep employees in their proper place or to lull them into a false sense of security. The work of British industrial sociologist Paul Thompson (Thompson & McHugh 1995; Ackroyd & Thompson 1999) typifies this critical–structuralist orientation. To Thompson and McHugh (1995: 361–87) it is the interaction of 'structure' (including economic inequality and institutional forces) and 'agency' (particularly the competing actions of managers and employees) that shapes the nature of the employment relationship across space and time.

Conversely, the critical post-structuralist approach focuses on the role of 'talk and text' or 'discourse' (i.e. language, disseminated ideas, ideology) in constructing employee and management perceptions of themselves, each other, the nature of the employment relationship, organisational power inequalities and, indeed, 'material reality' itself. Illustrative of critical post-structuralism is the work of British–Canadian acadamic Barbara Townley (1993a & b, 1994). Drawing on the work of French philosopher and historian Michel Foucault, Townley argues that human resource management discourse and practice is best understood in terms of the interplay of power, knowledge and subjectivity. Managers – the organisational knowledge-makers – simultaneously empower themselves and subjugate the managed by means of discourses and practices that individualise, objectify and discipline workers and shape their subjectivity and concept of self and work reality using complex regimes of surveillance (the 'panopticon'), classification and ordering ('taxonomia'), measurement ('mathesis') and, hence, knowledge construction: 'HRM . . . constitutes a discipline and a discourse . . . HRM serves to render organizations and their participants calculable arenas, offering, through a variety of technologies, the means by which activities and individuals become knowable and governable' (Townley 1993a: 526). As such, the central point at issue between 'realist' and 'post-structuralist' conceptions has to do with whether or not there is a single material reality that is ontologically given and therefore influential and epistemologically knowable distinctly and separately from what employees, managers and the rest of us say and think about that supposed material reality.

Perhaps this is all a little too abstruse for you, so let me briefly illustrate the differences between these four 'ways of seeing' human resource management by taking the example of 'performance management' itself.

From a prescriptive perspective, performance management is basically an objectively given function to be fulfilled. Employees are hired to deliver work effort. What is of most importance is advising management how to elicit this effort by the most effective means possible.

From a descriptive perspective, performance management still presents as an objectively given process, but what is chiefly at issue is why performance management seems to be more effective in some situations than others – something that must be ascertained through empirical inquiry rather than by means of normative deduction from first principles.

To a critical structuralist, performance management is a necessary and perennially problematic aspect of the employment relationship. Unlike a typical commercial exchange, which involves the exchange of things of agreed value equivalence, the employment relationship is seen as being both an unequal and an indeterminate exchange. When an employer hires an employee, what the employer is actually buying is that employee's *capacity* to perform. It is then up to the employer to secure a 'return' on the wage or salary outlay by eliciting as much work effort as possible from the employee for the wage or salary paid. To a critical structuralist, the consequent struggle over the 'effort–wage bargain' is both the reason for the ongoing performance management 'problem' and the *raison d'être* of performance management practices.

Finally, to a critical post-structuralist, performance management presents as a series of discursive interventions by management intended to construct 'performance' as an objective organisational truth, to shape each employee's self-concept, values, attitudes, beliefs and behaviour, to recast the employee as a resource object, and to legitimate and sustain organisational power inequalities between 'manager' and 'the managed'. In essence, critical post-structuralism sees performance not as an objective fact but, rather, as an artefact – even an artifice – of management power, and associated practices, such as performance appraisal, as a means of constructing organisational 'reality' in a way that ensures employee subordination to the will of management. For instance, to Barbara Townley (1993a: 531–5; 1993b; 1994: 72) individual performance assessment is not only a device intended to render the employee subject 'knowable' and 'amenable' by means of individual measurement, classification and ranking but also a discursive practice intended to problematise the performer and to shape their self-concept accordingly while simultaneously producing and legitimating managerial knowledge ('human resource information') and empowering the manager. Thus appraisal systems may operate 'to inculcate correct behavioural norms', to tie individuals to ' "appropriate" identities' and make their behaviour and performance 'predictable and calculable – in a word, manageable' (Townley 1993a: 537–8). At the same time, appraisal exemplifies how 'knowledge of the individual and the work performed articulates the managerial role as a directional activity' (Townley 1993b: 236).

So, which of these approaches informs this book? The short answer is that they all have a bearing on the approach taken and the recommendations made. Since this is first and foremost a book for management aspirants and practitioners, it would be quite misleading to offer a text that was bereft of prescriptive intent. The book's primary aim is to provide a consistent framework for effective management practice. To this extent, those taking a critical perspective may be tempted to dismiss this as 'prescriptive, functionalist and uncritical' (Watson 2004: 447). However, the approach taken is neither narrowly unitarist nor blithely uncritical. The prescriptions offered are grounded in the best available empirical evidence; they do not derive from some supposed normative higher truth. To that extent, the approach is descriptive and positivist. That said, the approach also embraces the normative tenets of a multi-stakeholder or pluralist position, as opposed to those of a unitarist world view.

Further, it would be disingenuous of me to pretend that the approach taken is not also coloured by both critical structuralism and post-structuralism. For all of the acrimonious and typically abstruse argument between exponents of these two variants of 'anti-managerialism' (see for example Contu & Willmott 2005; Reed 2005a & b; Tinker 2002) both camps still have much in common. Materiality makes discourse purposive; discourse makes materiality meaningful. Take the phenomenon of 'performance' again: just as management discourse about 'performance' would be quite pointless in the absence of desired tangible outcomes, so management 'talk and text' about 'performance' seeks to invest these tangible outcomes and the processes by which they are achieved with a particular set of human meanings; meanings that certainly do not emanate automatically from the product produced. Moreover, both critical approaches have much to offer a constructively critical approach to the study and practice of human resource management. In particular, while the structuralist critique reminds us of the ethical importance and analytical value of adopting an employee-centred approach to understanding the nature and influence of human resource management, critical post-structuralism alerts us to the extended socio-cognitive insights that may be obtained by interrogating organisational 'talk and text' about 'performance' and 'reward' matters, particularly in relation to what this may mean for how employees see themselves, their peers, their supervisors, their work and their organisation.

In short, then, this is a text written with prescriptive intent but from a pluralist and (constructively) critical perspective.

## Structure

The book comprises five thematic parts and a total of twenty-one chapters. The four chapters comprising part 1 explore the fundamentals of performance and reward management theory and practice. Chapter 1 examines the general nature and purpose of employee performance and reward management. Chapter 2 considers key issues in work psychology, chapter 3 explores the matter of motivation, and chapter 4 examines what is involved in practising performance and reward management strategically.

The chapters in part 2 cover the options and techniques for effective individual and group performance management. Chapter 5 deals with results-based performance management, chapter 6 managing behaviour and chapter 7 the management of competencies, while chapter 8 investigates the issues and techniques involved in performance review, planning and developing.

In part 3, the focus moves to reward management; specifically to base pay and benefits. Chapter 9 overviews the logic of base pay and the major options involved. Chapter 10 examines alternative base pay structures, chapter 11 details the considerations and methods involved in developing position-based base pay systems, while chapter 12 examines the options and requirements for developing person-based base pay systems. Chapter 13 then explores the rationale and varieties of employee benefit plans.

The chapters in part 4 detail the main varieties of performance recognition and reward, with special emphasis on pay-for-performance plans. Chapter 14 provides a general assessment of performance-related rewards (or 'incentive' plans), including matters of efficacy and fairness. Chapter 15 discusses merit pay for individual performance, chapter 16 explores cash and non-cash 'recognition' plans, chapter 17 considers old and new forms of individual results-based incentives, chapter 18 focuses on collective short-term incentives for large and small work groups, and chapter 19 details collective long-term incentives in the form of employee share plans. The final chapter in part 4 (chapter 20) considers incentive plans for those employees whose unique potential to influence organisational performance warrants distinct consideration, namely senior executives.

Revisiting the behavioural and strategic consideration examined in part 1, the chapter comprising part 5 (chapter 21) presents a 'best fit' approach to assembling the various concepts, evaluation techniques and practices explored in parts 2–5 into a coherent, cohesive and strategically aligned whole. Specifically, this final chapter examines the requirements for and challenges associated with performance and reward system review and the steps involved in system development; that is, system design/redesign and implementation.

Each chapter also includes discussion questions, while major case study exercises are included at the conclusion of parts 2–5. A list of references cited is included at the back of the book.

## Chapter summary

In a very real sense, this book represents a series of delicate balancing acts: between the research monograph and the teaching text; between the learning needs of students and those of practitioners; between manager and the managed; between the individual and the collective; between the financial and the non-financial; between the domestic and the international; between the empirical and the conceptual; between ideas and practice; and, most exactingly of all, between offering critique and recommending solutions. As to whether the text succeeds in striking an appropriate balance between these competing demands, I am content to await the reader's verdict. In the book's planning and writing, I have been especially mindful of the sobering observations made several years back by respected US industrial relations academic George Strauss (2001: 892) regarding what he sees as the general shortcomings of US texts on human resource management:

> (1) They are too cookbook-y. I would prefer less on how to do it and more on whether to do it. (2) Their approach is unitary rather than pluralist. They pay too little attention to the problems of implementation and largely ignore the possibility that workers, managers (and even vice presidents) will resist managerial policies they do not like. (3) In some cases the parts are poorly integrated . . . And (4) they largely ignore the impact of HRM policies on society.

To be sure, there is prescription aplenty in the chapters that follow, but, in line with Strauss's exhortation, I have striven to avoid the normative confines of a managerialist worldview and to assert the practical worth of a pluralist or multistakeholder approach. I have also endeavoured throughout to maintain faith with the best traditions of academic empiricism while also recognising the worth of the epistemological insights on offer in both genres of critical management studies: the structuralist and the poststructuralist.

My chief hope is that the approach taken and the analysis and arguments offered will serve both to challenge readers' preconceptions about these pivotal people management matters and to enhance their appreciation and understanding of the rewards to be gained from designing, implementing and managing performance and reward systems that are not only strategically aligned and organisationally effective but also supportive of employee well-being, work satisfaction, equity and felt-fairness. My overall hope is that, in readers' final analysis, *Managing Employee Performance and Reward* 'performs' as promised.

## Discussion questions

1 Why is performance pay such a problematic issue in public sector employment?
2 Was the H-P incentive experiment a case of good ideas but poor execution? If so, what should have been done differently, and why?
3 Why are performance management and reward management such closely related aspects of human resource management?
4 Why are rewards such a sensitive aspect of human resource management?
5 Compare and contrast the prescriptive, descriptive and critical approaches to human resource management. Which is more 'realistic', and why?

Part I

# THE FUNDAMENTALS

It is appropriate that we begin our journey by considering those ideas, concepts, propositions and debates that are fundamental to a rounded understanding of employee performance and reward management and, equally, to well-informed and effective practice in these fields.

The four chapters in part 1 are devoted to this end. Chapter 1 seeks to clarify the meaning, nature and purpose of our two focal human resource processes: performance management and reward management. While our treatment of the 'what' and 'why' of performance and reward management is written from an explicitly prescriptive–descriptive perspective, the treatment is neither wholly management-centred nor uncritical.

Building on this foundational knowledge, the three accompanying chapters consider, respectively, the psychological, motivational and strategic basics of performance and reward management. These chapters offer frameworks for practising performance and reward management in both a psychologically aware and a strategically informed manner. The development, implementation and maintenance of effective performance and reward management systems requires simultaneous attention to each of these fundamental dimensions.

By 'psychological' dimensions we mean the attitudes, perceptions, values and emotional (or 'affective') states that prefigure the observable actions – or behaviour – of individual employees, or at least that seem to predispose individuals towards certain behavioural actions rather than others. While 'motivation' is undoubtedly the most widely acknowledged and theorised of all work attitudes, as we shall see, there are others that may be no less salient or influential, including those that are grounded more in perception and in deeply held values and emotions than in dispassionate or rational cognition.

By 'strategic' dimensions we mean the plans, processes and actions involved in establishing and maintaining an alignment between an organisation's purpose, structure and objectives, on the one hand, and the individual and collective behaviour and achievements of its employees, on the other. You will notice that, on the basis of these definitions, employee behaviour is *the* key bridge between the psychological and the strategic.

Before considering these themes in detail, it is necessary for us to examine the general nature and purpose of performance and reward management.

## Chapter One

# PERFORMANCE AND REWARD BASICS

As a way of mapping the general terrain of performance and reward management, this chapter overviews the general meaning, nature and purpose of performance and reward management practice. We begin by examining the definition and dimensions of employee performance. Next we consider the possible purposes of performance management. Following this, we investigate the main requirements for the effectiveness of a performance management system. Attention then turns to the definition of employee reward, the non-financial and financial reward elements covered by a 'total reward' approach, and the three main categories of financial reward or 'remuneration'. Finally, we examine the general objectives of a reward management system.

## 'Performance'

What is 'performance'? The trite response is that it depends on who you ask. A critical post-structuralist may say that performance is whatever the dominant management discourse says that it is. To a pluralist, the answer will depend on the stakeholder concerned: a shareholder is likely to equate it with share price improvement and annual dividend payments, a manager on a profitshare plan may nominate annual net profit, a production manager may suggest labour productivity, and a customer might suggest product quality or cost-attractiveness, while to a production line employee performance may equate with job and income security and workplace health and safety. Such responses do indeed highlight two important facets of performance: first, it is a subjective, constructed (and hence frequently contested) phenomenon; second, and relatedly, it is open-ended and multidimensional. In short, what is important about performance is not just how 'high' or 'low' it is but also how it is defined and measured, by whom and for what purpose.

However, while these are important points in a general descriptive sense, they do not get us very far in a practical or applied sense. To conceptualise 'performance' as a manageable human resource phenomenon (and hence with prescriptive ends in mind), it is perhaps most useful to view performance in 'cybernetic' terms; that is, as a process-based work 'system'. Adapting insights offered by Wright and others (Wright & McMahan 1992; Wright & Snell 1991) on what has been described as the 'open system model' of human resource management, we can conceptualise work and work performance as a system comprising three main elements arranged in a linear sequence:

1 'inputs', including employee knowledge, skills and competencies (i.e. abilities and attitudes), as well as other tangible and intangible 'resources'
2 human resource 'throughputs' (i.e. activities that transform inputs into outcomes, including, most importantly, work effort and other behaviour); and
3 'outputs', including outcomes from work behaviour; i.e. results.

So, an employee provides work inputs in the form of knowledge, skills, abilities and attitudes, applies these through effort and related forms of work behaviour, and produces a certain quantity of products or services of a certain quality within a certain period of time. Strictly speaking, inputs in the form of knowledge, skills and competencies are not tantamount to performance; they have to do with the employee's *potential* to perform. Yet, as we shall see in chapter 7, since the early 1990s the competency-based approaches have become a prominent feature of performance management practice in many Western organisations.

Performance, however, is not just an individual phenomenon; as figure 1.1 suggests, it also has group and organisation-wide dimensions, each with inputs, processes and results that parallel those operating at the individual level. In this sense, performance can be thought of as having three horizontal (or sequential) dimensions and three vertical (or scalar) dimensions. So, for instance, a team or other work group might contribute a level of collective know-how (input), engage in cooperative teamworking

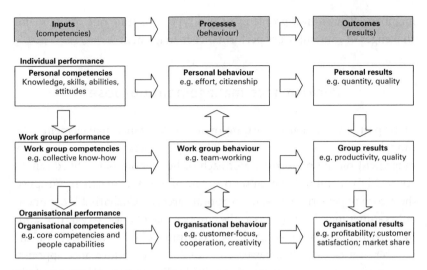

**Figure 1.1** What is performance?

(behavioural process) and achieve a certain level of group productivity (result). At the organisational scale, inputs would include the collective know-how, productive capacities, cultural values and work attitudes of the entire workforce, processes would include such collective behaviour as cooperation, creativity and customer focus, and results would include such outcomes as corporate profitability, market share and customer satisfaction. As we shall see, all of these vertical dimensions fall within the ambit of performance and performance management.

Moreover, as figure 1.1 indicates, these performance variables also have important cross-dimensional linkages. Individual knowledge and skill feeds into work group know-how, which in turn flows into organisational productive capabilities. Similarly, individual results flow into group results, which in turn contribute to organisation-wide results. This is not to suggest that group and organisational inputs, behaviour and results are simply the sum of individual contributions. As we shall see, other factors are at work that will influence the transmission and strength of these vertical associations. You will notice, too, that the vertical linkages associated with behavioural processes are bi-directional. This is because collective behaviour arises from and shapes individual behaviour. Just as a misbehaving individual team member may disrupt team cooperation, so a behaviourally dysfunctional team will almost certainly further impair the behaviour of individual team members. Behavioural problems of this type constitute one of the major challenges of contemporary performance management.

## Performance management purpose

In the past, it was not at all uncommon for performance management to be thought of as a once-a-year event in which the supervisor passed summary judgement on the performance of each of her subordinates, filled out an appraisal form, informed each subordinate of the outcome, then consigned the record of performance to the corporate archive. Uncharitable commentators sometimes describe this as the empty ritual of once-a-year 'tick-and-flick' performance appraisal. Management thinker W. Edwards Deming, the pioneer of total quality management, even decried performance appraisal as one of modern management's most 'deadly diseases' (Deming 1986). According to Deming, traditional appraisal 'nourishes short-term performance, annihilates long-term planning, builds fear, demolishes teamwork, nourishes rivalry and politics'. Deming labelled performance appraisal a lottery, with individual ratings emanating largely from random factors outside individual control (cited in Carson, Cardy & Dobbins 1991). Other critics argue that, by focusing on short-term, individual performance and by reinforcing top-down management, performance appraisal *per se* is too narrow and non-strategic to provide a comprehensive approach to performance management (Bach 1999; Beer 1981; Flannery, Hofrichter & Platten 1996; Lawler 2000).

Today, it is far more common for organisations to regard performance management as a continuous, future-oriented and participative system; as an ongoing cycle of criteria setting, monitoring, informal feedback from supervisors and peers, formal multisource assessment, diagnosis and review, action-planning and developmental resourcing (Bach 1999; Williams 2002). The basic elements and phases in this cycle are illustrated in figure 1.2. The cycle itself may be annual, six-monthly, quarterly or even monthly in nature. As participants in this process, all stakeholders – human resource managers, line supervisors, fellow workers and employees themselves – are expected to act responsibly and to accept accountability for their contribution and assessments. Whether or not this does actually happen will depend in large measure on the level of support shown by senior management, on how well the system is resourced, and how effectively the system's purpose is communicated to all involved.

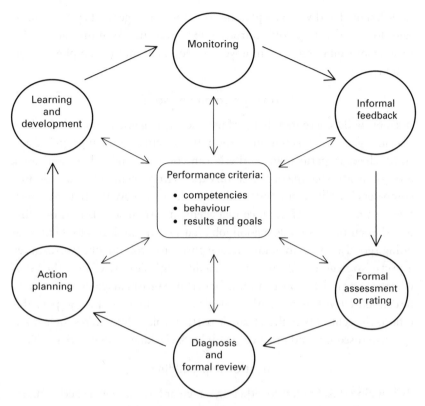

**Figure 1.2** The performance management cycle

Why is it necessary to 'manage' employee performance at all? On this count, at least, the prescriptive management writers and their ideological adversaries, the critical structuralists, appear to share some common ground (albeit with very different agendas in mind): without performance direction and recognition, employees will be at loss as to the nature and level of work effort required. Just imagine how work would likely be undertaken in an organisation that made little attempt to define how it wished its workers and managers to behave, what it wanted them to achieve, and what it meant by 'good' and 'bad' performance, as well as how it proposed to treat star performers, on the one hand, and under-performers on the other. In today's organisations, simply instructing employees to 'get on with doing a good job' is just not an acceptable option.

This, of course, begs a critical question: what should a 'good' perfor-mance management system seek to do? From a prescriptive perspective, a well-designed and well-accepted performance management system can be said to have a four-fold purpose: (1) strategic communication, (2) relationship-building, (3) employee development and (4) employee evaluation.

## Strategic communication

It is now widely accepted that performance management has a vital role to play in organisational communication. In particular, clear, appropriate and comprehensive performance criteria can convey to individuals and work groups exactly what the organisation expects from them in terms of desired competencies, behaviour and results in order to achieve its strategic objectives. An effective performance management system signals not only that it wishes employees to 'do a good job'; it also communicates to them what doing a good job actually entails in each position or role. In other words, a key aspect of strategic communication is facilitating 'role clarity'. Since the 1980s it has become much more common for performance management systems to be configured with an explicitly strategic purpose in mind. In large part, this reflects the centrality of the 'strategic partner' role in human resource management discourse and practice (Dunphy & Hackman 1988; Ulrich 1998).

## Relationship-building

By bringing stakeholders together on a regular basis to review performance achievements and plan for further development and improvement, systematic performance management stands to make a major contribution to the building of stronger work relationships within the organisation. This, in turn, can have a positive influence on work culture. Requiring supervisors, subordinates and peers to take an active, positive and accountable role in performance review and planning can help to widen multi-party dialogue and information-sharing, as well as to enhance the level of interpersonal trust. As the APS experience (see the Introduction) suggests, however, a poorly designed and implemented performance review system may be very disruptive of workplace relationships.

## Employee development

Performance management may serve a developmental purpose. This may include: providing formal feedback on recent performance, including strengths, weaknesses and areas for improvement; maintaining and improving motivation and performance; providing guidance on career development, identifying barriers to improved performance; and assisting in human resource forward planning, especially regarding the development of personal skills and competencies. As figure 1.2 indicates, the performance management and staff training and development functions are mutually supportive. Performance review provides an important means of evaluating outcomes from staff training and development initiatives. At the same time, it is the major means of identifying deficits in employee knowledge, skills and abilities that may require remediation. For similar reasons, the developmental purpose also aligns with the job or role assignment decisions that are a pivotal aspect of the staffing function.

### Employee evaluation

Performance management systems frequently also fill an evaluative purpose. In essence this has to do with determining individual 'merit' for selection, promotion and/or reward allocation. Assessment for job reassignment, promotion and demotion or retrenchment are among the most longstanding objectives of systematic performance management. The evaluative purpose also includes monitoring the effectiveness of other human resource policies, especially recruitment, selection, training and job evaluation. Another traditional purpose of individual performance assessment has been to obtain numerical ratings and rankings that can then be used as the basis for determining performance-related adjustments to pay. This, of course, is the critical bridge between the two human resource processes with which we are centrally concerned, and the nature of this association will be a recurrent theme in the chapters that follow.

Yet the relationship between the developmental and evaluative purposes is frequently a troubled one, and achieving and maintaining a harmonious relationship between the two is undoubtedly one of the single greatest challenges that awaits the unsuspecting human resource manager. In particular, employees may be left wondering whether the main purpose of their annual performance review is to help them to develop their future performance or to reward (or punish) them for past performance. The developmental objective recognises that the role of the manager is not just to evaluate and reward past performance but also to enhance employees' present and future capacity, motivation and performance.

Critics of traditional supervisory performance appraisal, with its focus on once-a-year assessment of past performance, have long argued that it privileges the evaluative purpose over strategic, relational and developmental

**Table 1.1** Aims of performance management in Australian private and public sector organisations, 2003

|  | Respondents ($N = 992$) nominating stated aim (%) |
|---|---|
| **Strategic:** |  |
| • align objectives | 75.5 |
| • change organisational culture | 28.0 |
| **Developmental:** |  |
| • determine training and development needs | 89.2 |
| • develop individual competencies | 56.6 |
| • assist career planning decisions | 56.0 |
| **Evaluative:** |  |
| • appraise past performance | 88.9 |
| • link pay to performance | 50.7 |
| • assess future potential and promotion prospects | 47.9 |
| • discipline or dismiss non-performing staff | 28.9 |
| • retain high-calibre staff | 27.5 |

*Source:* Nankervis & Compton 2006: 88.

considerations (Lawler 1994c; Mohrman & Mohrman 1995; Wilson 1994: 201–29). As we have seen, the preferred approach today is that of continuous 'performance management'. Does this mean, however, that the traditional evaluative purpose is becoming less important while the developmental is becoming more so? A 2003 survey of performance management practices in Australian organisations (Nankervis & Compton 2006) suggests some surprising findings in this regard. Table 1.1 summarises the main aims of performance management, as reported by the survey respondents, who numbered just under a thousand. The results indicate that while the evaluative purpose remains strong, strategic and developmental purposes are also now very much in evidence, with 89 per cent of respondents indicating the determination of training and development as an important purpose of their performance management practices – exactly the same proportion that nominated the evaluation of past performance as a major system purpose. These responses also differ significantly from a comparable Australian survey undertaken in 1995 (Nankervis & Leece 1997), which found that only 58 per cent of respondents indicated staff development as an important consideration, compared to 94 per cent nominating evaluation of past performance as a major system purpose. In other words, in Australia, the relative importance of the developmental purpose has risen substantially since the 1990s, although the evaluative purpose has certainly not been eclipsed entirely. A similar trend is evident in the UK, where a 2004 survey showed that 71 per cent of organisations surveyed operated performance management systems with a developmental focus, whereas just 43 per cent used performance ratings to inform performance pay decisions (CIPD 2005b: 2).

## Basic requirements for effective performance management

Irrespective of specific purpose, what are the main requirements for the effectiveness of a performance management system? Again, in prescriptive vein, the four key requirements are: (1) validity, (2) reliability, (3) cost-effectiveness and (4) felt-fairness.

### Validity

Validity relates, first, to the criteria by which employee 'performance' is defined or 'constructed' in terms of desired standards and, second, to how accurately the performance measures or 'indicators' applied to these standards reflect or predict actual performance. The more valid the performance construct and the measures associated with it, the more closely and comprehensively these will relate to what employees are actually required to do in their role. In other words, validity has to do with whether the standards set and the measures used are relevant to the specific work role involved, whether they measure enough of the right things, and whether the measures or indicators themselves accurately reflect or capture what is achieved in relation to desired standards (Drenth 1998: 68–9; Klein 1996).

In relation to performance measurement, validity can be disaggregated into three dimensions:

1  construct validity (= role relevance of performance standards)
2  content validity (= role representativeness of performance standards)
3  criterion-related validity (= the accuracy of performance measures or indicators used in reflecting and/or predicting the desired performance standards).

A performance management system is said to be construct valid if the performance standards and measures are directly relevant to what is required in the job, position or role involved; that is, construct validity is concerned with the role *relevance* of the performance standards and measures applied. The key system design question here is: are we really measuring the right things for this role?

Content validity refers to the extent to which the performance standards and measures provide a representative and comprehensive coverage of all desired facets of role performance. A system would fail the test of content validity if it recognised and measured some aspects of the job but ignored one or more other aspects that the job holder had been asked to address. So, for example, content validity would be compromised if the organisation desired to maximise both labour productivity and product quality but specified a standard and measure only for productivity. As such, the key system design question here is: are we measuring *enough* of the right things for this role?

Criterion-related validity refers to the closeness of the association between the performance measures used and what it is that the organisation actually says it wants from the employee. For example, a system would fail the test of criterion-related validity if it used, say, observations of personal grooming standards to measure the quality of customer service provided, or if it used observations of hours worked as a measure of work effectiveness. This is not to say that the measures used may not be valid in relation to other performance standards or criteria; the point is that in these instances neither measure is valid for the particular criterion specified. Here, then, the key design question is: are we really measuring what we say we are trying to measure?

## Reliability

Reliability has to do with the consistency and accuracy of the measurement task itself as opposed to the performance criteria and measures used. Equally, reliable measurement will be impossible where the measurement criteria themselves are wholly or partly invalid. Yet reliability itself is an elusive ideal. Since information is necessarily partial and selective, we can never know the true reliability of any measurement instrument; only its estimated or probable reliability, expressed as a correlation coefficient between $+1.0$ for perfect reliability and $-1.0$ for total unreliability. A measuring instrument will have high reliability, first, if it repeatedly produces the same scores over time for specific levels of performance and, second, if it produces the same scores for any given performer when administered by a different assessor. A system is more likely to have high reliability if the measurements made by assessors are free of unintended or intended mismeasurement or error. Unreliable measurement may arise where the measures themselves are not explained clearly and consistently beforehand and where one assessor therefore applies different standards over time or where different assessors apply different standards at the one time. Unreliability may also arise where assessments are based on partial, incomplete or invalid measurement data. As we have seen in the case of performance assessment in the APS (in the Introduction), assessors may also make deliberately inaccurate assessments for personal and/or political reasons. In sum, reliability requires construct- and criterion-valid performance measures, measurement based on full evidence, and the consistent application of measures between assessors and over time.

## Cost-effectiveness

As we shall see in the chapters in part 2, over recent decades a great deal of time and energy has been invested in the pursuit of ever more reliable performance measurement instruments, and while reliability is clearly a necessary condition for system effectiveness, it is debatable whether technical accuracy alone is sufficient for this purpose. Moreover, beyond a point, the time and expense involved in the pursuit of ever more reliable performance measurement instruments may well be cost-prohibitive (if not counterproductive) in terms of return on investment. Hence, cost-effectiveness is also an important consideration in designing and managing any performance management system.

## Felt-fairness

However, those who take a more employee-centred approach to performance management matters contend that a requirement of no less importance is system felt-fairness. The argument here is that, to be effective, a performance management system should meet the test of felt-fairness, both in terms of the decision-making processes involved, or procedural fairness, and the outcomes delivered, or distributive fairness. Clearly, felt-unfairness has been a significant issue in the APS experience – and the APS is certainly not alone in this regard. We will have more to say about the matter of felt-fairness, or 'organisational justice' as it is termed in the academic literature, in the next chapter. For now, we need only note that we are not dealing here with normative fairness in any absolute moral or ethical sense;

rather the focus is on perceived fairness, which, depending on the employees and organisations involved, and, indeed, on the national cultural context involved, may be informed by a variety of normative positions on the nature of fairness and equity.

In sum, validity, reliability, cost-effectiveness and felt-fairness are distinct but overlapping requirements. Without valid performance criteria, reliable measurement is impossible; without both of these, it is highly likely that employees will see the system as being inherently unfair. Further, even if the system is fully valid, reliable and felt-fair, the system will still be unsustainable if, over time, it does not deliver a positive return on associated costs and investments. Ideally, then, a performance management system should strive to be simultaneously valid, reliable, cost-effective and fair. As we shall see, however, balancing these competing requirements is an extremely challenging task.

## 'Reward' and 'total reward'

Let us now consider briefly the basics of reward management. What is a 'reward'? A reward may be anything tangible or intangible that an organisation provides to its employees either intentionally or unintentionally in exchange for the employee's potential or actual work contribution, and to which employees as individuals attach a positive value as a satisfier of certain self-defined needs. On this definition, rewards can be seen as including not only financial rewards (i.e. 'pay', 'remuneration' or 'compensation') but also rewards of a beneficial non-financial nature. Such a broad definition means that the options for configuring a reward management system are extremely wide. Such a definition also accords with what is referred to in the practitioner literature (e.g. Fuehrer 1994; Kao & Kantor 2004: Zingheim & Schuster 2000b) as a 'total reward' approach.

What types of reward fall within the scope of a total reward approach? As figure 1.3 indicates, rewards can be divided into two broad categories: 'intrinsic' and extrinsic'.

Intrinsic rewards arise from the content of the job itself, including the interest and challenge that it provides, the task variety and autonomy, the degree of feedback, and the meaning and significance attributed to it. It follows that one of the most important determinants of the level of intrinsic rewards in any organisation is the way in which its jobs are designed. Extrinsic rewards arise from the factors associated with, but physically external to, the

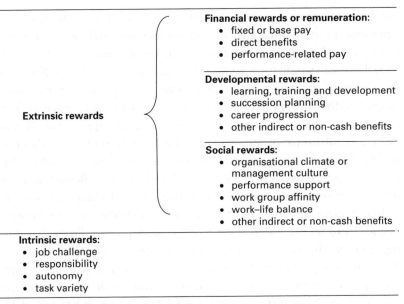

**Financial rewards or remuneration:**
- fixed or base pay
- direct benefits
- performance-related pay

**Developmental rewards:**
- learning, training and development
- succession planning
- career progression
- other indirect or non-cash benefits

**Social rewards:**
- organisational climate or management culture
- performance support
- work group affinity
- work–life balance
- other indirect or non-cash benefits

**Extrinsic rewards**

**Intrinsic rewards:**
- job challenge
- responsibility
- autonomy
- task variety

**Figure 1.3** Components of 'total reward'

job that the employee does; that is, from the job context. As we shall see in chapter 3, some theorists argue that intrinsic factors are the most powerful motivators of work effort.

Extrinsic rewards are of three main types: financial rewards, developmental rewards and social rewards. Developmental rewards cover those rewards associated with personal learning, development and career growth, such as skills training and performance and leadership coaching. Social rewards are those rewards and 'indirect' (or non-cash) benefits associated with the organisational climate, performance support, quality of supervision, work-group affinity, and opportunities for enhanced work–life balance, such as flexible work time arrangements, staff sabbaticals, fitness and wellness programs, and the like (considered further in chapter 13). Financial rewards (or pay, remuneration or 'compensation' to use the preferred North American term) are of three main types: base pay (the relatively fixed component of total remuneration); performance-related pay (which by definition varies with measured performance); and direct benefits, such as employer contributions to superannuation or pensions, health care, childcare and the like. We shall return to these categories of cash remuneration in a moment.

A key step in framing a total reward approach is to determine the respective roles of financial and non-financial rewards. This, in turn, may require an audit of the organisation to identify what non-financial rewards it provides and to ascertain whether these alone may be sufficient to promote desired behaviour. In some situations non-financial rewards may be able to play a role equal to, if not greater than, that of monetary rewards. This is very likely to be the case in voluntary not-for-profit organisations, such as welfare bodies, where workers may expect to receive little or no pay at all. Here the intrinsic rewards that flow from the work itself may be all that is expected. Indeed, paying people in such a situation may even prove counterproductive – it may extinguish intrinsic motivation. On the other hand, voluntary bodies may also need to hire employees for some tasks, in which case careful consideration would need to be given not only to the reward mix offered but also to differences in expectations and attitudes between paid and unpaid workers.

In other organisations, the need to strike an effective balance between financial and non-financial rewards will be ever-present. Firms that offer high job security, that enjoy a high level of prestige and public esteem or that provide opportunities for 'in-house' training and development might not have to offer as high a level of financial reward as do competitor firms that offer much less on the non-financial side. At the other end of the spectrum, a firm experiencing high labour turnover and low productivity because employees find their jobs boring and repetitive may opt to increase financial rewards substantially in order to meet staffing and performance requirements. Alternatively, it may choose to emphasise intrinsic rewards through job enrichment to make the work more interesting. In formulating an optimal approach to total reward management, then, each organisation will need to consider various combinations of intrinsic and extrinsic rewards.

## Remuneration

While non-financial rewards constitute an increasingly important aspect of a total reward management, financial rewards are almost always of primary importance in reward management practice. For this reason, in the chapters that follow, consideration of reward management options and methods will focus primarily, although by no means exclusively, on rewards of a monetary nature; that is, on remuneration.

What exactly do we mean by the term 'remuneration'? According to the dictionary definition, to 'remunerate' means to 'reward, pay for service rendered; . . . provide recompense for toil etc' (*Australian Concise Oxford Dictionary*, 7th edn, 1987, p. 935). The word most commonly used as a synonym for 'remuneration' is 'pay'. To 'pay' means to provide money in exchange from some other commodity or service deemed to be of equal value. In this respect, it is widely accepted that the two terms – 'remuneration' and 'pay' – can be used interchangeably. Employees receive pay in the form of a wage or salary in exchange for providing their labour (or, at least, their potential to perform labour) to the employer.

In the North American literature we also encounter another synonym, namely 'compensation'. In North America, this is the preferred term, partly because of its association with commercial and contract law. However, some commentators object that the term 'compensation' implies that employee remuneration has to do with 'making amends for the distasteful fact that people have to work for a living' (Armstrong 1996: 3); that pay is all about 'compensating' employees for sacrificing their leisure time by turning up to work. Thus the term 'compensation' carries negative connotations, whereas 'remuneration' and 'pay' are more value-neutral. So in this book the term 'compensation' will not be used at all, and the terms 'remuneration' and 'pay' will be used interchangeably.

In considering remuneration, however, it is also necessary to recognise that remuneration itself covers a number of distinct types of financial reward. Specifically, direct remuneration typically comprises three main categories of financial reward: (1) base pay, (2) direct benefits and (3) performance pay.

### Base pay

Base pay is the foundational component of employee remuneration. The traditional practice has been to fix base pay according to the *job* or *position* occupied, with periodic across-the-board adjustments to compensate job holders for increases in the cost of living. It is pay for the job rather than for the person in the job. Under this approach, employees increase their base pay by ascending a seniority-based promotional hierarchy of job pay grades, with each grade having only a relatively narrow pay range. Position-based base pay of this sort takes two distinct forms: wages and salaries. Waged remuneration is typically paid on the basis of a fixed rate of pay per hour, standard day or standard week worked, with a premium or 'penalty' rate for overtime (i.e. time worked in excess of standard hours). Time-based wages have traditionally been the main form of remuneration applied to manual and other 'blue-collar' jobs. In contrast, salaried employment involves annualised payment, typically carries no upper limit on hours to be worked, and is the main form of remuneration applied to executive, managerial and professional/'white-collar' positions. In recent times, however, the trend has been to structure base pay around the skills and competencies of the person rather than the 'size' of the job occupied, and to couple this to very different base pay structures. The differences between job-based and person-based approaches to managing base pay will be explored in detail in the chapters in part 3 of this book.

### Direct benefits

Direct benefits, which are essentially add-ons to base pay, include financial rewards, such as paid holiday leave, employer-funded superannuation, 'fringe benefits', such as employer-funded health care, life insurance, housing finance and the like, as well as provision of a company car, mobile phone and so on. The relative importance of direct benefits in the total remuneration package will depend very much on the nature of the prevailing tax regime and whether or not it encourages employees and employers to 'package up' benefits to minimise current and future tax liability. Benefits of a cash and non-cash nature are considered further in chapter 13.

### Performance pay

Performance pay covers incentives paid on the basis of performance delivered by employees either individually or collectively. An incentive is a payment made on the basis of past performance in order to reinforce and enhance future performance. Performance pay is usually an overlay to base pay, and it varies according to the level of measured or assessed performance. In short, performance pay is contingent or 'at risk', rather than fixed or guaranteed. There are many distinct forms of performance pay and they can be classified according to three key variables: the performance unit involved (individual, work-group, whole organisation); the performance criteria used (behaviour, results or both); and the time frame over which performance is measured (short-term or long-term). The main types of performance pay (as well as their non-cash alternatives) are detailed in the chapters in part 4.

## Purpose of reward management

What is it that organisations hope to obtain by offering rewards to their employees; that is, what should a system of reward management seek to do? In essence (and again in prescriptive mode) a reward system maintained by a work organisation is likely to have three primary objectives:

1  to *attract* the right people at the right time for the right jobs, tasks or roles
2  to *retain* the best people by recognising and rewarding their contribution
3  to *motivate* employees to contribute to the best of their capability.

Notice here the strong linkage between the reward and staffing functions (regarding the staff attraction and retention objectives) and between the reward and performance management functions (regarding motivation). In addition, a well-formulated and administered reward system is likely to have a number of important secondary objectives. In particular, it should seek to be:

- need-fulfilling: the rewards should be of value to employees in satisfying relevant human needs
- felt-fair, particularly in terms of offering rewards commensurate with contribution
- legal: it should comply with relevant legal requirements regarding employee rights and entitlements, including, of course, all mandatory benefits and minimum standards
- affordable: the rewards allocated, and any associated on-costs, should be within the organisation's financial means
- cost-effective: there should be an appropriate 'return on investment' from total reward outlays
- strategically aligned: as with performance management, reward management should support the organisation's corporate and business objectives.

Taken together, this is a particularly exacting set of objectives, and it is most unlikely that any organisation will be willing or able to achieve all of them simultaneously. Clearly the ill-fated H-P reward experiment of the mid-1990s (see the Introduction) fell well short of several of these objectives; not the least being motivation, felt-fairness, cost-effectiveness and strategic alignment. There is also considerable potential for conflict between the objectives themselves. For instance, one of the greatest challenges lies in reconciling the need for reward fairness with the objective of cost-effectiveness. Which is of greater importance? Dissatisfaction arising from perceptions of reward inequity can certainly lead to increased employee turnover and reduced motivation, but the costs and benefits of being a low payer will vary depending on the type of organisation involved. While some organisations may suffer serious performance impairment, others may be able to absorb these consequences and still meet their objectives. Tensions may also arise between the goal of cost-containment and that of offering rewards that are sufficient to attract and retain the right type and number of employees. From an organisational perspective, the optimal approach is not necessarily the cheapest. Rather, it is that which maximises the 'return' to the organisation for the 'investment' made, a point to which we shall return in later chapters.

The above checklist of generic objectives, then, represents a set of ideal reward system outcomes rather than a comprehensive blueprint for system effectiveness. Exactly how an organisation should set about configuring a reward system that best suits its needs and those of its employees is something that we shall explore in detail in subsequent chapters.

## Chapter summary

In this chapter, we have explored the multiple meanings of 'performance' and 'rewards', the main elements of performance and reward systems, and the possible uses to which such systems may be put. Central to this discussion has been the proposition that neither the meanings nor the composition of such systems are preordained. In a very real sense, the key challenges in managing such systems are not merely those to do with system structuring but, rather, those associated with investing them with clear purpose and meaning, especially for those more intimately affected by them. It is to these more complex matters of employee mindset that we must now turn.

## Discussion questions

1 Who or what defines 'performance' in an organisation?
2 Why might evaluative and developmental performance management come into conflict, and how can the potential for conflict be minimised?
3 A valid method of assessing performance may be either reliable or unreliable, but an invalid method can never be reliable. Why?
4 What is meant by the concept of 'total reward'?
5 What should a reward system seek to do?

## Chapter Two

# WORKING WITH PSYCHOLOGY

To be effective, performance and reward management systems should encourage employees to demonstrate consistently those types of work behaviour and results that are deemed necessary to support the organisation's strategic objectives and desired corporate culture. More so than other human resource practices, performance and reward management systems also exist to shape and reshape employee work behaviour in ways desired by the organisation. Yet, as the examples of performance and reward system dysfunction noted in the Introduction attest, establishing and maintaining the desired association between performance and reward practices, on the one hand, and behavioural outcomes, on the other, is no simple matter. Performance and reward practices sometimes go badly awry, eliciting not the wanted work behaviour but, rather, systemic misbehaviour. The means to avoiding such unfortunate behavioural consequences lie not in the behaviour itself but in understanding and influencing the factors that help to shape work behaviour – and, above all else, this requires close consideration of employee work attitudes and what has come to be known as the employee 'psychological contract'.

In this chapter, we explore the complex links between employee attitudes and behaviour. Drawing on the concept of the employee-centred 'psychological contract', the chapter also presents a basic employee-centred framework for better understanding and influencing employee attitudes and behaviour in ways beneficial to both the organisation and the employees themselves. The chapter opens with a discussion of the three main categories of work behaviour, then moves to an overview of the three key attitudinal categories, as well as considering some of the possible associations between the two sets of categories. With these propositions in mind, the chapter next introduces the reader to the nature and practical significance of the notion of the 'psychological contract'. This is followed by consideration of the set of perceptual factors that are widely regarded as lying at the centre of the employee psychological contract, namely perceptions of 'organisational justice' and injustice.

# Work behaviour

Work behaviour is the observable, describable and verifiable actions that directly influence work outcomes – or results – in either a desired or undesired way. But exactly what types of behaviour should performance and reward management systems seek to elicit? While the range of possible attitudes and behaviour is virtually limitless, it is possible to identify three broad types of behaviour that most organisations will require to some degree.

The three key types of behaviour that most organisations are likely to deem desirable are: 'membership behaviour', 'task behaviour' and 'organisational citizenship behaviour' (Long 2006: 79–97). The first two categories cover what might be termed job or role compliance behaviour, but organisational citizenship behaviour is qualitatively different and generally more elusive. Let us examine each of these three behavioural categories more closely, beginning with the most basic behaviour of all: membership behaviour.

## Membership behaviour

Membership behaviour is demonstrated when an employee decides to join and remain with an organisation. The observable characteristics of high membership behaviour include low absenteeism, low staff turnover, a high level of outsider interest in being recruited to the organisation, and longer internal job tenure; in other words, high levels of staff attraction and retention.

Note, however, that turning up to work regularly is not the same as actually doing work. Why, then, is membership behaviour important to the organisation? Simply because without it the organisation will lack access to an adequate and reliable supply of those human capabilities and contributions that it needs to survive and succeed. Membership behaviour, then, is a prerequisite for all other forms of work behaviour in all work organisations. This is so even where the work does not require the employee to be physically present on a regular basis in an office or other workspace, as in most forms of home-based working (telecommuting, outwork) and in field work (sales representatives, field maintenance). Whatever the actual workspace involved, the employee is still required to 'present' for work.

However, not all organisations will be interested in retaining the same employees for long periods of time. Indeed, in some cases, too much membership behaviour and too little turnover can be organisationally disastrous: too much 'old blood' and too little 'new blood'!

## Task behaviour

Task behaviour occurs when employees perform specific work tasks that have been assigned to them and which form part of the organisation's core work activities. The chief signifier of task behaviour is work effort: the actions that the employee takes towards completing assigned tasks. Indeed, the two are essentially one and the same. All organisations will naturally be interested in securing task behaviour since this, by definition, is associated with acceptable task performance. Borman and Motowidlo (1993: 73) define task performance as 'the proficiency with which job incumbents perform activities that are formally recognised as part of their jobs . . . activities that contribute to the organization's technical core either directly by implementing a part of its technological process, or indirectly by providing it with needed materials or services'.

As with membership behaviour, then, task behaviour has to do with compliance with the formal requirements of the job or role to which the employee is assigned.

## Organisational citizenship behaviour

By contrast, organisational citizenship behaviour occurs when employees voluntarily and altruistically undertake special actions that exceed membership and task compliance. This might involve extra effort, high cooperation with others, high initiative, high innovativeness, extra customer service, and a general willingness to make sacrifices for the good of the organisation.

The concept itself derives from research undertaken by Dennis Organ and colleagues on the sources of 'good soldier' behaviour in the US military (Bateman & Organ 1983; Organ 1988b). In common usage, voluntary, altruistic and conscientious behaviour of this sort is also known as 'discretionary effort' or simply 'going the extra mile'. In the academic literature it is also termed 'extra-role' or 'pro-social' behaviour. It is also linked to what Borman and Motowidlo (1993, 1997) term 'contextual' performance. This involves employees using their energy and ability to support the organisation's social, cultural and psychological environment in which the technical core functions, rather than supporting the technical core directly. Whereas task performance is job-specific, contextual performance is said to be common to many or even all jobs. According to Borman and Motowidlo (1993: 73, 82) contextual performance has five main components:

1 behaviour such as volunteering to carry out task activities that are not formally part of the job
2 persisting with extra enthusiasm or effort to complete one's own task activities
3 helping and cooperating with others
4 following organisational rules and procedures even when personally inconvenient
5 endorsing, supporting and defending organisational objectives.

Why might an organisation desire such behaviour from its employees? The answer is that discretionary effort of this type is frequently considered to be the defining characteristic of high work performance. Logically, employees who do more than their job description requires of them should contribute more to organisational effectiveness than those who adhere strictly to the task script. As we shall see in subsequent chapters, such behaviour tends to feature prominently in the high-range performance descriptors included in many contemporary individual performance assessment instruments.

Yet such behaviour may not always be beneficial to the organisation, and some organisations may even view it as undesirable or counter-productive. For instance, in a firm with a strict division of labour, narrow task assignments and a tightly controlled production process, employees who habitually go out of their way to assist others may well not fulfil their own assigned tasks.

By its very nature, organisational citizenship behaviour is also problematic to 'manage'. Borman and Motowidlo (1993: 93–4) highlight three main 'pitfalls' here. First, it is paradoxical to *require* employees to volunteer to do more than their jobs specifically call for, as opposed to *inviting* them to do so. Second, making such performance behaviour an explicit expectation could well be self-defeating since it may well lead employees to concentrate on helping others and to neglect their own tasks. Third, the requirement that employees will proactively and enthusiastically support organisational values, rules and procedures leaves little room for healthy dissent or the advancement of new ideas that may run counter to prevailing management wisdom. The upshot may be an organisation peopled by 'yes men' and paralysed by corporate 'group think'.

What is really at issue here is the appropriate balance between task behaviour and organisational citizenship behaviour. There is no doubt that citizenship behaviour is assuming greater importance in managerial work and for non-managerial work in service sector and knowledge-based organisations. In these cases, work is often self-managed, customer-focused, interdependent, fluid and underpinned by the need for considerable inter-personal skills. Such work is also likely to yield outcomes that are largely intangible and therefore not amenable to more objective measures of perfor-mance. However, even in such work settings, it is not at all clear that citizen-ship behaviour should be accorded *primary* importance. While endorsing strategies for encouraging citizenship behaviour, Borman and Motowidlo (1993: 95) note that even in managerial work, such behaviour may consti-tute no more than 30 per cent of the total performance domain. For line employees engaged in routine manual and mechanised task execution, the balance in favour of task behaviour would be substantially higher still.

## Work attitudes

No human resource practice will elicit any of the above categories of behaviour *directly*. Practices first affect employee attitudes, and it is these cognitions that will influence behaviour in some way, although not always in the desired manner. What is an attitude? In relation to work, an atti-tude is a conscious state of mind about aspects of the self, the work context and/or the relationship between self and context. Attitudes may also involve strong value orientations and emotions – that is, 'affective states' – about the self, relationships and/or the work context. Values and emotions are not necessarily consciously held, but they may still have a powerful influence on associated attitudes. In turn, attitudes may or may not have behavioural consequences. They may drive behaviour; they may lie dormant. For our pur-poses, work attitudes (and associated emotions) are perhaps best thought of as cognitive predispositions or inclinations towards certain courses of action (i.e. observable behaviour) and away from others. Exactly what attitudes are we talking about here? There are really three main attitudinal categories that we need to consider: 'motivation', 'job satisfaction' and 'organisational commitment'.

## Motivation

Motivation is the wellspring of task behaviour or effort, and it refers to the strength of a person's willingness to perform allotted work tasks – to undertake work effort. To motivate means to energise the individual to deliver work effort and task behaviour. The term itself derives from the Latin word *movere*, meaning 'to move' (Steers & Porter 1991: 5–6). However, motivation is not a homogeneous or indivisible phenomenon. It can be broken down into various elements. When we study motivation, then, we are really concerned with three related aspects of task behaviour:

1 the *direction* of that behaviour: why people take certain actions rather than others; e. g. emphasising product quantity over quality
2 the *intensity* of that behaviour: why the actions taken involve either a lot of effort, or a little
3 the *duration* of that behaviour: why some actions are more sustained and enduring than others (Kanfer 1998).

We shall explore the matter of motivation in more detail in the next chapter. For now, we simply need to note two basic points. First, the wellsprings of work motivation are more complex and controversial than we might imagine, and it is vital that we not allow our thinking on this subject to be dominated by *a priori* assumptions. What moves one individual to deliver solid and sustained work effort may have little motivational effect on other employees, or may have more behavioural impact in some work contexts and climates than in others. In fact, it is this very variety of possibilities that makes motivation such an absorbing field of academic study and management practice. Second, as our discussion so far suggests, motivation is by no means the only important work attitude. Its significance needs to be understood in context, not in isolation.

## Job satisfaction

Job satisfaction refers to the overall positive or negative attitude that employees hold towards the job and the job context. In other words, how contented or discontented are employees with the totality of their job assignment? In this sense, job satisfaction is also an affective state – that is, an emotional condition – as well as an attitude. As a holistic summative feeling about the job, it covers both the job content – or factors 'intrinsic' to the job – and the job context – or factors surrounding or associated with the job, such as work relationships, work culture and human resource practices, including those to do with performance and reward management. As such, job satisfaction can be said to subsume attitudes and affective states to do with more specific aspects of the job, such as satisfaction or dissatisfaction with performance management procedures and outcomes, reward determination processes and outcomes (i.e. reward satisfaction), career development opportunities and the like. As we shall see later in this chapter, job satisfaction also has a close but complex association with other affective states, particularly perceptions of organisational justice and injustice.

## Organisational commitment

Organisational commitment has to do with the strength of the employee's attachment to the organisation. This sense of attachment may be conscious and rational, or subconscious, non-rational and deeply emotional, or a mixture of both. In general organisational commitment covers one or more of the following: a sense of shared goals and values with the organisation; a feeling of organisational belongingness; and an intention to remain with the organisation.

The classic taxonomy of organisational commitment is that by Meyer and Allen (1991). This identifies three main attitudinal 'components' of organisational commitment: (1) affective commitment, (2) normative commitment and (3) continuance commitment. Affective commitment relates to the employee's emotional attachment to, identification with and involvement in the organisation. Employees with strong affective commitment will remain with that organisation because they want to; because they identify with it emotionally, and because their sense of self-identity and self-worth is closely intertwined with their involvement in the organisation. This is commitment that is genuinely 'from the heart'.

Continuance commitment, by contrast, is calculative and non-emotional; it comes from the head rather than the heart. People who feel only continuance commitment will remain with the organisation only because, for now, they perceive that the costs associated with leaving the organisation outweigh the anticipated benefits of leaving. Employees whose main link to the organisation is based on continuance commitment remain with it only because they feel that they need to, at least for the moment. So continuance commitment is about *needing* to stay with the organisation.

Normative commitment reflects a feeling of obligation to remain with the organisation. Employees with high normative commitment feel that they ought to stay with the organisation even though they may have little or no emotional attachment to it. It is about feeling a moral *obligation* to stay, at least for a time. For instance, an employee who has had the benefit of in-house training and development may feel an ethical obligation to stay with the organisation long enough to repay the perceived debt even though it may be in their best material interest to move to another organisation that is prepared to pay a higher price for their enhanced productive capacity – or 'human capital'.

It is important to note that these three dimensions are not mutually exclusive. In fact, an employee's overall commitment to the organisation can best be thought of as consisting of varying levels of all three components. It should also be recognised that, whatever its apparent attractions, affective commitment will not be universally desired. Not all organisations will want to be 'loved' by their employees; as we shall see in chapter 3, some may even prefer employees to leave both their hearts and their heads at the office or factory gate. An overweening commitment to the organisation may also be decidedly unhealthy for both parties, particularly if it leads to workaholism, work stress and staff burnout.

Further, it cannot be assumed that employee commitment is unidimensional. There is now ample evidence that employee outlook is informed by multiple and sometimes competing commitments. As well as – or perhaps in competition with – commitment to 'the organisation', employees may have strong emotional attachments to other work-related and non-work entities: their families, their fellow workers, their clients or customers, their profession or trade or their union. As such, and as recent interest in work–life balance matters attests, commitment to the organisation can neither be understood nor managed in isolation from other aspects of employees' life experience and outlook (Iverson & Buttigieg 1999).

## Attitudes and behaviour: associations and antecedents

I have suggested above that attitudes and associated affective states (i.e. values and emotions) prefigure behaviour and behavioural outcomes. But how might the above sets of attitudes and behaviour interrelate? Do certain attitudes predict particular types of behaviour? Moreover, in terms of behavioural effects, do certain attitudes prefigure or reinforce other attitudes? Building chiefly on theoretical and empirical insights from

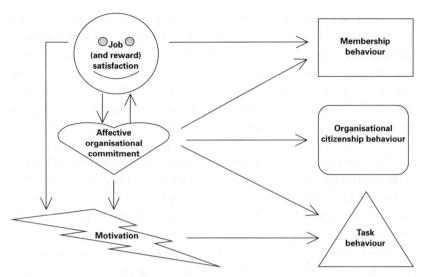

**Figure 2.1** Hypothesised relationships between work attitudes and work behaviour

organisational psychology (Heneman & Judge 2000; Long 2006: 66–70; Meyer & Topolnytsky 2000; Meyer & Herscovitch 2001; Meyer et al. 2002; Organ 1988a; Organ & Ryan 1995; Schappe 1998) we postulate a number of causal associations between work attitudes and work behaviour, as well as between attitudinal categories themselves. These are described diagrammatically in figure 2.1. We are not suggesting that these behavioural effects are inevitable; rather we are proposing that they are possible and, in the right circumstances, probable.

Turning first to motivation, as noted above, where the context is conducive, a willingness to deliver task effort is likely to lead to task behaviour that may in turn produce desired results. However, since motivation is specific to the task domain, it will not have a direct influence on either of the other two behavioural categories. Moreover, as figure 2.1 indicates, unlike the other two attitudinal categories, motivation is best thought of as a dependent attitudinal variable rather than an interactive variable. It may be enhanced or impaired by satisfaction and commitment but does not itself intensify or detract from these more deeply embedded attitudinal states. Beyond these generalities, however, there is considerable disagreement as to the main determinants of motivational strength, and we shall return to this central issue in the next chapter.

Second, job (and reward) satisfaction is likely to influence membership behaviour directly. Why? Because all else being equal, employees who are more satisfied with their rewards and job conditions are likely to engage in less absenteeism and to show a greater desire to remain with the organisation. Happier workers are likely to present for work on a more regular basis because they will be less stressed and will harbour fewer work-disrupting grievances. Satisfied employees will keep turning up to work because they judge that the extrinsic and/or intrinsic rewards on offer for doing so meet a substantial number of their material and/or emotional needs and significantly outweigh the costs associated with turning up to work, including the cost of lost leisure time. If the opposite applies, membership behaviour and affective commitment will be low and labour absenteeism and turnover correspondingly high.

Notice, too, that job (and reward) satisfaction may also have an indirect effect on organisational citizenship behaviour, via affective commitment, as well as on task behaviour, via motivation. In other words, the influence of job satisfaction on citizenship and task behaviour is mediated, respectively, by the strength of affective commitment and motivation. Hence, job and reward satisfaction will have a positive influence on citizenship behaviour only if the employee also has high affective commitment. Similarly, it will have a positive influence on task behaviour only where motivation is also high. This is because workers who are happy with their jobs (and their pay) are less likely to want to leave, which will certainly mean lower replacement costs, but they are not necessarily more productive in what they do. A satisfied employee may not be a more highly motivated employee at all (Organ 1988a). In fact, contentedness with the job and with rewards may foster task complacency. What we can be sure of, however, is that employees who are dissatisfied with their jobs and rewards will not only show less membership behaviour but will also feel less committed to the organisation and less highly motivated, which means that all three behavioural categories are likely to be negatively affected. Dissatisfaction with pay or other rewards can have disastrous consequences for work behaviour, workplace relationships and organisational effectiveness (Heneman & Judge 2000).

Finally, turning to affective organisational commitment, we suggest that it is likely to influence not only all three behavioural categories but also both other attitudinal categories. While Organ and others (Organ 1994, 1997; Moorman, Niehoff & Organ 1993) contend that citizenship behaviour is a function of multiple attitudinal, affective and contextual variables, affective commitment does appear to be a necessary condition for sustained citizenship behaviour (Organ & Ryan 1995; Meyer et al. 2002). When employees feel a strong sense of identification with the organisation, its values and objectives and its clients or customers, they are far more likely to exhibit citizenship behaviour. Equally, they will pursue organisational goals in an energetic and innovative way, will have low turnover, low absenteeism and low dissatisfaction, and will find the thought of 'cheating the boss' repugnant. More committed employees will not only exhibit a higher level of citizenship but are also likely to be both more satisfied and more highly motivated, which in turn translates to higher membership behaviour and greater task effort (Schappe 1998). In short, high affective commitment can intensify all other attitudinal and behavioural factors, whereas its absence can have a suppressive effect across all attitudinal and behavioural categories.

So the possible associations between work attitudes and behaviour seem relatively clear. But if attitudes shape behaviour, what is it that shapes attitudes themselves? We have noted that work attitudes interact with each other, so attitudes can be seen as mutually reinforcing, at least to a degree. But this really sheds little light on attitudinal *origins*. Where do work attitudes (and associated emotions) really come from? For instance, what determines the strength of an employee's affective commitment to the organisation and, hence, their predisposition towards organisational citizenship behaviour?

Some commentators suggest that the primary determinants of most if not all work attitudes and behaviour are personality traits. In terms of orthodox psychological theory, 'personality' may be defined as those conscious and unconscious attributes or 'traits' that shape individual being: how we see ourselves as individuals, how others see us, and how we think and behave in daily life. The most widely accepted and applied taxonomy of person-ality 'factors' or 'traits' is the 'five-factor model'. Also known as the 'Big Five', this identifies five primary factors that are said to underlie personality, namely emotional stability, extraversion, openness to experience, agree-ableness and conscientiousness. Of these, conscientiousness is frequently nominated as the most valid predictor of job performance, and there is considerable research evidence that it is positively related to a wide range of performance criteria across many occupational categories (Barrick & Mount 1991; Hurtz & Donovan 2000; Mount & Barrick 1998). Consci-entiousness is also commonly seen as having a positive association with citizenship behaviour (Hattrup, O'Connell & Wingate 1998; Hogan et al. 1998; Konovsky & Organ 1996; Organ 1994).

However, other studies indicate that the relationship between personal-ity and performance is mediated by situationally specific factors (Latham &

Pinder 2005: 489). Tett and Burnett (2003) propose a person–situation interactionist model of job performance in which trait-expressive behaviour is elicited and maximised only in situations where it is valued and encouraged by peers and management. A particular trait may be related to job performance positively, negatively or neutrally, depending on the situation. For instance, conscientiousness may actually inhibit desired results when timeliness and fast turnaround are at a premium, while agreeableness will be counterproductive in the context of robust business contract negotiation. In sum, personality traits appear to be important in predicting some work attitudes, behaviour and performance aspects, but job context and job characteristics will also have an important mediating or moderating effect (Latham & Pinder 2005: 490).

Of course, some critics question the relevance and worth of personality constructs and assessment to performance and performance management. For instance, Spillane and Martin (2005: 253, 255) assert that 'efforts to predict performance from personality tests have been consistently and spectacularly unsuccessful' and that 'personality and performance are not related'. While many would disagree with these assertions, at the very least they remind us of the need for caution regarding claimed associations between personality, behaviour and performance outcomes, especially propositions of a reductionistic nature. When it comes to work performance, personality certainly is not all-important; indeed, by itself, it may not be very important at all.

In the next section, we consider an explanatory model that, while recognising the potential influence of personality, arguably offers a better means of understanding and perhaps managing the complex associations between employee experience, expectations, perceptions, emotions, attitudes and behavioural performance – the concept of the employee-centred psychological contract.

## The psychological contract

While the notion of the 'psychological contract' can be traced to the writings of Argyris (1960), Levinson (1970), Schein (2004) and the social exchange theorists of the 1960s (Anderson & Schalk 1998; Conway & Briner 2005: 7–14), the concept has only recently found its way into the mainstream of academic and practitioner thinking about the employment relationship, due largely to its 'seminal reconceptualisation' in the late 1980s by the

US organisational psychologist Denise Rousseau (Conway & Briner 2005: 14–15; Cullinane & Dundon 2006; Rousseau 1989).

In a legal sense, of course, a contract is a written or verbal agreement about the mutual responsibilities of parties in an exchange relationship, involving a promise, an acceptance and a payment or other 'consideration'. A psychological contract, however, has to do with the perceptions and expectations by each party as to what they and the other party have undertaken to give and to receive in exchange. As such, it may overlap with, but also differ from, and extend beyond, matters codified in written contracts of employment. So a psychological contract both fills the perceptual gaps in the written employment relationship and shapes employer and employee behaviour in ways that cannot necessarily be discerned from a written contract. Why do such 'contracts' exist at all? The reason is that, as noted in the Introduction, the employment exchange is typically open-ended, imprecise and only partly codified, which necessarily leaves the parties to their own devices to 'fill in the gaps' in line with their perceptions of what is promised and what is required. Hence, for our purposes, the psychological contract may be defined as the subjective understandings or perceptions of the 'promissory-based reciprocal exchanges' between the employee and the employer or employing organisation (Conway & Briner 2005: 35; Rousseau 1989).

Following its reappearance in the mainstream management literature in the 1990s, the basis and scope of the psychological contract was the subject of considerable debate (Conway & Briner 2005: 20–36). However, there is now a broad consensus that while management is interested in shaping the content of the implicit employment 'deal' by means of an 'espoused' psychological contract, it is the nature of the psychological contract (or contracts) embraced by employees that is of primary importance and interest. There is also general agreement that the employee psychological contract is mutable and fragile. Moreover even those writing from a critical poststructuralist perspective (e. g. Cullinane & Dundon 2006; Grant & Shields 2006), who tend to see the construct as a managerialist device rather than as a descriptive tool, acknowledge its potential significance for management effectiveness.

Being perceptual and subjective, the employee psychological contract is characterised by limited rationality in that it reflects the employee's incomplete, selective and possibly distorted view of the basis of relationship and the exchange or 'deal' (Rousseau & Ho 2000: 277–9). Even if promises are made clearly, explicitly and consistently, this does not guarantee that both parties will share, or continue to share, a common understanding of all contract terms. The possibility of perceptual incongruence increases

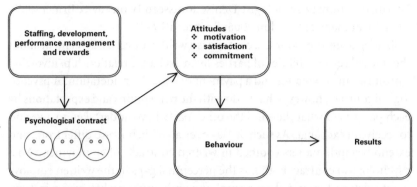

The psychological contract: *perceptions* of mutual obligations by which both parties to the employment relationship interpret, act and respond to each other.

**Figure 2.2** Behaviour, attitudes and the psychological contract

the likelihood of contractual disagreement and disharmony – or 'breach'. Employee perceptions may be influenced by self-serving bias and errors in causal attribution. Further, since psychological contracts are unwritten, subjective and transient, analysing and influencing them pose significant challenges for management (Robinson & Rousseau 1994; Rousseau 1989). Herein lies a major management dilemma, however, since the attitudinal and behavioural consequences of psychological contract mismanagement may be disastrous for an organisation (Morrison & Robinson 1997).

## A model of the employee psychological contract

Figure 2.2 illustrates a proposed general relationship between human resource management practices, the psychological contract, employee attitudes and behaviour, and work results. The notion of the psychological contract helps us to explain why, provided core management and employee expectations are met and promises and obligations are fulfilled, the employment relationship may be positive, harmonious and productive. Conversely, if expectations or promises and obligations are not met, the perceived contractual 'breach' may give rise to negative work attitudes, behaviour and relationships. A contractual breach occurs when one party experiences a discrepancy between the actual fulfilment of obligations by the other party and what that party has previously promised to do; that is, a perceived breach of promise and trust (Robinson 1996). The perceived breach may either be short-lived or develop into an enduring sense of injustice, betrayal or 'violation' (Pate, Martin & McGoldrick 2003; Robinson & Rousseau 1994). Breach may impair key attitudinal drivers, including satisfaction, commitment and motivation. Violation may produce a range of negative work behaviour ranging from lower levels of discretionary effort to higher absenteeism, sabotage and exit (Anderson & Schalk 1998: 643–4; Conway & Briner 2005: 63–87; Coyle-Shapiro 2002; Morrison & Robinson 1997; Robinson 1996).

Given the fragile nature of the employee psychological contract, breach and violation are relatively common (Morrison & Robinson 1997; Robinson & Rousseau 1994: 247). A number of factors may trigger a perceived contractual violation breach from the employee perspective. First, the employer may renege on a promise, say by cutting pay or withholding a promised increase or bonus, or by imposing longer hours of work. Second, there may be an incongruence of expectations between the parties, perhaps because the deal was not well explained at the time of hire or because it was misunderstood. For instance, an employee whose perception was initially positive may come to see the original deal as unfair in the light of new information received. Or a job applicant who may have received inaccurate information on the rewards or workload applicable to the position sooner or later realises that she has been misinformed, and sees this 'incongruence' as a breach of promise. Third, breach may arise from 'contract drift'; that is, a gradual divergence of perceptions between the parties involved as to what the exchange was, is and should be about. Some circumstances that may lead to contract drift include organisational change (restructure, merger, acquisition), downsizing and loss of job security, the substitution of casuals for permanent employees and other forms of workforce reprofiling, and a growth in pay inequality between the top and the bottom of the organisational hierarchy. Perceived violations of this type may affect all three key employee attitudes, but they will have an especially severe impact on organisational commitment.

Since our interest lies chiefly in identifying the factors that may influence employee expectations, outlook and actions, we need to consider what might lie within employee psychological contracts. In this regard, we believe that Guest's extended model of the psychological contract, from the employee perspective, represents a particularly useful way of understanding the attitudinal and behavioural impact of employment practices at the scale of the individual employee (Guest 1998: 659–60). Figure 2.3 presents a modified version of Guest's proposed model of the employee psychological contact. Rather than representing the phenomenon as a homogeneous state of mind, Guest identifies three factor categories linked in a linear fashion: causes, content and consequences. Causes, or inputs to the contract, include

**Figure 2.3** A model of the psychological contract (employee perspective)
*Source:* adapted from Guest 1998.

both organisational contextual factors (culture, climate, leadership style, human resource strategy and practices) and those specific to the individual employee (prior experience, work–life expectations, self-defined needs, socialised values and beliefs about work and the nature of the employment relationship and personality). Content, or the state and basis of the contract, has three main cognitive-affective components: trust, sense of 'delivery on the deal' and felt-fairness. Trust is essential to the maintenance of a positive psychological contact. It is also more easily destroyed than fostered or retrieved (Kramer 1999; Robinson 1996). As we shall see, felt-fairness can be disaggregated into three main 'organisational justice' perceptions: procedural justice, distributive justice and interactional justice. Consequences include key attitudes, such as job satisfaction or dissatisfaction, job security or insecurity, organisational commitment, and motivation, as well as the full range of work behaviour, from interpersonal and work relations and prescribed task performance to attendance or absence and organisational citizenship behaviour (Guest 1998: 660–1).

Guest's model is helpful to us in four main respects. First, by identifying three specific perceptions that are said to form the basis of the psychological contract, it allows us to overcome the limitations of having to view the psychological contract as an unknowable 'black box' of employee cognitions and emotions. Second, by recognising the influence of social 'inputs' it allows us to transcend the construct's otherwise highly individualised nature; to identify relationships between the psychology of the individual and the attitudes and behaviour of the group. Third, while recognising that management style and practice do constitute important 'inputs' to the process, there are also other causal factors over which management will have little or no control. Employee perceptions cannot simply be fashioned at will by management; the scope for shaping or reshaping employee attitudes will be limited (or perhaps even broadened) by the employee's prior experiences, socialisation, personality and expectations. Fourth, Guest offers us a way of thinking about work psychology as a dynamic rather than static phenomenon; specifically, it allows us to trace causal and other dynamic associations over time. This, of course, is of particular relevance to the management of change in human resource practice. In stable contexts, an existing psychological contract is likely to be reaffirmed by custom, practice and norms of contribution, with substantial convergence between employer and employee understandings of the basis of the exchange. However, a change in management practice heightens the possibility of incongruity between promise and fulfilment and, hence, the potential for perceived violation.

There is a growing body of research evidence in support of these propositions. The level of trust has been found to be a critical factor in employee outlook and behaviour. Robinson (1996) reports that when trust deteriorates, employee satisfaction and commitment falls, as does motivation and discretionary effort. Likewise, in their study of customer service employees, Deery, Iverson and Walshe (2006) find that psychological contract breach is related to lower organisational trust, which arises when employees perceive a discrepancy between the organisation's espoused behaviour and its actual behaviour, and that this, in turn, increases voluntary absenteeism. Trust is also affected by the consistency or inconsistency of management communication. In a study of change management in three large British organisations, Stiles et al. (1997) found that the presence of mixed messages from management regarding performance management practices eroded positive work relations. Regarding contractual inputs, Ho (2005) finds that social values and referents play a major role in shaping employee evaluations of psychological contact fulfilment. For instance, because of their social values or their choice of social comparators, under-performers may still believe that a performance reward should have been forthcoming and that the organisation has breached its promise. As we shall see below (in our discussion of equity theory), the choice of social referent or comparator group plays a major role in shaping the employee perceptions of reward satisfaction and distributive fairness. Similarly, employee contractual evaluations are likely to be informed by social and work group norms and, as Deery, Iverson and Walsh (2006: 167) suggest, psychological contracts thus have both individual and collective dimensions: 'Where individuals in a work unit have a shared understanding of the terms of their psychological contract, there will be a tendency for them to reinforce each other's assessments of it and perceive breaches by observing organizational practices affecting fellow employees . . . In such circumstances, individual attitudes can coalesce, and work groups can agree on their interpretation of their organization's behaviour.'

## Management-espoused psychological contracts

While Rousseau (1989: 126) suggests that psychological contracts are borne by the employee rather than management or the organisation, she also notes that organisations provide the context for the creation of the perceived contract or 'deal' and that management does seek to foster particular types of employee psychological contract by means of the reward and other human resource practices applied (1990: 399). In this respect, Rousseau (1990; Rousseau & Ho 2000) offers us a useful means of distinguishing between different types management-espoused deal. Rousseau identifies four contractual types: 'relational', 'transactional', 'balanced' and 'transitional'. Figure 2.4 summarises the main points of difference between the four in terms of their approach to employee performance and reward, with the two chief distinguishing dimensions being desired duration and degree of performance contingency. In essence, these describe differences in the unwritten or implicit employment relationship that senior management will wish employees to embrace.

Relational contracts are characterised as being long-term, entailing a promise of employment security and internal training and promotion opportunities in exchange for employee loyalty over the long term, with rewards that are primarily guaranteed rather than performance contingent and that emphasise internal equity. Benefit provision may be high but, overall, reward levels may not be particularly high by external market standards. Transactional contracts, by contrast, focus on short-term exchange, where there is no promise of long-term retention and where rewards are chiefly financial and tied explicitly to individual performance, particularly measured results. Since such contracts are characterised by high voluntary turnover, employers will generally need to offer high financial rewards in order to induce employees to stay. Balanced contracts are basically hybrids of the relational and transactional, emphasising recognition and reward of both

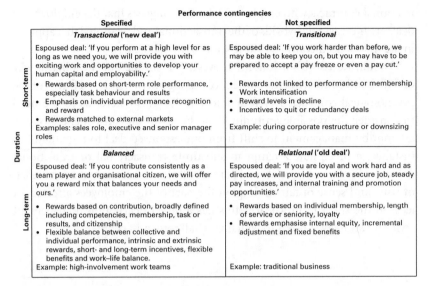

| | | Performance contingencies | |
|---|---|---|---|
| | | **Specified** | **Not specified** |
| **Duration** | **Short-term** | *Transactional* ('new deal')<br><br>Espoused deal: 'If you perform at a high level for as long as we need you, we will provide you with exciting work and opportunities to develop your human capital and employability.'<br><br>• Rewards based on short-term role performance, especially task behaviour and results<br>• Emphasis on individual performance recognition and reward<br>• Rewards matched to external markets<br>Examples: sales role, executive and senior manager roles | *Transitional*<br><br>Espoused deal: 'If you work harder than before, we may be able to keep you on, but you may have to be prepared to accept a pay freeze or even a pay cut.'<br><br>• Rewards not linked to performance or membership<br>• Work intensification<br>• Reward levels in decline<br>• Incentives to quit or redundancy deals<br><br>Example: during corporate restructure or downsizing |
| | **Long-term** | *Balanced*<br><br>Espoused deal: 'If you contribute consistently as a team player and organisational citizen, we will offer you a reward mix that balances your needs and ours.'<br><br>• Rewards based on contribution, broadly defined including competencies, membership, task or results, and citizenship<br>• Flexible balance between collective and individual performance, intrinsic and extrinsic rewards, short- and long-term incentives, flexible benefits and work–life balance.<br>Example: high-involvement work teams | *Relational* ('old deal')<br><br>Espoused deal: 'If you are loyal and work hard and as directed, we will provide you with a secure job, steady pay increases, and internal training and promotion opportunities.'<br><br>• Rewards based on individual membership, length of service or seniority, loyalty<br>• Rewards emphasise internal equity, incremental adjustment and fixed benefits<br><br>Example: traditional business |

**Figure 2.4** Management-espoused psychological contracts
*Source:* adapted from Rousseau & Ho 2000: 298 and Brown & Armstrong 1999: 300.

individual contribution and collective performance, and short-term and long-term exchange, as well as a flexible total reward approach combining intrinsic, financial, developmental and social rewards. Transitional contracts are essentially short-term crisis-driven deals emphasising work intensification and cost-cutting with little or no positive return to the employee apart from the possibility of selective job retention (Rousseau 1990; Rousseau & Ho 2000: 297–304).

According to Rousseau, the distinction between espoused relational and transactional psychological contracts captures neatly the marked changes in Western management thinking about the employment relationship since the 1980s, especially the abandonment of long-term employment obligations and position-based pay, and the pursuit of greater workplace 'flexibility' and reward systems that are strongly performance linked (Guest 1998: 659), or what Lawler (2005: 11) refers to as 'the death of the loyalty contract'. Some commentators (e.g. Tulgan & Greene 1999) have suggested that transactional contracts, and the performance-contingent rewards that typify them, are especially apposite to members of 'Generation X'. This is not to suggest that relational contracts are anachronistic. Rousseau suggests that there are many examples of highly successful organisations that maintain relational contracts with employees. She also suggests that the employment deals are increasingly hybrids of the transactional and relational that approximate to balanced contracts (Rousseau & Ho 2000: 300).

Overall, Rousseau's taxonomy represents a simple but meaningful way of fixing and comparing the content of management-espoused forms of the psychological contract. Her four-fold typology also alerts us to the need to consider the possible attitudinal and behavioural consequences of any attempt by management to shift from one espoused deal to the other. For instance, a precipitate attempt to substitute transactional or transitional contracts for those of a relational nature will almost certainly cause a breach of trust and sense of fair-dealing on the part of the employees affected, at least in the short term. Clearly, this has a direct bearing on management style and strategy, a point to which we shall return in chapter 4.

## Organisational justice perceptions

Fairness perceptions and how such perceptions are 'managed' are central to the state of the psychological contract. Employee perceptions about the fairness or unfairness of any human resource management practice will have a major influence on how they respond to that practice and how they relate to the organisation overall. Also known as 'organisational justice' perceptions, these feelings of fairness or unfairness are widely acknowledged as playing a central role in the shaping of employee outlook and behaviour. The growing body of academic literature in the 'organisational justice' genre (Colquitt, Greenberg & Zapata-Phelan 2005; Konovsky 2000) is concerned primarily with employee perceptions of fairness and with how such perceptions can be 'managed' in the organisation's interests.

Organisational justice perceptions can be thought of as having three distinct but overlapping dimensions: distributive justice, procedural justice and interactional justice (Beugre 1998). While there is some debate as to whether interactional justice is a distinct cognitive dimension or merely a subdimension of procedural justice (Bies 2005; Bies & Mogg 1986), as we shall see in chapter 8, the notion of interpersonal felt-fairness has obvious application to performance management practices, especially the provision of performance feedback and the conduct of performance reviews. For now, however, our discussion will focus on the procedural and distributive dimensions.

## Procedural justice

Procedural justice has to do with the perceived fairness of employment decision-making processes, including those associated with performance assessment and decisions relating to reward allocation. While such procedures will obviously influence reward outcomes, it is generally agreed that employee perceptions of performance management procedures are distinct from those relating to reward outcomes (Ambrose & Arnaud 2005; Greenberg 1987, 1990; Beugre 1998: 21–36).

Procedural justice considerations are especially pertinent to the procedures involved in measuring and assessing individual employee performance, with employees generally placing as much if not more weight on the felt-fairness of the assessment process as they do on the assessment scores or grades themselves (Gilliland & Langdon 1998). For instance, feelings of procedural injustice may arise where the performance assessments are seen as being based on incorrect or inconsistently applied criteria, inadequate performance information, biased judgements, or deliberate harshness or leniency. Less obviously, perhaps, perceived procedural unfairness may eventuate where those affected by the system are denied adequate notice of its implementation, some opportunity to contribute to system design and administration, adequate means for putting their own view of their performance, and/or access to a mechanism for refuting and appealing unfavourable judgements (Folger, Konovsky & Cropanzano 1992; Folger & Cropanzano 1998; Gilliland & Langdon 1998). It may take only one of these to impair the employee's sense of system trust and fairness and hence to cause a breach of the psychological contract.

Within the Western academic literature, the dominant construct of procedural fairness is that of 'due process'. In turn, the due process model draws on the concept of due process of law as it applies in those legal systems that share a common heritage in English legal principles and practice. According to Forkosch (1958), due process in law embraces three essential features: (1) adequate notice, (2) fair hearing and (3) judgement based on evidence. Drawing on these legal precepts, a number of writers (Folger & Bies 1989; Folger, Konovsky & Cropanzano 1992; Gilliland & Langdon 1998; Greenberg 1986; Leventhal, Karuza & Fry 1980; Taylor et al. 1995) have formulated sets of prescriptive rules or requirements for due process or procedural justice in individual performance assessment. What is particularly striking about these formulations is the consistency of their emphasis on the importance of meaningful employee input at all stages of system design, implementation and administration. This includes opportunities to challenge, test, refute and have corrected any assessment evidence or judgement that the assessee believes to be inaccurate, unrepresentative, biased, unethical or which is perceived as being unfair in any other way. It is also important to note that due process models posit assessment accuracy (i.e. validity and reliability) as a subfactor of procedural fairness (Folger, Konovsky & Cropanzano 1992: 167).

Field research (Taylor et al. 1995) supports the contention that a performance management system that complies with such requirements produces significantly more favourable reactions from line employees (ratees) and managers (raters) alike than one that is non-compliant. The same study found that this was the case even though employees in a due-process-compliant system received significantly lower performance ratings than those in the control group. In the USA, issues relating to due process have also been found to have more salience than any other criteria in influencing judicial decisions regarding performance appraisal (Lee, Havihurst & Rassel 2004; Werner & Bolino 1997).

## Distributive justice

Distributive justice perceptions are those related to the felt-fairness of allocative decision-making outcomes (as opposed to decisional processes). Clearly, reward outcomes are especially pertinent to distributive felt-fairness and, in particular, to feelings of reward injustice and dissatisfaction. As we shall see, employee cognitions here are likely to be informed by both absolute and relative considerations. Theories developed to explain distributive justice perceptions tend to highlight both considerations. The 'norm of contribution' – also known as the 'equity norm' – proposes that rewards should be commensurate with the effort or contribution made. To this, however, must be added the norm of relative or comparative worth. This asserts that for an employee to regard her rewards as fair she must see them as being proportional to the rewards received by some comparison group or individual. Importantly, the comparator individual may be another person altogether or an imagined past or future self. The stronger the perception that the rewards allocated are unfair in either absolute or relative terms, the greater the potential for breach of the psychological contract.

While there are a number of distinct social and psychological theories on distributive justice cognitions (Dornstein 1991), the most widely cited is that formulated in the 1960s by another social exchange theorist, John Stacey Adams (Adams 1963, 1965). Known as equity theory, Adams' formulation

| Focal person<br>or self<br>(A) | | Reference<br>person<br>(B) | | A's assessment<br>or attitude |
|---|---|---|---|---|
| Outcomes A<br>Inputs A | < | Outcomes B<br>Inputs B | ⟶ | Feeling of under-<br>reward inequity |
| Outcomes A<br>Inputs A | = | Outcomes B<br>Inputs B | ⟶ | Feeling of<br>reward equity |
| Outcomes A<br>Inputs A | > | Outcomes B<br>Inputs B | ⟶ | Feeling of over-<br>reward inequity |

**Perceived outcomes:**
Pay, benefits, recognition, status, achievement, satisfaction, security, etc.

**Perceived inputs:**
Knowledge, skill, ability, qualifications, experience, age, seniority, loyalty, effort, time, performance, responsibility, etc.

**Possible behavioural responses:**
- Leave for a more rewarding position elsewhere.
- Change outcomes within organisation.
- Change inputs.

**Possible cognitive responses:**
- Rationalise away the felt inequity by altering perception of 'self's' own inputs and outcomes
- Psychologically distort inputs and outcomes of 'comparison other' to eliminate felt inequity
- Change 'comparison other' or referent.

**But:**
- Which response?
- Which referents?

**Figure 2.5**  Equity theory (J. S. Adams)

proposes that employees assess the fairness or otherwise of their rewards (or 'outcomes') in relation to their effort and qualifications (or 'inputs') and that they do so by comparing their own input/outcome ratio against that of other individuals, typically those within the same organisation. Employees who believe their outcome/input ratio is either lower or higher than those with whom they compare themselves (the 'comparison other') will have feelings of reward inequity. Equity theory posits that inequity can arise from perceived over-reward as well as from perceived under-reward. The emotional state associated with perceived over-reward, however, is not one of dissatisfaction but of guilt. In sum, reward equity perceptions involve a continuing process of comparison with the outcome/input ratios of others seen as occupying a comparable position. Figure 2.5 summarises the main premises and predictions of equity theory.

Equity theory hypothesises that, in an effort to restore equity, an employee might take one or more of six possible courses of action:

1 leave the organisation for a more rewarding position elsewhere
2 change outcomes within the organisation
3 change inputs
4 rationalise away the inequity by altering their perception of their inputs and outcomes
5 psychologically distort the inputs and outcomes of others to eliminate felt inequity, or
6 change the 'comparison other' (referent).

You will note that the latter three responses are purely cognitive and accommodative in nature, whereas the first three are behavioural in nature and have clear implications for effort and performance. For example, employees who feel under-rewarded may seek to increase reward outcomes either outside the organisation or within it. They could simply quit for a more rewarding job elsewhere, or they might demand higher extrinsic rewards (including pay increases) within their current job. They could do this either as individuals or collectively through a union. Another option is for employees to reduce their contributions either overtly or covertly. They might formally request a reduction in task load or working hours, or transfer to a less onerous job. Alternatively, they could opt for covert reduction by increased absenteeism, longer coffee breaks, reduced service quality, ignoring paperwork or simply putting less effort into the job (Adams 1963, 1965; Mowday 1991).

Like all general theories, equity theory does have its shortcomings. How do we know which particular response pathway an employee is likely to take? When might behavioural responses prevail over purely psychological ones, and vice versa? In truth, this is actually very difficult to predict, and equity theory provides no reliable guidance as to why an employee who feels inequity might choose one course of action rather than another. This limits its potential as a guide to managing behavioural outcomes. We might also question whether all employees are as 'inequity' sensitive as equity theory assumes. Nor does it explain the choice of comparator person or group. Can it be assumed, as Adams did, that employees will tend to compare themselves with others in the same or similar occupations and at the same level in the organisational hierarchy? In this regard, such critics as Hyman and Brough (1975) have argued that equity theory and its progenitor, Homans' distributive justice theory (Homans 1961), are chiefly devices for limiting comparative horizons and for containing reward dissatisfaction and its consequences. However, exponents of a comparable theory – relative deprivation theory – suggest that the choice of social comparator may not be limited to social 'similars' and that line employees may well choose 'upward dissimilars' (i.e. managers and executives) as comparators (Dornstein 1991; Martin 1981; Runciman 1966). While employees may indeed make reward comparisons with 'dissimilar' others, including senior managers and executives (Martin 1982; Cowherd & Levine 1992), equity theory does seem capable of accommodating comparisons of this type. Arguably, a strength of equity theory is that it draws attention to the need to 'manage' the choice of referent group, since this may have a profound effect on justice perceptions and the attitudinal and behavioural consequences.

Whatever its conceptual shortcomings, then, equity theory makes two valuable points about whether or not employees are likely to see their reward outcomes as being distributively fair. First, it suggests that felt-fairness will be informed by the way employees estimate their reward outcomes and measure these against what they believe they contribute, very much like the age-old notion of a 'fair day's pay for a fair day's work'. Second, equity theory posits that feelings of distributive justice are also informed by a process of social comparison of perceived input/outcome ratios.

Equity theory, then, may well help us to solve some of the greatest conundrums of reward dissatisfaction and felt-unfairness. Let us put the theory to the test, using some Australian data on employee distributive justice perceptions. The second and most recent Australian Workplace Industrial Relations Survey (Morehead et al. 1997), which was conducted in 1995, asked employees whether they believed they were paid fairly for the things they did in their job. Of the 347,000 who responded, 47 per cent agreed that they were fairly paid whereas 32 per cent disagreed; that is, almost a third felt dissatisfied with their existing remuneration (Morehead et al. 1997: 557). But there were also some interesting variations in the degree of pay dissatisfaction between different categories of employee. Figure 2.6 presents the relevant survey results.

Overall, the employees who felt least fairly paid were male full-timers in their twenties and thirties working long hours in professions or trades, the public sector or service industries, in large workplaces and who belonged to a union. Those who were most inclined to feel fairly paid were women, teenagers, those aged fifty and over, casuals and part-timers, managers,

| '*I get paid fairly for the things I do in my job*' | *Percentage* |
|---|---|
| Agree | 47 |
| Disagree | 32 |
| Neither | 21 |
| | |
| '*I am fairly paid*' | |
| Employee categories with highest 'fairly paid' perception: | |
| Casuals | 61 |
| In top income quartile | 58 |
| Managers and administrators | 56 |
| Part-timers | 55 |
| Aged 15–20 | 55 |
| Aged 50 plus | 53 |
| Women | 49 |
| English-speaking background | 48 |
| Salesworkers and personal service workers | 52 |
| Non-unionists | 51 |
| | |
| '*I am not fairly paid*' | |
| Employee categories with highest 'unfairly paid' perception: | |
| Plant and machine operators | 37 |
| Para-professionals | 36 |
| Aged 21–29 | 35 |
| Tradesworkers | 35 |
| In bottom two income quartiles | 35 |
| Union members | 35 |
| Working 35+ hours a week | 34 |
| Permanent employees | 34 |
| Professionals | 34 |
| Males | 33 |

**Figure 2.6** 'Fair pay' perceptions of Australian employees, 1995
*Source:* Morehead et al. 1997: 556–7.

administrators and salespeople, those working in mid-sized workplaces in single-site organisations, in entertainment, recreation, business services and communication industries, and who were non-unionists.

What should we make of these differences? Obviously, the survey results suggest that the respondents had some strongly held, if intuitive, notions of what constitutes a 'fair' or satisfactory level of pay for the work they did. But the same evidence seems to offer valuable pointers to identifying some of the variables that may help to shape distributive justice perceptions. Unlike the women, the relatively well-paid males seemed to believe (1) that their rewards were not commensurate with their contributions, and (2) that they were under-rewarded in comparison with others with whom they chose to compare themselves. Age is also a major factor. Note that, compared to younger and older employees, 20- and 30-something males were particularly unhappy with their pay levels. In an all probability, this is attributable to the fact that employees of this age, who are likely to have large home mortgages and high promotion aspirations, generally have very different life goals and needs from younger and older employees. A similar explanation may apply to the marked attitudinal differences between full-time and casual employees. The significance of union affiliation may be that unions can be both cause and consequence of pay dissatisfaction.

In summary, distributive justice explanations for reward satisfaction or dissatisfaction suggest that perceptions of reward fairness are multidimensional – simultaneously individual and social, absolute and relative, interpersonal and intra-personal. Effective reward management requires that attention be paid to all of these dimensions of reward felt-fairness.

### Procedural or distributive justice: which is more important?

While procedural and distributive justice perceptions are linked, it seems that procedural justice effects may be stronger on some aspects of employee attitude and behaviour than others, as well as being stronger overall. Organisational justice researchers contend that procedural justice perceptions have a stronger influence on overall perceptions of fairness, a positive psychological contract, job satisfaction, organisational commitment and the demonstration of organisational citizenship behaviour (Beugre 1998: 79–90; Greenberg 1995: 327–41; Cropanzano & Folger 1991; Folger & Cropanzano 1998; Sweeny & McFarlin 1993; Terpstra & Honoree 2003). For instance, Folger and Konovsky (1989) found that while distributive justice had its greatest effects on pay satisfaction, procedural justice was far more influential in respect of organisational trust and commitment.

There is also evidence that, in relation to reward satisfaction, procedural justice perceptions can either moderate or amplify distributive justice perceptions. There is evidence that, where a pay reduction is accompanied by full and frank explanation of the reasons for the cut, the negative behaviour frequently associated with pay dissatisfaction (including employee theft!) is likely to abate; whereas in the absence of a formal justification dysfunctional behaviour is likely to increase. For example, employees will remain committed despite a perceived unfair pay outcome (from a biased supervisor) if they continue to believe that the decision-making procedures themselves (as opposed to the particular decision-maker) are fair (Greenberg 1990, 1993, 1995: 327–41). On the other hand, a belief that procedures themselves are unfair is likely to engender feelings of mistrust, an entrenched belief that the psychological contract has been irreparably breached and, consequently, an erosion of motivation, commitment and desired work behaviour (Brown & Armstrong 1999).

Whatever the precise nature of interaction between procedural and distributive justice perceptions, however, both clearly play a central part in shaping and reshaping the employee psychological contract. If employees feel that performance and reward management procedures and/or outcomes are unfair, they are likely to be less trusting and to believe that the psychological contract has been violated. In turn, the effects on employee behaviour and performance may well be disastrous.

## Chapter summary

In this chapter we have argued that it is not only necessary but also instructive to seek a meaningful way through the complexity of work psychology. We began by exploring three pivotal categories of work behaviour, namely membership, task and citizenship behaviour. Next we considered three key attitudinal categories, namely satisfaction, commitment and motivation. Then we mapped some of the possible associations between these attitudinal and behavioural categories. With these propositions in mind, we then examined the nature and practical significance of the notion of the 'psychological contract', as well as the perceptual factors that are widely regarded as lying at the centre of the employee psychological contract, namely organisational justice perceptions. The purpose throughout has not been to overwhelm you with psychological theory; rather, the point of the exercise has been to persuade you that these constructs are potentially valuable guides to informed and effective management practice. In the next chapter, we investigate in more detail the matter of motivation, again chiefly with a view to harnessing academic theories and debates to a conceptually informed and rigorous approach to performance and reward practice.

## Discussion questions

1  What are the main determinants of organisational citizenship behaviour?
2  How does personality influence individual performance?
3  Can psychological contracts be 'managed'?
4  Why is it that employees in low-paid jobs frequently demonstrate higher levels of reward satisfaction than those in more highly paid jobs?
5  Is the importance of organisational justice overstated?

Chapter Three

# MANAGING MOTIVATION

In chapter 2, we examined some of the possible associations between work attitudes, including task motivation, and work behaviour, including work effort or task behaviour. One of the key messages of that discussion was that work attitudes do not arise randomly or accidentally, nor are they a simple reflex of employee personality traits. This is good news for people managers since it means that it is to some degree possible to manage and, where necessary, to alter attitudinal states. We also noted the importance of the employee psychological contract and justice perceptions as crucial mediating influences between human resource practices and employee attitudes and behaviour. These are also useful conceptual devices for better understanding and perhaps influencing employee attitudes, perceptions and behaviour in a way that is beneficial to both the organisation and the employees themselves.

Of the attitudes considered in chapter 2, that which is generally accorded greatest importance as a determinant of employee performance is work (or task) motivation. In this chapter we examine the matter of motivation in greater detail. As we shall see, for all of its importance, and despite its being one of the most closely researched topics in the social sciences, the sources of task motivation remain a matter of longstanding and continuing debate in Western management thought. The chapter begins by reiterating the definition of motivation given in chapter 2. We then examine the assumptions and hypotheses associated with each of two main theoretical approaches to motivation: first, 'content' or 'needs' theories, and second, 'process' theories. The central argument of the chapter is that while neither approach provides a definitive account of the wellsprings of work motivation, each offers useful insights and practical messages for the management of this most important work attitude.

## Motivation: meaning and complexity

Pinder (1998: 11) defines work motivation as a set of energetic forces that originate both within and beyond an individual's being, to initiate work-related behaviour and to determine its form, direction, intensity and duration. As such, motivation is an important but problematic work attitude. The problem for management is that because work motivation is a state of mind, it cannot be observed directly; it can only be inferred (after the event) from observed behaviour. But inferring motivational strength from observed behaviour or measured results is also problematic since motivation is not the only factor shaping individual performance. You will recall from chapter 2 that other significant attitudinal influences include job and reward satisfaction and organisational commitment, while key perceptual and emotional influences include felt-fairness and trust, which, as we have argued, are core constituents of the state of the employee psychological contract. As such, how employees behave and perform is likely to be influenced as much by the nature of the relationships they have with their supervisor and peers – or more accurately their perceptions of these relationships – as it is by their inner willingness to work; indeed, it is highly likely that the quality of these relationships will also mediate their task motivation. A further complication is that what motivates employees differs widely, which makes it very difficult to generalise about the sources of motivation and, hence, task behaviour. In sum, an observed performance problem may or may not reflect a lack of motivation, and what motivates some individuals may leave others totally unmoved.

And there is a further complication that we have to deal with here. Despite many attempts, no one has yet come up with a tested and proven general theory of work motivation. What we have, in fact, is a range of alternative theories, each with its own assumptions about human nature and psychology; each with its own prescriptions for effective motivation management. It is now time for us to consider these competing theories of motivation – and to find a meaningful way to harness these conceptual differences to performance and reward management practice. As we work our way through the explanatory models associated with each of the two main theoretical approaches, it is important for you to note the differences in the basic assumptions on which each approach draws. One major difference is that whereas 'content' theories all assume that motivation is a product of the desire to satisfy underlying and universal human needs, 'process' theories are concerned less with primary (or primal!) causes than with the subtle cognitive processes that prefigure work effort; that is, with 'how', 'when', 'where' and 'how much' motivation occurs rather than with a search for any motivational constant.

## Content theories of motivation

Content (or needs) theories focus on the underlying human needs that supposedly shape motivational drive. The assumption is that people will behave in ways that they think will satisfy some or all of these needs. A *need* is a requirement for individual survival and/or well-being. Need satisfaction gives rise to feelings of pleasure and satisfaction. Need deprivation generates feelings of displeasure and dissatisfaction. All content theories propose that individuals are assumed to seek need satisfaction and avoid dissatisfaction. The logic is that an unsatisfied need generates psychological tension; the person then identifies an objective that will satisfy that need, and a behavioural pathway is chosen to attain that objective. In essence, then, all behaviour is seen as being motivated by unsatisfied needs and the desire for need satisfaction.

But what needs are we really talking about here? In broad terms, human needs can be categorised into two subsets: physical needs and psychological needs. Let us now examine the hypothesised associations between needs, motivation and need satisfaction in five of the classic content theories:

- Maslow's hierarchy of needs
- Alderfer's 'ERG' theory
- McClelland's achievement motivation theory
- Herzberg's two-factor theory
- Hackman and Oldham's job characteristics model.

### Maslow's hierarchy of needs

Abraham Maslow (1943) suggested that people have five types of need, arranged in a definite hierarchy of importance. According to Maslow's model, there are three 'lower-order' or 'deficiency' needs (physiological needs, safety needs and social needs) and two 'higher-order' or 'growth' needs (ego or esteem needs and 'self-actualisation' needs). Physiological needs include food, water, air, shelter, clothing, and . . . sex. (In regard to the last, we need to note here that Maslow's model was a general theory of human behaviour both within and beyond the workplace!) Safety needs cover security, stability and freedom from threat. Social needs include friendship, affection and acceptance. Esteem or ego needs include self-respect and respect from others, while self-actualisation is the need to fulfil one's human potential.

Maslow argued that lower-order needs had to be satisfied first. Only when these are met could the higher-order needs come into play. Each level in the hierarchy requires satisfaction before the next highest order can motivate behaviour. A lower-order need will always take priority over a higher-order need, until met. Only when a person's immediate physiological survival needs (for food, clothing, shelter, sex) are satisfied will that person become concerned about the next order of needs, namely safety and security needs, and only when these are met will they look to satisfying social needs, such as the need for friendship and acceptance by others – and so on, up the hierarchy, until we get to self-actualisation needs. Maslow called this phenomenon 'prepotency'. He suggested that organisations tended to be far more successful in providing opportunities for satisfying lower order needs than for meeting higher order needs.

It is tempting to believe that Maslow's hierarchy provides a comprehensive explanation of all human needs and motivational drives. It has a seductive simplicity and is still widely cited in the management literature. It forms the basis for all content theories.

But was Maslow right? There is little empirical evidence to support the assumption that there are five distinct, hierarchically ordered levels of human needs. The concept of prepotency is difficult to verify and has never been proven. Take the case of the 'starving artist' who persists in toiling away in the garret despite not having any bread on the table. Could it be that the artist is motivated more by higher-order needs despite lower-order ones remaining partly unsatisfied? It is also possible that people may be motivated to meet all needs simultaneously. Moreover, people may prioritise different needs at different points in their lifecycle. Single people may feel relatively little need for economic security and high need for social acceptance. By contrast, couples with a mortgage and a bank manager and children to support may subordinate social needs to security needs. The safest conclusion is that there will be considerable individual variation in the weight (or 'salience') that people attach to particular needs, depending on their situation and perceptions. This also means that any given type of reward may well have radically different need-satisfaction value for different employees.

## Alderfer's 'ERG' theory

Clayton Alderfer (1972) reduced Maslow's seven needs to three. Alderfer proposed that people are motivated to act so as to achieve individual satisfaction and that satisfaction depends on meeting three needs:

1  for 'existence': these needs are concerned with basic survival; they are akin to Maslow's 'physiological' needs
2  for 'relatedness': these represent needs for interpersonal and social affiliation; they are equivalent to Maslow's 'social' needs
3  for 'growth': these relate to the need to make optimal use of one's personal capacities; they parallel Maslow's need for 'self-actualisation'.

However, in a departure from Maslow's notion of prepotency, Alderfer suggested that several needs drivers might be active at any time. Moreover, Alderfer theorised that an already satisfied lower-level need could be reactivated if the individual was unable to satisfy a higher-order need. He termed this the 'frustration-regression' principle. Any contextual blockage to achieving higher needs could have profoundly negative motivational consequences. The chief implication for motivation management is that to minimise frustration-regression, managers should seek to eliminate any situational constraint that might restrict opportunities for personal growth and development (Cherrington 1991: 36–7).

## McClelland's achievement motivation theory

Whereas Maslow's model emphasised *innate* needs, achievement motivation theory points to the primacy of *acquired* needs. On the basis of research on managerial employees, David McClelland (1961) identified three acquired needs:

1  need for 'affiliation': the desire for friendly and close interpersonal relationships
2  need for 'achievement': the desire to excel and succeed
3  need for 'power': the desire to influence, control and direct.

McClelland's basic hypothesis is that these needs emerge over time, through experience. He also argues that all three needs can be drawn out via appropriate human resource development initiatives. Moreover, he contends that the salience of each need will vary according to the individual's position in the organisational hierarchy. According to McClelland, ordinary employees are motivated principally by the need for affiliation, junior and middle managers primarily by the need for achievement, and senior managers and executives by the need for power. McClelland proposes that those with high achievement need will prefer jobs that offer personal responsibility, feedback and moderate rather than high risk (since they want the opportunity to demonstrate achievement but also to avoid jeopardising their chances of success). As such, human resource practices should be tailored to suit these different needs. For instance, for line employees (with high affiliation need) the emphasis should be on using teamworking and collective incentives, for middle managers (with high achievement need) the emphasis should be on providing promotional opportunities and some level of reward that is contingent on individual high performance, while for executives (with high power need) the accent should be on recognising leadership impact, influence, authority and risk-taking (Boyatzis 1982). Overall, however, the need for power is seen as the ultimate motivator (Cherrington 1991: 39–43; McClelland & Burnham 1976).

This all sounds eminently sensible until we start to interrogate the underlying assumptions. The model assumes organisational hierarchy, but what if the organisational structure is flat, loose and relatively egalitarian rather than being a pyramid of status and power inequality? In such an organisation, the content of achievement and power would be very different. Further, there is a problem of Western cultural bias here. In some societies, the need for affiliation – for collective, cooperative work relations – will override the highly individualistic need for achievement and power. In such societies, an effective manager would be one who is supportive of collective rather than individualistic work practices, even though the culture may still privilege high 'power distance' between the manager and the managed (Hofstede 1984). We have to ask, then, just how valid McClelland's model might be for non-Western cultural contexts: say Indonesia, China or India. Incidentally, we shall encounter McClelland's work again in chapter 7 when we examine the competencies model of performance management.

## Herzberg's two-factor theory

Frederick Herzberg's two-factor theory (1966, 1987) seeks to overcome some of the practical shortcomings of Maslow's model by pinpointing the factors that cause job satisfaction and dissatisfaction. Essentially, two-factor theory underscores the significance of higher order need satisfaction to employee motivation and the importance of intrinsic rewards in meeting such needs.

Herzberg's model draws on evidence obtained in the 1960s from several hundred US professional engineers and accountants, who were asked to list work experiences that made them feel 'exceptionally good' about their jobs as well as those that made them feel 'exceptionally bad' about their jobs. Herzberg found that the two lists were very different; the factors that caused negative feelings were quite different from those that caused positive feelings. The factors that made the respondents dissatisfied had to do with pay, poor relations with supervisors and co-workers, and poor work conditions – things to do with the job *context*. The factors that elicited positive feelings about their jobs were those to do with job *content*, such as mastering a new task, learning a new skill or completing a challenging assignment. On the basis of this evidence, Hertzberg concluded that two distinct sets of factors influenced work behaviour: (1) 'hygiene factors' and (2) 'motivators'.

Hygiene factors relate to the job context, including working conditions, pay, supervision, status, security, interpersonal work relations, and employer policy and administration. According to Herzberg, hygienes do not motivate or satisfy; rather, they forestall dissatisfaction. Their absence causes dissatisfaction, but their presence does not cause satisfaction. They are 'dissatisfiers' and are equivalent to Maslow's 'lower-order' or 'deficiency' needs.

Motivators cover the individual's psychological need for achievement, recognition, intrinsic interest of work, responsibility and advancement. These five motivators determine positive job satisfaction and task performance. They are the 'satisfiers' and are congruent with Maslow's 'higher-order' or 'growth' needs.

Herzberg's point is that job dissatisfaction and job satisfaction or motivation are driven by quite distinct variables; they are not on the one continuum. The wellsprings of job dissatisfaction are those factors 'extrinsic' to the job; the sources of job satisfaction and motivation are those 'intrinsic' to the job.

So where does this leave extrinsic rewards like pay? Pay is represented as a 'hygiene' factor. At best, pay produces a situation of no dissatisfaction. But this does not mean that pay is unimportant. Employees must certainly be well paid so as to negate the possibility of dissatisfaction. In sum, to maximise satisfaction, and hence motivation, managers have to achieve two distinct outcomes simultaneously: first, to maximise satisfaction by improving job content variables; and, second, to minimise job dissatisfaction by improving job context variables.

Despite its continued popularity, however, Herzberg's theory has never been corroborated empirically. It also has a number of empirical and conceptual weaknesses. One problem is that Herzberg's own research may well be biased by the common tendency for people to take personal credit for positive feelings and attribute negative feelings to environmental factors. This may have been particularly so of Herzberg's informants. Another problem has to do with the suggestion that pay cannot be a satisfier. Indeed, Herzberg's own evidence (1987: 112) indicates that it can. In his own results, 'salary' is reported as a major reason for positive feelings lasting several months 22 per cent of the time, and unusually negative feelings of the same duration only 18 per cent of the time. This seems to directly contradict Herzberg's claim that money does not act as a long-term satisfier. Herzberg explains this inconvenient result away by suggesting that where pay does correlate with a feeling of satisfaction, it is really only serving as a surrogate for motivators like recognition and advancement. Other studies suggest that pay can indeed be a significant source of satisfaction and may even reinforce intrinsic motivation (Rynes, Gerhart & Parks 2005). The symbolic meanings attached to pay can be particularly powerful. Money can symbolise status, accomplishment and success, and it can certainly address ego and esteem needs. Of course, as we shall see in the chapters in parts 3 and 4, the specific attitudinal and behavioural effects will depend significantly on the level and type of remuneration involved, and on how pay decisions are made and communicated.

Yet Herzberg's model is useful for reminding us of the importance of intrinsic rewards in the overall scheme of things. Pay might be important, but it certainly is not everything. Intrinsic rewards, such as the challenge and diversity of the job itself, can be powerful motivators, particularly where professionals and knowledge workers are concerned.

## Job characteristics model

Building on Herzberg's model, Richard Hackman and Greg Oldham (1976) sought to identify the specific job characteristics that give rise to intrinsic motivation. Their job characteristics model identifies five core job dimensions:

1 'task identity': the extent to which the worker is able to perform a complete cycle of tasks
2 'task significance': the overall status and importance of the job

3 'skill variety'

4 'autonomy': the extent to which workers can decide for themselves how the job will be performed

5 'feedback': the extent of feedback from supervisors and co-workers on the quantity and quality of work.

Hackman and Oldham suggest that jobs high in these dimensions will induce three critical psychological states (meaningfulness, responsibility and identification with results achieved), which in turn will be intrinsically motivating. However, echoing the accent on higher-order needs in earlier needs theories, the job characteristics model also suggests that the motivational impact is moderated by the strength of the individual's need to achieve: only those with high achievement need will be motivated by the five core job dimensions.

The job characteristics model provides the rationale for motivational strategies based on job enrichment. In fact, its progenitor is the 'socio-technical systems' approach to motivation management advanced by Fred Emery and other researchers from the British Tavistock Institute in the 1940s and 1950s (Rose 1978). As noted in chapter 3, the satisfaction that flows from task variety and job autonomy is also linked to affective organisational commitment and organisational citizenship behaviour, as well as to membership behaviour. As we shall see in chapter 4, job enrichment also has direct relevance to organisations with (or aspiring to achieve) high involvement management cultures. However, this does not mean that such organisations can afford to ignore extrinsic rewards, such as pay.

## Summing up content theories

As table 3.1 (p. 75) indicates, there is a strong congruence between each of the five content theories that we have discussed. Lower-order needs correspond with existence and affiliation or relatedness needs and with hygiene factors (including pay). Higher-order needs are congruent with growth and achievement needs, and with the job content factors identified by Herzberg and Hackman & Oldham. The overall message from these constructs is that motivation is a by-product of the quest to satisfy our needs as people and workers and that effective motivation and performance management requires careful attention to which needs are most salient for any given group of employees and, hence, which rewards are therefore likely to be most highly valued as need satisfiers by these employees.

Perhaps the most useful element of need theories is the distinction between lower-order and higher-order needs. It does seem to be the case that higher-order needs require different modes of satisfaction from those of a lower-order nature and that they should be addressed and managed in different ways. In particular, the type of motivation and behaviour produced by an extrinsic reward like money is likely to be very different from that produced by rewards of an intrinsic nature.

However, need theories share some common shortcomings. They assume the existence of a universally applicable set of human needs. They tend to treat the workplace as the primary site of human need fulfilment. They underestimate the motivational potency of extrinsic rewards, including financial rewards. They assume that needs conform to a simple, ordered hierarchy of need importance when, in reality, needs seem to operate in a more flexible, less ordered and predictable way. Most importantly, however, they assume that the link between needs and behaviour is direct and automatic rather than mediated by human consciousness, values and choice. Even if we all have the same needs to satisfy, we may each prioritise them differently and choose different pathways to satisfying them.

The key point here is that the salience – or motivational pull – of a particular need cannot be taken for granted. The simple truth is that certain needs will be more salient to some people than to others. It is not needs *per se* that drive motivation but the *salience* of needs. To understand the link between needs and motivation, then, we need to understand what determines need salience. The salience of a particular need to a particular person will depend on two main variables: (1) the degree to which the person feels deprived of that need and (2) the importance attached to the need. Need deprivation is the difference between how much of something a person currently has and how much more of that thing they require to fully satisfy their need for it. Need salience will be strongly influenced by the person's circumstances. If their job requires them to work alone, they may feel high deprivation on social needs. Need salience is also influenced by personal characteristics, including personality traits. Some people may place far higher salience on ego and esteem needs than on the need to be liked by fellow workers. The individual nature of these preferences means that it may well be dangerous for organisations to take the needs of their employees for granted or to see these needs as being homogeneous or identical.

**Table 3.1** Summary comparison of content theories of motivation

| Hierarchy of needs (Maslow) | ERG theory (Alderfer) | Achievement motivation theory (McClelland) | Two-factor theory (Herzberg) | Job characteristics model (Hackman & Oldham) |
|---|---|---|---|---|
| *Higher-order needs:*<br>• Self-actualisation<br>• Ego/esteem | • Growth | • Power<br>• Achievement | *Motivators:*<br>• Achievement<br>• Growth<br>• Recognition<br>• Responsibility | *Intrinsic factors:*<br>• Skill variety<br>• Task variety<br>• Task significance<br>• Autonomy<br>• Feedback |
| *Lower order needs:*<br>• Social<br>• Safety<br>• Physiological | • Relatedness<br>• Existence | • Affiliation | *Hygienes:*<br>• Work relationships<br>• Supervision<br>• Work conditions<br>• Pay | *Extrinsic factors:*<br>• Relationships<br>• Job context<br>• Work conditions<br>• Pay |

# Process theories

Process theories of motivation differ from content theories in that they seek to explain (and exploit) the cognitive processes by which individuals decide to pursue particular pathways to reward attainment and need satisfaction rather than others. While the number of theoretical constructs in this genre is now vast, in the following discussion we confine our remarks to five of the most influential process theories:

1  reinforcement theory
2  expectancy theory
3  goal-setting theory
4  social cognition theory
5  cognitive evaluation theory.

## Reinforcement theory

This is the oldest and least complex of the process theories, and it derives from the work of such behavioural psychologists as Ivan Pavlov (of salivating dog fame), B. F. Skinner (of Skinner Box fame) and E. L. Thorndike. It is based primarily on E. L. Thorndike's 'law of effect', which posits that behaviour that results in a pleasurable outcome is likely to be repeated whereas behaviour that results in an unpleasant outcome is unlikely to be repeated. Through a process of learning and reinforcement, the individual comes to perceive a link between behaviour and consequence and can be programmed to behave in desired ways. Positive reinforcement of desired behaviour elicits more of the same; punishment of undesired behaviour (negative reinforcement) elicits less of the same (Skinner 1969; Steers & Porter 1991: 10–12).

Reinforcement theory makes four essential points about the association between motivation, effort and rewards:

1  Rewards do reinforce performance.
2  To reinforce desired behaviour, rewards must follow immediately after the behaviour.
3  Behaviour that is not rewarded will be discontinued ('extinguished').
4  Withholding rewards (or reward increases) is a powerful means of discouraging unwanted behaviour or misbehaviour.

Reinforcement theory provides the implicit or explicit rationale for all forms of performance-contingent extrinsic reward. In particular, it suggests that performance incentives have a positive and powerful role to play in reinforcing desired behaviour in situations where financial incentives are highly valued. The implications for effective reward management are quite clear: the behaviour and results expected from each employee should be clearly spelt out, and each time these are demonstrated an extrinsic reward of significant value to the recipient should follow immediately afterwards. The more instantaneous the reward and the reinforcement – that is, the sharper the cognitive 'line of sight' between the two – the better for all concerned.

The problem with reinforcement theory is that it takes a depressingly mechanistic view of the human condition. If the behaviour of rats can be programmed by means of extrinsic rewards and punishments, so too can that of people. The contrast with content theories could not be greater. Indeed, Herzberg (1987) refers derisorily to Skinnerian behaviourism as the 'KITA' ('Kick-In-The-Ass') view of employee motivation. Others (e.g. Kohn 1993a) argue that sole reliance on extrinsic rewards and punishments might well serve to extinguish intrinsic motivation by taking away the self-control that employees might otherwise be able to exercise in their jobs. It may well make employees feel manipulated, humiliated and powerless, and give rise to resentment and dissatisfaction. In short, reinforcement theory is probably applicable only to roles and task behaviour that are simple and routine.

### Expectancy theory

Expectancy theory draws on reinforcement theory but takes a more subtle and contingent approach to motivation. Pioneered by Victor Vroom (1964), and extended by Porter and Lawler (1967) and Lawler (1971), expectancy theory has for decades been regarded by many as offering the most practical insights on motivation management. Indeed, Lawler has been a leading contributor to the practitioner-focused literature on performance and reward matters since the 1970s.

Expectancy theory is based on the assumption that work behaviour is determined by individual expectations of the likely consequences of such behaviour. It seeks to explain and predict worker motivation in terms of *anticipated* actions and rewards. Employees' behavioural choices depend on the likelihood that their actions will produce a specific result that is attractive to them. It emphasises individual perception, judgement and choice in

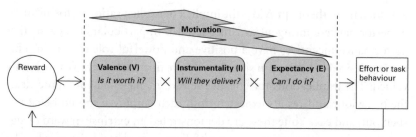

**Figure 3.1** Expectancy theory (Vroom)

particular contexts and assumes that people make rational decisions on the basis of accurately perceived economic realities.

In Vroom's model, motivation depends on three cognitions:

1 'Valence' (reward attractiveness). This is the value the employee places on the potential outcome/reward: *how much do I really want this potential reward?*
2 'Instrumentality' (perceived performance–reward linkage). This is the degree to which the employee believes that performing at the specified level will produce a positive outcome or reward. In common usage, instrumentality is also referred to as the 'line of sight' between performance and reward. This is partly related to the employee's level of trust in the organisation's reward promise: *if I achieve the required level of performance, how likely am I to be rewarded positively for it?*
3 'Expectancy' (effort–performance linkage). This is the employee's perception of the probability that a given effort will lead to a certain level of performance. In essence, this has to do with the employee's level of personal confidence about being able to perform: *can I achieve the required performance with the skills and resources at my disposal?*

The basis of Vroom's model is depicted in figure 3.1. According to Vroom, the strength of motivation ('motivational force') is a function of valence × instrumentality × expectancy (or V × I × E). The main implication is that management should act to maximise all three motivational elements. A performance-contingent reward will be effective only if the link between effort and reward is clear and the value of the promised reward is seen to be worth the extra effort. In short, expectancy theory predicts that employees will do what they think they are capable of doing in the way of task

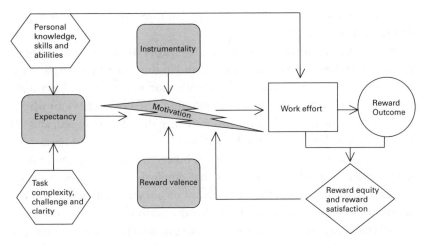

**Figure 3.2** Expectancy theory (Porter & Lawler)

performance (E) provided that they feel that the promise of reward is genuine (I) and that the rewards themselves are worthwhile (V).

The extended version of expectancy theory incorporates equity theory considerations (Pinder 1991: 150–2). You will recall from chapter 2 that equity theory proposes that employees assess the fairness or otherwise of their rewards (or 'outcomes') in relation to their effort and qualifications ('inputs') and do so by comparing their own input/outcome ratio to that of other individuals, typically those in the same organisation. Equity theory also equates reward equity (inequity) and reward satisfaction (dissatisfaction). So in Porter and Lawler's extended version of expectancy theory, which is summarised in figure 3.2, feelings about what constitutes a fair or equitable reward outcome interacts with the rewards actually offered or received to determine the overall level of reward satisfaction and, hence, motivational strength. The Porter and Lawler model also takes into account people's actual (as opposed to perceived) capacity to perform, in particular the mediating influence of individual capacities and organisational resources. Task performance also depends on factors other than imagined performance capability and sheer effort; such factors as personal knowledge, skill and ability, as well as task complexity and how clearly the employee actually understands what is required; that is, task and role clarity. Unless the employee does have the knowledge, skills, resources and task clarity required to transform raw effort into desired behaviour and results, no amount of self-delusion about being able to deliver what is required will result in performance achievement.

In its extended form, then, expectancy theory amounts to a complex, multifaceted theory of task motivation, and in this respect it offers a range of valuable and practical insights into motivation management. Essentially it proposes that a reward system will promote desired task behaviour where: (1) it offers valued rewards commensurate with the effort required, and (2) it establishes a clear and achievable pathway between effort and reward.

One problem with expectancy theory, however, is that it assumes rather than explains the differing valences that employees place on anticipated rewards. As we have seen, the value placed on a reward will depend on the salience of individual needs and whether the person believes the reward is capable of satisfying salient needs. Another problem is the assumption that behaviour is rational and premeditated when we know that much workplace behaviour is impulsive and emotional. A further limitation is that it fails to distinguish adequately between extrinsic and intrinsic rewards in determining reward valence. It simply assumes that they are additive (Pinder 1991: 152–4).

## Goal-setting theory

First formulated by Edwin Locke and Gary Latham (1984, 1990, 2002), goal-setting theory emerged over several decades on the basis of evidence gathered from extensive laboratory and field investigations covering a wide range of tasks and settings (Locke & Henne 1986: 17–20). Since its first comprehensive articulation in the mid-1980s, goal-setting theory has come to occupy a central position in both academic and practitioner thinking about motivation and performance and, according to some commentators, it is now the dominant theory in the academic literature on motivation (Latham & Pinder 2005: 496).

As defined by Latham and Locke (2006: 332), a goal 'is a level of performance proficiency that we wish to attain within a specified time period'. Goal-setting theory contends that individuals are most highly motivated when (1) they are set specific but challenging goals, (2) they have strong commitment to these goals and (3) they have a high sense of self-efficacy regarding goal achievement. It is based on the premises that (1) the more employees know about what is required of them performance-wise, the stronger their identification with the goals set and (2) the more precise and frequent the feedback on how well they are going in meeting these

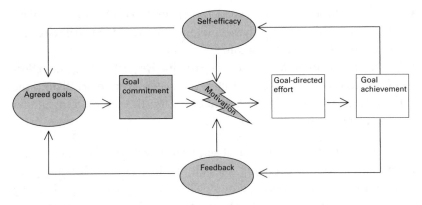

**Figure 3.3** Goal-setting theory (Latham & Locke)

requirements, the greater the motivational effect will be. The basis of goal-setting theory is illustrated in figure 3.3. Note, in particular, the role of goal commitment, continuous feedback and self-efficacy in sustaining motivational strength and, hence, goal-directed effort. It is important to note here that while the practice of goal-setting resembles the management by objectives (MBO) techniques popularised by US management writer Peter Drucker in the 1950s, goal-setting theory suggests that the mere imposition of goal-based tasks on employees may actually impair motivation. It posits, in fact, that goal achievement will be moderated, first, by the degree of employee acceptance of the goals set; second, by level of their commitment to goal achievement; and, third, by the strength of their confidence in being able to achieve the goals (Sue-Chan & Ong 2002).

Hence goal-setting theory has several practical implications for effective performance management:

- Clear and specific goals are more motivating than generalised and imprecise statements to do with performance requirements that simply exhort the employee to 'do a good job'.
- Difficult but attainable goals (i.e. 'stretch goals') motivate more than those which are easily attained.
- Feedback on task performance enhances motivational effect.
- For goals to produce higher performance, employees must have the knowledge, skills, abilities, materials and equipment (i.e. 'instrumentality') to accomplish them and must believe that they can accomplish the goals set (i.e. they must feel 'self-efficacy').

- Goals must be accepted or 'owned' by the employee. One way to achieve this goal commitment is to have employees participate in goal selection, measurement and interpretation.
- Self-regulation of performance (via participative goal-setting and reflection on feedback) is a more effective motivational approach than is the formula for reward and punishment characteristic of reinforcement theory behaviourism.

The instrumentality element in goal-setting theory derives from expectancy theory and is seen as operating through the linkage of challenging goals with valued rewards. Likewise, the emphasis on self-efficacy in goal-setting theory parallels that on expectancy in expectancy theory. However, there is one very important discrepancy between goal-setting theory and expectancy theory in this regard. According to expectancy theory, the higher the expectation of being able to achieve the required performance, the higher the motivational force will be. However, goal-setting theory suggests the opposite, namely that more challenging goals, which, by definition will be less readily attained, will actually be more motivating than those that are readily achievable. So how can the tension between these two pivotal process theories be resolved? The answer may well lie in the insights offered by content or needs theories. As we have seen, most needs theories highlight higher-order need drivers, including achievement and self-actualisation, as being the most potent motivators. Since high achievers are the ones most likely to respond favourably to stretch goals, we can say that, all else being equal, goal-setting will be best suited to employees with a high need to achieve and least suited to those who are low on the need to achieve (Locke & Henne 1986: 20).

## Social cognition theory

Like goal-setting theory, Bandura's social cognition theory (1986) also emphasises the positive role of self-regulation, as opposed to the use of controls applied by another party. Social cognition theory is akin to expectancy theory in that it asserts the importance of employees' belief that they can accomplish the task. Social cognition theory also resembles content or needs theories in emphasising the importance of higher-order needs – for achievement, esteem and self-actualisation – as well as the importance of task autonomy. However, it takes the logic further by highlighting the centrality of learned self-efficacy. Goal-setting alone will not necessarily produce stronger task motivation and performance. The effectiveness of goal-setting is mediated by goal commitment, feedback acceptance and self-efficacy. Employees must have ownership of the goal, confidence in their own ability to achieve the goal and confidence in the feedback provided, all of which are seen as socially acquired cognitions rather than immovable personality traits (Latham & Pinder 2005: 503). In essence, then, social cognition theory sees motivation itself as a developmental project; indeed as a personal development goal.

What does this mean for effective motivation management? Social cognition theory suggests that employees should be given considerable task autonomy as well as regular positive feedback on performance strengths and deficits. It is important not only that individual employees accept the goals set down but also that they are confident that they have the capacity to achieve them and have personal control over outcomes. This means assisting employees to overcome performance self-doubt and inhibition, to accept performance challenges and opportunities, to reflect on achievements and problems, and to establish and act on goals for performance enhancement. If a goal is not achieved, goal acceptance, self-efficacy and confidence in feedback accuracy predict whether employees will either redouble their effort to achieve or lose motivation. This process can be assisted by means of performance development practices, such as employee counselling, mentoring, role modelling, individual and group coaching, competency assessment, development programs and the like. The key here, however, is self-regulation and sustained learning and development. Social cognition theory also emphasises the importance of personal achievement and social and developmental rewards.

### Cognitive evaluation theory

Cognitive evaluation theory is something of a hybrid theory in that it actually supports some of the arguments advanced by content theories. In particular, it contends that the use of extrinsic rewards (and punishments) may destroy the intrinsic motivation that flows from inherent job interest. Unlike other process theories, it also focuses on the direction of motivational strength, rather than on its intensity and duration.

Developed by Deci and Ryan (1985), cognitive evaluation theory (also known as intrinsic motivation theory) reverses the cognitive sequencing typical of other process theories. For instance, as we have seen, expectancy theory posits that task motivation and behaviour involve rational premeditation: each employee will think through the possibilities before deciding on a course of action or inaction. In contrast, cognitive evaluation theory posits that people are much more likely to act first and evaluate, rationalise and ascribe meaning and motive to what they have done only after the event. The tendency is to confer motivational meaning on the behaviour – to attribute meaning and purpose to it – only in retrospect. People are more likely to ask 'Why *have* I done this?' than 'Why *should* I do this?' Cognitive evaluation theory suggests that individuals who *have* been deriving high intrinsic rewards for their work tasks may radically revise their self-attributed motives for doing the work once a financial incentive is offered to them. The point is that the initial motivation to do something is likely to be implicit and intrinsic rather than calculative and driven by the pursuit of some extrinsic reward. For this reason, Deci and Ryan (1985) argue that extrinsic rewards should not be applied to task performance because they may well dissipate the intrinsic motivation that may have driven performance initially (Deci 1992; Deci, Koestner & Ryan 1999). The perception of being 'controlled' extrinsically is assumed to be demotivational, a point embraced with some passion by opponents of performance incentives (e.g. Kohn 1993a).

As appealing as it may appear, however, cognitive evaluation theory also has its limitations. On the conceptual side, it is by no means clear that intrinsic and extrinsic motivation are antithetical; indeed, as critics suggest, the weight of evidence indicates that the two are, if anything, mutually reinforcing (Locke & Henne 1986: 8–10; Rynes, Gerhart & Parks 2005: 576–7). Further, it is questionable whether most work behaviour is impulsive rather than calculative; experience suggests that both play a part in work behaviour. This is a debate to which we shall return in chapter 14. On the practical side, while it may be quite appropriate for jobs and roles which are intrinsically motivating in the first instance, not all jobs will be intrinsically rewarding. In such cases, it would be necessary either to enrich the jobs or to apply extrinsic rewards.

## Summing up process theories of motivation

The main strength of process theories is that they emphasise the importance of perception and decision-making in individual work behaviour. Individuals behave as they do partly (if not chiefly) because they make conscious decisions as to the expected outcome and perceived value of such behaviour.

Process theories also appeal because, unlike content theories, they are not grounded in universalistic assumptions about employee needs or reward valence. Process theories also acknowledge the importance of social and job context as co-determinants of motivational strength, while those other than reinforcement theory also highlight the importance of self-efficacy, task or goal clarity and motivational learning. Finally, the accent on cognitive contingency makes process theories more compatible with the notion of the psychological contract and with organisational justice constructs.

What of the weaknesses? Process theories other than cognitive evaluation theory ignore the importance of work behaviour of an impulsive, unpremeditated sort. Because they are grounded in individual psychology they are of limited value in understanding and managing collective attitudes and behaviour, such as that associated with teamworking, although this not to suggest that the insights offered by, say, social cognition theory are not capable of being adapted to the management of work group performance.

## Motivation management: from theory to theoretically informed practice

Are these different theoretical approaches to task motivation mutually exclusive, or can they be aggregated into something that resembles a comprehensive theory of motivation? It all depends on whether you are a theoretical purist or a management pragmatist. Many practitioners adopt the pragmatic view that it is possible to combine the 'best' elements of each theory into a broad and balanced set of motivation precepts and principles. The truth is that many managerial approaches to motivation are highly eclectic, in just this manner. If anything, the dominant tendency is to combine need theories and the main cognitive theories into a contingency-type approach that seeks to identify the conditions under which extrinsic and intrinsic rewards *can* motivate individuals to achieve higher levels of task performance.

With these points in mind, it is appropriate to conclude this chapter by identifying some of the chief practical messages from these bodies of theory for effective motivation, performance and reward management. Although it is by no means exhaustive, the following lists sum up some of the more important implications of specific theories, respectively, for effective performance management and reward management.

Some key implications for effective performance management:

- Define and communicate the desired behaviour and results clearly (process theories).
- Identify the essential performance capabilities (knowledge, skills and abilities) for the position and ensure that employee capacities match these requirements (expectancy theory – expectancy).
- Encourage self-efficacy regarding task performance (expectancy theory, goal-setting theory, social cognition theory).
- Set tasks that are specific and challenging but attainable (goal-setting theory).
- Encourage employee ownership of performance criteria (goal-setting theory, social cognition theory).
- Ensure that performance achievement is accurately measured (expectancy theory – instrumentality).
- Provide timely and positive feedback (reinforcement theory; goal-setting theory, social cognition theory).
- Do not overlook the importance of intrinsic motivation (two-factor theory; cognitive evaluation theory).

Some key implications for effective reward management:

- Understand individual employee needs and how these differ between employee groups (content theories of motivation).
- Offer individuals valued rewards; i.e. rewards that address high salience needs (Maslow's hierarchy of needs; expectancy theory – valence).
- Link rewards clearly and directly to performance in a timely way (reinforcement theory).
- Deliver on the rewards promised (expectancy theory – instrumentality).
- Strike an appropriate balance between financial and other rewards (two-factor theory).
- Do not overlook the potential of intrinsic rewards (two-factor theory, cognitive evaluation theory).
- Manage perceptions of work inputs, reward outcomes and comparisons (equity theory).

# Chapter summary

As a state of mind, motivation is the most critical direct attitudinal determinant of work effort or task behaviour. As we have seen, although motivation is one of the most closely researched topics in the social sciences, the wellsprings of motivation remain a matter of great dispute in Western management thought. In this chapter, we have examined the assumptions and hypotheses associated with each of two main theoretical approaches to motivation: 'content' or 'needs' theories, on the one hand, and 'process' theories, on the other. Our central argument has been that although neither approach provides a wholly satisfactory explanation of the sources of work motivation, each offers useful insights and practical messages for the management of this most important work attitude. Content theories furnish helpful insights on *what* motivates whereas process theories help us to better understand *how* motivation arises. Process theories also offer useful guidance on how motivation can be sustained and strengthened via the maintenance of positive psychological contracts and favourable perceptions of organisational justice and trust.

# Discussion questions

1  Is all employee motivation need-driven?
2  Is Herzberg right or wrong about money not being a motivator?
3  What are the main differences between expectancy theory and goal-setting theory?
4  What are the implications of social cognition theory for effective motivation management?
5  How does cognitive evaluation theory differ from other theories of motivation?

Chapter Four

# BEING STRATEGIC AND GETTING FIT

As noted in the introduction to part 2, the factors that shape behavioural outcomes are at once psychological and strategic, and the development, implementation and maintenance of effective performance and reward management systems requires simultaneous attention to both of these basic dimensions. By 'strategic' dimensions we mean the plans, processes and actions involved in establishing and maintaining alignment between an organisation's objectives, on the one hand, and the individual and collective capabilities, behaviour and results of its employees, on the other. In this final chapter on the conceptual foundations of performance and reward management, we explore what is involved in managing employee performance and rewards strategically.

To suggest that employee performance and rewards should be managed 'strategically' sounds eminently sensible; after all, you would hardly want to propose that an organisation should manage its people in a non-strategic way! But what does managing human resources 'strategically' really mean? In broad terms, it can be said that taking a strategic approach to people management requires the identification and application of those human resource management principles, policies and practices that best align with and support the strategic objectives of the organisation as a whole as well as those of the relevant division, department and/or business unit. How should an organisation go about shaping its performance and reward policies and practices so that they do elicit the capabilities or competencies, behaviour and results that the organisation says that it must have in order to be successful in achieving its objectives? Is there really 'one best way' to manage human resources strategically? How can we tell whether an organisation is managing its people strategically? These are certainly important questions. Yet, as in the matters of work psychology and motivation, here too we encounter some major disagreements in the academic literature, this time as to what constitutes the 'best' approach to strategic human resource management.

When we turn to the academic literature for guidance here we find that there are really two different approaches to selecting the 'best' combination of human resource practices for achieving strategic ends. One approach, widely referred to as the 'best practice' approach, contends that there is 'one best way' to configure human resource practices for strategic success. The alternative approach, known as the 'best fit' approach, posits that there is no single superior set of human resource practices. According to the 'best fit' formulation, the bundle of practices that is likely to lend strongest support to organisational effectiveness will be that which best matches the organisation's specific strategic purpose, its external environment and its internal structure, culture and capabilities.

In this chapter, we examine each of these approaches in more detail, as well as weighing up the strengths and weaknesses of each. As with chapters 2 and 3, the aim of this chapter is to alert you to the key contentions and debates and to offer a theoretically aware yet practical way forward. While acknowledging the strengths and weaknesses of each model, we argue that the best fit approach offers the most meaningful and practical way forward. The chapter then proceeds to elaborate a basic framework for practising 'best fit' performance and reward management; a framework that we shall revisit frequently throughout the remainder of the book.

## The 'best practice' approach

The best practice approach posits that there is a particular set of human resource practices that can be applied in virtually any organisational context to increase performance and deliver outcomes beneficial to all stakeholders, including employees. The performance effect is said to be stronger when these practices are bundled together to complement each other and to create positive synergies between them; that is, with these best practice bundles the whole is greater than the sum of the parts. This approach actually covers a number of related prescriptive models of human resource management, including those variously described as the 'high-commitment', 'high-involvement', 'high-performance work systems', and 'mutual gains' models. These are all grounded in what British commentators (Storey 1995, 2001; Legge 1995a: 35, 1995b: 66–7) have characterised as a 'soft' or 'developmental humanist' prescription for human resource management effectiveness; an approach in which employees are seen as valuable human 'assets' or 'resources' warranting significant trust, involvement, empowerment and development.

Most of these models can be traced to the work of the 'Harvard School' writers of the 1980s (Beer et al. 1984; Walton 1985; Walton & Lawrence 1985) and to ideas formulated by the 'neo-human relations' writers of the 1950s and 1960s (Rose 1978; Wren 2005). In particular, best practice prescriptions owe a great deal to Douglas McGregor's theory Y/theory X dichotomy. In the theory X scenario, workers are depicted as indolent, untrusting and untrustworthy, low-achieving, and motivated only by the threat of punishment; under theory Y they are depicted as committed, trustworthy, high-performing corporate citizens and self-actualisers, worthy of empowerment and development (Rose 1978: 188; Wren 2005: 430–5). Building on McGregor's model, Walton (1985: 77), a leading proponent of the Harvard School, posited a moral dualism between 'control' and 'commitment': '. . . workers respond best – and most creatively – not when they are tightly controlled by management, placed in narrowly defined jobs, and treated like an unwelcome necessity, but, instead, when they are given broader responsibilities, encouraged to contribute, and helped to take satisfaction in their work.' High-commitment or high-involvement management is widely seen as the foundation of 'best practice' people management: 'High performance management practices provide a number of important sources for enhanced organizational performance. Simply put, people work harder because of the increased involvement and commitment that comes from having more control and say in their work; people work smarter because they are encouraged to build skills and competencies; and people work more responsibly because more responsibility is placed in hands of employees further down the organization.' (Pfeffer & Veiga 1999: 40.)

Typically, high-involvement 'best practice' is seen as entailing some or all of the following: job security; a well-developed internal labour market and promotion system; job enrichment; employee participation and involvement in decision-making; self-managed work teams; open two-way communication; extensive skill development; reduced status differences;

and reward practices that relate pay to employee skills or competencies and to group or organisational performance (Hiltrop 1996: 633). Leading US exponents of the best practice approach include Mark Huselid (1995; Huselid & Becker 1996), Edward Lawler (1986, 1990, 1992, 2000, 2005; Lawler & Mohrman 1989; Lawler, Mohrman & Ledford 1992) and Jeffrey Pfeffer (1994, 1996, 1998a; Pfeffer & Veiga 1999; Varma et al. 1999). The approach has also found support among some leading UK researchers, most notably in the more recent works of David Guest and colleagues (Guest 1999, 2002; Guest & Conway 1998, 2002; Guest & Peccei 2001). For instance, the bundle of practices recommended by US best practice exponent Jeffrey Pfeffer (1998a) – the so-called 'Pfeffer-digm' – includes:

- employment security
- selective hiring
- self-managed teams or team working
- high pay contingent on organisational performance
- extensive training
- reduction of status differences
- information sharing.

Guest and colleagues (Guest 1999, 2002; Guest & Conway 1998, 2002; Guest & Peccei 2001) have identified the following set of practices as having the most positive influence on employee work attitudes and behaviour:

- employee involvement programs
- job security
- job autonomy and challenge
- training opportunities
- single employment status
- high pay
- non-union workplace
- systematic and open communication.

The best practice approach appeals because it seems to offer a clear, consistent and ready-made solution – perhaps even the perfect solution – to age-old problems of labour management. The fact that there is wide agreement as to what constitutes 'worst practice' in people management also lends legitimacy to the approach. Involve, empower and develop employees and they will be dependable and motivated citizens of the organisation;

treat them as untrustworthy and expendable costs of production and the outcomes will be dismal. In this sense, best practice prescriptions also appear to accord quite closely with the requirements identified in chapter 2 for sustaining positive employee psychological contracts and justice perceptions (Guest & Conway 2002).

There is also a respectable body of evidence to suggest that best practice prescriptions do make a difference to organisational effectiveness. There is evidence from the United States (Applebaum & Batt 1994; Applebaum et al. 2000; Arthur 1992, 1994; Becker et al. 1997; Becker & Huselid 1998; Cutcher-Gerchenfeld 1991; Delery & Doty 1996; Huselid 1995; Huselid & Becker 1996; Ichniowski, Shaw & Prennushi 1997; Kochan & Osterman 1995; MacDuffie 1995; Pil & MacDuffie 1996; Varma et al. 1999) that firms implementing employee involvement and development practices do experience significant improvements in performance and tend to outperform comparable firms that do not. For instance, in a study of thirty US steel minimills, Arthur (1994) found that plants with such practices took 34 per cent fewer labour hours to produce one ton of steel, produce 63 per cent less scrap and experience 57 per cent less labour turnover. In a multi-industry study, Huselid (1995) found that high-performance work practices, including comprehensive recruitment and selection, incentive rewards and extensive employee involvement and training, have a positive effect on both employee performance (turnover and productivity) and organisational profitability. In a study of US banks, Delery and Doty (1996: 825) found that firms applying a combination of employment security, profitsharing and results-based individual performance assessment have superior financial outcomes to those that do not, with the best practice model explaining as much as 11 per cent of variation in firm performance. In a study of thirty-nine US organisations, Varma and colleagues (1999) find that high-performance work practices (such as team incentive plans, pay for skill and competency development, and rigorous staff selection) create cultural change towards greater cooperation and innovation, improve employee job satisfaction, and improve the firm's financial and operational performance. According to Pfeffer (1996: 36), such studies indicate that the best practice approach produces performance improvements of between 25 and 50 per cent.

Yet best practice prescriptions have been challenged on a number of grounds. Some have pointed to methodological shortcomings in studies purporting to confirm best practice predictions, including the validity of the practice and performance measures used, neglect of possible reverse causality, absence of controls for non–human resource influences and reliance on data gathered via single-respondent surveys (Becker & Gerhart 1996; Purcell 1999). Others have criticised best practice formulations as a management 'fad' that is overly idealistic and unrealistic. For instance, Purcell (1999: 36) warns that best practice precepts may cause managers to deliberately overlook major aspects of organisational specificity and difference and lead organisations 'into a utopian cul-de-sac'. In particular, Purcell argues that the approach is insensitive to differences in competitive context and national culture. Logically, best practice prescriptions and the associated technique of best practice benchmarking would lead to organisational isomorphism rather than competitive differentiation. Further, best practice prescriptions are expensive and are therefore unlikely to be feasible for firms operating in markets where entry barriers are low and competition is based on cost minimisation (Purcell 1999; Boxall & Purcell 2003).

Many commentators have also pointed to inconsistencies, contradictions and lacunae in what best practice advocates have to say about which particular practices and practice configurations are supposedly 'best' – a shortcoming acknowledged even by exponents themselves (Becker & Gerhart 1996: 784–5; Delery 1998; Delery & Doty 1996; Guest 1997). Delery and Doty (1997; Delery 1998: 292) note that there are countless permutations of practices and practice bundles that may conceivably produce a high-performance outcome. For instance, some versions include performance pay *per se* whereas others do not, and some nominate certain types of performance-related reward, such as group incentives and share plans, but omit others, such as individual piece rates and commissions. Pfeffer (1998b), for instance, espouses the use of profitsharing and other collective incentives but decries individual incentives, such as merit pay, as organisationally dangerous and destructive. Likewise some include individual performance assessment whereas others do not (Becker & Gerhart 1996: 784–6). There are inconsistencies even within the formulations advanced by individual proponents. Pfeffer's own best practice prescriptions are themselves something of a movable feast: in 1994 there were sixteen practices on his best practice list; by 1998 this had been reduced to seven (Boxall & Purcell 2003; Pfeffer 1994, 1998a; Purcell 1999). There are also some clear inconsistencies in what is proposed. For instance, take Pfeffer's recommendation for 'high compensation contingent on organisational performance'. Does this mean that the firm should maintain high pay levels even when firm performance falls? Logically, with performance-contingent rewards, reduced performance should result in reduced reward, but Pfeffer's formulation appears to ignore this unpalatable possibility. Further, in practice, the prescription for employment security may well come into conflict with that for high pay (Marchington & Grugulis 2000: 1112–15).

Then there is perhaps the greatest imponderable of all: how many practices are there – or should there be – in a best practice 'bundle'? Exponents typically identify between five and fifteen key practices, but does this mean that all are essential to best practice or, conversely, that a lesser number will suffice? Thus far, we have little guidance as to what might constitute a critical mass of synergistic practices. Are some practices more important than others? And how do practices interact? Do some practices complement others, while some substitute for others?

Finally, those writing from one or other of the critical management perspectives have decried high-involvement best practice (or 'soft' human resource management) as either a rhetorical mask for work intensification or a subtle discursive device to further subjugate the employee subject (e.g. Keenoy 1990a & b; Keenoy & Anthony 1992; Legge 1995a & b, 2001). Homing in on the 'win–win' implications of the 'Pfeffer-digm', Marchington and Grugulis label its unitarist and universalist precepts and prescriptions as a 'dangerous illusion' that 'actually lead to work intensification and more insidious forms of control' (2000: 1105–6). Specifically, they suggest that while best practice may benefit some 'core' workers, such as permanent employees in professional and skilled roles, it may simultaneously worsen the situation of 'non-core peripheral' workers. They also argue that the approach's unitarist underpinnings means that employee involvement or 'voice' will be granted only to the extent that it does deliver improved performance (2000: 119–21). Whatever the validity of these criticisms, as Guest (1997: 7) has observed, in the eyes of its critics it would seem that best practice human resource management is damned if it does and damned if it doesn't!

## The 'best fit' approach

The 'best fit' approach, as it is known in the British literature (Boxall & Purcell 2003), proposes that far from there being one superior and universally applicable set of human resource practices, such practices should be tailored differently so as to 'fit' each organisation's specific internal and external circumstances. In other words, what is best will be contingent on the organisation's precise strategic purpose, operating context, structure, size, age, management style, culture, workforce profile and the like. This approach is really an amalgam of two models of strategic human resource management that rose to prominence in the 1980s and 1990s: first, the 'contingency' model of strategic human resource management, and second, the 'resource-based' model. The key difference between these two models is one of emphasis: contingency theory emphasises the importance of configuring human resource practices to match the firm's business strategy and external competitive environment whereas the resource-based model stresses the competitive potential of aligning practices so as to achieve maximum leverage from the firm's internal resource capabilities, particularly its unique human resource competencies. Given that these two models can also be viewed as alternative ways to practice strategic human resource management, it is appropriate that we should consider each in a little more depth.

## The contingency model

The contingency model, which is also known as the 'matching' model, arose from the work of US writers associated with the 'Michigan School' (Devanna, Fombrun & Tichy 1981; Fombrun, Tichy & Devanna 1984; Tichy, Fombrun & Devanna 1982) and, more recently, from the work of fellow US writers Randall Schuler and Susan Jackson (Jackson & Schuler 1995; Schuler 1987, 1989, 1992; Schuler, Dowling & De Cieri 1993; Schuler & Jackson 2005; Schuler & MacMillan 1984). The contingency model also draws on precepts from the field of 'strategic management' as well as from 'strategic choice theory' (Kochan, McKersie & Cappelli 1984). Strategic choice theory highlights the pro-active role of management in decision-making and choice at three levels: workplace and individual relationships; collective bargaining and personnel policy; and long-term strategy and policy-making. While strategic choice theory acknowledges that management choices may be constrained by the firm's particular circumstances, regulatory requirements and other external environmental factors, it contends that management values and choices are key mediating variables between competitive context and human resource policies and practices. In short, it is management agency that determines the nature and degree of fit between practice and context.

In this vein, in their earlier writings, Schuler and Jackson (Schuler 1987, 1989, 1992; Jackson & Schuler 1995; Schuler & Jackson 1987) propose a contingency model involving two simultaneous dimensions of fit or alignment, each focused on eliciting the 'role behaviours' necessary to achieving specific strategic ends:

1 'vertical alignment', whereby human resource policies and practices are chosen and configured so as to match the behavioural requirements for competitive success in the chosen domestic or international product or service market(s), and

2 'horizontal alignment', whereby practices in each of the key human resource management functions (staffing, development, performance management and rewards) act in concert to elicit the desired 'role behaviours'.

Schuler and colleagues hypothesise that firms that attain and sustain vertical and horizontal alignment will enjoy a competitive advantage over firms lacking alignment, and to demonstrate the practicalities of their model they offer 'human resource practice "menus" ' listing alternative practice choices in each of six human resource processes (planning, staffing, appraisal, compensation, training and development, and labour relations). These practice choices are then matched to each of three types of business strategy ('cost reduction', 'quality enhancement', 'innovation') by identifying the types of role behaviour required by each strategy and the practices best able to elicit the needed behaviour (Schuler 1989; Schuler & Jackson 1987). For instance, firms with a quality enhancement business strategy will prefer to 'make' rather than 'buy' human resource capabilities, to have skill-based pay, to set pay levels above market rates, and to have a high level of employee involvement, whereas those with a cost reduction strategy will prefer the opposite.

In their early contributions Schuler and Jackson (1987; 1989: 172–5; Schuler 1987, 1989: 172–5) also highlight a further key contingency: that of business 'life-cycle stages'. As well as desired behaviour being contingent on the nature of external context and chosen competitive strategy, they propose that behavioural requirements and practice possibilities will depend on whether the firm is at start-up stage, in a growth stage, at maturity, in decline or undergoing turn-around. For instance, since a start-up firm would likely lack the cash flow to offer high monetary rewards, it could offer equity participation as a way to attract and retain high-quality staff, whereas a firm in decline (and hence shedding staff) would be likely to pay below-market rates.

In their more recent formulations, Schuler and Jackson (Jackson & Schuler 1995; Schuler, Dowling & De Cieri 1993; Schuler & Jackson 2005) offer an 'integrative' model that identifies a range of additional 'external' and 'internal' contextual contingencies. Among the key external contingencies, they include: the global environment; the legal, social and political environments; unionisation; labour market conditions; industry characteristics; and national cultures. Their main internal contingencies include: firm technology; structure (especially departmentalisation versus divisionalisation); size; lifecycle stages; and business strategy. Significantly, while in their 1995 survey piece Schuler and Jackson represented organisational culture as 'inextricably bound to HRM and therefore not meaningful if separated from it' (Jackson & Schuler 1995: 238), their most recent survey does identify organisational culture as a distinct internal variable (Schuler & Jackson 2005: 25). While these additions and modifications certainly acknowledge the significance of the firm's internal characteristics, the focus remains on the need to align practices with the external context: ' "lasting" competitive advantage from human resource management comes from developing HR practices that are appropriate for an organisation's specific context' (Schuler & Jackson 2005: 15).

## The resource-based model

In contrast, exponents of the 'resource-based' model (Barney 1991, 1995; Barney & Wright 1998; Wright, Dunford & Snell 2001; Wright, McMahan & McWilliams 1994; Wright & Snell 1991, 1998) propose that the key to achieving sustained competitive advantage lies primarily with internalities rather than externalities. In essence, the model highlights the strategic value of the organisation's internal resources, particularly those of an intangible nature, including workforce competencies and organisational knowledge, learning and embedded culture.

According to Jay Barney (1991, 1995), the key to sustained competitive advantage lies in having a workforce equipped with organisationally specific knowledge, skills and abilities that are difficult if not impossible for competitors to either duplicate or poach. Barney (1991, 1995; Barney & Wright 1998) proposes that to achieve 'sustained competitive advantage' a firm must have 'human capital resources' that meet all of the following four 'VRIO' requirements:

1  are valuable ('V'): resources that allow the firm to exploit opportunities and neutralise threats in the external environment
2  are rare ('R'): resources that are in very scarce supply to the firm's current or potential competitors

3 are difficult to imitate ('I'): resources that any competitor will find extremely difficult and costly to duplicate and for which there is no strategically equivalent or similar substitute, largely because they are embedded characteristics of the organisation's unique history and/or culture, and

4 are supported by organisation ('O'): resources with which the firm's structure, policies and practices are fully horizontally integrated and which are therefore able to be exploited to the full.

The implication is that it is only a combination of V + R + I + O that will deliver sustained competitive advantage. V + O will, at best, provide competitive parity, while V + I + O is likely to result only in temporary competitive advantage. Significantly, while these requirements acknowledge that internal resources are strong or weak only with reference to external opportunities and threats, the key to sustained competitive success lies in the manner in which the firm's human capabilities are identified, developed, differentiated from competitors, rendered immune from competitor emulation and fully organisationally integrated. A preoccupation with matching external contingencies will be inadequate to the task: 'In the end ... sustained competitive advantage cannot be created simply by evaluating environmental opportunities and threats, and then conducting business only in high-opportunity, low-threat environments. Rather, creating sustained competitive advantage depends on the unique resources and capabilities that a firm brings to competition in its environment. To discover these resources and capabilities, managers must look inside their firm for valuable, rare, costly-to-emulate resources, and then exploit these resources through their organization.' (Barney 2005: 60.)

Building on these propositions, Wright, Snell and others (Wright & McMahan 1992; Wright, McMahan & McWilliams 1994; Wright & Snell 1991, 1998; Wright, Dunford & Snell 2001) criticise Schuler and Jackson's behaviourally focused contingency model for neglecting the performance potential of human resource competencies (knowledge, skills, abilities). In terms of an open systems model, work competencies, they suggest, are logically prior to work behaviour and therefore of greater underlying importance to performance enhancement. Wright and colleagues also argue that the resource-based view offers a far more practical, flexible, dynamic approach to achieving fit than does an approach that emphasises accommodation to external contingencies. This is said to be particularly so for firms operating in unpredictable and rapidly changing environments.

## Balancing and internal fit

Despite considerable initial disagreement between exponents of the contingency and resource-based models, in recent years a convergence of sorts has emerged, one that emphasises the need for both external and internal fit (Youndt et al. 1996). This, in essence, is what has become known as the best fit approach. Thus, the best fit approach posits that effective strategic human resource management requires a set of people management policies and practices that, first, align with and support the organisation's particular external environment and competitive strategy ('external fit') and, second, fit with and support the organisation's *desired* structure, culture and workforce capabilities ('internal fit'). As such, management decision-makers are charged with making informed strategic choices as to which particular bundle of people management policies and practices best fits the organisation's internal and external circumstances. Taking this a step further, Delery and Doty (1996; Delery 1998) speculate that while both aspects of fit may be important, the most appropriate combination of human resource practices will vary according to whether competitive strategy is informed primarily by internal (resource-based) considerations or by external (market-based) considerations.

As figure 4.1 indicates, then, the best fit model prescribes a combination of external and internal fit. Human resource strategy, policy and practice should fit the competitive strategy and the external environment (external fit) by encouraging those forms of behaviour and results required to meet the organisation's strategic success factors. At the same time, human resource strategy, policy and practice should also fit the organisation's actual or desired structure, culture and human resource capabilities (internal fit).

In line with the tenets of mainstream strategic management theory, best fit practice is typically represented as a five-step process:

1 defining organisational mission and objectives
2 environmental ('SWOT') analysis
3 strategy selection
4 strategy implementation
5 strategy evaluation.

The key tool associated with best fit strategy-making is 'SWOT' analysis; that is, identification and analysis of the major opportunities and threats presenting in the organisation's external environment, and of the organisation's

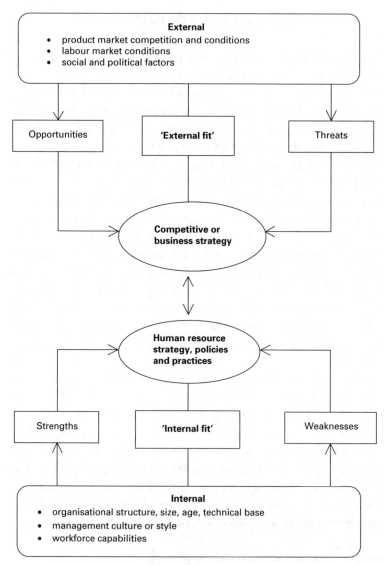

**Figure 4.1** A 'best fit' model of strategic human resource management

internal <u>s</u>trengths and <u>w</u>eaknesses relative to these key externalities. Only by this means can the organisation shape or reshape human resource practices so as to capitalise fully and effectively on emerging external opportunities while at the same time protecting itself against external threats. Specific strategies and practices should be chosen in light of the strengths, weaknesses, opportunities and threats identified by means of environmental analysis. Essentially, management produces a series of strategic options on the basis of the findings of the SWOT analysis. The aim is to select and implement the competitive and human resource strategies that provide the strongest 'fit' between the organisation's assessed external and internal circumstances. The chosen strategies should then be transmitted throughout the organisation, from the executive level to individual business units, divisions and/or departments.

Specific external factors that should be taken into account (as posing potential threats and opportunities) include:

- product market competition and conditions
- technology and new product or service innovation
- business environment
- capital market conditions
- labour markets
- general economic conditions (local, regional, national and global)
- political conditions
- legal requirements and changes
- industrial relations climate
- union presence, outlook and activity
- demographic profile and changes
- local and national social and cultural values, attitudes and beliefs.

Factors internal to the organisation itself that may be sources of strength or weakness (particularly in relation to external threats and opportunities) would include:

- the organisation's structure
- the organisation's culture
- the organisation's resources, including its technical base and the knowledge, skills and abilities of its workforce.

The best fit approach has particular appeal to human resource practitioners because it positions them as first-level 'strategic partners' in management decision-making. By definition, the rejection of a 'one size fits all' approach also widens the range of discretion and choice available to them. In fact, the model confers on all senior managers an extraordinary degree of responsibility and organisational knowledge, power and influence.

Best fit also injects greater flexibility into the system since it requires managers to be fully attuned to external and internal developments and to make appropriate changes to human resource strategy, policy and practice configuration. Moreover, best fit recognises the potential of human resource practices as 'enablers' of both organisational stability and organisational change. Most importantly, however, the formula is capable of accommodating both inter-organisational and intra-organisational diversity. As well as providing for differences between organisations, it also sanctions the multiple internal 'fits'; that is, the application of distinct configurations of human resource practices to different business units, according to the specific business strategy, unit structure and culture involved in each case.

Still, as a prescriptive formula, the best fit approach also has a number of conceptual and practical shortcomings. One problem is that best fit may overstate the rationality of management decision-making and choice. It assumes that management strategists always act rationally and with full and accurate knowledge of all relevant facts. Yet, as Marchington and Grugulis contend (2000: 1117), managers 'are not omniscient, omnipresent, and omnipotent, because they lack cohesiveness and typically engage in political behaviour'. In reality, managerial rationality is likely to be circumscribed by lack of information, time and ability to accurately interpret information. Managers are also fallible. They may read environmental factors wrongly. They may misunderstand corporate mission and strategy. They may fail to communicate their plans effectively. Their plans may go astray, or be ignored or undermined by those further down the line of control. Further, as agency theory suggests (see chapter 20 for elaboration), managers may not always act in the best interests of the organisation and its owners. In reality, managers are not merely loyal agents; they are intensely political players with their own interests and agendas. They play their own career games; they compete with each other for status and resources; they make trade-offs and compromises. For these reasons, it is just as likely that strategy will emerge accidentally rather than by way of rational and dispassionate deliberation by senior management. Equally, human resource strategy, policy and practice may be more a set of trade-offs between competing stakeholder interests than a pristine reflection of management planning. In this sense, strategy is something that is 'enacted' incrementally rather than being fully premeditated and 'intended' (Hiltrop 1996: 630). In the context of external flux and uncertainty, it is all the more likely that strategy will be retrospective rather than premeditated. An enacted strategy, then, will be emergent, evolutionary, iterative, flexible, adaptive and open-ended. It is also more likely to be reactive, negotiated, partial and short term in focus.

While both the behavioural-contingency and resource-based models hypothesise dynamic associations between practices, sets of desired competencies or behaviour and organisational effectiveness, the best fit approach actually provides only limited practical guidance as to how an organisation should ascertain whether it has achieved fit and as to how fit should be monitored and maintained over time. A related shortcoming is a propensity for short-termism and inconsistency. Altering human resource practices every time there is an observed change in the external environment may well be a recipe for administrative chaos and for serial breaching of the employee psychological contract. At the very least there is a need to strike a balance between practice consistency and recurrent 'refit'.

Finally, there is as yet only limited evidence that achieving fit does improve organisational performance. While there is considerable support for the proposition that the characteristics of a firm (i.e. external and internal contingencies) do influence the choice and configuration of human resource practices (Jackson, Schuler & Rivero 1989), the evidence that the alignment of strategy and practice then translates into improved performance is, at best, circumstantial. The evidence in support of resource-based prescriptions is somewhat stronger, although hardly conclusive (Becker & Gerhart 1996: 786–7; Hiltrop 1996). Overall, there is rather more evidence to support best practice prescriptions for performance enhancement (Huselid 1995). However, it must be said that the multivariate complexity of the best fit approach, and especially the 'integrative' model advanced by Schuler and colleagues, makes it far more difficult to test empirically than is the case with the best practice approach. Those propositions that are most readily tested are not necessarily those that are the most valid – or the most worthy guides to practice.

## Which is best?

So neither 'best practice' nor 'best fit' are beyond question. Best fit is mired in multivariate complexity; best fit in prescriptive and normative simplicity. Indeed, if the best practice approach were to hold all of the answers, this could have been a very brief book! Overall, while neither approach offers the perfect solution, each carries instructive messages for enlightened practice:

- Both approaches emphasise the importance of maximising cohesion (horizontal fit) between human resource practices themselves.
- Both approaches accentuate the need for alignment between organisational structure, culture and human resource practices.
- The contingency element of best fit highlights the importance of environmental surveillance to identify and respond to external opportunities and threats.
- The resource-based element of best fit emphasises the strategic potential of human resource capabilities within the firm, and the need to apply practices that maximise and capitalise on these capabilities.
- Best practice highlights the potential of employee involvement and development to organisational effectiveness.
- While best fit sanctions major change in human resource practices where circumstances require this, it may be impossible to sustain fit in situations of constant environmental instability and uncertainty. What is best fit today may be a poor fit tomorrow. Paradoxically, therefore, the best fit model may well be best suited to organisations operating in relatively stable environments.
- Conversely, while best practice emphasises consistency of approach, it may be best suited to situations of environmental change and uncertainty. At least with best practice there is less risk of an organisation becoming a slave to environmental flux or fashion.

Arguably, the two approaches still have much in common: both are prescriptive; both assume that people are the organisation's most valuable resources and that managing these resources strategically holds the key to organisational effectiveness; both emphasise the importance of 'horizontal integration' or practice complementarity. Thus, as Becker and Gerhart have noted (1996: 788), there does seem to be ample room for conceptual compromise and integration. Further, Youndt et al. (1996: 837) suggest that while 'the universal approach helps researchers to document the benefits of HR across all contexts, ceteris paribus, the contingency perspective helps us to look more deeply into organizational phenomena to derive more situationally specific theories and prescriptions for management practice . . . '. Indeed, there are signs of a conceptual convergence between the two, with some commentators proposing a blended approach in the form of a 'configurational' model (Boxall & Purcell 2003; Delery & Doty 1996).

In essence, this suggests that the practices applied by an organisation should be a tailored blend of best practice and best fit prescriptions. For instance, the configuration might include a selection of practices that accord with prevailing statutory requirements and social standards (say, for a minimum standard of guaranteed base pay and family-friendly benefits) plus practices chosen to best address the strategy for competitive success (such as performance incentives for individuals and work groups). Clearly the balance between the two will vary according to organisational circumstances, which, of course, is itself consistent with a best fit approach. Overall, while it may be open to strategy-makers to choose few or perhaps no options from the best practice repertoire, in line with the tenets of best fit, there should be valid external or internal reasons for taking such a course. As we shall see, there are valid strategic, structural and cultural reasons why an organisation may choose not to embrace proffered best practice prescriptions.

## A basic model for strategic performance and reward practice

With these points in mind, we now proceed to outline a basic model for strategic performance and reward management practice. While informed chiefly by the tenets of best fit, it is also mindful of the performance potential of best practice prescriptions, particularly those to do with employee involvement. Moreover, since being strategic is arguably more of an art than a science, the model is offered not as a set of all-encompassing rules for practice but, rather, as an illustrative guide to better strategic practice, irrespective of whether the strategy-making process itself happens to be intended, enacted or, as is much more likely, a combination of both.

Drawing on the insights offered by Heneman, Fisher and Dixon (2001), we propose that being strategic about performance and reward management requires careful analysis of and alignment between four key sets of factors: (1) competitive strategy, (2) organisational structure, (3) management culture and (4) performance and reward policies and practices.

A balanced and better approach to strategic practice requires close attention to the actual and desired associations between all four dimensions. These linkages are described in figure 4.2. Note that the associations are both multidimensional and bi-directional. The chief implication here is that competitive strategy is not necessarily superordinate to other factors but,

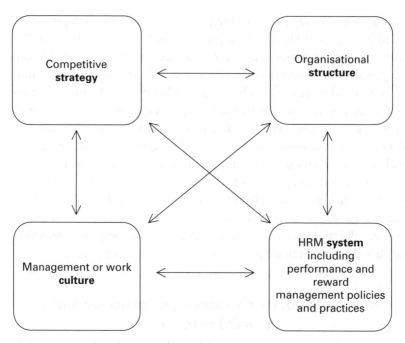

**Figure 4.2** Four key elements of 'best fit' strategic alignment

rather, may both shape and reflect structure, culture and human resource practice. There has been a great deal of debate in the academic literature about these associations. Most mainstream strategic management writers argue that it is strategy that determines structure and culture. Others argue that strategy 'follows' structure and/or culture. Our model recognises both possibilities; in other words, that strategy, structure and culture may be co-determinate.

A second implication is that to optimise their effectiveness, performance and reward policies and practices should be both compatible with and aligned with strategy, structure and culture – or more precisely, with strategy, *desired* structure and *espoused* culture. Indeed, misalignment between any of the four factors is likely to produce suboptimal outcomes. Equally, in the short term at least, misalignment is far more likely to be the rule than the exception, so a key (and perhaps constant) strategic challenge will be to determine appropriate ways of managing and perhaps accommodating a degree of misalignment. To this end, it is helpful to examine more closely some of the possible permutations of strategy, structure and culture, and how these may either align or misalign.

## Competitive strategy

What type of competitive strategy might an organisation adopt? Various management theorists have developed typologies to guide us here. Of course, all such typologies are abstractions from complex reality. In practice, few firms will be 'true' to any one 'pure' strategy. Most business strategies are hybrids. Nevertheless typologies are useful for helping us make sense of complex reality. The larger point is that organisations do have different strategic options to choose between.

Among the most widely cited typologies are those offered by US economist Michael Porter (1980), human resource management theorists Randall Schuler and Susan Jackson (1987) and US management theorists Raymond Miles and Charles Snow (1978, 1984). Porter's three strategies are: (1) 'low-cost leadership', (2) 'differentiation' and (3) 'focus'. Low-cost leadership attempts to gain market share by emphasising low product cost compared to competitors. A differentiation strategy involves seeking to distinguish the business's products from those of competitors, perhaps by manipulating brand image or emphasising quality. A focus strategy concentrates on a particular buyer group or market space.

Schuler and Jackson's typology includes: (1) 'cost reduction', (2) 'quality enhancement' and (3) 'innovation'. In a cost reduction strategy, a firm attempts to gain competitive advantage by being the lowest-cost producer. With quality enhancement, the firm seeks market share by emphasising quality rather than cost. An innovation strategy is used to develop products or services different from those of competitors.

The Miles and Snow typology also identifies three market competition strategies: (1) 'defenders', (2) 'analysers' and (3) 'prospectors'. Defenders act to protect and preserve their market share from existing and new competitors. They will have only one core product or service line and focus on improving the technical efficiency of their existing operations. Defenders are not diversifiers; they are risk-averse and reactive. A defender will seek to maximise the efficiency of existing technical methods and hence may emphasise cost minimisation or quality enhancement or a balance of the two. For instance, some automobile manufacturers tend to favour cost defender strategies, whereas others choose to compete on quality and to focus on high-end niche markets.

Analysers may have started out as defenders but have become cautious diversifiers. They may have one or two core products or services and one

| Miles & Snow | | Schuler & Jackson | |
| --- | --- | --- | --- |
| | Cost reduction | Quality enhancement | Innovation |
| Defender | ✓ | ✓ | ✗ |
| Analyser | ? | ✓ | ✓ (limited) |
| Prospector | ✗ | ✗ | ✓ (extensive) |

**Figure 4.3** An integrated typology of competitive strategies

or more non-core product lines that are spin-offs from the core business. An example would be a consumer electronics firm that has diversified into making movies; another would be an electricity supply firm that has added natural gas supply to its portfolio. Analysers are more likely to be market followers than market leaders and will also be inclined to compete on quality rather than cost, at least in the long term.

Prospectors are habitual diversifiers. They are proactive and perhaps aggressive market opportunists and risk-takers with a diverse and ever-changing portfolio of products and little loyalty to any particular type of product or service. They are constantly on the lookout for new and more attractive market opportunities, always trying to be first into a new product or service area. As such they will market a wide range of often unrelated products or services. The emphasis is on speed, agility, technological dynamism, flexibility and risk-taking, particularly to anticipate new customer needs and maintain a competitive advantage. The key success criteria are reduced product or service cycle times, adapting rapidly to environmental change and capitalising on new technical and product opportunities. The archetypal example is the US multinational General Electric, the one-time consumer white goods giant that now has a remarkably diverse business profile, ranging from jet engines to medical technology, insurance and consumer finance.

There is clearly considerable overlap between these typologies. For instance, low-cost leadership (Porter) bears a strong similarity to cost reduction (Schuler and Jackson), as well as to a cost-focused defender strategy (Miles and Snow). Likewise, there are similarities between differentiation (Porter), quality enhancement (Schuler and Jackson) and a quality-focused defender strategy (Miles and Snow). The innovator (Schuler and Jackson) and prospector (Miles and Snow) types also have much in common, and both have some resemblance to a differentiation strategy (Porter).

As figure 4.3 indicates, however, the sharpest similarities are those between the Schuler & Jackson and Miles & Snow typologies. As such, we propose an integrated typology that recognises four basic competitive strategies: (1) cost defender, (2) quality defender, (3) analyser and (4) prospector. The value of this typology is its recognition that firms may compete both within their existing market(s) and by moving between different markets. Moreover, as we shall see below, each approach will require a distinct approach to defining, measuring and rewarding employee performance.

## Organisational structure

For any organisation to have form and substance, it must possess a structure of some sort. In essence, organisational structure is the framework of roles, relationships and rules that provide the organisation's cohesion and integration. On this basis, structure may be broken down into four main elements: (1) job design, (2) internal differentiation, (3) a decision-making and communication system, and (4) a coordination and control system. These elements imply a range of structural possibilities and choices: should jobs be defined narrowly in terms of task range and with close supervision, or widely, with wide task range and significant autonomy? Should internal differentiation be by function, product, process or customer type? Should decision-making and communication be top-down, bottom-up, side-to-side or multidirectional? Should coordination and control be centralised and hierarchical or decentralised and devolved?

You will notice that we have not identified organisational size as a distinct structural feature. This is because size is best thought of as a product of the four elements we have identified. Hence, an organisation with more jobs, more internal units and more complex decision-making, coordination and control systems will necessarily be larger in size, whether size is measured in terms of workforce, assets or revenue.

Organisations come in a remarkable variety of shapes and sizes, and the organisational studies literature identifies an almost bewildering number of distinct organisational structures: from functional, divisional and matrix structures to process, network and virtual organisational forms. As is so often the case with detailed typologies, however, the purported differences can be meaningfully reduced to a much smaller number of archetypes. In this respect, Burns and Stalker (1961) offer us a typology that, despite its age and simplicity, still captures the fundamentals of structural difference in contemporary work organisations. Burns and Stalker propose that, in structural terms, all organisations can be thought of as occupying a point on a continuum between two poles: (1) 'mechanistic' and (2) 'organic'. Put simply, this can be thought of as the machine versus biological metaphor of organisational structure. Burns and Stalker propose that these two structural types vary greatly in terms of 'role formalisation', 'functional specialisation' and 'administrative intensity'.

Mechanistic structures have high formalisation, high specialisation and high administrative intensity. They comprise jobs that are narrowly defined and arranged in a formal hierarchy of size and significance, with jobs lower down the hierarchy being specialised, highly standardised and low skilled. Decision-making is highly centralised, communication is top-down, and coordination and control is via a tightly structured vertical command-and-control hierarchy. Staffing emphasises internal recruitment and promotion. Internal differentiation is typically along functional or departmental lines, with separate 'silos' for key business functions like sales and marketing, production, finance and human resources. These are classic pyramidal structures that are still commonplace in the military, in large firms in rapidly developing economies such as China and India, and in public sector bureaucracies. However, mechanistic structures may also be multidivisional in nature, in which case, while there may be a degree of decentralisation to constituent business units, these will still be subject to centralised planning, coordination and monitoring. According to Burns and Stalker, mechanistic structures are best suited to stable environments.

By contrast, organic structures rate low on formalisation, specialisation and administrative intensity. Such structures substitute flexibility, fluidity and horizontal relationships for formality, function and hierarchy, and their constituent parts are loosely coupled rather than tightly integrated. They entail wide job or role assignments, many with significant autonomy and high knowledge and skill requirements, as well as interdependence and team-working. Decision-making, coordination and control is devolved and decentralised, and communication is multidirectional. Consequently, organic structures lack centralised management hierarchies. In organic structures work is organised on the basis of process and customer focus rather than by task and function. Organic structures are also outward-looking, emphasising external labour market recruitment over internal selection and promotion and access to knowledge by means of outsourcing, networking arrangements, joint venture projects and temporary alliances. Firms that have been fully 're-engineered' to de-emphasise internal functional boundaries and accentuate customer-focused processes also exemplify an organic structure. The most extreme instances of organic structures are the so-called 'virtual' organisations in which expertise and tangible resourcing is wholly outsourced, and communication and coordination is either informal or internet-based. Internet retailers, software development consortia and film-making ventures are examples of virtual structures. Burns and Stalker (1961) propose that organic structures are a more effective fit for dynamic and less predictable operating environments.

As with any typology, this taxonomy simplifies reality and, again, few organisations will fit the mechanistic/organic distinction with pristine purity. As with competitive strategy, most organisations will have hybrid structures. For example, global network entities like Amway, Nike and McDonald's also have some of the organic structural characteristics, although such firms also exhibit many of the features typical of mechanistic structures. Structures that superimpose horizontal divisional or process-related relationships on a hierarchical functional structure, which are know as 'matrix' structures, are best thought of as mechanistic–organic hybrids. These are intended to allow greater internal autonomy and flexibility but without sacrificing overall centralised coordination. As such, it is important to remember that the mechanistic/organic distinction merely captures the range of structural possibilities. Again, however, simple typologies are a useful means of reducing organisational complexity to manageable descriptive proportions.

## Management culture

Management culture, the third factor in our proposed model, is in some ways the most complex and controversial of the factors with which we are dealing. It is also the strategic dimension that relates most closely to the employee psychological contract. Adapting Schein's definition of organisational culture (Schein 2004), management culture can be defined as the set of management-espoused assumptions, values, attitudes and beliefs about the nature of the employee subject and how employees should best be managed. The espoused management culture thus signals to employees how they can expect to be treated, how to behave in the workplace, how to relate to one another, to managers and to customers, what to value, what is recognised and rewarded, and what is not. Management culture is also bound up with what is known as management 'style'. A 'style' has to do with underlying values, principles and ideals. It is the style that shapes day-to-day managerial outlook and action. The 'style' exposes the normative essence – the heart and soul – of management outlook and mentality. It is the touchstone of management ideology – how managers, or at least senior managers and executives, think and act towards their employees on a day-to-day basis.

As is the case with strategy and structure, academic writers have produced a variety of typologies of management culture and style. Some of these are built around basic dichotomies; others identify a larger number of cultural styles. Among the most influential of the dichotomous formulations are those by US organisational psychologist Douglas McGregor (1960), 'Harvard School' exponent Richard Walton (1985) and British industrial relations academic Alan Fox (1974).

As noted earlier in the chapter, the two types identified in McGregor's model are 'theory X' and 'theory Y'. To recap: with theory X, employees are assumed to be untrusting, untrustworthy, uncooperative and motivated chiefly by extrinsic rewards and punishments; with theory Y they are assumed to be trustworthy and committed, corporate citizens, worthy of empowerment and development. Similarly, as we have also seen, Walton distinguishes between 'control'-based management and 'commitment'-based management.

The two people management styles identified in Fox's model are 'low trust' and 'high trust'. A low-trust culture involves an essentially authoritarian approach to the management of the workforce, demanding employee obedience and punishing non-compliance through strict disciplinary codes and the threat of dismissal. The approach hinges on the presumed inviolability of management prerogative and a marked hostility to any independent trade union presence.

Alternatively, in a high-trust culture, employees are given greater discretion over job decisions, performance is less strictly monitored and a greater commitment is given to employment security. The employer adopts a softer, more consultative approach in an attempt to win over employees and gain their consent and commitment. At the industrial relations level, the high-trust approach might involve employer acceptance of trade unions, direct negotiation with unions and possibly the adoption of joint consultative and regulatory procedures with unions or, alternatively, the use of non-union employee representation plans.

With these distinctions in mind, and in line with the template offered by Heneman, Fisher and Dixon (2001), our strategic framework recognises two distinct types of management culture and style: 'traditional' and 'high involvement'. In essence, a 'traditional' management culture accords with McGregor's theory X, Fox's 'low-trust' style and Walton's 'control'-based approach. This is characterised by low to moderate trust, a positive view of hierarchy, bureaucracy and power inequality, insistence on management prerogative, a hostility to independent employee representation, a perception of labour as a 'factor of production', an emphasis on the primacy of membership behaviour and task compliance, and espousal of a relational psychological contract along the lines detailed in chapter 2.

By contrast, a high-involvement culture will be characterised by high trust, a negative view of hierarchy and bureaucracy, advocacy of open communication and shared decision-making, a perceptions of employees as 'valued contributors', an emphasis on task autonomy and citizenship behaviour, and espousal of either a transactional or a balanced psychological contract of the type described in chapter 2. A high-involvement culture, of course, accords with the main normative assumptions that underpin best practice prescriptions for strategic effectiveness.

## What fits with what?

Having outlined a framework that describes the basic strategic, structural and cultural options, we can now examine, first, how these might best align with each other and, second, how we can go about determining best fit performance and reward requirements for some of the main structure–strategy–culture configurations. Of course, since we have yet to explore specific performance and reward practice options, at this juncture it would be premature for us to go into too much detail. Rather, our remarks will focus on requirements of a more general nature regarding desired employee attitudes, capabilities, behaviour and results. Then, in subsequent chapters we can identify specific performance management and reward management practices that may be best suited to the particular configurational requirements.

As figure 4.4 indicates, some combinations of organisational factors are viable whereas others are not. In particular, it is difficult to imagine a high-involvement culture being sustainable in the presence of a mechanistic structure or the absence of organic structural characteristics. Likewise, a traditional culture will be unsustainable except in the presence of a mechanistic structure. However, matters become rather more complicated once we factor in competitive strategies. On the one hand, a mechanistic structure and a traditional culture are the natural counterparts of a cost defender competitive strategy, while the same applies to a high-involvement–organic–prospector configuration. Yet when we turn to consider the structures and cultures that may be compatible with quality defender and analyser strategies, the issue is less clear-cut. Each of these competitive strategies could conceivably be supported by either type of organisational structure, although the choice

**1. Viable structure–strategy–culture configurations**

| Management culture | Organisational structure | Competitive strategy | Key performance requirements code |
|---|---|---|---|
| Traditional ✓ | Mechanistic ✓ | Cost defender ✓ | 1: TMCD |
| | | Quality defender ✓ | 2: TMQD |
| | | Analyser ✓ | 3: TMA |
| | | Prospector ✗ | ✗ |
| | Organic ✗ | Cost defender ✗ | ✗ |
| | | Quality defender ✗ | ✗ |
| | | Analyser ✗ | ✗ |
| | | Prospector ✗ | ✗ |
| High involvement ✓ | Mechanistic ✗ | Cost defender ✗ | ✗ |
| | | Quality defender ✗ | ✗ |
| | | Analyser ✗ | ✗ |
| | | Prospector ✗ | ✗ |
| | Organic ✓ | Cost defender ✗ | ✗ |
| | | Quality defender ✓ | 4: HIOQD |
| | | Analyser ✓ | 5: HIOA |
| | | Prospector ✓ | 6: HIOP |

**2. Key performance factors**

| | 1 TMCD | 2 TMQD | 3 TMA | 4 HIOQD | 5 HIOA | 6 HIOP |
|---|---|---|---|---|---|---|
| Transactional contract | ✗ | ✗ | - | - | - | ✓ |
| Balanced contract | ✗ | - | - | ✓ | ✓ | ✗ |
| Relational contract | ✓ | ✓ | ✓ | - | - | ✗ |
| Membership behaviour | ✓ | ✓ | ✓ | ✓ | ✓ | ✓ |
| Task behaviour | ✓ | ✓ | ✓ | ✓ | ✓ | ✓ |
| Citizenship behaviour | ✗ | ✗ | ✗ | ✓ | ✓ | ✓ |
| Individual results | ✓ | ✓ | ✓ | - | - | ✓ |
| Group/collective results | ✗ | ✗ | ✗ | ✓ | ✓ | ✓ |
| Quantity/productivity | ✓ | ✓ | ✓ | - | - | - |
| Cost minimisation | ✓ | ✗ | ✓ | ✗ | - | - |
| Quality | ✗ | ✓ | - | ✓ | ✓ | - |
| Timeliness | ✗ | ✗ | - | - | ✓ | ✓ |
| Creativity/innovation | ✗ | ✗ | ✗ | - | ✓ | ✓ |
| Risk-taking | ✗ | ✗ | ✗ | - | - | ✓ |
| Short-term results focus | ✗ | ✗ | - | - | ✓ | ✓ |
| Long-term results focus | ✓ | ✓ | - | ✓ | - | ✗ |

**Figure 4.4** Aligning strategy, structure, culture, espoused contracts and performance requirements

of structure would then rule out one or other of the cultural options. For instance, a quality defender organisation might choose an organic structure, but this would then require a move to a high-involvement culture. Equally, an analyser may choose to adhere to a mechanistic structure, but this would rule out the option of a high-involvement culture. Viewed from the reverse perspective, if an organisation was intent on adopting a high-involvement culture, it would necessarily also have to move towards an organic structure, although this would still leave open the choice between a quality defender, analyser or prospector competitive strategy.

As figure 4.4 also indicates, each of the six sustainable strategic configurations will also involve distinct combinations of key performance factors as well as compatible espoused psychological contracts. Those espoused contracts and performance factors most relevant to each case are marked with a tick; those that are inappropriate are marked with a cross; those without a strong association either way are marked with a dash. It is the identification, application, measurement and reward of these factors that really holds the key to achieving fit or alignment between the three organisational variables (i.e. strategy, structure, culture) on the one hand, and performance and reward practice, on the other, with the espoused psychological contract also encapsulating and communicating the aligned employment deal. This is best illustrated by briefly comparing three instances of configurational sustainability.

First, the case of a firm with a traditional culture, mechanistic structure and cost defender competitive strategy (i.e. case 1: 'TMCD'). For such a firm, the key competitive success factors will be functional and technical efficiency and cost minimisation, on the basis of job assignments that are narrow, individualised and closely supervised but also with long-term employment security. Employees will be required, above all else, to work to task. Accordingly, this firm will espouse a relational psychological contract and require membership and task behaviour, but not citizenship behaviour. It will focus on individual rather than collective results, and on productivity and cost rather than quality. Given that the firm's key goal is defence of long-term market share and stability, the performance focus will also be long term rather than short term.

Second, the case of a firm at the opposite end of the spectrum: a high-involvement organic prospector (i.e. case 6: 'HIOP'). For this firm, the keys to competitive success are agility, adaptability, timeliness and innovation. As such, it will require demonstration of all main behavioural categories, but particularly citizenship behaviour. It will also have to strike a positive balance between individual and collective results. Naturally, it will also need to encourage timeliness, creativity and risk-taking, although it will be less concerned (although not unconcerned) about productivity, cost and quality factors. Given the emphasis on diversification and short product or service cycle times, it will necessarily espouse a transactional deal, will prefer a short-term focus to all work activities, and will recognise and reward accordingly.

Finally, let us consider an intermediate case, that of a high-involvement quality defender (i.e. case 4: 'HIOQD'). How would its requirements differ from those of, say, an analyser firm with a mechanistic structure and a traditional culture (i.e. case 3: 'TMA')? The latter might simply be a cost defender that has decided to diversify into a second product or service area, whereas the former is much more likely to apply a 'total quality management' approach to value creation. As such, the HIOQD firm will be looking for greater flexibility and commitment from its workforce, hence its preference for a loose organic structure and greater employee involvement, perhaps via self-managing work teams and a high-skill, high-reward approach to human resource management. In turn, this means that, compared to its TMA comparator, a HIOQD firm is likely to place much more emphasis on fostering a balanced psychological contract and on eliciting citizenship behaviour. It will also emphasise collective rather than individual results, and product or service quality rather than cost minimisation and volume. Compared to the 'TMA' case, it will also be inclined to emphasise long-term rather than short-term performance.

## Managing misalignment and change

While best fit theory posits that misalignment is not sustainable in the longer term, at any given point in time, an organisation or one or more of its constituent business units may well be in a state of misalignment. In this sense, it is best to think of misalignment rather than alignment as being the natural state in the short term.

Mechanistic and organic structures are both susceptible to misalignment. Many large mechanistic organisations are internally differentiated, with multiple divisions and/or units each with their own strategic, structural and cultural settings. Entities forming a network organisation are even more likely to have distinct internal structures and management cultures. As such, within any given organisation, structure and culture may vary significantly from unit to unit. For instance, a multi-unit organisation that is predominantly traditional and mechanistic in nature may still include some units that are managed on high-involvement organic lines. Alternatively, a defender firm undergoing transition may spin off several high-flying business units that are essentially analysers or even prospectors.

Misalignment may also arise from corporate merger, acquisition and takeover activity, which can force together quite incompatible structures and cultures; executive turnover, with an incoming CEO perhaps deciding to push through a major restructure, a culture change program or a change of competitive strategy; and corporatisation and privatisation, which commonly sets new competitive strategies against old structures and cultures.

Perhaps the greatest single cause of misalignment, however, is time itself. Organisations can be thought of as having something akin to a natural 'lifecycle': they are formed, undergo youthful growth and development, attain 'maturity', experience decline and either die, are absorbed or are reborn. Each life stage involves different strategic priorities and performance requirements and, hence, different human resource practices. For instance, a start-up firm with limited market share and cash flow is likely to place considerable emphasis on cost-effectiveness as well as on membership behaviour, timeliness, short-term results and perhaps risk-taking, whereas a firm at maturity may accentuate citizenship behaviour, collective results and a long-term focus. A firm at renewal stage may well place strong emphasis on innovation, risk-taking and short-term focus. However, it is important here not to become overly anthropometric about organisational ageing. Some firms never make it to maturity; others are born, thrive and die within a matter of a few years.

There is no universally agreed prescription for addressing misalignment. On the basis of the strategic model outlined above, the appropriate point of departure would be a thoroughgoing SWOT analysis. Beyond that the best course of action will depend on the causes, nature and extent of misalignment.

Take the example of a traditional mechanistic cost defender firm, say a hitherto publicly owned telecommunications entity that is undergoing privatisation, and to which the new executive team has just applied an analyser competitive strategy involving diversification into the electronic media and a range of communications technology production activities. As suggested in figure 4.4, this is actually a sustainable configuration (i.e. case 3: 'TMA'). However, the executive team also wishes to install a high-involvement culture, so now we do have a classic case of misalignment. So what should change first, the structure or the culture, and what should drive the change? One option would be to 'go organic' first, say by restructuring the organisation into a network of loosely aligned product-specific business units. An alternative option would be to 'go high involvement' first, perhaps by introducing self-managing teams, employee participation plans and job enrichment. A third option would be to seek to change the structural and cultural settings simultaneously; however, change on this scale may cause confusion and uncertainty. A fourth option would be to roll out the changes one business unit at a time, but this may cause inordinate delay in the overall change process. The point is that there is no one best way to address misalignment. Moreover, whatever the path chosen, careful consideration must be given to selecting and implementing those performance and reward management practices that best support the change process both in terms of the attitudes and perceptions held by the employees concerned and in terms of the behaviour and results obtained.

## Chapter summary

What this chapter has offered, then, is a simple but useful framework for organisational analysis and an open-minded approach to best fit alignment; a framework for aligning performance, recognition and reward system practice with those human resource capabilities, behaviour and results that are most strongly mandated by the spatial and temporal interplay of competitive strategy, organisational structure and espoused management culture. Such a framework will provide us with critical guidance and direction as we work our way through the various methods and techniques available for building performance and reward management systems that have the greatest potential to satisfy the expectations, goals and needs of all organisational stakeholders.

## Discussion questions

1 Whose version of 'best practice' should we accept?
2 Could it be that 'best fit' is 'best practice'?
3 ' "Best fit" is good in theory but elusive in practice.' Discuss.
4 Think of a firm that you believe has a cost-defender competitive strategy and another that you see as having a quality-defender strategy, then compare the two in terms of (a) what they actually produce and market, (b) their public 'brand image', (c) their organisational structure, and (d) their management culture.
5 Name one firm that you believe to have a 'prospector' strategy, and consider whether its structure and culture are aligned with this strategy.

# Part 2

# PERFORMANCE MANAGEMENT IN ACTION

The four chapters in part 2 examine the key concepts, techniques and processes associated with the management of employee performance. In chapter 1 we observed that, from a descriptive cybernetic perspective, work performance may be thought of as having three horizontal or process dimensions – that is, inputs (knowledge, skills, and abilities), task effort and other types of work behaviour, and outcomes or results – and three vertical or scalar dimensions – that is, individual, group and organisation-wide performance. By definition, the methods that accentuate behaviour and competency have an individual focus.

Chapters 5, 6 and 7 examine the main performance management methods or techniques associated with each of these dimensions. Chapter 5 considers those approaches to performance management that are results-focused. Chapter 6 will then consider the methods and techniques that are behaviourally focused, while chapter 7 will examine the concepts and techniques that emphasise performance inputs or capacities in the form of performance competencies.

Chapter 8, the final chapter in part 2, examines both the provision of performance feedback to individual employees and practices directed towards performance development, including coaching.

The case study that concludes part 2 – 'Delivering fairness: Performance assessment at Mercury Couriers' – provides an opportunity to apply your knowledge of performance management concepts and assessment methods to a particularly problematic case of performance mismanagement. Once you have framed your responses to the case in question, you may wish to compare these with the model responses provided in the book's appendix.

## Chapter Five

# MANAGING FOR RESULTS

Since results are the most tangible and readily measurable of the horizontal dimensions of performance, we shall begin our discussion at the end, as it were, by examining in this chapter those approaches to performance management that are results-focused, including both those that focus on individual results and those that are associated with group and organisation-wide results. The chapter begins with an overview of those facets of work performance that are commonly characterised as 'results'. Next we consider some of the key concepts associated with defining and measuring results, the promise and perils of results measurement, and the requirements for measurement reliability. The remainder of the chapter is then devoted to a discussion of two of the most widely applied results-based performance measurement and management methods, namely goal-setting and the balanced scorecard.

## What are 'results'?

In terms of the (prescriptive or descriptive) conception of work as a linear value-adding process, 'results' can be defined as those tangible and intangible outcomes from work behaviour or activity that management deems desirable and valuable in achieving organisational objectives. Conceived thus, the results domain may be seen as covering six main outcome categories:

1 product or service quantity
2 product or service quality

3 financial outcomes
4 timeliness
5 innovation
6 stakeholder reactions.

Here, we have adapted the taxonomy of key human performance outcomes identified by Fitz-enz (2000: 91–128), which lists generic human resources 'value adding' factors: 'cost', 'time', 'quantity', 'error' and 'reaction'.

Quantity, quality and financial outcomes – the so-called 'hard' outcomes – are the defining features of traditional results-based approaches to performance definition and management. Product or service quantity includes such criteria as the total number of units produced or sold, number of new accounts created, labour productivity (number of units produced or sold per employee or per unit of labour time), and client or customer turnover or throughput. Quality covers such criteria as the attainment of maximum product reliability or standard of service proficiency and the minimisation of defect rates and customer complaints. Less obviously, quality-based results may also include the maximisation of workplace safety and the minimisation of detrimental environmental impact. Financial results cover a plethora of monetary outcome possibilities: from operating costs (materials, capital, human resources) to sales turnover, gross revenue, earnings before interest, tax, depreciation and amortisation (EBITDA), gross profit, profit net of operating costs, net operating profit after tax (NOPAT), to internal 'value added'; that is, gross monetary value of product sales or service provision less the costs of materials and resources involved in generating that gross value. There are also various financial ratio measures that may be used, including earnings per share (EPS), return on assets (ROA), return on equity (ROE), which considers combined return on total equity – that is, shareholders' funds plus capital debt.

In the wake of the silicon chip revolution and the globalisation of product and service markets, these more traditional categories of results have been supplemented by the categories of timelines and innovation. Timeliness, which as we have seen is a vital success factor for any prospector firm, would include such criteria as speed of response to customer demand, delivery time, new product or service development time and 'time to market', customer inquiry turnaround time, actual achievements compared to production schedule or timetable, and amount of unmet customer backlog.

Innovation – another key success factor for prospector firms – covers such criteria such as the rate of new product or service development and the degree and pace of plant and supply chain diversification.

Finally, stakeholder attitudes and reactions include such criteria as the level of product or service take-up, the level of external customer satisfaction, the level of external supplier cooperation and satisfaction, and the extent of employee satisfaction and commitment, as well as judgements made about the organisation by external shareholders, institutional investors, share markets, the media and the general community. As we shall see, internal and external stakeholder attitudes and reactions have assumed considerable prominence in organisational performance management practices that emphasise the importance of the underlying non-financial or intangible determinants of financial results, particularly the balanced scorecard and 'triple' or 'quadruple bottom-line' approaches that posit the joint significance of shareholder, customer, employee and community interests.

## Measuring results: KRAs, KPIs and goals

As with all approaches to performance management, the four most basic design considerations are (1) determining what to measure (a matter of construct validity), (2) how much to measure (content validity), (3) how to measure accurately (criterion validity), and (3) how to maximise measurement reliability, whatever the measures used. You will recall that validity and reliability considerations were introduced briefly in chapter 1. With a results-based approach, validity considerations are typically addressed by identifying a small number of 'key result areas' (KRAs) for the position or work group involved, while performance in each KRA is typically gauged or measured by means of 'key performance indicators' (KPIs).

Every position or role within an organisation will have a set of core tasks, the outcomes of which will contribute materially to the organisation's effectiveness. These core tasks constitute the KRAs of the position concerned. In essence a KRA is a significant, distinct area of work activity or accountability, the achievement of which determines or indicates performance effectiveness or success. Achievement must also be able to be defined in terms of quantifiable or measurable outcomes. While the number of KRAs will vary from position to position, it is common for each position to have around five KRAs. Note that these will not necessarily constitute the totality of the position's content, since any given position is likely to cover dozens of tasks, duties and responsibilities as well as a large range of work competencies and types of behaviour. However, the position's KRAs should cover each of the major desired outcomes from the position. For example, take the position of plant production manager. This will cover a wide variety of activities and responsibilities to do with planning, organising, controlling, directing, coordination, budgeting and the like. In terms of desired primary outcomes, the position may be reduced to, say, five KRAs, such as:

- KRA 1: Plant productivity
- KRA 2: Unit cost
- KRA 3: Product quality
- KRA 4: Plant safety
- KRA 5: Employee turnover.

In selecting KRAs, system construct and content validity requires that the KRAs represent the range of tasks, duties and responsibilities that the position-holder has been asked to perform. To illustrate: if the only KRA selected for measuring results achieved by our production plant manager was plant productivity (KRA 1), then it is likely that she would focus all of her attention on maximising short-term output and, in doing so, take actions that might compromise cost effectiveness, product quality, plant safety and employee retention rates, each of which would be to the organisation's long-term detriment.

But defining the performance domain in a valid and balanced way is just the first challenge. The next – and no less important – challenge is to decide how to measure actual results in each area, and this means selecting KPIs that are valid constructs for gauging outcomes in each KRA and that can be applied so as to produce reliable measurements. Depending on the nature of the KRA, a KPI may be either a direct measure of the results achieved in the area or an indirect or proxy measure; that is, a KPI may be either a direct or an indirect measure of what has been achieved in the relevant KRA. Returning to the case of our production plant manager, one option would be to measure of results achieved in the plant productivity KRA (KRA 1) by means of a simple, direct measure such as the number of units produced per employee over the course of the year. But what if the plant employs a high proportion of part-time employees? Such a KPI may yield a deceptively low productivity measure. In this situation, a more reliable KPI would be the number of units produced per person-hour worked.

Matters become more complicated still when we turn to those KRAs for which there is no obvious direct indicator and for which proxy indicators must therefore be used. Take the product quality KRA (KRA 3). One possible indicator of results here would be the number of defective components detected on the production line per month, another would be the number of defective end-products returned by customers each month, a third might be the number of customer complaints. Note that these are not identical measures, nor do they take into account faulty materials, as opposed to faulty work. Equally, many factors apart from work quality may contribute to the level of customer complaints. In short, there is no one wholly valid or reliable KPI for this KRA. As such, it is necessary to choose between a range of possible proxies and, again, this choice should be based on considerations of criterion validity and measurement reliability as well as felt-fairness. For instance, why should employees be penalised for product faults that arise from poor-quality materials? To do so would certainly fail the tests of validity and reliability, but it may also give rise to damaging perceptions of system injustice.

By definition, KPIs measure what has been achieved rather than what might be achieved, and this brings us to our third main results-based concept, that of goals. A goal is a target outcome for future achievement in a KRA and in terms of a specified KPI. So a goal quantifies a desired KPI result for a specific KRA. As such, each goal must be expressed in term of a specific KPI. A goal must also be time-framed. So, for our production manager, the goal set down for the product quality KRA (KRA 3) might be: 'to reduce the rate of work-related final product defects over the next six months to 1 per cent of total units produced'. Table 5.1 illustrates one configuration of KRAs, KPIs and goals that may be appropriate – that is, valid and reliable – for our production manager role.

Are 'goals' any different from 'objectives'? While it is sometimes suggested that goals have a longer time-frame than objectives, for practical purposes the distinction is simply semantic since the time frame itself is part of goal definition. As we shall see below, the two most widely used methods of results-based performance management, namely goal-setting and management by objectives (MBO), are essentially one and the same, except for one critical difference: with MBO, targets are typically imposed from above; with goal-setting, targets should be agreed, not imposed.

**Table 5.1** KRAs, KPIs and goals for a production manager role

| Key result areas | Key performance indicators | Goals for the next 12 months |
|---|---|---|
| KRA 1: Plant productivity | KPI 1: Units produced per person-hour | Goal 1: Increase productivity by 5% over the year |
| KRA 2: Unit costs | KPI 2: Operating costs per unit produced | Goal 2: Reduce unit costs by 5% over the year |
| KRA 3: Product quality | KPI 3: Defective products per 1000 units produced | Goal 3: Reduce defect rate over the year to 1% of total |
| KRA 4: Plant safety | KPI 4: Lost time injuries per month | Goal 4: Reduce lost time injuries to an average of 2 person-days per month over the year |
| KRA 5: Employee turnover | KPI 5: Voluntary separations per month | Goal 5: Reduce the voluntary turnover rate to 10% over the full year |

## The promise and the perils of measuring results

There is something inherently reassuring about results-based metrics; about being able to run a series of KPI measures over the achievements of individuals in their position KRAs and come up with a set of performance 'numbers'. Measuring results seems to be an objective and accurate means of assessing work performance. After all, all jobs produce results of some sort, and these can be measured in some way. Measuring results in each KRA focuses attention on the position's critical success factors, challenges employees to find more creative means of achieving desired outcomes, and provides immediate and continuous feedback on how performance is tracking. Moreover, as the popular management aphorism (commonly attributed to MBO pioneer Peter Drucker) suggests: 'You can't manage what you can't measure.' In similar vein: 'If you don't measure results, you can't tell success from failure', and 'What gets measured gets done'.

But measurement also has its own potential problems – even perils. Measurement decisions are fraught with potential sins of omission and commission. What gets measured is often what is easy to measure, not what is most important to the organisation. With results-based metrics, it is tempting to privilege the 'how much' over the 'how'. This is particularly relevant to service work, where it may be easy to quantify the number of clients or customers attended to but much harder to gauge the quality of the service provided, even though in a commercial context service quality is likely to determine the level of repeat business and customer loyalty. Further, what the organisation decides to measure is what it will get, since it may be only what gets measured that will get done. What is not measured is likely to be quickly forgotten. Moreover, managing numbers may become an end in itself and a substitute for effective management decision-making. The business world is awash with number fetishes; that is, with the dangerous assumption that a 'good number' necessarily means that the system is in robust good health. But for this to be the case, the measures used must not only be valid and reliable but also based on sound information and interpreted with precision and accuracy. Even then, the metrics are merely a partial reflection of a larger reality, rather than actually constituting that reality. In short, measuring results must never be regarded as an end in itself; rather results are a potentially useful means of achieving desired ends.

What, then, are the main requirements for measuring results validly, reliably and, hence, effectively? To be effective, results-based performance measures should be:

- related to appropriate strategic goals and objectives, with each measure weighted accordingly (i.e. construct validity)
- relevant to the objectives and accountabilities of the individuals and groups concerned (i.e. construct validity)
- comprehensive, covering all key result areas (i.e. content validity)
- accurate indicators of actual performance against the performance standards or criteria set (i.e. criterion-related validity)
- focused on measurable outputs that can be clearly defined and for which evidence can be made available (i.e. reliability)
- based on solid data or evidence that will be available as the basis of measurement (i.e. reliability)
- verifiable: provide accurate information that will confirm the extent to which objectives have been met (i.e. criterion-related validity and reliability)
- able to provide a sound basis for feedback and further performance development.

Consistent with these basic prescriptions, there are several design questions that should be asked of any performance measurement system, whether the focus happens to be on results, behaviour, competencies or some combination of these. In particular, it is necessary to establish whether the measures:

- accurately reflect current organisational priorities (i.e. construct validity)
- measure enough of the right things (i.e. construct and content validity)
- use measures that accurately reflect performance on the chosen criteria (i.e. criterion-related validity)
- are applied consistently and accurately using sound data (i.e. reliability)
- relate to goals or other performance standards that are realistic rather than too difficult or too easy (i.e. validity and procedural fairness)
- are understood and accepted by the employees concerned (i.e. procedural fairness).

Armed with these general insights and caveats, we can now turn to examining the main results-based performance management techniques currently available to system designers: goal-setting and the balanced scorecard.

## Goal-setting

In practice, goal-setting is a refinement of the management by objectives (MBO) technique pioneered by the celebrated US management writer Peter Drucker in the 1940s and 1950s. Current approaches to goal-setting, however, are informed by the process theory of motivation of the same name – that is, goal-setting theory – which, as noted in chapter 3, is of more recent origin (Locke & Latham 1984, 1990). The logic of both MBO and goal-setting is that better results will be achieved by directing employee task effort towards anticipated future achievement than by benchmarking only against what has been achieved in the past. The main difference between the two is that whereas MBO ordains that objectives should be set unilaterally by management (Levinson 1970), goal-setting theory prescribes a participative approach to establishing and reviewing performance standards, whether for individuals or groups. In short, goal-setting theory emphasises the importance of 'self-regulation' to effective motivation and performance management.

### Goal-setting as 'SMART' practice

To recap the discussion in chapter 3, goal-setting theory contends that individuals will be more highly motivated when they are set specific but

challenging levels of performance proficiency achievement within a specified future time frame, when they also have high goal commitment and
self-efficacy, and when feedback on progress towards goal achievement is
continuous. As also noted in chapter 3, this carries a number of practical
implications for effective people management. First, and most importantly,
clear and specific goals are more motivating than generalised and imprecise
statements about expected performance. Second, challenging but attainable goals will be more motivating, particularly for employees with high
achievement need, than will goals that are easily attained. Third, regular,
timely and specific feedback on the progress in achieving goals can have a
positive reinforcement effect on task focus and effort. Fourth, performance
self-regulation via participative goal-setting and reflection on feedback have
more positive motivational effect than do externally imposed standards,
controls and feedback.

The basic steps involved in goal-setting for individual employees are
tenfold:

1 the identification or clarification of KRAs for the job or position involved
   by means of joint discussion between employee and supervisor
2 joint agreement as to valid and reliable KPIs for each KRA
3 joint agreement on a specific quantitative goal for each KRA/KPI set
4 the pursuit of these goals by the employee over a pre-determined performance cycle
5 regular self-monitoring of, and informal supervisory feedback on,
   progress towards goal achievement during this performance cycle
6 at the close of the cycle, a formal comparison of the actual level of goal
   attainment over the period against each agreed KPI goal
7 a formal review of performance outcomes over the cycle, with both
   self-assessment and supervisory assessment of perceived performance
   strengths and weaknesses, and a joint analysis of the reasons for any goal
   shortfall
8 joint sign-off on the review outcomes
9 agreeing an action plan to address any performance deficits, including
   additional resourcing where necessary
10 further discussion of KRAs and KPIs to take account of any changes to
   position content, followed by joint agreement as to the goals for the next
   performance cycle.

Both in the practitioner-focused literature (Bacal 1998; Rudman 1995: 52–7)
and in practice, it has become customary to recommend that the setting

| S | *Specific and stretching:*<br>clear, unambiguous, straightforward, understandable and challenging |
|---|---|
| M | *Measurable and able to be monitored:*<br>related to valid quantifiable performance measures (KPIs) that will allow progress to be tracked during the performance cycle. |
| A | *Agreed and accepted:*<br>a target that the employee has co-determined and over which she/he feels a sense of 'ownership' |
| R | *Realistic and representative:*<br>challenging but position-valid and within the capabilities of the individual |
| T | *Timely:*<br>achievable within a defined time scale, with progress being subject to continuous feedback. |

**Figure 5.1** 'SMART' goals

of goals should be in accordance with what have become known as the 'SMART' criteria. Figure 5.1 summarises the criteria that typically underlie this acronym. You will note that, taken together, these five general requirements seek to uphold the tenets of validity, reliability and self-regulation.

In comparison with the typically detailed nature of performance management instruments designed to assess behaviour and/or competencies, goal-setting instruments are generally quite simple and open-ended in nature. Figure 5.2 is an example of an individual goal-setting instrument. Note that the instrument requires the employee to contribute to all key aspects of the goal-setting process: identifying and weighting KRAs, choosing valid KPIs, setting the specific KPI goals, and assessing and commenting on results achieved. Note, too, that in this case the overall score is the weighted sum of the degree of goal achievement in each KRA. The approach is also readily adaptable to business units and constituent work teams. It can also be linked to the payment of individual and/or collective incentives along the lines to be discussed in chapters 17 and 18.

## Goal-setting: the good, the bad and the ugly

As a method for managing employee results, goal-setting undoubtedly has much to commend it. By using seemingly 'objective' measures, it has the potential to avoid the subjectivity and susceptibility to unreliability inherent in behavioural assessment. It prescribes performance standards that are quantitative and highly specific and which can be aligned readily with the strategic objectives of the organisation or business unit. Since it is results-focused, goal-setting is also applicable equally to individuals, teams, business

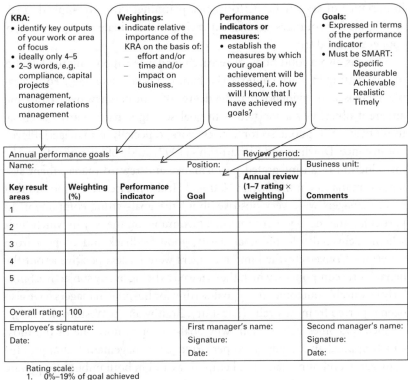

**Figure 5.2**  Individual goal-setting instrument

units and whole organisations, which certainly increases the possibility of achieving and maintaining vertical strategic alignment. At the same time, goal-setting is – or at least should be – highly participative and encourage self-management. As such, it is a natural complement to a high-involvement management culture. The emphasis on outcomes also allows employees discretion to find their own creative pathways to goal achievement, so the method therefore has particular relevance to firms with a prospector competitive strategy since, as noted in chapter 4, creativity and innovation are critical success factors for such organisations. At the level of the individual employee, goal-setting facilitates self-monitoring, feedback and performance improvement on a continuous basis, as well as highlighting the importance of systematic performance planning. Properly applied, goal-setting also encourages greater supervisor–subordinate communication, cooperation and trust.

There is also a solid body of research evidence supporting the benefits of goal-setting in work contexts (Latham & Locke 2006: 332). For example, there is some evidence that the degree of transparency, ownership and apparent objectivity associated with goal-setting is particularly beneficial to motivation in public sector service work, especially at managerial level. For instance, Dowling and Richardson's (1997) study of outcomes from the introduction of an integrated performance and reward management system for managers in the British National Health Service (NHS) found that NHS managers were very positive about the goal-setting component. In particular, the managers commented favourably on the way in which their scheme delivered role and goal clarity, good feedback and support from superiors. Conversely, the same managers were far less positive about the behavioural component, which they viewed as being overly subjective. Similarly favourable outcomes from goal-setting for hospital managers have also been reported from Australia (Lansbury, Braithwaite & Westbrook 1995).

Such outcomes help explain why goal-setting is now one of the most widely applied and highly rated performance management techniques for managerial and non-managerial employees and in both public and private sector organisations. For instance, in the UK, 62 per cent of organisations use 'objective-setting and review' and, of these, 82 per cent rate the method as an effective performance management technique (CIPD 2005a). In Australia, although the reported use of MBO *per se* has declined dramatically since the early 1990s (from 70 per cent in 1990 to just 7 per cent in 2003), most organisations employ 'objectives/targets' as a major aspect of performance management practice at all levels – from senior managers (85 per cent) to line staff (55 per cent) (Nankervis & Compton 2006: 88–9). What this indicates, in effect, is a substantial and widespread use of goal-setting techniques in Australian organisations.

Yet, as leading proponents Latham and Locke themselves acknowledge (Latham & Locke 2006: 334–7), goal-setting also has some potentially serious shortcomings. Being results-focused it downplays behavioural 'means'. Goals may also be too few in number. Tasks not subject to goal-setting may be ignored, and there may be a temptation to set easy goals, especially where goal achievement is linked to pay. Goals may be set in too many areas, perhaps giving rise to an obsessional angst over numbers. Equally, goals may be too generic, perhaps relevant to the organisational level but meaningless at the level of the individual employee. Goals may be weighted in a manner that is inappropriate to the balance of task activity within the job or position. Goals may be defined and measured using indicators that are invalid for the KRA concerned. Goal inconsistency and conflict are also real possibilities, particularly where moderator goals are applied in 'soft' KRAs such as quality, safety and customer satisfaction to temper a narrow focus on results in 'hard' KRAs such as output quantity and cost effectiveness. Further, as was customary during the heyday of MBO (Levinson 1970), goals may be imposed rather than agreed. Likewise, the focus on results may mean that contextual constraints on employees' performance capabilities are underestimated or ignored. For instance, setting the same loans business goals for retail bank branches in suburbs with different levels of average income and wealth will seriously disadvantage bank staff in poorer suburbs and may even encourage them to issue credit to borrowers with inadequate debt-servicing capacity. Conversely, employees may become so fixated on particular goals that that may engage in 'dysfunctional persistence' (Latham & Locke 2006: 337) despite a significant change in the work context. The pursuit of personal goals may have a detrimental effect on group cooperation and performance. Further, where failure to attain a specific goal is punished in some way, goal setting may discourage employees from being creative and taking reasonable risks in pursuing their goals. Employees who have a strong track record of meeting challenging goals may find the hurdle is eventually set so high that it is impossible to achieve. A focus on KRA results may also lead to the neglect of work–life balance considerations, although some organisations now specify work–life balance itself as a mandatory KRA for goal-setting purposes.

While the above problems are primarily matters of system design, and therefore amenable to remedy, there are other problems of a more intractable nature, including problems associated with time horizon, subjectivity and suitability. A focus on short-term individual goals may give rise to a form of strategic myopia, or endemic short-termism. Moreover, whatever the promise of system objectivity, the fact is that the selection of KPIs, the setting of specific KPI goals, the weighting of goals and the interpretation of outcomes against those goals are still matters for human judgement and, hence, subjectivity and possible error (Williams 2002: 88–90).

Perhaps most importantly, however, whatever its promise, goal-setting will not be a suitable fit for all situations. Since goal-setting is a formula for continuous performance enhancement, it also opens the possibility of employee stress and performance 'burnout', particularly where performance potential has technological limits. After all, only so much extra output can be extracted from a given mode of technology and mode of work organisation. In this respect, goal-setting may be inappropriate to narrow, routine jobs of the type commonly found in organisations structured on mechanistic lines. Here, it is likely that employees will be able to work only to a technologically determined standard of performance proficiency and not according to the dictates of 'continuous improvement'. In such situations, performance improvement targets may amount to 'snap' goals rather than 'stretch' goals. Further, goal-setting may be a poor fit in situations of contextual uncertainty, since the goals set today may well be rendered redundant tomorrow by changes that are beyond employees' control (Latham & Pinder 2005: 497–8). At the very least, then, in such situations – including those that are likely to prevail in high-risk/high-return contexts, such as those likely to be sought by prospector firms – provision should be made for goals to be altered or updated during the cycle if circumstances change.

## The balanced scorecard

Like goal-setting theory, the concept of the balanced scorecard is also relatively recent in origin; its authors, Robert Kaplan and David Norton, published their initial formulation in the *Harvard Business Review* (Kaplan & Norton 1992) soon after Locke and Latham released the first fully developed version of goal-setting theory. This close timing may not be entirely coincidental since, as we shall see, multifactor and multilevel goal-setting is a defining feature of the balanced scorecard model.

### The balanced scorecard ideal

The balanced scorecard is a holistic formula for managing organisational goals and results in an integrated and strategically aligned manner. It seeks to do so by recognising multiple stakeholder interests in organisational success and by systematically pursuing synergies between these stakeholder interests. It also sees human resource managers as vital 'strategic partners' and human resources as the key ingredient for business success.

Being results-focused, it subscribes to the assumption that 'what you measure is what you get', and it entails setting and communicating strategically aligned goals and measuring and rewarding goal achievement. As a multi-measure, multi-stakeholder approach to organisation-wide performance management, it recognises three key stakeholders – shareholders, customers and employees – and for this reason the approach is frequently confused with the so-called 'triple bottom-line' approach to defining and evaluating organisational performance. Both approaches certainly acknowledge that shareholder value creation is not the only legitimate organisational objective and, as such, both challenge that defining corporate mantra of the 1980s and 1990s, the doctrine of 'shareholder value creation'. However, rather than seeing shareholder, customer and employee interests as distinct and unrelated, the balanced scorecard sees all three as being bound together in the organisational 'value creation' process, or 'value chain' (Kaplan & Norton 1992, 1996a & b; Mooraj, Oyon & Hostettler 1999).

Figure 5.3 summarises the four facets of value creation identified in the balanced scorecard model, along with the associated stakeholder interests and functional responsibility areas for each. The first is internal learning and growth, which covers employee commitment, capability, learning, creativity and well-being. This, of course, is primarily a human resource management responsibility and, as the developmental accent suggests, the balanced scorecard is very much in line with the resource-based view of the firm and the Harvard School model of 'best practice', which we considered in chapter 4. The second area of value creation is that of internal business processes, which is predicated on employee learning and growth but where the immediate emphasis falls on production line and supply chain technical efficiency. In functional terms, this is the domain of engineers and other systems management professionals. The third facet is the realm of the external customer: the end user of the outcomes from these internal processes and the source of market value creation. Here, functional responsibility lies chiefly with sales and marketing professionals. The final facet is that of value realisation for the organisation's owners, which, in the case of listed companies, are the external shareholders. This could be said to be the functional realm of finance and accounting professionals. Overall, then, the hypothesised value creation process brings together not only employees, customers and shareholders but also professionals from all of the main functional fields. In this sense, it is a formula for the integration of both stakeholder interests and functional expertise, with human resource managers taking a lead role. The model is also said to enable the systematic evaluation of the 'downstream' impact of particular human resource development initiatives on process, customer and financial outcomes.

| Key phases: | Key stakeholders (and functional responsibility areas) | Strategic indicators (examples) |
|---|---|---|
| **4. Financial**<br>*How do we look to shareholders?* | Shareholders<br>(Accounting professionals) | Lag:<br>• Return on equity<br>• Revenue growth<br>Lead:<br>• New or existing product revenue mix |
| **3. Customers**<br>*How do our customers see us?* | External customers<br>(Sales and marketing professionals) | Lag:<br>• Market share<br>• Customer satisfaction<br>Lead:<br>• On-time delivery<br>• Customer-specific product development |
| **2. Internal business processes**<br>*What must we excel at?* | Internal 'customers' and others in supply chain<br>(Engineering, IT and other systems management professionals) | Lag:<br>• Product defect rate<br>• Unit product cost<br>Lead:<br>• Supply chain efficiency |
| **1. Internal learning and growth**<br>*How can we continue to improve and create value?* | Employees<br>(HR professionals) | Lag:<br>• Rate of new product development<br>• Employee job satisfaction<br>Lead:<br>• Develop strategic competencies<br>• New product development time |

**Figure 5.3** The balanced scorecard: four phases of value creation
*Source:* adapted from Kaplan & Norton 1992, 1996a & b.

**Balanced scorecard goals and results for year ended**
(Note: weightings – financial + customer + process + people = 100%)

| Financial perspective goals, weighting = _% | | | | |
|---|---|---|---|---|
| Key result area | Measure/indicator | Goal | Weighting (%) | Outcome (% of goal achieved) |
| Sales revenue | | | | |
| Stock loss | | | | |
| | | | | |
| **Customer perspective goals, weighting = _%** | | | | |
| Key result area | Measure/indicator | Goal | Weighting (%) | Outcome (% of goal achieved) |
| Satisfaction | | | | |
| Product return | | | | |
| | | | | |
| **Process perspective goals, weighting = _%** | | | | |
| Key result area | Measure/indicator | Goal | Weighting (%) | Outcome (% of goal achieved) |
| Accounts | | | | |
| Restocking | | | | |
| | | | | |
| **People perspective goals, weighting = _%** | | | | |
| Key result area | Measure/indicator | Goal | Weighting (%) | Outcome (% of goal achieved) |
| Training | | | | |
| Suggestions | | | | |
| | | | | |
| **Overall results, weighting = 100%** | | | | |
| Financial | | | | |
| Customer | | | | |
| Process | | | | |
| People | | | | |
| **Aggregate:** | | | | **% Goal achievement** |

**Figure 5.4** Example of an individual goal-setting instrument for a retail sales role based on the balanced scorecard

Kaplan and Norton propose that the model should be applied by means of strategic indicators and goals for each of the four areas of value creation that cascade through the organisation and seek to strike a balance, first, between 'lag indicators' (i.e. measures of past results achieved) and 'lead indicators' (i.e. KPI-related performance enhancement goals for future attainment) and, second, between short-term financial goals and long-term developmental goals. Goals that are transmitted from the apex to the base of the organisational structure will thus serve to communicate strategic business objectives throughout the whole organisation to the point where the goals of individual business units and individual employees at all levels align with the organisation's overall strategic success factors. Figure 5.4 provides an example of a personal scorecard applied to individual employees as part of the organisation-wide goal-setting process. Note that the instrument requires KRAs, indicators, goals and weightings to be set in each of the four generic KRAs prescribed by the balanced scorecard model.

## The balanced scorecard: for and against

The balanced scorecard is undoubtedly one of the most comprehensive and cohesive models of 'best practice' performance management to have emerged in recent decades, and its attractions are numerous and substantial. It is results-based, uses multiple measures, offers a means of thoroughgoing strategic alignment, and provides employees with a direct line of sight between the organisation's goals and theirs. It addresses the problem of functional boundaries and 'silos' typical of mechanistic organisational structures by integrating most if not all key business functions in the performance enhancement process while simultaneously having a practical focus on the importance of human resource 'deliverables' in this process. It balances financial and non-financial considerations, short-term and long-term goals, and past and planned results. It stands to facilitate customer focus and customer satisfaction as well as employee goal clarity, development, participation, satisfaction and well-being. Equally, it may encourage organisational creativity, innovation, flexibility and change. Further, the emphasis on performance metrics means that goal attainment can be readily linked to employee rewards in the form of individual goal-based bonus plans (see chapter 17) and/or collective goal-sharing (see chapter 18). Finally, although it is generally seen as a 'best practice' prescription, the model is also capable of being adapted to fit different organisational circumstances. Indeed, while the original model was designed for private firms, it has since been modified to better suit the strategic needs of public sector agencies.

For these reasons, the balanced scorecard and its numerous variants have enjoyed support in the practitioner and prescriptive academic literature (e.g. Huselid, Becker & Ulrich 2001; Manas 1999). In the United States the model has also been adopted by some iconic firms, including Sears Roebuck, AT & T, Motorola, BellSouth, Eastman Kodak, American Express, Mobil Oil, CIGNA, Dow Chemicals, Taco Bell and Tetra Pak (Manas 1999; Marquardt 1997; Mooraj, Oyon & Hostettler 1999; Yeung & Berman 1997). It has also been taken up by larger firms operating in a wide cross-section of industries in smaller developed countries. In Australia, versions of the balanced scorecard have been applied in a range of financial services and service sector firms. For instance, retail bank ANZ utilises an extended balanced scorecard covering five generic KRAs:

• Perform: financial measures
• Customer first: customer and community

- Well-managed: risk, productivity, constraints, operational quality
- Lead and inspire: people and leadership
- Breakout: innovation and transformation

Although these are organisation-wide criteria, each of the ANZ's business units is able to decide the weighting that it wishes to assign to each in assessing its own employees (Callus 2005: 19–20).

Yet it can hardly be said that the balanced scorecard has taken the corporate world by storm. While we still lack reliable data on its incidence internationally, country-specific data suggests that only a minority of organisations have thus far embraced the approach. In Australia, only a quarter of organisations responding to a 2003 survey reported using the balanced scorecard as the basis for their performance management systems (Nankervis & Compton 2006: 90). In the UK the incidence appears to be lower still, with only 3 per cent of organisations using the method as a means of linking team and organisational objectives (CIPD 2005a: 4).

What lies behind this reluctance to embrace the promise of the balanced scorecard? The short answer is that, like many a proffered holistic solution to the challenges of organisational performance enhancement, the balanced scorecard has its practical limitations and conceptual shortcomings, as well as a small but growing number of academic detractors (Andon, Baxter & Mahama 2005; Atkinson, Waterhouse & Well 1997; Norreklit 2000).

On the practical side, its ambitious scope means that its implementation will necessarily take considerable time, resourcing and commitment. Translating broad and long-term corporate objectives into accepted short-term individual goals also poses many practical challenges. The emphasis on strategic goal alignment means that it may easily come to be seen as a top-down control device rather than a genuinely participative practice. The model may also be too cumbersome to cope with sudden and unforeseen changes in the operating environment. The emphasis on internalities – especially human resources and internal process improvement – may also detract from a proper consideration of external developments. The fate of photographic film producer Eastman Kodak and mail-order retailer Sears Roebuck are classic cases in point. In the 1990s Eastman Kodak adopted the balanced scorecard as a means of improving its cost competitiveness in the face of growing global competition. However, its preoccupation with process improvement in the manufacture of high-quality film blinded it to the threat and the opportunity created by the rise of digital photographic technology. Similarly, Sears Roebuck was one of the first firms to take up the balanced scorecard, and it did so chiefly as a turn-around strategy and as a means of clawing back retail market share from aggressive low-cost supermarket stores like Wal-Mart (Wilson 1999: 155–61; Marquardt 1997: 20–1). Again, however, the preoccupation with internal business process improvement blinded the firm to the rise of internet advertising and shopping and, after a brief recovery, its fortunes soured once again. In 2004 it was taken over by a competitor, Kmart.

As to conceptual shortcomings, while Kaplan and Norton's model is commendably pluralist in its conception of stakeholder interests, there are at least three significant omissions: external suppliers, the community at large and the environment. Critics have also pointed to a number of logical flaws in Kaplan and Norton's value chain construct. First, the emphasis on the role of human resource development in value creation and business success may well be overstated, particularly in industries where capital:labour ratios are high and in firms operating in volatile markets with high risk/high return prospects. Second, the assumption of a linear causal relationship between people, processes, customers and profits is open to question. It may be more valid to assume that the relationship between these four facets of value creation is one of mutual interdependence rather than linearity. For instance, learning and development may contribute to financial results, but it is equally credible to suggest that the latter will determine the scope for the former. Finally, as Norreklit (2000) suggests, the Kaplan and Norton model entails a questionable set of assumptions as to the temporal associations between the four foci of value creation since the time horizons associated with each phase or facet are clearly different. For example, whereas improvement in internal processes and customer satisfaction may be accomplished within a matter of months, enhancing staff learning and improving underlying financial performance may take years. At the very least, these time differentials suggest that value creation is subject to multifactorial longitudinal influences rather than being determined in a unilinear fashion.

## Chapter summary

In this chapter, the first of four chapters dedicated to approaches and options for practising performance management, we have considered the concepts and practices associated with defining, measuring and managing employee and organisational results. We began by discussing the nature and importance of three concepts that are defining features of all results-based approaches, namely key result areas (KRAs), key performance indicators (KPIs) and goals. Next, taking up themes first raised in the Introduction, we examined the basic requirements for validity and reliability in results-based approaches in general. The later sections of the chapter were then devoted to an examination of two of the most prominent techniques for managing results, namely goal-setting for individuals and groups, and the balanced scorecard model for the strategically aligned and integrated management of results across four generic result areas: learning and development; internal business processes; customers; and financial performance. As well as noting the strengths of these approaches, in the interests of balance, we have also acknowledged possible practical and conceptual limitations. The evidence suggests that while goal-setting has enormous potential as a valid, reliable and felt-fair method of performance management, only a minority of organisations has as yet experimented with the balanced scorecard, perhaps with good reason.

Clearly, a results-based approach will have greatest relevance and potential where individual, group and/or organisational outcomes can be accurately specified, quantified and measured. Where this cannot be readily accomplished, it may be preferable to look to one or other of the two other horizontal dimensions of work performance – that is, to behaviour and competencies – as the focus of performance measurement and management or, as is more common, to an approach that balances results with behaviour and/or competencies. We shall turn to these two alternative approaches in chapters 6 and 7.

## Discussion questions

1  Is money the only result that really counts?
2  'When it comes to performance, the ends are more important than the means.' Discuss.
3  'You can't manage what you can't measure.' Right or wrong? Why?
4  'Goal-setting isn't really "smart" thinking.' Discuss.
5  What are the strengths and limitations of the balanced score card model?

Chapter Six

# MANAGING BEHAVIOUR

In chapter 2 we examined the nature and possible determinants of three major categories of work behaviour: membership behaviour, task behaviour (or work effort) and organisational citizenship behaviour. In this chapter, we examine the assessment processes and techniques associated with the management of work behaviour, the strengths, weaknesses and common problems of these behavioural assessment methods, and the situations in which each may be most and least appropriate.

Behavioural assessment can be defined as an approach to performance management that focuses primarily (although not necessarily exclusively) on observing, recording and measuring, appraising or assessing the work behaviour of individual employees over a designated period (typically annually, six-monthly or quarterly). Behavioural criteria are applied widely to both managerial and non-managerial employees in both the public and the private sectors. In Australia, for instance, 46 per cent of organisations use behaviourally based measures as part of their approach to performance management (Nankervis & Compton 2006: 88). Historically, behavioural assessment has been one of the hallmarks of individual 'performance appraisal', particularly in service work, and while results and competencies are assuming greater importance in performance management, behaviourally based assessment maintains a strong presence in performance management practices across a wide range of industries, organisations and work roles.

Since work behaviour must be measured and managed by means of human observation and judgement, behavioural assessment necessarily involves subjective judgement and, hence, is prone to human error and unreliability. You will recall from chapter 2 that, along with validity, felt-fairness and cost-effectiveness, reliability is a key requirement for the effectiveness of a performance management system. As we shall see, the subjective element is both the approach's greatest potential shortcoming and one of its main potential advantages, particularly where the performance management system is directed towards enhancing strategic communication, work relationships and employee development.

In this chapter, then, we examine four aspects of behaviourally based performance management: the alternative sources of behavioural information; the sources of potential unreliability in behavioural assessment and how these may be addressed; and the main behavioural assessment techniques available for use in contemporary organisations.

## Sources of behavioural information

Traditionally, the task of behavioural assessment fell largely to the employee's immediate supervisor. Today, however, it is becoming increasingly common for assessment to be undertaken by other stakeholders as well, including peers (especially in teams), subordinates, the assessees themselves, and external customers and clients. This is known generically as multisource assessment and feedback. Where sources include peers, and the assessee as well as the supervisor, the multisource method is known as 180-degree assessment and feedback; where subordinates and/or customers are also included, the method is commonly referred to as 360-degree assessment and feedback. We shall return to the issue of multisource assessment below.

The use of each of these behavioural information sources varies considerably from country to country. Tables 6.1 and 6.2 present recent data on the incidence of these and related assessment sources and methods in the UK and Australia.

### Supervisory assessment

Assessment by supervisors is still very much the norm in most medium- to large-scale organisations. Supervisors are assumed to have the greatest knowledge of job requirements and the most opportunity to observe how employees perform in these jobs. Supervisors also have a vested interest in how well their employees perform.

**Table 6.1** Incidence and perceived effectiveness of performance assessment methods in the UK, 2004: percentage of respondent organisations using each method

| | Organisations using method (%) | Organisations using method and believing it to be effective (%) |
|---|---|---|
| Peer appraisal | 8 | 12 |
| Team appraisal | 6 | 10 |
| Subordinate feedback | 11 | 17 |
| Self-appraisal | 30 | 53 |
| 360-degree appraisal | 14 | 20 |
| Individual annual appraisal | 65 | 83 |
| Biannual appraisal | 27 | 38 |
| Rolling appraisal | 10 | 21 |
| Continuous assessment | 14 | 20 |

*Source:* CIPD 2005a: 3–4.

**Table 6.2** Incidence of performance assessment methods in Australia, 2003: percentage of respondent organisations using each method

| | Organisations using method (%) |
|---|---|
| Behaviourally based measures | 46 |
| Behaviourally anchored rating scales | 20 |
| Competency criteria included | 66 |
| Ranking and rating | 12 |
| Team or workgroup input | 12 |
| Assessment by supervisor only | 6 |
| Self-assessment | 33 |
| Peer assessment | 36 |
| Assessment by subordinates | 9 |
| Multi-assessor feedback | 14 |

*Source:* Nankervis & Compton 2006: 88–9, 92.

On the other hand, in terms of their own career advancement prospects, supervisors have a vested interest in 'talking up' the performance of their subordinates. It is also common for personal bias to intrude into supervisory appraisals. Favouritism is a frequent feature of hierarchical relationships. Supervisory assessment also reinforces hierarchy itself and, while this may be desirable for organisations with mechanistic structures and traditional management cultures, it may be a poor – or at least problematic – fit for organically structured, high-involvement organisations. Such factors may explain the decline in supervisor-only assessment in recent decades. In Australia, for instance, single-source supervisory assessment is now used by just 6 per cent of organisations (see table 6.2).

## Assessment by peers

Assessment by co-workers is particularly well suited to teamworking situations where it may furnish more reliable behavioural information than that provided by supervisors and others further up the management hierarchy. Who better to provide feedback on an employee's performance than those who work beside him or her on a daily basis? Peer assessment is particularly well suited to teamworking contexts. Team co-workers are well placed to identify behavioural strengths and weaknesses easily overlooked by other information sources. This is particularly so of such behavioural criteria as team cooperation, information sharing and peer communication. For the same reason, peer input can be a useful source of information on the development needs of individual team members.

By the same token, peer assessment has some significant weaknesses. It has the potential for biased feedback, especially as a result of the operation of peer friendship networks, the possibility of peer enmity and the fear of peer retribution. Peer assessment may be quite dysfunctional in highly competitive work situations. Peers may also be reluctant to provide negative information when they know that the assessee's pay or promotion prospects may depend on what they report. For this reason, peer appraisal is probably better for developmental purposes than evaluative ones. It is also likely to be opposed by unions because of the anti-collectivist potential of peer surveillance (Bettenhausen & Fedor 1997; Fox, Ben-Nahum & Yinon 1989; Murphy & Cleveland 1995: 140–2; Peiperl 2001).

The incidence of peer assessment varies considerably from country to country. In Australia, it is used by 36 per cent of organisations (see table 6.2). By contrast, in the UK just 8 per cent of organisations use peer assessment, of which only a small minority (12 per cent) believe that it is actually effective (see table 6.1). The comparable figures for team-based appraisal in the UK are also low, with only 6 per cent of organisations using this method, and with a low approval rating (10 per cent) among those that do use it.

## Assessment by subordinates

Appraisal by subordinates – or 'bottom-up' assessment – focuses on elicit-ing information on how effectively supervisors manage downwards. It also supports employee involvement strategies. Feedback from subordinates can support two-way communication and management development, as well as being a potentially powerful means of reinforcing supervisors' accountabil-ity for their own judgements about subordinates (Bernardin 1986). As with peer assessment, the use of bottom-up assessment varies greatly between countries. Subordinates' assessment is applied in 9 per cent of Australian organisations (see table 6.2) and 11 per cent of UK organisations, although, as with peer appraisal, only a small minority of British users (17 per cent) believe that it is effective (see table 6.1).

Again, this may be because subordinates' feedback also has some signifi-cant shortcomings. While it can illuminate behavioural problems associated with managing downwards, it will shed little light on how the supervisor manages upwards, a set of behavioural dimensions about which subordi-nates are likely to have little direct knowledge or opportunity to observe. Subordinates may also be inclined to inflate assessments either to ingrati-ate themselves with supervisors or to avoid possible retribution (Antonioni 1994; Redman & Mathews 1995). Upward appraisal can also place super-visors themselves in difficult situations. For instance, it may inhibit them from taking tough decisions for fear that this may alienate their subordinates and make them uncooperative. For these reasons, it may be desirable that bottom-up feedback be given anonymously and on a rotating basis involving random assessor selection. Clearly this will be feasible only where the sub-ordinate cohort is relatively large (Bettenhausen & Fedor 1997; Murphy & Cleveland 1995: 136–7).

## Self-assessment

The rise of self-appraisal is undoubtedly one of the most important devel-opments in behavioural assessment techniques in recent times. In the UK, it is used by 30 per cent of organisations, of whom more than half rate it as being an effective performance management technique (see table 6.1). In Australia, too, self-assessment is now used by 33 per cent of organisations (see table 6.2), up from 25 per cent in 1990 (Nankervis & Compton 2006: 97).

Self-assessment is particularly valuable in identifying individual behavioural deficits and associated training and development needs. As such, it is particularly appropriate for systems with a developmental purpose. It is also compatible with a management culture that is high trust and high involvement in nature.

By the same token, self-assessment is prone to unreliability driven by self-serving bias. A meta-analysis by Harris and Schaubroeck (1988) found that while peer and supervisory ratings were relatively highly correlated, the correlations between self-supervisor and self-peer ratings were much weaker. The tendency to self-serving bias means that self-assessment would be inappropriate for systems with a predominantly evaluative purpose, especially where assessments are linked to pay. In such situations, self-assessments will almost certainly be inflated. For this reason alone, it would be inadvisable to use self-appraisal for pay determination purposes. Self-assessment can also be dysfunctional where a highly competitive individual performance pay system applies and there is low trust among peers. In sum, the method would be best suited to high-trust, participative work cultures that place a premium on staff learning and development. It is only in these circumstances that employees will be confident that their self-assessments will be respected and acted upon in a constructive manner (Atwater 1998; Meyer 1980; Murphy & Cleveland 1995: 137–40).

### External customers or clients

Behavioural feedback from external customers or clients has particular appeal to organisations seeking to develop a customer-focused culture of the type typical of quality defender and analyser competitive strategies.

Customer feedback typically takes the form of customer satisfaction surveys, and the focus is usually on the performance of units and divisions rather than individuals. Firms of all sizes now routinely use customer satisfaction surveys as part of their overall performance monitoring and management systems. However, where the work is service-based and individualised, as in retailing, financial services, customer service, hospitality and call centre operations, for example, customer feedback often focuses on the behaviour of the individual employee. Overall, customer feedback is most appropriate where employees are in regular contact with external customers, as in the case of sales representatives, staff involved in field maintenance and servicing work, and customer service staff.

Obviously, customer-based assessment cannot take all aspects of work performance into account, since the customer has only a limited knowledge of the person's behaviour and results. Hence, the validity and reliability of customer input is open to question. The reliability of customer responses is also open to doubt since customers have no accountability for their input. It can also be expensive to administer, although many organisations have automated the process using computerised customer satisfaction surveys.

One means of circumventing the cost and reliability problems associated with customer surveys is the so-called 'mystery customer' technique, also known in retailing as the 'mystery shopper' method. This approach, which has grown significantly in popularity in recent years, especially in retailing and call centres, involves a one-time observation and assessment of an actual employee–customer interaction by an in-house or external participant observer masquerading as an ordinary customer, client or shopper. The employee may have been informed that such a procedure is being used in the organisation, but she/he will be unaware of the assessor's identity and the time when the assessment occurs. Secretive assessment of this type may elicit highly accurate behavioural information, and the observer may well be more impartial than, say, a supervisor or peer. However, the method is also open to question on several important grounds, not the least being those to do with the ethically dubious and possibly illegal nature of secret surveillance. The methods may also violate employees' perceptions of procedural and distributive fairness and, hence, both compromise trust and cause a breach of the psychological contract. Indeed, while the technique remains under-researched, there is some evidence (Brender-Ilan & Shultz 2005) that the mystery customer method is viewed by service workers as being procedurally and distributively less fair than supervisory assessment, because the assessment is based on just one encounter, because of the anonymity of the judgement process itself and because the practice does not treat the employee with dignity and respect. Additionally, where the assessment is undertaken by an external agent, assessees may doubt the agent's competence to undertake a valid and reliable assessment.

## Multisource assessment

According to exponents, multisource rating has the potential to overcome many of the problems inherent in traditional supervisory rating. Put simply, the assumption is that the greater the number of knowledgeable assessors, the more accurate the overall rating is likely to be.

Typically, multisource assessment involves each assessee being assessed by the immediate supervisor, several peers and, where supervisory employees themselves are being rated, by several subordinates. Where the employee has direct contact with customers or clients, assessment by customers may also be included. Where the assessee is a line employee, between three and five assessors are generally involved; where the assessee is a supervisor, the number of assessors typically doubles. The aggregate assessment is typically a weighted average of the individual assessments, with the composite feedback being communicated by the direct supervisor.

Advocates (Antonioni 1996; Edwards & Ewen 1996a, 1996b) contend that multisource assessment offers a more participative, inclusive, balanced, development-oriented, valid, reliable and procedurally fair means of gauging employees' behaviour. Perhaps its greatest single attraction is its synergy with a high-involvement management culture and a relational or balanced psychological contract that emphasises staff development (Garavan, Morley & Flynn 1997).

However, the multisource approach does have several potential shortcomings. It multiplies the amount of information management involved. (One way to manage this additional information load is to use intranet-based assessment, online tutorials for assessors, computerised collation of appraisal results and computer-generated reports.) Moreover, one extreme rating can still influence the overall score. While 360-degree rating has the advantage of providing readings on each individual's performance from a range of different vantage points, assessor bias remains an ever-present possibility, and the impact of one aberrant rating can still be quite dramatic. One solution would be to eliminate extreme ratings automatically from the multiassessor collations. However, this overlooks the possibility that outlier ratings may occasionally reflect an assessee's performance quite accurately from the assessor's particular vantage point. Further, assessors, especially subordinates, may withhold negative ratings for fear of retribution, although again this may be addressed by means of assessor anonymity (Garavan, Morley & Flynn 1997). By the same token, peer and subordinate assessors are not accountable for follow-through with feedback or corrective advice and may therefore feel little accountability for ensuring that the judgements they make are accurate (Wood et al. 2000). For these reasons, multisource assessment may be better adapted to a developmental than to an evaluative purpose.

It may be that multisource assessment, particularly 360-degree assessment, is a technique whose time has passed. Enthusiasm for multisource assessment peaked in the late 1990s, but by the mid-2000s its incidence had become limited and fragmentary. In Australia, only 14 per cent of organisations report using multiassessor feedback, although a great many more do make use of at least some forms of non-supervisory input (see table 6.2). In the UK, 360-degree assessment is also used by just 14 per cent of organisations, and of these only a fifth rate it as being effective (see table 6.1). Indeed, there is little firm evidence that it does improve employee performance.

There are those who suggest that the multiassessor model is little more than an exercise in impression management. For example, British critical sociologist Keith Grint (1995: 68–89) argues that 360-degree assessment is concerned with creating a false impression of employee involvement and empowerment and greater objectivity. It merely replaces single-assessor subjectivity with multiassessor subjectivity. Moreover, at the end of the day, it is still the managers who determine reward and punishment. Interestingly, however, Grint concedes that upward appraisal does at least hold out the promise that managers may become more empathetic towards their subordinates and accountable for their well-being.

## Managing unreliability in behavioural observation and assessment

Of all of the problems associated with behavioural assessment, the most widely acknowledged is undoubtedly that of assessment error or unreliability. This is because behavioural assessment is, by definition, a subjective process – assessors are required to make judgements about the assessee's work behaviour. This means that the assessment process relies on consistent behavioural observation, accurate recall of observed behavioural incidents, and reliable summation and interpretation of these incidents. Each of these requirements is subject to the possibility of error.

Assessment error may be either unintentional or intentional. Unintentional errors arise from the limitations of human cognitive capacity, and especially from the fallibility of unaided memory. Errors of this type frequently happen because the information processing demands exceed the limits of cognitive capacity (Bretz, Milkovich & Read 1992: 323–6; DeNisi & Peters 1996; DeNisi & Williams 1988; Murphy & Cleveland 1995: 182–214). By contrast, intentional errors (also known as classification errors) arise from the conscious manipulation of assessment scores for the assessor's own personal or political reasons. Reliable assessment and classification may actually be the last consideration on the assessor's mind. They may be pursuing their own goals rather than those of the organisation. This is because assessors are players in the game of organisational politics rather than detached observers free of vested interest. Let us consider briefly some of the specific types of error that may arise in each of these two categories.

## Unintentional errors

Among the most widely acknowledged forms of unintentional inaccuracy are:

- halo and horns errors
- first impression error
- recency error
- similarity error
- attribution error.

Halo and horns errors occur because the assessor bases the assessment on just one positive or negative behavioural incident. If the assessor's cognitive processes allow one positive episode to overshadow all other behavioural observations, including those of a negative nature, the assessment will be distorted by what is known as a 'halo effect'; that is, the assessee is perceived in angelic terms – as being incapable of doing any wrong. If the assessor's cognitive processes permits one negative incident to colour the overall assessment, irrespective of any positive behavioural episodes, the assessment will be distorted by what is referred to as a 'horns effect'; that is, the assessee's behaviour is seen as being diabolical, complete with metaphorical horns. In effect, the assessor falls back on trait-like judgements of the person rather than the performance, a habit that is all the more likely where the assessor is required to process information relating to a large number of assessees. Either way, the totality of the assessee's behavioural performance is not reliably factored into the final judgement (Murphy, Jako & Anhalt 1993).

As the term suggests, first impression error occurs when the assessor develops an enduring negative or positive impression of the assessee at an initial encounter and allows that impression to colour the assessment of all subsequent performance. Clearly, first impression error bears a close relationship to halo and horns error.

Recency error amounts to last impression error. Without a written record of employee behaviour, the assessor may simply rate on the basis of the most recent and clearly recalled behavioural observations. For the assessor, this may simply be a reflection of limited long-term memory capacity and recall; to the assessee, however, it also presents an opportunity for conscious manipulation of the assessment process by engaging in attention-seeking behaviour immediately before the formal assessment round.

Similarity error occurs where the assessor habitually but unknowingly gives more favourable assessments to individuals whom they see as being like themselves in appearance, interests, behaviour and/or perceived personality, and lower assessments to perceived opposites. Similarity error may be a deeply embedded cause of unconscious discrimination on gender, ethnic, racial and age-related grounds in some organisations. For instance, there is some evidence that it has contributed to the persistence of the 'glass ceiling' and the continued under-representation of women in senior management positions.

Attribution error occurs when the assessor makes unreliable judgements regarding the causes of observed high or low work performance. One of the major problems of traditional supervisory assessment is that supervisors are far more likely to attribute the performance by their subordinates to within-person factors rather than to contextual factors, such as the level of resourcing or the quality of supervision itself. What supervisor would willingly admit that the quality of their supervision may be substandard? Attribution errors are immensely difficult to overcome. There is some evidence (Dobbins et al. 1993) that assessors frequently fail to distinguish between performance that is within the employee's control and performance that is not. In particular, assessors may fail to take into account situational factors that inhibit or enhance employee performance. Individuals can perform only within the opportunities and constraints set by the job context. For instance, a performance-enhancing factor might be access to leading-edge information technology or greater training in job relevant skills. Inhibiting factors might include poor materials, tools or information, organisational bottlenecks, unpleasant or dangerous work conditions, inadequate information flow or poor management direction. These are sometimes referred to as 'situational constraints' (Bacharach & Bamberger 1995; Peters, O'Connor & Eulberg 1985). Any assessment process that affords inadequate consideration to situational enablers and constraints is likely to result in assessments that are both invalid and unreliable.

Attribution error is also especially salient where self-assessment is involved. Exponents of attribution theory (Heider 1958; Jones & Harris 1967) argue that self-assessment judgements have a high propensity for self-serving attribution or bias. In particular, self-assessors are inclined to attribute high personal performance to factors within their control, or internal to 'the self', while ascribing low personal performance to situational factors that are beyond their control or external to themselves. This, of course, is one of the reasons why self-assessment is rarely applied as a stand-alone source of behavioural information and judgement.

These, then, are some of the most common forms of unintentional error. Such errors have the potential to erode system validity and reliability as well as employee trust in system fairness. While it is most unlikely that such errors could be eliminated entirely from the assessment process, there are several means by which such errors may be minimised. One strategy is to alert assessors to the possibility of such errors occurring by incorporating coverage of each error type in an appropriate prior training program. Since such errors are unconscious rather than calculative, drawing attention to the possibility of their occurrence is likely to serve as a means of error containment. A second strategy is to support observational recall by requiring assessors and assessees to record significant behavioural incidents as they occur using either a performance diary or what are known as 'critical incident' forms. This documentation can then be reviewed by both parties before undertaking a summative assessment (Greenberg 1987).

## Intentional errors

Intentional errors arise because the assessors concerned – whether supervisors, peers, subordinates or the self – see assessment as a tool for furthering their perceived personal interests within the organisation (Kozlowski, Chao & Morrison 1998; Longenecker, Sims & Gioia 1987). You will recall from the Introduction that conscious manipulation of this type appears to have been a significant feature of performance management within the Australian Public Service. These conscious attempts to manipulate assessment can be reduced to three main forms of intentional error: leniency error, harshness error and central tendency error.

Leniency error occurs when, to avoid interpersonal conflict or to attract more resources to her unit, an assessor may give some or all assessees an undeservedly high rating. To illustrate: if a supervisory assessor wishes to impress her own superiors, she may be inclined to inflate the assessments that she gives to her own subordinates because she perceives that truthful assessments may reflect badly on her own managerial performance. She may also be concerned that lower ratings will sour her relationship with subordinates or be tempted to give an overly generous assessment to some-one she wants to see promoted out of her section. Leniency is one of the most intractable of all assessment errors (Murphy & Cleveland 1995: 241–59).

Alternatively – although less commonly – the assessor may be unduly harsh with some or all assessees, perhaps to assert power over them or to drive them to enhance their real performance level further still. Harshness error of this type is a hallmark of the 'management by fear' approach to staff supervision. Harshness error may also occur where the assessor wishes to be rid of a capable but troublesome subordinate or to see off a pretender to their own supervisory position.

To avoid conflict either way, the assessor may be tempted to engage in central tendency error; that is, failing to distinguish accurately between high and low performers but locating all assessees at the midpoint of the assess-ment range. Central tendency error may buy the assessor a modicum of workplace harmony, but it may also have extremely negative consequences for the organisation. In particular, it may demotivate high performers while giving low performers no incentive or encouragement to change their ways.

Intentional errors are potentially both more destructive and more diffi-cult to eliminate than unintended errors. They are inevitable consequences of organisational power inequality and interpersonal politics. The primary means of controlling intentional error is to maximise assessor accountabil-ity for the judgements they make, as well as their belief in the validity and value of assessment outcomes (Marshall & Wood 2000; Murphy & Cleveland 1995: 259–66, 419–20). The use of subordinate assessors may be a useful means of combating harshness and central tendency errors, although it may also increase the probability of leniency error. Another potentially effective means to this end is the process of assessment verification. Typically, this involves the implementation of statistical cross-checking to ensure consis-tency between assessors. Many organisations now use external consultants and computer programs to collate, verify and standardise appraisal results. Forced distribution is another widely used means of combating deliber-ate distribution errors. Typically, this involves each assessor's results being ranked and then recalibrated to fit a bell curve, with preordained cut-off points between adjacent performance grades. However, assessment 'nor-malising' along these lines may give rise to problems of its own, particularly perceptions of procedural unfairness. We shall revisit the issue of forced distribution below.

## Behavioural assessment methods

In one respect, the history of behavioural assessment is best understood as the history of an unending quest for ever more accurate (i.e. valid and reliable) measurement methods. As the flaws in each approach have become more evident, new instruments have been developed in a bid to overcome these deficiencies. Yet the quest for the Holy Grail continues, and there is ongoing debate about which of the available methods offers the best solution to the general problems of validity, reliability and felt-fairness. The safest approach to adopt here is that some methods will be a better fit for some strategies, structures and cultures than for others, a point to which we shall return later in the chapter.

The behavioural assessment techniques developed to date can be grouped into two broad categories: comparative methods and rating methods. Comparative methods seek to develop a ranking of individuals within a given work group on the basis of assessments of relative performance. The comparison may involve either holistic person-by-person comparisons or comparison on a criterion-by-criterion basis, which are then aggregated into an overall ranking. Comparative techniques are perhaps most useful where the main purpose is to differentiate between individual performers in relatively small work groups. However, while they do allow the organisation to track changes over time in each employee's relative position in the ranking, they provide no absolute benchmarks on change over time in individual performance, generally lack specificity as to individual strengths and weaknesses, and are incapable of providing focused feedback on what individuals may need to do to improve their performance. Moreover, in the simplest of these comparative methods, the behavioural assessment criteria are generally unstated, which makes such methods particularly susceptible to validity and reliability problems. Comparative methods include:

- straight ranking
- alternation ranking
- paired comparison
- forced ranking or distribution.

Rating methods, by contrast, attempt to define behaviour deemed necessary to job effectiveness and to measure the extent to which each employee exhibits such behaviour. They thus differ from ranking approaches in that they seek to rate performance against a set of standard behavioural criteria and generally to determine an absolute numerical rating for each employee. Depending upon the system's purpose, these individual ratings may or may not then be used to determine a rank order. There are numerous variants of the rating approach, but the main types are:

- critical incident method
- Graphic Rating Scales (GRS) and Mixed Standards Scales (MSS)
- Behaviourally Anchored Rating Scales (BARS)
- Behavioural Observation Scales (BOS)
- weighted checklist
- forced choice.

Let us now examine each of these methods more closely so that we will be better placed to choose between them in an informed way.

### Straight ranking

With the straight ranking approach, all employees are ranked from 'best' to 'worst' on the basis of comparative overall performance. The primary attraction of straight ranking is its simplicity. It requires a minimum of bureaucracy and may be an acceptable solution for small enterprises with just a few employees. Since it involves rank ordering, it necessarily combats intentional assessment errors, particularly central tendency and leniency errors.

However, the emphasis on whole-person judgements and the absence of specific behavioural criteria mean that the assessment process is highly subjective and prone to both construct or criterion invalidity and assessment unreliability, especially via unintentional errors. The main source of potential invalidity is that ranking may be driven by impressionistic views of personality traits rather than by job-relevant behaviour. Nor does it permit meaningful comparisons between different work groups that are ranked by different assessors. Indeed, there is no way of knowing whether assessors have actually adhered to a consistent set of assessment criteria. It can really be applied with any degree of accuracy only to quite small work groups. Straight ranking also provides no measure of the degree of difference in performance, only relative position in performance ranking. This means that it is generally a poor means of identifying and remedying specific weaknesses in individual performance. The approach also assumes that no two subordinates have equal performance. It may be relatively easy to rank the top and bottom performers, but what of those who are middle-order

**Ranking scale for the behavioural criterion:**_____

*Instructions:*
1.  For the behaviour being assessed, list all of the employees to be ranked.
2.  Put the name of the employee who ranks highest <u>for this criterion</u> on line 1.
3.  Put the lowest-ranking employee <u>for this criterion</u> on the last numbered line (e.g. line 20, where there are 20 employees to be ranked).
4.  Then list the next highest ranking employee on line 2, the next lowest ranking employee on the next lowest line (e.g. line 19) etc.
5.  Continue until all employees have been ranked for this criterion.

| Highest-ranking employee | |
| --- | --- |
| 1. | 11. |
| 2. | 12. |
| 3. | 13. |
| 4. | 14. |
| 5. | 15. |
| 6. | 16. |
| 7. | 17. |
| 8. | 18. |
| 9. | 19. |
| 10. | 20. |
| | **Lowest-ranking employee** |

**Figure 6.1** Example of alternation ranking instrument

performers – typically the majority of the workforce? Since it does not provide an absolute rating, it is also difficult to link it to pay decisions.

## Alternation ranking

Alternation ranking is similar to straight ranking, except that comparison is criterion by criterion rather than whole of person. Figure 6.1 illustrates how the method works in practice. For each behavioural criterion, the assessor chooses the employee who has outperformed all others on this criterion and inserts their name at the top of the criterion ranking. She then selects the employee who has performed least well on this criterion than any other, and inserts their name at the bottom of the criterion rank order. The employees assessed as second highest and second lowest are then added to the ordering, and so on until all employees have been ranked on each criterion. An overall ranking is then determined, with the employee ranking highest most frequently being ranked first overall, and so on down the rankings until the employee achieving the greatest number of low rankings is accounted for.

Because alternation ranking does specify a set of desired types of behaviour, it is likely to achieve higher validity than straight ranking. Since it also involves standardised assessment criteria, it also affords greater inter-assessor reliability, which means that the method is more amenable to cross-group comparisons. For the same reason, it is also more capable of identifying specific behavioural deficits. However, there is still no measure of absolute performance difference between individuals and, notwithstanding the presence of behavioural standards, the method is still prone to unintentional assessor error.

## Paired comparison

Paired comparison is a more methodical variant of alternation ranking. Examples of criterion-specific paired comparison instruments are given in figure 6.2. Each employee is formally compared with every other employee, one at a time, for each performance criterion. Each is then ranked according to the number of criteria for which they were judged to be the higher performer in each pairing.

Paired comparison has the appearance of thoroughness and is likely to furnish more reliable rankings than either straight ranking or alternation ranking. However, the fact that hundreds and possibly thousands of comparisons may be involved heightens the possibility of unintentional error. Like simpler ranking methods, this method also fails to measure the degree of absolute performance difference between individuals.

## Forced ranking

Forced ranking (or forced distribution) is simply a variant of straight ranking and is typically applied in large organisations as a means of rank-ordering a large number of employees from best to worst, primarily for evaluative purposes. This is sometimes referred to as the 'totem pole' approach. Some major US firms, such as General Electric, have applied forced distribution as a recurrent means of routinely culling the lowest performing 10 per cent of their workforce. Under its previous CEO, Jack Welch, General Electric literally 'decimated' its workforce each year with the aim of fostering a 'true meritocracy', a practice that Welch (cited in Gerhart & Rynes 2003: 184) justifies as follows: 'A company that bets its future on its people must remove the lower 10 per cent, and keep removing it every year – always raising the bar of performance and increasing the quality of its leadership.' At least a quarter of the Fortune 500 firms in the United States – including Cisco Systems, Hewlett-Packard, Microsoft, Lucent and Intel – have incorporated forced distribution into their performance management systems (Scullen, Bergey & Aiman-Smith 2005: 1), although anecdotal evidence indicates that the method is now on the wane (Smith 2006).

**For behavioural criterion:** *team communication*

Key: + means superior to; − means inferior to. For each chart, sum the number of positives in each column to identify the highest-ranked employee on this criterion.

| Compared to: | Alan | Kate | Louise | Ahmed | Joy |
|---|---|---|---|---|---|
| Alan | | + | + | − | − |
| Kate | − | | − | − | − |
| Louise | − | + | | + | − |
| Ahmed | + | + | − | | + |
| Joy | + | + | + | − | |
| Total superior | 2 | 4 | 2 | 1 | 1 |

Kate ranks highest on team communication behaviour.

**For behavioural criterion:** *customer focus*

Key: + means superior to; − means inferior to. For each chart, sum the number of positives in each column to identify the highest-ranked employee on this criterion.

| Compared to: | Alan | Kate | Louise | Ahmed | Joy |
|---|---|---|---|---|---|
| Alan | | − | − | − | − |
| Kate | + | | − | + | + |
| Louise | + | + | | − | + |
| Ahmed | + | − | + | | − |
| Joy | + | − | − | + | |
| Total superior | 4 | 1 | 1 | 2 | 2 |

Alan ranks highest on customer focus behaviour.

**Figure 6.2** Example of a paired comparison instrument

With forced distribution, which is a more sophisticated variant of forced ranking, predetermined percentages of employees are placed in performance grades or categories so that the overall spread of performers conforms to a normally distributed curve; that is, to a 'bell curve'. Figure 6.3 illustrates the logic of forced distribution. The method is often applied to straight ranking as a way of establishing degrees of difference in performance for the purpose of determining individual pay outcomes. The assessor is required to assign ranked subordinates to different grades, with a specified maximum

| Performance grade | Specified percentage of employees in grade |
|---|---|
| Top grade | Top 2% |
| 9th grade | Next 4% |
| 8th grade | Next 7% |
| 7th grade | Next 17% |
| 6th grade | Next 20% |
| 5th grade | Next 20% |
| 4th grade | Next 17% |
| 3rd grade | Next 7% |
| 2nd grade | Next 4% |
| Bottom grade | Bottom 2% |

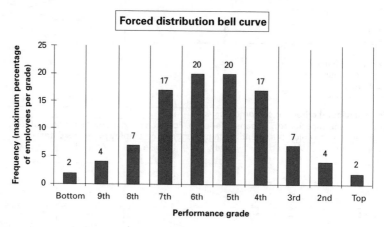

**Figure 6.3** Forced distribution

proportion per grade. Forced distribution may be applied in conjunction either with the above comparative techniques or with rating techniques such as those discussed below. With the latter, the raw scores produced by means of numerical rating techniques are 'normalised', with individuals being assigned to categories on a graded bell curve.

Forced distribution definitely serves to eliminate central tendency, leniency or harshness error since it forces assessors to differentiate between assessees. Some commentators (Grote 2005) argue that forced ranking offers a powerful means of differentiating between employees for the purposes of staff retention, retrenchment and performance enhancement. There is also some research evidence (Scullen, Bergey & Aiman-Smith 2005) that forced ranking can lead to significant improvement in workforce performance, at least in the initial year of application, with the performance improvement reportedly being stronger the greater the percentage of workers fired and the lower the level of voluntary staff turnover.

However, both forced ranking and forced distribution have some major shortcomings. Forced ranking assumes that the initial rankings are necessarily valid and error-free. However, validity and reliability cannot be taken as given, especially with the comparative methods we have considered so far. When used as a termination device, the benefits of forced ranking are likely to be short-lived. Over time, as with goal-setting, the constant raising of the performance bar is likely to produce diminishing returns, particularly as it becomes more difficult to recruit people who are able to outperform those who have been terminated. One study found that while the practice resulted in a 16 per cent productivity improvement in the first two years, by the third and fourth years, improvement was down to just 6 per cent and declined further thereafter (Smith 2006). Detractors such as Lawler (2002) contend that forced ranking is punitive and inherently unfair and that it promotes a form of ruthless, devil-take-the-hindmost individualism and a culture of 'survival of the fittest'. Other critics (Landry 2005, cited in Smith 2006) have characterised it as the so-called 'rank-and-yank' approach to performance management.

Clearly, forced distribution is unlikely to support a culture of high trust and high involvement and will have a high propensity to cause breach of the psychological contract. With forced distribution, the assumption that individual performance is normally distributed may itself be invalid, especially in high-performance workplaces and workgroups, where individual differences are likely to be slight and therefore subject to measurement error. With forced distribution, individual employees may meet all of the stated criteria for an A grading, but since only a limited percentage can be awarded an A, they may be forced down to a B. Naturally, this stands to undermine system trust and a sense of distributive justice.

## Critical incident technique

First developed as a social science research technique by John Flanagan in 1954, the critical incident method is the foundation of virtually all existing behavioural rating approaches. The technique outlines procedures for collecting direct observations of human behavioural incidents that are deemed to be of special significance in terms of consequences. According to Flanagan, for an incident to be critical 'it must occur in a situation where the purpose or intent of the act seems fairly clear to the observer and where its consequences are sufficiently definite to leave little doubt concerning its effects' (Flanagan 1954: 327).

In practice, with critical incident technique the assessor observes and records work behaviour that is deemed to be particularly effective or ineffective in achieving job requirements. The incident reports provide descriptions of the assessee's behaviour at its best and its worst and can be collated into a formal performance record using a diary format or purpose-made critical incident forms. Employees may also be required to undertake behavioural self-assessment along these lines or to provide written responses to incidents observed and reported by the supervisor. Critical incident method strengthens construct validity because it focuses on work behaviour rather than on, say, personality traits. Specific feedback can then be given on behavioural strengths and weaknesses. The use of diaries or critical incident forms serves to minimise the possibility of recency error and, hence, to strengthen assessment reliability. The method also identifies job-valid critical behaviour that can be used as criteria in more sophisticated behavioural rating methods of the type considered below (Fenwick & De Cieri 1995).

Strictly speaking, critical incident technique is not itself a behavioural rating method; rather it identifies performance criteria on which valid ratings may be based. As such, it may be difficult to convert the recorded incidents into an overall rating. Being non-quantitative, the method cannot be used by itself to determine performance ratings. The technique also presents a number of other problems. Most obviously, perhaps, the knowledge that a supervisor is keeping a running record (a 'little black book') of behavioural incidents can be intimidating. It is also time-consuming for the supervisor. Moreover, the incidents themselves are not weighted in terms of their relative importance to job performance. Unintentional error may still occur because, for certain employees, the supervisor may unwittingly record only positive behavioural incidents or, conversely, only behaviour of a negative type. Unless assessors have a clear awareness of the sort of behaviour they are required to look for, their observations and assessments may be idiosyncratic, inconsistent and, hence, unreliable. By the same token, the method is also open to intentional manipulation via the selective reporting of behavioural incidents.

## Graphic Rating Scales and Mixed Standards Scales

Graphic Rating Scales (GRS) are among the most widely used quantitative rating techniques. The behavioural categories deemed to be performance-related are listed in a graphic rating matrix of the type illustrated in figure 6.4. Each employee's performance is then rated against each one of these categories. The overall rating is typically against five or seven grades

| | 1<br>Unsatisfactory | 2<br>Needs<br>improvement | 3<br>Meets<br>expectations | 4<br>Exceeds<br>expectations | 5<br>Exceptional |
|---|---|---|---|---|---|
| Communication | | | | ✓ | |
| Judgement | | | ✓ | | |
| Planning | | ✓ | | | |
| Reliability | | | | | ✓ |
| Initiative | | | ✓ | | |
| Resilience and flexibility | | ✓ | | | |
| Problem-solving | | | ✓ | | |
| Supports company values | | | ✓ | | |
| Develops self | | ✓ | | | |
| | | | | | |
| **Overall assessment** | | | ✓ | | |

**Figure 6.4** Example of a simple graphic rating scale

of performance, from the most positive to the least so. For each behavioural criterion, the assessor is required to select the most appropriate grade of performance. The grades for each criterion are then aggregated arithmetically or intuitively to determine an overall performance rating.

GRS are relatively easy to develop and have the appearance of scientific objectivity. Because they enable all employees to be assessed against a common set of performance criteria, they stand to strengthen inter-assessor consistency and reliability. Being quantitative, they also provide an absolute measure of performance differences between employees rather than just a relative ranking. For the same reason, they also permit direct comparison of the ratings produced by different assessors. Since they require ratings across multiple criteria, they stand to strengthen content validity as well as to reduce the likelihood of halo and horns errors.

A minor variant of GRS are Mixed Standards Scales (MSS). With MSS, the assessor is required to rate each employee's performance on each stated performance criterion against a proficiency standard specific to that criterion; hence the term 'mixed standards'. Typically, the criterion-specific standard carries a simple one-word descriptor, such as 'average', 'acceptable' or 'proficient'. For each scale, the assessor is required to indicate whether the assessee's performance on that criterion is below, at or above the standard. Figure 6.5 illustrates a section of an MSS instrument.

Since they generally do not provide standard definitions for either the behavioural criteria or each performance grade, GRS and MSS instruments remain vulnerable to most forms of intentional and unintentional assessor error. Because they typically provide only one- or two-word

| | Inflexible | Normal | Highly adaptable |
|---|:---:|:---:|:---:|
| Flexibility | | ✓ | |

| | Low | Average | High |
|---|:---:|:---:|:---:|
| Initiative | | | ✓ |

| | Poor | Proficient | Strong |
|---|:---:|:---:|:---:|
| Communication | | ✓ | |

| | Substandard | Acceptable | Outstanding |
|---|:---:|:---:|:---:|
| Overall performance | | ✓ | |

**Figure 6.5** Example of a section of a mixed standards scale

descriptions of each behavioural criterion and each performance grade, there is still considerable scope for idiosyncratic interpretation and, hence, inconsistency and unreliability in the way performance standards are applied, both between different assessors and by any one assessor over time. The problem of unreliability will be compounded where the behavioural criteria specified encourage judgements based on personal traits rather than performance. This would certainly apply to such criteria as 'responsibility', 'loyalty', 'ethicality', 'trustworthiness', 'resilience' and 'independence'. In the absence of detailed criterion definitions, different assessors will almost certainly interpret trait-like criteria in different ways. For instance, behaviour that one assessor interprets as positive proxies for 'loyalty', another assessor may view as signifying a lack of 'independence'. Moreover, in the absence of detailed grade descriptors, what one assessor interprets as 'meeting expectations' or 'satisfactory' may be interpreted more positively or less so by another assessor. As we shall see, more sophisticated GRS seek to minimise these problems by providing standard descriptions of each behaviour and each rating grade. With MSS, the use of varying grade descriptors increases the possibility of inconsistent judgements being applied to different criteria (Dickinson & Zellinger 1980; Saal & Landy 1977). Finally, simple rating scales of these types are not particularly well suited to a developmental purpose because they give no detailed indication of areas in which improvements need to be made. To overcome this shortcoming, it is common for rating scales to be combined with short essay-style appraisals or, at least, with space for the inclusion of brief open-ended comments by the assessor and, occasionally, by the assessee as well.

**1. Positive anchors only**
*Communication*

- Persuasively communicates in a way that produces positive results
- Listens well and understands the needs of the customer and others
- Conveys confidence when communicating
- Expresses ideas clearly and directly

**2. Positive and negative anchors**
*Communication*

1. Persuasively communicates in a way that produces positive results
2. Listens well and understands the needs of the customer and others
3. Conveys confidence when communicating
4. Expresses ideas clearly and directly
5. Misunderstands customer needs
6. Fails to liaise with other team members regarding customer service issues
7. Provides insufficient or inaccurate information to customers and team members
8. Customers complain about communication style

**Figure 6.6** Behavioural anchors

## Behaviourally Anchored Rating Scales

Behaviourally Anchored Rating Scales (BARS) are so-called because they provide specific examples – or 'anchors' – to illustrate and describe each behavioural criterion. GRS aim to maximise inter-assessor reliability by providing all assessors with a consistent set of behavioural definitions. The method begins with a critical incidents approach, with job experts identifying specific instances of effective and ineffective behaviour. These critical incidents are then grouped into broad behavioural categories. The critical incident descriptors for each behavioural criterion are then incorporated into a graded rating scale similar to that used in Graphic Rating Scales. The rating scale is typically a 1–5, 1–7 or 1–10 scale. Unlike simple Graphic Rating Scales, however, behaviourally anchored scales typically provide detailed descriptions for each performance grade.

Both the anchors themselves and the rating scales that accompany them can be configured in several different ways. As figure 6.6 suggests, anchors may include positive behavioural examples only or a mix of positive and negative behavioural examples. The intention behind including negative anchors is to lessen the possibility of halo and central tendency errors. As figure 6.7 indicates, in terms of the rating process itself, behavioural anchors and rating grades may also be configured in two distinct ways. On the one hand, anchors may be used to describe the rating grades themselves, as in the first example. Here the assessor is required to choose the one anchor that best describes the assessee's behaviour in each performance category. In this example, the assessor selects '4. Conveys confidence when communicating' from the five possible most negative to most positive anchor choices. Clearly,

**1. Behavioural anchors or descriptors for grades**

*Select the grade corresponding to behaviour that best describes the person's behaviour regarding the stated performance factor.*

**Communication**

| 1 | 2 | 3 | 4 ✓ | 5 |
|---|---|---|---|---|
| Customers complain about communication style | Fails to liaise with other team members regarding customer service issues | Expresses ideas clearly and directly | Conveys confidence when communicating | Communicates persuasively in a way that produces positive results |

**2. Rated anchors with standardised grade descriptors**

| Communication | Rating |
|---|---|
| • Listens well and understands the needs of the customer and others | 4 |
| • Expresses ideas clearly and directly | 5 |
| • Conveys confidence when communicating | 4 |
| • Persuasively communicates in a way that produces positive results | 3 |
| Overall rating for this category | 4 |

| | |
|---|---|
| 1. Unsatisfactory | Your work performance does not meet basic behavioural requirements. |
| 2. Needs improvement | Your work performance falls short of basic behavioural expectations in some significant respects. |
| 3. Meets expectations | Your work performance meets basic behavioural expectations but generally does not exceed them. |
| 4. Exceeds expectations | Your work performance meets basic behavioural expectations and often exceeds them. |
| 5. Exceptional | Your work performance always meets basic behavioural expectations and exceeds most. |

**Figure 6.7** Examples of behaviourally anchored rating scales

this may be a difficult choice, especially where the assessor believes that several anchors may be appropriate for the assessee concerned.

Alternatively, as in the second example in figure 6.7, the assessor may be required to rate every anchor separately and then to produce a composite rating for the general behaviour to which the anchors relate. In this case, the anchors are assumed to be weighted equally, so the assessee calculates the category score by averaging the ratings for the constituent anchors. Requiring a rating for each anchor may enhance assessment precision, but it also increases substantially the number of judgements that each assessor is required to make, which in turn may actually compromise reliability by increasing the probability of cognitive overload and, hence, unintentional error.

By describing in detail both the behaviour itself and the grading scales by which behaviour is rated, a BARS method seeks to overcome the reliability problems inherent in a simple GRS. With BARS, all assessors work with standard definitions of each desired behaviour and each performance grade. A related advantage of BARS is that it focuses solely on relevant job behaviour, not personal impressions, so there is less likelihood of construct invalidity. Since behavioural standards are clearly defined, behavioural problems can be identified quite precisely for developmental purposes. Like GRS, BARS also yields a total score that can be applied to performance pay decisions.

Conversely, because the number of anchors applied to each behavioural criterion is necessarily selective – typically five to ten anchors per criterion – it is possible that some relevant behaviour may be overlooked. Some BARS require the assessor to select just one anchor that best describes the employee's behaviour on that dimension, when either none of the specified anchors might be appropriate or perhaps two or more might be equally applicable. Moreover, the selective use of anchors may actually induce content invalidity and unintentional error, since recall is likely to focus only on those behavioural incidents that are reflected in anchors. Assessors may also have difficulty in matching observed behaviour with the anchors used. As Murphy and Constans (1987: 573) suggest: '. . . behavioral anchors present a potential problem if they describe behaviors that are actually observed by assessors but that are not representative of the assessee's overall performance levels. For example: a truly good performer will sometimes exhibit ineffective behaviors. If behavioral anchors direct the assessor's attention to or facilitate the recall of those unrepresentative behaviors, ratings of that person may be unfairly low.'

Further, BARS takes no systematic account of the frequency with which particular types of behaviour are manifested, thus increasing the risk of assessor error. For instance, an assessor may make a judgement based on just one observed incident rather than on the basis of the frequency with which this and other behaviour is demonstrated. Moreover, by their very nature behavioural anchors invite attribution error, since the assessor is encouraged to hold assessees wholly accountable for their observed behaviour. Individualised attribution of this sort overlooks the point that employees should be held responsible only for performance that is job valid and within their control.

BARS is also costly since, if construct and content validity are to be upheld, separate behavioural scales must be produced for each job or work role. The cost aspect may explain why the use of BARS remains quite limited. In Australia, for instance, only one in five organisations uses BARS as part of their performance management system (see table 6.2).

### Behavioural Observation Scales

Behavioural Observation Scales (BOS) are similar to BARS except in two vital respects. First, whereas BARS focuses on a select number of behavioural anchors, BOS seeks to assess specific behaviour necessary to effective job performance using a uniform scale. This means assessment of every specific type of behaviour, including every behavioural anchor, which in turn means that the assessor may now have to rate each employee on upwards of a hundred behavioural criteria. Second, rather than asking the assessor to choose between a diverse set of behavioural statements, as in BARS, BOS requires the assessor to score *each* specified form of behaviour separately in terms of a standard scale measuring *frequency* of occurrence. Since a uniform scale is used, the behaviour-specific ratings can then be averaged to obtain an overall performance score. Using the previous example, figure 6.8 illustrates how a BARS instrument may be transformed into a BOS instrument designed to assess behavioural frequency. Note how the rating scale focuses on observed behavioural frequency.

BOS have the advantage of requiring each specific desired behaviour to be rated separately against a standard scale, rather than requiring the assessor to choose between behavioural examples or anchors, as in BARS. It is also useful for providing detailed feedback, since the specific behavioural deficits can be readily identified (Latham & Wexley 1977, 1994).

**Instructions**
For each statement, circle the number of the grade that best identifies the frequency with which the behaviour described in that statement occurs.

**8. Communication**

| | Almost never | Rarely | Sometimes | Usually | Almost always |
|---|---|---|---|---|---|
| Listens well and understands the needs of the customer and others | 1 | 2 | 3 | 4 | 5 |
| Expresses ideas clearly and directly | 1 | 2 | 3 | 4 | 5 |
| Conveys confidence when communicating | 1 | 2 | 3 | 4 | 5 |
| Persuasively communicates in a way that produces positive results | 1 | 2 | 3 | 4 | 5 |

**Rating scale**

| |
|---|
| 1 = 0%–25% of the time |
| 2 = 25%–44% of the time |
| 3 = 45%–64% of the time |
| 4 = 65%–94% of the time |
| 5 = 95%–100% of the time |

**Figure 6.8** Example of a section of a behavioural observation scale

The major drawback of BOS is the time and cost involved in its development, since a separate behavioural scale must be developed for each performance-related behaviour in every job or each work role. For this reason alone, the approach is used by only a small minority of organisations. The level of information required may be more than most assessors can remember or process mentally. Some BOS instruments specify upwards of a hundred forms of behaviour, and the manager is required to remember how frequently each employee exhibited each one over the entire rating period. This means that an assessor who is responsible for appraising, say, thirty assessees is required to make a total of 3,000 specific behavioural judgements. Even with the aid of detailed critical incident records, an information and decision-making load of this magnitude would be apt to test the cognitive capacities of even the most conscientious assessor. Ironically, because of its very complexity, BOS may be susceptible to invalidity and unintentional error, since assessors may be tempted to generalise behavioural frequencies from a global evaluation of the individual rather than first determining the actual frequencies for each form of behaviour. For this reason, some researchers (e.g. Murphy, Martin & Garcia 1982; Murphy & Cleveland 1995: 437–8) conclude that BOS may actually be the most error-prone of all behavioural rating approaches.

*Directions*
Place a tick next to each statement that accurately describes the employee's behaviour on each criterion.

*Behavioural criterion 8: communication*                                    (Weighting*)

| Statement | Tick | Weighting |
|---|---|---|
| Listens well and understands the needs of the customer and others | ✓ | (+2.5) |
| Provides insufficient or inaccurate information to customers and team members | ✓ | (–2.0) |
| Persuasively communicates in a way that produces positive results | | (+3.0) |
| Expresses ideas clearly and directly | ✓ | (+1.5) |
| Customers complain about communication style | | (–3.0) |
| Conveys confidence when communicating | | (+2.0) |

(Category score)                                                             (+2.0)

\* Weights are not normally disclosed to the assessor.

**Figure 6.9**  Example of a section of a weighted checklist

## Weighted checklist

The weighted checklist method derives directly from the critical incident technique, but overcomes one of the latter's major drawbacks by providing a numerical performance score that can then be used for performance comparison and pay calculation. It also makes use of selected behavioural statements or anchors to prompt and direct judgements. First, job-valid positive and negative behaviour is identified. Next, each is codified as a behavioural statement, and these statements are then grouped into sets relating to key behavioural criterion categories. Positive or negative numerical weightings are then attached to each behavioural statement in terms of its significance to the organisation, with the weightings typically being determined by internal or external work study experts. An example of an extract from a weighted checklist is provided in figure 6.9. For each criterion, the assessor is asked to check those statements that best describe the assessee's observed behaviour in the relevant behavioural category. Note that while each of the behavioural statements in the figure has a weighting attached to it, weightings would not normally appear on the assessor's copy of the form. Assessors merely check off the statements that they believe best describe the employee's behaviour, and the weightings are applied later by the human resources department, which also calculates the weighted total score for each employee.

Weighted checklists are therefore essentially instruments for rating critical behavioural incidents. The fact that the designated value of each behaviour is concealed from the assessor reduces the possibility of 'second guessing' and intentional error. The absence of a rating scale also removes one of the elements of unreliability that, as we have seen, is a common feature of graphic rating instruments.

However, because assessors are unaware of the weighting attached to each behaviour by the organisation, it is difficult for them to provide detailed feedback on behavioural strengths and weaknesses. Moreover, assessors' sense of accountability for system outcomes may be undermined by the fact that they are denied access to 'inside' information on the relative importance of the behaviour they are called on to assess. The instrument also provides assessors with little guidance as to how they should assess behavioural frequency. Moreover, weighted checklists are also still vulnerable to unintentional error because the supervisor may recall only negative or positive behaviour, and it is possible for assessors to manipulate ratings for their own purposes, albeit at one step removed from the final rating process.

## Forced choice

The forced choice method was developed to minimise the potential for unintentional halo or horns error and to combat deliberate misclassification (i.e. leniency, harshness or central tendency error) of the type common with standard rating scales like GRS and BARS. The method forces the assessor to choose one behavioural statement from two carefully paired statements by identifying the statement that more accurately describes the assessee's behaviour. The statements in each pair are matched so as to be equal in surface appeal or 'desirability'. Some pairs will contain statements relating to positive behaviour; others will carry statements relating to negative behaviour. In technical terms, both statements in each pair will occupy similar loci on a 'desirability' index; that is, they will both appear equally desirable or both equally undesirable. However, one of the two paired statements is seen by the organisation as having a stronger linkage to good performance; that is, it is said to have a higher 'discrimination' index value, since it distinguishes good performers more sharply from low or standard performers. Again, the desirability pairings and the discrimination index values are determined by experts, not by the assessor, who remains unaware of the differential index values applied. An example of a section of a forced choice instrument is given in figure 6.10. Note that while discrimination index values are disclosed in this example, in practice these values remain confidential.

Properly designed, a forced choice instrument has great potential to minimise assessor error and unreliable ratings. It stands to eliminate most

**Instructions**
1. Review the critical incident records for the person you are assessing.
2. Assess the person's behaviour one pair at a time.
3. Decide which of the two paired behavioural statements *more accurately describes* the person's observed behaviour, then tick the number of the statement that you have selected.
4. If you believe that both statements in a pair somewhat describe the person's behaviour, you must still select just one statement from the pair. In doing so, you should review your critical incident records for this person and consider the totality of the person's observed behaviour over the full rating period.

| | Check only one statement per pair: | | (Performance discrimination index value*) |
|---|---|---|---|
| Pair E | 1 ✓ or 2 | 1. Conveys confidence when communicating | (+2.0) |
| | | 2. Persuasively communicates in a way that produces positive results | (+3.0) |
| Pair F | 1 ✓ or 2 | 1. Provides insufficient or inaccurate information to customers and team members | (−2.0) |
| | | 2. Customers complain about communication style | (−3.0) |
| Pair G | 1 or 2 ✓ | 1. Listens well and understands the needs of the customer and others. | (+3.0) |
| | | 2. Expresses ideas clearly and directly. | (+1.5) |
| | | (Partial score) | (+1.5) |

\* Discrimination index values are not disclosed to the assessor.

**Figure 6.10** Example of a section of a forced choice behavioural assessment instrument

unintentional errors by forcing assessors to consider the full range of behavioural possibilities, from the most desirable to the least so, then to make fine choices between ostensibly similar behaviour. Since the importance attached to each behavioural statement by the organisation is unknown to the assessor, the scope for intentional error is also significantly reduced.

However, because of its sheer complexity, it is one of the least used assessment methods. Developing and implementing a forced choice instrument demands considerable subject matter expertise and funding. The fine behavioural distinctions required also make it imperative for assessors to maintain detailed critical incident records. Moreover, notwithstanding its apparent sophistication, the approach is not entirely foolproof. It is still possible that the system designers may overlook important behavioural dimensions or under- or over-value specific types of behaviour. Assessors' lack of knowledge of relative behavioural importance makes it difficult for them not only to defend their judgements but also to provide detailed performance feedback. Overall, forced choice is not an instrument for the faint-hearted or the cost-conscious.

## Some common flaws in behavioural rating instruments

By now it should be apparent that designing, implementing and maintaining a system of behavioural rating is no simple matter: it is difficult to do well, and extremely easy to do badly. While rating instruments have a legion of possible design flaws, some are especially common. By way of illustration, let us briefly consider examples of five such problems:

- conflation of behavioural criteria
- invalid behavioural statements or anchors
- inadequate differentiation between behavioural statements or anchors
- inadequate specification to behavioural frequency
- inadequate grade descriptors
- inadequate guidelines for determining an overall rating.

A common design flaw is the rolling of different behaviour into the one generic criterion. Take this example: 'Dependability: follows policy guidelines, is alert to problems, adapts well to change, and communicates well with the supervisor.' This composite statement really covers four quite distinct forms of behaviour: policy compliance, alertness, adaptability and upward communication. Since assessors will vary in their perceptions of the relative importance of these constituent forms of behaviour, rolling them into one generic criterion is likely to compromise consistency of judgement and, hence, rating reliability.

Behavioural statements or anchors may also be invalid for the criterion involved. For instance, the negative anchor 'Reluctant to accept change' may be valid for a criterion such as 'Adaptability' but not, say, for the criterion 'Dependability'. Likewise, the anchor 'Is willing to work outside ordinary working hours' may be valid for the criterion 'Willingness to work' but it would be inappropriate for a criterion like 'Punctuality'. Or again, the anchor 'Contributes ideas and seeks clarification' may be valid for a criterion like 'Communication' but would not be valid for a criterion like 'Listening skills' since verbalising is not necessarily a signifier of good listening; indeed, it may well signify quite the opposite.

Another common flaw is the absence of clear differentiation between anchors for adjacent grades. The degree of overlap between adjacent anchors

*Each grade is described in terms of Outstanding Performance (A) and Unsatisfactory Performance (F). The four intermediate grades (B, C, D, E) represent behaviour between the two extremes. The ratings of A or F should be given if it is believed that it is a generally true statement that could be supported, if necessary, by specific occurrences. A rating of B means that although A is not a generally accurate description of behaviour, there are marked tendencies in that direction, and C means some tendencies in that direction. A rating of E means that although F is not a generally accurate description of that behaviour, there are marked tendencies in that direction, and D means some tendencies in that direction.*

|  |  | A | B | C | D | E | F |  |
|---|---|---|---|---|---|---|---|---|
| Problem-solving | Gets straight to the root of the problem |  |  |  |  |  |  | Seldom sees below the surface of a problem |
| Judgement | Decisions are consistently sound |  |  |  |  |  |  | Poor perception of relative merits or feasibility in most solutions |

**Figure 6.11**  Inadequate grade descriptors

may be such that assessors will find it impossible to distinguish between them consistently and reliably. For instance, many assessors would have considerable difficulty in distinguishing between the following two proximal statements: '3. Consistently generates and shares ideas that are adopted by the team' and '4. Builds on others' ideas; encourages and owns implementation of ideas'. In other questions, the distinction between adjacent anchors is far from self-evident. The same applies to these two anchors: 'C. Does not waste resources' and 'B. Is careful about how they use resources'.

Many rating instruments either overlook the issue of behavioural frequency or address it in an inconsistent manner. For example, it is common for some anchors for a given criterion to acknowledge the frequency dimension whereas others do not. For example, how is the assessor meant to distinguish reliably between these two adjacent anchors: 'Inconsistently makes decisions with the right balance between quality, speed and risk' and 'Makes decisions with the right balance between quality, speed and risk'? Further, frequency-related terms such as 'regularly', 'consistently', 'often', 'generally', 'inconsistently' and 'rarely' are not self-defining, and it cannot therefore be assumed that all assessors will interpret such terms in the same manner.

Non-existent or imprecise grade descriptors are another frequent failing. Figure 6.11 exemplifies this problem. Note how the intermediate grade specifications are vague and relative rather than absolute. Since these are the very grades that will be most relevant to the majority of employees, the absence of precision will almost certainly compromise rating reliability.

Finally, while behavioural rating instruments may require assessment across more than twenty behavioural criteria, where the ratings are linked

Using the behaviour assessment framework, assess the behaviour that has been consistently observed in the workplace. On the basis of the assessment of each type of behaviour, determine the overall behaviour assessment.

| Core behaviour | Unsatisfactory | Needs improvement | Meets expectations | Exceeds expectations | Examples of behaviour |
|---|---|---|---|---|---|
| Clear and decisive | | ✓ | | | |
| Empowered and accountable | | ✓ | | | |
| Learn and grow | | | ✓ | | |
| Trust and team spirit | | | | ✓ | |
| Discipline and excellence | | | | ✓ | |
| Challenge and innovate | | | ✓ | | |
| Overall behaviour assessment: | | | | | |

**Figure 6.12**  Inadequate guidelines for determining overall rating

to reward determination assessors are typically also required to indicate a rating for overall behavioural performance or, more commonly still, a summative assessment of combined behaviour and results. In many cases, however, the relevant instrument is bereft of clear guidelines as to how assessment on the specific behavioural criteria should be combined to arrive at an overall rating. Should all criteria be weighted equally? Are some really more important than others? In the absence of specific guidelines as to how the summative assessment should be determined, the likelihood of inter-assessor unreliability will be all the greater (Saul 1992). Figure 6.12 illustrates this problem. In this case, the assessee achieves an equal number of ratings in each of the three adjacent grades: 'Needs improvement', 'Meets expectations' and 'Exceeds expectations'. But how should this be translated into an overall rating? Should the assessor simply opt for the average grade (assuming equal criterion weighing); that is, an overall rating of 'Meets expectations'? Or should she opt to accentuate the existence of behavioural deficits and opt for 'Needs improvement'? Conversely, should she accentuate the strengths? Without proper guidelines here, the decisions of different assessors are likely to be highly idiosyncratic. The potential for unreliability is compounded where the summative judgement must also cover results-based criteria.

The preceding discussion of possible shortcomings in rating instrument design is by no means exhaustive, and the examples considered are merely illustrative of some of the more common problems. The case study included at the end of part 2 allows you to try undertaking a constructively critical assessment of a performance rating instrument. See how many of the above problems you can identify, as well as any other aspects that you believe may compromise validity, reliability and fairness. On the positive side, many of these can be remedied by means of careful attention to instrument structure and wording, so also consider how you might set about amending the instrument, particularly to improve validity and reliability.

## Assessing behavioural assessment

In one sense, the history of behavioural assessment is that of an unending quest for the Holy Grail of performance management practice: an assessment instrument that has perfect job or role validity, eliminates unwitting and intended assessor error, determines relative and absolute performance differences in a consistently reliable manner, and does so in a cost-effective way. However, as must by now be readily apparent, no such method currently exists, nor is it ever likely to exist. As Landy and Farr (1983) have observed, no one rating technique is consistently better than all others, although it does not necessarily follow, as they and other commentators (Murphy & Cleveland 1995: 433) have implied, that rating formats *per se* have only limited capacity to enhance rating reliability.

As is evident from the above discussion, what is available to us is a range of behavioural assessment methods, each of which has its own particular strengths and weaknesses. Figure 6.13 offers an overall assessment of the strengths and weaknesses of each method in terms of cost-efficiency, validity and reliability. Generally speaking, comparative methods rate highly in terms of cost-efficiency and the control of intentional assessor error, moderately well in upholding construct and content validity, but very poorly in controlling unintentional error. Conversely, most rating methods are more effective in addressing validity and in countering unintentional errors, but also more costly to design and maintain, while only the weighted checklist and forced choice techniques are likely to match comparative methods in countering deliberate assessor error. In short, there is no perfect solution, and choosing between these behavioural assessment options therefore necessarily requires well-informed trade-off and compromise. The safest recommendation here is that comparative methods are a better fit for small, single-site workplaces

| | Cost efficiency | Validity | Reliability | |
|---|---|---|---|---|
| | | | In countering unintentional errors | In countering intentional errors |
| **Comparative methods** | | | | |
| Straight ranking | High | Low | Low | High |
| Alternation ranking | High | Moderate | Low | High |
| Paired comparison | Moderate | Moderate | Low | High |
| Forced distribution | High | Moderate | Low | High |
| | | | | |
| **Rating methods** | | | | |
| Critical incidents | Moderate–high | Moderate–high | Moderate–high | Low–moderate |
| Graphic rating scale | Moderate–high | Moderate | Low–moderate | Low–moderate |
| BARS | Low | Moderate-high | Moderate | Moderate |
| BOS | Low | High | High | Moderate |
| Weighted checklist | Low | High | Moderate–high | High |
| Forced choice | Low | High | Very High | Very high |

**Figure 6.13** Assessing behavioural assessment methods

whereas role-specific rating methods are more appropriate for larger organisations with multiple jobs, numerous employees and many assessors.

The larger 'best fit' question, of course, is whether behavioural assessment
should be used at all. Overall, behavioural approaches are best suited to two
distinct situations, with each requiring a different behavioural emphasis. The
first situation is where the work is prescribed, routine, closely supervised and
relatively stable, as would be the case in, say, a traditionally managed mechanistic market defender firm, of the type described in chapter 4. In such situations, it is possible to specify a single set of desired task-specific behaviour,
and assessment would therefore focus primarily on eliciting membership
and task behaviour.

Equally, behavioural assessment would also be appropriate to situations
where the work itself is non-routine and highly discretionary, where there
is minimal supervision, and where there are numerous behavioural pathways to the same end result, as in the case of much knowledge-based
work in organisations with (or aspiring to achieve) organic structures,
high-involvement cultures and either analyser or prospector competitive
strategies. In such contexts, the emphasis will be primarily on citizenship
behaviour and demonstration of core corporate values rather than on membership and task behaviour. However, as we shall see in the next chapter, in
such situations the performance measurement approach is more likely to
involve performance criteria in the form of high-performance (or 'differentiating') competencies that are measured by means of observable behavioural
proxies incorporated into BARS.

# Chapter summary

This chapter has examined the major sources of behavioural information within work organisations, as well as the two main categories of assessment methods associated with the management of work behaviour, namely comparative methods and rating methods. While acknowledging that no extant method surpasses all others in terms of instrument validity, reliability and cost-effectiveness, we have argued that each method has its own particular strengths and weaknesses that may make it a better fit for some work contexts than for others. We have also pointed out some of the more common design flaws in behavioural rating instruments. In general terms, comparative methods are a better fit for small, single-site workplaces whereas rating methods are more appropriate for larger organisations with multiple jobs, numerous employees and many assessors. Finally, regarding best fit considerations, we have suggested that behavioural appraisal may be appropriate for two different organisational contexts: the first involving traditionally managed and mechanistically structured organisations; and the second involving organically structured high-involvement organisations. In each case, however, the behavioural emphasis will be different, with the former focusing on task and membership behaviour and the latter on organisational citizenship behaviour and core values. However, as we shall see in chapter 7, some commentators suggest that a competency-based approach may have more to offer in these latter respects.

# Discussion questions

1  Why is behavioural assessment such a perennially troubled aspect of HRM?
2  What are the requirements for 'validity' in performance assessment?
3  'The pursuit of ever-more reliable performance measurement techniques is a self-defeating exercise.' Discuss.
4  Is forced ranking a necessary evil?
5  How can something as subjective as behavioural assessment ever be made fair?

## Chapter Seven

# MANAGING COMPETENCIES

Having examined the concepts, methods and processes associated with managing employee results and behaviour, we can now turn our attention to the last and, in many respects, most complex and controversial of the three horizontal dimensions of work performance, namely those performance inputs or capabilities that have come to be known generically as 'competencies'. Like the behavioural approach, with which it has a close affinity, the competencies approach is necessarily individual in focus; indeed, the competencies construct itself derives from studies of the psychology of individual difference. The competencies concept also has a close association with the resources-based view of human resource management, which we have argued (in chapter 4) is best understood as an internally focused prescription for 'best fit'.

This chapter opens with a discussion of the competencies concept. This is followed by an examination of the techniques and processes involved in competency analysis and identification and in modelling competency-based or competency-related performance management systems. Then we turn our attention to the techniques involved in assessing the competency profiles of individual employees, and a final section of the chapter assesses the strengths, weaknesses and 'best fit' aspects of the competencies approach.

## The 'competencies' construct and competency-based human resource management

As noted previously, at the level of the individual employee, performance inputs consist of a combination of job knowledge, skills and abilities, or 'KSAs', to use the commonly applied acronym. While the competencies approach acknowledges the importance of all three types of input, exponents also draw a strong distinction between position-specific knowledge and skill, on the one hand, and underlying performance abilities on the other. Sometimes this distinction is cast in terms of the difference between 'hard' (learnable, technical) skills or competencies and 'soft' (underlying or innate) skills or competencies.

Job knowledge and 'hard' motor and cognitive skills are seen as being associated with the base-line technical requirements of work performance; that is, with proficient task performance. Without these capabilities, the employee would not be competent to undertake the job or role at all. For this reason, these are sometimes described as 'threshold' competencies (O'Neill & Doig 1997). In general, assuming a requisite level of general knowledge, literacy and numeracy, and a willingness to learn, threshold competencies may be acquired relatively quickly. Such performance capacities can also be imparted through formal training programs.

However, exponents of the competencies approach (Dubois & Rothwell 2004; Lucia & Lepsinger 1999; Spencer & Spencer 1993) contend that the key to effective performance management lies less with these threshold competencies than with the 'soft', embedded or underlying attributes that appear to make the difference between performance proficiency and performance excellence. Competencies that distinguish between acceptable and exemplary performance are known as 'differentiating' competencies (Tucker & Cofsky 1994). Exponents of competency-based human resource management suggest that while differentiating competencies may be less visible and verifiable than 'hard' threshold competencies – and therefore more difficult to measure – they nevertheless hold the key to high performance. Exponents also suggest that while it is not possible to transform every employee into an outstanding performer, differentiating competencies are not immutable and are amenable to development and enhancement. According to Dubois and Rothwell (2004: 22), even a modest improvement in an employee's competency profile can lead to a significant increase in performance outcomes. As such, competency-based formulations have come to cover not only staff recruitment and selection functions but also development, performance management and reward management. According to Risher (2005: 22–3), another prominent advocate of the competencies approach, defining and communicating desired competencies not only indicates to every employee what it is that makes for outstanding performance but also 'gives employees the framework they need to plan their personal development and to enhance their performances'.

This conception of performance competencies was pioneered by psychologists Robert White and David McClelland. White (1959) identified a human trait that he labelled 'competence'. It was McClelland, however, who introduced and popularised the term 'competency'. As noted in chapter 3, McClelland, a professor of psychology at Harvard University, was also responsible for the approach to motivation known as achievement motivation theory, and the concepts of competency and achievement orientation are closely connected (Boyatzis 1982).

In the early 1970s, McClelland (1973) challenged the then widely held belief that intelligence *per se* was the key to high performance and high achievement. He argued that while intelligence may influence performance, other personal attributes, such as the individual's motivation and self-image, were primarily responsible for differentiating successful from unsuccessful performance (Dubois & Rothwell 2004: 17) and that, by extension, such non-technical attributes were also what distinguished high achievers or performers from ordinary performers. It was these achievement-oriented competencies, McClelland suggested, that organisations should seek to identify, encourage and reward. McClelland identified twenty competencies that he suggested would most often predict superior performance in professional and managerial jobs:

1  achievement orientation
2  concern for quality and order
3  initiative
4  interpersonal understanding
5  customer service orientation
6  impact and influence
7  organisational awareness
8  relationship building or networking
9  directiveness

10  teamwork and cooperation
11  developing others
12  team leadership
13  technical expertise
14  information seeking
15  analytical thinking
16  conceptual thinking
17  self-control and stress resistance
18  self-confidence
19  organisational commitment
20  flexibility.

In the 1980s McClelland's work was extended and refined by George Klemp (1980), Richard Boyatzis (1982) and others. Klemp defined job competency as 'an underlying characteristic of a person which results in effective and/or superior performance in a job' (cited in Dubois & Rothwell 2004: 18). Boyatzis was sometime president of McBer & Co., the firm founded by McClelland to disseminate the notion of performance-related management competencies and which was subsequently absorbed by the Hay Group, now one of the leading global consulting firms in the human resource management field. Boyatzis (1982) suggested that any competency-based human resource management system should include two crucial dimensions: (1) type of competency and (2) the level or degree to which the individual possessed each competency. Boyatzis identified twelve types of competencies relating to superior performance (including, *inter alia*, self-confidence, concern with impact, proactivity and efficiency orientation) and three levels of competency: (1) 'motives and traits' at the unconscious level, (2) 'self-image and social role' at a semi-conscious level and (3) 'skills and knowledge' at the behavioural level.

Building on the framework created by Boyatzis, Spencer and Spencer (1993) produced what has become the standard definition of performance competencies, as well as developing the so-called 'iceberg' model of competency levels. Spencer and Spencer (1993: 9) defined a competency as 'an underlying characteristic of an individual that is causally related to criterion-referenced effective and/or superior performance in job or situation'. A simplified version of the Spencer and Spencer iceberg model is presented in figure 7.1. The point of the iceberg analogy is that the bulk of individual performance capability is submerged, or 'below the waterline', whereas only

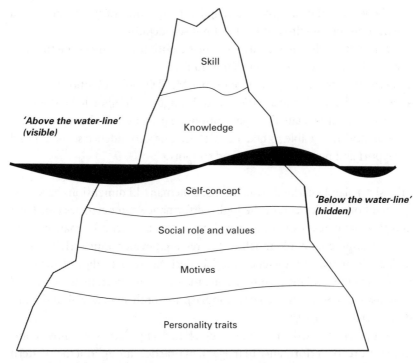

**Figure 7.1** Performance competencies: the Spencer and Spencer 'iceberg' model
*Source:* adapted from Spencer & Spencer 1993.

the technical knowledge and skills – the tip of performance capability – are visible and readily observable 'above the waterline'. On this basis, the individual's submerged attributes – personality traits, deep motives, social values and self-concept – are seen as the key predictors of high performance.

Extending McClelland's earlier work on high-performance management competencies, the Hay Group's Daniel Goleman has also formulated a model of leadership competency based on the notion of 'emotional intelligence' (EI). According to Goleman (1995), 'emotional intelligence' correlates strongly with superior performance at all levels – non-managerial as well as managerial. As a driver of performance, emotional intelligence, he suggests, has double the performance impact of job skills and intelligence quotient (or 'IQ') combined. Goleman identifies five key components of emotional intelligence. The first three are essentially to do with good 'self-management', the last two with interpersonal and social skills. Goleman's five EI dimensions are:

1 *self-awareness:* knowing one's strengths and weaknesses, values, needs and emotions; being self-confident but not self-deluding
2 *self-regulation:* being in control of one's emotions, and therefore the situation; being reflective rather than impulsive
3 *motivation:* the drive to achieve (as per McClelland's definition)
4 *empathy:* being able to see the world through one's subordinates' eyes so as to better appreciate their perceptions, expectations and emotions
5 *social skill:* being able to take people into one's confidence so as to build rapport and networks of trust and support.

Like McClelland's earlier formulations, Goleman's EI dimensions have now entered both the lexicon of the high-performance competencies construct and the mainstream of competency-based human resource management and development. While much of the research evidence underlying these high-performance competency models derived from studies of management attributes and behaviour, despite their complexity competency-based systems are now relatively commonplace for both managerial and non-managerial employees.

Competency-based or competency-related approaches are now common features of performance management practice throughout the Western world. For instance, in the UK competency assessment is used by almost a third of organisations (CIPD 2005a: 2). In Australia, two-thirds of organisations make some use of competency criteria in performance assessment, with 35 per cent now incorporating competency sets linked explicitly to organisational values in the assessment methods applied to non-managerial staff (Nankervis & Compton 2006: 88, 91). Here, as elsewhere, the adoption of competency criteria for performance management purposes appears to be a relatively recent development. Australian survey evidence from the mid-1990s (O'Neill & Doig 1997) indicated that although more than 80 per cent of Australian organisations were engaged in some initiative involving competencies, the main usages at that juncture were for training and development (48 per cent) and recruitment and selection (47 per cent). At that time, most of the competency initiatives were also directed at senior professional and managerial staff rather than at non-managerial employees, and less than a third had applied competencies throughout the whole organisation.

Although there is considerable variation in the content of competency-based performance management systems, the dominance of the McClelland–McBer–Hay formulation has also led to a degree of criterion standardisation, at least in relation to the more abstract competencies. Many of these also reflect the Boyatzis–Spencer focus on traits, motives, social role and self-concept. Table 7.1 (p. 186) lists some of the most frequently applied competencies under each of these attribute categories.

In practice, it has also become common practice to distinguish between 'role' competencies and 'core' competencies. Role competencies are position-specific and include both hard or threshold competencies and soft or high performance competencies for the particular job, role or function. They are intended to distinguish between superior performance and standard performance in specific tasks and result areas. By definition, role competencies will vary from position to position, since capabilities necessary for high performance in one role may be different from those necessary in another. For instance, effectiveness as a salesperson is likely to require such qualities as communication ability, self-confidence, empathy, customer orientation and composure, whereas effectiveness as a product designer is more likely to require creativity, problem-solving and persistence. Equally, however, trait-based competencies like conscientiousness and openness to new ideas and experiences will likely be valid criteria for both of these roles.

In contrast, core competencies are the essential organisation-wide competencies that the organisation believes all of its employees need to possess to make them effective contributors (Prahalad & Hamel 1990; Tucker & Cofsky 1994). These competencies are seen as setting the organisation apart in terms of its competitive capacities. They also define and convey key aspects of the organisation's mission, cultural values and competitive strategy. As such, they may serve to reinforce a common set of desired values, attitudes and behaviour. For instance, a firm with a quality-defender competitive strategy would certainly wish to include quality focus and customer focus among its core competencies. Core competencies may also be used to direct and support organisational change. For instance, where a mechanistic organisational structure is being replaced by an organic structure, it would be appropriate to include team-orientation and flexibility among the new core competencies applicable throughout the organisation. A firm making the transition from an analyser to a prospector competitive strategy may wish to add creativity, adaptability and results orientation to its list of core competencies.

## Competency analysis, modelling and validation

In this section, we will consider the methods involved in identifying relevant competencies and in developing and validating a framework for

**Table 7.1** Commonly applied performance competencies

| | |
|---|---|
| Self-concept | • Self-knowledge |
| | • Self-confidence |
| | • Developing self |
| | • Time management |
| Social role or values | • Communication ability |
| | • Relationship-building |
| | • Delegating and directing |
| | • Empathy |
| | • Integrity and trust |
| | • Motivating others |
| | • Team orientation |
| | • Conflict management |
| | • Political awareness |
| Motives | • Achievement or results orientation |
| | • Strategic or business focus |
| | • Decisiveness or action orientation |
| | • Customer focus |
| | • Quality focus |
| | • Leading and shaping |
| Traits | • Conscientiousness |
| | • Problem-solving |
| | • Creativity |
| | • Openness to new ideas and experiences |
| | • Dealing with ambiguity |
| | • Environmental alertness and awareness |
| | • Flexibility and adaptability |
| | • Composure |
| | • Patience |
| | • Perseverance |

competency-based assessment; or a 'competency model', to use the preferred practitioner term. A competency model is a written description of the competencies required for fully effective or exemplary performance in a particular job position or broad role category. A competency model should incorporate competencies relating to each of three main categories: (1) core competencies, (2) threshold role competencies and (3) differentiating role competencies. Whereas core competencies must necessarily be inferred deductively from the organisation's espoused culture and strategy, the identification of role competencies requires careful inductive analysis. The identification of threshold competencies involves analysis of requisite base-line position knowledge and skill using the traditional techniques of job and skill analysis, or perhaps by means of generic skill dictionaries. With differentiating competencies, the aim is to identify those role competencies that set high performers apart within the relevant role. This may be undertaken by means of a formal analysis of performance competencies associated with the relevant jobs or roles. The main challenge in doing so is that, by definition, these 'below-the-waterline' competencies cannot be observed or measured directly, and it is necessary to infer their presence by means of observable and measurable proxies.

Since competencies are demonstrated by means of performance behaviour and/or tangible results, this typically means analysing competencies by means of attitudinal, behavioural and/or results-based indicators. Similarly, once differentiating competencies have been identified and validated, their incorporation into valid and reliable instruments for assessing the competency profiles of individual employees also requires the identification of valid behavioural descriptors or indicators for each competency.

Identifying differentiating competencies and appropriate behavioural indicators in this way requires considerable expertise and scrupulous adherence to validity requirements, and in larger organisations these tasks are typically undertaken by specialist external consultants with expertise in organisational psychology and psychometric methods.

There are three main methods of data collection for competency modelling purposes: (1) behaviour event interviewing (BEI), (2) expert panels or focus groups and (3) competency menus. BEI is a refinement of critical incident technique, which we considered in chapter 6. It is also the centrepiece of the procedure developed by McClelland and others between the 1960s and 1980s to develop competency models, namely the job competence

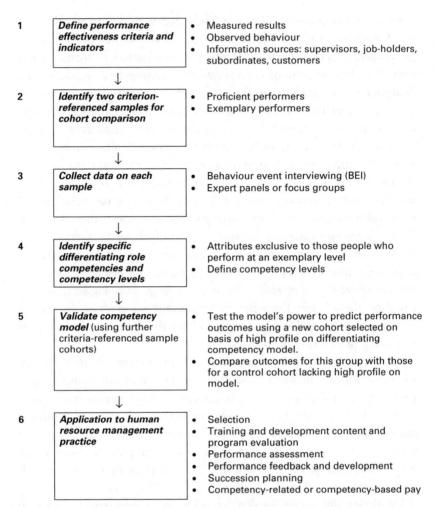

1  **Define performance effectiveness criteria and indicators**
- Measured results
- Observed behaviour
- Information sources: supervisors, job-holders, subordinates, customers

↓

2  **Identify two criterion-referenced samples for cohort comparison**
- Proficient performers
- Exemplary performers

↓

3  **Collect data on each sample**
- Behaviour event interviewing (BEI)
- Expert panels or focus groups

↓

4  **Identify specific differentiating role competencies and competency levels**
- Attributes exclusive to those people who perform at an exemplary level
- Define competency levels

↓

5  **Validate competency model** (using further criteria-referenced sample cohorts)
- Test the model's power to predict performance outcomes using a new cohort selected on basis of high profile on differentiating competency model.
- Compare outcomes for this group with those for a control cohort lacking high profile on model.

↓

6  **Application to human resource management practice**
- Selection
- Training and development content and program evaluation
- Performance assessment
- Performance feedback and development
- Succession planning
- Competency-related or competency-based pay

**Figure 7.2** Analysing and modelling differentiating competencies using behaviour event interviewing
*Source:* adapted from Spencer & Spencer 1993.

assessment method (Spencer & Spencer 1993). Figure 7.2 overviews the main steps involved in BEI-based job or role competence analysis.

Identifying samples of proficient and exemplary performers means first defining valid and measurable performance indicators for the job or role concerned. Then an appropriate number of subjects must be selected for analysis. For multiple incumbent jobs, the recommended minimum sample is six to ten high performers and six to ten average performers (Klein 1996). In theory, this should provide a database sufficient to differentiate between the two groups.

Next, data is collected on what it is that distinguishes superior performers from average performers. Essentially, this means identifying those attitudinal and behavioural characteristics that best predict outstanding performance. Remember that 'submerged competencies' cannot be observed or measured directly; they can only be gauged by means of presumed behavioural proxies.

The interview process typically involves employees identified as proficient or exemplary performers being asked 'a series of detailed questions about actions performed in the work setting that workers perceive to be successful or unsuccessful and the thoughts, feelings, and outcomes that accompanied them' (Dubois & Rothwell 2004: 28). To illustrate: the interviewee may be asked to respond to the following:

- 'Tell me about a time when you were asked to do X. What did you do? How did you handle it? Why did you do it this way?'
- 'Here is a situation we found ourselves in recently. What would you have done in a similar situation? Why?'

The responses from the interviewee sample cohorts may then be transcribed, coded and tabulated using an appropriate qualitative data analytical method, and subjected to detailed analysis. Three sets of attributes are then identified:

1 those demonstrated only by superior performers, which are categorised as differentiating competencies
2 those demonstrated by both proficient and superior performers, which are taken as constituting threshold competencies
3 those shown only by proficient performers, which are discarded as being unrelated to desired performance.

Among the advantages of the BEI method are that it produces data that is valid, highly reliable and generally free of method-related bias, provides a detailed understanding of the ways in which competencies are manifested, and enables the identification of highly abstract competencies that are unlikely to be identified by other means. The main disadvantages are that interviewing requires considerable expertise – typically sourced externally – and interview responses are costly and time-consuming to process. Moreover, since it relies on experiential data on past performance, the method cannot be used to identify competencies that may be required in new work roles (Dubois & Rothwell 2004: 29).

With the alternative data-gathering technique of expert panels or focus groups, specially selected groups with knowledge of the organisation and its people engage in 'brainstorming' sessions regarding the attributes that distinguish high performers. Panels or focus groups may also be used to supplement BEI-based data-gathering. In the US, 68 per cent of firms applying the competencies approach use expert panels or focus groups to create competency models, while 58 per cent use BEI and 8 per cent use competency menus (Rahbar-Daniels, Erickson & Dalik 2001: 72). Although they are easy to administer, focus groups may overlook less obvious competencies and participants may lack objectivity.

With competency menus, respondents are asked to select from a generic list of competencies those they believe are critical to high performance. To obtain a balanced data set, input is usually sought from supervisors, peers and subordinates.

Because of their cost-effectiveness and ease of administration, generic competency menus are becoming an increasingly popular means of identifying role competencies. However, because of their generic nature, menus are incapable of identifying competencies that may be unique to the one organisation. Moreover, menus do not identify the specific behavioural indicators that signify each differentiating competency, a critical requirement for the development of competency-based or competency-related assessment instruments. Further, competency menus developed by external providers may be deficient in relation to both validity and reliability.

Having obtained and analysed relevant data by one or other of the above means, the next step is to use the findings to develop a preliminary competency model. As well as identifying specific performance competencies, the model should include a definition of each competency and behavioural descriptors or examples by which the degree of competency possession may be measured.

The preliminary model should then be validated to ensure that the chosen competencies do in fact predict high performance. Ideally, this should involve the selection of new comparator cohorts using the model criteria, then comparing the two groups' longitudinal performance outcomes to gauge how accurately the model predicts observable differences in individual performance. Clearly, the larger the sample size, the more robust and reliable the statistical significance of the predictor coefficients will be, so it may be necessary to repeat the validation process several times to obtain sufficiently large sample sizes. The measures of predictor strength and significance will also allow the organisation to rank and weight the competency criteria in terms of performance impact.

## Competency assessment

Once validated, the competency model and behavioural indicators can then be codified into a competency assessment instrument for measuring the presence and degree of competency possession by individual employees. As with straight behavioural assessment, competency assessment can be undertaken by a number of different means: from focus groups, assessment centres and psychometric testing to behavioural observation and judgement by either single or multiple assessors. Irrespective of the assessment technique or techniques used, in order to maximise assessment reliability, all assessors should be trained comprehensively in the details of the competency model and associated behavioural indicators.

### Assessment centres

Initial competency assessment is often undertaken in special assessment centres operated either in-house or by outside experts, such as organisational psychology professionals. Activities typically involve six to twelve people at a time and are usually conducted off-premises over periods of one to three days, with information-gathering centring on behavioural observation, interviewing and psychometric assessment. Programs usually involve a mix of activities, including:

- structured individual or group simulation exercises designed to assess how competent individuals are at handling particular role demands, such as problem-solving or conflict management
- strategy games designed to assess strategic awareness and thinking abilities
- 'in-basket exercises' to assess threshold competencies and differentiating attributes, such as stress tolerance
- 'leaderless group discussion' to assess communication and decision-making abilities and interpersonal attributes

- team sports and games
- individual presentations
- personality assessment
- motor skills, cognitive and aptitude tests
- behaviour event interviewing.

Assessment centres are particularly appropriate for new hires since such employees as yet have no record on which assessment can be based. As we shall see in chapter 12, this is a particularly useful way for organisations with competency-based reward systems to determine an initial pay level for new recruits. However, because centre-based assessment is labour-intensive, expensive and time-consuming, and can accommodate only a small number of assessees at a time, it is still targeted primarily at managers and professionals. For these reasons, assessment centres are not a viable means of undertaking large-scale competency assessment.

### Competency rating instruments

In most organisations that have adopted the competencies approach for the bulk of their workforce, the preferred mode of competency assessment tends to be behavioural observation and rating. As noted in chapter 6, there is a range of behavioural rating techniques.

The simplest competency rating instruments are competency-based Graphic Rating Scales. These are identical to the behavioural counterpart except that the criteria being rated are core, threshold and differentiating competencies rather than directly observable work behaviour. The assessor is simply asked to rate the degree to which the employee possesses each competency, typically on a 1–5 or 1–7 rating scale. The scores are then tallied to give an overall competency rating. Input may also be sought from multiple raters, including employees themselves where the system's purpose is primarily development. However, as noted in chapter 6, in the absence of clear behavioural indicators for each competency criterion, and without clearly defined grade descriptors, the reliability of ratings obtained by this means must be open to doubt.

More reliable techniques in this regard are Behaviourally Anchored Rating Scales (BARS) and Behavioural Observation Scales (BOS). More sophisticated behavioural rating techniques, such as weighted checklist and forced choice instruments, may also be adapted for use with competency criteria, although anecdotal evidence suggests that BARS remains the preferred method. The BARS approach utilises scaled behavioural descriptors illustrating varying degrees of a given competency. Behavioural anchors are rank-ordered descriptions of the behavioural manifestations of the personal characteristics identified in the competency model. The use of explicit behavioural anchors enhances consistency of assessment judgements because assessors are all working from a common behavioural frame of reference. For this reason, BARS is usually seen as a more reliable and legally defensible approach than simple Graphic Rating Scales, which typically make little or no use of behavioural indicators or grade descriptors. As with its straight behavioural counterpart, a competency-based BOS measures the frequencies with which behavioural indicators associated with each competency are demonstrated.

With competency-based BARS and BOS instruments, it is usual for the degree of criterion presence to be assessed in terms of competency 'levels', with the rating scale configured accordingly. The instrument may identify as few as three or as many as ten competency levels, but the behavioural indictors or anchors that describe each level should be sufficiently distinct to enable assessors to differentiate reliably between adjacent levels for any given competency criterion.

Figure 7.3 provides an example of a rating scale for one competency criterion in a BARS instrument. Note that three levels of competence are identified, each with its own select behavioural indicators.

## Assessing the competencies approach

### Promise

Since differentiating competencies are held to be reliable predictors of future superior performance, the major promise of the competencies approach is that of guaranteed high performance. This, of course, has been an aspiration of human resource management system designers since the beginning of the modern era. For a time – in the mid-1990s – the competencies approach loomed large in practitioner discourse as the centrepiece of 'best practice' human resource management: '... competencies are sets of skills, knowledge, abilities, behavioural characteristics, and other attributes that, in the right combination and for the right set of circumstances, predict superior performance.' The same authors also suggested that competencies 'add value and help predict success' (Flannery, Hofrichter & Platten 1996: 93). Another

| Competency | Level | | | Your rating | | | Your rationale |
|---|---|---|---|---|---|---|---|
| | 1. Needs development | 2. Effective | 3. Highly effective | 1 | 2 | 3 | |
| **11. Composure:** *The ability to maintain task focus, team focus and emotional control, especially in the face of difficulties and setbacks* | • Gets rattled and loses cool under pressure and stress.<br>• Gets easily overwhelmed and becomes emotional, defensive or withdrawn.<br>• Is defensive and sensitive to criticism.<br>• Is knocked off balance by surprises and gets easily rattled.<br>• Causes others to lose composure or become unsettled.<br>• Lets anger, frustration and anxiety show. | • Is cool under pressure.<br>• Does not become defensive or irritated when times are tough.<br>• Is considered mature.<br>• Can handle stress.<br>• Is not knocked off balance by the unexpected.<br>• Doesn't show frustration when resisted or blocked. | • Can be counted on to hold things together during tough times.<br>• Is a settling influence in a crisis.<br>• Models calmness and collectedness to others.<br>• Coaches subordinates in remaining calm and focused.<br>• Encourages others to see setbacks as learning opportunities. | | | | |

**Figure 7.3** Section of a competency-based, behaviourally anchored rating scale for a mid-level manager role

enthusiast, management consultant O'Neal (1993), went so far as to describe competencies as 'the DNA of organizations'.

Competency-based performance management has also been seen as a way of encouraging employees to behave less as job-holders and more as valued contributors since the approach seeks to focus on those personal attributes that are most likely to deliver high-performance behaviour and results. Linking individual competencies to the organisation's espoused values, goals and strategies also stands to enhance strategic focus and alignment. Competency models may also serve to sharpen role clarity by clearly communicating desired role inputs (Rahbar-Daniels, Erickson & Dalik 2001).

As we have seen, the competencies model has its origins in McClelland's work on high performance at managerial level, and competency systems are now commonplace for selecting, developing, assessing, rewarding and promoting managers in a wide range of organisations. Despite this, the model's effectiveness in enhancing managerial performance has been subject only to empirical testing in the field (as opposed to the experimental laboratory). A field study by Levenson, Van der Stede and Cohen (2006) finds that competencies are positively related to manager performance at the individual level and that manager performance may be increased through competency development. However, the same study finds that the link between competencies and performance at business unit level is much weaker, which suggests that outcomes from competency-based management development programs are moderated by other organisational factors. In short, context matters.

Exponents also argue that the concept of differentiating competencies is applicable to employees at all level of the organisation. As competency exponent Howard Risher (1997a: 146) puts it: 'In contrast to the common reference to predominantly manual jobs in discussions of skills, competence is a concept applicable to every job and every employee.' The approach is also said to be especially compatible with the rise of service and knowledge-based work. The argument here is that the decline of manual jobs and the rise of the 'knowledge worker' has given rise to the need to recognise the importance of new, more diverse abilities than those associated with technical knowledge and skill, particularly those abilities associated with professional knowledge work, such as problem-solving and creative thinking.

Perhaps most importantly, however, the holistic nature of the competencies approach makes possible the development of a bundle of cohesive and tightly integrated human resource management practices. Competency assessment can be applied not only to performance management but also to each of the other three main human resource processes: recruitment and selection, development, and reward management. A fully integrated competency-based human resource management system holds out the promise of an organisation being able to nurture its own unique set of human resource capabilities. As such, the approach is highly compatible with the resource-based view of organisational 'best practice'. An emphasis on core competencies also stands to support the development a cohesive corporate culture.

## Possible pitfalls

Yet the competencies paradigm is not without its potential pitfalls and critics. Two obvious drawbacks are the approach's sheer costliness and complexity. The exacting methodology associated with BEI-based competency identification and modelling means protracted development times and high development costs, especially where external consultants are involved. As erstwhile advocate David Hofrichter (Hofrichter & McGovern 2001: 35) has conceded: 'Competency models grew to be bigger and more complex as well as more expensive and time-consuming to build than anyone had anticipated.' Further, the complexity of competency constructs increases the probability that the purpose of adopting this approach, as opposed to one that is, say, results-based, will not be clearly articulated to the stakeholders involved. In turn, this gives rise to the possibility of system non-acceptance and even distrust, particularly where employees themselves have little or no involvement in system development.

A related shortcoming is the continued lack of clarity and agreement as to what is and is not covered by the term 'competencies'. The distinction between threshold, differentiating and core competencies is itself apt to cause confusion. Assessors and assessees may also be uncertain as to what exactly is being assessed: behaviour, values, attitudes, personality traits or other factors of a still more abstract nature.

The competencies construct has also been the subject of considerable debate in the academic literature. Some critics have argued that the emphasis on differentiating competencies as opposed to technical knowledge and skills is both impractical and misleading. For instance, Lawler (1994a, 1996) has argued that the distinction between 'surface' and 'deep' competencies is little more than an exercise in 'semantic obfuscation'. He contends that the only meaningful competencies are those that are learnable and measurable. When

Lawler speaks of 'competencies' he really means learnable technical skills. Lawler argues that it is far better to concentrate on performance criteria that are readily measurable (i.e. results), and on capacities able to be imparted through training. He certainly acknowledges that organisations may have a legitimate interest in *recruiting and selecting* employees on the basis of personal traits, but adds that people should be *rewarded* for acquired skills and knowledge and for proven performance, rather than for personality traits and other highly abstract criteria.

Another problem is the potential to confuse competencies with performance – a possible source of construct and criterion related invalidity in system design. Competencies, of course, are performance inputs and, as such, equate with neither results nor behaviour. Yet if it is necessary to measure competencies by means of behavioural observation, would it not be simpler to opt for a more traditional behaviourally based approach? On this basis, competency models begin to resemble an unnecessarily circuitous means of recognising and developing desired work behaviour.

As with behavioural assessment, assessing individuals for the types and degree of competencies that they possess is necessarily subjective. This may cause competency-based pay systems to degenerate into systems for assessing personality and rewarding personality traits. The challenge here is to ensure that assessments are made in a consistently reliable manner using valid criteria and indicators. In the absence of these requirements, assessors may base their judgements on irrelevant traits and personal prejudice (Sparrow 1996). As we have seen, assessing employees on the basis of observable performance is difficult enough; assessing them on the basis of phenomena as abstract as core or differentiating competencies is likely to be all the more problematic.

Finally, the claimed link with performance is far from proven. Sparrow (1996) has suggested that the presumed link between competencies and exemplary performance is largely an act of faith. Again, as exponent Hofrichter (Hofrichter & McGovern 2001: 35) now concedes: 'The most difficult hurdle for competency advocates to overcome was that they offered relatively few success stories – fewer, probably, than either strategy or quality or culture could claim. To date, there are no known cases of a competency model single-handedly saving a company – and that seems to be the minimum qualification for achieving "silver bullet" status.' Despite the initial enthusiasm for competency-based human resource management, there are indications that many organisations remain sceptical about the claimed benefits. In the UK, although competency assessment is used by almost a third of organisations, only 39 per cent of users rate the method as being effective (CIPD 2005a: 2). Moreover, as we shall see in chapter 9, only a minority of organisations have thus far adopted competencies as the centrepiece of their reward management systems.

### 'Best fit' with competency-based performance management

In previous chapters, we have identified circumstances for which results-based and behaviourally based performance management may be appropriate fits. To recap: a focus on results may be most appropriate where the ends can be more accurately specified and measured than means, as in work of a highly discretionary nature, such as management work and many areas of professional knowledge work, and in work of a highly interdependent nature, such as teamwork. A focus on membership and task behaviour would be appropriate in routine, closely supervised service and administrative work, whereas an approach targeting citizenship behaviour would be compatible with service work of a more discretionary nature, as well as with most professional and managerial roles.

But with which work situations would the competencies approach be a solid fit? An accent on competencies would be appropriate where work has high knowledge content, as with, say, research and development roles. It would also fit where underlying traits and other personal attributes are seen as being just as important to high performance as are technical skills and knowledge, routine behaviour or measurable results *per se*, as is the case with much professional service work, emotional labour, such as teaching and health care work, and management work, all of which require strong interpersonal abilities. Competencies may also be a suitable choice where results are difficult to quantify but where the work itself is not closely supervised, as with teachers and other knowledge workers. A focus on role competencies may also be appropriate where narrow, closely supervised jobs have been replaced by more broadly defined work roles and where the organisation wishes to recognise and reward personal qualities rather than job content, a point to which we shall return in chapter 9.

In many cases, however, the best fit is likely to lie with a composite approach, involving a combination of results, behavioural and competency criteria. A composite approach will allow the organisation to manage all three aspects of the performance process: input, work actions and work outcomes. A mixed approach would be appropriate where inputs, means and ends can all be specified and measured to some degree and where all are considered important to overall individual and collective performance. In such cases, the main design challenge is to determine the relative weightings to be attached to each of the three performance components, and this, in turn, will be primarily a matter of relative importance in relation to the organisation's strategic and cultural priorities.

## Chapter summary

In this chapter we have explored the concepts, methods and processes associated with the last of the three main approaches to performance management: the competency-based approach. Competencies can be defined generically as individual performance inputs that are related positively and causally to desired work behaviour and results. The chapter identifies and discusses three main types of competency: (1) threshold role competencies, (2) differentiating role competencies and (3) core competencies.

A brief overview of the historical development of the differentiating competencies construct is also provided. The chapter then examines in some detail the main methods and processes associated with competency analysis and the development of competency models and competency assessment instruments, including competency-based behavioural rating instruments. The next section considers the promise and pitfalls of the competencies approach, noting in particular the potential problems arising from system complexity and cost. Finally, some recommendations are made as to the 'best fit' possibilities of stand-alone competency-based systems and systems incorporating a mix of competency, behavioural and results criteria.

## Discussion questions

1 'The distinction between competencies and behaviour is more apparent than real.' Discuss.
2 Should an organisation place more weight on core competencies or on role competencies?
3 What are the challenges involved in assessing individual competency levels?
4 Is the promise of the competencies approach overstated?
5 'Competencies do not equal performance.' Discuss.

## Chapter Eight

# PERFORMANCE REVIEW AND DEVELOPMENT

Thus far, we have considered the three main approaches to defining, monitoring and measuring work performance. However, as important as this is, it is only one phase of the performance management cycle. As noted in chapter 1, a rounded approach to individual performance management, whether the system's purpose is primarily evaluative or, alternatively, mainly developmental, also involves:

- diagnosis of the primary causes of any assessed performance deficits
- the provision of formal feedback on each employee's assessed strengths and weaknesses regarding results, behaviour and/or competencies; that is, a formal performance 'review'
- formal dialogue and planning to remedy any assessed performance deficits and to reinforce existing strengths; that is, an 'action planning' process
- application of appropriate performance development strategies and practices, ranging from counselling for assessed underperformance to mentoring for employees with high potential, and coaching to further enhance the achievements of high-performing employees.

Without these vital steps, the full potential of performance management is unlikely to be realised. Moreover, as with the processes of monitoring and assessment, without due attention to validity, reliability and felt-fairness requirements, it is most unlikely that feedback provision, action planning

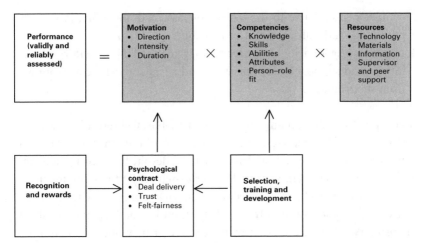

**Figure 8.1** A basic diagnostic tool for analysing individual performance deficits

and development initiatives will deliver the outcomes desired by either the organisation or the employee.

In this chapter, we examine the main options for completing the cycle of performance management by these means, beginning with the diagnosis of the likely reasons for assessed substandard performance.

## Performance assessment diagnosis

Whether the assessment criteria are primarily results-based, behaviourally based or competency-based, the assessment data will need to be subjected to careful analysis so as to identify and remedy the main causes of measured underperformance. This may be undertaken either by the supervisor alone before the formal review meeting or jointly by the supervisor and the assessee during the meeting. Proper diagnosis of the reasons for assessed underperformance requires that attention is paid to both the possible person-based causes as well as possible contextual influences.

Figure 8.1 illustrates a basic diagnostic tool for identifying the sources of underperfromance and for weighing up their relative influences. The central premise is that individual performance (validly and reliably assessed) is the multiplicand of three key variables:

1 motivation, including the direction, intensity and duration of willingness to furnish task effort

2 competencies relative to the job or role assigned, including job or role knowledge and skills, abilities and attributes
3 resources provided, including technology, material inputs, informational inputs, and support from supervisor and peers and, where appropriate, from subordinates.

A non-positive value on any one of these variables will result in a negative performance outcome, irrespective of the value of the other two. Thus, an employee whose motivational drive is lacking, despite being competent and well resourced, will demonstrate low performance. By the same token, an employee who is highly motivated, but who lacks appropriate role competencies and/or relevant resources, will also show low performance. In short, the primary cause of underperformance may or may not be low motivation; competency and/or resourcing deficits may be no less influential – and the crucial point here is that the latter factors are attributable chiefly to the organisational rather than individual factors (Bacharach & Bamberger 1995; Neal & Griffin 1999). For instance, if the employee's competency profile is a poor fit for the position to which she has been assigned, this is essentially a management responsibility rather than that of the individual, at least in the short term. An inadequate competency profile may reflect inappropriate job placement or inadequate provision of training and development opportunities – both of which are critical management functions. Likewise, inadequate resourcing cannot be attributed to the employee, since this is a management responsibility.

Equally, as figure 8.1 suggests, low motivation itself may have contextual rather than personal causes. Again, the pivotal consideration here is the state of the psychological contract. As noted in chapter 2, human resource practices themselves, including performance assessment, recognition and reward itself, as well as employee selection, training and development, will be major determinants of the state of the psychological contract. As such, low motivation may reflect dysfunction in human resource practices themselves. It cannot simply be assumed that low motivation is the 'fault' of the individual employee. The wellsprings may well be individually based, but this can be established only through careful interrogation and analysis of valid performance evidence. It is likely that the primary causes of underperformance will be clearly identified only through a searching process of information-sharing, analysis and consensus-building between the supervisor and the employee concerned. This is rightly one of the key functions of a formal performance review meeting.

# Performance review meetings

The performance review meeting is the crucial bridge between valid and reliable performance assessment, on the one hand, and focused, effective performance remediation and enhancement, on the other. The review meeting can be defined as a formal dialogue and exchange between individual employees and their supervisor regarding the employee's assessed performance over the review period for the purpose of reaching agreement about what had been achieved, what can be improved and how such improvements can be achieved.

While other knowledgeable stakeholders, such as the supervisor's immediate superior, may also participate in the meeting, it is generally the supervisor who is rightly assigned the task of reviewing, analysing, conveying and discussing the assessment evidence and outcomes, since it is the supervisor who should have the greatest understanding of the assessee's strengths, weaknesses and development needs, albeit informed by assessment input from additional sources, including peers and subordinates. In most cases, panel-based review sessions are inadvisable, since the assessee may regard the experience as inquisitorial rather than remedial and constructive.

## Review meeting content and timing

As we shall see, the 'style' of the meeting may take a number of different forms. However, in general terms, the meeting should ideally entail six main steps:

1 communication and confirmation of the details of the employee's assessed performance, including both criterion-specific ratings and the summative rating
2 provision of feedback on specific performance strengths and weaknesses in relation to desired results, behaviour and/or competencies
3 provision of positive reinforcement regarding assessed strengths
4 consideration of, and agreement on, the underlying reasons for any assessed performance weaknesses
5 exchange of views about what has been achieved and what needs to be addressed
6 agreement about what needs to be done next and how this can be accomplished (adapted from Armstrong 2000: 80–1).

While the content of the meeting will – and should – vary on a case-by-case basis, at the most general level, the meeting should cover the following matters of content:

- the employee's past and present performance level
- what the employee has learnt or needs to learn
- what the employee believes she/he is capable of
- where the employee is faring in terms of performance and career goals
- how the employee is going to get there
- what guidance and support can be provided to help the employee get there.

The frequency and timing of the formal review meeting must also be given careful consideration. Traditionally, formal reviews were conducted once per year. More recently, it has become increasingly common for such reviews to be undertaken half-yearly or even quarterly, although a common practice is to combine informal one-on-one quarterly meetings with an annual formal feedback session.

Timing should also be given close consideration. The traditional approach was to conduct all review meetings simultaneously, say, in the final week of the financial year, primarily so as to harmonise with the organisation's annual staff planning process. While this has the advantage of compressing the formalities into a narrow period for that time at least, it is highly likely that the organisation will be distracted from its core business activities. In all probability, this annual organisation-wide ritual will also witness much of the manipulative behaviour identified in chapter 6 as giving rise to halo and horns or recency error. In many organisations, the art of impression management attains its apogee at the time of the annual review round!

The alternative is to stagger the assessment and review meetings so that the formal review process is distributed more evenly throughout the year. One common means to this end is to conduct the assessment and formal review meeting around the anniversary of each employee's appointment. This has the advantage of distributing assessors' workloads in a more manageable way. However, it also means that some supervisors may be required to devote several hours each week to arranging and conducting review sessions.

A related consideration here is the timing of the review meeting in relation to any associated reward reviews. Many organisations still make use of the review meeting as a means of communicating decisions relating to annual base pay adjustment and/or performance pay levels. There is also some evidence that combining performance feedback and reward discussions may serve to reinforce the developmental messages, at least where low performers are involved (Prince & Lawler 1986). Yet it is also possible that simultaneity may have significant dysfunctional consequences. The problem here is that once reward outcomes are placed on the agenda, there is a high probability that the employee's attention will shift away from performance assessment and the messages associated with it to a singular focus on reward outcomes. Where this occurs, the process of performance planning may well be impaired. For this reason, many organisations now delay reward announcements until one to three months after the performance review meeting. A lag of this order allows ample time for assimilation of and reflection on the content of the review meeting before any financial consequences arise.

*Reinforcement theory?*

## Review meeting styles

Undoubtedly the single most important determinant of the effectiveness of any review meeting is the style and tenor with which it is conducted. The extent to which employees' experience in the review meeting accords with how they expect to be treated will have a major influence on their perceptions of justice, especially procedural and interactional justice cognitions and emotions. In turn, as noted in chapter 2, an alteration in fairness perceptions may influence the state of the employee psychological contract and therefore pivotal work attitudes and behaviour.

That said, however, it must also be acknowledged that there is no one best way to conduct a review meeting; no one feedback style that is right for all possible circumstances. What we have at our disposal is a range of approaches, some of which will be better suited to some management cultures and associated organisational contexts than others. In essence, the style should fit the espoused management culture, particularly regarding the degree of employee involvement, empowerment and autonomy. Most importantly, however, the review style must also accord with the expectations and needs of the individual assessee; that is, a 'best fit' approach requires that the review style should, wherever possible, be tailored so as to best address and accord with each individual employee's specific circumstances. With this latter point in mind, it is becoming more common for organisations to include simple taxonomies of general review styles in guideline documents prepared to assist reviewers in planning their approach to the provision of feedback to different individuals. For instance, one such guide to 'interviewing technique' (cited by Dessler, Griffiths & Lloyd-Walker 2004: 280–1) identifies three distinct styles of review meeting: (1) the 'tell and sell' style, (2) the 'tell and listen' style and (3) the 'problem-solving' style.

While there is as yet little reliable research evidence on this important aspect of performance management practice, anecdotal evidence from Australia indicates that the approach or approaches to the conduct of review meetings most commonly recommended in review guidelines are generally variants of one or more of these three styles. Indeed, in the practitioner literature, the 'problem-solving' style appears to have been elevated to 'best practice' status. As such, it is appropriate for us to examine each of these styles, and the circumstances to which each may be most appropriate, a little more closely.

The 'tell and sell' style is best suited to a mechanistically structured organisation managed on traditional low-trust lines. Here, the reviewer assumes the role of a sentencing judge with the aim of delivering the performance judgement to the assessee, obtaining their acceptance of the judgement dispensed, and persuading them to acquiesce in the reviewer's plan for improving their performance. An underlying assumption is that the reviewer is a superior able to undertake reliable performance assessment and diagnosis and with the ability to persuade and motivate. In turn, the assessee is assumed to be motivated to improve their performance by being made aware of their assessed weaknesses. Given the degree of power distance between the two parties, in 'tell and sell' situations, an assessee may seek to suppress defensive responses and to disguise hostility when presented with negative performance feedback; that is, with evidence and judgements regarding the nature and cause of performance weaknesses.

Such an approach may be time-efficient and cost-effective. It may also suit situations in which a low-involvement, low-trust management culture prevails and subordinates need and expect detailed and directive advice from a superior. By the same token, the 'tell and sell' approach does little to encourage employees to take greater responsibility for the management of their performance, leaves little room for employees' voice and contribution, and may lead to dysfunctional face-saving behaviour by either or both parties, as well as to a potential erosion of employee loyalty. Overall, the 'tell and sell' approach fails to address many of the commonly prescribed requirements for procedural justice.

With a 'tell and listen' style, the reviewer still adopts the role of a judge, although the approach is essentially that of an attentive judge prepared to hear the assessee's case. The reviewer advises the assessee of a tentative performance judgement, then allows the assessee to respond, considers both viewpoints, arrives at a conclusion and formulates a plan for improvement. The logic here is that allowing the employee an opportunity to voice feelings, especially those of a defensive nature, reduces the emotional barriers and blockages to change. The reviewer is assumed to believe that the employee's feelings should be listened to and respected, although not necessarily accepted, and should be able to listen attentively, be sufficiently flexible to allow the employee to respond, possess high emotional intelligence (as described in chapter 7), and be able to synthesise and summarise multisource information clearly and concisely.

The obvious advantage of the 'tell and listen' style is that it provides a safety valve for defensive reactions to be expressed and discussed. It also permits a flexible dialogue between the parties, harnesses the employee's own informational input, allows the employee some influence over remediation strategies, and may serve to elicit or reinforce a relationship of trust between the reviewer and the subordinate. A potential disadvantage is that the reviewer is required to defend his/her viewpoint, and this may lead to discussion wandering from the central issues of performance diagnosis and planning. There is also a strong possibility that one or both parties may view the provision for employee input as merely a token concession. Finally, the success of the 'tell and listen' approach will depend largely on the quality of the prior preparation undertaken by both parties, which in turn will require a considerable investment of time by both. Overall, the 'tell and listen' approach is likely to be a suitable fit for organisations with a mechanistic structure but which are undergoing transition from a traditional low-trust management culture towards one that entails higher involvement and a greater degree of trust.

The 'problem-solving' style represents a radical departure from the above approaches. Here, the reviewer plays the role not of a judge but of a counsellor, mentor and/or coach committed to a mutual and constructive approach to identifying and correcting agreed performance problems. The key aim is for both parties to discuss and analyse the performance evidence jointly, to draw out the employee's emotions and ideas, and to work together to identify solutions to performance problems. At the same time, the reviewer must seek to encourage and resource employee development and performance enhancement. Similarly, the employee must feel empowered, responsible and accountable. Self-assessment is also a standard feature of the problem-solving style. The underlying assumptions are, first, that performance enhancement arises from a full and frank discussion of assessed problems and, second, that open dialogue dissolves emotional barriers to remediation. Such an approach requires an exacting degree of reviewer competency: an ability to frame exploratory questions, to listen attentively, to generate insightful ideas and solutions, to evaluate arguments and counter-arguments in an open-minded and non-emotive manner, and to see matters from the employee's perspective, as well as to reconsider, refute, summarise and negotiate in a wholly constructive way. In sum, the reviewer must be fully informed, open-minded and intellectually agile, and have high emotional intelligence.

On the positive side, the constructive tenor of the 'problem-solving' style means that the probability of performance improvement is all the more likely. The approach also allows greater freedom for novel ideas and views to be aired without fear of judgement or retribution. It also stands to reinforce trust, cooperation and open communication between all concerned. In short, the probability of achieving a positive and genuine consensus is much greater with this approach. Equally, by its very nature, the 'problem-solving' approach is far better equipped to avoid attribution error and to facilitate 'double loop' learning; that is problem-solving that not only learns from past mistakes but also capitalises on them to identify and implement more effective work practices (Armstrong & Baron 1998: 218–27).

Yet a 'problem-solving' style is not without shortcomings. In particular, having enough reviewers with the requisite competency profile will require substantial investment in in-house competency development programs or rewards sufficient to attract and retain highly competent external recruits. Moreover, the approach is by definition more exacting and time-consuming than less inclusive approaches, and outcomes will also be less controllable. Given the accent on self-assessment and candid disclosure, a problem-solving approach also sits uneasily with an evaluative purpose. In the short run, at least, the problem-solving formula, with its avowedly developmental purpose, has little compatibility with performance-related rewards. In sum, then, this approach has strong synergies with a high-trust, high-involvement management culture, but its developmental focus and emphasis on self-assessment may also conflict with the use of performance pay and other forms of performance-contingent reward.

## Review meeting preparation

Irrespective of the style adopted, it is imperative that the reviewer is prepared thoroughly for each meeting. Accordingly, well before the scheduled meeting date, the reviewer should consider:

- all relevant performance information from all designated sources, including their own observations, those of peers, the assessee and, where appropriate, subordinates and/or clients or customers
- the assessee's existing position description and associated performance standards
- how well the assessee has done in achieving performance standards and objectives since the last review meeting
- the factors that have affected performance, both within and beyond the assessee's control
- the extent to which the assessee has implemented the personal development plan agreed at the last review
- the specific feedback that will be provided and the evidence used to support it
- points for discussion on possible actions by assessee and reviewer to improve performance
- whether the assessee has been given sufficient guidance and what extra guidance could be provided
- whether the best use is being made of the assessee's skills and abilities and any changes that could be made
- whether the assessee is ready for additional responsibilities in the current job
- whether the assessee and the organisation would benefit from the assessee being reassigned
- the direction that the assessee's career could best take
- any additional development the assessee may need to further their career in the organisation
- possible objectives for the next review period (adapted from Armstrong 2000: 80–3; Armstrong & Baron 1998: 330–1).

Where the purpose of performance assessment and review is primarily developmental, and certainly where the review meeting style accords with a 'problem-solving' approach, the assessee should also be required and resourced to undertake either a formal or an informal self-assessment well before the meeting date. Typically, both the reviewer and the assessee will be required to prepare preliminary assessments, which are then exchanged several days before the meeting date so that there are no surprises on the day of the meeting and both parties are informed and forewarned as to the nature and degree of agreement and discrepancy in the assessment record.

In undertaking self-assessment, each employee should be encouraged to consider:

- whether they have met performance standards and objectives
- examples of standards and objectives not being achieved and why
- problems that may have arisen and what could be done about them
- performance successes, with examples
- aspects of work where improvement is required
- progress in implementing the previous development plan
- any unmet development needs
- requirements for better support or guidance
- future work aspirations
- whether it is time to assume extra responsibilities
- whether it would be desirable to move to another role
- possible objectives for the next review period (adapted from Armstrong 2000: 82–3; Armstrong & Brown 1998: 331).

Whether the performance assessment is based chiefly on results, behaviour, competencies or, as is more likely, on a combination of these criteria, a requirement for formal self-assessment means that the employee is actively involved in the process, is able to provide potentially crucial input to the review process, and is less likely to behave defensively. Further, self-assessment increases the probability that the review meeting will proceed as a constructive and open dialogue rather than a judgement session. By the same token, self-assessment requires that each employee has a clear understanding of the relevant performance standards and objectives, that there is a climate of mutual trust between the parties, and that the employee does not fear being penalised for providing an honest self-evaluation. In essence, this means that employees as well as reviewers should undergo comprehensive prior training in the system's purpose, standards and processes.

## Conducting a problem-solving review meeting

Clearly, the manner in which a review meeting is conducted and the atmosphere in which it proceeds will depend primarily on the reviewer's preferred style. Where, as is frequently the case, the style adopted – or, at least, intended – is that of 'problem-solving', there are a number of critical requirements for review effectiveness.

Each employee should receive adequate notice of the meeting date and time, and sufficient time should be set aside for the meeting itself, with one hour generally being a reasonable benchmark in most cases. The review should proceed according to a clear structure, preferably agreed in advance. The meeting should also be conducted in private and in an atmosphere conducive to uninterrupted dialogue. Ideally, the venue should be a meeting room other than the supervisor's own office or workspace, so that the trappings and distractions of status are not present.

The reviewer should encourage the employee to do most of the talking and should invite self-appraisal. To encourage open dialogue, the reviewer should avoid aggressive interrogative questions that elicit only brief 'yes'/'no' responses; instead 'open' questions that invite the employee to elaborate perceptions, feelings and explanations should be used:

- 'How well do you feel you have done?'
- 'How do you feel about that?'
- 'Why do you think that happened?'
- 'What could you have done differently?' (adapted from Armstrong & Baron 1998: 334–5).

A problem-solving approach requires that the reviewer be an active listener and not interrupt the employee unnecessarily. The reviewer should also show empathy and understanding, and allow scope for mutual reflection and analysis. The dialogue should focus on performance, not on the person *per se*. There should be no surprises and no unexpected criticisms. According to Ulrich and Beatty (2001: 296) feedback is most effective if it:

- is based on behaviour
- is specific rather than general
- offers suggestions for improvement as opposed to unconstructive criticism
- focuses on the future rather than the past
- encourages active reflection rather than passive acceptance.

To maximise review accuracy – that is, assessment validity and reliability, and analytical precision – the parties should review the whole period, not just a select number of critical incidents. Moreover, the discussion should recognise performance achievements and strengths and not dwell solely on assessed deficits. Indeed, it is generally best to consider the positives before any negatives.

Once all significant areas of weaknesses have been identified, agreed and prioritised, the parties should jointly draw up an action plan to help address problems and accentuate strengths. This typically takes the form of a personal development plan incorporating both self-managed learning and, where appropriate, other forms of remediation and support, such as performance coaching.

Finally, the parties should review and revise the existing performance standards and measures wherever necessary, and certainly where there have been significant changes in job or role content. As noted in chapter 5, the joint review of performance criteria and indicators is a defining feature of the goal-setting process.

## Providing negative feedback

Few supervisory tasks in the position descriptions of a line manager are more emotionally and interpersonally fraught than that of having to provide negative feedback to subordinates. Providing negative feedback does not involve simply criticising the recipient; rather it entails the communication of information and judgements regarding low or reduced achievement against desired performance standards or expectations in a clear but constructive manner and with a view to facilitating appropriate remediation.

The barriers to the effective provision of negative feedback are often substantial. Most people do not like giving it. Most people do not like receiving it, partly because of perceived loss of 'face', the avoidance of which is of paramount importance in some non-European cultures. Negative feedback is typically received and interpreted less accurately than positive feedback because the emotional mechanisms aimed at protecting self-esteem serve to distort the messages received.

It is also highly likely that negative judgements will trigger emotive responses that may overwhelm the messages and the possibility of rational dialogue and action planning. One central aim of the feedback review, of course, is to persuade the recipient that a performance problem exists, that remedial action is warranted and that remedying the problem is within their power. The nature of the behavioural response is likely to be conditioned

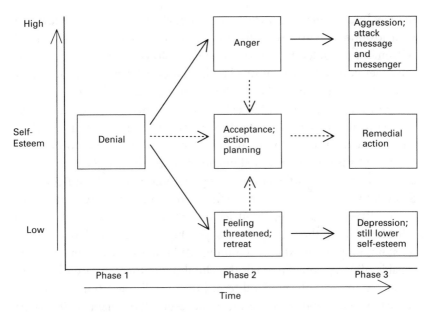

**Figure 8.2** Possible behavioural responses to receipt of negative feedback

by a range of cognitions and affects, particularly the individual's self-concept and degree of self-esteem. As figure 8.2 suggests, it is common for recipients of negative feedback to engage initially in acts of denial that reflect what is referred to by exponents of attribution theory (see chapter 3) as 'self-serving bias'. This happens when undesirable outcomes are attributed unreflectively to contextual factors rather than being accepted as falling within the control of the individual.

What happens next is likely to depend partly on how the reviewer responds to the act of denial but also on the level of the recipient's underlying level of self-esteem and the strength of their need for recognition and esteem. Individuals with low self-esteem may feel threatened, undergo a process of emotional withdrawal and end up in a downward spiral of depression and further loss of self-confidence and self-respect, perhaps to the point where self-blame overwhelms rationality and self-efficacy. However, as figure 8.2 suggests, high self-esteem may be just as problematic in this regard as is low self-esteem, especially where it is so high as to induce self-delusion. Individuals with high self-esteem, especially those with a history of high performance recognition, and perhaps over-exposure to praise, may move from a state of denial to one of anger and then to a state of aggression in which both the message and the messenger come under verbal attack, leaving the reviewer with no option but to close the meeting. Either way, these extreme emotional outcomes will render the feedback session wholly counterproductive unless the reviewer is sufficiently attuned to the emotional dynamics to anticipate and deflect such problems before they overwhelm the exchange.

According to Audia and Locke (2003) acceptance of negative feedback, and hence the recipient's potential to benefit from the information conveyed, will depend on three sets of cognitions. First, the recipient must believe that the reviewer is genuine and well intentioned; that is, that the reviewer has credibility, is trustworthy and is acting in good faith and with goodwill. Second, the recipient must have high 'elaboration' proclivity; that is, they must actively scrutinise the feedback information to verify its validity and reliability. Third, the recipient must have high 'self-efficacy'; that is, they must not only accept what is communicated but also believe that they are capable of doing something positive about it and that they are adequately resourced to do so. In practical terms, the overall suggestion here is that while these perceptions are specific to the feedback recipient, reviewers are also able to bring influence to bear on each so as to maximise the likelihood of acceptance and active remediation.

## Remedying under-performance: counselling and action planning

Within the review meeting context, performance remediation typically involves two interconnected steps: (1) performance counselling and (2) action planning. Performance counselling is simply the process of analysis and advising that the reviewer undertakes with a view to assisting substandard performers to improve their performance against valid criteria. The four key steps in the counselling process are as follows:

1 *understanding* the perspective of the other person
2 *recognising and agreeing* the existence, nature and extent of the problem
3 *reframing* the perspective from negative to positive; discussing the issues to help change perspectives and indicate possible solutions
4 *empowering* the employee to recognise the problem, propose solutions and take action to implement the solution (adapted from Armstrong 2000: 93–9; Armstrong & Baron 1998: 239–48, 344–8).

In this critical process, it is important that the reviewer is able to provide specific examples of negative behavioural incidents and/or results or competency shortcomings, which the assessee should then be allowed the opportunity to reflect on and respond to. The reviewer must also confine the discussion to valid and agreed performance criteria and seek to offer constructive suggestions and solutions. Equally, to minimise the possibility of defensiveness or loss of self-esteem, the reviewer should avoid dealing with more than one or two weaknesses at a time, avoid 'playing the person', and ensure that the recipient is treated at all times with dignity and respect so as not to elicit feelings of interactional injustice, even when firm refutation or counter-argument is warranted.

Once there is agreement as to the nature and extent of the performance deficits, attention should then turn to the process of planning remedial action. Where 'problem-solving' is the preferred review style, the parties jointly negotiate, formulate and agree on a suitable action plan, with the recipient being invited to produce their own ideas as to the most appropriate course of action. Where the style accords more with a 'tell-and-sell' approach, the reviewer formulates the plan, explains it to the recipient and requests their agreement. Irrespective of the degree of employee input, the reviewer must also ensure that the employee is adequately resourced to implement the action plan. In many organisations, action planning is systematised by means of personal development plan forms of the type illustrated in figure 8.3. Note that this particular instrument presents the parties with a range of possible performance development initiatives: from on-the-job training, mentoring and coaching, to networking and assessment centre activity. Action plans also typically incorporate goal-setting techniques of the type present in this example. The use of personal development or action plans is now a common feature of performance management practice throughout the Western world. In the UK, for instance, almost two-thirds of organisations incorporate personal development plans in their performance management systems, with more than 80 per cent of users rating the feature as being effective (CIPD 2005a: 2–3).

## Developing high performance: mentoring and coaching

While performance counselling is an intervention directed primarily at remedying assessed underperformance, mentoring and coaching are practices

**Performance development plan for the year 200X**

| | |
|---|---|
| Employee's name:..................................... | Supervisor:............................................. |
| Position:............................................. | Signature:............................................. |
| Signature:........................................... | Date:................................................... |
| Date:................................................. | |

All performance development planning should be based on:
1. a thorough and agreed analysis of the nature and scope of assessed performance weakness over the preceding year
2. agreement on the factors primarily responsible for these weaknesses and the main needs arising from these weaknesses
3. agreement on the steps that should now be taken to address these weaknesses and needs and the goals that should be applied to ensure that these needs are met in an effective and timely way.

In determining the steps to be taken and goals to be set, consider which of the following options may provide the most appropriate and realistic solutions.

| | | |
|---|---|---|
| ❑ On the job training | ❑ Further education | ❑ Formal training |
| ❑ Mentoring | ❑ Committee or task force participation | ❑ Self-learning programs |
| ❑ Secondment | ❑ Lateral transfer | ❑ Special projects |
| ❑ Coaching | ❑ Higher duties | ❑ Assessment centre activity |
| ❑ Job rotation | ❑ Online training | ❑ Networking |
| ❑ Reading and discussion of relevant publications | ❑ Conference/seminar attendance | ❑ Teamworking exercises |

**Performance development goals***

| 3–5 High-priority development needs for 200X: | Specific goal and measure to address each need |
|---|---|
| 1. | |
| 2. | |
| 3. | |
| 4. | |
| 5. | |

| 1–3 Longer-term career development needs or aspirations | Goal and measure for addressing each nominated long-term need or aspiration |
|---|---|
| 1. | |
| 2. | |
| 3. | |

*Note that each goal must be:
- ✓ specific
- ✓ measurable
- ✓ achievable within the time-frame
- ✓ relevant to the job or role
- ✓ time-framed.

**Figure 8.3** Example of an action planning and performance development instrument

intended chiefly to enhance the effectiveness of high-potential and high-performing employees, managers and executives. Both practices are widely applied in Western work organisations. In the UK, 36 per cent of organisations used coaching and/or mentoring, although, significantly, only 46 per cent of users currently rate these practices as being effective (CIPD 2005a: 3).

## Mentoring

Mentoring involves a part-time or full-time relationship of support and guidance between an experienced work colleague and a less experienced but high-potential colleague. The mentor provides support, advice, contacts and feedback to the protégé – or 'mentee' – regarding the latter's work role tasks, duties, responsibilities, and competency requirements, their personal and performance development, and their career planning (Ehrich & Hansford 1999). Mentoring relationships may last for just a few months, but it is more usual for them to run for between six months and two years. While mentoring may be applied at any level in the organisation, it is most commonly applied to junior professional and manager roles and is a longstanding practice in firms with partnership structures, particularly firms in accounting, the law and management consulting. In some cases the organisation compulsorily assigns one or more mentees to each mentor; in others, the organisation encourages and resources the formation of voluntary mentoring relationships, and there is some evidence that voluntary and self-selecting relationships are more enduring and effective than those involving mandated and arbitrary assignment. In mechanistically structured and traditionally managed organisations, the immediate supervisor may fill the role of mentor. However, in high-involvement organisations with more organic structures, it is equally likely that the mentor will be a more experienced peer rather than a superordinate. Indeed, peer mentoring has recently emerged as an area of significant experimentation and innovation in the service and information sectors.

Within the relationship, the mentor generally fills one or more of four main roles: (1) role model, (2) adviser, (3) broker and (4) advocate. As a role model, the mentor, who has attained a significant level of experience in the role or position concerned, passes on this experience to the mentee over the course of the relationship. As an adviser, the mentor provides guidance to the mentee on matters of organisational communication, protocol, persuasion and politics. In the broker role, the mentor provides the mentee with useful contacts, networking opportunities and information. As a personal advocate, the mentor champions the mentee's cause, recommending them for appropriate assignments and career advancement opportunities.

Mentoring stands to improve one-on-one communication within the organisation, facilitates close monitoring of performance capability and achievement, provides mentees with readily applicable 'hands-on' learning, accelerates the rate of organisational learning, provides valuable rewards of a developmental nature that will increase normative commitment and reduce turnover of high-potential employees, and builds networks of knowledge-sharing that can enhance organisational core competencies and competitive resources. Gender-specific mentoring and associated networking practices are also potentially powerful ways of addressing the particular career development and advancement challenges that still face many high-potential female professionals and managers in today's large organisations (Ehrich & Hansford 1999; Murray & Owen 1991).

At the same time, mentoring may also have a dark side. The relationship can easily fail because of unrealistic expectations by one or both parties. The relationship may promote an overweening dependence by the mentee on the one mentor. The relationship may be damaged by personality conflicts, even where the association is wholly voluntary. As such, a careful and tactful process of prior screening, selection and matching may be required to reduce the possibility of relationship breakdown. Where the mentor is also the mentee's immediate supervisor, perceptions of power inequality may inhibit open dialogue, and the supervisor's role as performance assessor may cause role confusion and misunderstanding. Cross-gender mentoring in particular may also give rise to rumours of sexual liaison that may damage the reputation of both parties. Co-workers may feel that the mentee is the beneficiary of favouritism. The mentor's peers may resent the presence of a more junior employee in their deliberations. The mentor may have extensive role knowledge and experience but lack the basic competencies in leadership and teaching needed to facilitate the mentee's trust and learning, including those associated with emotional intelligence (J. Long 1997; Ehrich & Hansford 1999). Finally, by definition, mentoring is not an appropriate developmental practice at senior manager and executive level. At these levels, the more appropriate intervention is coaching.

## Coaching

Whereas mentoring is a decades-old practice, coaching is of more recent origin, having risen to prominence only since the mid- to late 1990s (Kilburg 1996; Kampa-Kokesch & Anderson 2001). In general terms coaching may be defined as a solution- and results-based individual or small group learning facilitation process derived from behavioural theories of learning and change that is intended to help high-performing employees further enhance their performance focus, effectiveness and achievements. According to Skiffington and Zeus (2003: 129): 'Coaching, as opposed to managing, involves focusing on an individual's development and enabling him or her to become more self-reliant and to solve problems and make decisions independently. Coach managers promote reflection and insight and help individuals to become more self-managing and self-generating.'

As such, coaching may be viewed as a specialised method for developing those performance capacities defined in the competencies literature as 'differentiating' role competencies. In this respect, it is highly significant that the rise of coaching as a field of organisational and quasi-professional practice has been synchronous with that of competency-based performance management, which is explored more fully in chapter 7. The purpose of coaching is to examine areas for development and to assist the 'coachee' in thinking through their self-concept and work-related challenges and problems and identifying, applying and evaluating actions to effect appropriate changes in the coachee's competencies, attitudes, behaviour and impact.

The coach is neither a role model nor a teacher – that is, the coach does not assume a mentoring role – and, with the exception of business coaching, does not necessarily need to possess a detailed knowledge of the technical content of the coachee's job or role. The coach is there to help the coachee learn how to learn and self-develop. The coaching relationship involves day-to-day discussion of personal attitudes, outlook, emotions, work relationships, goals and personal development strategies. The coach helps the coachee to frame an appropriate development plan incorporating agreed development goals and attainment strategies and, if the relationship continues, the coach can track accomplishments in carrying out the plan. The role of the contemporary organisational coach includes the following tasks and actions:

- increasing the coachee's self-awareness
- managing self-esteem
- modelling desired behaviour
- teaching the coachee how to learn, how to be a better problem-solver, how to set and keep to personal goals
- getting the issues on the table for honest discussion
- dealing with conflict, stress, emotions and interpersonal problems
- targeting behaviour to change
- obtaining feedback from other stakeholders
- giving feedback (positive and negative)
- ensuring behavioural practice and rehearsal
- encouraging the coachee to take responsibility for their assumptions and actions
- keeping the coachee focused and on track
- helping to identify personal strategies that will work most effectively (adapted from Kilburg 1996: 140–1).

Coaching takes a wide variety of forms: from behavioural coaching, results coaching, group coaching and organisational coaching, to leadership coaching, executive coaching, business coaching and life coaching. Leadership and executive coaching are now among the most widespread and lucrative career management and leadership development activities in work organisations in Australia and elsewhere. Around 40 per cent of large Australian firms currently use coaching in some form, primarily for senior managers and executives (Souter 2005). There is also no shortage of practitioners in the field, particularly specialist external providers of one-on-one coaching to executive clients.

Current coaching practice has its conceptual roots in adult learning theory, psychodynamic theory (regarding self-awareness and defensiveness) and several key theories of work motivation, including goal-setting theory, social cognition theory and cognitive evaluation theory, as well as sports psychology, from which the practice, of course, derives its name.

Since coaching practice is still in the early stages of development, there is no one agreed or dominant model for the coaching process and coaching practice. However, in the realm of organisational coaching, one of the most widely disseminated approaches is the 'behavioural coaching model' formulated and popularised by Skiffington and Zeus (Zeus & Skiffington 2000, 2002; Skiffington & Zeus 2003). According to Skiffington and Zeus (2003: 123), behavioural coaching 'encapsulates personal development, beliefs, values, emotions, motivation and social learning, as well as personal and organisational dynamics and defenses'. Behavioural coaching, they add (2003: 123), has the following general characteristics:

- targeting and focusing on specific behaviour
- analysing behaviour in relation to its antecedents and consequences
- applying valid and reliable methods of behavioural assessment, data collection and data analysis
- goal development informed by goal-setting theory and research
- employing validated behavioural change techniques
- managing and maintaining behavioural change.

Skiffington and Zeus's behavioural coaching model, which is summarised in figure 8.4, identifies four stages of change, five distinct forms of coaching and a linear seven-step coaching process. The model also rests on a number of key assumptions, including the following:

- Coaching is widely accepted as a powerful tool for personal and professional growth.
- Successful coaching programs focus on individual, team and organisational business objectives and goals.
- Change lies at the heart of any coaching program.
- Changing behaviour involves learning.
- Coaching outcomes are likely to be most successful when coachees are voluntary, understand the basis of behavioural coaching and through the coaching partnership become strongly committed to the change process.
- The model can be effective only in a safe, open and trusting climate.
- Coaching outcomes should be measured against the stated objectives of the individual, team or organisation.
- Scope must be allowed for differences in coaching styles and techniques, and for individual differences among both coaches and coachees (Skiffington & Zeus 2003: 125).

In the first stage of change – the reflective stage – both the coach and the coachee are either unaware that there are problems to address or have

| Stages of change | Five forms of coaching | Seven-step coaching process |
|---|---|---|
| 1. Reflective | 1. Coaching education | 1. Education |
| 2. Preparation | 2. Skills coaching<br>3. Rehearsal coaching | 2. Data collection<br>3. Planning (target, goals, action plans)<br>4. Behavioural change |
| 3. Action | 4. Performance coaching | 5. Measurement<br>6. Evaluation |
| 4. Maintenance | 5. Self-coaching | 7. Maintenance |

**Figure 8.4** The behavioural coaching model
*Source:* Skiffington & Zeus 2003: 125.

this awareness and accept that changes have to be made but have yet to commit to moving forward. Here the prospective coach applies coaching education and assumes the role of teacher, alerting the prospective coachee to the possible benefits of coaching, as well as the rights, responsibilities and time requirements of each party. At this stage, the coach's own behaviour is critical, since the coach is 'walking a tightrope' between causing potential disillusionment with coaching and persuading the prospective coachee of the benefits it has to offer (Skiffington & Zeus 2003: 126, 127, 130).

In the second – or preparation – stage of change, the parties accept that change is required but are unsure how to proceed and are not as yet fully committed to a coaching intervention. At this stage the role of the coach is to take the preparatory step of collecting data, conducting assessments, targeting specific behaviour for change, setting goals and developing action plans. At this preparatory juncture, the prospective coach enacts the second and third steps in the coaching process, namely base-line data collection and action planning. Base-line data collecting techniques frequently include self-reflection, personality and leadership inventories, psychometric assessment, physical assessment, behaviour event interviews (BEI), the coach's own critical incident observations, multisource or 360-degree feedback, targeted attitude surveys and focus groups (Skiffington & Zeus 2003: 126, 130–46). Once the preliminary data-gathering is complete and the parties have agreed to establish a formal coaching relationship, the coach then initiates action planning, including the setting of agreed development goals and measures (Skiffington & Zeus 2003: 126, 146–51).

With the details of the action plan now finalised, the coaching process progresses to the fourth and critical step: that of behavioural change. Here, coaching initially takes the form of skills coaching, with the coachee learning new skills or competencies, such as those to do with planning, presentation, assertiveness, communication, management of difficult colleagues, networking and marketing. Coaching next takes the form of rehearsal coaching, with the coachee rehearsing the newly acquired competencies through simulation and role-play exercises in preparation for their application in the workplace (Skiffington & Zeus 2003: 126, 151–2).

In the third stage of change – the action stage – the coachee applies the learned competencies in the workplace. These are monitored, measured and evaluated continuously by the coachee and peers, with the coachee self-monitoring and the coach also shadowing the coachee as they apply the new competencies. At the same time, the coach is required to help the coachee to manage performance fluctuations and any new internal or contextual barriers to performance development (Skiffington & Zeus 2003: 126).

The data-gathering techniques applied at this point in the process – that is, post-intervention evaluation – are much the same as those used to gather the base-line or pre-coaching data. By means of formal measurement evaluation, the coachee's post-coaching behaviour can be compared with their pre-coaching performance to gauge the nature and degree of improvement:

- How has their level of self-awareness, self-esteem, self-efficacy and job satisfaction altered?
- Are they more in control of their emotions?
- How has their value orientation changed?
- Do they believe that their work–life balance has improved?
- Has their level of work stress declined?
- Has their level of physical wellness improved?
- Do peers and subordinates see them differently now?
- How has their level of business goal attainment improved?
- Has their time management improved?
- Have their communication and listening competencies improved?

In the fourth and final stage of change – the maintenance stage – the emphasis is on consolidating and sustaining the behavioural changes and ensuring that the coachee's behaviour does not regress or revert. Here, coaching takes the form of self-coaching. While the coach remains available to the coachee, the overall aim is to develop the coachee's performance competencies to the point where they are no longer reliant on the coach, have high self-efficacy and are able to self-coach by learning to 'recognize triggers for both desired and undesired behaviors and ways to self-correct and self-regulate' (Skiffington & Zeus 2003: 129, 160–1).

Since coaching is a results-based intervention, pre- and post-intervention measurement and evaluation is crucial to demonstrating coaching efficacy. Evaluating coaching outcomes, however, is a complex process. In part, this is because it is generally difficult to isolate the effects of coaching from other organisational influences, even with longitudinal data (pre- and post-coaching data), unless parallel control group data is also available. Moreover, since multiple stakeholders are involved (the coachee, the coachee's family, peers, subordinates, clients, the organisation), outcomes are widely diffused and therefore difficult to aggregate. Aggregation is problematic because outcomes are both tangible and intangible in nature. In fact, it is generally easier to gauge change in attitudes and associated intangible effects than it is to measure the financial 'return on investment' (ROI) accruing to the organisation.

Even so, it is financial ROI that is almost certainly going to be of greatest interest to most organisations. Conducting an ROI evaluation involves the comparison of coaching costs with estimated financial benefits. Costs may include:

- direct costs of program implementation, including research and development expenditure, search costs, sessional fees, travel and accommodation expenses
- costs associated with program administration
- work time commitments
- costs of short-term productivity reductions while coachees are in session.

Possible direct financial benefits include:

- bottom-line productivity
- improved sales or revenue figures
- reduction in staff turnover and replacement costs arising from improved staff retention
- greater cost efficiency
- improved product or service quality
- improved productivity.

While any organisation with an efficient human resource information system will be able to estimate these accounting benefits quite readily, the chief methodological challenge lies in estimating the financial value of intangible outcomes, including improvements in:

- leadership competencies
- management competencies
- conflict resolution skills
- relationships with peers and subordinates
- job satisfaction
- time management
- coachee organisational commitment
- relations with customers/clients (Skiffington & Zeus 2003: 153–8).

Whatever the promise of the coaching phenomenon, it must be conceded that to date the belief that coaching does deliver a significant ROI to an organisation remains more an article of faith than an empirically verified fact (Kampa-Kokesch & Anderson 2001: 213–23).

Apart from the matter of solid empirical corroboration, coaching in general, and executive coaching in particular, does have a number of practical shortcomings. The coaching process is necessarily painstaking and time-consuming while at the same time demanding high degrees of mutual patience, honesty and trust. Consequently, there are formidable psychological barriers to coaching effectiveness (Kilburg 1996: 142; Mone & London 2002: 100–2). The boundary between a 'coaching' problem and a 'clinical' psychological problem, such as depression, remains ill-defined, giving rise to the possibility of harm arising from the coach playing amateur psychologist or psychotherapist. Low barriers to entry and lack of effective accreditation leave the field open to incompetent service providers (Sherman & Freas 2004). Privately hired coaches may be viewed by other managers as corporate interlopers – as 'court jesters' or 'Svengalis'; as purveyors of 'simple answers and quick results' (Berglas 2002: 88–90) – providing advice that may influence executive decision-making yet being unaccountable to the organisation and having little understanding of strategic imperatives and decision-making. Equally, unlike in-house mentors, external coaches may lack adequate knowledge of the business and its strategy. Finally, sceptics argue that coaching is just another management 'fad' whose fall from favour will be no less spectacular than its meteoric rise. Yet it must be said that the coaching phenomenon, which is now entering its second decade, shows no sign of decline.

## Chapter summary

This chapter has examined the critical final steps in the individual performance management cycle: those of performance review and analysis, feedback and development planning. The chapter opened with a discussion of the possible internal and contextual causes of assessed underperformance, noting that low motivation may not be the only factor, or even the most important factor, here. Attention then turned to the conduct and content of formal performance review meetings, including a 'best fit' comparison of three distinct 'styles' of review meeting: 'tell and sell', 'tell and listen' and 'problem-solving'. Next, we canvassed the challenges involved in providing negative feedback to assessed underperformers, as well as recommendations for maximising positive outcomes from this process. The penultimate section then considered strategies for remedying underperformance, including counselling and action planning. The chapter's final section examined two strategies for enhancing the performance of high-potential employees: the more traditional method of mentoring, and the more recent practice of performance coaching.

This chapter concludes our examination of the concepts, methods, techniques and debates associated with the performance management process. Equipped with this understanding of general performance management theory and practice, we can now turn our attention to the second of the two pivotal human resource processes with which this book deals, namely reward management in general, and remuneration management in particular. While it is appropriate that our exploration of reward management matters should commence with the issues of base pay and benefits (part 3), the insights into performance management concepts and methods provided in this and the accompanying part 2 chapters will be especially helpful in allowing us to come to terms with the vexed matter of performance-related rewards, which is the central theme of the five chapters in part 3.

## Discussion questions

1 What factors other than low motivation may contribute to assessed low performance?
2 What are the main challenges in providing negative feedback, and how can these best be addressed?
3 What should a reviewer do to lessen the likelihood of a review meeting becoming unduly emotional?
4 'Behavioural coaching': what is it, how can its effectiveness be maximised, and how should associated outcomes be defined and measured?
5 What competencies should a good performance coach possess?

# DELIVERING FAIRNESS
## Performance assessment at Mercury Couriers

Mercury Couriers is a capital-city-based mid-sized firm that employs 600 people in its rapidly growing commercial parcel collection and distribution business, which it has operated successfully throughout Australia since the firm's establishment seven years ago. The firm has separate departments covering customer service, parcel collection and distribution, vehicle maintenance, accounts, legal, marketing and human resources. Most of its line employees and supervisors work in customer call centres, distribution centres and vehicle maintenance facilities located strategically across the country. The firm could best be described as having a cost-defender competitive strategy, a mechanistic organisational structure and a traditional management culture.

Don Cobb, Mercury's human resources manager, is proud of his and the firm's achievements. When it comes to people management, Don's approach is down-to-earth and pragmatic. Previously a despatch driver himself, Don has little time for managers who spend their time reading the latest management books, chasing university degrees or agonising about the options for 'best practice' people management. Don also believes in 'buying' rather than 'building' skilled staff. In-house training and development, he says, is just a waste of everyone's time – and of the firm's money.

He is especially proud of the one-page form that he has designed for use in the firm's once-a-year performance assessment round. The form, which is reproduced below, is applied to all of Mercury's non-managerial employees, including call centre staff, parcel despatch people, drivers, vehicle maintenance workers and administration staff. The form is straightforward and can be completed in just a few minutes, so that supervisors are not tied down in unproductive paperwork. The assessment outcomes are then used to determine which employees will receive the $5,000 annual bonus that the firm pays to its best performers and which employees will be dismissed. Under Don's system, the top 20 per cent of employees get the bonus and the bottom 10 per cent are 'let go'.

But this year's performance assessment round did not go as smoothly as Don might have hoped. This year, for the first time, three employees, all known to each other and all recruited from the same competitor firm less than eighteen months before, challenged the accuracy of their assessments, wrote a letter of complaint to the managing director, and threatened legal action unless changes were made to the way in which they and their fellow employees are assessed.

To Don's astonishment, the problem, they argued, lay in the form itself. Don's initial inclination was to dismiss the complaints as nothing more than sour grapes, since none of the complainants has made it into the bonus cut. Then, feeling that his integrity had been challenged, he decided to commission a human resources consulting firm to confirm the worth of his assessment form.

The firm he chooses is none other than the one for which you happen to work and for which you are the resident expert on performance management systems. So the task of providing an expert opinion on Don's form falls naturally to you. Specifically, you agree to provide brief (200–400 word) written responses to each of the following four questions:

1. What are the specific type or types of performance management technique(s) present in the instrument?
2. What are the instrument's main strengths?
3. Are there any features in the instrument that may compromise assessment validity, reliability and felt-fairness?
4. Are there any ways in which the instrument, and the approach to performance management that it reveals, might be improved?

Don is keen to receive your report. After all, his reputation as a 'can-do' manager has been called into question. So what do you report? Will your analysis be to Don's liking?

## MERCURY COURIERS

ANNUAL PERFORMANCE ASSESSMENT FORM

Name: _____

Position: _____

Branch & Division: _____

*Instructions: Draw a circle around the applicable number for each question.*
1. Quantity of work is the amount of work an individual does in a working day.

| 1 | 2 | 3 | 4 | 5 |
|---|---|---|---|---|
| Does not meet minimum requirement | Does just enough to get by | Volume of work is satisfactory | Very industrious; does more than required | Superior work production record |

2. Accuracy is the correctness of work duties performed.

| 1 | 2 | 3 | 4 | 5 |
|---|---|---|---|---|
| Makes frequent errors | Careless; makes recurrent errors | Usually accurate; makes only average number of mistakes | Requires little supervision; is exact and precise most of the time | Requires absolute minimum of supervision; almost always accurate |

3. Alertness is the ability to grasp instructions, to meet changing conditions and to resolve unexpected problems.

| 1 | 2 | 3 | 4 | 5 |
|---|---|---|---|---|
| Slow to catch on | Requires more than average instruction and explanation | Grasps instructions with average ability | Usually quick to learn and understand | Exceptionally keen and alert |

4. Respect and courtesy, the key to making his/her job opportunities.

| 1 | 2 | 3 | 4 | 5 |
|---|---|---|---|---|
| Blunt, discourteous, antagonistic | Sometimes tactless | Agreeable and pleasant | Very polite and willing to help | Inspiring to others in being courteous and pleasant |

5. How mentally flexible is this person in his/her thoughts and approach to any presented task?.

| 1 | 2 | 3 | 4 | 5  *True* |
|---|---|---|---|---|
| Rigid | | Average | | Flexible |

6. Dependability is the ability to do required jobs well with minimum of supervision.

*True*

| 1 | 2 | 3 | 4 | 5 |
|---|---|---|---|---|
| Requires close supervision; is unreliable | Requires prompting sometimes | Usually takes care of necessary tasks with reasonable promptness | Requires little supervision. Is reliable | Requires absolute minimum supervision |

7. How readily does this person offer to help out by doing that which is apart from his/her own job?

| 1 | 2 | 3 | 4 | 5 |
|---|---|---|---|---|
| Resists | | Normal | | Readily |

8. What is your appraisal for this person's overall performance in the past 12 months?

| 1 | 2 | 3 | 4 | 5 |
|---|---|---|---|---|
| Poor | Below average | Average | Above average | Excellent |

9. Attendance (state problems if any):

| | Rank order of this employee in this department: ........................ . | Rated by: |
|---|---|---|
| | | Name: .............. |
| | Total number of employees: ........... | Signature: ........... |
| | | Date: ............... . |

Model responses to this case study challenge are provided in the book's appendix.

# Part 3

# BASE PAY AND BENEFITS

Having considered the key psychological and strategic dimensions to understanding the employment relationship, as well as the three main approaches to managing employee performance, we can now turn our attention to the second of the two human resource management processes with which this book is concerned, namely the management of employee reward and, in particular, the management of employee pay or remuneration. As noted in chapter 1, a remuneration system typically comprises three main elements: base pay, benefits, and performance-related pay. In designing any remuneration system careful attention should be paid to three key considerations: first, the relative role that each of these three components will play in total remuneration; second, the practices that will be drawn on to configure each component; and third, the target level of total remuneration for each position. The chapters in parts 3 and 4 offer guidance in addressing these key design considerations.

The five chapters in part 3 cover base pay and benefits. Chapter 9 considers the rationale for base pay, the main options for configuring base pay, the general strengths and weaknesses of each approach, and the incidence of each. Chapter 10 then details the pay structures associated with each option, while chapters 11 and 12 discuss the evaluation methods and processes associated with the development of pay systems based on each of these approaches. Chapter 13 then examines the logic of employee benefit plans and the main options for configuring such plans.

The case study exercise that follows chapter 13 – 'Just rewards: Rethinking base pay and benefits at Court, Case & McGowan, commercial law partners' – provides you with an opportunity to apply the knowledge that you have acquired from the five chapters in part 3. Model responses are provided in the book's appendix.

## Chapter Nine

# BASE PAY PURPOSE AND OPTIONS

We begin our coverage of remuneration practice by considering what, for most employees, is the primary component of their total remuneration, namely base pay. The chapter opens with a discussion of the general nature and logic of base pay. We then consider the two broad alternative approaches to configuring base pay – pay for the position (or 'job-based' base pay), and pay for personal skills and personal competencies (or 'person-based' base pay) – and the general arguments for and against each. The chapter also examines evidence on the comparative incidence of job-, skill- and competency-based pay in various countries, noting that while the two person-based approaches have assumed growing importance in base pay practice since the 1980s, the take-up of person-based practices varies considerably from country to country, sector to sector, organisation to organisation and occupation to occupation.

## 'Base pay': what and why

Base pay is the foundational component of total remuneration, and it can be defined as the part of an employee's direct remuneration that is not performance-contingent. It is commonly viewed as the 'fixed' or 'guaranteed' portion of pay in that it is chiefly time-based rather than performance-based. For each quantum of time worked, the employee receives a predetermined amount of pay. In broad terms, time-based pay can be delivered either as an hourly, daily or weekly wage, or in the form of an annual salary. It is also typically the largest component of total pay for non-executive employees. As the primary or foundational component of cash reward, it serves as the benchmark for other cash components, including benefits and incentive pay, which are frequently expressed as a percentage of base pay. As such, the larger the amount of base pay, the greater the likely levels of benefit and incentive payments.

Some organisations make little or no use of fixed remuneration, with some paying workers purely on the basis of results achieved. For instance, some real estate agencies, automotive retailers and courier firms pay staff on a commission-only basis, while manufacturing plants sometimes place employees on pure piece rate systems. In such cases it is a straightforward matter to measure the results achieved by each individual, to put a price on each unit of output, and to pay the worker accordingly. High effort and high output delivers high earnings; no effort and no results produces zero earnings. These individual results-based pay practices are examined more closely in chapter 17.

From an organisational perspective, base pay does have some potential drawbacks. It commits the employer to fixed payments irrespective of performance contributed. By itself, it is unlikely to motivate task behaviour. Unlike performance-related pay, it is unlikely to discourage underperformers from remaining with the organisation; indeed, it may have the opposite effect.

Yet, whether by necessity or choice, paying base pay remains the rule rather than the exception. To counter the potential for exploitation in situations of labour oversupply, legislators in many countries require that employees be paid at or above a statutory minimum time rate; in other words, legislators have mandated payment of a guaranteed minimum level of base pay to each employee. However, there are also some solid economic reasons why organisations may choose to do so voluntarily. This is particularly the case in situations where qualified labour is in short supply. In such circumstances, base pay has a major role to play in attracting and retaining desired staff. Significantly, even where their use is permitted by law, results-only payment systems tend to be applied only in situations where competent labour is in abundant supply. So in many market contexts offering base pay makes sound economic sense.

Base pay also has profound psychological implications. A guaranteed amount of pay addresses employees' basic needs by providing a guaranteed minimum level of income security throughout their term of employment. In Maslovian terms (see chapter 3), meeting employees' security and safety needs is essential for sustained task motivation. Providing each employee with a guaranteed base pay also demonstrates the employer's commitment to the employee, which in turn means that the employee is more likely to reciprocate by demonstrating both membership behaviour and organisational citizenship behaviour. As such, base pay is both an important means of eliciting membership behaviour and a key foundation for the maintenance of a relational (i.e. long-term) psychological contract. Base pay also allows organisations to recognise work requirements that may be just as important as results, such as skill and competency development. Finally, base pay is not incompatible with performance pay, although, as we shall see, the relationship between the two does require careful thought, planning and management. For all of these reasons, base pay warrants our close attention.

## Pay for the position versus pay for personal skills or competencies

The traditional practice has been to fix base pay according to the job or position occupied. This amounts to paying for the job rather than for the person who happens to hold the job. A job can be defined as a group of related tasks, duties and responsibilities that are necessary to the effective operation of the organisation and which can be meaningfully combined and assigned to individual employees within the organisation. In the job-based approach, positions of larger 'size' – that is, with a greater content of tasks, duties and responsibilities – attract higher levels of base pay, and employees can increase their base pay chiefly by being promoted up a job hierarchy arranged by job 'size'.

More recently, however, the trend has been to develop base pay around the productive 'capacities' *of the person in the job* rather than the 'size' of the job itself. Personal 'capacity' can be defined in terms of traditional person-characteristics such as experience and seniority. Increasingly, however, it is being defined in terms of personal 'skills', 'knowledge' and 'abilities'. The premise here is that employees should be paid according to the work capacities that they possess, regardless of the particular job or role to which they happen to be assigned at any point in time. Some commentators (Klaas 2002; Risher 1997b, 2003) have gone so far as to suggest that traditional jobs are anachronistic; that effective human resource management now requires a focus on personal capacities and performance rather than on managing positions. The job, it is argued, is redundant; we live in the age of the 'jobless' or 'de-jobbed' organisation. Lawler (1991: 148), an outspoken critic of job-based pay argues: 'It is people that have market value, not jobs. Jobs are simply a bureaucratic structure that can be used to estimate the market value of an individual. The key compensation issue from a human resource management perspective concerns what an individual is worth: not what a job is worth.'

The two main options for pay for personal capacity are skill-based pay and competency-based or competency-related pay. Both of these person-based approaches seek to establish a stronger link between the amount of base pay and the degree of employee 'capability' or 'capacity'.

## Skills and competencies

At this point, it is helpful to pause to consider several important definitional distinctions: specifically, the difference between job skills and personal skills, and between the latter and personal competencies.

To carry out the tasks, duties and responsibilities associated with a job, a job-holder will need to possess certain skills. A skill is a learned capacity to perform a certain task in an accurate and timely manner. So skills are a constituent part of jobs. If this is so, however, what is so different about the 'job' and 'skill' approach to base pay? The critical distinction is between skills *in the job* (i.e. skills as job content factors) and skills *in the person* (i.e. skills as attributes of the individual employee). The job-based model seeks to identify and measure the type, and degree of presence in each job, of those skills that are essential to job execution. By contrast, the skill-based formulation is concerned with rewarding 'value-adding' skills possessed by each employee. This distinction between *positional* and *personal* skills is critical to understanding the rationale behind both the skill-based and the competency-based or related approaches to base pay. According to exponents of the person-based option, whereas the traditional positional approach focuses on job content *per se*, the newer person-focused models emphasise employee learning and the enhancement of the individual's 'human capital'.

Of course, pay for personal skill is nothing new. It underpinned traditional margins for skill paid to craft workers who had served a formal trade apprenticeship. Craft workers expected to be paid for their personal skills even when they were engaged on tasks that actually required little real skill. As craft work became more mechanised and subdivided, employers found that they were paying for skills that their workers were no longer required to exercise. This is what distinguishes new from old pay-for-skill systems. The new approach recognises and rewards only those personal skills that the organisation actually needs or may need in the foreseeable future. Even though the employee might not use all of these skills in every task performed, the portfolio of skills will reflect the range of task skills that employees may be called on to exercise over time.

There is a further definitional distinction that we need to reiterate here. This is the difference between 'skills' and 'competencies'. Some commentators (Lawler & Ledford 1985; Lawler 1996) contend that there is no difference at all here; that the two terms are interchangeable. Those who adopt this view tend to see personal capacity as an inseparable combination of work knowledge, skills and abilities – or 'KSAs'. The emphasis here is on recognising and rewarding bundles of knowledge, skills and abilities that are capable of being measured, built into training programs and learned. However, as noted in chapter 7, there is another school of thought that draws a very strong distinction between 'skills' and 'competencies'. To recap briefly: 'skills', it is said, are associated with technical capacities requiring relatively short learning times; 'competencies' are personal attributes that require development over a longer time period and which are tied to career advancement. Sometimes this distinction is cast in terms of the difference between 'hard' technical skills, which can be readily learned, and 'soft' abilities, which are more difficult to acquire but which, it is argued, are associated with high performance. As we have seen, these deep abilities – or submerged 'competencies' – include such attributes as self-confidence, achievement orientation, interpersonal empathy, persistence, problem-solving ability and the like. Base pay systems based on competency seek to recognise and reward individuals in possession of these and other abilities. In this chapter, and those that follow, skill-based pay systems are defined as those that seek to assess and reward 'hard' technical proficiencies, whereas competency pay is taken to mean pay systems that focus chiefly on assessing and rewarding 'soft' or 'submerged' abilities (Hofrichter & Spencer 1996).

| Options | Structures | Evaluation techniques | Modes of pay progression |
|---|---|---|---|
| **Position-based systems** | | | |
| • **Job- or position-based pay** | 1. Pay ladders<br><br>2. Narrow grades | Market surveys and/or job evaluation | Seniority and/or 'merit'-based increments and promotion |
| **Person-based systems** | | | |
| • **Skill-based pay** | Broad grades or job families | Skill assessment | Skill sets |
| • **Competency-based pay** | Broad bands | Competency assessment | Competency zones or levels |

**Figure 9.1**  Options for base pay

As well as making quite different assumptions about what base pay can contribute to an organisation, and how it can do so, the above three alternative approaches involve distinct pay structures, evaluation (i.e. pricing) methods and processes, and modes of pay progression. Figure 9.1 provides an overview of the main base pay options, including the structures, evaluation techniques and progression modes associated with each, which will be explored in detail in subsequent chapters.

## Pay for jobs, skills or competencies?

Let us now turn to consider the general advantages and disadvantages of each of these three broad options for base pay configuration. At this juncture, we are interested chiefly in comparing the broad potential and limitations of each approach. In subsequent chapters, we shall explore the structures, evaluation techniques and development processes associated with each.

Paying for the job or position has a number of possible advantages. It can provide the foundation for a stable pay structure and is a convenient way for large, complex organisations to build a coherent, integrated and competitive pay structure based on consistent criteria. In essence, the job-based approach is a formula for achieving distributive justice on the basis of the equality norm. It operationalises the norm of equality in the determination of pay structures by prescribing 'equal pay for equal jobs' and 'unequal but proportional pay for unequal jobs'. This may help to minimise dissatisfaction between employees over comparative pay levels, which, as equity theory suggests (see chapter 2), can impair motivation and effort. For similar reasons, job-based pay is generally preferred by unions because it permits the maintenance of common pay standards both within and between organisations, irrespective of differences in the profitability of firms. It also provides role clarity because each job position is usually accompanied by a detailed job description specifying exactly what the job entails and how it relates to other jobs in the organisation. Likewise, the promotion prospects and promise of long-tenure employment associated with an internal job hierarchy can elicit higher levels of employee commitment and citizenship behaviour. Perhaps most importantly for the organisation, however, job-based pay allows a ready assessment of the firm's competitive position in relevant external labour markets. This is because, for the most part, external labour markets themselves still revolve around price signals for whole jobs. For the same reason, the job-base approach offers organisations considerable certainty as to future labour costs because the actual costs per job are known in advance. This can reduce the uncertainty associated with payroll budgeting and forward planning.

However, critics, such as Lawler (1994a), contend that job-based pay has some serious shortcomings. Because pay is based on position rather than job-holder performance, there is little short-term incentive to improve performance. If you pay someone a fixed wage for each hour, day or week they perform a designated job, but they have no monetary incentive to perform beyond the customary effort level for the job. To be sure, promotion to a more important job will deliver a significant pay increase, but this also stands to reinforce organisational hierarchy. Employees are encouraged to increase their pay by securing promotion up the job hierarchy, which stands to make the organisation 'top-heavy' and to saddle it with a costly management structure. Paying the job rather than the person also provides employees themselves with little incentive to acquire skills and competencies that the organisation may need now or in the future. Pay for narrow job assignments is also incompatible with the multiskilling requirements of teamworking. Pay-for-the-job may also be too slow and inflexible to accommodate rapid changes in technology, work processes and product or service type requirements, such as those characteristic of prospector firms.

As noted above, in position-based systems, within-job and between-job pay progression is generally based on either seniority or 'merit', both of which entail person-based assessment of the job-holder. However, in both cases, person-based pay adjustment still occurs within the structural control points and limits set by the job-based approach. Moreover, both seniority- and merit-based pay progression have shortcomings of their own. Merit-based adjustment to base pay is considered in detail in chapter 15. Regarding seniority, while it certainly underwrites relational psychological contracts (see chapter 2) and rewards sustained membership behaviour and commitment, it can also exacerbate some of the general shortcomings of the job-based approach. In particular, it rewards time service rather than knowledge, skill or performance. It encourages top-heaviness, traditional hierarchies and even gerontocracy while simultaneously discouraging younger high performers. By emphasising internal age-related progression over external recruitment, it stands to deny the organisation access to new staff with fresh ideas. By the same token, depending on the dictates of the prevailing employment law regime, it may give rise to unlawful age-related discrimination in staff selection and progression, as well as to various forms of indirect discrimination, particularly against female employees.

Given these shortcomings, could it be that the skill-based approach is a superior means of structuring base pay? Again, it recognises and rewards individuals for the type, range and depth of skills that they have acquired and can use effectively, and which the organisation needs them to have. As such, the approach offers a number of advantages to both organisations and their employees.

For the organisation, skill-based pay encourages employees to develop personal skills in line with the organisation's changing needs. It allows organisations to ensure that employees have the appropriate type and level of skills *before* they are assigned to a position and receive a pay rise. The employee must demonstrate proficiency at the skills before receiving higher base pay. Pay-for-skill facilitates functional flexibility through multiskilling and teamworking. Multiskilling allows employees to be redeployed quickly without retraining delays and minimises 'downtime' arising from the absence of required skills. By facilitating a breakdown of rigid job demarcations, it enables a more flexible utilisation of the workforce as employees acquire a breadth and depth of relevant skills. It is especially relevant to teamworking or where maximum plant utilisation and speed of response are critical. By encouraging the acquisition of new knowledge and skills, skill pay allows organisations to respond rapidly to new skill needs arising from technological and product market changes. Skill pay also facilitates systematic organisational learning and continuous improvement by rewarding employees for developing their 'human capital'. The traditional practice of 'front-end' technical training for life in the form of adolescent apprenticeship is now largely anachronistic. In its place has come the concept of lifelong learning, to which skill-based pay is well suited. Skill-based pay also encourages a participative work culture by allowing for the devolution of decision-making tasks to line employees as they acquire the knowledge and skills to become more self-managing (Lawler 1990: 160–6; Murray & Gerhart 2000).

Well-managed skill-based plans can undoubtedly deliver positive outcomes for their organisations. A survey of management attitudes regarding outcomes from ninety-seven skill-based pay plans in seventy different US companies (Jenkins et al. 1992) indicated that, in a majority of cases, the plans were 'very successful' in achieving greater workforce flexibility and improved employee awareness and satisfaction, and 'somewhat successful' in delivering improved labour productivity, reduced absenteeism and voluntary labour turnover and lower labour costs. Significantly, more than two-thirds of the respondents indicated that pay rates had increased as a result of using skill-based pay. Even though it tends to increase payroll costs automatically as employees learn new skills, users saw this as being more than compensated for by improvements in labour flexibility and productivity, reduced absenteeism and greater workplace harmony.

For employees themselves, skill-based pay offers the prospect of more challenging, varied and enriched work, and the opportunity to enhance their 'human capital' and, hence, marketability. The approach also reinforces the use of developmental rewards by offering employees systematic opportunities to enhance skills and pursue skill-based career paths and pay increases within the organisation without the pressure to gain promotion to supervisory or managerial positions.

What of the negatives? From an organisational perspective, skill-based pay has a number of potential disadvantages. Equipping an employee with needed skills does not guarantee that the employee will apply them effectively. This is because skill-based pay rewards skill *acquisition* rather than skill *application* (Gerhart & Milkovich 1992: 505). Skill-based plans involve complex procedures for skill training, assessment and accreditation; administrative procedures that can be very costly. A related problem is that of escalating training and assessment costs. When skill acquisition becomes the key to pay and career progression, the demand for training will inevitably increase. If used as a stand-alone reward system it can create a work-force of perennial students, and training time is necessarily 'downtime' performance-wise. Since skills assessment is continuous individuals may need to be reassessed several times a year, which itself can be disruptive. Training 'bottlenecks' may be another problem, particularly in the initial stages, where there may be a short-term rush on available training facilities. The approach will also increase the pressure on supervisors, particularly regarding decisions about the allocation and scheduling of access to training programs (Dewey 1994; Greene 1993; Lawler 1990: 166–70). Finally, given its focus on hard, technical capabilities, skill-based pay will have limited application outside production line, maintenance and routine administrative work.

Skill-based pay also carries some possible negatives for employees themselves. One of these is 'topping out'. Once employees have acquired all the skills they are required to learn, their pay will plateau, and they may lose task motivation and organisational commitment unless additional rewards, such as performance incentives, are made available. Then there is the problem of skill obsolescence. Since pay increases are based on the repertoire of skills that each employee accumulates rather than those that they actually use, any mismatch between learning content and actual requirements will undermine the system's efficacy. In the absence of opportunity to retrain, employees whose skills are no longer needed, say because of changes to product range or technology, may be exposed to pay reduction or even redundancy. Thus, as Murray and Gerhart (2000) observe, the efficacy of a skill-based system will depend largely on employees' trust in the system, the strength of their desire to enhance their human capital, their expections of training and reward outcomes and, hence, the strength of their motivation to seek skills.

Turning now to the third main approach to base pay configuration, the competency-based or competency-related approach, our consideration need only be brief, since we have already explored the general advantages and disadvantages of the competencies model at length in chapter 7.

As with competency-related performance management, the appeal of competency pay lies chiefly in its focus on those personal attributes that are seen to be the most important and reliable drivers of high-performance behaviour and results. As such, the suggestion that competency assessment should apply not only to performance management and development but also to employee reward has intuitive appeal (Armstrong & Brown 1998;

Brown & Armstrong 1999; Cira & Benjamin 1998; O'Neal 1995; Risher 1997a). Likewise, the competencies model appears to be applicable to staff at all levels of the organisation, not just to skilled manual workers.

Yet, as we have seen in chapter 7, the competencies approach also has its critics, as well as a range of drawbacks. One general shortcoming worth reiterating here is that, whatever the claimed link between the two, competencies, like skills, are still simply performance inputs, not outcomes. Indeed, while there is now widespread acceptance of the application of the high-performance competencies model to employee selection, performance management and development, its extension to reward practice has encountered considerable resistance (Zingheim & Schuster 2003). This may be due in part to the problem of pricing competencies. Even if it were possible to accurately identify, select and assess deep competencies, there is no agreed or reliable way to price them. If pricing learnable skill sets on the basis of pay survey data is fraught with difficulty, then putting a price on a specific submerged competency becomes little more than an exercise in educated guesswork. Competencies of this sort are commodities that have yet to be recognised in external labour markets. The problem becomes all the greater where the competency in question is specific to an organisation.

## The incidence of job-based, skill-based and competency-based pay

Payment according to the job or position held remains the dominant mode of remuneration in most developed countries. For instance, in Australia, standard time-based rates of pay for specific job classifications were enshrined in the plethora of occupational and industry awards developed under the system of compulsory arbitration. While the award-based system is now in decline, its legacy runs deep in Australian remuneration practice and is one of the main reasons why job-based pay remains the norm in Australian workplaces.

Yet in Australia, as elsewhere, person-based base pay undoubtedly assumed considerable importance in base pay practice during the 1990s, although the degree of adoption also varied considerably from country to country. A study of base pay practices in Canadian and Australian private sector firms at the end of the 1990s (Long & Shields 2005a) reported that in Australia 59 per cent of firms applied skill or competency pay to at least some of their non-managerial workers, whereas in Canada the comparable figure was 25 per cent, perhaps because of that country's strong legislative requirement for adherence to job-based 'equal pay' practices and principles. While this study did not distinguish between the two person-based options, in the Australian case, the higher take-up of person-based pay would seem to be attributable chiefly to the encouragement given to skill-based pay systems during the era of 'award restructuring' in the late 1980s and early 1990s (Probert 1992; O'Neill & Lander 1993–94).

In the USA, the use of skill-based pay has historically been most pronounced in manufacturing firms, particularly those in paper-making, automobiles, electronics and food processing. However, it has also been taken up in service industries such as banking and insurance (Gupta et al. 1992). Whereas skill-based pay originally applied only to factory workers and technicians, it has been extended to employees in retailing, distribution, hospitality and other service sector industries. Most firms that have taken up skill-based pay in the USA have also been large organisations, firms like Johnson & Johnson, General Electric, General Motors, Motorola, Honeywell, Digital and Northern Telecom's US subsidiary. US experience also suggests a positive relationship between skill-based pay and a high-involvement management culture (Gupta et al. 1992; Lawler, Ledford & Chang 1993).

The competencies approach was also taken up with considerable enthusiasm in the United States – its place of origin – in the 1990s. A 1996 survey showed that just a quarter of US companies using or developing competency-based or related human resource management systems had linked competencies to pay or were developing competency-based or related pay (American Compensation Association Competencies Research Team 1996: 17–20). Between 1996 and 2000, the proportion of US organisations using competency-based pay rose from 8 per cent to 16 per cent (Rahbar-Daniels, Erickson & Dalik 2001: 73). During this period, hundreds of large US corporations introduced competency pay plans for some of their employees; the range of industries involved – from fast food and hospitality to manufacturing and finance – being indicative of the initial appeal of the competencies model. Prominent North American users of competency-related pay include Burger King, Campbell's Soups, Chase Manhattan Bank, Dow Chemical, General Electric, Holiday Inn Motel chain, IBM and Marriott (Ashton 1996; Sibson & Company 1997; Risher 2002). While some of these firms apply competency pay across the entire workforce, in many North

American organisations it is focused chiefly on professional knowledge-workers: managers, consultants, lawyers, actuaries, teachers and the like.

In the UK, too, competency-related pay was initially welcomed as the way forward in base pay practice, especially as a solution to the manifest problems of merit pay (see chapter 15). British firms followed the US lead, and by the mid-1990s 12 per cent of British firms had reportedly adopted competency-related pay, with 78 per cent of these users rating it as 'very effective' (Creelman 1995: 7). By 1996, 45 per cent of UK firms were reportedly considering linking rewards to competency assessment (Sparrow 1996). The take-up was especially marked in pharmaceutical firms such as GlaxoSmithKline, beverage manufacturers such as Guinness Brewing, and service sector and financial services firms such as the Bank of Scotland and National Westminster Bank (Armstrong & Brown 1998; Brown & Armstrong 1999: 104).

Yet the enthusiasm initially associated with person-based pay has, in recent years, been replaced by a healthy degree of caution. While Australian organisations are undoubtedly making greater use of competency-related human resource management, the chief applications to date appear to be in the areas of staff selection and performance development rather than pay determination. A 1997 survey of 146 Australian firms and public sector organisations (O'Neill & Doig 1997) found that although most were making some use of the competencies model, the main usages were for training and development (48 per cent) and recruitment and selection (47 per cent), and only 18 per cent used competencies for remuneration purposes.

As the survey data in table 9.1 indicates, only around 5 per cent of UK organisations now apply competency pay in its pure form, while just 6 per cent use skill-based pay progression in its pure form. The incidence of wholly skill-based progression is highest in manufacturing (11 per cent of firms) and clerical/manual roles (4 per cent) and lowest in managerial roles (2 per cent). Wholly competency-based progression is marginally more pronounced in the private sector than in the public service (6 per cent compared to 4 per cent), but the low overall incidence is common to all occupational groupings. This contrasts markedly with the incidence of competency-based assessment in the UK, which, as noted in chapter 7, runs at more than 30 per cent.

Caution has also become the watchword in US organisations. According to two prominent US remuneration commentators (Zingheim & Schuster 2002: 51): 'Skill-based pay and pay for competencies are struggling at best. Practicality and reasonable simplicity are not strong suits for existing pay solutions that profess to pay for relevant new skills and capabilities that add

**Table 9.1** Incidence of selected types of pay progression management in the UK, by sector and occupational group, 2004: percentage of respondent firms using each type

| | | Sector | | | | Occupational group | | | |
|---|---|---|---|---|---|---|---|---|---|
| | All sectors | Manufacturing and production | Private sector services | Voluntary sector | Public services | Senior management | Middle or line management | Non-manual non-management | Clerical/manual |
| Performance plus skills/competencies | 63 | 67 | 63 | 39 | 46 | 48 | 51 | 51 | 47 |
| Performance only | 27 | 30 | 31 | 18 | 26 | 25 | 20 | 18 | 15 |
| Service/seniority | 20 | 9 | 8 | 49 | 58 | 13 | 20 | 22 | 23 |
| Skills only | 6 | 11 | 5 | 3 | 3 | 2 | 2 | 3 | 4 |
| Competencies only | 5 | 6 | 6 | – | 4 | 3 | 3 | 3 | 3 |

*Source:* CIPD 2005b: 5, 33.

to the worth of the company. The concept of paying for skills rather than the job makes incredible sense. But we have had too many failures caused by complexity, overdesign, haste and poor communications to simply return to these solutions without study and consideration.' Similarly, Heneman and LeBlanc (2003: 8) observe: 'The reason that competency-based pay has not taken off is the cost/benefit uncertainty.' The practical difficulties and uncertainties involved in administering skill and competency pay will be explored in more detail in chapter 12.

However, this certainly does not mean that organisations have abandoned all interest in person-based options. As table 9.1 shows, rather than adopting either person-based approach in pure form, most UK organisations (63 per cent) prefer a hybrid approach to person-based base pay progression in which skill and/or competency criteria are combined with individual performance; an approach that Brown and Armstrong (1999) have termed 'pay for contribution'. Significantly, the proportion of organisations using this approach is much higher than the proportion that use individual performance (i.e. 'merit' increments) as the sole means of base pay progression (27 per cent). Interestingly, seniority-based progression also remains important in the UK, where length of service or seniority is used by 20 per cent of organisations overall; usage being particularly high (58 per cent) in public sector organisations.

In sum, the available evidence indicates that notwithstanding the initial enthusiasm for linking pay to competencies, the general approach outside the USA has been one of circumspection. While the competencies model figures centrally in staff recruitment, selection, development and performance management processes (Risher 2003: 16), it is clear that only a minority of firms have adopted wholly skill- or competency-based modes of base pay progression. Indeed, recent contributions to the US practitioner literature by erstwhile exponents (e.g. Hofrichter & McGovern 2001) acknowledge that the promise of competency pay may well have been overstated.

## Chapter summary

This chapter opened with a discussion of the general nature and logic of base pay. Next, we explored the two broad alternative approaches to configuring base pay – pay for the position (or 'job-based' base pay), and pay for personal skills and personal competencies (or 'person-based' base pay) – and the general arguments for and against each. We also examined available research evidence on the comparative incidence of job-, skill- and competency-based pay in various countries, noting that while the two person-based approaches have assumed greater importance in base pay practice through-out the Western world since the 1980s, the take-up of person-based practices varies considerably from country to country, sector to sector, organisation to organisation and occupation to occupation. Notwithstanding the initial enthusiasm for linking pay to competencies, the general approach is now one of caution.

## Discussion questions

1  Why should employees receive any base pay at all?
2  Is the notion of the 'rate for the job' outdated?
3  The 'jobless organisation' – fact or fiction?
4  Pay for the person is not a low-cost option. Why?
5  Why might organisations be reluctant to link competency assessment to pay?

Chapter Ten

# BASE PAY STRUCTURES

Having considered the general differences between position-based and person-based options, we can now turn to the more technical aspects of managing base pay systems. In this chapter we investigate options for structuring base pay. As we shall see, approaches based on the job, skills or competencies each have their own distinct structures and modes of pay progression. As well as coming to terms with these ways of structuring base pay, following the tenets of a 'best fit' approach to system design, we also seek to identify those organisational settings and management strategies for which each of these alternative structures might be most (and least) appropriate. Chapters 11 and 12 will then examine the steps involved in developing, implementing and maintaining position- and person-based systems.

Two considerations are crucial to the design of any base pay system. First, what will be the system's overall form or 'structure'? Second, within this structure, what will be the 'rules' that determine how and by how much each employee's base pay changes or progresses over time? Since the question of progression is necessarily subordinate to that of structure, it is appropriate that we begin by discussing the latter.

What, exactly, is a base pay *structure?* In essence, it is the 'architecture' of the base pay system. A base pay structure has three main purposes. First, it specifies categories or classifications to which particular jobs and job-holders are assigned. Second, it specifies either the exact pay *rate* applicable to each position or a pay *range* (i.e. the minimum and maximum pay rates) for each category. Third, it establishes the criteria and mechanisms for pay progression either from rate-to-rate or within and between pay ranges.

While there are many possible permutations of base pay structure, most of these will approximate to one or other of four main types:

1  pay scales (or pay spines)
2  narrow grades (or job grades)
3  broad grades (or job families)
4  broad bands (or career bands).

Pay scales and narrow grades are both traditional means of structuring base pay, and both are associated with the position-based approach to base pay. However, broad grades and broad bands are more recent in origin, having risen to prominence during the 1980s and 1990s. Broad grades tend to be applied as the structural basis for skill-based pay whereas broad bands are associated most closely with competency-based or competency-related base pay positioning and progression. As we shall see, as a reward practice, broad-banding is no less controversial than the concept of competency pay itself.

## Pay scales

Pay scales (or pay spines) are the simplest position-based structures, as well as being among the oldest. As the example in figure 10.1 illustrates, pay scales typically consist of a hierarchy of position-specific pay levels, each consisting of a sequence of flat pay rates, steps or points. Movement from level to level involves merit-related promotion. Traditionally, however, step-wise pay increments within each level were based on seniority or service, with the increase occurring automatically after each year of service. In the past, service-based increments of this type were a defining feature of public sector salary structures in many countries. With increments for service and seniority, the base pay rate is typically incremented annually in recognition of an additional year's experience in the job and to reward continued loyal service in the job or role. Until the 1990s, this was the norm in most large organisations, both Western and non-Western. Seniority scales are still relatively common in large Western work organisations. However, seniority-based progression does have some substantial drawbacks, especially in relation to the non-recognition of short-term performance, but also regarding the possibility of unlawful age-based discrimination. For such reasons, in recent decades many organisations in both the public and the private sectors have adopted the practice of making within-level increments dependent on individual performance assessment; that is, the practice of 'merit increments'.

| Step<br>(increment for seniority, service and/or 'merit') | Level<br>(promotion) |
|:---:|:---:|
| 5<br>4 ↑<br>3 ↑<br>2 ↑<br>1 ↑ | E |
| 5<br>4 ↑<br>3 ↑<br>2 ↑<br>1 ↑ | D |
| 5<br>4 ↑<br>3 ↑<br>2 ↑<br>1 ↑ | C |
| 5<br>4 ↑<br>3 ↑<br>2 ↑<br>1 ↑ | B |
| 5<br>4 ↑<br>3 ↑<br>2 ↑<br>1 ↑ | A |

**Figure 10.1** Simple pay scale or spine

So pay for performance is assuming greater significance even in this most traditional of position-based structures. Even so, when coupled with a pay scale structure, merit increments are a blunt instrument for recognising short-term performance, since there is no scope to reward job-holders for differing degrees of performance. It is a matter of the job-holder's base rate either being increased fully to the next pay rate or not increased at all.

Despite the existence of more sophisticated structures that do allow for greater short-term differentiation between individuals, pay scales retain much of their importance, especially in public sector organisations. For instance, as the data in table 10.1 (p. 253) indicates, pay spines are still used by 20 per cent of organisations across all sectors in the UK, as well as by 58 per cent of public service organisations. In the public sector, at least, pay scales remain popular because they are a simple, transparent and convenient way for an organisation to manage the remuneration of large numbers of job-holders in particular work roles, such as clerical and administrative work. When rates need to be adjusted for inflation or to accommodate new across-the-board collective bargaining outcomes, the entire structure can be adjusted upwards by the relevant percentage amount.

## Narrow grades

A narrow grade (also known as a 'job grade') is a receptacle housing a group of jobs of similar value to the organisation and specifying a pay *range* for these jobs rather than a scale or spot rate. Each grade will cover a group of jobs regarded as being of similar value to the organisation and therefore worthy of roughly the same range of base pay. Each grade will allow for some variance in pay, but the range over which pay can vary is usually quite narrow. Each grade has a pay range that defines the minimum and maximum rates of pay for all jobs in the grade, with the pay range for each grade typically being around 20 per cent. Each grade also has a range midpoint that usually serves as an internal 'control point' intended to regulate pay increases. As figure 10.2 (p. 254) indicates, the grade midpoint typically defines the pay rate for acceptable proficiency in the job, and the range is then split into two subranges. Pay progression below the midpoint is linked to job learning and/or experience in the job. The longer it takes to achieve job proficiency and the more the organisation wishes to reward job performance via base pay increases rather than via promotion or stand-alone performance pay, the greater the range spread should be. In general, the range spread is likely to increase the further up the position hierarchy we go.

You will notice, too, that there is a degree of overlap between adjacent grades, and it is this that marks an important difference between grades and scales. The degree of overlap is often 20 to 50 per cent, but it can vary considerably both between organisations and within an organisation's pay structure. The degree of overlap carries implications for the organisation's overall management strategy, its structure and culture. The greater the overlap, the flatter the pay structure, the lower the degree of difference in value between jobs in adjacent grades and the less the emphasis on job promotion as a means of pay progression. In other words, the greater the overlap between adjacent grades, the greater the scope to award a high-performing

**Table 10.1** Incidence of methods for managing base pay structure in the UK, by sector and occupational group, 2004: percentage of respondent firms using each type

| | | Sector | | | | Occupational group | | | |
|---|---|---|---|---|---|---|---|---|---|
| | | Private | | | | | | | |
| | All sectors | Manufacturing and production | Private sector services | Voluntary sector | Public services | Senior management | Middle or line management | Non-manual non-management | Clerical or manual |
| Individual pay rates, ranges or spot salaries | 46 | 58 | 54 | 55 | 35 | 44 | 27 | 24 | 23 |
| Narrow grades | 27 | 39 | 24 | 43 | 34 | 16 | 20 | 21 | 28 |
| Pay spines | 20 | 5 | 4 | 35 | 58 | 11 | 17 | 18 | 18 |
| Job families | 14 | 12 | 14 | 10 | 7 | 5 | 7 | 9 | 10 |
| Career grades | 12 | 7 | 10 | 5 | 18 | 6 | 6 | 9 | 6 |
| Broadbands | 36 | 37 | 38 | 28 | 25 | 26 | 27 | 27 | 22 |
| Mix of broadbanding and job families | 19 | 10 | 18 | 10 | 9 | 7 | 11 | 10 | 10 |

*Source:* CIPD 2005a: 5, 32, 35.

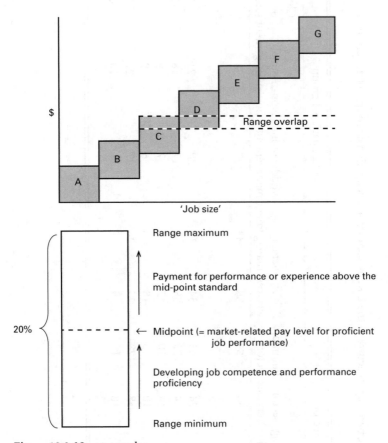

**Figure 10.2** Narrow grades

job-holder currently holding a job in the lower of two adjacent grades a level of base pay above that of an individual holding a job located in the higher of the two grades. Alternatively, the smaller the overlap, the greater the difference in adjacent job grade values, the steeper the pay structure, the greater the emphasis on promotion, and the more closely the graded structure resembles a traditional perpendicular pay scale. Too much overlap can cause problems, as can too little overlap. Normally, when an employee is promoted one grade, she will be located below the midpoint of the new grade (because she will not yet be fully proficient in the new job). However, if the range overlap is excessive, and the promoted employee was previously at the top of her old grade, grade promotion may well mean taking a cut in base pay, at least in the short term. To avoid this situation, the maximum of any given grade should generally be lower than the midpoint of the next highest grade.

But why use grades at all? Why not simply have a spot rate of pay for each and every job and job-holder? The reason is that when an organisation has a large number of distinct jobs or positions, it is not practical to specify precise rates for each job. Rather, with grades, jobs of similar 'value' or 'size' are grouped together for the purpose of base pay management. Having a system with unique rates for each job would be difficult to administer. Grouping jobs into grades also means that employees can move sideways between jobs in the same pay grade without having to go through a promotion process. Moreover, if a job changes, providing the change is relatively limited, the job-holder can be compensated without the need for promotion. Most importantly, however, the pay ranges that are a defining feature of a graded structure allow the organisation some scope, first, to recognise and reward performance development (via progression up to the grade midpoint) and, second, to reward sustained high performance (via progression above the midpoint). The application of merit pay in grades systems is considered in detail in chapter 15.

These are some of the reasons why narrow grades remain one of the most common building blocks for position-based base pay systems in many countries. As table 10.1 shows, in the UK more than one in four organisations make use of narrow graded structures, with the highest incidence being in manufacturing and production (39 per cent) and the voluntary sector (43 per cent), and the lowest usage being in private sector services (24 per cent). The same data also shows that narrow grades are most widely applied in clerical and manual positions and least applied at senior management level.

Narrow grades do pose a number of management problems. One challenge is getting the cut-off points between adjacent grades right in terms of relative job size and 'felt-fairness'. No matter where you draw the line, some jobs will always be on the margins of their grade, and the job-holders concerned will naturally be keen to have their job upgraded. The most significant drawback with narrow grades, however, is the still quite limited scope they provide to recognise and reward short-term performance differences between individual job-holders. A grade pay range of 20 per cent offers little scope to award significant base pay increases to high-performing staff, short of their applying for promotion to a position in the next highest grade. A related problem is the generally narrow content of each job assignment itself, which leaves little leeway for significant job enrichment and personal skill development and diversification.

## Broad grades

The broad grades approach (also known as the 'job families' model) involves combining a number of traditional job grades into a smaller number of grades, each with wider pay ranges. This may simply involve reallocating related jobs to a new wider grade in which relevant position holders are able to undertake a greater variety of tasks and to master a greater range of skills. Broad grades tend to have a pay range of up to 75 per cent, compared to up to 20 per cent in narrow grades. Typically, the minimum pay range value for each new broad grade represents the minimum pay level for the lowest narrow grade whose jobs have been placed in the new grade, while the maximum range value equates to the maximum pay level paid in the highest narrow grade whose positions have also been assigned to the same broad grade. The band minimum then becomes the competitive entry-level rate, and the band maximum is reserved for outstanding performers with wide competency in the job family.

Broad grades tend to retain many of the 'cost-control' features of traditional grades including midpoints, grade quartiles and internal steps or levels. Within a broad grade, person-based pay progression assumes primary importance, albeit within a specific job-family context. Where production line and routine administrative jobs are reconstituted into broad grades, pay progression is typically governed by the formal acquisition of additional knowledge and skills, so that broad-grading provides the structure for skill-based pay progression and, hence, the basis for multiskilling and career paths for manual, technical and administrative workers.

Figure 10.3 illustrates part of a broad-graded (or job family) structure. Note the way in which related narrow grades housing positions from the same family of jobs (in this case production line machining jobs) and their respective pay ranges are reconstituted into one broad grade covering the whole job family. The extremities of the old grade ranges now become the minima and maxima for the new broad grade. The same process would be repeated for other job families within the organisation (such as clerical or administrative job groupings) to build up a structure composed of multiple broad grades and arranged semi-hierarchically.

The broad grades approach has been widely implemented in Western work organisations since the late 1980s. In essence, it represents a compromise between traditional narrow grades and broad bands; between position-based pay and pay that is primarily (if not wholly) person-based. The more radical option of broad-banding has assumed particular importance in the

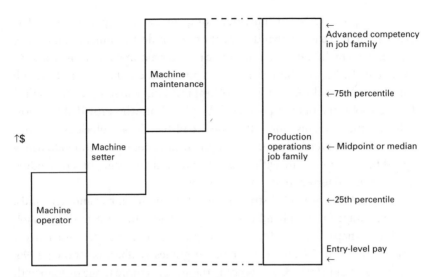

**Figure 10.3** From narrow grades to broad grades

United States, yet in other countries more interest has also been shown in the broad grades alternative. In the UK, for instance, 'job families' are used by 14 per cent of organisations to structure base pay, while 12 per cent use 'career grades'. (For details, see table 10.1.) As Armstrong and Brown (2005: 47–9) note, some British organisations have a preference for 'fat-graded' structures of this type because they represent a more cautious and evolutionary alternative to broad-banding. As Brown (1996: 46) has observed, a gradual approach to organisational change may well be more effective over the longer term: 'Moving towards an empowered, open and trusting company culture happens gradually, and it takes time to build the level of confidence needed to operate fully flexible pay management within broad pay bands. HR staff have to learn to trust line managers: and employees need to trust their own managers.'

## Broad bands

Broad bands do indeed represent a radical break from traditional job-based pay practice. Broad-banding involves doing away with a large number of narrow jobs arranged in a steep hierarchy in favour of a much smaller number of job bands. Pay ranges are substantially wider and the mode of pay progression is radically different. With broad bands, base pay progression is based not on job position, but on individual competency and/or performance. The critical difference is the abandonment of job grade assignment in favour of an emphasis on broad work roles and career development in those roles. As exponents Risher and Butler (1993: 56) put it, the emphasis shifts from job value to individual value: 'Instead of emphasising who has the most points for their jobs, the new emphasis will be placed on who provided the most value for their organisations.' Because broad-banding emphasises horizontal as opposed to vertical career development, and because an individual may spend their entire tenure with an organisation in one band, broad-banding is sometimes referred to as 'career banding'.

A typical broad-banded structure will have between five and ten bands. The pay range for each band is significantly wider than for traditional job grades, perhaps 100 to 300 per cent compared to 20 per cent for narrow grades and 50 to 75 per cent for broad grades (Gilbert & Abosch 1996; Abosch & Hand 1994a & b). Typically there is also more range overlap with broad-banding. The greater the overlap, the less the emphasis on hierarchy. It would be quite possible for an employee in a 'lower' band to be earning at least as much as many of those in a 'higher' band. The internal architecture of a broad band also tends to be very different from that of grade-based structures. Unlike broad grades, broad bands tend to have few if any internal 'control points', such as midpoints or quartiles. The objective is unimpeded pay progression based on personal worth to the organisation.

In the simple example given in figure 10.4 there are five bands, each covering distinct occupational roles: customer service, administrative support, engineering, strategic management and executive. Note the wide pay ranges and the high level of band overlap. This means, for example, that a committed production engineer can remain in this role and still receive base pay substantially above that received by other professionals who are positioned in the strategic management band or even in the executive band.

How many bands should there be? This will depend on the organisation and the work roles within it. On average, however, the number of bands tends to be about a third of the number of old job grades. Research conducted in the 1990s found that, on average, broad-banding by US firms resulted in thirty job grades being converted into between seven and eleven bands (Abosch & Hand 1994a & b, 1998; Enos & Limoges 2000; Tucker 1995). According to exponents, the appropriate number of bands is best ascertained by determining the number of distinct levels of employee 'contribution' in the organisation that 'add value' to the organisation. Value-adding tiers are

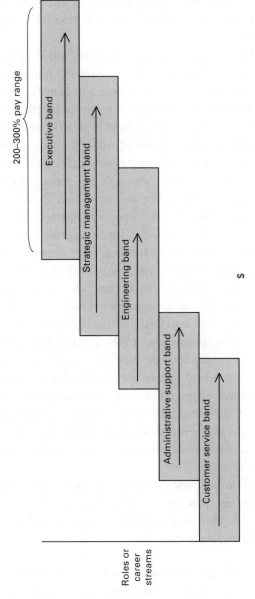

**Figure 10.4** Broad bands

clusters of roles that have common responsibilities and accountabilities. The original job hierarchy is recast so as to group together positions seen as having a similar influence on the organisation's success. In this way the new structure is made to reflect desired contribution rather than job size (Gilbert & Abosch 1996).

How can this be achieved in practice? Banding might be based on the number of distinct levels that exist in the organisation. It might be based on natural job clusters or work roles: for example, one band for technical staff, another for administrative support staff. It might be based on key areas of accountability or competency. As Hofrichter (1993: 56) notes: 'Whatever the number, each band must include a group of individuals who are contributing value added at a certain level. Otherwise, employees will view the entire approach simply as an attempt to wipe out pay-grade boundaries.' The aim here is to de-emphasise hierarchy and accentuate ability and personal development without promotion. As exponents Flannery, Hofrichter and Platten (1996: 100) put it: 'By de-emphasising titles, grades, job descriptions, and ever-upward movement, broad-banding helps organisations advance the values of group or team performance along with that of the individual. Frequently, for example, both supervisors and their subordinates will be placed in the same band. And, as their duties and roles change, they can very naturally move slightly "back and forth" within the band, without the need for an attention-grabbing promotion or the stigma of demotion.'

Another common feature of broad-banding is that much of the responsibility for day-to-day reward management is devolved to line managers. Typically, line managers are given discretion to manage their subordinates' pay adjustments within limits set by budget allocation and broad pay policy guidelines. In this sense, broad-banding underscores the wider trend in HRM practice towards the devolution of human resource management decision-making and responsibility.

The aim, then, is to reorient the remuneration system from a vertical emphasis on rewarding frequent job promotion to a horizontal emphasis on rewarding individual ability and encouraging career development. According to exponent Ken Abosch:

Broadbanding . . . collapses many salary grades into a few wide bands for purposes of improving organisational effectiveness . . . With fewer levels of bands: the compensation system is better positioned to respond to the needs of today's flatter organizations. Properly designed, broadbanding creates the framework for a remuneration system that de-emphasizes structure and control and places greater importance on judgment and flexible decision-making. It promises to add value by supporting employees' efforts to improve their competencies and skills – which ultimately helps the organization to shift business direction quickly. (Abosch 1995: 54)

Exponents such as Abosch (1995, 1998a), Brown (1996), Gilbert (1994), Hofrichter (1993), Risher (1995, 1997c, 1999b), Tucker (1995) and Rosen and Turetsky (2002) contend that broad-banding has many advantages over traditional graded structures. By flattening job hierarchies, it can redirect employees' attention away from competition for jobs and promotion and towards individual and group contribution to organisational success. Uncoupling promotion from individual career development and base pay progression redefines career 'success' from a vertical to a horizontal trajectory. This means that individuals no longer have to aspire to a managerial role in order to further their careers and base pay. Further, by promoting the self-management of personal capacity and contribution, broad-banding is said to empower employees. At the same time, because it devolves much of the day-to-day decision-making about base pay determination, this added responsibility for pay decisions is said to empower line managers.

By linking career development and pay progression to individual performance capability and achievement, broad-banding also supports a more strategic approach to reward management. The wider pay possibilities that it makes available also allow greater scope to reward employees for contributions that go beyond their standard role descriptions; that is, to reward organisational citizenship behaviour. Finally, broad-banding is said to emphasise external labour market competitiveness over internal pay equity considerations. This is because the focus is on using external market data to determine pay ranges that maintain overall competitiveness rather than on upholding equitable internal pay relativities between specific jobs: 'When organizations move to bands, they make the statement that internal equity is less important than it was under the traditional approach. Without salary grades and midpoints, internal equity simply is harder to define and, as a result, over time receives less emphasis . . . With their lack of definition, bands help people experience an internal culture that more closely mirrors the external, competitive environment and, as a result, makes it easier for employees to reorientate themselves to the marketplace.' (Gilbert 1994: 50.)

Although broad-banding was pioneered in the US public sector in the early 1980s (Schay 1996), it was only after its adoption by two major North American corporations, General Electric in 1989 and Northern Telecom in

1991, that it rose to prominence. Northern Telecom reduced the number of pay levels from fifty-four to thirteen. Under former CEO Jack Welsh, General Electric collapsed its old fourteen-level job graded structure for non-executive salaried employees into just four overlapping broad bands: 'associate professional', 'professional', 'lead professional' and 'senior professional'. The four bands had an average pay range of 130 per cent. The aim was to transform the entire organisation from a bureaucracy into a 'boundaryless' organisation in which employees were challenged and encouraged to 'take control of their own destinies' (Gilbert 1994; Hofrichter 1993; Tucker 1995).

The practice was also linked directly to the defining management precept of the mid-1990s, namely 'business process reengineering' (Hammer & Champy 1993; O'Neal 1996) and, as such, came to be seen as a change management device (Haslett 1995). US studies undertaken in the 1990s revealed that firms that had introduced broad-banding had done so primarily as a means of supporting organisational change and, in particular, with a view to achieving greater functional flexibility, a flatter organisational structure, and a greater emphasis on external labour market competitiveness (Enos & Limoges, 2000; Reissman 1995: 82). A 1996 study by consulting firm Towers Perrin found that 19 per cent of US companies were using broad-banding and 27 per cent were planning to introduce or extend it (Brown 1996). Between 1993 and 1998 the use of broad bands by US companies rose by more than 200 per cent (Abosch & Hmurovic 1998), and it is now widespread in large US public and private organisations.

The practice is now also widely applied in other Western countries. In the UK, it is used in stand-alone form by 36 per cent of organisations across all sectors, with the highest usage being in service firms (38 per cent) and the lowest in the public service (25 per cent) (see table 10.1 for details). For instance, the firm-wide structure introduced by the UK retail chain Tesco saw twenty-two grades replaced by just six 'work levels' (Armstrong & Brown 2005: 48). Survey research undertaken in 2000–01 indicates that broad-banding was used by 29 per cent of medium-sized to large firms in Canada for non-managerial employees, and by 44 per cent of firms in Australia for this purpose (Long & Shields 2005a: 72).

Yet it would be incorrect to conclude that broad-banding has taken the world by storm. Outside the USA, organisations evidently still prefer the 'evolutionary path to broad-banding' – via broad grades. According to Abosch and Hmurovic (1998: 44), the global preference for the broad grades approach arises from 'the need to accommodate country-specific cultural and socio-economic issues'. Organisation-wide broad-banding is still the exception rather than the rule, with its application frequently being limited both horizontally (to select divisions or units) and vertically (typically confined to salaried managerial or professional employees only). As table 10.1, indicates, in the UK, 19 per cent of organisations prefer to combine broad-banding with job families. Here, firms that have experimented with broad-banding, including pharmaceutical firm GlaxoSmithKline, have gradually reintroduced internal control points and zones to contain costs (Armstrong & Brown 2005: 48). Moreover, in many developing countries, the practice has long been regarded as too radical a departure from traditional pay practice (Abosch & Hmurovic 1998: 44–5).

Has broad-banding lived up to its initial promise? The limited evidence that we have on the success of broad-banding initiatives is positive, although the record is hardly unqualified. By far the most comprehensive studies of outcomes from broad-banding to date were those undertaken in the 1990s by consulting firm Hewitt Associates in conjunction with the American Compensation Association. The first of these studies was undertaken in 1994; a second follow-up study was undertaken in 1998. The 1994 study examined outcomes from broad-banding in 116 US organisations. The results indicated that broad-banding was rated as effective by 78 per cent of the firms surveyed. The respondents indicated that broad-banding was particularly successful in delivering greater flexibility, promoting lateral development, supporting business goals, developing skills and competencies, encouraging a team focus, and focusing employees' attention away from vertical promotion. The 1994 research also provided revealing insights on stakeholder perceptions of broad-banding's impact: 71 per cent of executives and 68 per cent of employees felt that boadbanding was effective, while 91 per cent of executives and 75 per cent of employees felt that broad-banding should be maintained or expanded in their organisations (Abosch & Hand 1994b). The 1998 study covered seventy-three US firms (including thirty-three participants in the 1994 survey). According to the researchers (Abosch 1998a; Abosch & Hand 1998), the results of the later study indicate that broad-banding continued to live up to its promise. Between the first survey and the second, the percentage of firms reporting a cost-neutral impact rose from 76 per cent to 90 per cent. While the change of job titles that accompanied broad-banding caused considerable initial dissatisfaction, only 12 per cent of employees remained negative about the loss of job title.

Yet the same survey results also indicated some significant shortcomings in the way in which broad-banding had been implemented. Few firms had installed mechanisms for monitoring the effectiveness of broad-banding.

The proportion of firms with no formal approach to career development fell only slightly between the two surveys – from 45 per cent to 41 per cent. Of those firms that had introduced broad-banding in conjunction with an extensive communication program, 73 per cent had provided very little formal communication following the launch. Moreover, only 27 per cent of employees indicated that they understand broad-banding (Abosch 1998a).

Even its strongest supporters concede that broad-banding is anything but problem-free. Exponents (Hofrichter 1993; Risher & Butler 1993; Abosch & Hand 1994a; Armstrong 1996) point to a number of potential pitfalls. From the organisation's perspective, far from simplifying payroll administration, broad-banding stands to make it more complex and challenging, and requiring considerably greater levels of remuneration expertise (Stoskopf 2002: 32). As we shall see in chapter 12, evaluating individual capacity in order to determine band position and progression is every bit as complicated as evaluating jobs. Moreover, moving to bands does not obviate the need to evaluate markets. Indeed, it makes it all the more important. The devolution of base pay decisions to line managers may actually threaten cost competitiveness and inflate payroll costs, particularly where there are no control points for managing in-band position and progression. Line managers may be unwilling or inadequately trained to assume responsibility for pay administration and may be too generous. In the absence of clearly defined limits and guidelines for pay progression, there is a danger of runaway payroll inflation. Another problem is that of inappropriate or unduly hasty implementation, since banding necessarily requires careful preparation and prior communication. Restructuring forty or fifty narrow grades into just five to ten broad bands necessarily takes time – perhaps two to three years to accomplish fully. Indeed, in the first flush of enthusiasm for the practice in the early to mid-1990s, critics (e.g. Neubauer 1995: 52) repeatedly urged caution: '. . . too many executives are willing to grasp at every new idea, without thoroughly analysing the problem, hence, the broadbanding "fad". Like any fad, broadbanding is a concept that seems right for the time but whose long-term worth remains unproven.'

The radical nature of broad-banding also has considerable potential to damage employee psychological contracts and justice perceptions. Extremely wide pay ranges can create unrealistic expectations of pay rise opportunities, and this too can cause breach of trust and feelings of distributive injustice, especially if these expectations remain unfulfilled. One critic (Armitage 1997: 25) suggests that recruitment advertisements for banded positions may specify 'a decent top salary to tempt as many applicants as possible, but with no intention of paying more than the bottom figure . . . Once inside the company, one discovers than nobody within the organisation doing that job is paid more than the median figure. The top figure is revealed as nothing more than a cynical "come on": a number plucked from the air.' Similarly, Armstrong and Brown (2005: 48) report that in the UK the practice 'created impressions for progression that could not be met in an environment of low inflation' and that in one public sector organisation it was calculated that it would take a high performer fifty years to reach the top of their band.

The removal of promotional opportunities may also rupture trust, while, according to Budman (1998: 25), stripping away promotion-related pay increases can lead to a significant long-term reduction in employee earnings. Armitage (1997: 25) contends that the reclassification that accompanies a move to broad-banding may also lead to disguised pay cutting: 'Pay banding is increasingly being used as part of a modern vogue for flatter management structures. In theory, it allows substantial salary increases without having to recreate junior or middle management layers. In practice, it often allows unscrupulous employers to do away with annual pay increases of any kind.' Overall, then, while broad-banding does hold considerable promise as a means of structuring person-based pay, its very complexity requires that it be handled with care, caution and, not least, patience.

## 'Best fit' considerations

Returning to the tenets of our 'best fit' model, and bearing the points made in this chapter and chapter 9 in mind, it is possible to identify certain synergies between each of the three main approaches to base pay determination, the four main base pay structures and the key dimensions of organisational structure, culture and strategy detailed in chapter 4. These are summarised in table 10.2.

Given their accent on service and seniority, traditional pay scales will have greatest appeal to those organisations that place a high premium on employee loyalty and workforce stability. As such they will have particular relevance to traditionally managed organisations structured on mechanistic lines, with large numbers of narrow, routine job assignments, operating with hierarchical internal labour markets (i.e. based on promoting within

**Table 10.2** 'Best fit' with base pay structures

| | **Pay scales and narrow grades** |
|---|---|
| Strategy | Cost defender |
| Structure | Mechanistic |
| Culture | Traditional; unionised |
| Roles | Line- and middle-level positions |
| | **Broad grades** |
| Strategy | Quality defender |
| Structure | Semi-organic |
| Culture | Semi-high involvement; some unionisation |
| Roles | Process; technical; maintenance; administrative |
| | **Broadbands** |
| Strategy | Prospector |
| Structure | Organic |
| Culture | High involvement; non-union |
| Roles | Service work; knowledge work; managerial roles |

the organisation), and seeking to foster long-term relational psychological contracts with their employees. In such contexts, pay scales would be an appropriate choice for all line employees and line managers, as well as middle managers. Firms with cost-focused defender strategies will also be attracted to the tight control that scaled structures allow over payroll costs, as well as to the assumption of long-term stability in technology and job content. By the same token, the simplicity and transparency of pay scales, as well as the ease of across-the-board rate adjustment, also means that pay scales will generally be compatible with a strong union presence and collective bargaining. In general, the same observations also apply to narrow grades structures. For the same reasons, however, pay scales and narrow grades will hold little appeal to organisations with organic structures, teamworking and either analyser or prospector competitive strategies. The emphasis on hierarchy would certainly be incompatible with a high-involvement culture.

As we have seen, broad grades offer the base pay flexibility required for more diverse and highly skilled task assignments, multiskilling, greater self-management and teamworking. As such it is well adapted to organisations with semi-organic structures involving interdependent work assignments and teamworking. Given the emphasis on skill development and process improvement, broad grades will be particularly well suited to a quality defender strategy. The scope to facilitate skill diversification means that broad grades and skill pay are also well suited to an analyser competitive strategy. Equally, broad grades and skill pay would be a poor fit for mechanistic organisational structures, in which tasks are narrowly specialised, low-skilled and individualised, as well as for cost defender strategies, since pay for skill is necessarily a high-cost option. Moreover, broad grades and skill pay would have only limited application to a prospector business strategy since in such organisations product cycles may well be too short to accommodate internal training and retraining. Such organisations are more likely to 'buy' rather than 'build' the skills they require.

Broad grades and skill pay are also likely to be compatible with a union presence, although, as Ledford has argued (1991a: 14), the emphasis on training, multiskilling and teamworking also points to compatibility with a degree of employee involvement. Skill-based approaches also lend themselves to employee involvement in pay system design and administration. However, a fully developed high-involvement culture arguably requires a greater degree of employee autonomy and empowerment than a skill-based system by itself is capable of providing.

The combination of broad grades and skill-based pay will be especially appropriate for roles with significant technical knowledge and skill requirements, such as process work, technical or quasi-professional roles, maintenance work and administration. In such roles, skills are relatively easy to identify, impart, assess and price. Ledford (1991a) suggests that skill pay suits continuous process technology, such as that present in chemical and steel plants and petroleum refineries, because it provides employees with incentives to learn about the entire production flow. This enables them to respond quickly and effectively to disruptions in the process, regardless of where in the production flow they may be working at the time. Clearly, skill pay is also well suited to teamworking (Bergel 1994: 35). By the same token, broad grades will be less appropriate to higher-level professional knowledge work and managerial roles, since the chief performance capabilities here are 'soft' competencies rather than formal task-specific technical skills.

Broad-banding is certainly not suitable for every organisation. The emphasis on wide role assignments and devolution of decision-making make it incompatible with mechanistic organisational structures, traditional management styles and a unionised workforce; indeed, it has been represented as the antidote to such 'rigid' and 'antiquated' phenomena. Conversely, where employee empowerment, adaptability, risk-taking and timeliness are required – as would be the case in high-involvement organic prospector firms – organisation-wide broad-banding and competency-based or competency-related pay would seem to hold particular relevance. As suggested in chapter 7, the competencies model is especially applicable in service, knowledge work and managerial roles. Such competencies as timeliness, creativity, lateral thinking and problem-solving are also particularly pertinent to organisations with prospector business strategies. Moreover, the emphasis on self-management and individual accountability under the competencies model is directly relevant to devolved, high-involvement organisations. In short, competency-based or -related broad-banding is of special relevance to organisations of the high-involvement prospector type in which speed and risk-taking are of the essence. As its origins indicate, the competencies approach is also particularly well suited to managerial and knowledge worker roles.

## Chapter summary

This chapter has examined the options for structuring base pay, noting that the job-, skill- and competency-based or -related approaches each have their own distinct structures and modes of pay progression. The following structures were considered: pay scales, narrow grades, broad grades and broad bands. As well as coming to terms with the specifics of each of these ways of structuring base bay, following the tenets of the 'best fit' approach to system design, we also identified those organisational settings and management strategies to which each of these structural alternatives might be best and least suited.

## Discussion questions

1 Why does base pay need to be 'structured' at all?
2 Why might an organisation prefer to use job grades rather than pay scales or spines?
3 From an employee perspective, what are the attractions and drawbacks of skill-based pay progression within a broad-graded structure?
4 Is broad-banding just a pay fad whose time has now passed?
5 Why would broad-banding be a poor fit for a firm with a mechanistic structure?

## Chapter Eleven

# DEVELOPING POSITION-BASED BASE PAY SYSTEMS

In chapter 10, we examined the two main alternatives for structuring position-based base pay (pay scales and narrow grades), as well as the two chief options for structuring person-based base pay systems (broad grades, with skill-based progression, and broad bands with competency-based or -related progression). In this chapter, we consider the main evaluation techniques associated with position-based pay, as well as the key steps in developing and implementing position-based systems, with particular emphasis on the design of narrow grades structures, since these are the more common of the two position-based structures. We begin with an examination of the two main techniques associated with pricing job positions, namely market pricing and job evaluation. As we shall see, the key difference between these two methods is that market surveys focus on maintaining an organisation's competitiveness prevailing in external labour markets whereas job evaluation methods are concerned primarily with establishing 'internal equity'; that is, with determining felt-fair job rates and rate differences within an organisation. Once we have a solid understanding of these evaluation techniques, we can proceed to consider how they may be applied to develop a position-based pay structure. Then, in chapter 12, we canvass the techniques and processes involved in developing person-based systems.

## Market surveys

Market surveys involve setting pay rates for particular jobs and positions according to what other employers are paying for the same or similar jobs in external labour markets. This typically entails some form of multi-employer survey to ascertain the 'going rate' for each job type. The organisation ascertains what other employers are paying for jobs similar to its own, then makes a strategic choice about whether it will pay the median rate, a lower rate or a higher rate. Regular market surveys also allow organisations to monitor changes in market rates and adjust their own pay rates accordingly. An organisation can either conduct its own market surveys or purchase survey data generated by an external provider, such as a remuneration consultancy firm or an industry or professional association.

If an organisation wishes to conduct its own survey, there are six main steps that should be followed:

1  deciding which jobs to survey
2  determining which outside organisations to survey
3  determining the method of data collection
4  determining what information to collect on each position
5  processing and analysing the raw survey data
6  deciding a policy on pay level relative to external market rates.

### 1. Deciding which jobs to survey

It is rarely necessary to include all of the organisation's jobs in every survey. Typically, each survey will cover a representative sample of 10 to 20 per cent of the organisation's jobs. This should be enough to calibrate the whole system for external pay movements. The sample would be changed each year so that all jobs will eventually be surveyed in their own right. It is also crucial that like is compared with like, and this requires going beyond mere position titles; it requires the use of current, concise job descriptions to ensure comparability of positions between firms, and this, in turn, requires proper job analysis beforehand.

### 2. Determining which outside organisations to survey

Defining the relevant external labour markets, and hence the relevant organisational competitors, is not as straightforward as it might seem. Competitors will be of two broad types: those in the same product or service market, and those in the same labour markets. In some cases firms in quite different industries will compete for the same type of labour. In general, the surveying organisation will need to identify the occupational groups for which it will collect data, the geographic extent of each group and the industry scope of each. It would also be advisable to focus on organisations of comparable size since firm size is an important determinant of pay mix, pay levels and labour cost ratios. Large firms tend to pay more for the same job than smaller ones; firms in some localities will have to pay more for the same job than those in other localities where the supply of labour is more plentiful.

## 3. Determining the method of data collection

There are three main means of collecting survey data: personal interviews, questionnaires and telephone interviews. Personal interviews are probably the best means of data collection since the interviewee can keep a running check on job match and data quality. However, it is also a costly and time-consuming method. Questionnaires are generally far cheaper to administer. The main problem with questionnaires is that they are not a particularly reliable means of data-gathering since there is no control over who completes the form. Telephone interviews probably deliver the best of all possible outcomes: they are relatively cheap, yet enable instant monitoring of job match and data accuracy.

## 4. Determining what information to collect on each position

Data on wage and salary levels should include the average level of base pay paid in each job and the pay range (i.e. minimum and maximum paid) for each job. But this alone will not be enough. For a proper comparison, it is important to ascertain not only the level of base pay by scale step or year of service but also the level of performance pay, the amount of employer superannuation contributions and other types of remuneration, particularly benefits, and the total amount of remuneration involved. This is because a low (or high) level of base pay does not necessarily translate into a low (or high) level of total pay, and in making decisions about external competitiveness it is important to know how other organisations configure the mix of total remuneration.

## 5. Processing and analysing the raw survey data

The chief complication here is that all employers sampled are most unlikely to be paying the same level of pay for any given position; it is far more likely that there will be a diversity of pay rates, so the raw survey data will require additional statistical analysis to enable an accurate overview of market rates and trends. Essentially, this means aggregating the firm-specific data using descriptive statistical procedures to identify the data sample range (minima and maxima), range distribution and range median for each recognised position. The range median is simply the rate that occupies the middle position (fiftieth percentile) in the range when the position data from each survey respondent is ranked from lowest to highest. Distribution can then

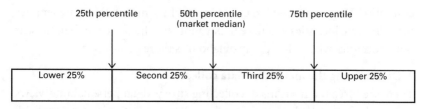

**Figure 11.1**  Salary survey data presentation: range percentiles and quartiles

be summarised in terms of the mean (average) rate for particular segments of the ranked range, such as percentile, decile or quartile means. Quartile means allows us to identify, for example, what the average amount of base salary paid by the highest paying 25 per cent of respondents (the upper quartile mean) and the lowest paying 25 per cent (the lower quartile).

Figure 11.1 illustrates the aggregation of survey data into range quartiles, and figure 11.2 offers an example of how summative data of this type can be presented. In this example, the data relates to the position of generalist human resources manager. Note that selected percentile values are presented for all main remuneration components (not just base salary) as well as for total employment cost. In addition, means are provided by firm size ('annual revenue'), location and industry.

**6. Deciding a policy on pay level relative to external market rates**

The summative data is really only a guide to establishing and maintaining pay competitiveness; it will not tell the organisation what amount it should pay for each position. This is a matter of strategic choice. A decision must be made as to how high or low the organisation's pay levels should be positioned, and this will be a matter of weighing up the projected costs and benefits. If, say, it decides to pay at the 75th percentile, it will need to be sure that the additional payroll costs will be more than offset by positive outcomes such as lower staff turnover, improved recruitment and retention, and stronger membership, task and citizenship behaviour. Conversely, if it decides to set base pay below the 50th percentile, there needs to be some assurance that the cost savings will not be eroded by negative attitudes and behaviour.

Market surveys are among the most widely utilised remuneration management techniques. In the UK, 75 per cent of organisations in all sectors of the economy link base pay levels to market rates, and 44 per cent link pay progression directly to market rates, with the highest usage being in private sector firms (CIPD 2005b: 5). In Canada, 74 per cent of such firms use market survey data for non-managerial employees, as do 66 per cent of Australian firms (Long & Shields 2005a: 72).

| Position Title: | Senior Human Resources Officer |
|---|---|
| Position Code: | 4175 |
| Career Level: | 3 |
| Sample Size: | 256 |
| No. of Organisations: | 76 |

| | | | | Percentiles | | | |
|---|---|---|---|---|---|---|---|
| Remuneration Component | % Rec | Average | % of TFR | 25th | 50th | 62.5th | 75th |
| TAXABLE BASE SALARY (TBS) | 70674 | 88% | 100% | 59715 | 70250 | 74117 | 79270 |
| Salary Sacrifice Superannuation | 4563 | 6% | 16% | 1500 | 2850 | 3614 | 4800 |
| NOMINAL BASE SALARY (NBS) | 71404 | 89% | 100% | 60327 | 70600 | 74500 | 80000 |
| Annual Leave Loading | 876 | 1% | 54% | 784 | 881 | 881 | 951 |
| Other Cash | 5930 | 7% | 5% | 2007 | 3283 | 3386 | 5245 |
| TOTAL FIXED CASH | 72151 | 90% | 100% | 61293 | 71885 | 75069 | 80294 |
| Company Superannuation | 6930 | 9% | 100% | 5779 | 6759 | 7358 | 7800 |
| Car Allowance | 18300 | 23% | 2% | 18000 | 18500 | | 18500 |
| Other Non FBT-able Benefits | 464 | 1% | 7% | 368 | 414 | 470 | 500 |
| Company Car/Novated Lease | 12215 | 15% | 4% | 8258 | 13080 | 15387 | 16181 |
| Health Insurance | 1553 | 2% | 2% | | 1500 | | |
| Other FBT-able Benefits | 987 | 1% | 4% | 327 | 349 | 420 | 1110 |
| TOTAL PACKAGE | 80014 | 100% | 100% | 67368 | 79516 | 83723 | 90032 |
| FBT Car | 6075 | 8% | 4% | 2815 | 6236 | 7726 | 9424 |
| FBT Other | 1076 | 1% | 5% | 352 | 448 | 758 | 1764 |
| TOTAL FIXED REMUNERATION (TFR) | 80306 | 100% | 100% | 67368 | 79516 | 83828 | 90128 |
| Total Variable Pay | 5358 | 7% | 70% | 1500 | 4855 | 6812 | 7324 |
| TOTAL REMUNERATION COST (TRC) | 84053 | 105% | 100% | 69602 | 83630 | 88790 | 94530 |
| Overtime | 1909 | 2% | 2% | | 1810 | | |
| Shift/Standby/On-call Allowance | | | | | | | |
| TOTAL EMPLOYMENT COST (TEC) | 84082 | 105% | 100% | 69602 | 83630 | 88790 | 94530 |

**Average Data**

| Industry | Sample Size | NBS | TFR | TRC |
|---|---|---|---|---|
| Transport & Shipping | 5 | 64806 | 78951 | 80229 |
| Computer & High Technology | 86 | 71166 | 79462 | 83076 |
| Manufacturing | 5 | 78695 | 105992 | 106332 |
| Banking & Finance | 121 | 72090 | 80688 | 84373 |
| Agriculture & Energy | 7 | 80777 | 91600 | 102400 |
| Other | 32 | 67294 | 74856 | 78567 |

| Organisation Size | Sample Size | NBS | TFR | TRC |
|---|---|---|---|---|
| Less than $25 million Annual Revenue | 3 | 72957 | 82826 | 82826 |
| $25 – $100 Million Annual Revenue | 22 | 72722 | 82126 | 85144 |
| $101 – $250 Million Annual Revenue | 29 | 60973 | 69218 | 71107 |
| $251 – $500 Million Annual Revenue | 24 | 70460 | 83273 | 87261 |
| $501 Million – $1 Billion Annual Revenue | 35 | 68496 | 75675 | 82045 |
| Over $1 Billion Annual Revenue | 143 | 74155 | 82857 | 86488 |

| State | Sample Size | NBS | TFR | TRC |
|---|---|---|---|---|
| New South Wales | 115 | 69439 | 77838 | 81891 |
| Victoria | 109 | 73438 | 82669 | 86214 |
| Queensland | 12 | 68760 | 77728 | 80140 |
| South Australia | 13 | 78489 | 88868 | 93367 |
| Western Australia | 5 | 63726 | 70697 | 73088 |

**Figure 11.2** Example of salary survey data presentation format: 'senior human resources officer' position
*Source:* CSi – The Remuneration Specialists, Australian General Industry Remuneration Report, June 2005. Reproduced with permission.

Valuing positions by means of market surveys has several clear advantages. It is usually neither costly nor administratively complex. Surveys provide an automatic means of keeping job rates in line with market conditions, thus allowing the organisation to remain competitive in both its labour and its product markets. Most importantly, market surveys support a focus on competitive external recruitment. This is crucial for organisations that accentuate a transactional rather than a relational psychological contract and recruitment from outside the organisation.

However, market pricing also has its shortcomings. Surveys are necessarily selective, and the data is only as valid and reliable as the survey methodology that produces it. Surveys are subject to sampling errors. Surveys do not capture the full range of rewards offered by organisations, including those of a non-financial nature, and this may give a false reading of competitors' strategies. Moreover, rates for similar jobs will also vary according to firm size, industry and region. Different organisations will define their jobs in different ways. Even where the same job title is used, the job content may be different (Cook 1994). The organisation needs to be sure that, as far as is possible, it is comparing like with like. The problem of job matching will be especially difficult where the organisation has many jobs that are unique in terms of content. This relates to the problem of 'compensation averaging': merely taking the average rate paid externally for seemingly comparable jobs as the pay-setting benchmark may either under- or over-value the tasks, duties and responsibilities that are included in some or all of the organisation's jobs. Market rates are rarely a pure reflection of job worth. They usually reflect *both* job value *and* job-holder characteristics and contribution. As such, the rates that organisations indicate they pay for a particular job often includes both base pay for the job and performance-rated pay for job-holder contribution, and special care needs to be taken to separate the two elements. Further, pricing to market implies a loss of organisational autonomy and control. In effect, it allows competitors to determine an organisation's internal pay structure, which means that the employer sacrifices autonomy over pay structure.

Moreover, external markets do not always value jobs rationally and equitably. Going rates are frequently contaminated by dominant social norms and value judgements about the worth of the person holding the job. The classic instance of this is the undervaluation of traditionally female-dominated occupations, such as nursing, teaching and childcare work. Labour markets have tended to ascribe lower economic value to the 'soft' (but arguably socially more important) interpersonal competencies required in such roles than to the 'hard' technical skills associated with positions historically dominated by men. This is one of the main reasons why governments in various countries have introduced pay equity legislation – to mitigate historical market inequities of this type.

Finally, a purely market-focused job pricing strategy will not address the issue of internal fairness. It rules out the possibility of building a base pay system that prices jobs according to their specific value *to the organisation*. Jobs that are more important to the firm in practice may have to be paid less than jobs of lesser importance simply because that is what external markets dictate. The thrust of the main alternative to market pricing – that is, job evaluation – is the maintenance of a base-pay structure that achieves internal equity.

## Job evaluation: purpose and methods

Job evaluation involves determining position pay rates according to the content or 'size' of each position within the organisation with a view to rewarding each job according to its 'value' or importance to the organisation. How? By analysing the descriptions for each job in the organisation and measuring the relative 'size' or importance of each job to the organisation by some systematic means. The end result of job evaluation is a hierarchy of jobs in which all jobs of similar 'size', no matter how different they might be in other respects, are placed at the same scale or grade in the job-based pay hierarchy.

The ostensible purpose of job evaluation is to provide a rational and fair basis for the determination and management of internal pay relativities between jobs. The aim is to price jobs 'fairly' according to their relative importance in adding value to the organisation.

In the UK, 51 per cent of organisations use job evaluation in determining base levels; usage is most pronounced in the public sector (CIPD 2005b: 5, 25). Usage is similar in Australia, where more than half of private firms apply it to non-managerial positions. In Canada, however, where provincial legislation mandates formal adherence to pay equity principles and practice, job evaluation is used by 75 per cent of private firms (Long & Shields 2005a: 72).

Generally, job evaluation involves four main steps:

1  undertaking a job analysis, which provides data on the content of specific jobs

2 producing job descriptions, which summarise the core tasks, duties and responsibilities of each job
3 selecting and applying the most appropriate job evaluation method, then using job descriptions to evaluate the relative worth of each job to the organisation
4 creating pay scales or grades based on job evaluation scores.

Job evaluation methods themselves come in two generic forms: qualitative methods and quantitative methods. Qualitative methods generally involve non-analytical and whole-job comparisons and tend to rely on impressionistic and quite subjective judgements about comparative job value. They are usually applied unilaterally by management without any consultation with employees. The two main qualitative methods are job ranking and job grading or classification, both of which are discussed below.

## Job ranking

Job ranking compares whole jobs only. It does not attempt to disaggregate jobs into component parts (or job 'factors'). Whole jobs are ranked in a hierarchy according to the perceived overall value of each. There are two main ways of doing this:

1 alternation ranking, which takes the jobs considered most valuable and least valuable and ranks them first and last, then moves to the next most and least valuable, and so on; and
2 paired comparison, which compares every job with every other job, then those with the highest number of favourable comparisons are ranked on top.

Ranking is quick and simple and well suited to small organisations with just a few job classifications. However, it has some distinct drawbacks. There is no defined standard or formal rationale to defend rank ordering; hence it is difficult to justify pay decisions. Ranking may be based on incomplete information. Rankings are just as likely to be based on the person doing the work, or on prevailing pay rates for the job, than on actual job content. Ranking assumes that the person doing the ranking has valid, accurate and up-to-date knowledge of all jobs being ranked, an impossible requirement in all but the smallest organisations. Moreover, since there is no formal standard for comparing jobs, inconsistencies are likely to arise where ranking is undertaken by more than one evaluator. Finally, ranking itself gives no indication of the degree of difference between jobs, and it is difficult to slot new positions into the right order once the ranking is done (Long 2006: 253–4).

For these reasons, ranking is generally used only in small organisations with simple job structures and well-accepted pay differentials. It is not practical in large organisations with many different jobs in many different workplaces and where job content itself is subject to frequent change.

## Job grading or classification

Job grading (also known as 'job classification') applies the reverse procedure to quantitative methods in that job grades and pay ranges are created at the commencement of the evaluation process rather than at the conclusion. For instance, a manufacturing organisation might identify a series of grades for production-line positions, say 'G1 – machine operation', 'G2 – machine set-up', 'G3 – machine maintenance' and 'G4 – line management'. Then a series of general content descriptions are created that cover the range of tasks, duties and responsibilities most closely associated with each grade. The descriptions for specific jobs are compared with the grade descriptions to identify the best match within the relevant job class. Jobs are slotted into the relevant grade, and all jobs in that grade are assigned to the same pay range.

With job grading, grade pay ranges are determined by identifying market rates for 'benchmark' jobs in each grade. This involves identifying the job that best typifies a grade. A benchmark job must have several essential characteristics. Its contents must be well known and relatively stable. It must not be unique to the organisation concerned but common to other organisations and have a widely recognised price in the external labour market. It must be representative of all jobs in the class.

Job grading is a convenient and inexpensive way of slotting new jobs into an existing pay structure. It is often used by organisations that have separate pay classifications for managerial, professional, clerical and manual jobs. Since the basis of the grading is spelt out it is easier to defend than simple ranking.

However, the grading approach also has its problems. It is difficult to produce generic grade descriptions applicable to a wide range of jobs. In the absence of systematic quantitative job analysis, grade definition may be little more than educated guess work. It cannot accommodate complex, multifaceted and non-routine jobs like those of many knowledge workers, which might be so wide-ranging that it is next to impossible to slot them into just one job classification. It is also inflexible since it takes the job grades as given and is insensitive to changes in the content of jobs within each grade. Like other non-quantitative methods, it does not measure degrees of difference between individual jobs (only differences between grades) (Long 2006: 254–6).

Quantitative methods, by contrast, seek to break jobs down into common denominators – or job 'factors' – that can be used to measure and compare jobs in terms of how much of each factor each possesses. There are many different quantitative evaluation techniques, including many proprietary methods marketed by specialist remuneration consulting firms. Here we focus on two generic quantitative methods – factor comparison and the points-factor technique – and on one of the most widely applied proprietary points-factor methods, the Hay guide chart profile method.

### Factor comparison

The simplest quantitative method is known as factor comparison. A 'factor' can be any attribute of a job that is considered to be of value to the organisation. Factor comparison is really a refinement of job ranking. The difference is that rather than whole jobs being compared, comparison focuses on differences in specific factor presence between jobs. Factor comparison focuses on building up a whole job price using monetary values for individual job factors. To do this, it identifies a number of major job factors against which all jobs can be assessed. It then takes a number of 'benchmark' jobs that have these factors and for which the current rate of base pay is considered appropriate, estimates the relative importance of each factor in these benchmark jobs, and ascribes a monetary value to each factor.

To illustrate, assume that the benchmark job is that of an electrician, for which the organisation pays base pay of $40 an hour. Using factor analysis, it is estimated that $15 is for technical knowledge, $5 for manual skill, $10 for responsibility, $5 for task planning and $5 for adverse working conditions. The job is then placed on a 'factor comparison chart', with a separate entry for each factor. Other benchmark jobs are then placed in the chart in the same way. Once all of the benchmark jobs are included, other jobs can then be compared with these jobs and located at the appropriate place on each factor pay scale. The factor pay rates for each job can then be tallied to provide the overall base pay for the job (Long 2006: 256).

One advantage of factor comparison is that it can easily be tailored to each organisation. It also allows explicit factor-by-factor justification for differences in job rates. However, it also rests on the questionable assumption that benchmark jobs are already appropriately remunerated. The process of determining factor presence in each job is also subjective. Unless the process is assisted by complex statistical software and computer technology, there is also a cognitive limit to the number of supposedly generic factors that factor comparison can handle.

## Points-factor job evaluation

The 'points-factor' approach works not by seeking to assign a monetary value directly to each factor but, rather, by assigning points based on degrees of factor presence. The method seeks to disaggregate jobs into relevant job factors, such as skill and knowledge requirements, decision-making, reporting and supervision responsibilities, and the like, by means of detailed job analysis. Points are assigned to each job according to the degree to which each designated job factor is present in the job, then the points scores are tallied to give an overall numerical score for each job. This provides not only an absolute ranking of jobs by score size but also precise measures of relative difference in job size or value. Point factor methods are also widely believed to be more acceptable to employees, since they are more transparent and generally more open to employee participation in the evaluation process. Points factor systems are typically administered by means of joint management–employee committees, sometimes with the assistance of outside job evaluation experts.

Points-factor instruments come in two main forms: (1) tailor-made (or 'policy-capturing') instruments developed by or for one organisation, and (2) off-the-shelf or proprietary instruments, of which one of the oldest and most widely applied is the Hay guide chart profile method.

An example of a simple policy-capturing instrument is given in table 11.1. The policy-capturing approach is so-named because it allows an organisation to weight factors according to their perceived relative contribution to meeting the organisation's own strategic objectives. There are three main steps involved in developing a policy-capturing points-factor approach:

1 identifying 'compensable factors'
2 developing rating scales for these factors based on degrees of factor presence, and
3 weighting the factors.

Compensable factors typically cover four broad facets of job content:

- job inputs (such as skill, knowledge, education, training, experience)
- job requirements (such as mental effort, physical effort, decision-making and supervision)

**Table 11.1** A simple 'policy capturing' points-factor job evaluation instrument

| Factors | A | B | C | D | E | Factor weights (total points) |
|---|---|---|---|---|---|---|
| | | | *Degrees* | | | |
| *Skill* | | | | | | |
| Work experience | 40 | 80 | 120 | 160 | 200 | |
| Qualifications | 20 | 40 | 60 | 80 | 100 | |
| Education | 8 | 16 | 24 | 32 | 40 | 400 |
| Initiative | 12 | 24 | 36 | 48 | 60 | |
| *Work content* | | | | | | |
| Difficulty of work | 10 | 20 | 30 | 40 | 50 | |
| Complexity | 20 | 40 | 60 | 80 | 100 | |
| Physical demand | 14 | 28 | 42 | 56 | 70 | |
| Mental demands | 10 | 20 | 30 | 40 | 50 | 300 |
| Hours | 6 | 12 | 18 | 24 | 30 | |
| *Responsibility* | | | | | | |
| Supervision of others | 16 | 32 | 48 | 64 | 80 | |
| Care of materials and equipment | 4 | 8 | 12 | 16 | 20 | |
| Decision-making | 12 | 24 | 36 | 48 | 60 | |
| Record keeping | 4 | 8 | 12 | 16 | 20 | 200 |
| Security | 4 | 8 | 12 | 16 | 20 | |
| *Working conditions* | | | | | | |
| Work environment | 10 | 20 | 30 | 40 | 50 | |
| Hazards or risks | 5 | 10 | 15 | 20 | 25 | 100 |
| Interpersonal relations | 5 | 10 | 15 | 20 | 25 | |
| | 200 | 400 | 600 | 800 | 1,000 | 1,000 |

*Source:* Clark 1992: 295.

- job outputs (such as product accuracy, consequences of error, responsibility for cash and assets)
- job conditions (work environment, hazards and so on).

These are usually broken down into more specific subfactors. A typical scheme will identify four factors, each with three or four subfactors. Commonly used factors include skill, effort, responsibility and working conditions.

The second step involves developing rating scales for each factor. The degree to which each factor is present in each job is measured by means of a rating scale. Typically a scale will recognise up to seven degrees of factor or subfactor presence. The larger the number of degrees of judgement required, the greater the cognitive challenge involved in discerning differences between adjacent degrees. Likewise, reliable judgements require the provision of factor, subfactor and degree descriptors so that assessors can make judgements against a set of valid and clear generic job content standards. The incremental progression in the degree scoring scale may be either arithmetic or geometric; the latter having the advantage of amplifying the scores attached to the factors considered to be strategically most valuable.

The third step involves weighting each factor according to its relative importance to the organisation. This is a critical step in the design process and is central to the 'policy-capturing' aspect of the evaluation process. Should all factors be weighted equally, or should they be weighted differently? The weight attached to each factor must reflect the organisation's strategic objectives; that is, the perceived relative importance of each job factor to organisational effectiveness. For instance, a firm with a quality defender strategy is likely to weight skill more highly than would a cost defender, whereas a high-involvement prospector will place high weight on factors such as decision-making and problem-solving.

In the example given in table 11.1, there are four job factors, all weighted unequally. Each factor is broken into various subfactors. For each factor and subfactor, there are five degrees; each degree representing an arithmetic multiple ($\times$ 2, $\times$ 3, $\times$ 4, $\times$ 5) of the points awarded for the lowest degree. Note that the maximum points that may be awarded to any position is 1,000. In an organisation structured on mechanistic lines, the highest scoring jobs should logically be the most senior executive positions.

## Hay guide chart profile method

With 'off the shelf' points-factor instruments, factors and factor weights are determined externally by the instrument designers on the basis of their judgement as to which factors are deemed to add the most value in any organisational context. By far the most widely used generic point-factor methods is the Hay guide chart profile method, which was first developed by the US-based consulting firm the Hay Group in the 1950s (Armstrong & Murlis 2004: 634–43; Holmes 1980–81; Patten 1988: 192–201; Skenes & Kleiner 2003).

With the Hay method, jobs are evaluated by means of special guide charts. These provide for the evaluation of jobs according to three generic job factors, namely 'know how', 'problem-solving' and 'accountability'. These are claimed to be components of all jobs. More recently, a fourth factor – 'working conditions' – has been added to the instrument criteria.

'Know-how' is defined as the total sum of every kind of knowledge and skill, 'problem-solving' is defined as the amount and nature of thinking required in a job, and 'accountability' is defined as being answerable for action and consequences. These three key factors are assumed to be sequentially related in the work process, such that 'know-how' is the major work input, 'problem-solving' is the principal work process, and 'accountability' is the major work contribution or outcome. The fourth factor, 'working conditions', scores the physical and psychological environment in which the work process occurs.

Each of the four factors is divided into several subfactors, as follows:

1 know-how:
   (a) cognitive know-how: practical procedures and knowledge, specialised techniques, and learned skills
   (b) managerial know-how: real or conceptual planning, coordinating, directing and controlling of activities and resources associated with an organisational unit or function
   (c) human relations know-how: active, practising, person-to-person skills in the area of human relationships
2 problem-solving:
   (a) thinking environment
   (b) thinking challenge
3 accountability:
   (a) freedom to act
   (b) magnitude of decisions, measured in monetary terms
   (c) impact of decisions
4 working conditions:
   (a) physical effort
   (b) physical environment
   (c) sensory attention: the intensity, duration and frequency of required job concentration using one or more of the five senses
   (d) mental stress: degree of tension or anxiety inherent in the work process or environment.

The presence of each subfactor is defined in terms of 'levels', to which particular scores are attached. For example, for cognitive know-how, eight levels are identified:

(A)  primary
(B)  elementary vocational
(C)  vocational
(D)  advanced vocational
(E)  specialised or professional
(F)  seasoned professional
(G)  professional mastery
(H)  unique authority.

For managerial know-how, there are five levels:

  I  task (i.e. wholly task-based)
 II  activity
III  related
IV  diverse
 V  broad.

And for human relations know-how, there are three defined levels: (1) basic, (2) important and (3) critical. The presence of each subfactor is assessed by means of special job profile 'guide charts', one for each factor, with scores being given for each subfactor level.

An extract from a Hay guide chart for evaluating the 'know-how' factor is provided in figure 11.3. Know-how points are calculated by identifying the best match for the job across the three subfactors: cognitive ('technical') know-how, managerial know-how and human relations know-how. Note that the three-way subfactor matrix is broken down into levels: eight for cognitive know-how, five for managerial know-how and three for human relations know-how. The points scores in the levels are based on a geometric scale, with the score values increasing in increments of around 15 per cent going down and across the matrix. The 15 per cent increments are said to represent 'just noticeable' differences in the degree of a subfactor's presence.

To illustrate: in this example, a cognitive know-how scoring of 'F' ('seasoned professional'), combined with a management know-how scoring of 'III' ('diverse'); and human relations know-how of '3' ('critical') – or an integrated know-how score of 'FIII3' – translates to numerical score in the range

Column group definitions:

- **T. Task:** Performance of a task (or tasks) highly specific as to objective and content and not involving the supervision of others.
- **I. Activity:** Performance or supervision of work which is specific as to objective and content with appropriate awareness of related activities.
- **II. Related:** Internal integration of operations which are relatively homogeneous in nature and objective, and which involve external integration with associated functions.
- **III. Diverse:** Operational or conceptual integration of activities which are diverse in nature and in objective in an important management area, or central co-ordination of a strategic function.
- **IV. Broad:** Integration of major functions in an operating complex.

Row categories (••• HUMAN RELATIONS SKILLS across top):
- **1. BASIC:** Ordinary courtesy and effectiveness in dealing with others is required.
- **2. IMPORTANT:** Understanding, influencing and communicating with people are important, but not overriding considerations.
- **3. CRITICAL:** Skills in influencing, developing and/or motivating people are critical to the achievement of job objectives.

Left axis (•• DEPTH AND RANGE OF TECHNICAL KNOW-HOW):

PRACTICAL PROCEDURES / SPECIALISED TECHNIQUES / PROFESSIONAL DISCIPLINES

- **A PRIMARY:** Jobs requiring elementary plus some secondary (or equivalent) education; plus work indoctrination.
- **B ELEMENTARY VOCATIONAL:** Jobs requiring familiarisation in uninvolved, standardised work routines and/or use of simple equipment and machines.
- **C VOCATIONAL:** Jobs requiring procedural or systematic proficiency, which may involve facility in the use of specialised equipment.
- **D ADVANCED VOCATIONAL:** Jobs requiring some specialised (generally non-theoretical) skills gained by 'on the job' experience or through part professional qualification.
- **E SPECIALISED/PROFESSIONAL:** Jobs requiring sufficiency in a technical, scientific or specialised field based on an understanding of concepts and principles normally associated with a professional qualification or gained through a detailed grasp of involved practices and procedures.
- **F SEASONED PROFESSIONAL:** Jobs requiring proficiency in a technical, scientific or specialised field gained through broad and deep experience built on concepts and principles, or through wide exposure to complex practices and precedents.
- **G PROFESSIONAL MASTERY:** Jobs requiring determinative mastery of concepts, principles and practices gained through deep involvement in a highly specialised field or through comprehensive business experience.
- **H UNIQUE AUTHORITY:** Jobs requiring outstanding knowledge and command of a profound discipline at a pre-eminent level.

Legend: Most likely Evaluation / Less likely Evaluation

| Know-How | HR | T.Task 1 | T.Task 2 | T.Task 3 | I.Activity 1 | I.Activity 2 | I.Activity 3 | II.Related 1 | II.Related 2 | II.Related 3 | III.Diverse 1 | III.Diverse 2 | III.Diverse 3 | IV.Broad 1 | IV.Broad 2 | IV.Broad 3 |
|---|---|---|---|---|---|---|---|---|---|---|---|---|---|---|---|---|
| A | 1 | 38 | 43 | 50 | 50 | 57 | 66 | 66 | 76 | 87 | 87 | 100 | 115 | 115 | 132 | 152 |
| A | 2 | 43 | 50 | 57 | 57 | 66 | 76 | 76 | 87 | 100 | 100 | 115 | 132 | 132 | 152 | 175 |
| A | 3 | 50 | 57 | 66 | 66 | 76 | 87 | 87 | 100 | 115 | 115 | 132 | 152 | 152 | 175 | 200 |
| B | 1 | 50 | 57 | 66 | 66 | 76 | 87 | 87 | 100 | 115 | 115 | 132 | 152 | 152 | 175 | 200 |
| B | 2 | 57 | 66 | 76 | 76 | 87 | 100 | 100 | 115 | 132 | 132 | 152 | 175 | 175 | 200 | 230 |
| B | 3 | 66 | 76 | 87 | 87 | 100 | 115 | 115 | 132 | 152 | 152 | 175 | 200 | 200 | 230 | 264 |
| C | 1 | 66 | 76 | 87 | 87 | 100 | 115 | 115 | 132 | 152 | 152 | 175 | 200 | 200 | 230 | 264 |
| C | 2 | 76 | 87 | 100 | 100 | 115 | 132 | 132 | 152 | 175 | 175 | 200 | 230 | 230 | 264 | 304 |
| C | 3 | 87 | 100 | 115 | 115 | 132 | 152 | 152 | 175 | 200 | 200 | 230 | 264 | 264 | 304 | 350 |
| D | 1 | 87 | 100 | 115 | 115 | 132 | 152 | 152 | 175 | 200 | 200 | 230 | 264 | 264 | 304 | 350 |
| D | 2 | 100 | 115 | 132 | 132 | 152 | 175 | 175 | 200 | 230 | 230 | 264 | 304 | 304 | 350 | 400 |
| D | 3 | 115 | 132 | 152 | 152 | 175 | 200 | 200 | 230 | 264 | 264 | 304 | 350 | 350 | 400 | 460 |
| E | 1 | 115 | 132 | 152 | 152 | 175 | 200 | 200 | 230 | 264 | 264 | 304 | 350 | 350 | 400 | 460 |
| E | 2 | 132 | 152 | 175 | 175 | 200 | 230 | 230 | 264 | 304 | 304 | 350 | 400 | 400 | 460 | 528 |
| E | 3 | 152 | 175 | 200 | 200 | 230 | 264 | 264 | 304 | 350 | 350 | 400 | 460 | 460 | 528 | 608 |
| F | 1 | 152 | 175 | 200 | 200 | 230 | 264 | 264 | 304 | 350 | 350 | 400 | 460 | 460 | 528 | 608 |
| F | 2 | 175 | 200 | 230 | 230 | 264 | 304 | 304 | 350 | 400 | 400 | 460 | 528 | 528 | 608 | 700 |
| F | 3 | 200 | 230 | 264 | 264 | 304 | 350 | 350 | 400 | 460 | 460 | 528 | 608 | 608 | 700 | 800 |
| G | 1 | 200 | 230 | 264 | 264 | 304 | 350 | 350 | 400 | 460 | 460 | 528 | 608 | 608 | 700 | 800 |
| G | 2 | 230 | 264 | 304 | 304 | 350 | 400 | 400 | 460 | 528 | 528 | 608 | 700 | 700 | 800 | 920 |
| G | 3 | 264 | 304 | 350 | 350 | 400 | 460 | 460 | 528 | 608 | 608 | 700 | 800 | 800 | 920 | 1056 |
| H | 1 | 264 | 304 | 350 | 350 | 400 | 460 | 460 | 528 | 608 | 608 | 700 | 800 | 800 | 920 | 1056 |
| H | 2 | 304 | 350 | 400 | 400 | 460 | 528 | 528 | 608 | 700 | 700 | 800 | 920 | 920 | 1056 | 1216 |
| H | 3 | 350 | 400 | 460 | 460 | 528 | 608 | 608 | 700 | 800 | 800 | 920 | 1056 | 1056 | 1216 | 1400 |

**Figure 11.3** Hay guide chart: 'know-how'

Source: Hay Group Australia. Reproduced with permission.

460–608 points. Taking into account the precise degree of cognitive know-how involved, the evaluators must then select between the three prescribed scores: 460, 528 or 608. For illustrative purposes, let us assume that the evaluators choose the middle option and score the position at 528 for know-how.

Once a score has been determined for know-how, the evaluators then turn to the second factor set, to do with problem-solving. An example of the guide chart for problem-solving is given in figure 11.4. Here, each of the two subfactors is broken down into levels as follows:

1 thinking environment:
  (a) strict routine
  (b) routine
  (c) semi-routine
  (d) standardised
  (e) clearly defined
  (f) broadly defined
  (g) generally defined
  (h) abstractly defined
2 thinking challenge:
  (a) repetitive
  (b) patterned
  (c) variable
  (d) adaptive
  (e) uncharted.

Again, the evaluators are required to identify the level combination that best describes the job on these dimensions. Continuing with the above example, the position being evaluated might be assessed as involving a 'broadly defined' thinking environment (F) and an 'adaptive' level of thinking challenge; that is, an integrated problem-solving score of 'F4'. Here you will notice that the numerical values are expressed quite differently from those given in the know-how chart; that is, they are expressed as percentage values rather than as absolutes. In our example, a problem-solving score of F4 translates to a percentage score in the range 50 to 57 per cent. This means that evaluators still have to determine a specific score in this range, so let us say that they choose a score of 55 per cent. Why, however, is the scoring here given in percentage terms, and how can it be combined with the score for

**••THINKING CHALLENGE**

| THINKING ENVIRONMENT – FREEDOM TO THINK | 1. REPETITIVE<br>Identical situations requiring solution by simple choice of things learned. | | 2. PATTERNED<br>Similar situations requiring solution by discriminating choice of things learned. | | 3. VARIABLE<br>Differing situations requiring the identification and selection of solutions through the application of acquired knowledge. | | 4. ADAPTIVE<br>Situations requiring analytical interpretative and/or constructive thinking and a significant degree of jevaluative judgement. | | 5. UNCHARTED<br>Pathfinding situations requiring creative thinking and the development of new concepts and approaches contributing significantly to the advancement of knowledge and thought. | |
|---|---|---|---|---|---|---|---|---|---|---|
| **A STRICT ROUTINE:** Thinking within detailed rules, instructions and/or rigid supervision. | 10% | 12% | 14% | 16% | 19% | 22% | 25% | 29% | 33% | 38% |
| **B ROUTINE:** Thinking within standard instructions and/or continuous close supervision. | 12% | 14% | 16% | 19% | 22% | 25% | 29% | 33% | 38% | 43% |
| **C SEMI-ROUTINE:** Thinking within well defined procedures and precedents, somewhat diversified and/or supervised. | 14% | 16% | 19% | 22% | 25% | 29% | 33% | 38% | 43% | 50% |
| **D STANDARDISED:** Thinking within substantially diversified, established company procedures and standards, and general supervision. | 16% | 19% | 22% | 25% | 29% | 33% | 38% | 43% | 50% | 57% |
| **E CLEARLY DEFINED:** Thinking within clearly defined company policies, principles and specific objectives, under readily available direction. | 19% | 22% | 25% | 29% | 33% | 38% | 43% | 50% | 57% | 66% |
| **F BROADLY DEFINED:** Thinking within broad policies and objectives, under general direction. | 22% | 25% | 29% | 33% | 38% | 43% | 50% | 57% | 66% | 76% |
| **G GENERALLY DEFINED:** Thinking within general policies, principles and goals under guidance. | 25% | 29% | 33% | 38% | 43% | 50% | 57% | 66% | 76% | 87% |
| **H ABSTRACTLY DEFINED:** Thinking within business philosophy and / or principles controlling human affairs. | 29% | 33% | 38% | 43% | 50% | 57% | 66% | 76% | 87% | |

Most likely Evaluation

**Figure 11.4** Hay guide chart: 'problem-solving'
*Source*: Hay Group Australia. Reproduced with permission.

know-how? The logic is that the relationship between knowledge level and required degree of problem-solving is multiplicative rather than additive. That is to say, the level of position knowledge is value-adding only to the extent that the position requires the application of that knowledge to solve problems, while problem-solving is necessarily limited by the level of know-how required in the job. Hence, in our example, the scores for know-how (528) and problem-solving (55 per cent) are multiplied to give a combined score of 290 for these two factors.

The numerical scores calculated using the guide charts for accountability and working conditions (not illustrated here) are then added to give an aggregate score for the position. By these means, the Hay guide charts allow the evaluators to develop points scores that allow comparison between individual positions in both absolute and relative terms as well as to determine 'size'-related base pay differentials for all positions evaluated.

## Points-factor evaluation: for and against

As a means of valuing jobs and developing position-based pay structures, the points-factor approach has much to commend it. It can introduce order, rationality, strategic focus and consistency into potentially arbitrary pay structures by using transparent and clearly defined measures of job size, by allowing measurement of the degree of difference between jobs, by permitting evaluation against a range of strategically relevant factors, by allowing each organisation to ascertain the relative importance of its own specific jobs using those criteria most relevant to its strategic purpose, by helping to identify and eliminate inequities in the existing pay structure, and by providing a rational basis for setting pay rates for new or changed jobs. Quantitative evaluation also lends itself particularly well to the application of human resource information systems technology. Equally, points-factor methods have the appearance of objectivity and may help to establish job pay relativities that employees perceive as being fair and equitable. For Arthurs (1996): 'job evaluation . . . continues to provide the best legitimation of pay differences. In the process it usually can be expected to minimise discontent about pay.' Points-factor methods can also provide employers with a solid defence against claims of pay discrimination. The approach also lends itself to employee involvement in system design and the evaluation process itself.

However, the points-factor approach also has some weaknesses and drawbacks (Lawler 1988; Long 2006: 289–96). In focusing on internal relativities and generic job content factors, it may downplay or even ignore critical market-related strategic success factors, a point actually conceded by commentators who assert its continuing relevance to contemporary reward practice (Heneman & LeBlanc 2002). Where an evaluation exercise leaves some jobs underpaid or downgraded relative to prevailing external market rates, the organisation's ability to attract and retain individuals to fill the positions may be affected. Points-factor evaluation can also be expensive, time-consuming and laborious. Further, it may be too inflexible to cope with rapid changes in technology and job content, since a change to technology and product or service type will necessitate re-evaluation, which in turn means that it may be unsuitable for organisations other than those with defender competitive strategies.

According to Lawler (1988; 1990: 135–52), points-factor methods privilege job size over job-holder contribution, emphasise internal equity over external competitiveness, and reinforce bureaucracy and hierarchy. Similarly, Emerson (1991) contends that the Hay method has an inbuilt tendency to reinforce managerial hierarchy and traditional bureaucracy. How? By assigning large point scores to *managerial* 'know-how' as opposed to line-employee 'know-how'; by allocating large scores to jobs that directly affect financial results; and by awarding high points for supervising large numbers of people. According to Emerson (1991: 46–7): 'When positions are rewarded for having subordinates and spending funds, an organisation's most energetic employees will embrace subordinates and budgets.' Gupta and Jenkins (1991: 137) make a similar point, noting that the scoring process 'raises the suspicion that job evaluations are used for "window-dressing" to provide a facade of credibility and objectivity to otherwise self-serving decisions'. They add that, whatever the claim to scientific objectivity, invalid and unreliable judgements remain distinct possibilities, especially in instrument design: in factor selection, in enumerating the degrees of factor presence, in establishing weightings between factors, and in interpretation of job descriptions in relation to factors and factor levels.

Poststructuralist critics, such as Quaid (1993) and Townley (1994), suggest that such methods may be little more than sophisticated but self-serving management control devices in which quasi-scientific analytical procedures and technical discourse create false impressions of pay structure objectivity, justice and equity. Townley sees points factor job evaluation in terms of its role in reinforcing and legitimating power inequalities within organisations. According to Townley, quantitative job evaluation is a management technique more concerned with controlling employees than with establishing objectively fair pay structures; a 'disciplinary technique' that uses classification ('taxonomia') and quantification ('mathesis') to create divisions and hierarchy within a workforce. Townley argues that those critics who merely attack job evaluation for its apparent technical shortcomings or its illusory promise of pay equity miss a vital point about its *raison d'être*, which is that it is essentially a 'disciplinary practice' meant to compartmentalise job-holders and keep them in their place.

According to Quaid (1993), the elaborate terminology, techniques and rituals associated with an expert-driven job evaluation process like that of the Hay method are directed primarily to reconstructing employees' collective perception of organisational reality to make them internalise the belief that both the procedures and the outcomes are scientific, objective and fair. In this sense, suggests Quaid, the Hay method amounts to a 'rationalized institutional myth'. Drawing on her own experiences of the use of the Hay guide profile method in a Canadian provincial government organisation in the mid-1980s, Quaid contends that points scoring is shrouded in mystery and complexity that only the external 'expert' is capable of comprehending and that employee involvement programs and evaluation committee meetings are merely elaborate 'resocialisation' rituals. This cognitive conversion, she contends, is a three-stage process involving 'externalisation' (ritualised involvement), 'objectification' (acceptance of the accuracy of systematic quantification) and 'internalisation' (acceptance of the outcomes as a better and fairer 'reality').

Still other critics have raised the question of the method's role in work intensification and job enlargement (as opposed to enrichment), particularly where supervisory, quality control and decision-making tasks previously performed by middle managers have been devolved to teams but without proper sizing of the new responsibilities for factors like 'problem-solving' and 'job knowledge'. According to Kates and Tuttle (1996), scores for these job factors have been diluted as the factors themselves have devolved down the job hierarchy, leading to a combination of work intensification and job devaluation.

## Job evaluation and gender-related pay discrimination

We argued earlier that job rates in external labour markets reflect longstanding evaluative biases against the tasks, skills and responsibilities typically found in female-dominated occupations. Yet commentators are divided on whether formal job evaluation is more a help or a hindrance in addressing gender pay inequity. In theory at least, the method offers a means of redressing pre-existing gender pay inequities. Indeed, since the 1960s, the approach has been the centrepiece of the campaigns by feminists and the union movement for genuine pay equity between the sexes. Such advocates as England and Kilbourne (1991) argue that, providing proper care is taken to avoid gender bias intruding into the technique, quantitative job evaluation does have the potential to deliver pay equity between the sexes. Conversely, in practice evaluation has occasionally served to perpetuate gender-related pay disparities.

There are a number of ways in which gender discrimination and bias may intrude into the evaluation process, in both instrument design and administration. First, existing bias may be perpetuated by male-dominated and female-dominated jobs being evaluated separately and by means of distinct sets of compensable factors rather than on the basis of a common factor set. Second, factor identification may ignore skills found in female-dominated jobs. The classic example is the exclusion of 'soft' social and interpersonal skills as opposed to 'hard' technical skills. Third, job factors may be valued on gender stereotypical lines. For example, certain job skills may be undervalued because they are seen as inherently and innately 'female'. Fourth, degree statements and scores may exaggerate the value-adding importance of factors found in male-held positions while understating those in female-held jobs (Gupta & Jenkins 1991; Long 2006: 292–5; Lander & O'Neill 1991; Walker & Bowey 1989; Weiner 1991: 127–31). As such, it is possible that gender bias may compromise both the validity (i.e. job relevance and comprehensiveness) of a points-factor instrument and/or the reliability of points score determination.

Perhaps the most appropriate conclusion here is that while points factor job evaluation can never provide a totally objective or absolutely accurate way of valuing jobs, and while a poorly conceived and executed system of job evaluation can impair both internal equity and external competitiveness, carefully designed and properly administered and maintained, points-factor job evaluation still has much to offer, certainly in comparison with relying solely on market rates or impressionistic job ranking. As we shall see shortly, however, in practice a well-managed system of job-based pay requires simultaneous attention to both internal equity and external competitiveness considerations (Sibbald 1993). And of course, this is all predicated on the assumption that a position-based base pay structure is the most appropriate choice for the organisation concerned.

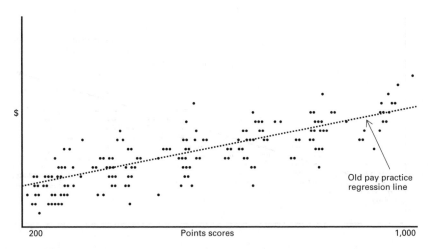

**Figure 11.5**  Developing job grades using points-factor scores: (1) Plotting point scores and existing pay practice line
*Source*: Adapted from Armstrong & Murlis 1998: 223–33.

## Developing a narrow-graded base pay structure

Having now weighed up the main evaluation techniques, we can proceed to consider how they may be applied to develop a position-based pay structure. Here we shall focus on working with points factor evaluation scores to develop a new narrow-graded structure. How do we get from numerical point scores indicating the relative 'size' of each job in the organisation to a job-based pay structure? There are six basic steps, and these can be best explained by means of the hypothetical examples in figures 11.5, 11.6 and 11.7.

As indicated in figure 11.5, the first step is to plot the evaluation scores against current rates of pay for each job using a scattergram. This gives an overview of the relationship between job size and what the organisation currently pays for each job. In this example, jobs have been scored on a points-factor scale ranging up to a maximum of 1,000 points.

The second step is to identify the current pay practice line. A trend line is drawn through the scattergram to produce a line indicating current pay practice. This can be done either by line of sight or, where a large number of job scores are involved, by means of linear regression analysis. The pay practice line may be straight or curved, depending on the nature of the correlation. Typically, the line is an upward sweeping curve. This is because

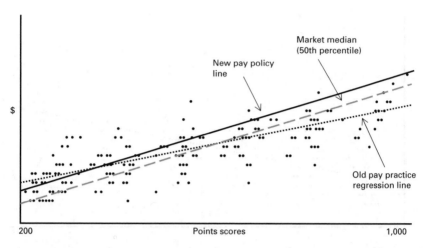

**Figure 11.6**  Developing job grades using points-factor scores: (2) Developing a new pay policy line
*Source*: adapted from Armstrong & Murlis 1998: 223–33.

pay rates for the most important jobs tend to be exponentially higher than for jobs of smaller size. In this example, however, the pay practice line is straight.

Step 3 (figure 11.6) involves deciding on a pay policy line. Using market survey data, a line indicating the median market rate for comparable jobs is superimposed on the pay practice line. The market pay line (or curve) sum-marises the market rates for the various jobs in question. The organisation then has to decide whether it is going to pay 'over' market, 'under' market or 'at' the market median – and a pay policy line is added on the basis of this decision. If the organisation decides to pay at the market median, the market rate line becomes the pay policy line. In this example, the organisation has been paying well above the market median for small-sized jobs but well below the market median for large jobs. Now, it takes the decision to pay 10 per cent above the market median for all jobs. Alternatively, the organ-isation could have decided to pay well over market for the most important jobs and well under for the least important ones. In that case, the pay policy line would intersect the market line and have a steeper slope.

The fourth step (figure 11.7) is determining the number of grades in the new structure and the boundaries between adjacent grades. In some cases, grade boundaries are set quite arbitrarily. For example, the organisation in our example might decide to have four evenly spaced grades. Given that the

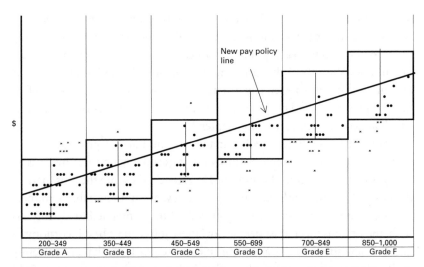

**Figure 11.7** Developing job grades using points-factor scores: (3) Establishing grade boundaries and pay ranges
*Source*: Adapted from Armstrong & Murlis 1998: 223–33.

range of scores is 1,000 less 200, or 800, this would mean that each grade would have a points range of 200, and the grade boundaries would be set accordingly. The width of each grade is measured in terms of a job points score range, in this case 200. The lowest grade would cover jobs with point scores between 200 and 400, the next jobs with point scores between 400 and 600, and so on. The problem with this approach is that it might well end up separating jobs of similar size into different grades.

A more acceptable approach is to identify natural clusters of jobs of the sort revealed by the point score scattergram in our example. This can be undertaken either by simple observation or by means of formal statistical analysis. In this example, six grades are established on the basis of natural clustering. Of course, if no clustering is evident, then determining grade numbers and boundaries will necessarily have to be arbitrary.

The fifth step is determining the pay range for each grade (figure 11.7). This involves establishing range midpoints and range spreads (minima and maxima). The range midpoint – the reference point for each range – is normally the point at which the score range for each grade intersects with the pay policy line. As we saw in the previous chapter, the midpoint usually corresponds to the rate of pay appropriate for a competent employee performing the job at a satisfactory level. Once the basic grade structure is finalised, the organisation needs to establish mechanisms for regulating progression through each grade. As noted in the previous chapter, many organisations use the 'split-range' approach, with the midpoint serving as the cut-over point between pay progression based on job learning and further progression based on performance-related merit raises or increments, which are considered further in chapter 15.

The sixth and final step involves managing anomalies in grade placement (figure 11.7). In this example, a number of jobs (now symbolised by crosses) fall outside the new grade boundaries. In essence, these are the jobs that, on the basis of the organisation's new pay policy, are not equitably remunerated – precisely the positions that job evaluation is intended to identify. As such, the organisation must decide how these jobs can be best incorporated into the new structure. As a general rule, those positions that are currently under-remunerated compared to other jobs in the same size range should have their base pay rate increased to the relevant grade range minimum. In this example, this would entail upward adjustment in the base pay for a total of thirty-three jobs: three to the grade B minimum, five to the grade C minimum rate, seven to the grade D minimum, ten to the grade E minimum, and eight to the grade E minimum. Those jobs that are over-remunerated relative to size pose rather more of a dilemma. One option would be to require the job-holders concerned to take a cut in base pay but, as equity theory predicts, such a move may prove counter-productive. A more circumspect option, especially where there is some buffer in the payroll budget, is to 'red circle' these positions, which means holding pay at the current level until they are absorbed into the relevant grade through general upward movement of the grade structure arising from, say, inflation adjustment, recalibration with external market rate shifts or across-the-board collective bargaining increases. In the example given, the jobs affected are chiefly those that need to be managed over time into grade A, the lowest grade. Of course, the reasons for any pay freeze must be justified in full to the job-holders concerned.

## Chapter summary

We began this chapter with a comparison of the market survey and job evaluation approaches to pricing jobs – two approaches that are frequently represented as antithetical means of determining base pay levels. It is appropriate that we conclude this chapter, however, by reiterating an important message conveyed in the above example, and this is that, far from being opposing approaches, market surveys and job evaluation in practice should and must work in tandem in the building of position-based pay structures that are simultaneously externally competitive and internally equitable. This appears to be what Heneman and LeBlanc (2003), Bowers (2003) and others have in mind in arguing for what they term a 'work valuation' approach, which, as Heneman and LeBlanc (2003: 9) put it, 'involves placing a value on jobs based on both internal and external considerations': 'Job evaluation and market pricing can actually complement one another. The right job evaluation system will identify those roles that are worth more to the enterprise. Once this is done, market pricing can be effectively used to peg the job higher or lower than the competition, reflecting performance challenges and other relevant factors.'

Notwithstanding their respective shortcomings, and despite the appeal of the person-based alternative to base pay configuration, *both* job evaluation and market surveys remain central features of remuneration practice in most developed countries. Moreover, despite the chorus of criticism and recurrent suggestions of its imminent demise, systematic job evaluation does indeed appear to be 'here to stay' (Hilling 2003).

## Discussion questions

1 What are the dangers in 'pricing jobs to market'?
2 What is more important in setting pay levels, internal equity or external competitiveness? Why?
3 'Points-factor job evaluation is just a pseudo-scientific means of legitimising pay inequality.' Discuss.
4 When it comes to gender-based pay equity, is it more accurate to say that job evaluation is part of the solution or part of the problem?
5 Is job evaluation an outdated reward practice? If not, why? If so, what should take its place?

Chapter Twelve

# DEVELOPING PERSON-BASED BASE PAY SYSTEMS

As we have seen, configuring base pay structures and pay progression according to the capabilities of the person holding the position rather than on the basis of the attributes of the position held represents a very different way of managing employees' base pay. Having considered the main tenets of the person-based approach, and the general characteristics, advantages and disadvantages of the two person-based options, namely skill- and competency-based or -related pay, in this chapter we examine the steps and design challenges associated with the development, implementation and administration, first, of skill-based systems and, second, of competency-based or -related systems. Since the processes of competency analysis and assessment have already been addressed in detail in chapter 7, in the present chapter our treatment of these aspects of competency-based and competency-related pay systems is necessarily brief.

## Developing a skill-based pay system

As noted in chapter 10, a skill-based pay system is one in which the base pay structure generally takes the form of broad grades, with in-grade pay level and progression being linked to the acquisition of desired 'hard' technical knowledge and manual skills and the formal assessment of individual employees' knowledge and skill learning and proficiency. Skill-based pay progression in broad grades is analogous to development-based pay increments up to grade midpoint in narrow-graded systems (discussed in chapter 11), except that skill learning covers the full range of skills covered by the job family rather than just one job, and the range of development-related pay is substantially greater.

Establishing a skill-based base pay system typically involves five main steps:

1  determining which employees are to be covered
2  conducting a skills analysis of the jobs or roles selected for coverage
3  configuring the skills identified into learning modules known as 'skill sets' and providing training in module content
4  pricing specific skills and skill sets, and
5  assessing, accrediting and rewarding individuals for the skills they have acquired.

## 1 Determining coverage

As we have seen, skill-based pay is particularly well suited to multiskilled teamwork and continuous process operations where there is high task inter-dependence. It is unlikely, however, that an organisation with these char-acteristics will want to extend skill-based pay to all employees. The most common roles likely to be considered for coverage are production line work-ers, skilled tradespersons and administrative or clerical workers. For man-agerial and professional employees, the competencies approach is likely to be a more appropriate choice for a person-based system.

## 2 Conducting a skills analysis of jobs

Skills analysis is concerned with identifying distinct skills embedded in whole jobs and regrouping these skills into meaningful, logical constellations of skills that can be packaged into distinct skill sets. Skills analysis is really a person-focused adaptation of job analysis and involves similar analytical techniques. Typically, information on skill needs is obtained by questioning employees and their supervisors about what specific skills are required to perform their work. As with job analysis and job evaluation, what has to be established is the nature of the technical requirements of the work – or, more accurately in this case, the desired technical capabilities of the worker – that are considered 'value-adding' for the organisation. As with job analysis, employees selected to participate in skills analysis are sometimes known as 'subject matter experts'.

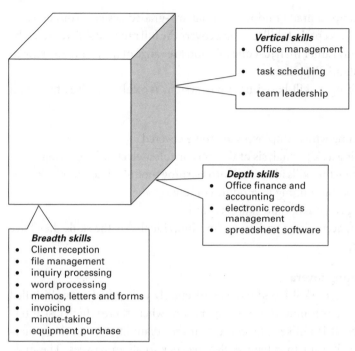

**Figure 12.1** Skills analysis: skill dimensions for an administrative support role
*Source*: adapted from O'Neill & Lander 1993–94: 20.

In undertaking skills analysis, it is important to remember that skill and skill development is a multidimensional phenomenon. Learnable skills may be thought of as having three dimensions: (1) breadth skills, (2) depth skills and (3) vertical skills (Jenkins et al. 1992: 22–4; Martocchio 2006: 175; O'Neill & Lander 1993–94: 18). Multiskilling involves the acquisition of additional skills on one or more of these three dimensions, and a skill-based pay structure will naturally emphasise one or more of these three learning dimensions. Figure 12.1 illustrates the nature of the relationship between breadth, depth and vertical skills that may be required in an administrative support role.

Breadth skills are task-specific skills associated with the one broad position or role. For instance, an administrative support employee might be trained to perform a range of communication, account-keeping, document production and record-keeping tasks: directing external inquiries; client reception; directing incoming correspondence, phone calls and emails;

advising staff on forms, procedures and information sources; issuing invoices, maintaining petty cash and paying small monthly accounts; word-processing; minute-taking; maintaining office equipment inventories, daily attendance and leave records, and the like. An administration support worker might extend her breadth skills by learning minute-taking. This is skill extension within the one broad role. It is the developmental dimension to which the term 'multiskilling' is most commonly applied, although the addition of extra breadth skills alone is perhaps more accurately described as 'multitasking'.

Depth skills are associated with the degree of skilled expertise that each employee brings to his or her particular position. It is also known as specialist skill. For instance, our administrative support worker might undertake formal training in accounting or computerised records management.

Vertical skills are those traditionally associated with supervisory and line management functions, work scheduling, coordination, control, decision-making and the like. This dimension is emphasised in self-managed team-working, since team members need to learn how to be self-managing and to be problem-solvers. To illustrate: our administrative support person may embark on training programs in advanced office management, work scheduling or team leadership.

### 3 Configuring skill sets and providing training in skill set content

Once the main breadth, depth and vertical skills in eligible work roles have been identified, these can be packaged into bundles of related knowledge and manual skill elements that, in turn, may be learned as distinct skill sets. A skill set (sometimes termed skill 'blocks' or 'units') consists of a bundle of related tasks and activities – or 'skill elements' – the mastery of which constitutes a finite and verifiable unit of learning on which training content can be developed and delivered (O'Neill & Lander 1993–94). Each skill set becomes a training module that must be completed successfully to warrant a further increase in the amount of base pay.

How many skill sets should there be? A typical US skill-pay plan of the early 1990s involved ten skill sets, each with an average learning time of twenty weeks and a combined learning time of around three years (Jenkins et al. 1992). The aim is to make the elements in each set challenging enough for employees not to progress too quickly through the sets and 'top out'. By the same token, the skill sets should not be so demanding that few workers get past first base. In the USA in the early 1990s, the average employee mastered about two-thirds of the available skill sets and did so in about two years (Jenkins et al. 1992: 25), which suggests that most participating employees at that time were either limiting their skill development relative to training opportunity or were limited in some way in pursuing further training.

Skill set systems come in a range of shapes and sizes; some are simple, others are complex. In some systems, the learning content and process are fully prescribed or 'sequenced'. In these sequential systems, skill sets are configured in cumulative and increasingly challenging learning steps, and each successive set builds on the previous one. Lower skill sets are prerequisites for those higher in the sequence; the former typically focusing on developing breadth skills and the latter on depth and vertical skills. For this reason, such models are sometimes referred to as 'stair-step' systems.

In the example of a sequential structure provided in figure 12.2, the three skill sets for the administrative support role are cumulative, with set 1 – the entry set – comprising basic breadth skills, set 2 comprising a combination breadth and depth skills relating to team-based office management, and set 3 consisting of quasi-managerial vertical skills. As each skill set is mastered, the employee's position in the administrative support broad grade also increases in a step-wise way: in the example, from an entry point level of $30,000 to $35,000 when set 1 is completed, to $41,000 when set 2 is completed, and to $48,000 when set 3, the most challenging set, is mastered. Failure to complete any step in the sequence means that further skill-based pay progression is suspended until certification in the relevant skill set is achieved. Stair-step models of this type generally apply to specific job families, so the organisation using skill pay would normally have a separate stair-step model for each of its job families.

The North American communications and information technology firm Nortel (previously Northern Telecom) introduced a system similar to this for its US field service technicians in the 1980s (before taking up broadbanding). This involved four skill sets arranged in a hierarchy of difficulty, from associate field technician through field test technician and field system technician to field system specialist. An employee could move from one set to the next, receiving an increase in base pay for each set accomplished. Within each set, skills were designated as either 'mandatory' or 'elective', and certification required that all mandatory skills and a certain number of elective skills had to be acquired before the employee advanced to the

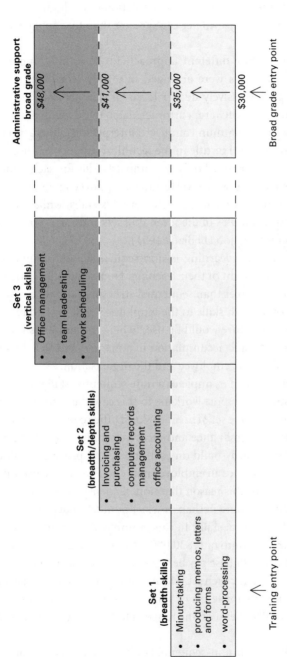

**Figure 12.2** Sequential skill-based pay progression in a broad-graded structure: a 'stair-step' model for an administrative support role

*Source*: adapted from Martocchio 2006: 183, 186.

Within the figure:

**Administrative support broad grade**

$48,000

$41,000

$35,000

$30,000

Broad grade entry point

**Set 3 (vertical skills)**
- Office management
- team leadership
- work scheduling

**Set 2 (breadth/depth skills)**
- Invoicing and purchasing
- computer records management
- office accounting

**Set 1 (breadth skills)**
- Minute-taking
- producing memos, letters and forms
- word-processing

Training entry point

next set. Completion of each set brought an increase in base pay. The higher the set, the higher the pay increment. Completion of the highest set yielded a potential base pay increase 40 per cent greater than that applicable to the lowest set.

Nortel used a slightly different approach for technical support engineers. For this role, skills were arranged into four sequential sets, with each set covering progressively deeper levels of skill across seven key job dimensions: hardware, software, customer database, documentation, network interface, written communication and interpersonal interaction. Each set corresponded to a level or title in the technical support engineering job family. The lowest set included only the simplest skills for each dimension and corresponded to the lowest-level technical support engineering job, and the second set included somewhat more complex skills, while the highest set covered the most complex of the seven skill sets and corresponded to the highest-level engineering job (LeBlanc 1991).

In other systems, skill learning is non-sequential, and employees can choose the order and extent of their learning. Non-sequential structures of this type tend to be simpler than sequential structures and to focus mainly on the addition of breadth skills to the employee's skill repertoire. A non-sequential skill set structure would be used where the emphasis is on task-widening and breadth skill accumulation in a manner and to a degree that is mutually suitable to the employee and the organisation.

Figure 12.3 provides an example of a non-sequential skill set configuration for administrative support workers. In this case there are four possible skill sets, each covering one set of breadth skills: office communication, document production, office finance and record-keeping. Note that the skills involved do not necessarily build on each other, and progression does not have to be sequential. Hence an employee may choose to learn just one set or more than one. It is for this reason that non-sequential structures typically emphasise breadth skills and perhaps a select number of depth skills, rather than 'higher-order' vertical skills. In this example, the employee enters the broad grade at the minimum rate, $30,000, and may take any combination of sets in any sequence, with base pay being increased for each set mastered, in this instance, by $2,500 for each set. More sophisticated systems may involve payment of increments for levels of skill achievement within a given skill set, although this will depend on the range of tasks and activities covered by each set.

An example of a simple non-sequential skill sets system is that introduced by US food and beverage manufacturer General Mills at one of its fruit juice

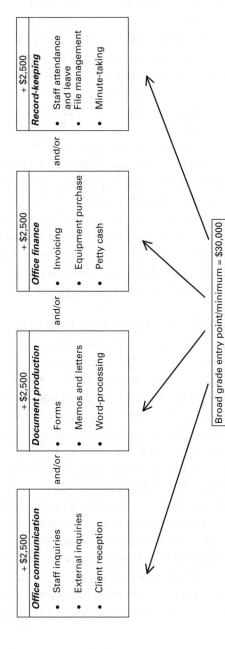

| Office communication | and/or | Document production | and/or | Office finance | and/or | Record-keeping |
|---|---|---|---|---|---|---|
| + $2,500 | | + $2,500 | | + $2,500 | | + $2,500 |
| • Staff inquiries<br>• External inquiries<br>• Client reception | | • Forms<br>• Memos and letters<br>• Word-processing | | • Invoicing<br>• Equipment purchase<br>• Petty cash | | • Staff attendance and leave<br>• File management<br>• Minute-taking |

Broad grade entry point/minimum = $30,000

**Figure 12.3** Non-sequential skill-based pay progression in a broad-graded structure: breadth skill sets for an administrative support role

plants in 1988. A skill set was configured for each of the four main steps in the plant's production process, namely 'materials', 'mixing', 'filling' and 'packaging'. Within each set there were three recognised skill levels: level 1 covered limited ability; level 2, partial proficiency; and level 3 full proficiency in the area. Employees received a base pay increase for each level completed, and all levels were considered of equal value in both training time and pay. A new employee could be assigned to any skill set and either complete all three levels in that set or move to another set after mastering two levels within the original set, although only when an opening became available in the new area. Employees unable to achieve at least level 2 in each set were subject to dismissal (Ledford & Bergel 1991).

A variation on the non-sequential approach is the skill points accrual model. This allows employees to move beyond the one job family: to move between roles within the organisation and to accrue skill points for each new skill mastered. In such schemes, the skill modules are less job-specific and tend to be defined in terms of strategic goals. So, for instance, there might be a skill module for 'customer relations' with a range of possible points being assigned to it according to its relative strategic importance and the depth of skill acquired and utilised. The more points the employee accrues, the higher the level of strategic skills and, hence, pay will be (Martocchio 2006: 185–6).

No system of skill-based pay will function effectively in the absence of appropriate and accessible training opportunities, and these are typically made available to employees either in-house or through a suitably qualified external training and development provider. As noted in chapter 9, where skill-based pay is introduced in the absence of adequate and accessible training, the consequences for the organisation and the employees concerned may be disastrous. The choice of training methods should reflect the learning content. Training methods are generally of three main types: presentational methods, hands-on methods and group learning methods. Many training regimens combine all three approaches.

Whatever the method or methods used, it is critical to ensure that eligible employees are motivated to participate in training and adequately prepared and resourced to do so. For instance, training exposure will have little positive impact on employees lacking basic literacy and cognitive skills. Equally, whatever the monetary incentive to succeed in training, effective learning requires the existence of a positive learning environment; one in which learning objectives are made clear, where training content is directly meaningful to participants and their current work, where participants receive frequent feedback on learning and where they have ample opportunity to put their learning into practice. A vital requirement for any viable skill-base pay system, then, is an effective training program. This necessarily requires careful design, implementation and maintenance, which in turn requires considerable investment of time and money. Skill-based pay is not a low-cost option.

The evidence also suggests a strong link between employee involvement in system design and administration, including skill analysis and certification, and overall satisfaction with the system itself. For example, in the case of the General Mills systems, staff attitude surveys indicated substantial employee approval of and satisfaction with the system. In both of the plants involved, employees undertook most of the design work themselves, receiving only general guidance from management and outside consultants. According to Ledford and Bergel (1991: 38), 'There is no doubt that the high level of support for PFS [Pay For Skill] at these facilities results partly from employee involvement. Employees see it as their plan to a large degree.'

### 4 Pricing skills and skill sets

How should personal skills be priced? This is potentially problematic because it is not possible to obtain accurate market prices for disembodied skills. External market rates provide only an approximate guide to pricing since they generally relate to whole jobs rather than specific skills (Schuster & Zingheim 1996: 100–4). Comparing external market rates may also be misleading, especially where skills are firm-specific.

For these reasons, it is generally the overall pay structure, rather than each particular skill or skill set, that is priced on the basis of external market rates. The simplest approach here is known as the 'high–low' method. This involves taking the market rate for the 'entry-level' job family position and the market rate for the most complex job and using the dollar difference between the two to set the overall pay range for the job family broad grade. In-grade pay increments can then be assigned to each skill set according to the number of sets involved and the degree of learning challenge associated with each set. This, of course, is hardly an exact science, but care should be taken to ensure that difficult-to-learn sets are not undervalued relative to more easily mastered sets.

Another method of skill pricing is to set the base pay increment for each skill set according to the learning time required, with a dollar value being attached to each hour or day of necessary learning time.

A more 'scientific' approach would be to pool market and skill content data on a large number of relevant positions, then use statistical analysis (such as factor analysis) to identify the monetary contribution that each skill element makes to the going rate for whole jobs. The values relating to the skill elements present in each skill set would then be summed to give an overall value for the set. However, analysis of this type will require a large number of job price observations as well as comprehensive and accurate detail on the skill content of each job in the data pool, and a database of this magnitude will be beyond the reach of most organisations.

So how is skill pricing undertaken in practice? In the USA in the early 1990s, around half of plans used 'relative worth' or skill set 'size' as the pricing criteria, while about 20 per cent used learning time. However, only 13 per cent used market value as the main skill pricing criterion (Jenkins et al. 1992: 29). This means that typical skill plans of that time tended to emphasise internal rather than external pricing criteria. While an internal focus may result in more positive distributive justice and pay equity perceptions, it also creates the danger of a firm positioning its skill pay ranges far above or far below the market medians for comparable jobs, with all of the attendant hiring and cost consequences that this may bring.

### 5 Skill assessment, accreditation and reward

An effective skill-based system, of course, also requires the implementation and maintenance of a valid and reliable program for assessing and accrediting individual learners for skills acquired. This means introducing assessment and accreditation for all employees covered by the system. This may be undertaken either 'on demand' or at regular intervals. In some schemes all employees must be reaccredited annually.

The mode of assessment and accreditation will vary according to the nature of the skills involved. In the case of breadth skills, assessment might take the form of work observation, work samples and other practical tests involving detailed task proficiency checklists. In the case of depth skills, it may be necessary to ascertain the depth of expertise attained by using written or oral examinations. In some skill-based systems, assessment is continuous, with employees' learning being subject to regular, on-going review. For vertical (quasi-managerial) skills, testing may involve written examinations, simulation exercises, assessment centre exercises and perhaps attitudinal and psychometric assessment. Depending on how the skill sets are configured and on the frequency of task rotation, it may be necessary to retest employees for proficiency in some or all skills. Annual or biannual performance assessment also represents a systematic means of both measuring and monitoring performance outcomes from training and development programs and of identifying knowledge and skill deficits requiring rectification (see chapter 8).

Who should do the assessing? One option is to use internal assessors from the organisation's human resources department; another would be to employ external training consultants. However, skills assessment also offers much scope for employee involvement, since peers will have considerable knowledge of task proficiency requirements and standards. In the skill-based pay system implemented in a US munitions manufacturing plant run by Honeywell in the late 1980s, annual accreditation was based on input from the team supervisor, a technical expert such as a production engineer, the team leader and peers (Ledford 1991a: 18; Ledford, Tyler & Dixey 1991: 68–70). However, it is important that peer assessors are not left open to the possibility of ostracism by fellow workers.

Of course, peer assessment raises the possibility that assessors may be overly lenient towards one another. US manufacturer General Mills came up with a novel solution to this problem. Where employees were found to be unable to perform tasks for which they had been peer accredited, both the assessee and the assessor were required to forfeit their next pay increase (Ledford & Bergel 1991: 31). The typical compromise approach is to appoint a joint management–employee accreditation committee. Such bodies may also be empowered to adjudicate appeals over withheld accreditation. Whatever assessment mode is used, it is also necessary to audit assessment outcomes to safeguard against unreliable assessment decisions.

As noted in chapter 9, a major administrative challenge with skill-based systems is the need to assess the skill profiles of all eligible employees at the outset. Unless proper planning is in place, the assessment system may simply be overwhelmed. To avoid such problems, it may be necessary to stagger the system's introduction or conduct initial assessments before the system's roll-out.

What happens if the initial assessment reveals that employees are overpaid or underpaid relative to their assessed skill levels? The challenge with overpayment is to find a means of aligning pay with skills in a way that does not demotivate. If pay is reduced, employees may be dissuaded from learning new skills, but they may also feel unfairly treated. It may be preferable to maintain the pre-existing level of pay and absorb any over-payment until upgrading of skills occurs.

## Developing competency-based and competency-related base pay systems

Whereas skill-based systems are typically configured on the basis of broad grades, in competency-based systems the defining structure is the broad band. As we have seen, broad bands commonly involve pay ranges several times wider than that of a typical broad grade, while in-band pay progression may be based on competency assessment alone or, alternatively, on a combination of assessed personal competencies and individual performance. Although progression of the former type is 'competency-based', the latter is best described as 'competency-related'. Either way, the challenges of competency analysis, definition, pricing and assessment are no less exacting – and arguably more demanding – than are the comparable system development challenges in position- and skill-based systems.

Developing a competency-based or related pay system involves four main steps:

1 competency analysis
2 configuring competency broad bands and pricing competency zones
3 assessing the competency profiles of each eligible employee on a regular basis.
4 determining each employee's zone position and pay progression.

### 1 Competency analysis

Even more so than with skill-pay, an organisation contemplating a move to competency pay and broad-banding must undertake the necessary groundwork before initiating system change. As noted in chapter 10, broad-banding represents a radical shift in reward principles and practice, as does competency-based performance management and reward. Accordingly, all relevant stakeholders, but particularly those likely to be most affected (line managers, professional employees and line employees) should be fully consulted beforehand as to the purpose and nature of system change – and the process of competency analysis affords ample scope for this. Like job evaluation and skills analysis, competency analysis provides considerable scope for employee involvement, both as 'subject matter experts' and as co-designers. The techniques associated with competency analysis, such as behaviour event interviewing, necessarily require detailed input from employees. Moreover, a shift to broad-banding will certainly increase the need for consultation with, training of and communication with employees. Competency-related broad-banding is likely to function effectively only in a culture of high trust and open communication. In short, competencies and broad-banding are not suitable options for organisations that persist in seeking to manage staff along traditional low-involvement lines – and there is some evidence that this was a contributing factor to the negative outcomes from some of the initial experiments with banding in the 1990s.

As discussed in chapter 7, competency analysis involves ascertaining which personal attributes and attitudes set superior performers apart from average performers, then incorporating these criteria in competency assessment and development programs. The techniques and processes involved in competency analysis are covered in depth in chapter 7. You will recall that the two chief competency categories identified in chapter 7 were 'core' competencies and 'role' competencies. To reiterate: core competencies are the essential organisation-wide competencies that the organisation believes all of its employees should possess in order to make them effective and committed performers. Differentiating role competencies are those personal attributes that are most closely associated with high task performance in any given position or role. Competency-based or related pay systems typically recognise both core competencies and differentiating role competencies.

## 2 Configuring competency broad bands and pricing competency zones

Competency zones are to broad-banded pay structures what skill sets are to broad grades; they constitute both the stepping stones and the control points of base pay progression. Competency zones thus provide the internal architecture for competency-based and competency-related broad bands.

As noted in chapter 7, competency-based assessment instruments commonly recognise between three and five levels of competency development in any given role. The descriptors attached to these levels typically seek to capture the essence of each particular level. For example, the descriptor sequence applied in a five-level system might be 'minimal', 'developing', 'proficient', 'advanced' and 'shaping'; and the descriptor sequence for a three-level system might be 'developing', 'applying' and 'shaping'. These level criteria constitute the standard for assessing competency levels on each core and role competency included in the assessment instrument. They also provide the categories for an overall assessment across all competency dimensions. Where competency assessment is linked to competency-based or -related pay, the competency levels are commonly transposed directly on to each broad band, so determining automatically both the number of zones within the broad band and the zone descriptors. Each competency zone then becomes the target placement position for employees consistently assessed as having that overall level of competency (Tucker & Cofsky 1994). So, for instance, an individual whose summative assessments consistently put her at the 'applying' level in overall terms would be placed in the 'applying' zone of her role broad band rather than in a higher or lower zone.

Determining a pay range for each broad band, and for each of its constituent competency zones, is even more challenging than the pricing of skill sets since personal competencies are still further removed from the job-based rates that prevail in external labour markets. As with skill-based pay, the simplest pricing method is the 'high/low' approach. Again, this involves using market rates (or pre-existing internal rates) for benchmark jobs and roles covered by the relevant competency band to establish maxima and minima for each band. The band is then segmented into the requisite number of 'zones', each with its own pay range. Although evidence on organisational practice in this regard is limited, the 'high/low' method appears to be among the most commonly used competency evaluation methods.

Returning to the theme of employee communication and involvement, the nature and logic of band configuration must be communicated to eligible employees well in advance of system implementation. In particular, the reasons for allocating positions and position-holders to one band rather than another must be fully disclosed. The basis of the band structure, particularly the nature of zones and zone pay ranges, should be communicated fully and openly to all employees to minimise any uncertainty surrounding the change. To lessen the possibility of damage to the psychological contract, and especially of erosion of distributive justice perceptions, employees should be fully informed in advance as to how their pay will be determined in the new structure and, most importantly, how their base pay will progress (Hofrichter 1993).

### 3 Competency assessment

Again, since the process of competency assessment has been covered in detail in chapter 7, it is not necessary for us to revisit this matter in any depth here. However, given the subjective nature of this process, it is appropriate to reiterate the need to maximise reliability and felt-fairness in the assessment process. In essence, this requires an assessment instrument that minimises error and unreliability, comprehensive prior training in assessment criteria and procedures, and application and review procedures that are accepted and well understood by assessors and assessees alike (Klein 1996).

Where the organisation has a pre-existing competency-based performance management system, the information required for initial band and zone placement should be already available, at least for existing employees. However, where competency assessment and broad-banding are being introduced simultaneously, it will be necessarily to conduct initial competency profiling for all eligible employees. Since each employee's financial fate and attitude to the new system hinges on the outcomes from this first round of profiling, it is crucial that the process is well resourced and not undertaken in haste.

### 4 Positioning each employee in a band and zone

Existing employees are assessed against the competencies applicable to their work role, assigned to the appropriate role broad band, and placed in the band zone most applicable to their overall competency level. Positioning new recruits poses an additional challenge, since the organisation will not yet have competency or performance data consistent with that used to place other employees. One solution here would be to conduct psychometric core competency assessments of all new hires, the results of which are then used to determine an initial zone placement. This would then be subject to formal review after new staff members undertake their first full competency assessment.

With competency banding, pay increments are not automatic and progression to the upper zones is not guaranteed. In fact, both in-zone and between-zone progression becomes increasingly difficult as competency requirements become more demanding. Where each employee is initially positioned within a zone pay range and how their pay subsequently progresses within and between zones will, of course, depend on the specifics of the banded structure. The key distinction here is between a system that is competency-*based* and one that is competency-*related*. The operational differences between these two approaches are best indicated by means of examples.

Figure 12.4 illustrates the workings of a purely competency-based plan. In this case, the employee's band and zone position is determined by a

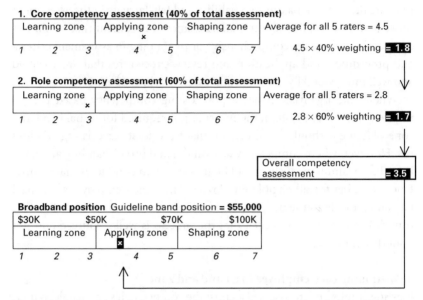

**Figure 12.4** Competency-*based* pay progression in a broad-banded structure
*Source*: adapted from Rahbar-Daniels 2002: 79.

combination of core and role competency multisource assessments on a seven-point rating scale, with the two competency categories weighted at 40 per cent and 60 per cent respectively. The broad band itself has a pay range of $30,000 to $100,000 and is segmented into three zones: learning ($30,000–$49,999), applying ($50,000–$69,999) and shaping ($70,000–$100,000). The weighted total score determines both the zone placement and the specific base pay amount. A total score of from 1 to 3 equates to a learning competency profile; a score of from 3 to 5 to an applying profile; and a score of 5 to 7 to the shaping profile. In this example, the multisource competency assessment involves five assessors – the supervisor, two peers and, for managers, two subordinates – with the assessor scores being averaged to give composite scores for each of the two competency categories. In this case, the average score for core competencies is 4.5, which translates to a weighted score of 1.8. Similarly the average score for role competencies is 2.8, which converts to a weighted score of 1.7. These two scores sum to a total score of 3.5, a score in the lower range of the applying profile. This in turn translates to placement in the median (applying) zone and to a specific pay level of $55,000, a quarter of the way along the relevant zone pay range (i.e. a zone penetration of 25 per cent and a band penetration of 36 per cent).

This example of a purely competency-based pay plan has two other note-worthy design features. Most importantly, it is not only the periodic adjustment to base pay amount that is determined by competency assessment but also the individual's absolute base pay level. Hence, any decline in the overall competency profile score will result in a reduction in total base pay. System efficacy and felt-fairness is thus crucially dependent on the maintenance of a valid and reliable regimen of regular competency profiling. Second, the broad bands in such a system have few if any internal cost control points, which means that the system is vulnerable to payroll cost blow-out in the event that competency assessments are contaminated by, say, leniency error.

A further example of a competency-based plan is that introduced by British pharmaceutical firm Glaxo Wellcome (now GlaxoSmithKline) in the 1990s. Figure 12.5 provides a diagrammatic representation of the original system. There were five overlapping broad bands (A and B for executives, C for directors and managers, D for professional and technical staff, and E for administrative staff), with individual roles being slotted into the appropriate band by comparing the competency profile with the profiles for the bands. Competency assessment was configured around twenty core competencies in five major categories:

1 personal qualities
2 planning to achieve
3 business and customer focus
4 supportive leadership
5 working with others.

Not all of the twenty core competencies were used for remuneration purposes. Those that were not – called 'unidimensional competencies' – were monitored solely for developmental purposes. These include all six competencies in the personal qualities category and the competencies for teamworking and giving feedback. The remainder, however, were used for pay purposes, with each having between three and five 'dimensions' or levels (Stredwick 1997). Much was made of this firm's innovative approach when it was first introduced. Yet several of the system's main design features, including the absence of internal control points, proved problematic, and the firm's successor, GlaxoSmithKline, has subsequently introduced more structure into the system, including increasing the numbers of zones and incorporating grades into the band and zone architecture. For example, in the administrative band (band E) there are five zones and a total of thirty-nine grades (Armstrong & Brown 2005: 48).

As we have seen, another potential shortcoming of competencies models generally is the assumption that competencies equal performance. Clearly, this is a dangerous premise on which to operate. Recognising this, many organisations that do see merit in applying the competencies construct to pay practice have opted for base pay systems that are competency-related rather than wholly competency-based.

Figure 12.6 details a simple competency-related system in which overall competency assessment determines which of the three band zones (learning, applying, shaping) an employee is assigned to, but where in-zone position and in-zone pay progression are determined by a combination of competency assessment and results-based performance grading (each on a 1–5 scoring scale). In this case, the criteria for scoring competencies in any given zone are adapted to the overall competency standard for that zone and will thus vary from zone to zone. Once scores are determined for competency profile and performance outcomes, these are then combined using the pay progression matrix for the zone to which the employee is currently assigned to give an annual pay adjustment figure, which is then added to the employee's pre-existing base pay figure. For instance, an employee in zone 1 who achieves a learning zone competency score of 4 and a performance score of 3 receives a base pay increase of $1,000, whereas an employee receiving scores of 5 and 5 receives $3,000.

Note, too, that in this example neither a high performance score nor a high competency score will by itself deliver a substantial increase. What is important here is, first, how well employees have developed their competency profile relative to the standards for the zone, and, second, how effectively they have applied the competencies they have at their disposal to produce desired outcomes. Logically, if the organisation finds that many employees are scoring high on performance but low on competency levels, it should check the validity and reliability of both sets of measurement criteria.

This example also serves to highlight another major design consideration common to all of the base pay options that we have now explored, namely what should be the nature of the relationship between base pay and pay for performance. In competency-related systems of the type just described, the traditional distinction between these two key components of total remuneration is essentially removed. By itself, this is not necessarily an undesirable outcome. However, by conflating the two, there is a risk that the distinct

*Core competency profile chart*

| Core competency | Competency descriptor | Dimension or level | | | | |
|---|---|---|---|---|---|---|
| Personal qualities | 1. Personal accounting | Unidimensional | | | | |
| | 2. Personal organisation | Unidimensional | | | | |
| | 3. Staff development | Unidimensional | | | | |
| | 4. Creativity and innovation | Unidimensional | | | | |
| | 5. Flexibility | Unidimensional | | | | |
| | 6. Continuous improvement | Unidimensional | | | | |
| Planning to achieve | 7. Gathering, analysing and interpreting data | 1 | 2 | 3 | 4 | 5 |
| | 8. Problem-solving and decision-making | 1 | 2 | 3 | 4 | |
| | 9. Establishing a plan | 1 | 2 | 3 | 4 | |
| | 10. Implementing and monitoring achievement | 1 | 2 | 3 | 4 | |
| Business and customer focus | 11. Company environment | 1 | 2 | 3 | 4 | |
| | 12. Business environment | 1 | 2 | 3 | 4 | |
| | 13. Customer focus | 1 | 2 | 3 | 4 | |
| Supportive leadership | 14. Effective leadership | 1 | 2 | 3 | 4 | |
| | 15. Empowering | 1 | 2 | 3 | 4 | |
| | 16. Teamworking, being supportive | Unidimensional | | | | |
| Working with others | 17. Developing colleagues | 1 | 2 | 3 | 4 | |
| | 18. Giving and receiving feedback | Unidimensional | | | | |
| | 19. Networking and building relationships | 1 | 2 | 3 | 4 | |
| | 20. Communication | 1 | 2 | 3 | | |

$\longrightarrow$

$

**Figure 12.5** Competency-based pay at Glaxo Wellcome
*Source*: adapted from Stredwick 1997: 36.

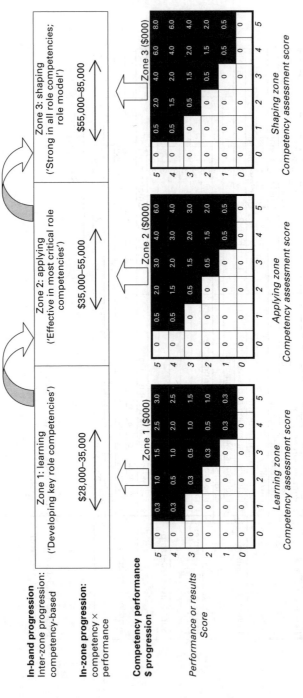

**Figure 12.6** Competency-related pay progression in a broad-banded structure

*Source:* adapted from Rahbar-Daniels 2002: 73.

'messages' customarily associated with each component will be confused or lost. Such a possibility should be an abiding concern of total reward management, irrespective of which component happens to the main focus of attention in the short term.

## Chapter summary

In this chapter, which completes our coverage of options for building base pay, we have detailed the steps and design challenges associated with the development, implementation and administration, first, of skill-based systems and, second, of competency-based or related systems. As we have seen, each of these two person-based approaches has promise and potential pitfalls. Broad-graded skill pay offers line employees multiskilling and skill-based career progression, but it is resource intensive, expensive and vulnerable to 'topping out' and to skill redundancy. Broad-banded competency pay promises high reward for high capability irrespective of seniority or status, but it is also expensive and poses particular problems in terms of managing pay progression, upholding internal equity and establishing external competitiveness. Overall, as suggested in chapter 10, each approach is better suited to some circumstances than others. In general, person-based options are better suited to high-involvement cultures, with skill pay being particularly suitable for quality defender and analyser competitive strategies and competency pay being a better fit for organisations with a prospector strategy.

## Discussion questions

1 Why is skill-based pay such a good option for firms with a high-involvement culture?
2 Why is skill pay such an expensive reward option?
3 What should a firm do if it no longer needs the skills that it has been rewarding its employees for acquiring?
4 How should an organisation determine the number of bands that it should have in its broad-banded pay structure?
5 What are the dangers of determining pay progression by means of a combination of competency assessment and performance results?

Chapter Thirteen

# EMPLOYEE BENEFITS

The rise of the concept of 'total reward management', which was canvassed in chapter 1, owes a great deal to the growing importance of benefit plans in reward practice. Benefits are among the most variegated, complex and rapidly changing aspects of contemporary reward management practice. Because of their constantly evolving nature, benefits almost defy definition (Lengnick-Hall & Bereman 1994). Known originally as 'fringe benefits', today the term 'employee benefits' covers both 'indirect pay' – that is, financial rewards that do not take the form of direct cash payments, such as employer superannuation and health care fund contributions – and non-financial rewards, ranging from special unpaid leave provisions to the provision of wellness programs and advisory services. Rewards in the form of company shares also fall partly within the scope of benefits programs. As such, benefits are a remarkably heterogeneous phenomenon. Their nature and significance varies considerably from country to country, organisation to organisation, role to role and person to person.

Benefits were once the least glamorous of all aspects of reward management – and were literally referred to as 'fringe' reward practices – yet many organisations now consider them to be an important means of gaining a competitive advantage in labour markets where key 'talent' is in short supply. As the workforce becomes more diverse and as the level of employee education and reward expectation rises, financial and non-financial benefits are likely to assume an increasingly critical role in the reward management system's ability to attract, retain and motivate high-potential and high-performing employees.

In many developed countries, benefits now comprise a growing proportion of total remuneration costs. In the USA, benefit costs rose from 10 per cent to almost 30 per cent of total remuneration costs between the mid-1960s and the mid-1990s. In large Canadian firms, benefits comprised around 20 per cent of total remuneration costs in 2004 (Long 2006: 443). In Australia, benefit programs now typically absorb more than 30 per cent of total payroll expenditure (Stone 2005: 517), with benefits comprising between 10 and 20 per cent of the typical employee's total pre-tax remuneration, including a compulsory 9 per cent employer superannuation contribution. So the importance of benefits to cost-effective human resource management is undeniable.

At the same time, however, benefit plans pose a major strategic dilemma for many organisations. In part, this is because such plans occupy an uneasy middle ground between the two different types of the management-espoused psychological contract described in chapter 2, namely the 'relational' and 'transactional' forms; that is, between the priorities of traditional needs- and service-based people management over the long term, and the more recent imperative for strategically aligned human resource management with a short-term focus. Benefits, then, can be a strategic minefield. They may either support the strategic intent of other reward practices or fundamentally compromise the objectives of staff attraction, retention and motivation. For instance, benefits packages that privilege a person's length of service over their performance potential and contribution may inhibit organisational dynamism and competitive success.

Benefits may also be a double-edged sword when it comes to equal employment opportunity, anti-discrimination and associated principles. Benefits may uphold the objectives of diversity management, equal opportunity and affirmative action, or they may lead the organisation quite unwittingly into the dangerous waters of direct or indirect discrimination. This is because eligibility for certain benefits is frequently determined, albeit by default, by age, marital status, carer status, gender, state of health and the like. Moreover, packages with eligibility provisions configured according to a person's family responsibilities may not only be seen as discriminating against those without such responsibilities but may also make the organisation unattractive to younger employees.

Benefit plans, then, warrant our close consideration. Towards this end, this chapter opens with a brief examination of the general rationale of benefit plans and the factors that have served to elevate their importance in reward strategy and practice. Next we investigate the main benefit plan types, beginning with retirement or superannuation benefits, followed by health care and other forms of personal insurance, leave and carer benefits, miscellaneous financial benefits and other non-financial benefits, including the fast-growing areas of flexible work time, wellness programs and employee assistance programs. Finally, we consider the differences between fixed and flexible benefit plans and the factors that must be taken into consideration in choosing between the two.

## Benefit plans: purpose and drivers

Like other elements of the reward system, benefits can serve a variety of purposes. You will recall from chapter 1 that the three primary aims of any reward management system are: (1) to attract the right people at the right time for the right positions or roles; (2) to retain the best people by recognising and rewarding their contribution; and (3) to motivate employees to contribute to the best of their capability. Organisations generally provide benefit plans to employees with one or more of these objectives in mind.

As supplements to base pay, financial benefits may enhance the organisation's ability to attract and retain high-value employees. Such benefits may also have particular taxation advantages over straight cash payments. Provision of particular non-financial benefits also allows organisations to address specific employee needs in a more targeted manner. This, in turn, may reinforce membership behaviour (i.e. attraction, retention and attendance), enhance employee well-being, work–life balance, job satisfaction and organisational commitment, and, albeit indirectly, improve work motivation and performance (Williams & MacDermid 1994). The provision of targeted non-financial benefits, such as childcare facilities, may also support diversity management and equal opportunity. Finally, the provision of some benefits is a matter of legal compliance. For instance, in Australia, employers are obliged to provide superannuation contributions equivalent to at least 9 per cent of the employee's regular wage or salary, long-service leave and workers compensation coverage to all full-time and part-time permanent employees, as well as casual employees who are employed on a regular basis. Until recently, permanents were also entitled to four weeks paid annual leave with a special leave loading, parental leave and personal or carer's leave (Stone 2005: 51), although most paid leave entitlements can now be cashed out or otherwise bargained away. In Canada, mandatory benefits for permanent employees include paid annual leave, rest breaks, employment insurance and workers compensation (Long 2006: 425).

For all their rising importance, employee benefit plans are among the least well-researched aspects of contemporary reward practice. Today there is still only a handful of academic studies on employers' motives for offering more comprehensive benefit plans and on employees' attitudinal and behavioural outcomes (Barber, Dunham & Formisano 1992; Rabin 1994; Tremblay, Sire & Pelchat 1998; Williams 1995; Williams & MacDermid 1994). Nevertheless it is possible to identify a number of factors that have contributed to the growth in benefits in many Western countries.

Obviously, the growth in mandatory benefits is attributable to new or additional legislative requirements. In Australia, this certainly explains the extension of employer superannuation contributions to all permanent employees since the 1980s. Changes in taxation law have also been influential here. High marginal tax rates on regular cash remuneration have placed pressure on employers to allow employees to 'sacrifice' cash for a range of benefits: from subsidised health and dental care, school fees, personal education expenses, subsidised holiday travel and accommodation and gym fees, to additional employer superannuation contributions, concessional personal and housing loans, 'company cars', mobile phones and notebook computers. The introduction of 'fringe benefits tax' provisions in many Western countries in the 1980s and 1990s certainly reduced the tax advantages of such cash-substitution practices, at least for employers. For instance, under the fringe benefits tax that has applied in Australia since 1986, while the employee receives the benefit, the tax liability is levied on the employer at the top marginal rate of income tax. The employer is also prohibited from claiming the cost of fringe benefits as a deductible expense. The upshot is that the full value of any fringe benefit is routinely deducted from the employee's notional total remuneration. Under the Australian system, the only significant benefits that are exempt from fringe benefits tax are employee amenities, employee share plans, superannuation contributions, workers compensation, accident-related medical care and income protection, and occupational health and counselling (Stone 2005: 518).

A further factor underlying the growth in benefits has been pressure from trade unions. For instance, in recent decades, Australian unions have successfully sought improved benefit entitlements in the following areas: annual leave, sick leave, unpaid and paid maternity, long-service leave, annual leave loadings, payment of union fees, provision of uniforms and safety clothing, and non-contributory superannuation benefits (Stone 2005: 518).

Perhaps the more important factors behind the growth in benefits, however, are demographic and workplace changes. The decline of extended family networks and the rise of a regionally and globally mobile workforce have created pressures for employers to support employees' child- and elder care responsibilities. The same is true of rising workforce participation by women, which has also added to the pressure for unpaid and paid maternity leave. Workforce ageing, at least in Western countries and Japan, has focused far greater attention on retirement savings and support, while growing skill shortages have impelled organisations to adopt innovative benefit programs designed to delay retirement and retain older, more experienced workers for longer. In knowledge work, the imperative to acquire graduate and post-graduate qualifications has increased expectations of employer support for further personal education. Longer hours of work, greater work pressure and higher levels of work stress have increased interest in special illness prevention, wellbeing and work–life balance programs. In many countries, the dismantling of the welfare state and the tightening of eligibility for social security benefits have added to the pressure for employers to provide health and unemployment insurance and greater retirement savings support.

## Retirement or superannuation plans

In developed countries, employer-funded retirement or superannuation plans are the single most important form of benefit provision for employees as well as one of the largest additional costs to employers on top of wages and salaries. It is therefore appropriate that consideration of such plans should head our discussion of the major forms of financial and non-financial employee benefits.

The last half century has also witnessed a slow but inexorable change in the nature and importance of retirement savings planning and provision. Traditionally, superannuation took the form of a gratuity paid to select staff in recognition of their long and loyal service and with the objective of retaining key staff, particularly managers and other male white-collar professionals. For other employees, post-employment security rested on support made available by the welfare state via aged pension programs. Since the mid-twentieth century, however, superannuation has increasingly assumed the form of deferred income for the purpose of long-term retirement planning, with both the employer and the employee contributing to the employee's personal fund, which is generally held in a trust until retirement.

In most developed countries, all but a small minority of employees are covered by superannuation provided by their current employer. However, coverage still varies considerably by employee category. For instance, in Australia in 2004, while 90 per cent of employees were covered by employer-provided superannuation, coverage was significantly higher for full-time employees than for part-timers (96 per cent and 77 per cent respectively). Employees in the public sector also had a higher rate of coverage than those in the private sector (97 per cent and 89 per cent, respectively) (ABS 2004).

Access to accumulated contributions is generally restricted by vesting requirements that limit entitlements until a certain period of service or age is attained. Employees who leave before this time are generally entitled only to the contributions that they themselves have made. Vesting provisions vary from fund to fund, with some being fully vested, others unvested or partly vested. In Australia, the minimum vesting age is typically set at 55 years, and until recently employees had little freedom of choice in selecting a fund. However, since 2005 Australian employees have had the right of portability, which allows them to transfer their entitlements between funds. Such a change is a belated recognition of the decline of long-term employment with one employer and the rising importance of shorter job tenures and greater employee mobility, especially in service and knowledge work. With the population ageing in most developed countries, and with aged pension eligibility in these countries becoming more restricted, this trend is certain to continue.

However, there is also considerable variation between countries in the nature of superannuation plans. In North America, 'pension funds' are almost always employer-specific. By contrast, in Australia the largest contributory superannuation funds are industry-based and have been promoted vigorously by trade unions. Such funds have generally performed extremely well and now cover more than a third of the Australian workforce (Stone 2005: 529). They also have the advantage of protecting employees from loss of entitlements through the mismanagement of trust funds by individual employers.

From the employer perspective, generous superannuation plans have solid potential to enhance recruitment effectiveness, reduce turnover and strengthen membership behaviour. They may also allow the organisation to retain valued employees for longer periods. Of particular importance here is the discouragement to separation arising from restrictive vesting arrangements – a form of 'golden handcuff'.

Superannuation plans are of three main types: defined benefit plans, defined contribution plans and hybrid plans. Each may be contributory or non-contributory, or both. In recent decades, defined contribution plans and hybrid plans have begun to replace defined benefit plans as the dominant mode of retirement planning in many developed countries. Of course, such changes are necessarily long term in nature, meaning that defined benefit plans still retain considerable importance. For instance, in the UK, 56 per cent of organisations operate defined benefit plans for existing staff, but only 39 per cent do so for new staff. For defined contribution plans, the comparable figures are 24 per cent and 26 per cent respectively (CIPD 2005b: 7). By contrast, in Australia, 80 per cent of firms offer defined contribution plans (Stone 2005: 528). Non-contributory plans – that is, plans that are fully funded by the employer – are also becoming far less common. These changes are attributable to a range of factors, including longer life expectancy, inflation, ballooning fund liabilities, especially in the USA, and the desire to redirect risk from the employer to the employee.

### Defined benefit plans

Defined benefit plans provide a predetermined amount of retirement income either as a lump sum or as a regular pension for the remainder of the person's life. Such an approach provides certainty as to the amount of entitlement at the point of retirement. Because such arrangements are not fully funded by contributions, it is necessary for the organisation to use actuarial calculations to ascertain the level of funding necessary to meet promised benefits.

The annual pension amount is typically based on:

1 the employee's average earnings over a set number of years retirement, commonly either the last three years of paid employment or the highest income years
2 the number of years of employment with the organisation, and
3 an actuarially determined percentage factor, typically in the range 1.25 to 1.5 per cent, based primarily on predicted life expectancy.

Thus, if an employee retires at age 65 after thirty years of service and he has received total eligible remuneration averaging $70,000 over the last three years of service, and if the actuarial factor applied is 1.5 per cent, then his annual pension will be $32,500; that is, $70,000 × 30 ×1.5 per cent. In this case, where the estimated life expectancy is, say, ten years, the amount that may be taken as a once-only lump sum at the point of retirement would be $325,000; that is, $32,500 × 10.

Clearly, defined benefit plans pose particular challenges for employers, especially in times of rapid change. Where remuneration levels are rising rapidly as a consequence of inflationary pressures, under a defined benefit plan, the employer's liability will be all that much greater at the point at which the employee retires. Rising life expectancies will have a similar effect. In such countries as the USA, these factors have given rise to a large number of chronically underfunded plans. These are some of the main reasons why employers have turned away from such plans in recent decades and towards defined contribution plans.

### Defined contribution plans

Defined contribution plans, also known as accumulation plans, specify the amount of employer and/or employee contributions but not the actual retirement benefit. Contributions are expressed as percentage of the employee's annual remuneration, and employee contributions typically range between 5 and 10 per cent, with the employer often contributing an equal or greater amount. The benefit may be paid either as a lump sum or as a pension where the employee uses the accumulated fund to purchase an annuity. The entitlement is calculated on the basis of accumulated contributions plus fund earnings over the period of contribution, with the latter determined largely by the changing state of returns on shares, real estate and other investments and, of course, the investment decisions made by the relevant fund managers. As such, employees have no guarantee of what their entitlement will be, so under such plans the employee assumes most of the risk.

### Hybrid plans

A widely applied compromise approach is the 'hybrid' pension plan. To illustrate: an organisation may operate a defined benefit plan while also making it possible for employees to contribute to a defined contribution plan. The employer may also match these contributions up to a predefined maximum. Employees are typically allowed to deduct their contributions from taxable income, while tax on plan earnings is deferred. In Canada, more than half of defined contribution plans operate in tandem with defined benefit plans (Long 2005: 429).

# Health care and other forms of personal insurance

Notwithstanding the continued importance of state-provided health and income security provisions in many developed countries, benefits that provide financial support to employees and/or their dependants during times of ill-health and high medical expenses, as well as in the event of accident, disability or premature death, are among the most highly valued types of financial benefits. Such benefits may include health care insurance, workers compensation insurance, and disability and group life insurance.

## Health care insurance

These plans either supplement the basic health and medical protection provided by the state, as is the case in most European Union countries, Canada and Australia, or provide for basic and additional benefits where provision by the state is minimal or non-existent, as is the case in many developing countries, as well as in the USA, where it is customary for employers to bear the cost of medical insurance. Such plans include additional medical and hospital benefits, plus full or part reimbursement for dental, optical, chiropractic and other specialised personal care services, as well as paramedical services. Generally, such plans cover both employees and their nominated dependants or immediate family members.

In many cases, the provision of supplementary health and medical benefits is by way of salary sacrifice; that is, the provision is expensed against total potential cash remuneration. However, depending on the prevailing provisions for income and fringe benefits tax and tax deductibility, it may still be more advantageous for the employee to obtain extra health coverage by means of salary trade-off than by taking the benefit in cash, which would be fully taxable, then purchasing their own additional coverage and claiming the cost as a tax deduction, which at most would only return a fraction of the total cost.

## Workers compensation, disability and life insurance

In many developed countries it is mandatory for employees to be insured against injury, disability and death arising from work-related causes. Such plans generally provide a specified proportion of the employee's current total remuneration until the employee is able to return to work or retires. Where the injury results in the employee's death, the benefits usually flow to the legally recognised partner and/or dependent children. Workers compensation premiums constitute a significant component of employment on-costs. In Australia, such costs comprise 3 per cent of total labour costs (Stone 2005: 520).

Some organisations also provide additional insurance to cover total and permanent disability or death arising from non-work-related causes, including vehicle accidents. Others provide life insurance benefits to provide financial protection for dependants on the employee's death. It is also common for special disability and death benefits to be included in superannuation packages.

## Leave and carer benefits

As working hours have increased, benefits relating to paid and unpaid leave, and to the recognition of employees' family and carer responsibilities, have assumed increasing importance in organisations' reward management practices. Some such benefits are required by law; others are wholly voluntary. In Australia, the chief mandatory benefits of this type are paid annual leave, long-service leave, sick leave and unpaid parental leave. Most such benefits fall into the category of benefits known (somewhat awkwardly) as 'payment for time not worked'.

### Payment for time not worked

Benefits involving payment for time not worked include annual leave, long-service leave, sick leave, paid maternity and paternity leave, bereavement leave, compassionate leave, public holidays, paid study leave, jury duty, volunteer emergency services work and the like.

The extent to which leave-related benefits are legally mandated varies considerably from country to country. Take the example of annual leave. In the USA, full-time employees are entitled to two weeks of paid annual leave. In Australia, the minimum is four weeks, although it is now possible for employees to bargain away some or all of this entitlement for a cash commutation. Provision for paid long-service leave also varies greatly from country to country. In Australia, permanent full-time employees are entitled to take three months of leave on full pay after ten years of service and a further three months after fifteen years of service. Casual employees are now also eligible for long-service leave in Australia. In many other countries, there is no provision for long-service leave.

Compulsory paid maternity leave is another benefit about which there has been considerable debate in recent years (Baird 2006: 39–59). Although a steadily rising number of Australian firms now voluntarily offer their female employees between one and three months of paid maternity leave, Australian legislators have thus far baulked at mandating paid parental leave. The only compulsory parental leave provisions for Australian employees are of an unpaid nature.

Table 13.1 details the proportion of Australian employees covered by paid leave and other financial benefits. As the table data shows, just under 71 per cent of Australian workers are eligible for paid holiday leave, 71 per cent are eligible for paid sick leave and 63 per cent for paid long-service leave, while 27 per cent are eligible for paid parental leave. This data also highlights the continuing gap between part-time and full-time employees in these respects. In all cases, the proportion of full-timers covered by these benefits is more than double the proportion of part-timers covered. With the exception of paid parental leave, the proportion of male employees covered is also higher than that of female workers. A third of female workers are eligible for paid parental leave compared to a fifth of male employees.

An increasing number of organisations are recognising the potential benefits of offering paid parental leave. Survey data compiled by Australia's Equal Opportunity for Women in the Workplace Agency (EOWA 2006) reveals that, in 2005, 46 per cent of Australian organisations provided some degree of paid maternity leave and 32 per cent offered paid paternity leave. For 2001 the comparable proportions were 23 per cent and 15 per cent, respectively. However, the duration of such leave remains relatively brief. Of those organisations offering any paid maternity leave in 2005, only 6.6 per cent offered fourteen weeks or more, with 40 per cent offering six weeks and just under 20 per cent offering twelve weeks.

## Childcare and elder care

As more and more women enter paid employment, and as the populations of developed countries age, working parents are being 'sandwiched' between work commitments, the need to care for young children and the need to care for elderly parents. To help their employees here, a small but growing number of organisations now offer employer-provided childcare facilities, assistance with childcare fees and/or special elder care programs.

**Table 13.1** Employee benefits: percentage of employees covered, Australia, 2004

|                                          | Persons | Full-time | Part-time | Male | Female |
|------------------------------------------|---------|-----------|-----------|------|--------|
| Employer-provided superannuation         | 90.1    | 95.7      | 76.7      | 90.4 | 89.6   |
| Paid leave benefits:                     |         |           |           |      |        |
| Holiday leave                            | 70.9    | 84.9      | 37.4      | 74.0 | 67.4   |
| Sick leave                               | 71.2    | 84.9      | 38.3      | 74.0 | 67.9   |
| Long service leave                       | 63.3    | 75.3      | 34.8      | 64.9 | 61.5   |
| Maternity or paternity leave             | 26.6    | 31.1      | 15.7      | 20.2 | 33.8   |
| Other financial benefits:                |         |           |           |      |        |
| Goods or services                        | 18.0    | 17.7      | 18.8      | 17.1 | 19.1   |
| Transport                                | 13.3    | 17.2      | 4.1       | 19.6 | 6.2    |
| Telephone                                | 9.1     | 11.5      | 3.4       | 13.0 | 4.7    |
| Shares                                   | 5.9     | 7.0       | 3.4       | 6.9  | 4.8    |
| Study leave                              | 4.2     | 3.6       | 5.7       | n.a. | n.a.   |
| Holiday expenses                         | 3.8     | 4.7       | 1.5       | n.a. | n.a.   |
| Medical                                  | 2.1     | 2.6       | 0.9       | n.a. | n.a.   |
| Housing                                  | 1.9     | 2.4       | 0.7       | n.a. | n.a.   |
| Low-interest finance                     | 1.5     | 1.9       | 0.6       | n.a. | n.a.   |
| Union or professional association dues   | 3.0     | 3.9       | 0.9       | n.a. | n.a.   |
| Electricity                              | 2.0     | 2.3       | 1.2       | n.a. | n.a.   |
| Entertainment                            | 1.7     | 2.3       | 0.3       | n.a. | n.a.   |
| Club fees                                | 1.9     | 2.4       | 0.7       | n.a. | n.a.   |
| Child care or education expenses         | 0.6     | 0.6       | 0.5       | n.a. | n.a.   |

Source: ABS 2004.

In Australia, a small number of organisations either offer in-house child-care or meet employee childcare expenses in some other way. Despite the high establishment and running costs, exacting accreditation standards and difficulty of making such facilities available to employees in multisite organisations, in-house facilities have the advantage of reducing parents' commuting time and increasing their access to children during the working day. In Australia, one of the first companies to offer in-house childcare was the Sydney-based property and financial services firm Lend Lease, which has a longstanding high-involvement culture. Lend Lease provides on-site childcare at its Sydney head office; in other capital cities, it assists staff to find suitable off-site childcare and then pays a rebate equal to the benefit available to its Sydney staff (Russell 2004a). Yet the provision of free childcare remains uncommon. As table 13.1 indicates, less than 1 per cent of Australian employees receive the benefit of employer-funded childcare.

For many employees, care of elderly parents is an equally demanding family responsibility; a responsibility for which the time demands may be both considerable and quite unpredictable. According to one Australian study, an employee with elder-care responsibilities loses on average three full working days per year, and a further four days are significantly disrupted (Stone 2005: 521). With a view to reducing the affect on attendance, performance and morale, some organisations have introduced special elder-care leave arrangements or have made provision for such leave in more general leave arrangements.

## Other 'fringe' financial benefits

There is also a wide range of miscellaneous financial benefits that employers may provide. Although some such benefits are mandatory in certain countries, the vast majority are 'fringe benefits' provided on a wholly voluntary basis.

### Severance pay

In many developed countries, including Australia, it is mandatory either to provide the employee with a specified period of notice of redundancy-related termination or to pay a predetermined quantum of severance pay to employees in lieu of such notice. Such payments are additional to accumulated superannuation entitlements. Severance pay entitlements are generally set on the basis of the employee's length of service with the organisation; for example, an extra one to four weeks pay for each year of full-time service, with set minima (typically one to four months) and maxima (typically one to two years, depending on the position held). Age may also be taken into account in determining the mandatory payout amount.

Termination payment arrangements may also be voluntary in nature, as is generally the case with salaried executives. As we shall see in chapter 21, in recent years designated termination payments made by company boards to departing senior executives in such countries as Australia have generally been equivalent to one to two years of base salary, and in some cases considerably more. The apparent generosity of these so-called 'golden parachutes' has attracted considerable criticism in the media and from large institutional investors, including major superannuation and life insurance funds.

## Other financial benefits

Other 'fringe benefits' that employers may choose to incorporate in a benefits package include:

- free grants of company shares, or share purchase plans involving low-interest or no-interest company loans. Such plans frequently supplement or substitute for employer superannuation contributions and have similar tax advantages. Employee share plans, which are both a fringe benefit and a form of 'long term incentive', are explored in detail in chapter 20
- discount loans
- housing or mortgage subsidies
- discount travel and accommodation
- product or service discounts
- free clothing
- subsidised canteens
- company cars and/or free parking
- club and gym membership
- self-education expenses
- school fees for dependent children
- notebook computers
- mobile phones.

Most such benefits are liable to taxation as a fringe benefit where such taxes exist. As figure 14.1 reveals, in Australia, the most common of these financial benefits are the provision of free or discount goods and services (covering 18 per cent of employees), provision of free or subsidised transport (13 per cent coverage), telephones (9 per cent coverage), company shares (7 per cent coverage), paid study leave (4 per cent coverage) and holiday expenses (just under 4 per cent).

# Other non-financial benefits

In addition to monetary benefits, many organisations now offer employees a range of non-financial benefits. In essence, these are intended to make the organisation a more appealing place to work as well as to increase employee morale, job satisfaction, membership behaviour, organisational commitment and task motivation. In recent years, longer-working hours and rising levels of workforce stress have prompted growing recognition of the importance of work–life balance and spurred some organisations to introduce non-financial benefits carefully targeted at enhancing employees' wellbeing. These benefits include, *inter alia*, flexible work-time arrangements, wellness programs and employee assistance programs. In part, these non-monetary plans are also targeted at reducing costs associated with compulsory financial benefits, including statutory sick leave and stress leave entitlements.

### Flexible work-time and work–life balance programs

Flexible work hours and schedules allow the organisation to respond more effectively to variable production and service provision requirements while also promising employees greater choice regarding the hours that they work. Such arrangements may be of special benefit to working parents, dual-career families and employees with study or community commitments.

Flexible work-time arrangements are virtually limitless in their variety. With variable day arrangements, employees are able to vary the number of hours worked on any given day, providing they work the required number of standard hours per week and are at work each day during designated 'core hours'. Similarly, with a variable week arrangement, employees may work a long week or a short week, provided that they complete a standard number of hours each fortnight or month. Another variant is the rostered day off. A further option is flexible start and finish times, whereby employees nominate a daily start time and adhere to it for an agreed period. Job-sharing and permanent part-time work also increase the degree of time flexibility available to each employee, as, of course, do telecommuting and other work-from-home arrangements, which also give employees greater scope to better integrate family and work responsibilities both spatially and temporally. Unpaid parental and carer leave arrangements also fall into this category.

However, flexible work schedules may also operate to employees' disadvantage. Flexible shift arrangements may be especially disadvantageous to working parents, since they stand to diminish predictability and regularity, so making it more difficult to plan family commitments and childcare arrangements. For instance, a combination of extended shift arrangements and frequent non-participative work rescheduling may make it impossible for working parents to make adequate childcare arrangements.

Thus temporal flexibility alone may actually have dysfunctional outcomes both for the organisation and for employees, and 'best practice' prescriptions highlight the need to ensure that variable hours arrangements are fully informed by work–life balance considerations – and the available evidence does indicate that the business case for flexible work-time arrangements configured along such lines is reasonably strong. A 2005 study of 377 Australian organisations showed that those applying 'best practice' work–life balance initiatives had enjoyed considerable returns on investment, including an average 3.6 per cent reduction in staff turnover, a 3.8 per cent decline in absenteeism, a 21 per cent improvement in the rate of return from parental leave, and a 13 per cent improvement in the level of employee satisfaction (Brown 2005).

In the highly competitive legal profession, such flexible work time and work–life balance programs are emerging as an important means of attracting and retaining high-potential female lawyers. In the past, women's ability to progress to partnership in law firms has been hindered by a masculinist work culture, a narrow focus on results in the form of 'billable hours', and the view that any career break for parenting purposes is literally career-breaking. One organisation that has consciously set out to counter these obstacles to women's career progression is the mid-sized Sydney law firm, Henry Davis York. Its benefits program includes flexible hours, part-time hours, job share, work from home and twelve weeks paid maternity leave for women who have been with the firm for more than two years. Several of the firm's female partners work part-time. Its employees are also able to participate in a wellness program that includes classes in yoga and Pilates (Brown 2005).

## Wellness programs

Also known as preventive health programs, employee wellness programs are designed to promote employees' physical and mental health and fitness. Examples include free medical check-ups, in-house gyms or subsidised gym membership, personal trainers, aerobics, yoga, Pilates and tai chi classes, in-office massages, stress reduction and relaxation sessions, ergonomic consultations, meditation rooms, staff health food canteens, nutrition seminars, weight control programs and quit smoking programs. As well as being inherently beneficial to employees themselves, health and fitness initiatives such as these can make a significant contribution to reducing absenteeism and raising productivity (Wells 2004).

Health and fitness programs may be run internally by specialist staff, as is the case in many large US firms, or outsourced, as is typically the case in Australian firms (Wells 2004: 42). In Australia, eligibility for such programs still tends to be selective, with access typically being confined to managers, professionals and other white-collar employees. However, some Australian firms have rolled out health and fitness programs for their entire workforce. One such firm is the large Australian building resources materials company Boral Ltd, which employs 10,000 people Australia-wide in production and logistics. Boral's workforce is predominantly male and blue collar and has an average age of 45. In 2004 the firm introduced free confidential health assessments for all employees, primarily with the aim of reducing illness-related absenteeism and sick leave costs, as well as fatigue-related accident and workers compensation costs. In 2005 this was followed by free health seminars on such topics as nutrition, men's health, exercise and sleep. The Boral Health Resources Centre also provides information to staff and their families on a wide range of topics: from asthma, diabetes and back care to drug and alcohol abuse, financial health, relationships and sleep management for shift workers. Known as 'Bwell', the program is one of the most ambitious employee health promotion programs to date in Australia. The business case for such programs appears to be quite solid; studies of similar programs run by comparable businesses in the United States showing an average return on investment of almost 300 per cent (Russell 2006).

## Employee assistance programs

The purpose of employee assistance programs is to help employees to cope with and remedy personal problems that are interfering with their performance. Participation in an assistance program may be one of the items included in an action plan designed to remedy under-performance arising from a major personal problem.

Assistance may involve counselling on such matters as drug or alcohol abuse, marital or other family relationship problems, financial problems and advice, time management problems, depression or other mental health problems, bereavement, stress management or work-related trauma. Trauma counselling is commonly offered in industries where employees are at high risk of experiencing violence, armed robbery or accidents, including banking, liquor stores, transport, mining, construction, police and emergency services.

Drug and alcohol abuse is a growing problem throughout the developed world, and organisations that do not have well-maintained programs for detecting and remedying substance abuse run the dual risks of increased workplace accident and injury and crippling litigation costs. In many industries, particularly road, rail and air transport, random drug and alcohol testing programs are now mandatory. Likewise, employers who do not take active steps to curb smoking on their premises run the risk of legal liability for injury caused by passive smoking.

Data on employee assistance referrals to one of Australia's leading employee assistance providers, Davidson Trahair Corpsych, reveals both the great diversity of problems for which professional assistance is sought and the high incidence of problems originating outside the workplace itself. Of 11,000 new counselling referrals to the firm from individuals from more than 300 organisations over a twelve-month period, 71 per cent presented with personal problems, of which 53 per cent involved family and relationship problems, including separation and divorce, and 40 per cent involved emotional wellbeing problems, including anxiety, depression, grief and loss of self-esteem. Of the total number of referrals, only 29 per cent related directly to work problems (Russell 2003). The key point is that all of these referrals related to problems that were affecting work wellbeing and performance.

## Fixed plans, flexible plans and plan design

Benefits packages are of two main types. They may have a standard content, with the composition being determined by legal requirement and employer choice. Alternatively, they may be flexible in content, with employees having a degree of choice in how best to configure their package within a range of options made available voluntarily by the employer. The latter are also known as 'flexible' or 'cafeteria' benefits plans.

### Fixed benefits

The traditional approach of offering one standard benefits package to all eligible employees has numerous advantages. The 'one size fits all' approach is simple, delivers economies of scale, is easy to communicate to employees, and has relatively low administrative costs.

Conversely, the approach assumes workforce homogeneity in an era when workforce diversity and the tenets of diversity management are in the ascendant. By definition, fixed benefits plans are incapable of adequately accommodating significant changes in employee needs and expectations. For the latter reason, some organisations now offer semi-flexible plans, involving a fixed core of, say, compulsory benefits, and a limited range of additional benefits from which employees may choose.

In general, fixed plans are likely to be better suited to organisations with stable workforce profiles, for whom problems of staff attraction and retention are not of major importance, and which place a high priority on cost minimisation. On this basis, fixed schemes will be particularly well suited to traditionally managed mechanistic organisations with cost-defender competitive strategies and which espouse a relational psychological contract. Such plans may also be preferred by firms with a traditional culture and a quality defender strategy. The administrative ease of standard plans is also likely to have particular appeal to small- to medium-sized firms.

### Flexible benefits

With fully flexible benefits plans, employees are allocated a sum – or benefits credit – that can be used to 'purchase' benefits from a 'menu' made available by the organisation. Such packages have increased in popularity since the 1980s, particularly in professional and other white-collar employment, although, as we shall see, in some developed countries they are still the exception rather than the rule.

The logic of flexible packages is that one size does not fit all. Differences in age, family responsibilities, financial circumstances and lifestyle preferences mean that different employees will have different benefit needs, and the needs of any one employee will change considerably over time. For instance, employees in their twenties may prefer to load their benefits in favour of study support, a company car and leisure or travel benefits while downplaying the superannuation option. However, a 30-something employee with young children may wish to skew benefits in favour of a concessional housing loan, supplementary health benefits and childcare support, and a 50-something employee may well be happy to forgo the preceding benefits in favour of salary sacrificing for higher superannuation contributions.

Overall, flexible schemes are likely to have greatest appeal to organisations with large, highly diverse workforces, for which staff attraction and retention concerns are of paramount importance, which place a strong emphasis on flexibility, and which espouse a transactional or balanced psychological contract. As such, cafeteria plans will be particularly appropriate to organisations with high-involvement cultures (Long 2006: 446) and competitive strategies of the analyser or prospector type.

For instance, under the flexible benefits plan offered by Australian property and financial services company Lend Lease, an analyser firm with a well-established high-involvement culture, employees receive their packages either wholly as cash or as cash plus benefits. Benefits include car leasing, in-house childcare, laptops, salary sacrifice superannuation payments, access to financial planning services and an employee share acquisition plan. As the firm's Asia-Pacific human resources manager explains (cited in Russell 2004a): 'their benefits package has to be flexible, so that people can choose benefits that are meaningful to them at certain stages of their lives.'

Still, flexible benefits packages have some significant drawbacks for both parties. For the employer, cafeteria plans have high administrative costs simply because of the wider range of options that have to be made available, the sheer technical complexity of multiplan schemes and the need to micro-manage each employee's package and frequent changes in their preferences. For the employee, the array of choice available may be daunting and confusing. Poor or ill-advised choices may also result in employees having inadequate health care coverage or insufficient retirement savings and so on. Clearly, a poorly communicated cafeteria scheme may jeopardise the financial wellbeing of employees and their dependants. Canadian research (Tremblay, Sire & Pelchat 1998) indicates that procedural justice considerations, including transparent and consistent communication, have a stronger influence on employee satisfaction with flexible benefits plans than do employee perceptions of the distributive fairness of plan outcomes. Employees and trade unions may also be opposed to flexible schemes out of a fear that flexibility may just be a smokescreen for reducing entitlements and shifting cost and risk to employees themselves.

For these reasons, in global terms, flexible plans are still relatively uncommon, although the incidence varies considerably from country to country. They are most popular in North America, where they originated in the 1960s. In the USA, where flexible benefits are tax-favoured, 85 per cent of large firms had flexible schemes by the mid-1990s. In Canada, where tax treatment is less favourable, flexible schemes were being used by 29 per cent of firms in 2004 (Long 2006: 443). Elsewhere, adoption has been slower. For instance, in the UK the approach is offered by just 8 per cent of organisations, with the highest incidence being in private sector service firms (12 per cent) and the lowest in the public and not-for-profit sectors (both 3 per cent). An organisation's size, however, is the key determinant, with flexible plans being used by almost a quarter of organisations with more than 5,000 employees (CIPD 2005a: 27–8). Again, the higher usage rate in large firms would seem to be due to the high administrative costs associated with complex and comprehensive benefits menus.

## Plan design

Designing an effective benefits plan is undoubtedly one of the most challenging of all reward management tasks. Plan design requires that close attention be paid to the following ten questions:

1  Which of the compulsory benefits must be made available to permanent full-time employees, to permanent part-timers, to casuals and to employees on short-term contracts?
2  What proportion of total remuneration should benefits comprise, and how should the proportion vary from role to role?
3  What specific financial and non-financial benefits do employees want the organisation to provide voluntarily?
4  Which of these voluntary benefits best align with the organisation's strategic needs and objectives, and which benefits are to target which strategic priorities?
5  Which employees (and dependants) should be eligible for these strategically aligned benefits, and what eligibility criteria will apply?
6  What is the estimated net benefit of providing these strategically aligned benefits to eligible employees?
7  Which benefits will be provided on a non-contributory basis, on a fully contributory basis (as with salary sacrificing), and by means of partial contribution or cost-sharing?
8  Should the benefits scheme for individual employees be fixed, semi-flexible or fully flexible (beyond what is mandatory)?
9  What role will internal and external experts and employees play in scheme design?
10 How will the overall benefits system be communicated, implemented, administered and evaluated over time so that it remains current and relevant?

# Chapter summary

This chapter began with a brief examination of the general rationale of employee benefits plans and the reasons for their growing importance to reward strategy and practice in developed countries, particularly the decline of extended family networks, increasing workforce diversification and rising education levels and expectations, workforce ageing, longer working hours and greater job mobility. Attention then turned to the main benefit plan types, beginning with retirement or superannuation benefits, followed by health care and other forms of personal insurance, leave and carer benefits, and other financial and non-financial benefits. Special attention was paid to the distinction between defined benefit and defined contribution superannuation plans and to the reason for the global trend from the former to the latter. Attention then turned to non-financial benefits in the form of flexible work-time arrangements, wellness programs and employee assistance programs, since these are now at the leading edge of innovation in benefits practice. Finally, we considered the differences between fixed and flexible benefit plans, the factors that must be taken into consideration in choosing between the two, and the factors to be considered in designing an effective and strategically aligned benefits system.

This chapter concludes our coverage of base pay and benefits plans, the foundational elements of any total reward management system. Recalling the discussion of generic reward system objectives in chapter 2 and our overview of 'needs' or 'content' motivation theories in chapter 4, we can generalise that in most organisations base pay and benefits programs are directed primarily (although not exclusively) to attracting and retaining the desired number of high-potential employees by providing rewards addressed chiefly at meeting 'lower-order' needs for security and safety and, to a lesser extent, for social affiliation.

In the chapters that follow in part 4, we turn our attention to those reward practices that are explicitly contingent on performance; practices the primary purpose of which is less to attract and retain *per se* than to motivate higher levels of desired work behaviour and results.

## Discussion questions

1 Why are employee benefits becoming an increasingly important component of employee reward practice?
2 What is the difference between defined benefit and defined contribution superannuation plans, and why are plans of the latter type becoming more popular?
3 What sort of organisation is likely to gain most from offering employees flexible or 'cafeteria' benefits schemes?
4 What are the advantages of non-financial benefits?
5 What are the pros and cons of 'flexible' benefits plans?

# JUST REWARDS

## Rethinking base pay and benefits at Court, Case & McGowan, commercial law partners

You could have cut the conference room air with a knife. James Court, chief national partner of Sydney commercial law firm Court, Case & McGowan, had just delivered an address to the firm's 600 Sydney-based solicitors informing them that the previous financial year had been one of the firm's best profit-making years ever. For all of Court's upbeat assessment, his announcements showed remarkably poor judgement and timing. Just two weeks earlier, the firm had completed its annual pay reviews, which had resulted in increases lower than for any of the previous five years. As the caterers rolled out the post-address refreshments, many of the solicitors present muttered darkly to each other that the time and effort that they had put into achieving this outstanding financial result had not been adequately recognised or rewarded. Several 20-something high achievers who had put in long hours on difficult legal cases grumbled about leaving the firm (and possibly the legal profession altogether) to work for an organisation where their contribution would be far better rewarded. One of the firm's most successful female corporate tax lawyers spoke of going to work for a merchant bank renowned for the five-figure bonuses it paid to its commercial litigation team.

Such utterances do not bode well for Fiona Fenton, the firm's new director of human resources. Court had invited Fiona along to his address to introduce her to the firm's core workforce. However, the conversations she overheard had left her feeling quite unnerved – and she had every reason to suspect that unless she did something to address this undercurrent of reward dissatisfaction her recent career move would end in disaster. With five years experience as a senior HR administrator in a large non-profit organisation – a job that she greatly enjoyed – Fiona had taken a gamble by making a career move into a mainstream corporate HR position. Whatever her initial expectations of her new job, however, she was now under no illusions as to the magnitude of the challenge that awaited her.

## The firm's strategy and structure

Court, Case & McGowan is one of the country's largest national commercial law firms, employing more than 800 people in its Sydney office alone. It also has offices in most other Australian capital cities. Its mission is to be 'the provider of choice of commercial legal services to Australian corporations', and its chief goals are to double its business in the highly profitable fields of corporate mergers and acquisitions, insurance litigation and tax law over the next triennium.

Like most other large legal firms, Court, Case & McGowan has a hierarchical structure based on seniority. Being a partnership, the firm is not listed on the stock exchange, and responsibility for its governance resides with its twenty-five partners, all highly experienced and respected members of the legal profession. The firm's 1,200 solicitors nationwide are categorised into the following four position grades:

- graduate at law, currently numbering 200
- junior solicitor (one to three years of experience), currently numbering 400
- senior solicitor, currently numbering 500
- senior associate, currently numbering 100.

This legal pecking order is also heavily gendered. Although women comprise 50 per cent of the firm's first-year graduates and junior solicitors, they make up only 35 per cent of the senior solicitors, and just 25 per cent of senior associates, and only five of the firm's twenty-five partners are women. In addition to qualified solicitors, the firm employs a large number of legal support staff, including administrative and secretarial staff, librarians and human resource practitioners, more than 80 per cent of whom are female.

While these workers make a major contribution to the firm's success, they are left in no doubt as to their lowly status in the firm's packing order. As a woman, Fiona, too, has quickly come to realise that she faces an uphill battle to invest HR with 'voice' and influence in such a male-dominated authority structure.

## Pay for position; promotion for performance

At present, remuneration for Court, Case & McGowan's solicitors consists solely of a base salary, which is subject to annual review. To date, these reviews have been overseen by the 'staff partner', Simon Goodchap QC, with only limited input from the HR section, which has hitherto mainly handled routine recruitment and payroll administration matters. No one else in the firm apart from Goodchap and his fellow partners seems to know just how these annual base pay decisions are arrived at. Employees are simply informed that 'a variety of factors will be taken into account' in determining their annual pay rise. Similarly, while pay levels for each of the four non-partner grades are obviously geared to some combination of seniority, experience and competence, just how pay relativities between grades are fixed remains something of a mystery, with the partners evidently assuming that solicitors learn as they go, adapting and improving their legal knowledge and skills over time.

Solicitors in any given grade receive 'more or less' the same base salary, irrespective of whether their performance is exceptional or just acceptable, with promotion to a higher grade being the firm's preferred way of rewarding consistently high performance. In the absence of any formal system of performance appraisal and review, a solicitor's performance is defined and measured in terms of 'billable hours' worked. As is the norm in the legal profession, to ensure that the firm obtains value for money from these base salary payouts, each solicitor is expected to meet a minimum budgetary requirement for the number of hours billed to clients each day. The minimum budgetary requirement is set at an average of 7.5 hours per day, with charge-out rates ranging from $150 per hour for a new graduate to $500 for a senior associate. No additional rewards are in place for those solicitors who exceed their annual billable hours budget. Budget underperformers are simply 'managed out'.

## What Simon says

Wishing to discover more about the firm's remuneration practices, Fiona arranges an interview with Simon Goodchap, who informs her that the solicitors' base salaries are determined 'by a variety of things such as the market rate in other major law firms, level of seniority and certain extraordinary qualities a solicitor may possess'. When pressed, Goodchap volunteers that the 'market' information used to set pay levels for each grade is actually limited to one Melbourne-based law firm with a similar grade structure but also with a reputation for doing insurance litigation 'on the cheap'. Somewhat sheepishly, Goodchap also revealed to Fiona that until last year he had shared information on pay ranges with his counterparts in two Sydney-based commercial law firms but that cooperation had now come to an acrimonious end. To Goodchap's dismay, despite having reached a gentlemen's agreement to set the same pay levels for the ensuing financial year, the two other firms held off announcing their annual pay reviews until after Court, Case & McGowan had done so, then they introduced base pay levels 30 per cent above those offered by Goodchap's firm. As a result, the two competitor firms were able to poach some of Court, Case & McGowan's best high-flyers in the highly lucrative areas of mergers and acquisitions and taxation law, and it has also encountered increasing difficulty in attracting any of the latest batch of top-notch law graduates.

Goodchap also confides to Fiona that while the existing pay system does incorporate grade-specific pay ranges for the purpose of recognising solicitors with 'extraordinary skills and talent', the range is never more than 10 per cent. Goodchap explained that this was because the firm wished to avoid internal conflict over pay inequality and because having a uniform rate of pay encouraged teamwork, a common feature of much of the firm's litigation work. Ironically, the fact that the firm encourages secrecy in pay administration actually serves to amplify the negative effect of the small pay disparity within each grade. The outcomes of the annual pay reviews are communicated to solicitors in sealed envelopes marked 'private and confidential' and, as a consequence, there is a great deal of rumour (much of it ill-founded) about disparity in pay for solicitors in the same grade.

Finally, Goodchap admits to Fiona that the absence of systematic performance appraisal makes it all the more difficult to justify pay differences between individuals in any given grade. He remains convinced, however, that individual performance appraisal is 'more trouble that it is worth and a totally unproductive exercise, especially when it comes to billable hours'.

## Fiona's challenge: a new reward approach

The more she hears, the more she wonders whether she has made the right career move; but Fiona is not faint-hearted and she also knows that she has much to do and little time to lose. It is clear that the firm's existing approach to reward management has serious shortcomings. The firm is failing to attract top talent and is losing some of its star performers to competitors and other industries. There is growing dissatisfaction in its core workforce with existing base pay levels and employee benefits, as well as with the absence of adequate rewards for high performance. No one really understands or can justify the annual pay review outcomes, and pay secrecy simply exacerbates the distrust. Promotion alone cannot motivate solicitors adequately. The limited number of senior associate and partner positions means that the firm cannot reward all high performers with promotion to the top – unless, that is, it wishes to become a 'top-heavy' organisation, which, in any case, would simply devalue the prestige of senior positions.

Fiona's meeting with Goodchap has had one important positive outcome: he has agreed to give her a free hand to implement change to the firm's performance and reward management systems and to guarantee support for her change program at partner level. So what exactly should she propose? Should she recommend a 'scorched earth' approach involving radical change to base pay? Should she concentrate on changing the firm's position-based approach to base pay – but, if so, should she simply adjust pay levels for each grade, or should change be more thoroughgoing, entailing, say, a move to broad-banding and base pay progression based not on seniority but on personal contribution? Alternatively, should Fiona focus on specially targeted benefits plans? Should she propose the introduction of performance-related incentives – but of what type, and using what performance measures? And what should she do first? Finally, how can she ensure that whatever changes she opts for constitute a cohesive approach capable of assisting Court, Case & McGowan to achieve its mission and strategic goals?

*Source:* adapted from Shields 2005. Reproduced with permission.

Model responses to this case study are provided in the appendix.

# REWARDING EMPLOYEE PERFORMANCE

Having considered the main options and processes associated with base pay and benefits, we can now turn to consider the remaining major area of reward practice, namely performance-related rewards. Also known as 'incentive plans', these are rewards that are contingent or 'at risk' in some way, rather than being 'fixed' or 'guaranteed', as is the case with more traditional forms of base pay. For this reason, such rewards are also commonly referred to as 'contingent' or 'variable' pay plans. Moreover, while many such rewards are financial in nature (i.e. performance pay or cash incentives), performance related-rewards may also take a non-financial form.

The seven chapters in part 4 offer a detailed coverage of the main types of individual and collective performance-related rewards and of key themes and debates associated with such rewards. Chapter 14 outlines the main types of performance-related reward, considers some of the general motives for adopting performance-contingent rewards, and overviews the main arguments and supporting evidence for and against such plans. Chapters 15 to 19 examine specific types of performance-related reward plans that are commonly applied to line employees and managers, with particular emphasis on plan usage, strengths and weaknesses. Plans covered include individual merit pay (chapter 15); recognition awards (chapter 16); results-based individual incentives (chapter 17); collective short-term incentives (chapter 18); and collective long-term incentive plans in the form of broadly based employee share plans (chapter 19).

While these chapters focus chiefly on ways of recognising and rewarding the performance of those who comprise the majority of a typical organisation's workforce, namely line employees, supervisors and line managers, middle managers and professionals, the final chapter in part 4 (chapter 20) considers the special case of incentive plans for executive-level employees. By virtue of the positions they occupy, senior executives exercise considerable individual influence over an organisation's performance. Hence executive rewards typically apply organisation-wide performance criteria as proxies for the performance of the individual executive. As we shall see, the processes and practices associated with executive incentives are among the most complex and controversial of all reward management issues.

The case study accompanying these chapters – 'Beyond the hard sell: Redesigning performance-related rewards at Southbank' – invites you to apply your new-found knowledge of individual and collective incentive plans to remedy some fundamental shortcomings in an existing employee incentive system. Model responses to this case are provided in the book's appendix.

## Chapter Fourteen

# OVERVIEW OF PERFORMANCE-RELATED REWARDS

As we have seen, there is considerable debate about the link between money and other types of extrinsic reward on the one hand and employee satisfaction, motivation, work effort and performance on the other. By way of introduction to part 4, this chapter identifies the main categories and types of performance-related reward, and considers some of the general motives for adopting performance-contingent rewards, as well as examining the evidence on the incidence of the main types of performance-related reward plans, particularly cash incentives or performance-related pay. The chapter also overviews the main arguments and supporting evidence for and against such plans, taking into account both effectiveness and felt-fairness.

## What is performance-related pay?

All forms of paid employment, including those where remuneration consists entirely of base pay, have performance standards or expectations of some sort attached to them. As Behrend (1957, 1961) and others have suggested, every form of paid employment involves an effort bargain as well as a pay bargain. In some cases, this will involve a set of implicit mutual expectations – *à la* a psychological contract – between employee and employer about a pay–effort deal – about the basis of 'a fair day's pay for a fair day's work'. In other cases, it might entail the imposition of specific task quotas for each unit of hiring time. This is the case with the practice known as 'measured day work', whereby employees receive a fixed daily wage but are required to work to a standard output quota. In most time-based pay systems, however, including waged and salaried employment, the link between pay and performance is neither direct nor explicit. Effort levels are frequently set according to custom and practice. Typically, performance standards are implicit and therefore open to contestation, misunderstanding and perceived breach of the psychological contract.

Pay for performance plans seek to reduce the sphere of uncertainty associated with the nature of the employment exchange by specifying the basis of the transaction in more explicit terms. Performance pay can therefore be defined as any remuneration practice in which part or all of remuneration is based *directly* and *explicitly* on employees' assessed work behaviour and/or measured results. As noted in chapter 2, performance-related reward plans are thus one of the defining characteristics of a transactional psychological contract. Equally, on the basis of the above definition, it is inappropriate to classify plans that focus on assessing and rewarding personal skills and competencies as performance-related reward plans since they focus on rewarding employees' productive 'inputs' rather than work behaviour or outputs. As indicated in part 3, such plans are best thought of as forms of base pay.

## Types of performance-related reward

While performance-related reward plans can themselves be classified in many different ways, the four crucial considerations, we suggest, are:

1 What is being measured: behaviour, results or both?
2 Whose performance is being measured: individuals, large work groups (business units, plants, divisions), small work groups (teams) or the whole organisation?
3 Over what time frame is performance being measured and rewarded: over a short term (twelve months or less) or a longer term (more than twelve months)?
4 What form does the contingent reward take: cash, company equity, non-monetary?

Importantly, as well as incorporating the 'horizontal' and 'vertical' dimensions of employee performance discussed in chapter 1, this taxonomy also takes account of the temporal dimension of performance definition and measurement, and the form taken by the reward itself. Using these dimensions, we can identify three main categories of performance-related reward:

1 Individual performance-related rewards. These are based either on the individual employee's assessed work behaviour or results or on a combination of the two. These typically have a time-frame of no more than one year and as such may also be described as a form of 'short-term incentive' (STI). They may also be of a cash or non-cash nature, or both.

2 Performance-related rewards based on the measured results of large or small work groups internal to the organisation as a whole. These may also be described as STIs, since the performance time-frame is typically between one month and one year. While rewards for group performance are generally monetary in nature, recognition for group performance may also be of a non-cash nature.

3 Collective performance-related rewards based on results achieved by the organisation as a whole. Where an organisation's results are defined in terms of financial accounting criteria (such as annual net operating profit) and the resulting payment is cash-based, the organisational performance plan would amount to a short-term incentive. However, where organisational performance is defined in terms of share market criteria (i.e. movements in ordinary share prices and/or dividend payments to shareholders over a number of years) and the reward takes the form of actual or potential company equity, the plan equates to a 'long-term incentive' (LTI).

Essentially, then, these are the three main performance-contingent reward options available to reward system designers. Figure 14.1 identifies the main methods associated with each category. Each of these plan types is considered in detail in subsequent chapters.

## The use of performance-related rewards

Performance pay has for many years been a defining feature of reward practice in many developed countries. A survey of 770 North American organisations, conducted in 2000, indicated that more than two-thirds operated variable pay plans of some sort (Lowery et al. 2002: 100). Performance pay is now a global phenomenon, and there is evidence of a substantial increase in the use of performance-related rewards in developed and developing

| Who (= performance entity or unit) and when (= time frame for payout)? | How? (= behaviour) | How much? ( = results) |
|---|---|---|
| Individual | • Merit raises or increments<br>• Merit bonuses | • Piece rates<br>• Sales commissions<br>• Goal-based bonuses<br>• Discretionary bonuses<br>• Individual non-cash recognition awards |
| Large group short-term incentives (STIs) | | • Profitsharing<br>• Gainsharing<br>• Goalsharing |
| Small group STIs | | • Team incentives<br>• Team non-cash recognition awards |
| Organisation-wide long-term incentives (LTIs) | | • Share bonus plans<br>• Share purchase plans<br>• Share option plans<br>• Share appreciation and other rights plans |

**Figure 14.1** Performance-related reward options

countries since the 1980s, and in both private sector firms and public sector organisations. Equally, the pattern of plan adoption has also varied considerably from country to country, and there has been considerable debate as to whether global business imperatives are causing a convergence in human resource practices, including performance pay practices, throughout industrialised countries.

A number of studies have compared the incidence of performance pay practices across national borders (Cin, Han & Smith 2003; Brown & Heywood 2002; Lowe et al. 2002; Poutsma, de Nijs & Poole 2003; Long & Shields 2005b; Pendleton et al. 2001; Tremblay & Chenevert 2004) and, although these studies have produced mixed findings regarding the extent of convergence in pay practices, they do nevertheless confirm that performance pay plans of various types now constitute a major element of overall reward practice in many countries. On the basis of eight country-specific studies, Brown and Heywood (2002: 272) conclude that 'the country studies demonstrate the importance of specific historical, cultural, and institutional factors in understanding the form and incidence of performance pay schemes across countries'. It is clear that national cultural factors exert some influence on pay plan choice, yet institutional, industry- and organisationally specific factors appear to be no less important. Legal compulsion and local custom and practice are also significant factors. For instance, profitsharing, the oldest of the collective incentive plans, has been compulsory in medium- to large-sized firms in France since 1967 (Fakhfakh & Perotin 2002: 96–100), while Brazilian employees have customary and constitutional rights to participate in profitsharing or gainsharing (Zylberstajn 2002: 241–6).

A comparison of the incidence of performance pay plans in Canadian and Australian private sector firms (Long & Shields 2005b) found that at the beginning of this decade the great majority of firms in Canada (94 per cent) and Australia (87 per cent) utilised at least one performance pay plan for their non-managerial employees. The median number of performance pay plans utilised in both Canada and Australia was three. As table 14.1 shows, plans geared to individual performance were by far the most commonly used category of performance pay in both countries, being used by about 88 per cent of Canadian firms and 81 per cent of Australian firms. The majority of firms had one or two individual performance pay plans. Group performance pay plans were used much less frequently than individual performance pay plans, as only 36 per cent of Canadian firms and 37 per cent of Australian firms used any type of group pay. Divergence between the two countries was most marked in relation to organisational performance pay. In Canada, just over half of firms (52 per cent) used some form of pay geared to organisational performance, whereas only 40 per cent of Australian firms did so.

As the annual surveys of reward practice in the UK by the Chartered Institute of Personnel and Development illustrate, there are also major variations in plan incidence within particular countries. Table 14.2 summarises the main findings regarding the use of performance pay from the institute's 2005 survey (conducted in 2004). The UK data reveals strong variations in plan incidence between economic sectors. Note, in particular, the higher incidence of performance pay in general in service sector firms (69 per cent), especially schemes driven by business results (71 per cent). Note too the relatively high emphasis in the public sector on both stand-alone, individually based plans (59 per cent – primarily merit pay) and team-based plans (25 per cent). These marked sectoral variations in plan incidence provide circumstantial support for the proposition that organisations' pay plan choices are informed primarily by 'best fit' considerations rather than by 'best practice' prescriptions.

## General objectives of performance-related reward plans

Why do organisations choose to use performance-related rewards at all? In general terms, such rewards can be seen as being directed at achieving one or both of two main objectives:

**Table 14.1** Incidence of performance pay plans in Canadian and Australian firms, c. 2000: percentage of sample firms using each plan type for non-managerial employees

|  | Canada | Australia |
|---|---|---|
| **Using one or more performance pay plans** | 94 | 87 |
| **Individual performance pay plans** | | |
| Any individual plan | 88 | 81 |
| Merit raises | 72 | 64 |
| Merit bonuses | 37 | 32 |
| Piece rates | 11 | 6 |
| Sales commissions | 27 | 28 |
| Special incentives | 29 | 29 |
| **Group performance pay plans** | | |
| Any group plan | 36 | 37 |
| Gainsharing | 14 | 17 |
| Goalsharing | 18 | 20 |
| Other group plans | 16 | 14 |
| **Organisational performance pay plans** | | |
| Any organisational performance pay plan | 52 | 40 |
| Profitsharing | 32 | 11 |
| Share bonus plans | 4 | 6 |
| Share purchase plans | 21 | 21 |
| Share option plans | 10 | 3 |
| Other organisational plans | 5 | 4 |

*Source*: Long & Shields 2005b: 1798.

1 the economic objective of increasing employee task motivation and work effort and, hence, of increasing desired performance outcomes
2 the cultural objective of transforming employee values, attitudes and behaviour so as to elicit higher levels of organisational commitment, membership behaviour and/or organisational citizenship behaviour.

Economic objectives can be broken down into three more specific purposes:

1 *Increasing task motivation.* This involves using performance-linked rewards to motivate or 'incent' greater work effort per unit of time worked, which should translate into increased labour productivity and reduced labour costs.

**Table 14.2** Incidence of performance pay plans in the UK, by sector, 2004: percentage of respondent organisations using each plan type

| | | Sector | | | |
|---|---|---|---|---|---|
| | All sectors | Manufacturing and production | Private sector services | Voluntary sector | Public services |
| Any cash-based bonus or incentive plan | 52 | 62 | 69 | 23 | 22 |
| Scheme driven by business results | 65 | 65 | 71 | 46 | 41 |
| Individual-based | 44 | 37 | 45 | 27 | 59 |
| Combination individual and collective | 38 | 37 | 40 | 55 | 22 |
| Team-based | 16 | 12 | 16 | 9 | 25 |
| Ad hoc or project based | 14 | 8 | 16 | 27 | 16 |
| Profitshare | 14 | 15 | 14 | – | 13 |
| Gainshare | 2 | 4 | 1 | – | – |
| Employee share scheme | – | 39 | 40 | – | – |

*Source:* CIPD 2005b: 6, 39–40.

2 *Altering performance standards.* This entails using a combination of formal performance measurement and performance-contingent rewards to renegotiate pre-existing performance criteria or standards.
3 *Increasing labour cost flexibility.* Also known as 'financial flexibility', this involves using performance-contingent pay to vary pay levels and aggregate labour costs in line with changes over time in the organisation's 'capacity to pay'.

The assumptions underlying the motivation objective are those that inform the main process theories of work motivation discussed in detail in chapter 3. To reiterate, these theories, which include reinforcement theory, expectancy theory and goal-setting theory, all emphasise the centrality of employee cognitive processes to understanding and managing the relationship between rewards and task motivation. For instance, reinforcement theory posits that a timely reward for a given desired action will motivate employees to repeat the rewarded action. Expectancy theory holds that a valued performance-related reward will motivate improved performance because performance is seen as being instrumental to achieving that reward. Goal-setting theory suggests that employees will be motivated more strongly by goals that are agreed and challenging and by feedback that is timely and precise. Agency theory (a model much favoured by economic theorists and considered in more detail in chapter 20) posits that if an organisation's owners are to overcome the propensity of their hired 'agents' (i.e. managerial and non-managerial employees) to pursue their own interests rather than those of the owners, or 'principals', then the rewards that agents receive should be contingent on delivering behaviour and results that align directly with the owners' material interests.

In addition to incenting greater motivation to perform to current performance standards, performance rewards may also be used to engineer a change in performance standards themselves. For instance, drawing on evidence on the introduction of individual performance pay throughout the British public sector during the 1990s, Marsden (2004) notes that although many employees found performance pay dissatisfying and divisive, labour productivity nevertheless rose. According to Marsden, this was because management was able to use a combination of individual performance assessment (especially via goal-setting) and performance pay to renegotiate performance standards and the 'effort bargain'.

In addition to direct economic motives, organisations often have another and, in many ways, more subtle objective in mind: that of using performance-related rewards to influence employee attitudes, values and behaviour and, hence, to shape or reshape the organisation's culture. Performance-related pay has been used symbolically to assist in developing a market-oriented, entrepreneurial and individualistic work culture, particularly by reinforcing a change in the espoused psychological contract. According to Kessler (1994), such change strategies may also have a number of corollary aims. In particular, they may aim to:

- weaken trade union influence
- undermine collective bargaining as the main means of pay determination
- revitalise and strengthen the role of the line manager by devolving reward decision-making from the human resources department to line managers themselves
- enhance employee commitment to the organisation by encouraging employees to 'buy in' to the organisation's success.

Brough (1994) goes further still, arguing that the organisational change objective explains the growth in employer interest in applying performance-related pay to manual workers in the UK since the 1980s. Performance-related rewards are seen as a potentially powerful means of articulating and achieving a new managerial culture and a new psychological 'deal'. For instance, the introduction of performance-related pay to privatised instrumentalities like British Rail and British Telecom was seen as a device for driving change in organisational culture and deunionisation (Kessler 1994; Kessler & Purcell 1995; also Heery 1997a & b). As noted in the Introduction to this book, the introduction of individual performance pay to the Australian Public Service was also informed by an explicitly cultural intent.

On this basis, in assessing outcomes from performance-related pay, it is important to distinguish between plan effectiveness in meeting short-term economic objectives, such as productivity and labour cost improvement, and success in facilitating attitudinal and cultural change over the longer term. Economic considerations may not be the only reason – or even the main reason – why organisations use performance-related rewards Management may be quite prepared to accept mediocre or even negative outcomes on the economic front, at least in the short run, provided that performance-related pay delivers greater success on the cultural front.

## Economic effectiveness of performance-related rewards

The belief that incentives have a powerful effect on work effort and results has been with us since ancient times (Peach & Wren 1992). Performance pay has certainly been on the rise in Western work organisations since the 1980s, and many senior managers from all sectors embrace incentive pay and its claimed benefits almost as an article of faith (Beer & Katz 2003).

As Gerhart (2000) and others have pointed out, a considerable body of research evidence points to a positive association between financial incentives and employee performance, at least in the North American context. A meta-analysis of studies of pay-for-performance plans indicated that two out of three such plans deliver performance improvements of some sort (Heneman, Ledford & Gresham 2000). Other US research suggests that the average monetary return on investment in performance pay plans is 134 per cent, while a 1998 survey of 500 US companies indicated that those actively using such plans achieved double the shareholder returns of those companies that were not active users (Beer & Cannon 2004). Earlier studies of US plans by Lawler (1971), Blinder (1990) and others suggest that performance-related pay schemes can increase productivity by as much as 15 to 35 per cent. US researchers Gerhart and Milkovich (1990) examined outcomes from managerial incentives in 200 companies and found that for every 10 per cent increase in the size of managers' rewards, the firm's return on assets rose by 1.5 per cent. Put slightly differently, every dollar spent on performance pay returned $2.34 in an organisation's earnings. Gerhart and Milkovich also found that the variable component of the managers' pay had a greater influence on both individual and organisational performance than did the size of the managers' base pay.

Overall, the evidence of a positive incentive effect is stronger for results-based plans than for plans based on behavioural assessment. Citing US examples, Gerhart and Rynes (2003: 170–1, 175) note that there are 'compelling examples of the effectiveness of results-oriented plans' and there is 'ample evidence that results-based incentive plans can greatly increase performance'. Further, they suggest (2003: 195) that strong individual results-based incentives not only have a positive incentive effect but also a potentially powerful 'job sorting' effect, whereby poor performers are actively 'managed out' while high-performing individuals will actively seek positions that offer high reward for high effort; in other words, individual incentive plans that are strongly pay-performance sensitive will attract those individuals who are favourably disposed towards a transactional psychological contract and repel those who are not.

There are also some celebrated cases of long-term success with results-based incentive plans, and although we shall consider the evidence relating to specific plans in subsequent chapters, it is instructive to pause here to detail one of the most widely cited success stories: that of the results-based incentive system operated by the US-based multinational electric welding equipment firm Lincoln Electric for its production employees in the USA and further afield for many decades now. This firm is wholly non-union, relies largely on existing employees and family networks to fill job vacancies, has a paternalistic work culture and operates a limited form of employee participation in the form of an employee advisory board. Lincoln Electric's incentive system is the cornerstone of its approach to human resource management. The main features of the Lincoln Electric system are:

- a piece rate system, with payment made only for goods that meet quality standards
- the absence of any guaranteed base pay (i.e. no hourly wage)
- an end-of-year individual merit bonus, involving twice-yearly performance ratings on four criteria: dependability, work quality, quantity of output, and workplace cooperation and contribution of ideas
- a profit-share bonus pool determined by the level of cash reserves remaining after the distribution of dividends to shareholders
- a restricted share purchase plan for employees with two or more years of service
- a strict policy of internal promotion
- job security for workers with at least two years service.

In effect, then, Lincoln Electric's espoused psychological contract is a hybrid of the relational and transactional contractual forms. According to company representatives, the firm has been successful for decades in meeting its economic objectives and being able to pay high bonuses without going into debt. The results are indeed impressive. Historically, bonuses have constituted more than 50 per cent of the total pay of the firm's US employees, and down to the 1990s the firm never failed to pay bonuses. In 1985 the average productivity was 2.5 to 3 times higher than that of workers in similar manufacturing plants. At the same time, average employee wages and bonuses were nearly 3 times the average pay for US manufacturing employees (Handlin 1992; Chilton 1993; Hastings 1999; Hodgetts 1997). The system also encourages strong membership behaviour; absenteeism and turnover rates being no higher than 2 to 4 per cent (Hastings 1999: 170).

In part, the Lincoln Electric approach works because it addresses three of the main problems traditionally associated with individual payment-by-results schemes: namely, fear of job loss, poor quality and constant rerating. The scheme guarantees that higher productivity will not result in job loss, rewards only work that meets quality standards, and has performance standards that have changed very little over time. Lincoln also has a low ratio of supervisors to line workers – 1:100 compared to a ratio of 1:25 in a typical US factory (Hastings 1999: 170). Company officials suggest that this is because piecework makes line employees more self-managing. In turn, the savings on supervision means that the company has more to spend on bonuses. (As we shall see below, however, the very success of the Lincoln Electric inventive system almost brought about the firm's undoing during the recession of the early 1990s.)

Not all mainstream management writers are enamoured of incentive pay. On the basis of survey responses from 200 senior executives from thirty countries, Beer and Katz (2003: 31–4) even suggest that executives' belief in incentive efficacy is a 'socially constructed myth'; a myth chiefly of US origin. Further, while advocating 'high pay contingent on organisational performance', best practice advocate Jeffrey Pfeffer (1998b; see also chapter 4) is highly critical of individual performance pay plans, arguing that they are antithetical to teamworking and cooperative work relationships.

Undoubtedly the most outspoken and influential critic of performance-related rewards in general in recent times, however, is the US social psychologist Alfie Kohn. His argument, in essence, is that all incentive schemes are necessarily dysfunctional because they are based on supposedly invalid psychological assumptions. His chief target (Davis 1995: 13) is Skinnerian behaviourism, with its mechanistic conception of reinforcement-driven motivation: 'We've turned American industry into a giant Skinner box with a parking lot.' In line with Deci and Ryan's cognitive evaluation theory of work motivation (1985; see chapter 3), Kohn contends that extrinsic performance-related rewards are antithetical to intrinsic motivation.

Kohn (1993a & b; Davis, 1995) makes six main points against incentive plans in general:

1 *Incentives undermine intrinsic interest in the job.* Employees may see financial incentives as a 'bribe' and therefore suspect that 'If they have to bribe me to do it, it must be something I wouldn't want to do'. According to Kohn, workers not receiving any special reward may outperform those who do. Following Deci and Ryan, Herzberg, and others, Kohn argues that the only genuine motivators are intrinsic; that is, interest in the job itself and enjoyment and satisfaction from a job well done. Pay bribes may actually cause people to lose intrinsic interest in what they do and reduce the quality of their work.

2 *Rewards motivate people to pursue one thing above all else: the reward.* Employees will demonstrate only the type of behaviour that attracts a reward. All unrewarded behaviour, including desired behaviour, is likely to be ignored. The resulting behaviour may well be wholly rational from the employees' perspective, but wholly dysfunctional for the organisation. The unintended consequence may be to encourage misbehaviour.

3 *Rewards punish.* No one likes to be manipulated, and rewards, like punishments, are essentially instruments for manipulating behaviour.
4 *Rewards rupture cooperative work relationships.* By rewarding individuals and fostering individual competitiveness, merit pay may serve to undermine cooperation and teamwork.
5 *Rewards ignore underlying reasons for work problems.* Incentive pay addresses symptoms rather than underlying causes. Managers fall into the trap of relying on incentive pay as a substitute for effective management strategies, such as appropriate job design, providing meaningful performance feedback, providing adequate opportunity to develop skills and competencies, and giving employees more discretion and autonomy to be creative: 'If you want people motivated to do a good job, give them a good job to do.'
6 *Rewards discourage risk-taking.* Incentives reduce risk-taking and creativity and reinforce a narrow focus on expected behaviour – on compliance rather than creativity and initiative.

It is important to note here that Kohn is not arguing that pay *per se* is unimportant. In line with Hertzberg's conception of pay as a 'hygiene factor' (chapter 3), Kohn argues that, when it comes to total pay, people should be paid well and paid fairly in base pay terms, but that the aim should then be to 'do everything possible to take money off people's minds' (Kohn 1998: 35). What Kohn is attacking is performance-contingent rewards, not generous base pay.

Kohn's arguments have themselves been challenged on both theoretical and empirical grounds. The proposition that incentive plans cannot be used to motivate desired performance is certainly contestable. Research shows that, under certain conditions (such as those prescribed by expectancy theory), incentives can exert a positive influence on behaviour. Challenging Kohn's logic, Gupta and Shaw (1998: 28) contend that money has motivational potential because of its 'economic and symbolic meanings': 'Money motivates because it can get us things – better houses, clothes, cars . . . Money [also] signals our status in and worth to society.' Invoking reinforcement theory, they contend that 'money motivates by rewarding certain behaviours; it also motivates by showing people what is valued in the organisation – it provides a cognitive map of the path people must take to succeed: i.e. to make more money' (1998: 28).

The assumption that extrinsic and intrinsic factors are dichotomous rather than complementary is also open to challenge. Kohn's claim that incentives displace intrinsic rewards draws mainly on research by Deci and Ryan (1985) that focused not on financial incentives for adult employees but on the behavioural responses of children in play situations. This research revealed that children who had been given intrinsically rewarding and enjoyable tasks but who were then offered extrinsic rewards in the form of money stopped doing these things for the fun of it and continued to perform only when monetary rewards were forthcoming. To extrapolate these findings to adult employees in work settings is, to say the least, questionable. Other research suggests that extrinsic and intrinsic rewards can make a joint contribution to job satisfaction. So it does appear that incentives can work directly to increase both job satisfaction and task motivation (O'Neill 1995; Evans et al. 1995; Gupta & Shaw 1998; Barton & Locke 2000; Rynes, Gerhart & Parks 2005). Canadian psychologists Cameron and Pierce (1997) use a meta-analysis of a hundred studies of reward–performance effects to argue that intrinsic and extrinsic motivation combine in an additive way to produce overall motivational force. They find that people generally enjoy performing a task more rather than less when they receive an extrinsic verbal or tangible reward. In particular, Cameron and Pierce find that praise leads to greater task interest and performance. The negative effects of extrinsic rewards, they suggest, are limited and easily prevented.

Kohn also assumes that all jobs are intrinsically rewarding when, in reality, this is not always so. For better or worse, many manufacturing and service organisations succeed quite effectively with job assignments that have limited skill content, narrow task range and low autonomy. This would certainly apply to organisations having what we have characterised in chapter 4 as a mechanistic structure.

A further criticism of Kohn's case is that he underplays the distinction between individual and collective incentives (Cumming 1994; Bennett Stewart 1993; Evans et al. 1995). His argument, if only by implication, is that the case against extrinsic incentives applies as much to collective schemes, such as team incentives and gainsharing, as it does to individual plans. Yet collective schemes rate only a passing mention in his argument. In asserting that rewards disrupt work relationships, Kohn points out that such plans are permeated with one of the most insidious forms of work pressure, namely peer pressure, and that group incentives are among the most 'transparently manipulative strategies used by people in power' (Kohn 1993a: 56). What we have here, however, is a grudging acknowledgment that such schemes may well be effective in achieving economic objectives. Moreover, Kohn overlooks the fact that group incentives are consciously directed towards encouraging the very attitudinal, behavioural and cultural characteristics that Kohn himself appears to endorse: teamwork, cooperation, shared effort and employee participation. Again, there is some evidence that appropriately designed group incentives can work. The available evidence points to a positive link, with the only question being the magnitude of the relationship.

Gupta and Mitra have attempted to discredit Kohn's arguments empirically by drawing on the results of a meta-analysis of thirty-nine published case studies of forty-seven distinct financial incentive–performance relationships; results which they suggest shows that 'the salutary effects of financial incentives are quite robust' (1998: 65). The results, they argue, also belie Kohn's claim that incentives erode intrinsic motivation: 'financial incentives are just as potent in inherently interesting and challenging jobs as they are in more boring and mundane jobs' (1998: 62). Indeed, Gupta and Mitra contend that their findings systematically debunk Kohn's 'myths' about incentive plans.

Yet even the findings of studies of apparently effective performance pay initiatives lend only qualified support to the case for such practices. For instance, while Gupta and Mitra's meta-analysis suggests a strong positive correlation between incentives and performance *quantity*, they concede (1998: 61) that the link to performance *quality* is far less robust: 'This information implies that financial incentives have a strong effect on how much an employee produces, but may not affect how well an employee does the job.' This is hardly what an organisation priding itself on customer focus and product quality would want to hear!

Overall, then, the evidence on the economic efficacy of performance-related pay is inconclusive. If Kohn is unduly pessimistic, then his opponents seem, at times, to be overly optimistic. Perhaps the safest conclusion to be drawn is that while performance rewards do have strong motivational potential, the key consideration is not whether they are applied but rather when, where and how they can be applied to best economic effect.

## Performance-related rewards and the management of culture

When it comes to the impact of performance-related rewards in the cultural sphere, the evidence is much clearer. Incentive pay can indeed be a powerful means of transforming employees' attitudes and beliefs. However, as illustrated in the Introduction, cultural change does not always unfold in the manner intended! As Hewlett-Packard discovered to its cost, organisational change strategies that use performance pay as a change-driver have their own design and implementation challenges. As such, should performance-related pay be used to drive cultural change, or should it be used only to reinforce such change? The conventional wisdom is that it is inadvisable to use pay to drive organisational and cultural change; rather it should be used to support and reinforce change (Flannery, Hofrichter & Platten 1996).

Are performance-related rewards more supportive of some desired cultural forms than others? Following the typology of managerial cultural orientations identified in chapter 4, can we say that performance pay is more likely to support a traditional low-trust approach or, alternatively, a high-involvement approach? On the one hand, it may be that performance pay – with its underlying logic of extrinsic control, reward and punishment – is most compatible with a traditional management culture; on the other, it is possible that, by encouraging employees to identify more closely with the organisation's financial success, as well as the chance to participate in that success, some performance pay plans may be conducive to high-involvement management.

As we have seen in chapter 4, Pfeffer and many other advocates of high-involvement 'best practice' propose that high pay linked to group or organisational performance is a key part of the best practice bundle (Becker & Gerhart 1996: 784–5; Huselid 1995; MacDuffie 1995). Group or organisational pay is deemed essential to foster the teamwork, cooperation and employee commitment necessary to make high-involvement management successful (Huselid 1995). In fact, Lawler (1986: 42) argues that the use of participative practices 'without rewards for organisational performance are dangerous because nothing will ensure that people will exercise their power in ways that will contribute to organisational effectiveness'.

However, the situation may be quite different when it comes to individual incentives. A major concern is that pay based on individual performance may encourage employees to place their personal interests ahead of those of the organisation. Another concern is that individual performance pay – particularly such forms as piece rates or sales commissions – may focus employees' attention narrowly on just one or two result areas, discourage employees from taking a broader view, and detract from the teamwork and interdependence essential to high-involvement management. Further, as Kohn argues, attempting to single out and reward individuals, in a context of high interdependence, may cause perceptions of inequity and create discord between employees.

The available empirical evidence on the relationship between management culture and particular types of performance pay – with the exception of profitsharing and share plans – is both relatively sparse and inconclusive. In his study of pay practices and 'high-commitment' management in British manufacturing firms, Wood (1996) found that while individual bonus plans were negatively related to high-commitment management, there was no significant relationship with the use of group or organisational incentives, including profitsharing. In contrast, a study comparing predictors of pay practice in Canadian and Australian firms (Long & Shields 2005b) found that high-involvement management was significantly related to profitsharing and other organisational performance plans and that high-involvement firms were neither more nor less likely than were more traditionally managed firms to use plans geared to individual or work-group performance; these results being common to both countries. As such, it may well be that the potential for individual and group incentives to support high-involvement management depends on the precise type of plan chosen.

Overall, the most consistent evidence is that relating to the synergy between high-involvement and organisation-wide incentives. Studies undertaken in North America, Europe and Australia (Drago & Heywood 1995; Freeman, Kleiner & Ostroff 2000; Heywood, Hubler & Jirjahn 1998; Long 1989, 1994, 1997; Osterman 1994; Wagar & Long 1995) point to a positive association between high-involvement management and profitsharing. Studies undertaken in the UK (Guest & Peccei 2001) and the United States (Blinder 1990) also suggest a positive relationship between high-involvement practices and employee share plans.

However, there is a further aspect of cultural fit that must be considered here: that of compatibility with national cultural values. Although other countries have certainly followed the trend, until recently incentive pay schemes were widely regarded as a Western phenomenon. Hofstede's classic research findings on cross-cultural differences (Hofstede 1984) indicates that US culture places a high value on individualism and tolerance of uncertainty (or acceptance of risk), both factors that are highly compatible with 'at risk' performance-related rewards. Yet, as others have suggested, performance-related rewards may not be compatible with the cultural values prevailing in other countries. As Beer and Katz (2003: 33) note: 'Compensation practices that abide by US logic may have unpredictable or undesirable effects when transplanted to other nations' soil.'

Lincoln Electric is one US multinational that had to learn this cross-cultural lesson the hard way. In the late 1980s, Lincoln Electric's management decided to respond to a loss of its US and global market share by engaging in a wholesale acquisition of competitor firms in Germany, Norway, the UK, the Netherlands, Spain and Mexico, as well as building 'greenfield' sites in Japan, Venezuela and Brazil. Having previously transplanted its traditional management culture and individually focused incentive system to plants in other Anglophone countries, including Canada and Australia, the firm's executives simply assumed that these tried-and-true practices would work equally well in these new sites and allow the company to quickly amortise its acquisition debts. That assumption, coupled with the overly ambitious expansion program, pushed the company to the brink of financial collapse during the recession of the early 1990s. Lincoln Electric's mistake was to assume that it could translate its individualistic management culture and reward practices to non-Anglophone workplaces with little if any alteration (Chilton 1993, 1994; Hastings 1999). As the firm's CEO at the time, Donald Hastings (1999: 178), subsequently observed: 'We had long boasted that our unique culture and incentive system . . . were the main source of Lincoln's competitive advantage. We had assumed that the incentive system and culture could be transferred abroad and the workforce could be quickly replicated.'

So Lincoln learnt about the importance of cultural fit the hard way. In 1993 it scaled down its operations in Europe and closed its plants in Brazil, Venezuela and Japan. The only new plant to which the incentive system was successfully transplanted was that in Mexico. This is all the more remarkable because piece work runs against the collectivist nature of Mexican culture, and the plant, which was acquired in 1990, had been highly unionised. What was different here? In a word, the *pace* of change. Individual incentives were introduced slowly to the Mexican plant: 'It took about two years: but the entire operation eventually adopted piece work. If it is done slowly and properly, the system can be introduced into some existing organisations or cultures where it might not seem to fit.' (Hastings 1999: 178.) The key lesson to be drawn from such experiences is that performance incentives can be used to support and reinforce cultural change but that the introduction of such systems itself requires cultural groundwork and preparation and, perhaps most importantly, patience and persistence.

# Just rewards?

So far we have considered the arguments and evidence relating to the effectiveness of performance-related rewards in delivering the results and behaviour desired by the organisation; that is, as to whether such plans can and do 'work'. From the employees' perspective, however, an equally important – if not more important – consideration, as outlined in chapter 2, is whether such plans meet the tests of perceived procedural and distributive justice.

One of the most common rationales for performance-related pay is that it operationalises the 'equity' norm of distributive justice. To reiterate: equity theory proposes, in part, that reward satisfaction stems from establishing congruence between employee inputs and outcomes. This is a common normative justification for performance-related pay. Here, for instance, is the rationale offered by Armstrong and Murlis (1994: 249): '... perhaps one of the most powerful arguments for performance pay is that it is right and proper for people to be rewarded in accordance with their contribution. It is equitable to differentiate rewards between employees performing at different levels in the same job. Employees should not be paid simply for being there: irrespective of how well they do.' Elsewhere, Armstrong (1996: 246) contends: 'It is right and proper for pay to be related to the contribution individuals make to achieving organisational objectives. High performers should be paid more than low performers.'

Reward relative to contribution; what could possibly be fairer? Yet there are those who argue that performance-related rewards stand to violate both distributive and procedural justice requirements. For instance, Heery (1996) argues that performance-related pay poses a threat to employee well-being because it contradicts employees' need for a stable and secure income; a need that is both economic and psychological. Without some level of guaranteed income, workers are likely to overwork and experience work-related stress and anxiety. This may lead to mental and physical health problems, which are bad not only for the individual but also for the organisation and society in general.

Heery also suggests that performance-related pay exposes employees' pay to disproportionate risk. Writing before the surge in executive reward levels in the late 1990s (see chapter 20), Heery (1996: 60) remarked that employee pay was being put more and more at risk at a time when executive rewards had risen to unprecedented heights: 'Despite the rhetoric of partnership which flows through the new pay literature, it is possible to discern a fairly hard-edged set of proposals for transferring the risks inherent in economic activity from those who are powerful to those who are less able to bear them.' To Heery, then, with such plans, there is a fundamental imbalance between the distribution of risk and the distribution of rewards. A performance-related pay scheme that is distributively just, Heery proposes, would be one that aims for a situation of 'acceptable risk'; one in which the interests of the employer in making pay contingent upon contribution is balanced against the interests of the employee in having a reasonably stable and predictable income.

Critics suggest that performance pay may also be procedurally unjust. According to Heery, such plans typically leave little scope for the independent representation of employee interests, or 'voice'. The assumption of shared interests means that performance pay leaves little scope for trade unions or collective bargaining (Heery 1996: 61): ' . . . employees have separate and opposing interests regarding remuneration to those of employers and therefore require a representative channel to secure the expression of those interests. This is not to say that shared interests also exist or that the new pay cannot foster complementary interests, but that the overlap between employer and employee will never be complete.' Procedural injustice may arise if pay is linked to performance measures that are either invalid or only partly within employees' control. Equally, procedural injustice may result from the use of performance criteria that, while being position valid, are not reliably applied. As noted in chapter 6, behaviourally based performance assessment is especially prone to unreliability.

Performance pay has also been questioned on the grounds that it may be especially disadvantageous to female employees. For instance, Rubery (1995) argues that women are likely to be worse off under performance-related pay, particularly where it takes the form of individual merit pay (see chapter 15). In the context of the greater discretion available to line managers, the subjectivity inherent in behavioural assessment is likely to disadvantage women relative to men, especially in service work, where supervisory positions tend to be male-dominated. Further, where individual incentives apply, the individualisation of the employment relationship stands to weaken women's bargaining power further still. At least with job-based pay and job evaluation, the prospects for reducing the gender pay and earnings gap are somewhat greater, partly because the process of pay determination is relatively open, transparent and amenable to employee 'voice' (Rubery 1995).

## Weighing up the arguments and evidence

Perhaps the most meaningful conclusion to draw from these debates on the efficacy and fairness of performance-related pay is that pay for performance may have the potential to elicit higher levels of desired behaviour and results from participating employees but that the effectiveness and felt-fairness of any such plan will be contingent on the mode of application, particularly the way the pay–performance linkage is configured, how effectively this linkage is communicated and accepted, and how appropriate it is for the organisational context involved.

On this basis, it is possible and meaningful to nominate a number of essential requirements for success with performance-related pay:

- The plan or plans used must be an appropriate 'fit' for the type of work, the espoused management culture, the expectations and values of the employees themselves, and the wider cultural context.
- The nature and purpose of each plan, and the performance criteria involved, should be communicated to employees well in advance of implementation.
- The performance criteria should be both valid (job relevant) and reliably (consistently and accurately) applied.
- Employees should believe that they have control over their performance as measured and, ideally, also have a sense of ownership over the performance criteria.
- The rewards should be commensurate with validly and reliably measured individual and/or group performance, and linked to such measures in a clear and transparent fashion.
- The plan must be administered in a procedurally fair manner.
- The rewards on offer should be of value to the employees covered.
- Promised rewards should be delivered in a consistent and timely manner.

## Chapter summary

This chapter has outlined the main types of performance-related reward, considered the general motives for adopting performance-contingent rewards, and overviewed the main arguments and supporting evidence for and against such plans, taking into consideration both plan effectiveness and felt-fairness. The chapter has also explored evidence on the general incidence of performance-related reward plans in a range of developed countries. The evidence overall indicates that there is certainly potential for a positive incentive effect but that the magnitude of the link varies significantly by plan type, plan context and plan administration, including the clarity and achievability of collective performance expectations, how much control employees have over performance measures, the degree of employee participation in system design and management, and the like. Whether the desired aim is performance enhancement or cultural change, performance-related reward plans are difficult to get right and extremely easy to get wrong. Incentive plans may not always backfire in the manner suggested by Kohn and other critics, but they can certainly create their own problems in relation to efficacy and fairness. As we work our way through each of the main types of performance-related reward in the chapters that follow, it is most important that we keep this caveat firmly in mind.

## Discussion questions

1 Should performance pay be used to drive change to an organisation's culture?
2 Is Kohn right or wrong about incentive plans?
3 Is Heery right in arguing that the pay of ordinary employees should not be put at risk?
4 Why do incentive plans so often fail?
5 Why might an organisation choose to use both individual and group incentives?

## Chapter Fifteen

# MERIT PAY FOR INDIVIDUAL PERFORMANCE

Merit pay is the most widely applied of the individual performance pay plans, and it takes two main forms: merit increments and merit bonuses. With merit increments – also known as merit raises – each employee typically receives an increase in base pay based on their annual performance assessment ranking or rating. These payments are referred to as merit raises or merit increments because they take the form of a permanent addition to base pay. By contrast, merit bonuses take the form of stand-alone payments that do not flow into the individual's base pay and must be re-earned each performance round. In this chapter, we examine each of these two variants of merit pay, beginning with merit increment plans, which are the more traditional of the two.

## Merit increments

In a typical traditional merit pay system, merit payments are delivered in the form of cumulative annual increments to the individual's base pay. The practice rewards employees for performance in a previous time period – typically one year – and, once given, each merit increment is 'folded' into base pay. In the USA and many other Western countries, annual merit increments still constitute the main form of regular base pay adjustment.

There are two distinct approaches to linking assessed performance to merit increments: (1) straight increments and (2) the merit grid approach.

### Straight increments

The straight increments option involves paying all employees who fall within the same performance grade an equal increment. You will recall that, where the system has an evaluative purpose, the aim of a typical behavioural assessment technique is to assign each employee to one of a predetermined number of performance grades, typically between five and seven grades. Those assigned to a particular performance grade then receive the same merit increment or raise. However, the increment may be expressed either as an equal dollar amount or as an equal percentage increase to base pay. Where a percentage increment is used, people who are in the same performance grade may well receive different dollar amounts because they may be on quite different levels of base pay. So even with straight increments, the organisation still has to decide whether the principle of equal reward for equal performance will be adhered to absolutely or only nominally. Why express the increment as a proportion of base pay rather than as a flat money amount? The assumption is that perceptions of the value of the merit increment will depend partly on how large it is in relation to base pay. Remember, the increment actually flows into base pay.

In the example in table 15.1, the five performance levels are: minimal, developing, proficient, outstanding and exceptional. Those rated as exceptional receive a 10 per cent increment; those rated as outstanding receive a 6 per cent increment; those rated as proficient receive 4 per cent; those rated as minimal receive no increment. The percentage increments for each performance grade will depend on the total merit pay budget, the number of employees in each performance level and their current level of base pay. All of these factors will need to be taken into account if the merit payout is not to overrun the budget allocation. For instance, if the total merit budget is 4 per cent of payroll, it would be problematic to have too many employees receiving increases of 6 or 8 per cent. Typically, an organisation will begin by allocating a quantum of the total merit budget to each performance grade; for example 20 per cent of the total amount available might go to the top grade, 40 per cent to the next highest grade (to cover the larger number of individuals involved), 60 per cent to the middle grade rating, and so on. The amount of funding allocated to each level is then divided by the number of employees in that grade to determine an average dollar payout. This average is then compared to the average base pay of employees in the relevant level to give an average percentage payout for the level.

**Table 15.1** Straight merit increments

| Performance grade | Base pay increment (%) |
|---|---|
| Exceptional | 10 |
| Outstanding | 6 |
| Proficient | 4 |
| Developing | 2 |
| Minimal | 0 |

The main problem with the equal percentage approach is that, in absolute dollar terms, it actually penalises those employees who, while assessed, say, as outstanding performers, may currently be on a lower amount of base pay amount simply because they are relative newcomers to the organisation or the position. They may well receive a lower dollar increment than those who are rated as proficient performers but who have been with the organisation for a longer period and therefore have a higher base pay. By default, then, straight increments privilege length of service or seniority. This may lead to dissatisfaction and demotivation among the organisation's rising high performers – a serious problem, indeed.

## The merit grid approach

The merit grid approach seeks to overcome the shortcomings of the straight increment option. The merit grid (or merit 'matrix' or merit 'guide chart', as it is also known) specifies the precise link between the assessed performance grade, the employee's current position in the base pay range and the percentage performance increment. In essence, the merit grid is a 'ready reckoner' for awarding merit increases based, first, on assessed performance and, second, on current position in the pay range. The chief aim, then, is to facilitate 'felt-fairness' in merit pay outcomes by specifying a precise link between performance level, existing base pay level and the merit increment. Merit grids are also designed to ensure that pay increases are applied consistently by supervisors throughout the whole organisation. Another important purpose is to communicate to managers and employees alike a clear linkage between assessed performance and merit pay outcomes.

There are three main steps involved in developing a merit grid:

1 constructing what is referred to as a compa-ratio index
2 drawing up a performance index and compa-ratio targets for particular levels of performance
3 constructing the merit grid itself.

Constructing a compa-ratio index involves plotting where all employees are currently positioned in their base pay range. The compa-ratio (short for compensation comparison ratio) indicates where employees sit in relation to the midpoint of their pay range. This is often referred to as the 'pay range penetration'. The compa-ratio is calculated by taking the individual's current base pay rate and dividing it by the midpoint of the relevant pay grade range.

As figure 15.1 indicates, an employee whose base pay is right on the midpoint of his pay grade range would have a compa-ratio of 1.00. In narrow graded structures, you will recall, the grade range midpoint is the desired level of pay for acceptable performance in the job or role concerned. An employee whose base pay equates to 90 per cent of the midpoint amount would have a compa-ratio of 0.90. An employee with base pay equal to 110 per cent of the midpoint would have a compa-ratio of 1.10.

Once individual compa-ratios have been calculated, these can then be aggregated into a weighted average compa-ratio for all employees in each particular grade. This summarises the ratio between the average amount actually paid to people in a particular base pay grade and the midpoint of the pay range for that grade. This statistic has many uses. It is a convenient tool for payroll forecasting and budgeting purposes. It is also a useful indicator of how effective and consistent the organisation is in managing base pay progression within and between pay grades. The compa-ratio average is a control index used for overviewing and assessing current base pay distribution and spread. Assuming a pay range of plus or minus 20 per cent around the midpoint, a compa-ratio of 1.00 equates with the midpoint of the pay range, 0.80 with the range minimum and 1.20 with the range maximum. A low aggregate compa-ratio might reflect underpayment, a large number of new employees, harsh performance assessment or all of these things. An average compa-ratio of 1.00 might indicate an acceptable distribution of employees through the pay range, assuming that employees are relatively evenly spread in terms of experience, seniority,

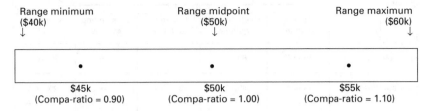

**Compa-ratio (or position in base pay range)**

| Range minimum ($40k) | Range midpoint ($50k) | Range maximum ($60k) |
|:---:|:---:|:---:|
| ↓ | ↓ | ↓ |

| $45k (Compa-ratio = 0.90) | $50k (Compa-ratio = 1.00) | $55k (Compa-ratio = 1.10) |
|:---:|:---:|:---:|

**Performance index and target compa-ratios:**

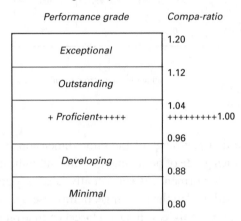

| Performance grade | Compa-ratio |
|:---:|:---|
| Exceptional | 1.20 |
| Outstanding | 1.12 |
| + Proficient+++++ | 1.04 <br> +++++++++1.00 <br> 0.96 |
| Developing | 0.88 |
| Minimal | 0.80 |

**Figure 15.1** Compa-ratios

competency and performance. An average compa-ratio of more than 1.00 would reflect a large number of senior, experienced employees in the grade, overly generous performance ratings, an uncompetitive salary midpoint or all of these.

The next step in developing a merit grid is drawing up a performance index and compa-ratio targets for particular levels of performance. The targets provide benchmarks for where individuals should ultimately be positioned in their pay range, given a particular level of sustained performance. Let us say the performance assessment system again identifies five broad categories of overall performance: minimal, developing, proficient, outstanding and exceptional. This performance range can be matched with target compa-ratios for each of the five levels. In the example in figure 15.1, the five levels of performance are given a spread of plus or minus 20 per cent from the midpoint, which equates with a compa-ratio of 1.00. This

| Current performance grading ↓ | 'Base pay range penetration' = current position in base pay range (quintiles) → | | | | |
|---|---|---|---|---|---|
| | Minimal quintile | Developmental quintile | Qualified quintile | Outstanding quintile | Exceptional quintile |
| Exceptional | 6%–8% | 6%–8% | 4%–6% | 3%–5% | 2%–4% |
| Outstanding | 6%–8% | 4%–6% | 3%–5% | 2%–4% | 2%–4% |
| Proficient | 4%–6% | 3%–5% | 2%–4% | 2%–4% | 0% |
| Developing | 2%–4% | 2%–4% | 2%–4% | 0% | 0% |
| Minimum | 0%–2% | 0% | 0% | 0% | 0% |

↑
Pay range mid-point (compa-ratio = 1.00)

**Figure 15.2** The merit grid

can then be aligned with a pay range of the same dimensions to give an ideal compa-ratio for each grade of performance. This will indicate where, say, an employee whose performance is consistently rated as outstanding should ultimately be positioned in the pay range. In this case, a consistently outstanding performer, for example, will have a target compa-ratio of 1.04 to 1.12. By this means, the organisation can identify, in broad terms, where employees who perform consistently at a particular level should ultimately be located in their pay range.

The merit grid allows the organisation to match the employee's current compa-ratio and performance grade with a specific merit increment. Figure 15.2 provides an example of a merit grid. In this case, the pay range compa-ratios are broken into quintiles and merit increments for each performance rating are specified as percentages of base pay rather than as flat dollar amounts. Note that for each level of performance, progressively smaller percentage increases are given for higher compa-ratio groups. This means that the better the performance rating and the lower the existing position in the pay range, the larger the percentage increase. Conversely, the higher the existing position, the lower the percentage increase, which means that employees with the same level of performance should receive around the same dollar amount no matter how large or small their existing base pay happens to be.

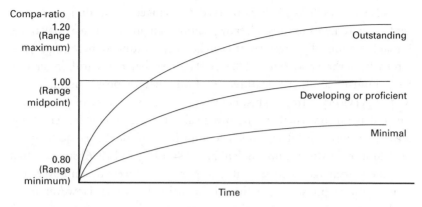

**Figure 15.3** Merit increment curves

What is the logic behind lower percentage increments for those on high base pay? The aim is to promote fairly rapid pay acceleration for new job incumbents to the competitive midpoint but, at the same time, to control pay costs at the top end of the range so that the organisation does not become uncompetitive. Remember, the midpoint (compa-ratio 1.00) is designed to provide a competitive level of pay for acceptable performance within the job or role concerned. If all employees in the same performance grade received the same percentage increase, there would be an inbuilt tendency for ever-wider pay inequality since those beginning with a high base pay level would necessarily receive greater absolute increases and those on a low start base would be progressively demotivated because they would always receive lower absolute amounts for the same level of performance. The idea of the discounted percentage increment for high performance is to ensure that, over time, employees within the one base pay grade or band and with a similar level of *sustained* performance end up receiving the same amount of base pay in their grade.

The overall logic of the merit grid is perhaps best captured by means of merit pay curves, such as those in figure 15.3. The higher and more sustained the performance (consistently outstanding), the steeper the initial rise and the higher the ultimate position in the pay range. Conversely, the weaker the underlying performance (minimum), the lower the rate of increase and the lower the ultimate position in the range. For sustained competent performance (consistently proficient) the ultimate range position is the midpoint, or a compa-ratio of 1.00.

As Lawler (1990: 74–5) has observed, the danger in awarding lower percentage increments to those already positioned high in their base pay range is that the nominally lower reward can be demotivating to these employees. Similarly, Gerhart and Rynes (2003: 169) remark that 'merit grids inherently have a built-in "antimerit" feature, aside from whatever problems might exist with supervisory ratings'. This, however, is largely a matter of perception. Much depends on whether employees value the increments in percentage terms or in absolute dollar terms. The empirical evidence here is quite equivocal. Research (Mitra, Gupta & Jenkins 1995, 1997; Teel 1986) suggests that it is the percentage increase that is important in terms of employee perception and response, rather than the actual dollar value. However, other studies suggest that what is ultimately important is the monetary amount itself, not its ratio to base pay. For instance, a study of the impact of merit pay in a large US transit authority (Scott, Markham & Vest 1996) suggests that the motivation and job satisfaction of high performers does not suffer because their actual dollar increments, coming off a higher base pay level, will still be as high as or higher than the money increments obtained by lower performers. It would seem, then, that the crucial issue here is how – and how effectively – the logic of the merit grid formula is communicated to the employees affected.

While the merit grid approach is widely used in large organisations, it is really suited only to pay structures based on narrow job grades and possibly broad grades. It does not lend itself well to use with broad bands since the emphasis on compa-ratios, current pay range position and range control points is incompatible with broad-banding's philosophy of flexible contribution-based pay progression.

## The merits and demerits of merit increments

From an organisational perspective, merit increments have many potential advantages. First, since pay increments are linked to achieved individual performance, the risk of the employer receiving no return on a pay increase is less than would be the case where pay is not directly performance-related, as in a traditional structure involving seniority-based pay scales. As such, merit increments increase performance-contingent flexibility in base pay adjustment. Reduced or withheld increments can send a strong signal to substandard performers that improvement is required. Although the reward is retrospective, increments can act as an incentive for higher future performance. The associated performance assessment process can also improve vertical communication between management and staff.

Second, merit increments signal the organisation's willingness to 'invest' in employees over the longer term and, as such, support internal career paths and relational psychological contracts. Likewise, because they increase base pay, merit increments can also increase membership behaviour and reduce labour turnover.

Third, from the employees' perspective, there is no 'downside' risk to total pay level. Upward pay adjustment may fall off if performance also declines, but total pay will not shrink. Merit increments, then, do not place employees' economic security at absolute risk.

On the other hand, there is no shortage of evidence that the merit increment approach is a problematic remuneration practice. First, merit increments are prone to the problems associated with individual performance assessment. Behavioural assessment, in particular, is subjective and prone to unreliability. Moreover, given the link to pay, assessors are often reluctant to give hard ratings because they know that this will deprive the employee of a pay rise.

A second problem is that merit increments conflate performance-contingent pay and base pay. Typically, base pay rises are made up of three elements rather than one: an individual performance component, a cost of living component and a market adjustment component to maintain a competitive position in relevant labour markets. Obviously, such an approach runs the danger of conflating performance rewards and needs-based adjustments to base pay. This means that employees may fail to see a clear and objective link between performance and pay outcomes. Virtually everyone gets an increase, and the tendency has been for employees to see the merit increment as a cost-of-living *entitlement* rather than as a performance reward.

A third disadvantage for organisations is that each merit increment amounts to an 'annuity'; that is, it becomes a permanent addition to base pay. This results in a compound growth in base salary, and the employee continues to receive past increases as annual entitlements irrespective of subsequent performance. While the merit grid approach can control this to some extent, the annuity problem is especially pronounced in straight increment systems. Figure 15.4 illustrates the nature of the annuity problem in the absence of regressive increments along merit grid lines. In this example, a

378    Rewarding employee performance

**Case**
- 5% merit increment paid each year to an employee on a commencing salary of $50,000 and who consistently achieves a 'proficient' performance grading over five consecutive years

**Consequences**
- $2,500 increment paid for performance in year 1 multiplies to $12,500 over five years.
- Employee receives cumulative merit increment payments totalling $40,097 over five years, equivalent to 13.8% of accumulated five-year salary payments of $290,097.

| Annual increments | Year 1 (start salary = $50,000) | Year 2 | Year 3 | Year 4 | Year 5 | Cumulative Payments over 5 years |
|---|---|---|---|---|---|---|
| +5% year 1 | $2,500 | $2,500 | $2,500 | $2,500 | $2,500 | $12,500 |
| +5% year 2 | | $2,625 | $2,625 | $2,625 | $2,625 | $10,500 |
| +5% year 3 | | | $2,756 | $2,756 | $2,756 | $8,268 |
| +5% year 4 | | | | $2,895 | $2,895 | $5,790 |
| +5% year 5 | | | | | $3,039 | $3,039 |
| | | | | | | $40,097 |
| Annual base salary | $52,500 | $55,125 | $57,881 | $60,776 | $63,815 | $290,097 |

**Figure 15.4** Merit increments: the annuity problem

5 per cent annual increment paid to an employee on a commencing salary of $50,000 for sustained proficient performance over five years produces accumulated merit payments over the five years totalling $40,097, equivalent to 13.8 per cent of accumulated five-year total salary payments of $290,097. In this example, the employee does continue to deliver an acceptable level of performance. The key point, however, is that past increments are retained and compounded, irrespective of current performance. Consequently, an employee could remain at the top of his pay range even though his performance may have tapered off. Once granted, a merit pay increase ceases to be contingent on assessed performance and becomes a permanent addition to payroll costs. The cost of the merit increment in year 1 is compounded into base pay in all subsequent years that the employee remains with the organisation. In other words, the employee is rewarded every year for performance given in one year. Critics tend to single out the annuity problem as the principal shortcoming of traditional merit increments (Lawler 1990, 2000; Schuster & Zingheim 1996; Zingheim & Schuster 2000a).

A fourth shortcoming is that the size of the traditional merit increase is often too small to have any effect on motivation and performance. This is usually a symptom of inadequate budget allocation. An important point of contrast between both types of merit pay on the one hand and many other forms of performance-related pay on the other is that merit pay plans are not self-funding. This is because merit pay is generally based primarily on assessed behaviour rather than on 'hard' financial results. The total amount available for payout is not driven by a formula for measuring financial performance. Rather, the schemes must be funded by means of a special payroll budget allocation. The size of this budget allocation will, of course, determine the total pool of funds available for distribution as individual rewards. Therefore, in designing individual incentive schemes of this type, organisations must consider not only how payouts will be allocated but also the overall size of the individual performance pay budget. While the absence of a funding formula means that management retains autonomy to control the overall cost of such programs, the result is often budget allocations that are too parsimonious to enable adequate reward differentiation between high and low performers. The amount set aside for distribution is usually small, typically 2 to 5 per cent of total payroll (Budman 1997). Employees also tend to have no understanding of how the merit budget is determined, and the lack of transparency can engender distrust. Generally, the size of the merit budget is linked to changes in external market conditions over which employees have little or no control. In times of market downturn, merit funding may be cut back to zero, which may mean that no employee receives an increment, not even the star performers. This too can be demotivating, since it stands to violate the 'instrumentality' requirement and is likely to be seen as a breach of the psychological contract. As expectancy theory posits (see chapter 3), where employees are promised a reward for achieving a certain level of performance, and where the specified performance standard is achieved, failure to deliver the promised reward is likely to erode trust, instrumentality cognitions and hence work effort and performance outcomes.

A related problem is the absence of adequate reward differentiation between high and low performers. This frequently arises from central tendency error in the performance rating process, which is considered in chapter 6. It is not unusual for the merit increases received by high performers to be no more than 5 percentage points above that received by average performers, a degree of differentiation that critics suggest is too small to be meaningful (Budman 1997: 33; Heneman 1992: 151–4; Lawler 1990: 72). In individualistic work cultures, such as that prevailing in the USA, failure to differentiate adequately between high and low performers can have adverse consequences for an organisation. Research on merit pay for faculty members in US colleges and universites (Terpstra & Honoree 2005) indicates that individuals who receive the same merit pay as co-workers who are performing at a lower level were most likely to resign in response to the perceived inequity.

So what is the range over which merit increments are most likely to be motivational? Mitra, Gupta and Jenkins (1995, 1997) suggest that the minimum increment large enough to be motivational is 6 to 7 per cent of base pay. Anything less than this is seen as non-performance-related. Workers who receive rises above this threshold are far more likely to believe that the increment is genuinely merit-based and to be satisfied with the results. The same research also suggests that the perception of a linkage between performance and pay steadily weakens as increments fall below 10 per cent. Interestingly, Mitra, Gupta and Jenkins also find that percentage increases beyond 15 per cent are unlikely to improve motivation and performance any further. Payments above 15 per cent are likely to be seen as a windfall rather than as a reward for contribution. Of course, it is highly likely that such perceptions will also vary according to the prevailing rate of consumer price inflation, which necessarily places a floor on the level of expected inflation-related (as opposed to performance-related) base pay adjustment. If the prevailing rate of price inflation is 5 per cent, annual increments of a lesser amount are not likely to be accepted as being performance-based.

## Merit bonuses

The main alternative means of linking pay outcomes to individual performance assessment is the merit bonus approach, also know as the 'lump sum' method. A bonus is a payment made quite separately from base pay. Merit bonuses do not become annuities and, to be retained, they must be re-earned. The critical difference between this approach and traditional merit increments is that the payments made are conditional rather than cumulative. In short, they avoid the annuity problem. This may be one of the reasons for the increasing popularity of the merit bonus alternative (Lawler 1990: 82; Schuster & Zingheim 1996: 144–7).

In fact, many merit pay plans now combine increments and bonuses. As illustrated in figure 15.5, a merit pay plan may limit regular assessment-based increments to the midpoint of the relevant pay range (a compa-ratio of 1.00). The logic here is that a compa-ratio of 1.00 equates to a proficient level of performance, whereas compa-ratios of less than 1.00 signify that the employee is still in a developmental phase. The aim, then, is to use merit increments as a means of recognising and rewarding development towards the level of job or role proficiency. Once this level is attained, however, merit increments cease, and any increases in total pay beyond this level take

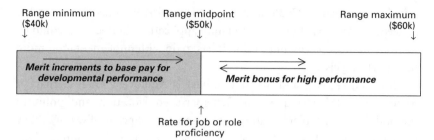

**Figure 15.5** Merit bonuses

the form of stand-alone bonuses that have to be re-earned each year to be retained. This means that while no employee can have a base pay greater than the midpoint value, there is still opportunity to receive additional amounts of pay related to individual performance. Of course, the system must remain attuned to the market, with the midpoint being adjusted in line with market movements rather than with changes in the cost of living.

## The effectiveness of merit pay

What evidence is there that merit pay does improve individual performance? Even advocates like Heneman concede that while the link to such instrumental outcomes as employee satisfaction, motivation and performance is positive, the performance effect is, at best, modest. Drawing together the results of twenty-two studies that examined the influence of merit pay plans on employee satisfaction, motivation and performance, Heneman (1990: 243) found that 'the relationship between merit pay and performance does not appear to be particularly strong'. He found that merit pay plans are more likely to influence employee attitudes than outcomes and that somewhat more favourable outcomes were attained in the private sector than in the public sector. In a meta-analysis of research covering forty-two merit pay plans, Heneman (1992) identified ten studies that claimed to address the relationship between merit pay and performance. Heneman noted that five of these studies reported a statistically significant correlation, whereas the remaining studies reported non-significant associations. Even where outcomes were significantly positive, the magnitude of the relationship between pay and performance was not large. From this, Heneman (1992: 258) concluded: 'The results to date on the relationship between merit pay and subsequent motivation and performance are not encouraging.' Heneman (cited in Budman 1997: 36) attributes this not to any inherent flaw in the concept of merit pay but rather to faulty application: 'it doesn't seem to be working in most places, but I think it has to do with implementation more than anything else.'

However, Gerhart and others (Gerhart & Milkovich 1992; Gerhart & Rynes 2003: 187–92) question Heneman's equivocation and point to methodological problems with his meta-analysis. Specifically, only a few of Heneman's studies used any control cases, and only six examined longitudinal associations; that is, performance levels after the implementation or removal of a merit pay plan. However, of these six, four indicated that the effect of merit pay on performance was indeed positive. Arguing that the 'actual evidence on merit pay is primarily positive', Gerhart and Rynes (2003: 189–92) make two main observations. First, they suggest that the stronger the link between assessed performance and merit pay outcomes, the higher the level of employee satisfaction and motivation. Second, they argue that the relationship between merit pay and subsequent performance outcomes is 'almost exclusively positive, although not always statistically significant'. They also suggest that to gauge the full effect of merit-based rewards, it is necessary to take account of the promotion-based increases to base pay as well as annual within-grade increments: 'Not surprisingly, studies that ignore the importance of promotions are less likely to find a strong link between pay and performance.' This assumes, of course, that promotion itself is validly and reliably related to performance.

Most of the research evidence to date regarding merit pay relates explicitly or implicitly to traditional merit increments. Could it be that the newer form of merit pay, namely the merit bonus approach, is more effective than merit increments in motivating individual performance? If expectancy theory assumptions hold, then bonuses should be more effective, because they establish a more direct line of sight between performance level and a level of reward that is not absorbed into base pay. Further, in line with reinforcement theory, fear of bonus loss should sustain a high level of performance. There is some research evidence in support of these motivational assumptions. For instance, a study of managerial pay by Kahn and Sherer (1990) found that those managers who had previously had the strongest link between bonuses and performance continued to have the highest performance levels, even after controlling for previous performance.

As suggested in chapter 14, however, performance improvement may not be the only criterion – or even the main criterion – by which organisations prefer to assess outcomes from a merit pay plan. Even if merit pay plans fail to deliver 'hard' economic gains, this does not necessarily mean that they have failed. Indeed, if the economic track record of merit pay is so lacklustre, why does it remain so widely used? The answer may well lie in what Heneman (cited in Budman 1997: 34) refers to as the 'John Wayne factor'. Merit pay epitomises the corporate culture of rugged individualism. Despite its instrumental shortcomings, it can have a powerful symbolic effect on an organisation's culture: the symbolism of individual effort and excellence.

## Merit pay in the public sector

Some commentators (Risher, Fay & Perry 1997) suggest that assessment-based merit pay is well suited to reward management in public sector organisations. In part, this is because formal supervisory assessment has long been part of public sector human resource practices. Indeed, some of the most valid, reliable, robust and long-standing systems of individual performance assessment are to be found in public service agencies, albeit primarily for the purpose of staff development and promotion. Another reason here is the strong emphasis on work behaviour in public sector performance criteria.

However, the available research evidence also sounds a clear note of caution regarding attempts to link performance assessment to individual merit increments or bonuses in public service contexts. As noted in the Introduction, research by O'Donnell and colleagues (O'Donnell 1998; O'Donnell & O'Brien 2000; O'Donnell & Shields 2002a) on the application of merit pay in Australian Public Service agencies since the early 1990s highlights many of the problems that may arise from such initiatives, particularly the possibility that altering the purpose of performance assessment from a developmental to an evaluative or reward focus may actually serve to undermine the integrity of the assessment system itself. The experience with merit pay in the Department of Finance, one of the most powerful agencies in the Australian Public Service, is a case in point. On the basis of employee testimony, it would appear that the department's merit pay system failed the twin tests of procedural and distributive justice. Perceptions of distributive injustice seem to have compounded an underlying lack of trust and faith in the department's performance assessment practices. For instance, although the initial rating scores provided by supervisors were moderated by senior management ostensibly to ensure consistency throughout the organisation, many employees believed that these initial ratings were moderated downwards for budgetary reasons to limit the overall cost of the performance management scheme (O'Donnell & Shields 2002a).

Similar findings have been produced by studies of outcomes from merit pay initiatives in the British public sector during the 1990s. Marsden and Richardson's survey of the performance-related pay scheme in operation in the British Inland Revenue Service found that it had, at best, limited motivational effect because of widespread employee concerns regarding the procedural fairness of the system (Marsden & Richardson 1994: 253–4). For example, many employees believed that a quota applied to the number of top-rating scores and that there was favouritism in the allocation of ratings (Marsden & Richardson 1994: 257–8). A study of managers' and professionals' perceptions of an individual performance management and reward system in a British National Health Service hospital (Redman et al. 2000) found that although a majority of employees felt that performance assessment with and one-on-one feedback from their supervisor contributed positively to their personal motivation and job satisfaction, views about the merit pay component were largely negative. A particularly strong theme to emerge from this study was the tension between the fact that, whereas the performance pay was individually based, performance itself was highly dependent on team effort.

In sum, the application of merit pay in public sector contexts appears to have several major pitfalls, each of which would need to be addressed for such systems to be effective and procedurally fair. One obvious problem is that of budget constraint. Where the pool of merit pay funds is strictly limited, reward distribution may amount to a zero-sum game in which securing a payment necessarily comes at the expense of other employees. As we have seen, this can also lead to the integrity of the performance assessment system itself being compromised by the moderation of ratings. Then there are wider questions to do with the suitability of individual merit pay for public service work. Individual short-term incentives, including merit pay, may be incompatible with the high degree of task interdependence and cooperation required in the provision of services to the public. Such rewards may also be incompatible with the values and attitudes that underlie the motivation and commitment of public servants.

The clearest message from the available research evidence is that a combination of behaviourally based assessment and individual merit pay may be incompatible with the values and attitudes of public sector employees. As we shall see in chapter 17, it may be that, if individual performance-related rewards are to be applied to public sector employees, a more acceptable approach may be to combine individual performance rewards with a more transparent, results-based approach to performance management in the form of goal-setting.

## Best fit with merit pay

In general terms, then, where might it be appropriate to use assessment-based merit pay? Merit increments based on supervisory appraisal would be especially applicable to traditionally managed and mechanistically structured organisations where the work is closely supervised and individualised, where work performance is focused more on behaviour than results, where it is possible to identify a valid set of task behaviour, and where the base pay structure consists of narrow job grades. Where results are readily quantifiable, however, it may be more appropriate to use results-based reward plans, such as goal-based bonuses, in such organisations. Merit bonuses based on multisource assessment may be a better fit in organisations with an analyser strategy and managed along high-involvement lines, especially in helping to recognise and reward behaviour relating to quality and customer focus. In such organisations, merit bonuses would be quite compatible with broad grades and skill-based base pay progression. However, care would also need to be taken here to ensure that individual rewards do not undermine teamwork and cooperation. Merit bonuses could also be applied in high-involvement organisations with prospector business strategies, where the emphasis is on risk-taking, creativity, innovation and timeliness, rather than on behavioural compliance, although such organisations will be more inclined to look to results-based incentives.

As we have seen, assessment-based merit pay may be a poor choice for public sector organisations. Indeed, some of the most striking examples of dysfunctional merit pay are those concerning attempts to apply merit bonuses to employees in public sector organisations. The emphasis on measurable performance over-emphasises certain aspects of the job and may be detrimental to overall service provision. The emphasis on individualism may undermine collective commitment to the ideal of public service, trigger petty jealousy, inhibit cooperation and erode motivation and morale.

In the absence of an adequate merit budget, the resort to rerating may also undermine perceptions of procedural and distributive fairness, with potentially dire consequences for staff motivation and retention.

## Chapter summary

This chapter has focused on merit pay, which is the remuneration corollary of individual behavioural assessment and remains the single most widely used form of individual pay for performance. We have examined each of the two main variants of merit pay, namely the more traditional merit increment (or raise) approach, and the increasingly widely used merit bonus approach. With merit increment plans, we noted the problem of payments becoming annuities. We also considered the pros and cons of the merit grid method of increment determination. Merit bonuses, which take the form of stand-alone payments, address the annuity problem and establish a clear distinction between base pay and performance pay and, as such, are likely to have a stronger incentive effect. However, since they are based chiefly on behavioural assessment, both types of merit pay stand apart from many results-based incentive plans in not being self-funding. Both require a dedicated budget allocation and, as we have seen, funding levels are frequently too low to enable adequate recognition to be accorded to high performers, a problem that is especially pronounced in public sector merit pay plans. Overall, merit increments are better suited to traditionally managed and mechanistically structured organisations, whereas merit bonuses would be a better fit for high-involvement analysers and prospectors.

## Discussion questions

1 Should something as subjective and error-prone as behavioural assessment be used to determine reward outcomes?
2 What advantages do merit bonus plans have over merit increments?
3 What is a compa-ratio, and what purpose does it serve in remuneration management?
4 What are the merits and demerits of the merit grid?
5 Should performance pay be used in a public sector context? If not, why not? If so, is merit pay the best choice?

## Chapter Sixteen

# RECOGNITION AWARDS

As noted in chapter 15, one of the chief shortcomings of merit pay as a means of recognising and rewarding individual performance is its formalistic basis and once-a-year payment regimen. To address these problems, in recent times many organisations that are committed to rewarding individual performance have opted for a range of more flexible and timely practices known generically as 'recognition awards'. This chapter considers the rationale of such plans and the variety of recognition practices, especially the competing claims of cash and non-cash plans. We then canvass the arguments for and against such plans, and conclude by considering the situations to which special recognition plans may be best suited as well as least appropriate.

## The logic of recognition plans

Recognition award exponent Donald Hay (1998: 1) notes: 'The primary goal of a recognition program is to express appreciation for the efforts and achievements of employees. Recognition can be as simple and informal as a verbal or written thank you or as sophisticated and formal as an organization-wide nomination process.' A key attraction of recognition awards is that they represent a flexible, low-cost and potentially effective alternative to regular merit increments or bonuses, and it is no accident that recognition awards have risen to prominence during the era of shrinking merit pay budgets. Hay (1998: 1) suggests that while recognition cannot replace pay, it can be a significant adjunct to a well-designed reward system: 'Regular and frequent acknowledgment of employee contributions can be a powerful addition to an organisation's reward strategy. The development and use of simple, low-cost recognition vehicles can help create a more flexible and robust reward strategy.'

McAdams (1999: 242) defines 'recognition plans' as those that 'honour outstanding performance after the fact and are designed for awareness, role modeling, and retention of recipients'. McAdams (1999) also distinguishes between 'recognition plans' and 'performance improvement plans' in that the former are retrospective and generally discretionary in nature whereas the latter are formula-driven and specify both performance expectations, targets or goals and potential reward outcomes in advance of actual performance. Recognition for immediate past performance may involve rewards that are either financial or non-financial in nature. However, the cash and non-cash approaches are by no means mutually exclusive and, as we shall see, the two frequently go hand and hand in a 'total reward management' approach.

Recognition awards can be categorised according to six main dimensions:

1 the frequency with which rewards are given (day to day, weekly, monthly, quarterly, yearly)
2 whether recipients are individuals or groups
3 how award recipients are determined (by supervisors, peer nomination or customers)
4 the performance criteria (membership behaviour, task behaviour, organisational citizenship behaviour, results)
5 the degree of plan formality and structure: informal plans include *ad hoc* awards issued at the discretion of the supervisor; more formal or structured plans include 'employee of the month' awards that cascade through to 'employee of the year' ceremonies
6 the form that the award takes (cash, non-cash, or combined cash and non-cash).

While many recognition plans are based on supervisory assessment of employee excellence, in many cases decisions about award recipients are made by peers. Peer nomination is said to invest awards with greater credibility and reward valence. Peer nomination also allows the employer to sidestep the need to find objective criteria for measuring employee performance.

Schemes in which award winners are nominated by customers also appear to be growing in popularity. In some cases, high-value customers are provided with books of gift vouchers. A client who is especially impressed by the service provided by one of the organisation's employees can issue a gift voucher on the spot, meaning that reinforcement is personalised and instantaneous. There is anecdotal evidence that customer-driven recognition awards are becoming widely used in the financial services, travel and hospitality industries, particularly retail banks, airlines, hotels and restaurants.

Recognition awards are more often directed primarily at reinforcing membership behaviour and encouraging organisational citizenship behaviour than at motivating higher levels of task behaviour. For instance, some schemes focus on encouraging membership behaviour in the form of regular attendance and timeliness. Other schemes seek to elicit higher levels of organisational citizenship behaviour by recognising and rewarding employee suggestions and inventiveness.

As a general rule, the more formal and highly structured the recognition program, the more likely that it will be cash-based, focus on individual or group results, have infrequent, high-cost rewards, involve supervisory nomination and have relatively few recipients. Conversely, the less formal the program, the greater the number of recipients, the more frequent the rewards, the greater the use of non-cash rewards, the greater the use of peer and customer nomination, and the greater the emphasis on individual behaviour.

Advocates (e.g. Nelson 1994: 73) argue that recognition should be both celebratory and fun: 'If you can reward a person and have fun in the process, you will satisfy two important desires of most employees: to be appreciated for the work they do and to enjoy their jobs and workplace.' The more formal schemes run by some large firms occasionally incorporate an element of serendipity in the selection process. For instance, the 'Reward and Recognition' scheme run globally by American Express includes fifteen specific recognition award plans: a 'Thank You Note' plan (leading to cash prizes), cash-based 'Achiever of the Month' and 'Achiever of the Year' awards in each of its offices, as well as a regional 'Great Performers Award', 'Chairman's Award for Quality' and an international 'Great Performers Grand Award'. Under the Amex 'Thank You Note' plan, staff get a wad of printed 'Thank You' notes to send along to any colleague who displays 'Blue Box Value'; that is, a high focus on customers and quality, being a team player and being a 'good citizen'. Each month, there is a draw of 'Thank You' note senders *and recipients*, and the winning pair each receive travellers cheques and have their award written up in the in-house journal. All senders and recipients also become eligible to participate in an annual Christmas party draw for a further round of more high-value prizes. While winning is a function of both performance excellence and the luck of the draw, the Amex plan also incorporates significant recognition and reward for the recognisers as well as the recognised (Freeman 1996).

## Cash recognition

The simplest and one of the most widely applied forms of cash recognition plan is the discretionary bonus. Discretionary bonuses are irregular lump sum awards for outstanding performance made at the discretion of the supervisor and/or senior management. Payment is kept completely separate from base pay, and the size of the payment is not tied in any arithmetic way to a performance measurement formula. Such payments can be used as a substitute for base pay increments, so that total pay itself can actually fall if performance is deemed by management to be substandard. The attraction of this approach is that it avoids bureaucratic procedures, across-the-board payouts and mechanistic formulas, and maximises management discretion about the frequency and amount of reward for meritorious performance.

A growing number of organisations regard irregular bonuses of this type as a means of making individual performance pay more flexible and targeted. While lump sum bonuses were once confined almost exclusively to senior management and sales staff whose performance could be easily quantified, they are now spreading to non-managerial employees.

Discretionary lump sum payments, being highly visible, can communicate a strong performance message. They are often spent in different ways from smaller, if more regular, merit increments. For example, a lump sum bonus may be used to take a holiday or to purchase a piece of valuable furniture or a new stereo, and may therefore have a more enduring effect on motivation than smaller but more frequent cash increments that become lost in base pay.

Discretionary bonuses have a number of advantages for organisations:

- The reward is payable immediately so there may be a clear and instantaneous reinforcement effect.
- The organisation is not committed to making payouts on a regular basis.
- The payment does not become an annuity.
- Lump sum rewards are highly visible.

- Additional rewards can be given to those at the top of their pay range without inflating future base pay costs.
- They are simple and easy to administer.

On the other hand, discretionary bonuses have these potential drawbacks:

- They are difficult to apply to people whose jobs have less tangible outcomes (e.g. sales support staff).
- They are individualistic and may impair team cooperation.
- The discretionary and arbitrary nature can mean that there is little clear link between performance and pay.
- If paid regularly (as with the 'end-of-year bonus'), they may come to be seen as an entitlement and a form of base pay adjustment – just like merit increments.
- Because they do not always differentiate between employees, high performers may feel that their contribution is not fairly recognised, which can be demotivating.
- They may discriminate against those working on long-term projects where tangible outcomes and rewards may be months or even years away.

## Non-cash recognition

The reward systems of many Western firms now incorporate relatively sophisticated, low-cost incentives in the form of non-cash recognition plans. Leading exponents like Bob Nelson (1994, 1996, 1997) and Jerry McAdams (1996, 1999) argue that cash has lost much of its cachet as a motivational device, particularly when it takes the form of traditional appraisal-based merit increments. They suggest that organisations are looking increasingly to other, more imaginative and enduring ways to recognise and reinforce individual and team performance. Recognition of a non-monetary type is said to provide instant reinforcement, increase the flexibility and spontaneity of the reward system, and enable 'high-visibility' recognition of desired behaviour and results. Non-cash rewards for high performance are also said to have a longer 'shelf life' than cash; that is, they have enduring 'trophy value'. A further potential advantage of such rewards is that they can be readily applied to work teams as well as to individuals.

The days when non-cash recognition was limited to a gold watch for long service or at retirement are long gone. McAdams (1999: 245–51) identifies seven basic forms of non-monetary recognition in current use:

1 social reinforcers: a pat on the back, respect, positive feedback, staff involvement in planning and decision-making
2 in-house learning and development opportunities
3 merchandise: either pre-selected items of significant monetary value or access to self-selected goods and services by means of shopping vouchers or certificates, retailer-specific debit cards, or printed or on-line catalogues from which specific items can be acquired by accumulating sufficient recognition points over a period (Russell 2004b)
4 travel: all-expenses-paid trips for individuals, families or groups
5 symbolic awards: plaques, personal letters from the CEO, flowers, books, 'thank you' notes, publicity in in-house journals or the staff intranet, pins, gold watches, pens and desk-sets, books, CDs and DVDs, restaurant meals, theatre tickets, tickets to sporting events, access to corporate 'boxes' at entertainment venues, T-shirts, embossed mugs, company umbrellas or hats, gym or sporting club membership, concierge services, massages, free parking spaces and the like
6 earned time off: time-off with pay additional to normal paid leave entitlements
7 flexible or family-friendly work schedules: ability to adjust working hours to fit personal needs and family commitments.

McAdams notes (1999: 246) that in the USA merchandise, travel and earned time off are the most popular non-monetary means of recognising outstanding performance. Indeed, recognition award merchandising is now something of a boom industry in the USA and elsewhere, and a number of major web-based providers are servicing the growing demand, including Hinda Incentives, Carlson, Maritz Inc. (McAdams' own firm), Wishlist and others.

Many merchandise-based plans incorporate both peer nomination and reward self-selection. For example, under a non-cash recognition program introduced for 400 staff at the Australian National Credit Union (ANCU) in 2004, staff accumulate points that can be redeemed on the Wishlist merchandise website. Any employee can nominate a peer for 'demonstrating and living ANCU's core values'. The employee's supervisor is then required to approve the nomination and to decide the number of points to be awarded. Wishlist manages the nominations and fulfilment and reports on the program to ANCU management. One obvious benefit of this approach is that it passes the test of reward valence since the employee can choose from a wide range of merchandise. The ANCU plan has evidently enjoyed stellar success. In its first nine months of operation, there were 500 instances of points being awarded (Russell 2004b).

Some large US-based multinationals operate highly formalised symbolic recognition systems in their global operations. For example, fast-food giant McDonald's applies a highly structured regimen of symbolic awards throughout its many thousand franchises around the globe. The McDonald's system includes, *inter alia*, a Quality Service pin, a Cleanliness pin, a Drive Through pin, a Back Area pin, a Front Counter pin, a Crew of the Month Award, awards for Employee of the Month and the Quarter, an Outstanding Performance Award and a McDonald's ring for ten years service. The more prestigious awards carry a valuable gift or prize of some sort as well as some corporate glory (Freeman 1996).

Non-cash recognition programs have undoubtedly become much more widely used in Western (especially Anglophone) countries since the 1990s. In 1985, only 2 per cent of recognition plans in US firms had non-cash awards; by 1992, 16 per cent were using awards of this type (McAdams 1995: 372). It appears that a majority of US firms now use such plans. While it might have first come to the fore in the USA, non-cash recognition is no longer a peculiarly American practice. Firms based in other Western countries such as Canada and Australia are also making greater use of non-cash rewards. A recent Towers Perrin (2003: 13) study of performance and reward practices in 240 US and Canadian businesses notes: 'Non-cash rewards are on the rise, probably because of their role in helping employers manage costs, engage employees and differentiate top performers.' Almost half of the firms surveyed offered non-cash rewards to high performers, and a further 12 per cent planned to do so with the next two years. Significantly, more of these firms (49 per cent) offered non-cash awards than special lump sum cash recognition awards (39 per cent).

Australian firms also seem to have turned to non-cash recognition with considerable enthusiasm in the past few years. According to survey data compiled by Mercer Human Resource Consulting (2004), the proportion of Australian firms offering non-financial recognition awards rose from 55 per cent in 2002 to 76 per cent in 2004. A number of local specialist providers of non-cash recognition have also emerged, such as RedBalloon Day (Simpson 2005). However, Australian practice would appear to be mainly symbolic and top-down, with on-the-spot 'Thank You' notes and acknowledgement in company publications being the most widely used practices, and decisions regarding reward allocation reside largely with supervisors and senior executives. According to the Towers Perrin study, most Australian plans were also 'irregular' and results-based, with the majority of plans being geared to goal achievement. Significantly – and perhaps ominously – the proportion of Australian organisations assessing the effectiveness of their non-cash reward plans is both small (only 13 per cent) and declining, although US and Canadian firms show a similarly low level of formal plan evaluation (Towers Perrin 2003: 14). Moreover, a considerable proportion of Australian firms remain sceptical about the claimed benefits of non-cash plans. Three-quarters of surveyed Australian firms reported that non-cash plans were effective in motivating employees, but the remainder doubted the efficacy of non-cash incentives (Russell 2004b).

## Non-cash recognition: for and against

Supporters of non-cash rewards (Hay 1998; Nelson 1996; McAdams 1999; Patrickson 2001) argue that traditional cash incentives, particularly merit raises, quickly lose motivational strength, partly because employees come to see 'merit' adjustments to base pay as entitlements rather than as rewards. Advocates of the non-cash option suggest that organisations should seek to recognise and reward performance excellence in more personalised, imme-diate and exciting ways. McAdams (1995: 372) asserts: 'It is easier and more effective to promote the excitement of a noncash award than its cash equiv-alent. Noncash awards have built-in excitement and recognition factors that cash simply doesn't have.' According to Nelson (1996: 68), firms should 'dump the cash' and 'load on the praise': 'Today's employees may not need a pay raise as much as they need a personal thanks from their manager for a job well done.' Exponents also point out that unlike cash rewards, which are quickly spent, non-cash awards have enduring 'trophy value', serving as a constant reminder of the recognition reveived (Brooks 1994: 39; McAdams 1999: 373). Non-cash recognition is also said to be just as applicable to teams as to individuals (McAdams 2000).

Advocates of non-cash recognition tend to invoke a (sometimes uneasy) combination of the needs-based motivation theories and reinforcement the-ory (à la Skinner and Thorndike). As noted in chapter 3, reinforcement theory posits that behaviour which attracts timely recognition and consis-tent reward is likely to be repeated. At the same time, advocacy of non-cash recognition programs frequently resonates with the needs-based models of work motivation formulated by Maslow, Herzberg and others (Cherrington 1991). As we have seen, Maslow's widely invoked 'hierarchy of needs' identifies social affiliation, esteem and self-actualisation as the three 'higher-order' human needs; the satisfaction of each requiring acknowledgement and recognition of the individual's acceptance, worth and achievement (Maslow 1943). Similarly, Herzberg (1966, 1987) included psychosocial 'recognition' as one of the key 'motivators', while monetary rewards, he suggested, were 'hygiene' factors; that is, necessary but not sufficient for high job satisfaction and hence high performance. Employee surveys do indeed indicate that being recognised for a job well done is one of the most frequently identified sources of job satisfaction, commitment to the organisation, and task motivation.

McAdams claims that non-cash rewards are both more motivating and less costly than cash bonuses. He has produced research findings on the cost-effectiveness of different types of reward for sales staff in 600 organisations, which, he suggests, reveal a major difference between cash and non-cash incentives. Cash incentives apparently improved sales performance by 13 per cent and cost 12 cents for every additional dollar of sales. Non-cash incentives also improved sales performance by about 13 per cent, but cost only four cents per dollar of sales (McAdams 1995: 373–4). There is also some evidence that non-cash plans are associated with higher performance by firms. For instance, Towers Perrin (2003: 17) reports that high-performing US and Canadian companies (i.e those with average five-year total shareholder returns above the relevant industry average) make significantly greater use of non-cash recognition (57 per cent) than do low performers (36 per cent). Of course, this data does not *prove* that non-cash plans pay; it may simply be that high-performing companies have more scope to offer additional rewards of this type. However, a longitudinal study comparing the influence of financial incentives and non-financial (social) recognition on profitability, customer service and employee turnover in twenty-one fast-food franchise stores found that while cash incentives had the stronger initial influence on all three result areas, over time non-financial incentives had an equally significant influence on profit-levels and customer service, although not on membership behaviour (Peterson & Luthans 2006). Therefore it may be that, over time, non-cash recognition practices have just as much influence on motivation and task behaviour as does monetary recognition.

Conversely, critics such as Kohn (1993a; Davis 1995) argue that, like all forms of performance-contingent reward, non-cash recognition is doomed to failure. Arguably, however, the key to understanding why non-cash recognition plans succeed or fail lies not in high theory but in matters of plan design, communication, roll-out and upkeep.

To be sure, non-cash recognition plans are not necessarily problem-free. In particular, such plans may:

- create an atmosphere of 'winners' and 'losers' (when the same few employees repeatedly get the award) or, alternatively, of 'everyone a winner' (where everyone takes a turn at receiving recognition) (McAdams 1999)
- be demotivating where employees feel that the reward is tokenistic and patronising ('beads and trinkets') and not worth the effort
- lead to charges of favouritism
- be seen as a substitute for regular pay
- do little to motivate underperformers.

Some rewards may also convey unintended messages. For instance, McAdams (1999: 254) cautions against using earned time off to reward high performers since this may reinforce the perception that leisure is pleasure and work is pain. Moreover, even the most ardent supporters of non-cash recognition acknowledge that it cannot replace cash. Indeed, the conventional wisdom among leading remuneration writers (Lawler 2000: 53, 76, 96–9; Zingheim & Schuster 2000a: 189, 195, 197; Armstrong & Murlis 2004: 371) is that, at best, non-cash plans represent a potentially valuable complement to financial rewards in a well-integrated 'total reward management' system. A study by Applebaum and Kamal (2000: 733) of job satisfaction predictors and non-financial reward efficacy in small business contexts finds that recognition and other non-financial rewards 'are most effective when supplemented with an income that allows employees to meet physiological and security needs for themselves and their families'. To say the least, then, cash retains much of its importance in the total reward mix.

## Best fit with recognition plans

In general, cash recognition plans are likely to have greatest appeal in organisations espousing a transactional psychological contract whereas non-cash recognition will be a better fit for cost-defender organisations favouring relational contracts and a traditional management culture. By instituting formal systems of symbolic recognition and praise, traditionally managed organisations can enhance employee commitment without compromising the power and prerogative of management. In quality defender and analyser firms, individual non-cash recognition may also encourage a cooperative workplace atmosphere, particularly in conjunction with peer nomination. However, in such situations, it would be more appropriate to apply non-cash awards of a group rather than an individual nature.

Are recognition plans also better suited to some roles than others? Given the paucity of published research evidence on the incidence of recognition plans, our observations here must remain speculative and tentative. Overall, individual non-cash recognition seems particularly well suited to service sector organisations, such as retail banks, retail stores, data processing firms, fast-food chains and hospitality firms, where staff perform routine tasks under close supervision and where performance itself is measured primarily in terms of customer-focused behaviour, including via voluntary customer satisfaction surveys. If the existing anecdotal evidence is any guide, formal non-cash incentive plans may have greatest appeal to staff performing routine task work or team-based work rather than those undertaking highly discretionary work or those located further up the organisational hierarchy. This does not necessarily mean that non-cash recognition is inappropriate for senior professional, managerial and executive level employees. However, both mainstream motivation theory and current reward practice suggest that the reward expectations of such individuals will focus primarily on promotion, pay and wealth acquisition rather than on rewards of a social and symbolic ('trophy value') nature. As we shall see in chapter 20, at executive level, the dominant and preferred forms of performance recognition are cash and company equity. After all, professional and managerial employees with large mortgages, high acquisitiveness and high achievement motivation will be looking for rewards in the form of pay, status and promotion rather than rewards of a social and symbolic nature.

## Chapter summary

In this chapter we have examined some of the more exotic and novel forms of performance reward: special cash and non-cash recognition awards. We began by contemplating the rationale for such plans, then turned to examine the variety of recognition practices, including both cash recognition and non-cash recognition. Next, we covered the arguments for and against such plans, reprising many of the general points made in chapter 14. Finally, we considered the situations to which special recognition plans may be best suited as well as those for which they would be least appropriate. In general, individual non-cash rewards are more likely to strike a chord among employees in traditionally managed organisations than among employees in high-involvement organisations. They are also more likely to be effective in the service sector where staff perform routine tasks under close supervision and where performance itself is measured primarily in terms of customer-focused behaviour. Group non-recognition would be a better choice for employees in high-involvement organisations, although for managerial and professional staff, cash recognition in the form of discretionary bonuses would be more appropriate.

## Discussion questions

1 Has cash really lost its cachet as a motivational device?
2 What are the advantages and pitfalls of discretionary cash bonuses?
3 What motivation theories underpin the argument for special recognition?
4 Is non-cash recognition just motivation on the cheap?
5 'A little praise can go a long way.' Discuss.

Chapter Seventeen

# RESULTS-BASED INDIVIDUAL INCENTIVES

This chapter considers some of the oldest and most enduring (although not necessarily the most endearing!) of all performance pay plans, namely results-based individual incentives. Also known as individual 'payment-by-results' plans, these include piece rates, task-and-time bonus plans (where employees are rewarded for completing a specified volume of work or a task in less than a 'standard' time), sales commissions and bonus payments to individuals for achievement of goals. We consider each of these plans in turn, noting the advantages and drawbacks of each.

With such plans, the result–reward relationship can be either standardised (i.e. a single rate of reward per unit of output) or configured according to a sliding scale, as in the case of progressively scaled payments, whereby the *rate* of payment itself increases as output rises. Sometimes these systems are used in conjunction with a guaranteed minimum base pay; sometimes, as in the case of pure piecework and commission-only work, there is no guaranteed base pay at all. Piece rates and task-and-bonus plans were developed primarily for labour-intensive manufacturing jobs and had their heyday in the early to mid-twentieth century, when they were at the forefront of innovation in reward theory and practice in industrialised economies. However, interest in individual output-based incentives of this type has waned with the relative decline in manufacturing activity in Western economies since the 1970s. Sales commissions, of course, remain widely used in such sectors as retailing, finance, insurance and real estate. Goal-based individual reward plans have become an increasingly important feature of white-collar professional and managerial work. A major attraction of these results-based plans for employers is that they offer greater certainty, immediacy and objectivity in the pay–performance relationship than that offered by other pay plans. However, as we shall see, results-based incentives can themselves be problematic and should be handled with caution.

## Standard piece rates

Straight or standard piece rates are the oldest form of performance pay, having been the principal form of payment to craft workers in the pre-industrial guild system (Peach & Wren 1992: 8–9). The practice also assumed considerable importance in the industrial era, both in new skilled occupations, such as printing, engineering and iron-moulding, and in mass production industries, such as clothing and shoe manufacture, where both factory employment and outwork were common.

In a standard piece rate plan, the employee receives a flat rate of payment for each unit of output produced, irrespective of the volume of output or the time taken. Hence, in a stand-alone standard piece rate system, if the rate of payment per unit produced is $10, the employee's gross earnings for nil output is zero, $50 for 5 units, $100 for 10 units, $200 for 20 units, and so on. Hence, for each additional unit produced, individual earnings rise arithmetically.

Such a system has a number of advantages for the employer. Most obviously, it establishes a clear and simple linkage between effort, results and reward. Workers who are paid by the piece are also less likely to require close supervision, since the payment system itself impels them to be more self-managing in relation to work effort, which in turn may significantly lower supervision costs. Straight piece rates may also eliminate the need for organisations to pay base pay.

By the same token, standard piece rate plans have a number of widely acknowledged disadvantages, particularly to do with the determination of an output standard by which the payment rate itself is fixed (Marriott 1957). First, output standards by which the payment rate is fixed have frequently been based on historical work effort norms rather than on the basis of what is technically possible with any given mode of technology. Even where an attempt is made to ascertain the technically optimal rate, the employees affected may reduce their work effort temporarily with a view to securing a rate that is too low – or 'loose' – so they can earn just as much or more with no more effort. Second, and conversely, a rate set according to the output of the best performing worker may be too 'tight', which in turn may cause employees to sacrifice quality and workplace safety in order to preserve earnings levels. Third, there is the fear of rerating. Workers may suspect that once they begin to exceed the set standard management may decide that that standard is too loose and may thus engage in rate reduction. In essence, this would mean that most of the benefits of productivity improvement would flow to the employer, with little of the gains going to employees themselves. Fourth, and relatedly, workers may fear working themselves out of a job if their productivity increases. Finally, straight piece rates are not well suited to situations where technology and work design are in a state of flux, since this will require frequent rerating, which would be costly and would corrode employee trust.

## 'Scientific' piece rates

The development of a 'scientific' approach to piecework that would avoid the problems of straight piece rates was one of the defining concerns of the first generation of modern labour management thinkers, none more so than the founder of scientific management, US mechanical engineer Frederick Winslow Taylor (1856–1915). Taylor's 'differential piece rate system', unveiled in 1895, was just one element of what Taylor claimed to be a revolutionary and comprehensive approach to labour management: the 'scientific management' approach, which called for a complete reorganisation of work and payment systems.

Taylor saw two fundamental weaknesses in standard piece rate systems. One problem was that of 'systematic soldiering'. The other had to do with employers' habit of cutting the piece rate every time employees lifted their effort level. In effect, this habitual and short-sighted rate-cutting simply penalised employees for working more efficiently, so their natural response was to engage in collective output restriction, or 'goldbricking' – or what Taylor preferred to call 'systematic soldiering'. Taylor's solution was to urge that piece rates should be set 'scientifically'. This meant using job analysis and systematic 'time study' to identify what output a worker working at peak efficiency was actually capable of producing task by task, then aggregating these optimal output figures to set the productivity benchmark and calculate the payment rate per piece.

The form of piece payment that Taylor recommended was far more sophisticated than the traditional flat rate per unit of output. Taylor devised what he called a 'differential' piece rate system. The 'high' rate was set such that the employee who met the standard earned 125 per cent of the base standard pay; the 'low' rate, for those who failed to meet the standard, was set at 80 per cent. This penalised workers who produced less than the scientific benchmark while offering a premium reward to those who beat the exacting standard. Taylor argued that both management and workers would be better off under his system: management through increased efficiency and productivity; workers through the exponential increase in earnings made possible by improved productivity (Peach & Wren 1992: 14–15; Taylor 1895; Cole 1918: 55–60). Even so, the implementation costs associated with Taylor's scheme were such that his piece rate plan found little favour among employers. Taylor's plan has the added disadvantage of being incompatible with any form of base pay.

## Task-and-time bonus plans

Rather more popular were the modified results-based schemes developed by several of Taylor's contemporaries, including Halsey and Gantt, and by later scheme designers like Emerson and Bedaux. Like Taylor, all were mechanical engineers. While their schemes differed significantly from Taylor's, they all shared Taylor's opposition to standard piece rates, and most embraced systematic work study methods as the best means of setting output standards. However, these later schemes had more appeal to employers because they could be superimposed on existing time-based systems of job pay. The main difference between these schemes was the way earnings varied with output. Some plans, like Halsey's, proposed a regressive link; some proposed a progressive link; some, following Taylor, advocated a differential link.

The 'premium bonus' system unveiled by US engineer F. A. Halsey in 1891 (four years before Taylor's own plan) was essentially a negatively geared, or regressive, scheme designed to reduce unit labour cost as output rose and involving a time-based incentive linked to standard time based on past output times, with a premium paid for beating past time standards. The premium was to be a third higher than the hourly rate, so delivering two-thirds of any productivity gain to employer. In other words, a worker who

**Table 17.1** Individual payment by results: standard piece rates, differential piece rates and premium bonus plans

| Types | Standard piece rate | | Differential piece rate | | Premium bonus | |
|---|---|---|---|---|---|---|
| Units produced | Rate per unit | Daily earnings | Rate per unit | Daily earnings | $ bonus @ 33.3% rate | Daily earnings |
| 15 | $10 | $150 | $12.50 | $187.50 | $16.67 | $116.67 |
| 14 | $10 | $140 | $12.50 | $175.00 | $13.33 | $113.33 |
| 13 | $10 | $130 | $12.50 | $162.50 | $10.00 | $110.00 |
| 12 | $10 | $120 | $12.50 | $150.00 | $6.67 | $106.67 |
| 11 | $10 | $110 | $12.50 | $137.50 | $3.30 | $103.30 |
| 10* | $10 | $100 | $10 | $100 | $0 | $100 |
| 9 | $10 | $90 | $8 | $72 | $0 | $0 |
| 8 | $10 | $80 | $8 | $64 | $0 | $0 |
| 7 | $10 | $70 | $0 | $0 | $0 | $0 |
| 6 | $10 | $60 | $0 | $0 | $0 | $0 |
| 5 | $10 | $50 | $0 | $0 | $0 | $0 |
| 4 | $10 | $40 | $0 | $0 | $0 | $0 |
| 3 | $10 | $30 | $0 | $0 | $0 | $0 |
| 2 | $10 | $20 | $0 | $0 | $0 | $0 |
| 1 | $10 | $10 | $0 | $0 | $0 | $0 |

* Daily output standard.

produced a greater number of pieces than provided for in the set standard time was paid for the standard hours plus a third of the hourly standard time equivalent for the extra pieces produced (Cole 1918: 47–54; Halsey 1896; Peach & Wren 1992: 13).

Table 17.1 illustrates the basis of Halsey's premium bonus plan and the main points of difference from both standard piece payment and Taylor's differential piece rate plan. Say the standard time is 10 pieces for an eight-hour day, for which the base pay is $100. A worker who actually produced 11 units in that time, under a 33.3 per cent premium bonus plan, would receive total daily earnings of $103.30, calculated as follows. The savings on the standard unit labour cost equals $0.90; that is, $10.00 ($100 ÷ 10) less achieved unit labour costs of $9.10 ($100 ÷ 11). Total labour cost savings are thus 11 times $0.90 × 11, or $9.90, of which 33.3 per cent (i.e. $3.30) accrues to the employee. For the day in question, the worker thus receives the fixed rate ($100) plus a third of the standard labour hours saved ($3.30), or a total of $103.30. For each extra unit produced beyond the standard output, the firm would receive *two-thirds* of the value added, which means that the *unit* labour costs must necessarily fall. As table 17.1 indicates, the returns to the employee would thus be far lower than under either standard piece rates or Taylor's differential scheme, and the returns to the employer would be commensurately higher. This would certainly mean that the employer would be less inclined to cut rates after any productivity improvement. Of course, it might also explain why premium bonuses of various sorts enjoyed considerably more popularity than the Taylorist alternative during the early to mid-twentieth century (Patmore 1988).

Gantt, one of Taylor's contemporaries, suggested that Taylor's scheme offered no real incentive beyond meeting the standard. His alternative was the 'task-bonus' system. Unlike Taylor's plan, it did not include a lower piece rate for substandard performance, but the task performance standard was still set using Taylor's work study methods. A worker who reached or exceeded the standard received a bonus additional to the standard piece rate, which amounted to a de facto higher piece rate for above-standard performers. Like Halsey's system, the Gantt formula included a guaranteed minimum hourly wage, but the time rate was set well below the rate paid for standard output, so that there was a strong incentive for workers to achieve the task standard (Cole 1918: 60–1; Gantt 1913; Peach & Wren 1992: 16).

Another contemporary scheme, the Emerson 'Efficiency' Plan, devised by US engineer Harrington Emerson, also provided guaranteed base pay, but emulated Taylor's method by prescribing a graduated differential 'efficiency bonus'. Every range of output was graded as a degree of 'efficiency', with standard output – that is, 100 per cent efficiency – being determined by means of time study and each level of lesser output graded as a smaller percentage proportion of full efficiency. At a specified level of efficiency, commonly 66 per cent, a bonus additional to base pay would be granted. The bonus rate then increases geometrically as a worker approaches standard efficiency, but above the 100 per cent efficiency standard it proceeds only arithmetically, so the gains accruing to the employer are exponentially greater for all output above the 100 per cent efficiency standard. In essence, this regressive scale was the reverse of that recommended by Taylor (Cole 1918: 61–3).

The most widely embraced of these early-twentieth century plans, however, was that devised by Charles Bedaux in the USA just after World War I. The 'Bedaux Point' system was similar in principle to a premium bonus system, but it also incorporated a regressive bonus scale. The system uses time units, called 'Bedaux Points' or 'B Points', rather than task times or output units to evaluate jobs and set effort standards. Calculation of these time units takes into account the requirement for both effort and rest pauses in working efficiently (a major oversight in Taylor's scheme). A B Point is a fraction of a minute of work plus a fraction of a minute of rest and, while the proportion will vary from task to task, the two must always sum to one minute. Each task is valued at a specific number of B Points (again using time study). Labour savings per hour is measured by the number of B Points by which the total exceeds 60, which is equivalent to a standard hour's work. Incentive payments increase according to the number of B points by which the worker exceeds the standard 60. In Bedaux's formulation, the employee receives a bonus equal to 75 per cent of the value of the time represented by the points saved, with the remaining 25 per cent being distributed to supervisors and management in recognition of their contribution to productivity improvement. Bedaux suggested that because the method was not task-specific, it could be applied to any employees in any occupation or industry (Bedaux 1921; Cole 1918; Marriott 1957). Indeed, in the interwar period, the Bedaux system was applied to both factory employees and clerical workers, particularly in Europe (Littler 1982: 108–15).

Although other variants of the time-and-task bonus approach exist, these are the classic formulations in the genre. Most drew directly on Taylor's job analysis and time study techniques, yet differential rate schemes, like Taylor's, Gantt's and Emerson's, have tended to be little used because of their sheer complexity and administrative difficulty. In contrast, because of their relative simplicity and adaptablity, the Halsey and Bedaux systems were applied quite widely, particularly in the 1920s and 1930s.

Whatever their technical differences, however, these schemes shared the same individualistic behaviourist assumptions. Some commentators (e.g. Marriott 1957: 36) suggest that the claimed differences between these plans are more apparent than real: '. . . all of the many plans are similar in a number of features. The name of their designer, generally attached to them, frequently appears to be the biggest single difference.' Taken together, they exemplify the combination of low-trust management culture and proto-typical transactional psychological contracting that characterised the employment relationship in the early industrial era. Although such firms as Lincoln Electric continue to swear by the worth of individual piece rate plans (see chapter 14 for discussion), their appropriateness to all but the most traditionally managed and labour-intensive firms must remain a matter of doubt.

## Sales commissions

Sales commissions are the retail sector equivalent of piece payment and, like the latter, they may be flat-rate, scaled progressively (or in rare cases regressively), stand-alone (commission-only payment) or paid as an overlay to base pay. Typically, a commission payment will be expressed as a percentage of the sale made. This might be a flat rate of, say, 5 per cent of the value of each sale. Alternatively, the rate may be configured according to a progressive scale, say 3 per cent of the value of the first ten sales per week, then 5 per cent for the next 10 to 19 sales, then 7 per cent of each sale over 20. Commissions may also be expressed as flat dollar amounts rather than as percentages of sales revenue achieved.

Whether the system is commission only or base pay plus commission will depend primarily on the nature of the product or service market involved, as will the proportion of total reward that is at risk via commission. Figure 17.1 summarises four such scenarios and the reward mix that may be most appropriate to each. Where the seller is required to expand sales of an existing product in an established market space – that is, to attract customers from current competitors – it may well be appropriate to apply either a commission-only approach or one in which base pay constitutes only a small proportion of potential total remuneration, since little or no time lag in new sales will be possible. Conversely, where the seller is required to engage in wholly new market development – that is, to sell new products to new customers – it may be advisable to configure rewards so that base pay constitutes either all or the bulk of total remuneration, at least until the new market is well established. Situations in which the seller is required to sell a new product range to existing customers, or to expand the market for an existing product, may warrant greater emphasis being placed on commission payments. However, the time required for consumer education may be such that base pay should still contribute a substantial proportion of total remuneration. In sum, decisions regarding the relative importance of

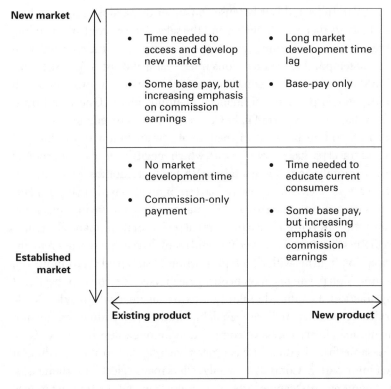

**New market**

| | |
|---|---|
| • Time needed to access and develop new market<br><br>• Some base pay, but increasing emphasis on commission earnings | • Long market development time lag<br><br>• Base-pay only |
| • No market development time<br><br>• Commission-only payment | • Time needed to educate current consumers<br><br>• Some base pay, but increasing emphasis on commission earnings |

**Established market**

**Existing product**         **New product**

**Figure 17.1** Product market context and sales commission configuration: four scenarios

commission earnings in the total reward mix should depend on the nature of the product market brief involved (Martocchio 2006: 295–310).

In general, commissions have the attraction of being simple to set and measure. They institute automatic task clarity and provide instant feedback and reinforcement. They substitute for direct supervision of sales staff, which is especially significant where staff are operating in the field rather than on the shop floor. Commissions are also likely to have a strong 'sorting effect' on staff profile, in that only the most effective salesworkers are likely to stay on. Unlike pieceworkers, employees on commissions are unlikely to fear that increasing sales performance will precipitate a rate reduction or job loss.

Like other forms of payment by results, however, commissions do have some general drawbacks. One obvious limitation is that commissions are limited to sales roles. Commission earnings are also notoriously uncertain and irregular. In part, this is because consumer demand is influenced by a range of factors that are wholly beyond the salesworker's control, including the interest rates on consumer credit, the general state of the economy, and spatial and temporal variation in consumer wealth and tastes. To assist commission staff to cope with income irregularity some firms provide staff with free independent professional financial planning advice. One such firm is the Australian air travel firm Flight Centre. Flight Centre employees receive between 25 and 50 per cent of their total remuneration in the form of ticket and travel package commissions, which inevitably leads to substantial month-to-month variations in total pay. Within three months of commencement, every new employee receives a free individualised financial planning session covering budgeting, debt management and savings planning. Employees are also entitled to a free annual review of their financial circumstances (Russell 2004c). However, it would seem that such assistance remains the exception in firms with a high proportion of staff paid on commission.

Commission payments may encourage aggressive, deceptive or negligent selling practices, including the sale of goods to consumers who may be unable to service a consumer credit or loan debt. Similarly, individual commission payments may foster excessive competition among salesworkers working for the same firm, leading to customer poaching and to the hoarding of market information. Commission-only sellers may neglect important tasks, such as good record-keeping, after-sales follow-up and the training of new salesworkers. Finally, unduly narrow definitions and measures of sales performance may damage the employer's interests. For instance, a focus on gross revenue generation rather than on profitability of sales may lead to suboptimal pricing and the erosion of profit margins.

## Goal-based individual bonuses

As noted in chapter 15, with merit pay plans, performance-related payments are based primarily on subjective performance assessment in which behavioural criteria are to the fore. One increasingly popular alternative to this is to base individual performance payments not on behavioural assessment but on individual goal achievement. In essence, these plans, which we shall call goal-based individual bonuses, entail annual or quarterly bonus payments linked directly to individual goal-setting. Although they were initially confined mainly to executives and senior managers, individual

**Table 17.2** Goal-based individual bonuses: simple and sliding scale plans

| Goal achievement | Simple flat scale* | | Progressive sliding scale | |
|---|---|---|---|---|
| | Rate of bonus payment | Amount of bonus paid | Rate of bonus payment | Amount of bonus paid |
| 130% | 100% | $1000 | 300% | $3000 |
| 120% | 100% | $1000 | 200% | $2000 |
| 110% | 100% | $1000 | 150% | $1500 |
| **100%** | **100%** | **$1000** | **100%** | **$1000** |
| 90% | 0% | $0 | 60% | $600 |
| 80% | 0% | $0 | 30% | $300 |
| 70% | 0% | $0 | 0% | $0 |
| 60% | 0% | $0 | 0% | $0 |

*Bonuses are paid out only if the performance target is achieved, which means that the organisation retains 100% of under-target performance improvement.

goal-based bonuses have become common features of reward practice for managerial and other salaried professional employees.

As with other results-based incentives, goal-based bonuses may be based on either a flat scale or a sliding (progressive or regressive) scale. Table 17.2 illustrates the difference between flat scale and progressive sliding scale bonuses. In each case the bonus paid for full goal achievement is $1,000. With the flat bonus plan, no bonus is paid unless the goal is met, and no additional bonus is offered for exceeding the goal. Either way, the absence of recognition for both 'near-miss' and 'over-achievement' performance may be demotivating to the individuals affected. An added problem with 'sudden death' plans of this type is that individuals falling just short of the target may engage in calculated dishonesty in order to improve their reward prospects. As one former chief executive of the Ford Motor Company observed, tying money to goal attainment in this way is 'a prescription for very smart people to find ingenious ways to make easy goals appear difficult, so as to ensure the receipt of their bonus' (cited in Latham & Locke 2006: 336). Sliding scale bonuses seek to avert this possibility. A threshold (or reduced) bonus applies where performance falls marginally short of the goal; the full bonus where the goal is fully achieved; and a premium bonus paid where the goal is exceeded. In the example shown in table 17.2, the bonus cuts in at 80 per cent of goal achievement, with a bonus payment being equal to 30 per cent of the full bonus ($300). For 100 per cent goal achievement, the employee receives 100 per cent of the $1000 bonus. A premium bonus is paid for performance in excess of full goal attainment, so that if goal achievement is 110 per cent, the bonus payout is 150 per cent of the goal achievement bonus – or $1500. For a 120 per cent level of goal achievement, the bonus payment is double the standard rate. In line with goal-setting theory (see chapters 3 and 5) the logic here is that full goal achievement must be challenging, so that any goal overrun connotes exceptional performance warranting a premium level of recognition.

Typically, bonus payments are based on aggregate performance across a series of goals measured by means of KPIs. For maintenance workers, for example, the goals and KPIs might include a mix of productivity, quality, work safety and customer satisfaction targets. At the end of each performance period (say, one month), workers would be assigned a performance index number based on the way their actual performance measured up against each agreed target. If actual monthly performance equalled, say, 90 per cent of the target, the index for that indicator would be 0.9. Rather than simply summing the performance indices for each goal to arrive at an overall result, the indices might be multiplied together and the resulting figure then used to calculate what proportion of the promised target bonus entitlement the employee will actually get. The logic is that it is more difficult to achieve three performance goals than one or two. Therefore employees should be rewarded proportionately more for overreaching their targets than for falling short. To illustrate: say the monthly bonus entitlement for meeting all three goals is $1000. Then if the actual performance indices are 0.9, 0.9 and 0.9, the multiplier would be $0.9 \times 0.9 \times 0.9$, or 0.729, and the actual bonus entitlement would be $1000 \times 0.729$, or $729 – a shortfall of $271. On the other hand, if all three goals are exceeded and the resulting performance indices are 1.1, 1.1 and 1.1, then the multiplier will be 1.331 and the bonus paid will be $1,331, or $331 over the target bonus. This amounts to a progressive individual bonus payment scheme.

The advantages and disadvantages of goal-based bonuses are essentially the same as those for goal-setting *per se* (see chapter 5). On the one hand, goal-setting introduces a degree of transparency, ownership and apparent objectivity rarely possible with a behaviourally based appraisal. In these respects, there is some evidence that goal-based approaches to individual performance-related pay may well be more effective in achieving instrumental objectives than those driven by performance appraisal. For instance, a study of a merit pay scheme for managers in the British National Health Service (NHS) (Dowling & Richardson 1997) reported that, unlike many other pubic sector schemes, the NHS scheme appeared to be 'modestly successful'. Using the results of an attitude survey of the managers affected, the study suggested that the NHS scheme had a positive motivational effect. The NHS scheme combined performance appraisal and individual goal-setting to determine performance pay levels. The NHS managers were particularly positive about the way their scheme delivered role and goal clarity, good feedback and support from superiors. They saw it as a clear and relatively objective means of performance measurement and reward. Interestingly, the NHS managers were far less positive about the qualitative or behavioural appraisal element, seeing it as inherently subjective. So it seems to have been the goal-setting element that was the scheme's saving grace.

Even so, as we have argued in chapter 5, goal-setting is not without its risks. Where goals are either too loose/easy or too tight/hard, too few or too many, a goal-based bonus plan is unlikely to be effective. Where the goals are financial in nature, such plans are self-funding, which means that they avoid one of the major shortcomings of traditional merit pay plans, namely that of budget underfunding. By the same token, where the plan incorporates non-financial goals, such as those related to site safety or customer satisfaction, goal achievement on these criteria will require special funding, with all of its attendant challenges. A further potential problem with the goal achievement approach is that it focuses the employee's attention and effort solely on goals that attract a reward. As with sales commissions, rewarding only the hard, measurable results may encourage employees to ignore equally important but less quantifiable aspects of the job or role. For instance, using only quantity-based goals may compromise product quality and site safety. Again, the key requirement is the setting of goals for each key result area (KRA) in the job or role, not just in those KRAs that are easiest to quantify and measure.

## Chapter summary

This chapter considers some of the oldest and most enduring of all performance pay plans, namely results-based individual incentives or individual 'payment-by-results' plans. We began by examining the oldest plan of all: standard piece rates, then turned our attention to more 'modern' adaptations, including 'scientific' piece rates plans and task and time bonus plans (where employees are rewarded for completing a specified volume of work or tasks in less than a 'standard' time). We then examined sales commissions, paying special attention to the distinction between commission-only plans and fixed pay plus commission arrangements as well as the factors to be considered in determining the mix of fixed and commission-based remuneration. Finally, we considered the option of individual goal-based bonuses. Despite their many differences, individual results-based incentives are relevant only to those situations where results can be validly defined, reliably measured and meaningfully attributed to individuals. Where this is not possible, group incentives of the sort considered in the next chapter may be a better fit.

## Discussion questions

1 Why do piece rates have such a high propensity to cause a breach of the psychological contract?
2 How do 'scientific' piece rates differ from standard piece rates? Are they any better – and for whom?
3 In what circumstances would it be appropriate to incorporate a high proportion of fixed pay in the total remuneration of sales staff working on commission?
4 'The main benefit of commission-only plans is not the incentive effect but, rather, the fact that such plans attract the right sort of person for the role.' Discuss.
5 'With results-based rewards, what does not get rewarded gets neglected.' Discuss.

Chapter Eighteen

# COLLECTIVE SHORT-TERM INCENTIVES

Performance pay plans that focus on recognising and rewarding short-term performance – that is, performance over a period of a year or less – fall into one or other of two broad categories: those that focus on assessing and rewarding individual performance; and those that focus on rewarding the collective performance of business units, work groups and/or teams. Having now considered the main options and techniques associated with rewarding individual performance, in this chapter we consider short-term incentive (STI) plans of a collective nature. We begin by outlining the general rationale for such plans and by overviewing the four main plan types: profitsharing, gainsharing, goalsharing and team incentives. Subsequent sections explore each of these four plan types in more detail, noting the advantages and disadvantages of each. Consistent with the approach taken in earlier chapters, a final section considers the circumstances in which each approach would be most and least appropriate.

## Collective incentives – rationale and options

Rewarding employees for their collective performance represents a fundamental departure from a focus on rewarding individual performance. In certain contexts, collective rewards may have decided advantages over individual incentives. Indeed, individual incentives may be quite dysfunctional in organisations where work is organised on interdependent and cross-functional lines and where results are predicated on a high degree of inter-employee cooperation. Interdependence of this type is one of the hallmarks of an organic organisational structure and a high-involvement management style. In such organisations, it may be neither possible nor logical to attribute performance to specific individuals, since what counts is collective effort and contribution. Collective incentives may encourage employees to work collaboratively to achieve goals that require teamwork and cooperation. Moreover, they may provide the basis for a 'win–win' situation in which all stakeholders – employees, management, clients or customers, and owners or shareholders – benefit by means of a meaningful co-partnership aimed at all-round performance enhancement. Accordingly, collective incentive schemes are more likely to elicit organisational citizenship behaviour than are schemes of an individual nature. In addition, collective incentives may empower employees by giving them more control over how they work and what they achieve. Collective plans are also likely to encounter less opposition from trade unions than are individual incentive plans. This is primarily because collective incentives focus on transparent results-based performance criteria rather than on individual behavioural assessment. In general, collective plans are also amenable to collective bargaining, employee involvement and more egalitarian pay outcomes. Indeed, the future of collective incentive plans seems assured. As work itself becomes more interdependent, and as the need for cooperation increases, so the need for reward systems that reinforce group cohesion and collective effort and effectiveness will increase.

This is not to suggest that collective incentive plans are problem-free. Nor is it the case that collective incentives are necessarily incompatible with individual performance plans. With careful planning, it is possible to combine the two approaches in such a way that they are mutually reinforcing. For instance, while the funding of a performance pay pool might be based on measures of improvement in collective results, the distribution of payments from the pool could be based on assessed individual contribution. Clearly, however, such an approach would have to be designed, implemented and communicated with considerable care in order to ensure that the collective and individual reward messages were harmonious rather than discordant.

While collective STIs can be categorised in various ways, most fall into one or other of four plan types, differentiated by the performance measure used, the time orientation (past versus projected performance) and the size of the employee cohort covered. The four collective STI types are:

1 *Profitsharing.* This is the oldest type of collective incentive plan, having been first formulated and applied at the outset of the industrial era. Here the performance measure is historical profit and the employee coverage is typically organisation-wide, although profitsharing can also apply to specific business units and profit centres within multidivisional firms.

2 *Gainsharing.* Although developed in the late nineteenth century, partly to remedy some of the shortcomings of profitsharing, gainsharing came to prominence only in the mid-twentieth century and has been quite widely applied in Western firms since that time. Gainsharing plans, which generally cover specific production plants in manufacturing firms, recognise and reward employees for productivity or cost improvements – 'gains' – over and above an historical benchmark.

3 *Goalsharing.* This type is a product of the 1970s and 1980s and, like gainsharing, tends to cover specific business units within the organisation. Unlike gainsharing, however, it uses forward indicators of performance, in the form of group goals, rather than being reliant on retrospective indicators.

4 *Team incentives.* These were first widely applied during the 1990s, and are essentially small group adaptations of gainsharing and/or goalsharing for permanent, part-time or temporary teams.

## Profitsharing

A profitsharing plan typically involves a formal arrangement under which bonus payments additional to base pay are made to some or all employees on a regular (usually annual) basis, based on a formula that links the size of the total bonus pool to an accounting measure of periodic (typically annual) profit, such as net profit (total income less operating costs) or net profit after tax. As such, profitsharing is applicable only to profit-making organisations and is not relevant to public sector organisations or non-profit entities. Payments usually take the form of a cash bonus, but they may also be in the form of restricted company shares, in which case the short-term profitsharing plan provides the platform for an employee share ownership plan (discussed in detail in chapter 19). Some profitshare plans cover all employees in the organisation; others cover select groups, such as managerial employees.

Profitsharing plans are of three main types: (1) current distribution plans, (2) deferred payment plans and (3) combination plans. With current distribution schemes, the firm distributes a proportion of its profits directly to its employees, usually on an annual basis, but sometimes half-yearly or even quarterly. The payment can be in the form of cash or unrestricted company shares. If the latter, the plan also qualifies as an employee share plan. In motivational terms, cash-based current distribution plans have the advantage of providing rewards in a relatively timely fashion, although payments may vary considerably from year to year in line with variation in the relevant profit measure.

With deferred schemes, each employee's share of the profitshare bonus pool is held in trust for distribution at a later date, typically when the employee leaves the firm through retirement or termination. In essence, deferred plans are retirement savings plans. Again, the payments can take the form of either cash or restricted company shares. Because payouts are held over, such plans have a long-term equalisation effect in that the impact of short-term profit fluctuation is less obvious to eventual recipients. Such plans typically also have substantial tax advantages since deferral of access also means deferral of tax liability and, quite possibly, a lower overall tax impost. Again, then, we see how easily profitsharing can be extended to become a long-term incentive plan. Deferred plans also seek to encourage long-term membership behaviour by placing a reward premium on long and loyal service and perhaps by applying a penalty for early departure.

Combination plans allocate payments partly in the form of current payments and partly in the form of deferred payouts. Such plans therefore combine the best of all possible worlds: an immediate cash incentive, a long-term retirement fund and a deferred and/or reduced tax liability.

While profitshare plans can be configured in a number of ways and according to a variety of formulae, there are four key plan design issues: (1) plan type, (2) formula for determining bonus pool size, (3) eligibility and (4) method of distributing payments. Two critical questions here are whether the payouts will be current or deferred and whether payments take the form of cash or equity. In many countries, deferred plans now predominate, primarily because of their advantages as a means of tax minimisation (or deferral) and retirement planning. A problem here is that deferred payouts may strengthen membership behaviour but dilute task motivation, since there is no immediate reinforcement effect.

The bonus pool can be specified either as a fixed proportion of profits or as a variable proportion. In a typical fixed proportion plan, the bonus pool is calculated as a fixed percentage (perhaps 5 to 10 per cent) of annual net profit. This clarifies the link between profits and payouts, but lacks flexibility and may commit a firm experiencing a windfall profit to making a massive cash payout. Variable proportion plans seek to overcome such inflexibility, typically by using a sliding-scale formula under which the employee share falls as profit levels progressively exceed certain benchmarks. The main problem with the variable approach is that employees may come to feel that they are not receiving a fair share of high profitability.

Eligibility may be organisation-wide or confined to specific groups. In the past most schemes have restricted eligibility to select groups of employees, particularly middle and senior managers whose actions are seen as having the greatest influence on overall financial performance. In more recent times, it has become more common for eligibility to be extended to non-managerial employees. Moreover, while eligibility may extend to the entire workforce, it is also common for profitsharing to be confined to specific plants, divisions or business units, providing these are autonomous profit-making centres.

In relation to the distribution of profitshare payments, there are four main alternatives: (1) equal dollar amounts, (2) as a proportion of base pay, (3) on the basis of seniority and (4) on the basis of individual 'merit'. Equal dollar amounts signal the firm's belief that all eligible employees have contributed equally to profitability. Distributing the bonus as a proportion of each employee's base pay means that the higher the individual's base pay, the higher the dollar amount they will receive. The assumption here is that shares should be distributed unequally according to individual value to the organisation, as measured by each person's base pay. The seniority approach, whereby payments are distributed as a percentage of earnings with payments being related to length of service, rewards loyalty to the firm (i.e. membership behaviour) but also reinforces a hierarchy of age. The individual merit approach, whereby payments are linked to individual performance appraisal, is the approach used by the multifaceted incentive scheme operated by US welding equipment firm Lincoln Electric. The profitsharing component has operated since 1934 and is paid in the form of an annual bonus. The size of the bonus pool is determined by the board of directors and is based on the level of annual profits. Payments are then distributed to individual employees on the basis of twice-yearly individual merit ratings based on four criteria: dependability, quality of work, output, and ideas and cooperation. During the 1980s, bonus payments amounted to more than half of the firm's total wages payout (Handlin 1992). Lincoln Electric's management claimed total success with this scheme. However, the danger in mixing collective and individual performance criteria is that the two can easily come into conflict.

From an organisational perspective, profitsharing offers a number of potential advantages:

- It can improve employee task motivation. By rewarding employees collectively for achieved or anticipated financial outcomes profitsharing is seen as a direct means of inducing improved effort and performance and, hence, higher productivity.
- Total labour costs vary with capacity to pay. By allowing overall labour costs to be varied automatically according to the employer's 'capacity to pay', profitsharing is seen as providing a form of organisational insurance against external contingencies, particularly fluctuations in product market demand and prices. As such, profitsharing is wholly selffunding.
- It can contribute to employment stability by reducing the need for retrenchments in times of downturn since overall labour costs are adjusted downwards automatically as profits fall.
- It can reduce the need for supervision, since employees will be more willing to be self-managing, leading to reduced costs of supervision.
- By increasing total employee remuneration, it can enhance membership behaviour (including reducing absenteeism and turnover).
- It can increase employees' identification with and understanding of the organisation. By strengthening employee interest in the organisation's long-term financial well-being, it focuses employees' attention on the financial state of the organisation and how they can contribute to its improvement. It also encourages employees to take a long-term view of the organisation and their role in it.
- It may contribute to the development of positive work group norms, especially cooperation and information-sharing. Hence profitsharing encourages organisational citizenship behaviour.
- It can improve labour–management relations and reduce industrial conflict, since all parties perceive a common interest in organisational success. The culture of commitment and cooperation associated with profitsharing can reinforce a high-trust employment relationship and a union- and conflict-averse workforce. Studies of the origins and early development of profitsharing indicate that industrial objectives were often at the forefront of employer reasons for turning to profitsharing. In many cases, union avoidance and the minimisation of strikes and other forms of industrial disruption were high on the profitsharing employers' agenda (Church 1971).

- It can be used as a retirement or superannuation plan and may carry tax advantages for both the company and its employees, especially in the form of deferred plans.
- Compared to other collective plans such as gainsharing, it is relatively easy to set up and maintain. There is no need to work with historical benchmarks or to have to place a money value on non-financial factors like customer satisfaction or workplace safety records, as there is with, say, multifactor gainshare and goalshare plans.

At the same time, however, profitsharing has a number of potential drawbacks:

- The line of sight between individual performance and reward is likely to be weak; that is, the 'instrumentality' nexus between effort and reward, as prescribed by expectancy theory, is at best very weak. Why? Because profitability is influenced by many variables that are beyond employees' collective control. For instance, employees generally have little influence over the accounting procedures used to calculate costs and profits, product pricing strategies, and prevailing conditions in product and capital markets. As such, employees may feel that they have little control over reward outcomes. The perceived link between effort and reward is lost and, hence, so is any positive motivational potential. This is why gainsharing may sometimes be a better alternative, since it seeks to reward only those factors that are within employees' control.
- Profitsharing may give rise to 'free riding' or 'social loafing', especially where payments are allocated on an equal basis irrespective of individual contribution. Free riding occurs when individuals receive the benefits of group membership without contributing proportionally to the costs of achieving these benefits. Similarly, social loafing describes the tendency for individuals to exert less effort when their outputs are combined with those of others (Gerhart & Rynes 2003: 178–9). Such problems, of course, may arise with any type of collective STI.
- The larger the eligible workforce size, the weaker the likely line of sight between effort and reward. This is sometimes referred to as the '1/N' problem. The larger the workforce (i.e. the larger the denominator 'N'), the smaller or weaker the notional line of sight (i.e. the lower value of the fraction), and *vice versa*. Thus, the greater the number of co-workers, the less likely the individual will be to believe that their effort level will have any impact on company performance and the less likely they will therefore be to contribute further task effort. This may be doubly problematic, first,

because, *ceteris paribus*, the potential for concealment of social loafing is greater in larger work groups and, second, because the efforts of individual contributors will have less marginal impact on group outcomes. The main implication is that profitsharing (and indeed many other collective STI plans) may be unsuitable for large business units or firms.

- A run of low profitability can cause significant reward dissatisfaction and demotivation among employees and actually compound the firm's troubles.
- Profitsharing is a blunt instrument for rewarding collective perfor-mance, particularly where eligibility is organisation-wide. Where it is organisation-wide, by definition, profitsharing cannot differentiate between operating units within the organisation in terms of differential contribution to overall profit.
- Ideally, profitsharing requires 'open-book' management, with the organ-isation having to share financial information with employees. This may not suit organisations with a traditional labour management culture.
- Profitsharing may attract union opposition. Unions tend to be suspicious of profitsharing, seeing it as a way for employers to substitute variable pay for fixed base pay and to undermine worker support for unions (R. Long 1997). Profitsharing also makes it more difficult for unions to maintain standard pay rates; that is, equal pay for the same jobs across different organisations.

There is certainly some evidence that profitsharing can improve a firm's financial fortunes. Long's research on profitsharing in Canada (R. Long 1997) indicates that more than 90 per cent of CEOs in profitsharing firms believed that profitsharing had a positive effect on employee interest in the company: on employee motivation, loyalty and job satisfaction. But how much of an incentive effect does profitsharing have? A meta-analysis of more than twenty econometric studies by Weitzman and Kruse (1990) indicated that, on average, profitsharing improved productivity by 7.4 per cent, with the median increase being 4.4 per cent. In a study covering 275 US firms, Kruse (1993) found that firms with profitsharing had productivity growth between 3.5 and 5.0 per cent higher than that in firms without profitsharing. Further, Kruse found that the decline in employment during business down-turns was lower in firms with profitsharing than in those without (2 per cent as against 3.1 per cent). Profitsharing may also reduce the cost of supervision.

However, there is cause for caution here. Much of the available evi-dence appears susceptible to sample bias in that observation is confined to successful plans simply because ineffective plans are less likely to survive. Further, Kruse's research (1993) indicates that profitsharing is not always effective; more than 25 per cent of firms with profitsharing showed no productivity increase at all. Kruse (1993) also found that productivity growth was far higher in small firms than in larger firms, indicating that size is an important mediating variable. Kim (1998) found that overall labour costs were higher in profitsharing firms than in other companies. Moreover, even where the evidence indicates that firms with profitsharing perform better than those without it, it is still necessary to establish the actual nature of the causal association involved. It may be that firms with profitsharing experience better results because they were better performers anyway and that this was why they introduced profitsharing in the first place. Indeed, Kim (1998) found that once the possibility of reverse causality is taken into account, any positive incentive effect of profit levels is removed. Overall, then, sympathetically disposed commentators tend to conclude that incentive effects from profitsharing are generally weak, although Gerhart and Rynes (2003: 220) also note that well-administered plans also have high potential for encouraging cooperation and commitment.

## Gainsharing

Gainsharing is a form of collective performance-related pay in which management shares with all employees in a particular production plant or business unit the financial gains associated with specific measures of improvement in the results achieved by that work group as measured against an historical benchmark of the group's performance. Gainshare plans thus have four defining features:

1 a focus on measurable results that are within employees' collective control, such as labour productivity, unit labour costs, reduced materials wastage and the like
2 the specification of a historical baseline of financial performance against which subsequent financial gains can be determined
3 the use of a predetermined formula for sharing the monetary gains between the organisation and the participating employees
4 a formal system of employee participation in making suggestions and decisions about ways to improve work group performance. In many (although not all) cases, gainshare schemes are designed, implemented and administered by joint management–employee committees.

Gainshare plans fall into two main categories:

1 *Traditional,* single-factor schemes. These emphasise 'hard' single-factor performance measures like labour cost reduction or labour productivity improvement. A key feature of these schemes is that they are self-funding. The greater the gain, the greater the total payout pool; the smaller the gain, the smaller the pool.
2 *Multifactor schemes.* These seek to combine a range of 'hard' performance measures, such as sales value, productivity and materials wastage rates, with the aim of striking a balance across relevant key result areas. Sometimes multifactor schemes also incorporate non-financial results measures, such as customer satisfaction, environmental compliance and workplace accident rates, but, by definition, this means that the scheme ceases to be fully self-funding.

The three most important of the traditional single factor, cost-saving schemes are the Scanlon, Rucker and Improshare plans. All of these focus on a single cost improvement measure, although each emphasises a different cost measure.

The Scanlon Gainshare Plan, formulated in the USA in the late 1930s by Joseph Scanlon, is sometimes described (incorrectly) as the 'first' such plan. Although the concept was pioneered by Towne in the 1880s (Peach & Wren 1992: 13; Schloss 1898), its more recent popularity owes much to the marketing zeal of Scanlon and his supporters. An erstwhile boxer, accountant, steelworker and union official, Scanlon eventually become a professor of management at the Massachusetts Institute of Technology. In 1938, while serving as a local branch president of the then powerful United Steelworkers' Union, Scanlon devised a high-involvement, joint union–management efficiency enhancement plan to rescue the steel mill where he worked from the verge of bankruptcy (Hammer 1991; Lesieur 1958).

Under a Scanlon plan, productivity gains are measured in terms of shifts in the ratio of overall labour costs to the value of total sales, set against a carefully determined historical benchmark ratio. The lower the measured ratio in relation to the benchmark, the greater the labour saving and, hence, the greater the gain. Gains are calculated on a monthly basis and shared between employees and the organisation on the basis of a predetermined formula, typically in the ratio of 75 per cent to 25 per cent. Typically, all employees get the same percentage payout on their base pay, and payments are made on a weekly, monthly or quarterly basis. In many Scanlon plans, only 50 per cent of the gain is distributed automatically to employees. The remaining 25 per cent is placed in an equalisation fund to reimburse the company for any future 'negative gains', with any excess remaining in the fund being distributed at the end of the year.

The Scanlon model also places a strong emphasis on cooperative relations between management, workers and any unions that might be present and on employee participation in productivity improvement. A joint labour–management 'productivity committee' oversees the design, implementation and maintenance of the scheme. Workers are also encouraged to submit suggestions for improving productivity and reducing costs, which are vetted by a special joint screening committee. This committee deliberates on suggestions and implements those considered worthwhile. Scanlon schemes generally involve an agreement that no existing employee will be retrenched as a consequence of improvements made. Devised by a unionist, the model is union-friendly and well suited to bargaining in a strong union context.

Figure 18.1 provides a simple example of a Scanlon Plan formula. In this example, the benchmark period ratio of labour costs to sales value is 20 per cent and the gainshare pool in the subsequent period is $400,000, of which 75 per cent is distributed to the employees involved.

Another single-factor scheme, the Rucker Plan, is also based on a labour:cost ratio, but rather than using total sales value as the key performance variable, it measures 'value added'. Value added equals the value of total sales less the cost of purchased inputs, such as raw materials, equipment and components made by outside suppliers. The rationale here is that material and supply costs are independent variables over which employees have no control. Alan Rucker, the scheme's US inventor, devised this approach after observing that the ratio of labour costs to value added in the US manufacturing sector had remained remarkably stable over a fifty-year period, at about 40 per cent. So a labour cost:value added ratio of 40 per cent seemed to be the natural and appropriate benchmark for measuring real gains in labour productivity and costs. As with the Scanlon model, the bonus pool is typically distributed on the basis of a predetermined formula. The Rucker plan also places a heavy emphasis on the importance of employee involvement (Hammer 1991; Welbourne & Gomez-Mejia 1995: 563).

Figure 18.2 provides an example of a Rucker plan. Note that the benchmark ratio of labour costs to value added is 40 per cent. In this case, a sixth

**Performance focus**

❖ Improvements in <u>labour costs relative to value of sales</u>

**Principles**

❖ 'Open-book' management: employees must understand the business
❖ Employee involvement in decision-making (e.g. with suggestion schemes or joint consultative committees)
❖ Reward equity: recognising and rewarding employee contribution to improvement in business performance
❖ High competence and high trust.

**Example**

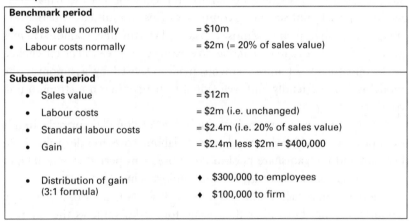

| **Benchmark period** | |
| --- | --- |
| • Sales value normally | = $10m |
| • Labour costs normally | = $2m (= 20% of sales value) |

| **Subsequent period** | |
| --- | --- |
| • Sales value | = $12m |
| • Labour costs | = $2m (i.e. unchanged) |
| • Standard labour costs | = $2.4m (i.e. 20% of sales value) |
| • Gain | = $2.4m less $2m = $400,000 |
| • Distribution of gain (3:1 formula) | ◆ $300,000 to employees |
| | ◆ $100,000 to firm |

**Figure 18.1** Scanlon Plan gainsharing
*Source*: adapted from Wilson & Bowey 1989: 358.

of the bonus pool is retained in an equalisation fund so that payouts can continue to be made in those periods when the benchmark is not reached.

A third and still more recent single-factor scheme, the Improshare Plan, was formulated in the 1970s by industrial engineer Mitchell Fein. Improshare differs from Scanlon and Rucker schemes in two main ways: first, it is not based on financial cost savings and, second, employee participation is not a major feature of the system. To measure gain in group performance, it focuses on sharing physical productivity gains measured in terms of labour *hours* saved. Why? To circumvent the effects of price inflation, over which employees have no control. It must be remembered that the decade in which it was developed – the 1970s – was a decade of high price inflation, and rapid price movements wreak havoc with gainshare formulae based on financial

**Performance focus**

❖ <u>Improvements in payroll costs relative to 'value added'</u> to materials used in the production process.

❖ Assumes payroll costs should = 40% of value added (US historical data)

**Example**

| **Benchmark period** | |
|---|---|
| • Output or sales value normally | = $10m |
| • Cost of materials used | = $5m (= 50% of sales value) |
| • Thus, benchmark value added | = $5m |
| • Benchmark payroll cost | = $2m (i.e. 40% of value added) |
| **Subsequent period** | |
| • Sales value | = $12m |
| • Cost of materials used | = $6m |
| • Added value | = $6m |
| • Benchmark payroll costs | = $2.4m (i.e. 40% of value added) |
| • Actual payroll costs | = $2.1m |
| • Thus, total bonus pool size for period | = $2.4m less $2.1m = $300,000 |
| • Distribution of gain | $200,000 paid out in bonuses<br>$100,000 retained in equalisation fund |

**Figure 18.2** Rucker Plan gainsharing
*Source*: adapted from Wilson & Bowey 1989: 355.

cost measures (Fein 1999; Hammer 1991; Kaufman 1992; Welbourne & Gomez-Mejia 1995: 563–4).

Under Improshare, work measurement techniques are used to establish the standard number of hours it takes to manufacture a product. A bonus is paid when workers produce the product in less than the standard time, with gains again being shared according to a predetermined formula. Because it focuses on time required to produce physical output, Improshare is really suited only to manufacturing firms – the sort of firms for which it was originally devised.

A simple Improshare model is illustrated in figure 18.3. In the benchmark year, the workgroup takes 4 hours to produce each unit. In the subsequent period, the workgroup produces 1300 units in 4080 hours, which represents a productivity gain of 1120 hours compared to the benchmark period performance. The gain is split 50/50 with the firm, which means that the total bonus pool is 560 hours multiplied by the standard hourly rate of pay, and

**Performance focus**
❖ Improvement in labour productivity (units produced per hour of labour time expended)

❖ Physical rather than dollar measure (hence factors out the effect of exogenous price movements or inflation)

**Example**

| Productivity benchmark |
| --- |
| • Over the previous year the workgroup has taken an average of 4 hours of labour time to produce each unit. |
| • i.e. 4 hours per unit |

| Subsequent gainshare period |
| --- |
| • Workgroup produces 1,300 units in 4,080 hours |
| • Benchmark time for this output is $1,300 \times 4.0 = 5,200$ hours |
| • Productivity gain is therefore 1,120 hours |
| • Gain split 50/50, so total bonus pool for workgroup = 560 hours × the standard hourly rate of pay |
| • Equal dollars bonus payment to each member of the workgroup. |

**Figure 18.3** Improshare Plan gainsharing

in this example equal dollar shares are distributed to each member of the work group.

Traditional single-factor gainsharing plans like the Scanlon, Rucker and Improshare plans are said to have a number of advantages, particularly compared to the older practice of profitsharing:

- Like profitsharing, they are self-funding.
- They can be targeted to particular plants, departments or divisions, or to discrete business units in the wider organisation. This compares with profitsharing, which is generally organisation-wide.
- They can be applied in public sector and other non-profit organisations. Again, this contrasts with profitsharing, which, by definition, can be applied only in profit-making firms.
- They seek to reward only those results that are within the group's control. This too contrasts with profitsharing since a firm's profitability will be influenced by a range of variables that are largely beyond employees' control, such as materials costs, rents, cost of capital, depreciation rates and fluctuations in product demand and price.
- Being productivity-focused, they emphasise cost effectiveness, not just the value or quantity of production.

- They promote work group norms favourable to cost savings and productivity improvement, make employees more accepting of technological change, and harness employee expertise, knowledge and ideas on ways to improve cost efficiency.
- Payouts are frequent and timely. Bonuses can be paid very soon after the performance is delivered – perhaps quarterly, monthly, even fortnightly – and can therefore be varied more closely with changes in group performance. This too contrasts with profitsharing, in which bonus payments are normally deferred until the end of the financial year.
- They may reduce supervision costs by instituting group self-monitoring, with employees engaging in 'mutual monitoring' to minimise 'social loafing'. In a study of forty-four large Canadian firms, Long (1994) found that firms with gainsharing had 31 per cent fewer managers than those without such plans.
- They may strengthen employee commitment and membership behaviour and so reduce labour absenteeism and turnover. They may also encourage organisational citizenship behaviour by enlisting the support of all employees to help improve performance, not just a select few top performers.
- They can support a high-involvement culture through employee involvement programs and devolution of decision-making. Formal employee participation in plant decision-making is widely regarded as both an essential feature and a key strength of productivity gainsharing (Arthur & Kim 2005).
- They can support a high-trust culture by improving two-way communication between management and employees and increase employees' understanding of the organisation.
- There is considerable evidence that such plans are compatible with a unionised workforce and collective bargaining (Dalton 1998; Kim & Voos 1997; Ross & Ross 1999).

However, such plans also have a range of potential drawbacks. In particular:

- They can be costly to establish and administer. Both managers and employees will have to devote considerable time to system design, implementation and maintenance.
- They may encounter resistance from middle managers because employee participation programs may be seen as posing a direct threat to the status and jobs of middle managers (Collins 1996).

- They may be unsuited to situations of continuous change. Each change in technology, work organisation and product type will require recalibration of productivity benchmarks.
- They may still encourage free riders and social loafing. Individual employees will still share in the benefits of collective performance improvement no matter how little they themselves contribute.
- Given the focus on 'hard' measures of cost and productivity improvement, traditional plans ignore non-financial or 'soft' aspects of group performance.

Although single factor plans of the above type are relatively straightforward, they may well overlook other factors that may be critical to the work group's overall financial performance. For this reason, most gainshare plans now typically incorporate multiple measures of group performance incorporating both 'hard' and 'soft' criteria. Most multifactor plans take losses into account as well as gains. Losses on any one measure are deducted from the bonus pool. One of the shortcomings of single-factor schemes is that they overlook the possibility of an increase in labour productivity being achieved by running up other costs, such as the costs of materials and equipment. For instance, workers may seek to improve their output by replacing equipment sooner than is economically necessary. Lawler (1990: 120) gives the example of a sheet-glass and mirror firm that had a plan focused solely on labour costs; in this case, on glass-cutting rates. Employees boosted their cutting rates by replacing expensive diamond-tipped cutting disks long before they were worn out. Labour productivity rose, but so did the cost of materials. So the formula should factor in all controllable factors and have a multiple-cost focus. For this reason, multifactor gainshare schemes frequently incorporate cost factors other than direct labour costs, such as the cost of materials and equipment used.

Multifactor schemes may also incorporate measurement of non-financial results. For instance, a service organisation might factor in not only the controllable cost of service delivery but also service delivery time and the level of customer complaints. Other significant non-cost variables may include product or service quality, workplace safety and accident rates, and environmental compliance (Belcher 1995). Thus, a multifactor gainshare plan for a building products company might include a range of financial criteria, such as machine changeover time, machine run speed, plant downtime and materials utilisation or wastage, as well as non-financial criteria such as site safety, hazardous waste and customer satisfaction, with separate historical benchmarks set for each criterion. Generally, measures that are difficult or impossible to quantify in financial terms, such as customer satisfaction or workplace accident rates, are used as 'modifiers' to expand or reduce the size of a bonus pool determined by means of traditional financial measures.

Although non-financial performance criteria are, by definition, not self-funding, group performance on these criteria is measured in exactly the same manner as for financial criteria; that is, by means of historical benchmarks. For example, a work group may have had an average of five lost time injuries per year over the past five years, and this could become the specified standard for the subsequent year. If there is an improvement on this standard over the ensuing year (say, only three lost time injuries occur), the self-funded component of the gainshare bonus pool may be supplemented in line with a specified formula; if performance on this criterion is substandard, the bonus pool may be reduced proportionally, or perhaps withheld altogether for a significant violation of the workplace safety standard. A firm might choose to deduct an amount from a labour savings gain if these savings are also accompanied by an increase in accident levels above a predetermined target. In this case, the assumption is that labour cost improvements should not be achieved by means of resorting to unsafe work practices.

Multifactor gainshare plans, then, have several advantages over single-factor, cost-based plans. They incorporate performance variables that are not directly cost-based but which may be critical elements of group performance. They have greater scope for focusing on those factors that are within employees' control. They have wider application than productivity and labour cost measures and, for this reason, are applicable to service sector organisations as well as to manufacturing firms.

Although the multifactor approach provides greater flexibility and a non-cost focus, it also has some disadvantages. The design is more complex and requires careful identification and selection of performance criteria. The design team will necessarily have to sift through a greater number of potential performance measures, and that will mean additional administration costs. The major disadvantage, however, is that the incorporation of non-financial goals means that the scheme ceases to be self-funding. Where payout levels are made conditional on the achievement of certain non-financial standards, employees can easily come to see total payout levels as arbitrary and quite possibly unfair, particularly if they believe that the standards themselves are unrealistic. There is no objective way to ascribe a monetary value to

non-cost variables. What dollar amount should be placed on an improvement in customer satisfaction or accident levels?

The evidence that gainsharing does improve performance outcomes is
relatively solid. Schuster (1984) reports solid success in terms of productivity
improvement. Hatcher and Ross (1991) found that substituting gainsharing for individual incentives produced a marked improvement in product
quality. Bullock and Lawler's (1984) study of outcomes from thirty-three
gainshare plans found that 75 per cent of organisations reported positive
effects, including improvements in productivity and quality, reduced labour
costs, and improved labour–management cooperation and employee pay.
Two-thirds of the plans were rated as successful. But *how* successful? A study
of Improshare schemes found that the median productivity increase was
8 per cent in the first year, with cumulative gains of 17.5 per cent by the
end of the third year (Kaufman 1992). A further US study, conducted in
the early 1980s, found that firms that had operated gainshare plans for at
least five years achieved an average annual saving of 29 per cent in labour
costs (Mitchell, Lewin & Lawler 1990: 67). A longitudinal study of a new
gainsharing plan in a large US automobile components plant (Arthur & Jelf
1999) found that cost savings ran to $US15 million while absenteeism fell
by 20 per cent and grievances by 50 per cent.

These are impressive results, with Gerhard and Rynes (2003: 201, 211)
concluding that gainsharing has a 'medium' incentive effect and a 'good'
impact on cooperative behaviour. Again, however, one problem with such
survey data is sample bias: most report outcomes only from surviving and
successful plans; cases of failure are not taken into consideration. As with
profitsharing, size and 1/N effects also appear to be important. Kaufman
(1992) found that a doubling of eligible workgroup size (from 200 to 400
employees) halved the productivity gain. Free riding is also no less an issue
here than it is in profitsharing, except that gainshare plans tend to cover
smaller work groups. As Gerhart and Rynes (2003: 201) caution, the incentive effectiveness of such plans appears to be contingent on administrative
and contextual factors. In short, the devil appears to be in the detail.

Clearly, gainshare plans require careful attention to plan choice, design
and implementation. Here there are at least eight key considerations:

1  work group compatibility
2  performance criteria
3  performance benchmarks

4 method of payment distribution
5 size of bonus payout
6 management attitudes
7 employee involvement
8 union attitudes.

Lawler (1990: 116) suggests that, because of the 1/N phenomenon, gain-sharing works best in work units of less than 500 employees. In larger groups, the perceived link between individual effort and group reward is likely to be lost. The group must also have functional cohesion. For this reason, organisations often have separate gainshare schemes for each operating unit, division or department. Except in smaller firms, it is rare for a gainshare scheme to be organisation-wide. It then becomes a question of which groups within the organisation will be subject to a gainshare scheme. Moreover, gainsharing is unlikely to be effective in an organisation where the work culture is highly individualistic. Another key requirement is that changes in technology and product base should be gradual rather than rapid; otherwise historical benchmarks will soon become obsolete.

The performance criteria should be clear, controllable and comprehensive. Except in the simplest of production processes, single-factor plans should probably also be avoided. Plans that focus only on labour savings may also lead to the neglect of quality and of other elements of overall costs. By the same token, while seeking to cover as many key controllable variables as possible, the formula should be as simple and transparent as possible, so that employees understand and trust it. A typical multifactor gainshare plan will probably focus on three to five key result areas. Further, the performance criteria must be flexible so as to accurately reflect what is occurring in the organisation and, in particular, must be adjusted in line with changes in the organisation's products, technology and activity mix.

The performance benchmarks should be accepted and agreed by the work group, not arbitrarily imposed. Choosing an appropriate benchmark year is crucial, since selecting one in which performance was unusually low or high will result in bonuses being negligible or excessive. In setting the standard, it is common for plans to use a moving average for the preceding three to five years, although a constant raising of the performance standard may also create motivational problems of its own.

Turning to bonus distribution, there are three main alternatives here. The bonus could be distributed as an equal dollar amount to each member of the group; as an equal percentage of each employee's base pay; or unequally according to the assessed contribution of each individual. The choice will depend on whether the organisation wishes to recognise and reward the special contribution of individual employees and on how much emphasis it wishes to give to individual as opposed to group performance. Either way, the payment mode will have to be managed and communicated carefully to avoid employee misunderstanding and dissatisfaction. Equal dollar amounts may demotivate top individual performers, while unequal payouts may be seen to favour individualists and to unfairly disadvantage team players. A preferable approach may be to distribute an equal dollar amount to each group member and to use other methods to recognise and reward individual excellence. Even then, however, individual factors will still have to be taken into account. In particular, payouts to individuals will need to be adjusted for the amount of time actually worked by each employee. Casual and part-time employees would not normally receive the same amount as full-timers, while those who only worked for part of the bonus period would also have their bonus reduced accordingly.

The organisation has to decide the target contribution of gainshare bonus payments to employees' total pay. Should bonuses be capped to control the total payout? Some plans impose a maximum percentage cap per individual, such as 25 per cent of total pay; others impose a limit on the size of the overall bonus pool. What happens if performance falls below the benchmark and no bonus is paid? Even though such payments are 'at risk', zero bonuses may demotivate. As with profitsharing, one way around this problem is to establish a buffer in the form of an equalisation fund that withholds a portion of the employees' share in good times to cover times when there is no gain or a loss. Some schemes withhold as much as 25 per cent of employees' share for this purpose.

Gainsharing is unlikely to work unless it has the full support of senior management. Senior management must be prepared to devolve some decision-making responsibility to workers. Middle managers must also be prepared to accept more participative decision-making. If they are unwilling to do so, the plan can easily falter. One reason why middle managers, in particular, may resist gainsharing is their fear that it will see them lose status and, quite possibly, their jobs. Collins' (1996) research on the collapse of a Scanlon-style scheme in a large US packaging firm provides a graphic illustration of what can go amiss when line managers themselves seek to undermine a gainshare plan. Collins' study demonstrates the dangers of seeking to impose such a plan as a means of transforming a hierarchical and adversarial work culture from above. The plan itself became a new battlefield for old rivalries and differences.

Gainsharing is unlikely to succeed without the opportunity for employee involvement in system design, implementation and maintenance. This was Scanlon's main point. Participation should go well beyond suggestion box schemes and should incorporate genuinely inclusive practices, such as permanent joint consultative committees. Managers and supervisors must support high involvement. This requires participative planning and joint management. A supportive, high-trust management style would seem to be essential. The bonus by itself is unlikely to motivate for very long. The research evidence (Arthur & Kim 2005) suggests that it is the participative element, rather than the group incentive *per se*, that delivers the most substantial and lasting outcomes.

Finally, gainsharing is less likely to succeed if on-site unions are not supportive. Unions are likely to regard gainsharing rather more favourably than most other modes of performance pay. This is because gainsharing rests on agreed, open and non-subjective performance measurement and reward distribution criteria, with union members being able to actively participate in the formulation of the share strategy. Unions have traditionally resisted alternative forms of performance pay, such as merit pay and profitsharing, because of their predisposition to subjectivity and management manipulation. A further reason why unions may be favourably disposed towards gainsharing is that, as a group incentive, it does not pit employees against each other. Remember, the architect of the Scanlon Plan was himself a one-time union official.

## Goalsharing

Goalsharing is the collective equivalent of individual goal-based bonuses (discussed in chapter 17) and, like the latter, it draws on the technique of goal-setting. While goalsharing also resembles gainsharing, it has two major differences. First, goalsharing is future-oriented, whereas gainsharing uses historical performance benchmarks. Second, with goalsharing the bonus pool is not self-funding. Rather than creating a pool based on dollar value improvements above a performance baseline, goalsharing allocates a predetermined amount geared to the achievement of specific goals. A series of goals or performance indicators are established for the work group and a fixed, predetermined amount is paid to the group for each goal achieved or exceeded. Another point of difference with gainsharing is that employee participation is not always a feature of goalshare plans, although it can be.

Goalsharing, then, is a collective incentive plan whereby group performance is measured and rewarded in terms of goal achievement over short time frames, typically monthly, quarterly or annually. For example, a firm might set annual goals for productivity, quality and customer satisfaction, with achievement of each goal leading to payment of a $500 bonus to each workgroup member. Such an approach is both simple and flexible, and includes the ability to add group goals for any relevant result area. Since the focus is on future rather than past performance, and since forward targets can be adjusted much more readily than historical benchmarks, goalsharing is better adapted to situations of technological and product change than is traditional productivity gainsharing.

As with goal-based individual bonuses, payments can be flat-rate or geared. In some goalshare schemes, the bonus is on a sliding scale, with performance falling just short of the goal receiving a discounted bonus, and performance in excess of the goal attracting a premium bonus. Again, the logic of a sliding-scale payout is that employees will not go unrewarded for falling just short of a challenging goal.

While goalsharing is generally not fully self-funding, some plans do have a formula for determining bonus pool size. Typically, the pool size is determined by an accounting measure of group or unit performance such as net operating profit. As such, it is not unusual for goalshare plans to resemble profitsharing. The difference is that payout from the pool is linked to specific, controllable group performance goals.

As with gainsharing, the mode of bonus distribution is another design issue of considerable importance. Bonuses may be distributed either on an equal dollar basis or unequally. Again, the organisation must determine whether it wishes to emphasise group accomplishment or individual contribution.

Figure 18.4 provides an example of a multifactor goalsharing plan for a business unit. In this case, there are two financial criteria (controllable expenses and net revenue) and three non-financial criteria (on-time delivery, customer satisfaction and product quality), with different weightings being attached to each of the five criteria. Achievement of each goal attracts a raw points score of 100, which is then multiplied by the percentage weighting for the relevant criterion to give the weighted points score. In this example, the work group meets the goals for net revenue and product quality, which

| Performance indicators | Weight | 50 | 60 | 70 | 80 | 90 | Target 100 | 110 | 120 | 130 | 140 | Weighted points score |
|---|---|---|---|---|---|---|---|---|---|---|---|---|
| Controllable expenses as percentage of unit revenue | 30% | 70% | 68% | 66% | 64% | 62% | 60% | 58% | 56% ✓ | 54% | 52% | **36** |
| Net revenue – $ million | 20% | $9 | $9.5 | $10.0 | $10.5 | $11.0 | $12.0 ✓ | $13.0 | $14.0 | $15.0 | $16.0 | **20** |
| On-time delivery – percentage meeting due date | 30% | 60% | 65% | 70% | 75% | 80% | 85% | 88% ✓ | 90% | 92% | 96% | **33** |
| Customer satisfaction score – average survey score | 10% | 70 | 75 | 80 | 85 | 87 ✓ | 90 | 93 | 96 | 98 | 100 | **9** |
| Product quality or non-defect rate | 10% | 85% | 87% | 89% | 91% | 93% | 95% ✓ | 96% | 97% | 98% | 99% | **10** |
| | | | | | | | | | | | Total points score: | **108** |

**Bonus scale**

| Total score | Payout (as percentage of base pay) |
|---|---|
| 0–69 | 0 |
| 70–79 | 2% |
| 80–89 | 3% |
| 90–99 | 4% |
| **100–109** | **5%** |
| 110–119 | 7% |
| 120–129 | 9% |
| 130–140 | 12% |

**Figure 18.4** Business unit multifactor goalsharing
*Source:* adapted from Wilson & Phelan 1996: 11.

translate into weighted scores of 20 and 10 points respectively (i.e. 100 × 0.2 and 100 × 0.1). The goals for expenses and delivery time are exceeded, translating to 36 and 33 points respectively (i.e. 120 × 0.3 and 110 × 0.3), which falls just short of the customer satisfaction goal, resulting in a score of 9 points (i.e. 90 × 0.1). The total weighted score for the five goals, then, is 108, for which the bonus scale prescribes a bonus payment to each member of the group equivalent to 5 per cent of their current level of base pay. Note that the bonus payments are progressively scaled, but also capped at the upper end. No bonus is payable where the weighted points score sums to less than 70, and the maximum payment (for total scores of 130 or more) is 12 per cent. Note, too, how the combination of strategically aligned goal-setting and multiple results-based criteria is well suited to the balanced score-card approach to performance management explored in detail in chapter 5.

Although goalsharing can be organisation-wide, in organisations that are internally diverse, construct and content validity requires that distinct sets of goals are set for each division or business unit. In such cases, applying a single set of performance goals to the whole organisation takes inadequate account of operational differences between the various divisions, departments and business units within the organisation. For this reason, it is not unusual for large organisations to have multiple goalsharing plans in place. For instance, in the mid-1990s, the US glass and ceramics manufacturer Corning Technologies had almost sixty separate unit-specific goalsharing plans in operation, having first experimented with the approach in 1988. Altmansberger and Wallace (1995) report that the Corning plans were highly successful, showing a strong correlation between payout level and performance achievement on business unit goals. On average, the plans delivered a return on investment of almost 500 per cent, a return that compares particularly favourably with reported outcomes under gainsharing.

Goalsharing, then, has some important advantages over traditional gainsharing:

- It is future-focused rather than retrospective.
- It is generally simpler to develop, offers more flexibility, has wider application and can better accommodate changes in technology and product or service type.
- It has more potential to be strategically aligned because it can be focused on specific business unit goals.
- It can be targeted at smaller work groups within business units, unlike gainshare plans, which typically cover whole business units.

Still, goalsharing is not problem-free:

- It is not self-funding, so the size of the bonus pool has to be determined by other means.
- There is no automatic or objective basis for determining a payment level for meeting each goal, and employees can easily come to feel that bonus levels are inadequate and inequitable.
- Goal-setting itself can be seen as arbitrary. Goalsharing can easily lose credibility in the eyes of employees if they perceive that the goals are set at unrealistically high levels. Some groups may feel that their goals are unfairly demanding compared to those of other groups.
- Goals can be changed too easily, and too many changes may undermine the plan's credibility.
- Goal fixation may cause employees to focus on rewarded goals only, to the detriment of other performance dimensions. The challenge is to select goals that capture all key aspects of group performance.
- Social loafing is still a possibility.
- Simple flat-rate plans may discourage groups who fall just short of goal achievement while providing no incentive to exceed the goal.

## Team incentives

Thus far, we have considered collective incentive plans that cover medium to large-scale work groups. With team incentives, however, the emphasis is on recognition and reward for small work groups of perhaps just five to ten members. In fact, team incentives tend to be small group adaptations of multifactor business unit gainsharing or goalsharing. Team incentives emerged – or, more accurately, re-emerged – in the 1990s as the reward corollary of teamworking. As noted in chapter 4, teamworking is commonly taken to be one of the defining features of high-involvement/high-performance best practice models. Although work teams have been a prominent feature of work organisations for many decades, it was only in the mid-1990s that organisations began systematically to link team performance directly to short-term incentive payments.

It is also important to recognise, however, that teams themselves take a number of quite different forms and that the form of any incentive plan used should match or 'fit' the nature of the team(s) involved. We shall return to the issue of matching incentive techniques to team type shortly. First, however, we need to consider the main types of team and the structural characteristics that determine team type.

Adapting insights offered by Lawler (2000: 193–7), Montemayor (1994; Balkin & Montemayor 2000) and Zingheim and Schuster (2000a: 203–25), we suggest that there are five main dimensions to team structure:

1 the degree of team autonomy (from closely supervised to fully self-managing)
2 the nature of the work flow between teams (from production line inter-dependence to wholly independent)
3 the degree of functional diversity within the team (from homogeneous or multiskilled to highly diverse)
4 the degree of time commitment required (full time or part time)
5 the time frame of team existence (permanent or short term).

Although these structural variables suggest a multiplicity of team types, on the basis of the above dimensions, it is possible to identify three main team types: (1) process teams, (2) parallel teams and (3) project teams.

Process teams are permanent entities involving membership on a full-time basis. Teams of this type tend to be found in manufacturing and service provision processes, where they constitute key elements of organisational production or service delevery. In most cases such teams will involve mul-tiskilling, with each team member crosstrained to be able to undertake all of the work done by the team. Examples here include permanent teams in engine assembly plants, claims processing teams in insurance firms and cus-tomer inquiry teams in call centres. In such teams, workers perform various tasks in a predetermined sequence and a semi-integrated way. Because there is substantial task interdependence, team performance will be a function of the lowest individual performance in the team. Such teams are also likely to have a high level of interdependence with other teams involved in performing related tasks in the same process line. Although such teams may be accorded a degree of autonomy ('semi-autonomous' teams with designated 'team leaders'), especially where a high-involvement culture prevails, the norm for such teams, particularly in the presence of a traditional management style, will be close external supervision by line managers, with team per-formance perhaps also being controlled by automated production line technology and/or electronic monitoring. For these reasons, whether or not it is appropriate to attribute results to any particular team and, hence, to distinguish between work teams for reward purposes will depend primarily on the nature of the work flow and the degree of external supervision and control.

Parallel teams are part time in nature, with members spending only a portion of their work time in a team context, with the remainder being spent in their standard job or role assignment; that is, teamworking parallels rather than replaces the employee's 'normal' work assignment. Such teams may be crossfunctional, although they may also involve employees from a single occupation or role. Depending on the brief, they may also be either short term or semi-permanent. In general, parallel teams have low to moderate autonomy. Examples here include teams that meet periodically to consider ways of improving product quality or workplace safety. Another would be a team of employees and managers drawn together on a part-time basis to provide input to a new job evaluation process.

Project teams exist to complete a specific finite work task, require members to relate to each other frequently and may involve some interaction with other teams. However, interactions between project team members and teams cannot be defined in advance. Project teams are also likely to be crossfunctional in nature and have diverse knowledge, skill and ability requirements, which means that team performance is critically dependent on member cooperation. Project teams also have a high degree of autonomy. While membership will be on a full-time basis, the team's existence may range from short term to virtually permanent, depending on the nature and recurrence of the project work. For instance, a policy development team may exist to fulfil just one project brief or a series of briefs over several years. In such cases, the key performance criterion will be fulfilling the project brief in a timely and proficient manner. On the other hand, some project teams will have a near-permanent existence. Examples include crossfunctional surgical teams, in which radiologist, anaesthetist, surgeon, theatre nurses and other team members undertake theatre procedures on a recurrent basis, and client case management teams in welfare agencies, in which psychologists, social workers, financial advisers, legal officers and other professional specialists address the needs of a succession of clients on a more or less permanent basis. Here, too, timeliness and proficiency will be the key – although certainly not the only – team performance criteria. Whatever the time frame involved, however, most project teams will operate with a substantial degree of independence from other work units and, hence, it is generally appropriate to attribute results to the team and, as such, to recognise and reward

performance on a team-by-team and project-by-project basis. Crossfunctional project teams are a defining characteristic of organic organisational
structures (see chapter 4).

Bearing these points in mind, let us now turn to consider the key issues
in the design and implementation of team incentive plans. Here we shall
concentrate on four key design questions:

1  Why choose team incentives at all?
2  How should the performance of particular team types be measured?
3  What are the main options for distributing rewards to team members?
4  What incentive approach is best suited to each type of team?

The choice of team incentives rather than another collective incentive
plan, such as business unit gainsharing or goalsharing, will depend primarily
on how self-managing and autonomous the work teams are in relation to
the rest of the organisation. If teams are largely self-managing, there is little
interdependence between teams and the emphasis is on cooperation *within*
individual teams, then team incentives may well be appropriate since each
team will exercise considerable control over what it does and what it achieves.
This would certainly be true of most project teams. Conversely, where teams
are highly interdependent and the emphasis is on cooperation *between* teams
to achieve divisional, departmental or organisational goals, as is typically
the case with process teams, then a gainshare or goalshare plan pitched at
capturing and rewarding the performance of the larger group may be more
appropriate. In short, the greater the degree of inter-team dependence, the
wider the coverage of the group performance scheme should be.

How should team performance be measured? Performance criteria and
measures should obviously be aligned with organisational objectives and
within employees' collective control. Many exponents of team pay recommend goal-setting rather than historical benchmarking as the best way
of measuring team performance, mainly because goal-setting is forward-
focused rather than retrospective and easier to communicate and adjust
than historical formulae.

As to performance criteria, there are two main alternatives: single-
factor and multifactor schemes. As with traditional gainshare schemes,
single-factor models focus on a 'hard' criterion like labour productivity
or labour cost savings. As we have seen with gainsharing, the disadvantage
of a single measure is that it encourages the team to focus on only one variable. However, this might be quite appropriate for purpose-designed teams
like project teams. In such cases, it is common to use a sliding-scale bonus

to reward the degree of goal attainment. Once the appropriate result areas and performance indicators are identified, performance targets should be set for determining incentive levels. As in goalsharing, the objective is to set performance levels that are challenging yet achievable. An alternative approach, particularly relevant in service sector firms, is micro-scale multi-factor goalsharing plans that combine financial goals with those relating to non-financial criteria, such as customer satisfaction.

The main options for distributing rewards to team members are as follows:

- team bonuses paid as an equal dollar payment to each team member
- team bonuses paid as a percentage of individual base pay
- individual merit bonuses based on performance appraisal (typically involving peer and 360 degree appraisal)
- team non-cash recognition awards.

Each approach sends distinctive signals as to the relative importance of group and individual performance. In the USA, it is not uncommon for team incentive plans to vary payments between individual team members. One circumspect way to recognise individual contribution is to pay team bonuses as a percentage of individual base pay. Exponents of individual merit pay, such as Heneman and Von Hipple (1995), argue for a more explicit recognition of individual contribution. To overcome the possibility of free riding, Heneman recommends the use of merit pay linked to multirater assessment of individual performance consistent with team values and goals. If individual incentives are to be used, however, the challenge is to develop an individual pay system that does not erode team cohesion by creating competition for individual rewards among team members. Non-cash recognition is also an increasingly popular means of recognising both team performance and that of individual team members (McAdams 2000). Ultimately, however, the choice of distribution method should depend primarily on the architecture of the teams involved.

What collective incentive approach may be best suited to each of our three main team types? The chief recommendations, adapted from those made by Lawler (1996; 2000: 202–18; Lawler & Cohen 1992), are summarised in table 18.1.

If there is a high degree of interdependence between process teams, it may well be inappropriate to seek to reward team-level performance at all. In such cases, a more suitable performance cohort for collective reward purposes would be the plant, business unit or division. This means that business

**Table 18.1** Matching collective incentives to team type

|  | Process teams | Parallel teams | Project teams |
|---|---|---|---|
| *Incentive plan type* | | | |
| – Business unit profitsharing | Yes | Yes | No |
| – Plant-level gainsharing | Yes | Yes | No |
| – Team multifactor gainsharing | No | No | Yes (for long-term teams) |
| – Team multifactor goalsharing | No | Yes | Yes |
| *Reward distribution mode* | | | |
| – Equal dollar bonus | Yes | Yes | Yes |
| – Equal non-cash recognition | Yes | Yes | Yes |
| – Bonus as percentage of base pay | Yes | No | No |
| – Individual merit pay | Yes | No | No |
| – Individual non-cash recognition | Yes | No | No |

*Source*: adapted from Lawler (1996; 2000: 202–18; Lawler & Cohen 1992).

unit profitsharing or plant-level gainsharing or goalsharing may be a better choice, perhaps supplemented by team-specific non-cash recognition. Yet it would still be appropriate to recognise the capacity of individual team members via skill or competency pay, particularly where knowledge, skill and ability requirements are the same throughout the team, as well as individual performance within the team, either by means of bonuses paid as a percentage of base pay, via individual merit pay, or using individual non-cash recognition.

Notwithstanding their part-time nature, team-level goalsharing could also be applied to parallel teams, although it may be less costly administratively to apply collective incentives at plant or business unit level, with non-cash recognition being used to acknowledge the team's particular contribution within the larger work group. Given that the time frame of parallel teams is typically short term, gainsharing would not be an appropriate option. As with project teams, the need for a high degree of cooperation between members of parallel teams means that it would be advisable to adopt an egalitarian approach to performance recognition and reward for members of these teams.

A suitable choice for short-term project teams would be team-level goalsharing, since goal-setting is not reliant on historical or long-term performance data and is ideally suited to project work, with bonuses being paid for project completion or the achievement of specific goals. Team gain-sharing may also be relevant, although only to project teams of a more permanent nature where it is possible to establish part-performance benchmarks. Project teams, however, will require an egalitarian approach that rewards collaborative teamworking rather than individualism. In essence, bonuses should be distributed in equal amounts to all members. The same applies to non-cash recognition. If bonuses are to be distributed on the basis of individual merit, then the accompanying performance appraisal system should include behavioural criteria that acknowledge the importance of teamwork, such as collaboration, coordination, mentoring and communication with other team members.

In sum, team incentive plans offer a number of general advantages over other performance-related reward practices:

- They have a micro-focus, targeting the performance of small work groups, and as such have greater potential to overcome the 'line of sight' problem so common in large group plans.
- Since they can be tailored differently for each team, they allow performance-related rewards to be configured more finely to particular forms of group work.
- They can improve team performance by encouraging cooperative behaviour, clarifying team goals and rewarding goal achievement.
- They can help to align organisational and team objectives (in line, say, with the tenets of the balanced score-card).
- Peer monitoring is likely to be more intensive with small-group incentives, which may help to reduce or eliminate free riding by intensifying the level of peer pressure brought to bear on perceived under-performers.

These general strengths notwithstanding, team incentives also share some of the possible pitfalls of large-group incentive plans, as well as having several drawbacks of their own. In particular:

- They may have a perverse effect on team member 'sorting' and team performance. Extrinsically motivated workers will seek to join those teams receiving the highest rewards, while none will want to belong to those teams receiving the lowest rewards. Thus, as was the case at Hewlett-Packard's San Diego site in the 1990s, employees may be unwilling to move between teams, making it even more difficult to address team underperformance (Beer & Cannon 2004: 8).

- Employees may feel that team incentives undervalue individual contribution and may become demotivated and leave. This may be a major problem where team bonuses are paid in equal dollar amounts rather than as a percentage of individual base pay.
- Team incentives can give rise to conflict over peer surveillance and peer pressure to perform. A study of teams and group incentives in US manufacturing firms (Cooke 1994) found that far from reinforcing teamworking, the application of group incentives caused excessive mutual monitoring by employees and an increase in conflict rather than cooperation.
- Team performance criteria can easily fall out of alignment with the goals of the business unit and organisation, leading to suboptimal performance.
- Team incentives cannot, by themselves, deliver effective teamworking. As the failed Hewlett-Packard experiment with collective incentives indicates (see Introduction), where a culture of teamworking is not well developed, the imposition of team incentives as a culture change strategy may have profoundly dysfunctional consequences (Beer & Cannon 2004). Again, performance-related pay can be used to reinforce organisational change but not to initiate or drive it.

## 'Best fit' with short-term collective incentives

Clearly, some collective incentive plans will be better suited to some work situations than to others. As we have seen, profitsharing is likely to be a better fit for small- to medium-sized establishments than for large organisations. Many proponents of the best practice approach also suggest that profitsharing is well suited to organisations with a high-involvement management style, with a high level of cooperation and interdependence throughout operating units, between managers and employees and between employees themselves. Remember, high-involvement firms place a high premium on organisational citizenship behaviour of the sort that profitsharing is designed to foster. Such firms will also be willing to provide employees with extensive communication and information about both the plan itself and company finances. By the same token, profitsharing may also have a role to play in organisations managed along more traditional lines and with a cost defender strategic focus. Indeed, this is where profitsharing first took hold, primarily as a means of dampening industrial conflict. Of course, in such firms profitsharing will not be accompanied by employee involvement programs or 'open book' management, so that much of its motivational potential may therefore be lost, but then again the primary objectives for such firms in pursuing profitsharing are likely to be cultural and industrial rather than economic. In such firms, the application of profitsharing for economic purposes is likely to be confined to salaried executives and other senior managers.

The conventional wisdom is that gainsharing also functions most effectively in small- to medium-sized entities. Equally, gainsharing will suit some management strategies more than others. Although it would be incompatible with a traditional low-trust management style, it is well suited to a high-involvement style, since it encourages participation, two-way communication, teamwork and cooperation. Equally, its emphasis on continuous improvement means that it is well suited to firms with quality enhancement and analyser strategies. However, since it assumes a given product base and mode of technology, gainsharing would generally be a poor fit for firms with a prospector business strategy.

Conversely, goalsharing is well suited to high-involvement prospector firms and business units. Multifactor goalsharing allows greater scope to factor in key success factors such as quality enhancement and customer satisfaction, while high-involvement prospectors may also look to multifactor plans to furnish the flexibility needed to accommodate ongoing changes in technology and product or service type. Goalsharing's future-oriented vision also holds particular attractions for prospector organisations. Its capacity to incorporate non-financial criteria also means that it is well suited to use in public sector organisations.

Team incentives are well suited to organisations characterised by task interdependence, crossfunctionality, project work and participative management. This means that it is appropriate for both high-involvement analysers and prospectors, especially the latter, which are typically structured on organic lines, with networks of autonomous project teams. It may also be the case that team incentives will be less effective in a unionised setting. One reason for this may be that unionised employees are more reluctant to engage in peer monitoring and surveillance than non-unionists. Another reason may be that unionised organisations tend to be managed along traditional lines, leaving little scope for the potential benefits of employee participation.

## Chapter summary

We began by outlining the rationale behind collective STI plans, noting in particular their potential to strengthen organisational commitment and citizenship behaviour. We then progressed to more focused discussion of each of the four main plan types: profitsharing, gainsharing, goalsharing and team incentives, noting the advantages and disadvantages of each. Profitsharing, the oldest of these plans, has the advantage of linking total payroll costs to the firm's capacity to pay, but the larger the workforce and the more volatile the firm's operating context, the weaker the line of sight between individual contribution and reward. Since gainsharing, goalsharing and team incentives focus on measuring and rewarding those results that are within the control of the work group, the line of sight does tend to be stronger with such plans. However, like profitsharing, these plans are also prone to the problems of free riding and social loafing and, in the absence of adequate recognition for individual performance, may demotivate those who have contributed most to collective outcomes. Overall, such plans appear to be most effective in small to medium-sized work units. Profitsharing may be adaptable to both traditionally managed and high-involvement organisations; gainsharing appears best suited to quality defender and analyser organisations, and goalsharing would be most effective in a prospector firm, while team incentives would be relevant to all high-involvement organisations, although, as we have argued, the details of the incentive plan would need to be tailored to the type of team involved.

## Discussion questions

1 What do firms hope to achieve by introducing profitsharing? How likely are they to get what they are after?
2 Is profitsharing better suited to traditional mechanistic firms or to those with high-involvement cultures?
3 Why might an organisation choose goalsharing over gainsharing and profitsharing?
4 Why and how should the incentives applied to project teams differ from those applied to process teams?
5 'Collective STIs do not distinguish adequately between "performers" and "passengers".' Discuss.

## Chapter Nineteen

# COLLECTIVE LONG-TERM INCENTIVES

In this chapter, we examine collective long-term incentives in the form of broadly based employee share plans. Employees may acquire equity in their company by two distinct means: either by being granted shares in lieu of a cash bonus, or by purchasing the shares over time using their own funds or funds provided by the company itself. Although there has been considerable innovation in equity plans for salaried executives in recent years (discussed further in chapter 20), plans for other employees generally fall into one of three main plan types: (1) share grants, (2) share purchase plans and (3) share option plans.

We begin with an overview of the general nature and extent of employee share ownership in developed countries. Next we consider the potential and possible pitfalls of equity-based rewards in general and major theoretical perspectives on how share plans might influence employee attitudes and behaviour. We then turn our attention to the nature and incidence of each of the three main share plan types, as well as considering the strengths and weaknesses of each. Finally, we consider the best fit options for employee share plans.

## Overview of employee share ownership

An employee share plan is any type of plan that allows some or all employees to acquire shares in the organisation that employs them. Such plans have a number of key features in common. First, rewards accrue in the form of share dividends and share price appreciation rather than in the form of a direct cash payment. Second, because share plans measure and reward organisational performance over longer time frames, they are appropriately categorised as long-term incentive (LTI) plans. The reward time frame may be as long as five or ten years, depending on the period of time the employee holds shares or has the option of acquiring shares. Third, by their very nature, share plans are applicable only to share issuing ('public') companies, particularly firms that are listed on a public stock exchange. As such, share plans cannot generally be applied to public sector organisations or to private sector firms that are not incorporated, such as partnerships. Some unlisted private companies operate plans that emulate the effects of employee share plans, but these plans (commonly referred to as 'replicator' or 'phantom' plans) are generally complex and remain relatively uncommon, except at senior management level. Fourth, the shares issued are typically only those of the employing firm. In other words, the equity involved is limited to that of one company rather than comprising a diversified share portfolio of the type typical of, say, superannuation or managed trust funds.

Such plans have been a common feature of remuneration practice for both managerial and non-managerial employees in many Western countries since the 1970s. In part, the rising level of employee share ownership reflects an underlying increase in share ownership in the overall population. In 2004, 44 per cent of adult Australians owned shares directly, compared to just 20 per cent in 1997. Australia now has a level of share ownership comparable to that in the USA and Canada, where around half the population holds shares, and substantially above that in the UK and other European Union countries, where the rate of ownership is generally 20 to 30 per cent (Australian Stock Exchange 2005).

However, the use of employee share plans *per se* also varies considerably from country to country, due mainly to differences in concessional taxation arrangements and other legislative provisions. In the UK, approximately 7 per cent of employees are share plan participants, in France the figure is 23 per cent, and in the USA 10 per cent, although some estimates (Gerhart & Rynes 2003: 206) put the level of US private sector employee ownership at around a third of the workforce. In the USA, in particular, favourable tax treatment makes share plans attractive to both employees and employers. By contrast, in Australia, where concessional tax provisions are extremely modest, the comparable figure is just under 6 per cent (Lenne, Mitchell & Ramsay 2005;

TNS Social Research 2005). There is also a marked sectoral unevenness in plan incidence in Australia, with share plan participation being far higher in communication services (30 per cent), finance and insurance industries (29 per cent) and mining (15 per cent) than in other industries (House of Representatives Standing Committee 2000: 23; Lenne, Mitchell & Ramsay 2005; TNS Social Research 2005). Despite these inter-country and inter-industry differences, however, overall it is clear that share plans are assuming greater importance in reward practices throughout the Western world.

## The potential of equity-based rewards

From an organisational perspective, employee share plans have a number of general advantages. In particular, they can encourage an 'ownership' mentality, greater employee interest in a company's success, closer integration of individual and company goals and better organisational citizenship behaviour. Share plans may encourage long-term commitment and membership behaviour, especially where disposal of the shares is subject to a time restriction. They may also create pressure 'from below' for improved management practice and greater employee involvement in decision-making.

Similarly, for employees themselves, share plans offer a number of benefits: long-term financial gains through dividend earnings and share price appreciation; a secure means of retirement saving; tax advantages arising from income deferral and lower tax on capital gains than on direct income; greater job security resulting from high organisational success; and greater involvement in, and influence over, company affairs.

Employee share plans have been shown to have a positive influence on organisational results, with estimates of labour productivity improvement ranging from 1.5 to 26 per cent. One 1980s study estimated that firms with share plans were 1.5 times as profitable as firms without such plans (Aitken & Wood 1989: 161). Rosen and Quarrey (1997) reported that firms introducing broadly based share plans experienced stronger sales and employment growth than comparable firms without such plans. However, as with other incentive plans – and in line with the 'best fit' model assumptions and predictions – performance outcomes from share ownership appear to be contingent rather than assured. One of the most extensive studies, by Blasi, Conte and Kruse (1996), compared 562 US firms with employee share plans with 4716 non-share-plan firms. In the share plan firms, the median proportion of company equity held by employees was 10 per cent and the mean 13.2 per cent. The study found that the use of share plans *per se* had no main effect on performance (measured in terms of profitability and price:earnings ratio). Rather, the link between plan use and performance depended primarily on firm size. In line with the 1/N and free rider phenomena (see chapter 18), performance returns diminished as firm size increased.

How, then, can and does the ownership (or prospective ownership) of company equity affect employee attitudes, behaviour and results? As we have seen in chapter 3, there are a range of theoretical perspectives on the association between monetary rewards and employee task motivation. With equity-based rewards, too, there are a range of explanatory models on offer, including those by Klein (1987), Long (1978) and Pierce, Rubenfeld and Morgan (1991). All draw more or less directly on process theories of motivation, but particularly on expectancy theory and equity theory (see chapters 2 and 3).

Klein (1987) identifies three distinct psychological effects of employee equity ownership: (1) extrinsic reward/satisfaction, (2) instrumental reward/satisfaction and (3) intrinsic reward/satisfaction. The extrinsic reward/satisfaction dimension suggests that behavioural outcomes will depend on how financially rewarding employees perceive share ownership to be. The critical variables here would be the size of the company contribution to employee share holding, the returns on shares held in terms of dividend levels and capital gains and the reward valence that each employee ascribes to these returns.

The instrumental reward/satisfaction dimension highlights the behaviour-shaping role of employee participation in organisational decision-making. The more the plan empowers employee-owners to make decisions, the more positive their behavioural responses are likely to be. The key variables here would be employee voting rights, the proportion of company equity in employee hands, management's employee involvement philosophy, openness and communication.

The intrinsic reward/satisfaction dimension points to the role of ownership *per se* in eliciting positive behavioural responses; that is, the direct effects of 'pride of ownership'. Owning shares in the employing organisation may create a perception of common interest among employees and foster stronger employee 'engagement'; that is, greater affective commitment, membership behaviour and organisational citizenship behaviour, as well as higher task motivation. In particular, ownership may lead to reduced absenteeism, lower labour turnover and fewer industrial disputes. What this dimension is really highlighting is the 'psychology of ownership'.

On the basis of a study of the attitudes of employees in thirty-seven different share ownership plans, Klein (1987) concludes that share plan effectiveness is best accounted for not in terms of the intrinsic rewards of ownership but rather in terms of the extrinsic and instrumental rewards on offer. Klein finds that satisfaction and commitment is highest, and employee turnover lowest, when the plan provides substantial financial benefits to employees, when management is highly committed to employee ownership, and when the company maintains an extensive communication program. In essence, Klein's findings suggest that the secret of success does not lie in ownership itself but rather in other programs designed to draw out and focus the commitment that can come with being a part-owner.

Other researchers have proposed more complex explanatory models that focus on the cognitive linkage between employee ownership and organisational commitment and the behavioural outcomes that may flow from them. These models also highlight the role of a range of mediating variables in the motivation process. In short, these studies suggest that the behavioural impact of share ownership is mediated and contingent rather than guaranteed. Merely issuing a parcel of shares to each eligible employee will not guarantee the desired response; indeed it may have some quite unintended and undesired consequences.

Long (1978) offers an explanatory model that conceptualises the behavioural dimensions of ownership in terms of expectancy theory, equity theory, cooperative behaviour and peer pressure against free riding. Ownership has the potential to increase the employee's expectancy perceptions, engender more cooperative behaviour and heighten co-owners' concern for the behaviour of others in the group. Long hypothesises that the closer integration of individual and organisational goals through employee ownership leads to stronger reward and performance expectations, improved work group norms and heightened motivation. At the same time, heightened psychological involvement in the fate of the organisation is said to lead to more cooperative behaviour and higher satisfaction, while greater commitment leads to reductions in turnover, absenteeism and discontent.

Long's model also distinguishes between cognitive processes to do with the 'self' and 'other' employees. How individual employee owners think and behave will depend on how they perceive the strength of the linkage between their own performance, the performance of the organisation as a whole and the ownership rewards that flow back to the individual from organisational performance. Equally, these expectations will be mediated by how the 'self' perceives the contribution that co-workers make to organisational performance and rewards. If employee shareholders (the 'self') regarded their fellow employees (the 'other') as engaging in free riding then their ownership status is unlikely to translate into high individual effort. Similarly, the larger the number of 'others', the weaker 'self's' line of sight between their own effort and overall organisational outcomes, as registered in the financial market. Here again, then, we encounter the problem of workgroup size, or 1/N.

Pierce, Rubenfeld and Morgan (1991) suggest that the relationship between the fact of share ownership and employee work effort is mediated by a range of cognitive variables. These variables will either enhance or reduce the individual employee's sense of 'psychological ownership' and the degree to which employees collectively demonstrate a sense of shared interest with and commitment to the organisation. According to Pierce, Rubenfeld and Morgan, the key variables include:

- management commitment to employee ownership and how this is interpreted by employees
- the extent of ownership; that is, eligibility, take-up rate, volume and spread of shares held by the workforce
- employee expectations of the material and psychological benefits that ownership *should* confer; for instance, are employees more interested in the dividends and capital gains (extrinsic rewards) or in being involved in decision-making (instrumental rewards)?
- whether employee involvement programs are in place and how they are perceived. If employees are attracted to instrumental rewards, the offering of shares without also implementing a genuine employee involvement program may be damaging to motivation and morale.

Without doubt, the clearest finding, in the extant research evidence on share plan efficacy relates to firm size and opportunity for genuine employee involvement. As Gerhart and Rynes (2003: 219) conclude, share plans '*can* have a positive impact on firm performance under the right conditions (i.e. small company size, strong two-way communications and employee participation, and high financial pay-in by employers)'. There is strong evidence of positive outcomes when share plans are introduced in conjunction with employee participation programs that give employees more voice in organisational decision-making. Similarly, research by Long (1981, 1982) suggests that the chief benefits in terms of employee satisfaction, commitment and motivation derive more from the presence of a genuinely participative management style than from employee ownership alone. Long's (1982) longitudinal case study of declining motivation and satisfaction under a share plan introduced by a Canadian electronics firm in the late 1970s seems to bear this out. Employee owners felt increasingly cheated because they were not given adequate opportunity to participate in day-to-day decision-making.

The level of personal shareholding is also likely to be important here. A British study of employee-owned bus companies (Pendleton, Wilson & Wright 1998) found that levels of commitment and satisfaction were strongest among those employees who had both substantial personal shareholdings in the firm and a strong perception that they were genuine participants in the firm's decision-making processes. A study by Rosen and Quarrey (1997) compared the performance of a number of firms before and after they introduced employee share ownership with a matched sample of non-share-plan firms and found no significant difference between the two sets of firms. However, when they compared non-share-plan firms with those that had introduced both share ownership *and* employee involvement practices, they found a major difference. The latter grew 11 to 17 per cent faster than the former.

How much formal involvement is necessary to reinforce the positive motivational potential of employee ownership? The answer seems to depend partly on what is implemented first. Research by Ben-Ner and Jones (1995) suggests that greater employee participation increases performance only when participation is limited to begin with. They suggest that where employees already enjoy considerable involvement and empowerment, organisational performance depends primarily on the material rewards that flow from share ownership.

In sum, the above models all suggest that merely making shares available to employees is unlikely to deliver positive benefits to the organisation. The key message is that realisation of the full potential of an equity plan will depend, *inter alia*, on:

- the pre-existing organisational culture and management style, especially regarding employee involvement (traditional/low trust or high involvement/high trust): do employees trust management and each other?
- plan configuration, including plan type (especially whether shares are issued free, in lieu of cash, or have to be purchased) and eligibility (especially whether eligibility is broadly based or selective)

- supporting policies and practices, especially 'open book' management, employee consultation and involvement programs
- how the plan and supporting practices are communicated to eligible employees
- the breadth, depth and duration of share take-up
- the reward preferences or valences of the employees concerned (extrinsic, instrumental, intrinsic)
- employee expectations of ownership risk and return: recent share price volatility or an expectation of share price decline may negate any potential benefits from an equity plan
- employee perceptions of reward 'instrumentality' or 'line of sight' between effort and financial rewards from equity holding: whether employees believe that their individual and collective effort influences dividends paid (from net profit) and how the external share market evaluates the company's performance.

While these considerations are common to all equity plans, each of the three main types of equity plan have their own potentialities and possible shortcomings.

## Share grants

With share grants, or share bonus plans as they are also known, employees receive a gift of fully paid shares in the firm. Shares are 'fully paid' if the price of the shares has been fully met and no acquisition debt is incurred by the recipient. The distribution of shares to each employee is commonly based on a predetermined allocation formula; perhaps according to years of service with the company, position in the organisational hierarchy, on the basis of individual performance, or as an equal number or value of shares to each employee where the size of the grant is determined by group or organisational financial results, as in, say, a profitshare scheme.

Share grants usually carry similar rights to those enjoyed by external shareholders, including full dividend payments, entitlement to the capital gains flowing from share price appreciation, eligibility for any issues of special bonus shares, and voting at the company's general meetings. It is also common for dividend payments to be 'fully franked', which means that the company absorbs any tax liability associated with dividend distribution. Some grants can also be traded immediately, which means that the grant is technically 'unrestricted'. However, it has become increasingly common for share grants to have certain limitations attached, which generally means that ownership does not transfer ('vest') immediately and/or that the shares are not tradable immediately in the same way as 'common stock' (i.e. ordinary shares held by external investors). Conditional share grants of this type are known as 'restricted' share plans. While employees are not required to outlay any of their own money, they usually cannot sell their shares until a specified minimum period has elapsed. Where the grants are linked to a retirement plan, the shares may be held in trust until the employee leaves the company. Dividend earnings can either be distributed annually to participating employees as income or paid into a trust fund, where they will continue to generate investment income for the shareholder until the period of restriction ends. Other restrictions may also apply. For instance, some or all shares awarded may be subject to forfeiture if the employee leaves employment with the company before the expiry of a specified period.

As we shall see in chapter 20, it is also now common for share grant plans for company executives to make the award of free shares subject to the satisfaction of a performance hurdle within the specified period of restriction. Although performance restrictions are still uncommon in plans targeted at non-managerial employees, there are not unknown. For instance, one major Australian company with a performance-based share grant plan for line employees is the National Australia Bank (NAB), one of the country's 'big four' retail banks. The first of its type in Australian retail banking, the NAB plan was initially introduced in 1987 as an interest-free share purchase plan (see following section for discussion), and in 1992 it was transformed into a share grant scheme, with each employee receiving twenty-five free shares per year. However, in 1995, in response to a senior management perception that the grant scheme was overly generous, NAB converted the plan to a performance-contingent grant plan: the 'enterprise value added' employee share ownership scheme. Under this plan, which remains the bank's current approach, each eligible employee stands to receive up to $1000 worth of shares depending on NAB's overall performance relative to its peers and the wider market. Shares are not held in trust and carry no restrictions, which means that they can be sold at will, although disposal also carries significant transaction costs. Ninety-five per cent of the bank's employees participate in the scheme, which maximises the tax concession currently available to broadly based employee share plans under Australian taxation law (discussed in the following section). It also complements the bank's cash

STI plans and is administered with informal input from the relevant union, the Finance Sector Union (Barnes et al. 2006).

In the USA, share grant plans are an important element of employee retirement savings, and exacting trust arrangements for this purpose are mandated under the federal *Employee Retirement and Income Security Act* (ERISA) 1974, which regulates private employer pension and welfare programs. This Act requires every company opting for a share plan to establish an independent trust to purchase shares on employees' behalf and to hold those shares in trust until the employee leaves, dies or retires. Typically, the trust borrows funds externally to purchase shares in the company. The company then contributes money to the trust over a number of years, which the trust uses to repay the loan. Both the principal and the interest on contributions to the trust fund are tax deductible to the company. From the employees' perspective, income earned from shares is not taxed until the shares themselves are distributed from the trust, usually at retirement. Even then, tax can be further delayed by rolling over the funds from the sale of the shares into other investments.

For the company, share grants may encourage long-term employee commitment and membership behaviour, particularly where restricted shares and trust arrangements are involved. A firm may also issue shares as a way of securing employee acceptance of an organisational change strategy. In smaller companies, restricted share grants may also be a means of locking up company equity to prevent hostile takeovers. Equally, issuing share grants to employees may require a company previously managed along traditional lines to institute a new management system that is more 'open book' and participative.

From the employee's perspective, share grants have the obvious advantage of being notionally cost-free, although grants are sometimes in lieu of an increase in cash remuneration, which means that an opportunity cost is involved. Regular share grants can serve as a convenient means for employees to supplement retirement savings. Depending on the prevailing taxation regimen, share grants may also carry tax advantages for share recipients, particularly where shares are received in lieu of additional cash remuneration and where tax liability on shares received can be deferred until retirement by being held in a managed trust. By the same token, employee shareholders will still be exposed to loss of capital and income if the company's share price and dividend levels fall. Indeed, given that their equity holdings are concentrated in the one firm, employee shareholders may well have a far higher risk exposure than will external shareholders since the latter are more likely to have a diversified share portfolio covering a range of sectors, industries and firms.

## Share purchase plans

With share purchase plans, employees have the opportunity to purchase part or all of a specified quota of shares in the company. Employees typically pay a small deposit on the full share purchase price – say, 10 per cent – with the balance of the purchase price repayable over a specified term. The plan typically includes favourable purchase terms, such as a purchase price set below the prevailing market value and/or a low or zero interest loan from the company to fund the purchase. Some schemes allow the share purchase loan to be repaid from dividends so that the repayment period is open-ended and there is no employee outlay from personal savings. Other schemes involve employee savings plans and pay deductions to fund purchase. Shares are typically held in trust until the loan is repaid or the minimum holding period has elapsed. Legal ownership of the shares vests to the employee over time as the loan is paid off. Share purchase plans generally prohibit the selling of shares until a minimum period has passed, or until the loan is fully repaid and the shares have vested fully to the employee. Share purchase entitlements are usually fixed according to position in the salary hierarchy or by seniority, the logic being that lower-paid employees will have less debt-servicing capacity.

In many countries, share purchase plans also attract concessional tax treatment. Subject to certain conditions, Australian taxation law allows employees a tax exemption on any shares provided free (or at a discount) by their employer each year up to a value of $1,000. For example, where a company's shares have a market value of $1.01, in one financial year it could issue up to 1000 shares to employees at a purchase price of one cent and the employees would be exempt from tax liability on the $1,000 purchase discount. However, for the full exemption to apply, the share plan must be offered on a 'non-discriminatory' basis to at least 75 per cent of the company's permanent employees with at least three years service. Further, the shares must not be subject to any forfeiture condition and must be held for a minimum of three years (or until termination) before disposal (House of Representatives Standing Committee 2000; Barnes et al. 2006). Any shares provided free or at a discount above the $1,000 maximum remain subject to the full marginal tax rate, as are dividends received on the concessional shares and any appreciation in their market price. Critics argue that these modest provisions, first introduced in 1995, fall well short of the more generous tax treatment afforded to employees and employers for such plans in many other developed countries. In 2000 the Commonwealth Parliamentary Standing Committee on Employment, Education and Workplace Relations (House of Representatives Standing Committee on Employment, Education and Workplace Relations 2000) recommended an increase in the tax-free threshold and tax concessions on proceeds of shares reinvested in superannuation or unit trusts or used to fund retirement, but to date these recommendations have not been acted upon.

In most Western countries, including the USA, the UK, Canada and Australia, share purchase plans are the dominant form of employee equity participation. In Australia and Canada, more than a fifth of firms operate share purchase plans for non-managerial employees. By contrast, share grant plans were used by only 4 per cent of Canadian firms and 6 per cent of Australian firms (Long & Shields 2005b: 1798). The most common means of financing share acquisition appear to be employer loans and salary deduction or sacrifice. Salary sacrifice, whereby the employee accepts a lower level of taxable cash salary in exchange for company shares of an equivalent value, has special appeal as a means of tax reduction and deferral. For instance, the Australian property and financial services firm Lend Lease, a company with a highly participative management culture, has a long history of employee financial participation. In its current employee share plan, employees can receive up to 5 per cent of their base salary in shares, which are held in trust. Employees receive annual dividend payments but have access to the shares only when they leave the company, at which point deferred tax becomes payable (Russell 2004c).

Discounted share purchase plans are also the preferred means of providing Australian employees with an equity stake in organisations undergoing privatisation and demutualisation. This is one of the main reasons for the growth in the popularity of employee share plans in Australia since the 1980s, particularly in banking and insurance, utilities supply and communications. For instance, when the previously fully publicly owned telecommunications provider Telstra was partly floated on the Australian Stock Exchange in 1997 the organisation's employees were offered a number of ways of becoming part-owners. All eligible employees were able to buy up to 2000 shares, which, based on the price cap of $3.30, would have meant an outlay of $6,600. If they purchased the full quota, they became eligible for 500 extra shares free of charge. Employees were also able to purchase the shares using an interest-free company loan and to use the dividends paid on these shares to help repay the loan. However, they were also required to hold all shares acquired in this way for at least three years (Baker 1997).

Purchase plans provide companies with access to an additional and otherwise untapped source of capital-raising, namely employee income and savings. For companies in financial difficulties, a full or partial employee buyout may be one of the few survival options available to a firm and its employees. One case in point here is the partial employee buyout of the US air carrier United Airlines in 1994. Before its near collapse in the wake of the terrorist attack of 11 September 2001, United Airlines was the largest majority employee-share owned firm in the USA. Under the 1994 rescue scheme, United's employees traded an average of 15 per cent in pay for 55 per cent of company equity and three seats on the twelve-member company board. The share purchase was funded by means of interest-free loans from the company for the purchase of 'preferred stock' to be held in trust until the person ceased to be a United employee. Two-thirds of United's 81,000-strong workforce participated in the scheme, and the initiative gave the company a second lease of life – until the share market collapse of 2000 and the terrorist attacks of 2001 (Chandler 1996; Zuckerman 2001).

Some of the main advantages accruing to companies from such plans may well be of an industrial and cultural nature. Unlike share grants, share purchase funded by a company loan means that employees are literally in the company's debt for the duration of the loan and may thus be more accommodating of management initiatives. Also, where employees have had to pay for the shares, intrinsic or 'ownership' motivation is likely to be considerably stronger and more enduring than would be the case where shares have been received as a gift. By the same token, share purchase plans entail greater risk all round than is the case with share grants. Employees committed to repaying the principal on a company loan at a fixed purchase price will experience severe financial difficulties if the share price collapses and the debt is not renegotiated or forgiven.

Ironically, the United Airlines experience also highlights another and perhaps more fundamental problem with share purchase programs, namely that equity ownership that is not accompanied by genuine employee involvement may prove to be doubly dysfunctional. Employees will not necessarily cease to be wage-earners merely because they happen to own company shares, particularly if they are denied anything other than token participation in organisational decision-making. In 2000, with the United Airlines share price falling precipitously, two of the largest employee shareholder groups in the company – the pilots and the maintenance engineers – took industrial action against the company during negotiations for a new industrial agreement. United's management took the engineers to court, and their union threatened strike action in retaliation. As journalist Laurence Zuckerman (2001) observed at the time: 'What happened? In retrospect, it seems obvious: while everybody agreed to call workers "owners", they did not act like owners, and management did not treat them like owners. If the two sides had worked hard to create a true ownership culture throughout the company, the experiment might have succeeded … Instead, labor and management displayed a lack of commitment from the start.' The point is that share plans implemented chiefly with a view to achieving labour cost reduction or reinforcing managerial control are likely to have different outcomes from those introduced with a view to increasing genuine employee participation.

## Share option plans

An option plan gives the employee the right to buy a specified number of company shares at a predetermined price at a specified future date, such as the third anniversary of the option grant date. The price payable to exercise the option to acquire some or all of the shares – the 'strike price' – is commonly set at or below the market value of the shares at the time the option is granted. If the market price increases after the option is granted, the option-holder stands to make a net gain by exercising the option to acquire the shares, then selling some or all of them on the general market. An employee who expects a further rise in the share price may retain some or all of the shares acquired. Unexercised options carry no shareholders' rights and, unlike fully vested shares, options are not normally transferable.

Although previously confined largely to senior executives' reward packages, since the mid-1990s option plans have also been extended to non-executive employees, including line managers, salaried professionals and line employees. In some cases, all-employee option plans are linked to special savings arrangements. For instance, under the Blair Labour government's

'Save-As-You-Earn' scheme initiative in the UK, companies are able to grant employees options to acquire shares three, five or seven years hence at a discount of up to 20 per cent on the grant date price. To this end, employees enter into a monthly savings plan to fund the future purchase. When the option vests, the employee can either apply the accumulated savings to acquire the shares or take the savings plus interest in cash (Armstrong & Murlis 2004: 332–3).

In the US information technology sector, all-employee option plans have been used extensively by both start-up firms and established firms such as Microsoft as a cash substitute and as a means of attracting and retaining high-value knowledge workers. Until 2003 Microsoft ran a broad-based option scheme for its professional employees, and several thousand have become millionaires as a result of exercising their option to buy (Seaman 2004). In line with agency theory prescriptions (see chapter 20) extending eligibility to managers, professional and line employees in this way may serve to strengthen employee focus on and alignment with the interests of external shareholders. As we shall see in chapter 20, executive option plans have been and remain a central element of the management dictum of maximising 'shareholder value'.

Figure 19.1 illustrates the workings of a simple option plan for line employees. On the option grant date (1 July 2007), employees receive the right to purchase up to 1000 shares in the company at the grant date share price of $10 per share using their own funds. No performance hurdle is imposed, but the option to buy at the specified strike price cannot be exercised until three years have passed (i.e. until 1 July 2010) and will lapse completely if not exercised within the subsequent two years (i.e. before 1 July 2012). By the time the three-year non-exercise period has ended, the company's share price will have done one of three things: risen above the $10 strike price, fallen below $10, or remained at or returned to $10. If the market price is above $10 (i.e. the options are 'in the money'), employees may decide to exercise their option to buy some or all of the options and either hold the shares thus acquired in anticipation of a further share price increase or (where the shares are not also subject to a restriction on disposal) sell the shares immediately to achieve a capital gain. Immediate disposal is most likely where employees believe that the company's share price may have peaked. Alternatively, an employee who expects a further substantial rise in share price may delay outlaying funds on share purchase until a later point in the two-year exercise window, when the capital gain per share may be

**At the grant date:** *1 July 2007*
- The prevailing company share price is $10.00 per share
- Option terms: each eligible employee may purchase up to 1,000 shares in the company at $10 per share no earlier than 1 July 2010 and no later than 1 July 2012, at which time the option to buy lapses.
- No performance hurdle restriction.
- Share purchase is self-funded rather than company-funded.

**At the earliest exercise date:** *1 July 2010*

| Scenario 1: options 'in the money'<br>Prevailing share price is $15.00 | Scenario 2: options 'underwater'<br>Prevailing share price is $8.00 |
|---|---|
| • Employees may either do nothing or exercise their option to buy some or all of the 1,000 shares at $10 per share.<br><br>• An employee who expects that the company's share price has peaked may decide to exercise the full option and sell the 1,000 shares immediately at a pre-tax profit of $5 per share.<br><br>• An employee who expects a further rise in the share price may decide not to exercise the option just now (given that this will involve an opportunity cost and that the option to buy still has two years to run). | • The employee does nothing in the short term but decides to wait and see what happens to the share price over the course of the following two years. |

**Figure 19.1** How does a share option plan work?

higher. A further reason for holding off on exercising the purchase option is that self-funded acquisition necessarily involves an economic opportunity cost since it will require either a commitment of personal savings or the taking out of a loan to fund the purchase. Conversely, where the market price is at or below the $10 strike price on the first possible exercise date, there is little prospect of a short-term gain (i.e. the options are 'underwater'), so the employee may decide simply to sit out part or all of the two-year exercise period to see how the share price tracks. If the options remain 'underwater', the employee will just allow the option to lapse.

Note that the granting of an option does not confer immediate equity ownership, so there will be no 'ownership' effect on motivation unless and until the option is exercised. Until the options are exercisable, the main behavioural effects will be twofold. First, restriction on exercise will strengthen membership behaviour, since the options are likely to be forfeited if the option-holder leaves the company. Second, during the holding period, the incentive effect will be largely extrinsic; that is, the holder will be motivated to improve company performance so as to strengthen market perceptions and lift the market share price with a view to maximising any capital gain when it becomes possible to exercise the option to buy and sell the shares involved. Some option plans – but especially those applied to senior managers and executives – now incorporate premium pricing whereby the strike price is set above the market share price at the grant date. Premium pricing increases the performance challenge associated with realising a potential capital gain. In recent years, it has also become increasingly common for companies to issue zero exercise price options, or 'ZEPOS', to company executives. These resemble restricted share grants in that, although they involve no purchase cost to the option-holder, they typically have performance hurdles attached to the exercise right. These and related executive-level equity instruments are explored further in chapter 20.

Until recently, a key attraction of option plans was that new option grants were widely believed to involve no net cost to the company. Such an assumption did have a degree of face validity. The company avoided the need to finance the share purchase directly, while the employee avoided the need to make any outlays at the date grant. Unlike cash rewards or share grants, then, option grants appealed as an apparently cost-free means of motivating and rewarding employees; that is, they did not leave employees out of pocket and did not constitute a recognised operating cost needing to be expensed against company profits. To many public company boards, options thus loomed as the perfect means of employee financial participation.

However, as is now widely recognised, option plans do have a number of shortcomings. Such plans may foster a purely speculative outlook on equity ownership, since employees are encouraged to sell as well as buy company shares. In the absence of a restriction on the trading of newly acquired shares, any ownership effect may be transient. At executive level in particular, option plans, especially those without restrictions attached, may be subject to various forms of collusive manipulation, including reduction of the initial strike price ('repricing'), softening of any performance hurdles, the calculated release of information to the marketplace in order to reduce the strike price or drive up the sale price for the purpose of personal gain ('insider trading'), and the automatic replenishment of option entitlements following the exercise of an option ('reloading'). These potential problems are considered further in chapter 20.

Moreover, the 'line of sight' between employee effort and financial reward is even more remote than is the case with share grant and purchase plans, since the realisation of any market-related rewards are significantly delayed.

In 'bull' share market conditions, in which most companies are experiencing share price appreciation, options may confer unearned ('windfall') gains on some option-holders. As with all equity plans, options are 'fair weather' reward instruments; they may work well in time of share price growth, but can also compound a firm's problems if the share price falls, say in a declining ('bear') share market. This is one of the reasons why Microsoft, one of the pioneers of broadly based option plans in the 1990s, abandoned options after the share market crisis of 2000–02 in favour of restricted share grants (Seaman 2004).

Morever, the contention that option plans are cost-free is no longer sustainable. First, the sale of option-acquired shares may impose a cost on external shareholders, especially where the plan involves the issue of additional company shares. *Ceteris paribus*, the greater the supply of shares on offer, the greater the downward pressure on the market share price. When employees seek to dump large numbers of shares on the market, the effect will be to 'dilute' the value of shares held by external shareholders. This is clearly a cost to shareholders. Second, as such commentators as Bodie, Kaplan and Merton (2003) have argued, options are not a cost-free form of remuneration for the organisation itself. Whenever a company issues options to an employee, an economic opportunity cost is involved: the cost of not using the options in some other way, such as selling them to an external investor, to generate additional revenue for the firm. For this reason, corporate regulators and international accounting standards authorities now require public companies both to expense new option grants to senior executives as an operating cost and to report the 'fair value' of such grants as an element of executive annual reward. A counter-argument here is that this stands to reduce profits and hence dividend payments to external shareholders, but expensing may just amount to internalising a cost that is already borne by external shareholders through the process of equity dilution.

## 'Best fit' with collective long-term incentives

The research evidence on share plan efficacy suggests that, in general, they are best suited to companies with a high-involvement culture and an organic rather than a mechanistic structure. For such firms, share ownership has strong potential to provide the intrinsic and instrumental rewards that will enable them to elicit high levels of commitment, task effort and organisational citizenship behaviour. Indeed, it may be that a prudently applied share plan may serve as a catalyst for transforming traditional firms into high-involvement firms. In general, however, share plan eligibility will be more broadly based in high-involvement cultures than in those of a traditional nature, where eligibility may well be confined to the executive level.

Like other collective incentives, share plans may also be better suited to small to medium-sized firms than to large corporations. Lawler speculates (1990: 127–8) that share plans work best in smaller firms with participative management styles: ' . . . in a small organisation in which participative management is practiced, employee ownership has a good chance of increasing organisational performance. The key here is combining ownership with employee involvement so that a line of sight exists.' In larger organisations the linkages between individual effort and organisational performance are obscured by the sheer number of employees involved.

An organisation's age is also likely to be an important determinant. Firms at start-up and in the initial stages of growth, when remuneration budgets are limited, are likely to be strongly attracted to broadly based option plans as a means of attracting and retaining high-performing knowledge workers. Mature firms may be more attracted to share grants, while those in decline or undergoing turnaround may opt for share purchase plans as a means of retaining high performers, mobilising additional capital and fending off takeover.

Long-term collective incentives may also be a better fit for some business strategies than others, but the permutations here are less clear-cut and the reward choices are likely to be driven mainly by factors associated with firm structure, culture and lifecycle stage. The longer time frame may be better suited to defender and analyser strategies than to the shorter cycle times typical of a prospector approach. On this basis, defender and analyser firms may find restricted share purchase plans to be an appropriate reward choice. Conversely, the accent on entrepreneurship, risk-taking and alignment with shareholder value means that a broadly based option plan may be a more appropriate choice for a firm pursuing a prospector business strategy.

## Chapter summary

This chapter has examined collective long-term incentives in the form of broadly based employee share plans. First we considered the general nature and incidence of employee share ownership in developed countries. We then investigated the potential and possible pitfalls of equity-based rewards in general and major theoretical perspectives on how share plans might influence employee attitudes and behaviour. With these general points in mind, we then turned our attention to the nature and incidence of each of the three main employee share plan types, namely share grants, share purchase plans and share option plans, as well as considering the strengths and weaknesses of each. While share grants and options expose employees to little absolute risk, this is not so of share purchase plans, which, even with price discounting and concessional loans, may still expose employees to considerable risk of capital loss. There is some evidence that share plans can have a positive effect on firm performance, but this appears to be mediated by the scale and depth of equity ownership and by the presence of a genuine employee-owner 'voice' in organisational decision-making. Overall, the strongest effect may well be that on organisational culture. In general, broadly based LTI plans are best suited to firms with a high-involvement culture. Indeed, it may be that a prudently applied share plan may serve as a catalyst for transforming traditional defender firms into high-involvement analysers or prospectors.

## Discussion questions

1  What pay-off can an organisation anticipate from granting free shares to its employees?
2  What makes for an effective employee share ownership plan?
3  'Shareholders willingly expose themselves to speculative risk, but employees should not be expected to do so.' Discuss.
4  Employee share purchase plans: safe bet or risky business?
5  What are the particular challenges of introducing a broadly based option plan?

## Chapter Twenty

# EXECUTIVE INCENTIVES

In this chapter we examine the trends, practices and debates associated with incentives for those employees at the apex of the management hierarchy, namely senior executives, but with particular attention to incentive plans for chief executive officers (CEOs). We begin by considering the place and role of hired executives in corporate governance as well as three influential theories of executive motivation, behaviour and reward: tournament theory, agency theory and managerial power theory. We then review the main components of executive reward, as well as trends in CEO reward level and composition in a number of developed countries in recent years. Following this, attention turns to the various short-term and long-term incentive plans and associated techniques, including performance targets or 'hurdles', currently applied to executives. Next, we examine the academic research evidence and arguments regarding the effectiveness of executive reward practices, particularly the extent of the association between company performance and executive pay outcomes. Applying a multistakeholder perspective, the final section canvasses some of the main implications for effective executive reward practice.

## Corporate governance and executive motivation and reward

The defining feature of the modern publicly listed company is the separation of ownership and control (Berle & Means 1932) and the consequent need for a formal system of internal 'corporate governance' aimed at maintaining alignment of interest between (1) the firm's owners (i.e. the shareholders); (2) those appointed to oversee the firm's operations in the shareowners' collective interests (the directors); and (3) executives hired by the board to manage the firm's day-to-day affairs. As such, the essence of 'corporate governance' is the maintenance of a constructive relationship between these three key 'stakeholder' groups, but particularly between shareholders and their boardroom representatives on the one hand and salaried executives on the other.

To ensure that boards are able to negotiate executive remuneration 'at arm's-length' with an incumbent or incoming executive, company laws in many developed countries now require the establishment of compensation or remuneration committees where either all or a majority of members are 'independent' directors; that is, directors who are free of any business or other relationship with incumbent executives that could materially inter-fere with – or could reasonably be perceived to materially interfere with – the exercise of their unfettered and independent judgement (Australian Stock Exchange Corporate Governance Council 2003: 19–20). For instance, independence may be compromised where a director is or has been an employee of the company, has a business relationship with the company, or has significant external relationships with the company's executives, includ-ing cross-directorships. In particular, a director of firm A who is also CEO of firm B could not be considered independent if the CEO of firm A is also a director of firm B.

The mainstream descriptive or prescriptive literature on the nature of the firm offers a number of alternative theoretical perspectives on executive motivation, behaviour and reward. For our purposes, the most significant of these are tournament theory, agency theory and managerial power the-ory. Each approach offers a distinctive explanation for executive motivation as well as a particular normative position regarding the most appropriate means of managing or regulating executive behaviour and reward.

## Tournament theory

Tournament theory sees the governance relationship as being essentially unproblematic and hierarchical management reward structures as desir-able and effective. Specifically, it focuses on the way in which executive reward hierarchies are structured and how and why such structures are nec-essary for attracting, retaining and motivating executive 'talent'. Tournament theory suggests that the steep hierarchy of senior manager pay levels is both explained and justified by the contest for promotion, status and power and the struggle to secure the ultimate corporate prize: the position of CEO. To the victor goes the ultimate material prize: remuneration unmatched by that given to any other 'player' in the game of corporate talent. The high rewards available for the CEO position act as an incentive for those lower down the management scale to accept rewards less than their current contribution (Lazear & Rosen 1981; O'Reilly, Main & Crystal 1988). Moreover, as victors ascend the management hierarchy, tournament theory predicts that rewards should include both a large payout (for prior contribution) and a significant incentive-based component (for current contribution) (Conyon & Sadler 2001; Gordon 2005: 680).

## Agency theory

Agency theory has for many decades been the most widely embraced theoretical perspective on corporate governance matters (Gomez-Mejia & Wiseman 1997: 259–300; Jensen & Meckling 1976; Jensen & Murphy 1990). In contrast to tournament theory, it focuses on the motivational and material separation between the firm's owners and its executive employees and, in particular, on the latter's propensity for risk aversion and self-serving behaviour. In large organisations, individual owners – or 'principals' – are incapable of exercising day-to-day control over organisational affairs. So they appoint salaried executives and managers to act as their agents. However, the interests of the owner-principals and the executive-agents are not necessarily identical; there may be significant 'goal incongruence'. Managers may well pursue activities that benefit themselves rather than the owners. For instance, executives may focus on personal gain rather than on shareholder gains, or on short-term goals that advantage themselves rather than on long-term goals that are more likely to advantage shareholders.

The 'moral hazards' and 'agency costs' attending managerial delegation constitute the core of what agency theorists term the 'principal–agent problem'. According to traditional agency theory, one specific way to reduce 'agency costs' and increase alignment between executives' material interests and those of ordinary shareholders is to make as much of the executive's rewards as possible contingent on the organisation's performance and financial returns to the owners (Levinthal 1988; Gerhart & Milkovich 1990; Barkema & Gomez-Mejia 1998; Bloom & Milkovich 1998). In other words, for chief executives, agency theory prioritises psychological contracts of a transactional rather than a relational nature (Kidder & Buchholtz 2002).

## Managerial power theory

The third major theoretical perspective, that offered by the managerial power thesis, has much in common with agency theory but challenges its assumptions in two key respects. First, it emphasises the contradictory position occupied by the company board itself, its vulnerability to executive influence, and the potential for board complicity in offering overly generous or suboptimal levels of remuneration. Second, managerial power theory is much less sanguine regarding the possibility of 'arm's-length bargaining' over the terms and conditions of executive employment and, hence, the likelihood of 'optimal contracting'. Exponents of the managerial power perspective (Bebchuk & Fried 2004; Crystal 1988, 1991a & b; Finkelstein & Hambrick 1989; Finkelstein 1992) argue that despite statutory requirements in many developed countries for boards in general, and executive remuneration committees in particular, to be composed of directors who are independent of incumbent salaried executives, many boards are still too readily swayed by the executives they hire.

These propositions have triggered a series of robust exchanges between agency theorists and proponents of the managerial power perspective. Indeed, academic debate about executive reward now centres largely on the relative explanatory worth of these two overlapping but competing constructs. Agency theory is much favoured in the economics and finance literatures, while the managerial power perspective is at the fore of the corporate law and organisational behaviour literatures. We shall return to this debate later in the chapter.

## Executive incentives: components and trends

An executive remuneration package typically has five main components:

1 *Annual base salary.* Fixed annual pay is the guaranteed, no-risk, element of the total pay package. The size of this guaranteed proportion generally reflects firm size (generally defined in terms of market capitalisation) and the complexity and challenge of the position itself, including the perceived degree of 'risk' involved.
2 *Benefits.* This includes recurrent company contributions to retirement or superannuation, special retention payments, low-interest or interest-free company loans, company cars, health insurance, medical and dental care, life insurance, club membership fees, leisure, holiday, travel,

entertainment and concierge expenses, children's school fees, financial and investment services, executive coaching costs, spouse travel and survivor benefits, and other 'fringe' benefits.

3 *Short-term incentives (STIs).* These are awarded on the basis of one or more aspects of organisational performance over a short period, generally one year. Payments typically take the form of an annual cash bonus, and it is increasingly common for payment to be contingent on the executive achieving one or more targets related to the firm's absolute or relative annual financial or accounting performance. Some firms also now require that an annual incentive payment either be deferred or taken in the form of company shares.

4 *Long-term incentives (LTIs).* These tend to relate to organisational performance over a three-, five- or ten-year period, with rewards generally taking the form of company equity rather than cash, although cash payments based on multiyear performance would also qualify as an LTI. The aim is to encourage a longer-term focus on improving organisational performance, particularly in terms of total returns to shareholders. Increasingly, LTI plans include both market-related performance targets and restrictions on the disposal of equity-based rewards.

5 *Termination and post-employment payments.* These may include severance payments geared to length of service (also known as 'golden parachutes'); payments for early contact termination, typically expressed as a proportion or multiple of annual base salary; post-employment consulting fees; and other special retirement benefits, such as spouse pensions, free air travel and accommodation.

Base salary and benefits are customarily described as constituting the 'fixed' component of annual remuneration while STIs and LTIs constitute 'at risk' components. Until the late 1980s, fixed pay (base salary plus benefits) comprised the major element of executive pay in most Western firms. However, since the early 1990s, in the USA and many other Western countries, there has been a marked shift of emphasis in the composition of executive remuneration from base salary to incentives, particularly LTIs in the form of option plans. The increased importance of incentive plans has also driven an unprecedented growth in the absolute level of executive total remuneration.

The changes in the level and composition of executive pay have been led by developments in the USA. Figure 20.1 (a) shows the average annual remuneration level and composition of the CEOs of the Standard & Poors 500 firms in the decade to 2002, based on data reported in these firms'

**(a)   Total reward level (2002-constant dollars)**

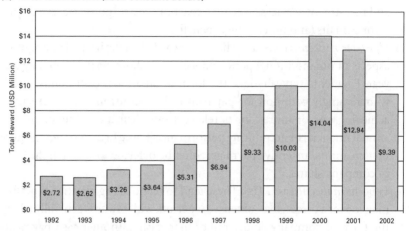

**(b)   Total reward composition (%)**

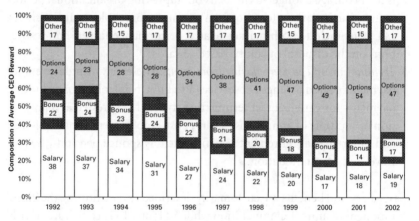

**Figure 20.1** Average remuneration of US CEOs in Standard & Poors 500 firms, 1992–2002

*Source:* adapted from Jensen, Murphy & Wruck 2004: 31.

annual proxy statements. Over this period, average total CEO remuneration in these large firms (expressed in 2002 constant US dollar terms) rose from $2.7 million to a peak of $14.0 million in 2000 – a cumulative increase of 420 per cent – but then declined to $9.4 million in the wake of the share market downturn of 2001–02. As figure 20.2(b) indicates, the primary contributor to the pay surge of the later 1990s was share option plans, which by 2000 contributed just under half of average total remuneration, compared to just on a quarter in 1992.

While the absolute levels of CEO reward remain significantly lower in smaller developed countries like Australia (primarily because of smaller firm size), the trends in total remuneration growth and reward composition have mirrored those in the USA. Data compiled by consulting firm the Hay Group and presented in figure 20.2 details the Australian trend. Between 1990 and 2004 the contribution of LTIs to total annual CEO remuneration rose, on average, from 13 to 39 per cent, and that of STIs increased from 5 to 21 per cent, while the contribution of fixed pay fell from 82 to just 40 per cent. Similar, although less pronounced, changes were also recorded for other senior executives, with the LTI proportion rising to 30 per cent and the STI proportion to 20 per cent, while the contribution of fixed pay fell to 50 per cent.

The turn to incentive-based rewards has been paralleled by an increase in CEO turnover and a reduction in average CEO tenure. According to research commissioned by the Business Council of Australia (2004), these changes in CEO employment have been more pronounced in Australia than elsewhere. Large listed Australian companies have a higher rate of CEO turnover than do firms elsewhere (14 per cent compared to 9.7 per cent), while Australian CEOs now have relatively short tenures (5.6 years compared to 7.6 years). Overall, the combination of variable pay and shorter tenure connotes a shift from relational to transactional psychological contracting at the organisational apex.

Having reviewed the major trends in the level and composition of executive reward practice, particularly the greater emphasis on performance-related incentives, we can now consider in more detail the specific types of short- and long-term incentive plans that firms may choose for their CEOs and other senior executives.

## Short-term cash incentive plans

These take the form of bonuses paid annually on the basis of profit- or revenue-related performance achieved over the previous financial year. Short-term incentives for executives are of two main types: (1) discretionary bonuses and (2) results-based bonuses.

### Discretionary bonuses

Discretionary bonuses involve payments additional to base pay made at the discretion of the company board. They can take three main forms:

**(a) CEOs**

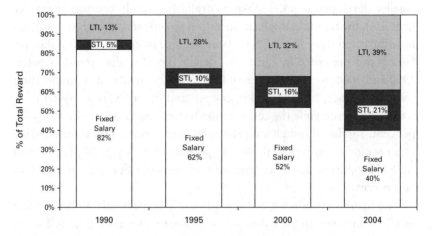

**(b) Senior executives**

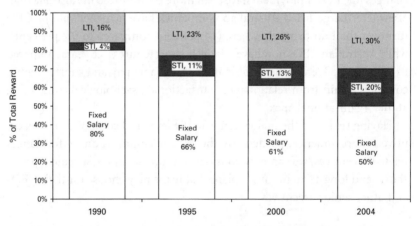

**Figure 20.2** Average percentage composition of total reward of Australian CEOs and other senior executives, 1990–2004
*Source:* Neuhold & Hay Group 2005; O'Neill & Berry 2002: 232.

cash, fully or partly paid shares, or additional company contributions to the executive's superannuation fund. By definition, discretionary bonuses are not paid out at regular intervals. The main advantage is that the board retains discretion not to award a bonus when 'windfall' profits occur. However, a problem is the absence of any objective link between executive performance and the amount and frequency of bonus payments. The lack of criterion transparency here may lead external shareholders to suspect that payments made are not genuinely performance-based and that the board is displaying unacceptable largesse.

## Results-based bonuses

Results-based bonuses seek to overcome some of the problems of discretionary bonuses by linking rewards to one or more predetermined performance targets. They amount to reward-linked executive goal-setting and, as noted in chapter 17, bonus payouts of this type may be flat rate or sliding scale in nature. With a flat-rate bonus, the full bonus is paid out for achieving the set target. If the target is not achieved, no bonus is forthcoming. With a progressive sliding-scale bonus, the rate of payment increases as measured performance approaches the target, and a premium bonus is paid if the target is beaten.

The targets themselves generally focus on one or more indicators of the firm's annual financial performance; that is, on its internal accounting performance. Some widely applied financial measures include:

- operating expenses compared to budget
- revenue growth
- net earnings, or net income
- net operating profit after taxes (NOPAT)
- earnings before interest and taxes (EBIT), or operating income
- earnings before interest, taxes, depreciation and amortisation (EBITDA)
- earnings per share (EPS), or net income divided by the average number of shares outstanding
- return on assets (ROA), or net income divided by total assets
- return on equity (ROE), or net income divided by total shareholder equity
- economic profit or economic value added (EVA®).

EVA® targets are among the most challenging of all short-term financial performance criteria. EVA® measures net economic profit by deducting the cost of capital from post-tax net operating profit (NOPAT). It is a measure of wealth creation that takes into account the opportunity cost of shareholder capital used in the business. In other words, it focuses on how much wealth creation executives generate with the capital that shareholders place at their disposal as compared with the wealth that could have been generated had the capital been invested elsewhere, say, in government bonds (Dolmat-Connell 1999a: 476–9). The simplest way to structure an EVA® bonus is to give the executive a fixed percentage of EVA®. More sophisticated schemes reward achieved EVA® improvement in excess of an expected EVA® improvement.

For the firm itself, the two main advantages of accounting-based STIs are high 'instrumentality' (i.e. the relatively clear line of sight between executive behaviour, the performance indicator and the resulting reward) and the immediacy of the 'reinforcement' effect. The chief drawback of accounting-based STIs is their susceptibility to manipulation. Profit- and cost-related bonuses have particular problems in this regard. Indeed, they highlight particularly sharply the possibility that incentive plans may actually exacerbate rather than curb the principal–agent problem. For instance, in order to achieve a bonus, the executive may be tempted to inflate the firm's paper profits artificially by postponing infrastructure investment, cutting back on research and development, retrenching staff to reduce payroll costs or divesting assets to raise revenue. Such actions will deliver a short-term personal gain but only at the cost of longer-term organisational performance and sustainability. It is partly for this reason that firms typically apply LTIs as well as STIs to their executive-level employees.

## Long-term equity-based incentive plans

As we have seen, the rapid growth in the remuneration of senior executives employed by public companies in many developed Western countries since the early 1990s was driven chiefly by an explosion in the use of equity-based LTI plans. Such plans come in an almost limitless variety of forms, but most existing plans fall into one of the following categories:

- restricted share plans
- mandatory share purchase plans
- option plans
- performance shares (or zero exercise price options)
- share rights plans
- share surrogates (including share appreciation rights, performance units, share warrants, and phantom share plans).

### Restricted share plans

Restricted share plans are variants of straight share bonuses or grants. The executive receives the share free of charge, but full shareholder entitlement is 'restricted' in some way. For instance, the shares may be subject to forfeiture if the executive leaves the firm before the expiry of a specified period; a restriction commonly referred to as a 'golden handcuff'. Alternatively, or additionally, full ownership ('vesting') of the shares may be subject to the meeting of a performance target or 'hurdle' within this period. Such hurdles may involve internal financial indicators, external share market indicators or a combination of the two. A commonly used market indicator is total shareholder return, which measures the additional wealth per share accruing annually to ordinary shareholders in the form of share price appreciation, dividend payments and any bonus share issues. Further, disposal of the shares may be prohibited for a specified period of time, typically three to five years. During the period of restriction, the executive may still receive dividends arising from the shares and be entitled to exercise a full shareholder vote.

## Mandatory share purchase plans

Mandatory share purchase plans require the executive to acquire ordinary shares in the company, typically on a regular basis and frequently at a substantial discount on the prevailing market price. For example, each year the executive may be required to acquire shares equivalent to 25 or 50 per cent of their notional base salary. To enhance the tax advantages to the executive, the purchase is commonly funded by means of salary sacrifice, meaning that tax on the salary forgone is deferred until the shares fully vest. For this reason, such plans are frequently termed 'tax-deferred share plans'. It is also common for companies to make low-interest or interest-free loans available to the executive to facilitate the purchase, with the loan being repaid from dividend earnings. The shares vest progressively as the loan is paid off.

The objectives of compulsory share acquisition are threefold: first, to encourage a psychology of ownership on the part of the executive; second, to avoid the impression that the executive is receiving something for nothing; and third, to align the executive's material interests more closely with those of ordinary shareholders by exposing them to downside risk as well as potential upside gain. Many commentators believe that compulsory share acquisition is the most effective way of addressing the principal–agent problem. An added advantage to the firm is that, unlike share grants, the full value of the shares is not expensed against profits, since the only accounting costs are those related to the provision of any share price discount and interest subsidy.

## Executive option plans

Share option plans give the executive the right to buy a specified number of company shares at a predetermined price – the 'strike price' – at some point in the future, typically between two and five years. Options to purchase shares are given to employees at nil or minimal cost. The price payable to convert the option to a share is usually set at the market value of the shares at the time the option is granted. If the market price increases after the option is granted, the employee stands to make a capital gain by exercising the option to buy, then disposing of the shares acquired. The chief incentive, then, is to act in such a way as to drive up the company's share price over time, an outcome directly beneficial to ordinary shareholders. The non-exercise period also serves as an executive retention device.

Apart from the no-exercise period itself, simple option plans of the type that predominated throughout the 1990s had few or no caveats, restrictions or hurdles. In the 1990s such plans were widely seen as involving nil cost to the firm since, unlike share grants and discounted and/or subsidised share purchase plans, there is ostensibly no associated *direct* cost to the firm. At the same time, simple option plans involve no downside risk to the executive. The executive avoids the need to make upfront outlays, and there is no exposure to actual wealth loss since, if the share price happens to fall below the strike price, the option to buy need not be exercised.

However, in terms of principal–agent alignment, simple unconditional option plans also have a number of significant weaknesses. The executive may not be exposed to loss of currently held equity if the share price falls, but ordinary shareholders themselves will certainly be worse off in absolute terms. The link between performance and reward is also quite unclear. So many uncontrolled variables influence share price that it represents a very remote measure of the executive's own performance. In a bull market, executives whose performance is mediocre still stand to make a large capital gain, whereas in a bear market, even the best-performing executives may be penalised. It is only where share price is primarily a reflection of company performance rather than external factors that options are likely to have the desired effect (Johnson 1999). Moreover, ownership itself is usually transient. If the option is exercised, the shares are often resold immediately to realise a capital gain. In effect, simple option plans encourage share speculation rather than ownership.

Options also invite market manipulation. Simply by releasing overly optimistic forward profit figures or by raising the possibility of a takeover, the executive can make a windfall gain. Yermack (1997) furnishes evidence that executives do seek to maximise their returns from option grants by timing the exercise of the grant to coincide with favourable earnings releases. A five-year study of US firms with executive option plans (Aboody & Kasznik 1998) found that many executives used their power to make corporate disclosures, especially immediately before options are granted and exercised, to maximise their gains. Corporate disclosures and earnings forecasts tended to be less optimistic immediately before option grants were made and more optimistic immediately before options were exercised.

In line with agency theory predictions, option plans are also susceptible to a range of other risk-avoidance actions, including repricing, uploading and conversion. Using US data on 1998 option repricing events in the computer software industry, Pollock, Fischer and Wade (2002) explore how CEO power affects the repricing of executive options and find that powerful CEOs have a greater ability to change the strike price to remove the downside risk faced by ordinary shareholders. Using US data for 1995–2004, O'Byrne and Young (2006) find that when the firm's share price falls, boards typically compensate the option-holder by increasing the number of new options granted. Australian evidence indicates that executives are able to lock in their gains by cashing in options and related equity instruments before they have vested. Some major financial institutions now market special derivative products, also known as 'cap-and-collar' schemes, which allow the executive to lock in a guaranteed minimum value for any LTI equity held in exchange for agreeing to assign any gains above this minimum to the scheme provider. In effect, the executive trades away the risk that may arise from any future fall in the firm's share price. As such, such schemes subvert the basic tenet of performance-contingent reward by protecting the executive from the downside risk faced by ordinary shareholders (West 2006; Stuart 2006).

Moreover, since option plans generally involve the issue of new shares rather than the purchase of existing shares by the company, the executive's subsequent disposal of option-acquired shares may also dilute ordinary shareholder wealth. When options are exercised and the shares then sold, the resulting increase in share supply may depress share values, which again can be detrimental to ordinary shareholders. At the same time, the greater volume of shares means, *ceteris paribus*, that earnings per share (EPS) are likely to fall. The extent of the dilution effect will depend on whether the option plan involves the issue of additional shares or a buyback of existing shares, with the latter generally being non-dilutive.

Finally, as is now recognised by legislators and international accounting standards requirements, unvested options do represent a prospective wealth source to the recipient as well as a cost to the company both administratively and in terms of opportunity cost. Instead of issuing executives with an option over future share issue, a company could just as easily sell them for cash in a relevant equities market. As critics (e.g. Bodie, Kaplan & Merton 2003) have argued, this forgone revenue is a cost to the company. The non-expensing of options during the 1990s may also have contributed to the overstatement of corporate earnings and the overheating of equities markets before the market downturn of 2000–02 (Klinger et al. 2002: 9). In the absence of proper expensing, it is next to impossible for shareholders and potential investors to gauge accurately the underlying financial performance of companies with generous executive option plans.

Equally, without a reliable estimate of the probable financial value of new option grants, it is extremely difficult for external investors to gauge accurately the total current financial reward flowing to executives each year by virtue of their status as hired employees. For this reason, under the current International Financial Reporting Standards, which apply in most developed countries apart from the USA (which applies parallel standards), listed companies must disclose the estimated present value of new and unvested equity-based LTIs for the top executive grouping. We shall return to the issue of LTI valuation below.

To overcome such potential weaknesses, and especially in the wake of the global share market slump of 2000–02 and the subsequent tightening of corporate governance requirements in many developed countries, it has become increasingly common for boards to apply hurdles and restrictions to executive option plans. Four widely used devices here are premium pricing, longer vesting periods, disposal restrictions and market-based performance hurdles.

Premium pricing involves granting options at a strike price above the price prevailing at the date of grant. This means that the market share price must rise before the options are 'in the money'. Whereas traditional option plans involved no vesting period, it is now common for the minimum vesting period to be at least two years and, in a growing number of cases, three, five or even ten years, with some or all of the entitlement being forfeited for early departure. The longer the vesting period, the stronger the 'golden handcuff'. Some plans also entail vesting in instalments, with say 20 per cent of the grant vesting after one year, 40 per cent after two years, 60 per cent after three years, 80 per cent after four years and 100 per cent after five years. Restrictions are also being placed on share disposal following exercise of an option. The imposition of a one- or two-year non-disposal requirement is a means of minimising speculative behaviour and potential dilution effects, as well as increasing ownership mentality.

Increasingly, firms are also tying options to performance targets and hurdles, particularly to the achievement of a specific increase in shareholder returns. Such targets may be absolute or relative in nature. An absolute hurdle would be one whereby, for instance, the option grant cannot be exercised at all unless the firm achieves an increase in total returns to shareholders (in dividends plus share price growth) of at least 60 per cent over a three-year period. By contrast, relative targets take account of performance net of that of the general market or of select comparator firms. A company's share price can be dragged down or pushed up by market-wide share price movements that have little or no relationship to executive or company performance. Unless account is taken of such general movements, the executive may incur an undeserved penalty or make an equally undeserved windfall gain (Johnson 1999). One way to allow for these general movements is to index the company's share price against overall market trends using a recognised share price index. A more precise measure of a company's *relative* share performance would be to index its share price against that of peer companies in the same industry. A growing number of executive option schemes now use relative performance measures of this type.

One of the most commonly used relative performance hurdles in current executive option plans is the achievement of total shareholder returns (TSR) in excess of the 50th (i.e. median) percentile of returns achieved by a specified group of peer companies. That is, if the firm achieves TSR better than half of the comparator group, the options vest. Relative hurdles of this type also commonly incorporate performance-conditioned vesting. For instance, if the firm achieves TSR equivalent to the peer group median, the executive may receive 50 per cent of the full potential option entitlement; if its TSR performance exceeds the 75th percentile of peer group performance, 100 per cent of the entitlement may vest.

Table 20.1 indicates the LTI plan types and hurdles used by companies operating in Australia. The most commonly used plans are now restricted

**Table 20.1** Long-term incentive plan types and hurdles, Australia

| LTI plan type | Percentage of companies | |
|---|---|---|
| Restricted shares or ZEPOs | 57 | |
| Options | 45 | |
| Share purchase loan plan | 9 | |
| Cash plan | 4 | |
| More than one LTI plan | 23 | |
| No LTI plan | 11 | |
| **LTI hurdles** | **Share plans (%)** | **Option plans (%)** |
| Total shareholder return (TSR) | 64 | 64 |
| Earnings per share (EPS) | – | 4.5 |
| Dual hurdle (TSR & EPS†) | 11 | 4.5 |
| No hurdle | 25 | 27 |

† Dual hurdles may be 'either/or' or 50/50.

*Source:* Neuhold & Hay Group 2005.

share plans and ZEPOs, followed by options. For both share and option plans, TSR is by far the most commonly used hurdle criterion. Although one in four executive option plans still have no hurdle attached, unhurdled options are confined almost exclusively to international companies (Neuhold & Hay Group 2005).

Vesting may also be performance-accelerated, meaning that the stronger the firm's performance relative to the comparator group, the faster the rate and/or level of vesting. Of course, the use of relative performance measures of this type may also result in a substantial payout to the CEO in circumstances where company performance is actually declining, albeit at a lower rate than that of comparator firms. On this basis, Pass (2003: 18, 27) concludes that the LTI relative hurdles applied in UK companies are 'undemanding' and reward 'average rather than exceptional performance'.

Ascribing an annualised value to unvested options and related equity instruments for remuneration expensing and reporting is not without its challenges – or its opponents. It is true that options relate more to long-term executive wealth creation than to annual income generation and that income is realised when options are exercised and the acquired shares are disposed of. Further, attributing an annual income flow to holdings of unexercised options is not a precise science; rather, it is a matter of probability modelling and estimating. Yet current option holdings do constitute potential future income and should therefore be factored into any estimate of annual total remuneration. As we have seen, in many countries it is now mandatory for firms to report the estimated present – that is, current year – value of new

The value of a single option is

$$c = Se^{-qT}N(d_1) - Xe^{-rT}N(d_2)$$

Where:
c = present value
$d_1 = \{\ln(S/X) + (r - q + \sigma^2/2)\,(T)\} / \{\sigma T^{1/2}\}$
$d_2 = \{\ln(S/X) + (r - q - \sigma^2/2)\,(T)\} / \{\sigma T^{1/2}\}$
S = Current share price
X = Strike or exercise price
e = 2.71828 (exponential constant)
q = Expected dividend yield
$\sigma$ = Volatility of returns
T = Time to expiration of grant
r = Risk-free interest rate
N(.) = The cumulative probability distribution function for a
standardised normal variable

**Figure 20.3** Black-Scholes option pricing formula
*Source:* Conyon & Sadler 2001: 167–8.

option and related equity grants and to include these values as an operating
expense. The 'present value' approach takes the projected future value of
the options granted and discounts it to a present value in order to estimate
the level of annual total remuneration.

The most widely used approach to estimating the present value of unexercised share options – and the approach now ordained under the International
Financial Reporting Standards – is the Black-Scholes model. Essentially, the
model seeks to predict the full future value of the option grant for the
period of the grant, then apportions a notional amount of income for each
year of the grant. Towards this end, the model takes account of the following variables: option strike price, price of an underlying security, share price
volatility, risk-free rate of return, dividend yield, expected term of the option
grant, and, where a performance hurdle applies, the estimated probability
that the hurdle will be met.

The standard Black-Scholes formula for estimating present value is
described in figure 20.3. Another approach, the binomial model, uses a similar formula. A simpler variant is the minimum option value method, which
excludes consideration of the firm's share price volatility. Black-Scholes and
similar methods tend to place a greater value on options the higher the
specified strike price, and some critics argue that Black-Scholes is prone to
over-valuation (Ellig 2002: 373–6). Options granted to executives generally
have an expected cost to the firm of 30 to 40 per cent of the estimated fair
market value (Conyon 2006: 27). Still, the valuation process itself at least

acknowledges that new option grants are both a cost to the company and wealth-generating for the recipient.

### Performance shares and zero exercise price options

In recent years, many firms have replaced simple option plans with performance shares or zero exercise price options (or ZEPO plans). With such plans, the executive is allowed to take up shares at no cost but only on condition of a performance hurdle being satisfied over a designated performance period. In other words, the executive receives a free grant of shares subject to a hurdle. Since fewer ZEPOs will be needed to deliver a level of reward comparable to that of a fixed price option plan, there is less potential for dilution of ordinary shareholder wealth, especially when the shares themselves are market purchased rather than new issue. Unlike options, performance shares do not encourage speculative behaviour.

### Share rights or warrant plans

Share rights or warrant plans are essentially non-compulsory share purchase plans with option-like characteristics. A rights plan gives the holder the right, but not the obligation, to buy shares in the company. The purchase price is typically the market price at the date of grant. Some rights plans emulate direct grant and ZEPO plans by allowing shares to be acquired without payment, but such plans generally involve performance hurdles. A warrant gives the executive the right to buy a stated number of ordinary shares in the company at a prescribed price over a set period. Typically, they are packaged with bonds or preferred stock so that the executive is able to participate in any increase in the value of the ordinary shares. Warrants are similar to options in that they allow the warrant holder the opportunity to participate in an increase in share value, but the paper gain can be commuted to cash or equity at the end of the period specified.

### Share surrogates

Share surrogates include a range of plans that emulate or substitute for plans that confer equity ownership. Surrogate plans include share appreciation rights, performance units and phantom share plans. Such plans are a direct cost to the firm but, unlike options, they do not dilute shareholder wealth.

Share appreciation rights differ from option plans in two main respects. First, they take account of dividend earnings as well as share price appreciation *per se* over the designated grant period. Second, the executive is not required to take ownership of the shares; rather, the executive receives cash equivalent to the wealth that would accrue to ordinary shareholders via share price appreciation plus dividend earnings over the grant period, with the base line typically being the market price at the date of grant. While rights payments are a direct cost to the firm, unlike unexercised option holdings, they allow the executive to share in the dividend stream flowing to ordinary shareholders during the period of the grant. Figure 20.4 illustrates the difference between gains from a rights plan and a simple option plan. The executive stands to receive a cash payment geared to the total returns to shareholders over a specified period in the form of share price appreciation plus dividends, whereas rewards flowing from an option plan will reflect share price movements only. Appreciation rights are frequently granted as a companion to share options in order to cover the holder for capital gains tax liability arising from an option gain. In short, appreciation rights plans replicate the financial gains accruing to ordinary shareholders but avoid the dilution effect common with option plans.

Likewise, performance units confer financial gains commensurate with those that flow from equity ownership but without actually transferring equity. The one major difference between performance units and share appreciation rights is that the grant date price of the performance unit is zero rather than the prevailing market price. Many such plans now also incorporate performance hurdles, meaning that reward is contingent rather than assured.

Variants of such plans are also occasionally applied in unlisted companies in the form of phantom share plans. The executive is credited with a number of fictional shares to which the firm assigns a notional price. On retirement, or at the end of the vesting period, the participant receives a cash amount equal to the appreciation in the value of the notional share plus the amount of any declared dividends. For example, if each unit of equity is worth $30 at grant and $80 at the end of the vesting period, the firm pays the executive $50 per unit. Such plans operate like share appreciation rights but focus on growth in notional share value as determined by a formula. Such plans allow privately owned companies to permit executives to participate directly in equity ownership and to think like owners but without giving them board voting rights. The main drawbacks are that firms often find it difficult to value the stock appropriately and there is less flexibility since the valuation date is generally set in advance.

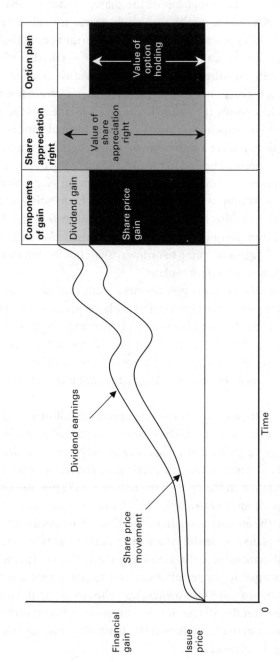

**Figure 20.4** Share appreciation rights
*Source*: Egan 2004. Reproduced with permission.

## External regulation and mandatory reporting

In many developed countries, executive reward now stands apart from all other aspects of employee reward management in publicly listed firms in that the details of reward level and composition, as well as the underlying justification for reward setting, must be placed on public record via company annual reports. In relation to the remuneration of executives and non-executive directors, company boards and auditors now face a degree of mandatory reporting and public accountability considerably more exacting than was the case before the share market slump and consequent corporate failures of 2000–02. These most recent disclosure requirements are also part of a long-term trend towards a more exacting approach to corporate governance by both legislators and stock exchange regulators. Indeed, since the 1980s, new rounds of governance regulation have followed a clear cyclical pattern, with each economic downturn, spate of corporate collapses and upsurge in public and media 'outrage' about executive (mis)behaviour and 'reward excess' triggering a further tightening in reporting requirements, including initiatives intended to ensure greater objectivity and transparency in procedures that determine executives' pay. These developments have also followed a particular international course, with changes in smaller developed countries emulating those in the USA and UK.

### The USA and UK

In the USA, the economic downturn of the early 1990s precipitated sweeping new pay determination and disclosure rules by the Securities and Exchange Commission and the New York Stock Exchange (NYSE) designed to make CEO pay more transparent and arm's-length, including the creation of remuneration committees composed fully or predominantly of independent directors. Similar measures were applied in the UK by the London Stock Exchange following the reports of the Cadbury and Greenbury committees in 1992 and 1995 respectively, including more detailed reward disclosure and a non-binding provision that there should be no executives on the remuneration committee (Lowry & Dignam 2006: 416–21).

Then, in the wake of the Enron and WorldCom corporate scandals and share market slump of 2000–02, the US Congress passed the *Public Company Accounting Reform and Investor Protection Act 2002*, also known as the Sarbanes-Oxley Act. Sarbanes-Oxley transformed US corporate governance practices, particularly those relating to auditor independence. It also tightened dramatically the accountability requirements imposed on the boards of US public companies in relation to executive remuneration, including their subsidiary entities operating in other countries. In particular, Sarbanes-Oxley prohibits executives from selling company shares when pension fund holders are precluded from doing so, curtails the use of executive loans, and requires repayment of incentives received on the basis of company earnings statements that have subsequently to be restated. In 2003 the NYSE introduced a new rule requiring that all new executive equity plans and any 'material revision' of existing plans, which generally includes option repricing and hurdle softening, be subject to formal shareholder approval (Golden 2004). The UK also introduced a shareholder approval requirement in 2002, albeit on an 'advisory' or non-binding basis (Lowry & Dignam 2006: 421).

### Australia

While Australian reporting requirements remain less exacting than those in the USA and UK, change here has followed the international trend. The *Company Law Review Act 1998* significantly strengthened the disclosure requirements for both the directors and the executives of listed corporations. Under this Act, and Section 300A of the *Corporations Act 2001*, the annual director's report was required to detail 'the nature and amount of each element of the emolument of each director and each of the 5 named officers of the company receiving the highest emolument' (Stapledon 2006). However, most companies continued to report the cash and equity components in separate sections of the financial statements. Moreover, until 2003 only a minority of companies reported both the number and the estimated current fair value of new option grants. The fragmentary nature of the reporting meant that it remained difficult to accurately gauge the total reward level of each named executive.

   The collapse of leading Australian insurer HIH and telecommunications carrier One.Tel in 2000–02, and the associated public outcry over unwarranted payments to underperforming CEOs, spurred a further tightening of both voluntary and mandatory disclosure standards. In March 2003 the Australian Securities Exchange (ASX) Corporate Governance Council issued a new voluntary code: the ASX *Principles of Good Corporate Governance and Best Practice Recommendations*. Principle 9 (Australian Stock Exchange Corporate Governance Council 2003: 51–7) states that the corporation should ensure that the level and composition of executive remuneration is 'sufficient and reasonable and that its relationship to individual performance is defined'. The ASX recommends five means to achieving 'best practice' in executive reward:

1 continuous disclosure of the company's remuneration policies and remuneration levels and mix for company directors and the five highest paid non-director executives, including all annual fixed remuneration, performance-based remuneration, 'the value of shares and options granted, according to an established and recognised method of valuation' and any other equity-based remuneration, and any termination payments
2 establishment by the board of a remuneration committee, chaired by an 'independent' director and with a majority of 'independent' directors
3 structuring remuneration of non-executive directors differently from that of executives
4 application of shareholder-approved performance thresholds to equity-based executive remuneration
5 full reporting of remuneration policies and remuneration committee membership in the 'corporate governance' section of the annual report, including an explanation for any departure from ASX 'best practice' recommendations.

While these recommendations are not legally enforceable, they now constitute a key element of Australian reporting standards, and any firm failing to provide reasons for non-compliance runs the risk of being suspended or delisted. Regarding remuneration committee composition, it is noteworthy that the ASX requires only a majority of non-executive directors whereas comparable provisions by the London Stock Exchange, for instance, require that there should be no executives on such committees.

Despite the ASX initiatives, Australian legislators clearly believed that more stringent mandatory reporting requirements should also be applied. The upshot was the *Corporate Law Economic Reform Program (Audit Reform and Corporate Disclosure) Act 2004* (also known as CLERP 9), which became law on 1 July 2004. In addition to the pre-existing reporting requirements prescribed by Section 300A of the Corporations Act, this legislation requires each public company to:

• prepare an integrated and comprehensive annual 'remuneration report' on director and executive remuneration policy and practice, including details on the application of performance targets and any consequences for shareholder wealth in the relevant financial year

- put the remuneration report to shareholders for a non-binding vote
- disclose the remuneration details of all directors, the five named executives of the company who receive the highest remuneration for the relevant year and, where consolidated financial statements are required to cover subsidiary entities, the five named relevant group executives who receive the highest remuneration
- disclose the following additional aspects of executive remuneration in the annual remuneration report:
  - the proportion of remuneration that is fixed and performance-related pay, and the justification for each
  - the value of equity granted, vested and exercised during the financial year and the sum of these values
  - the value and proportion of total remuneration consisting of options
  - duration of service contracts, notice periods and termination payments.

As such, CLERP 9 has strengthened Australian shareholders' collective influence over remuneration packages, including termination payments, by providing an opportunity to discuss the remuneration report during the annual general meeting and to vote on the package, although, as in the UK, the board is not legally bound by the outcome of the vote. Shareholder approval is also required for termination payments that exceed seven times an executive's annual average salary over the previous three years (Blake Dawson Waldron Lawyers 2004: 7–10).

Mandatory disclosure requirements were made more stringent still by the release in January 2004 of Australian Accounting Standard Board (AASB) Standard 1046 ('Director and Executive Disclosures by Disclosing Entities'). As a formal Accounting Standard, AASB 1046 is legally enforceable under the Corporations Act. This standard mandates disclosure of options values using a recognised valuation method (Stapledon 2006).

Some critics argue that ever more exacting disclosure requirements are essentially self-defeating. The more onerous the reporting requirements, the greater the administrative cost ultimately borne by the shareholders. It is also possible that the more information CEOs have about how their peers are remunerated, the more likely they may be to demand comparable treatment. On this basis, disclosure may have a 'ratcheting' or accelerator effect on pay levels, particularly where boards insist, as a matter of pride, on paying their CEO above the market median for peer firms. While this may be so, the case for comprehensive disclosure and accountability is arguably more than justified, in terms of both shareholder rights and the ideal of corporate social responsibility.

# Firms' performance, executives' reward and managerial power

Whatever the pros and cons for organisations of mandatory public reporting, the public availability of detailed information on the level and mix of senior executives' and directors' annual reward has presented reward management researchers in many developed countries with time series data of unparalleled comprehensiveness and richness; data spanning one, two and, in some cases, three decades. These data pools have enabled researchers to explore the cross-sectional and longitudinal associations between pay and performance in a way that is rarely possible for other categories of employee. This has stimulated a robust empirical and conceptual debate, especially regarding the relationship between CEO reward outcomes and prior company performance and the extent to which this relationship is influenced by the day-to-day power exercised by CEOs themselves (Gerhart & Rynes 2003: 142–8).

## Pay-performance sensitivity

Pay-performance sensitivity is typically defined as the dollar change in CEO wealth associated with a dollar change in shareholder wealth. Studies conducted in the USA (Hall & Liebman 1998; Jensen & Murphy 1990; Lilling 2006; Tosi et al. 2000), Canada (Zhou 2000), the UK (Conyon & Sadler 2001), and Australia (Merhebi, Swan & Zhou 2006) indicate that executive reward levels are sensitive to prior changes in company performance, although in most cases the reported associations are quite weak, particularly on the downside. In their classic study of 2,213 US CEOs for the period 1969–83, Jensen and Murphy (1990) report that CEO wealth increased $US3.25 for every $US1,000 increase in shareholder wealth, whereas CEOs lost 24.4 cents for every $1,000 lost by shareholders. From a basic agency theory perspective, the higher the sensitivity, the closer pay-setting practice approximates to optimal contracting.

Significantly, the evidence on which most extant sensitivity studies are based predates the ascendancy of option plans. The first UK study to include estimates of LTI values (Buck et al. 2003) finds that the use of LTIs actually reduces pay-performance sensitivity. For CEOs, the presence of LTI plans reduces the level of reward increase per £1,000 of shareholder return from £1.81 to £1.55. Such findings appear to challenge classical agency theory assumptions regarding the benefits of performance-contingent incentives, although other studies informed by agency theory (Jensen & Murphy 1990; Jensen, Murphy & Wruck 2004; Kay 1999) note that share option plans are far less effective than ownership per se in aligning executive and shareholder interests.

One particularly revealing finding arising from more recent pay-performance sensitivity research is that sensitivity is related inversely to the degree of business uncertainty and risk. Several recent studies (Bloom & Milkovich 1998; Aggrawal & Samwick 1999; Mishra, McConaughy & Gobeli 2000; Zhou 2000) have found that the pay-performance association is non-linear; firm performance being linked positively to incentive plans at lower levels of risk (especially share price volatility) but then diminishing, and perhaps turning negative, as the degree of CEO risk exposure increases. As agency theory implies, executive risk aversion is likely to be intensified in situations of high uncontrolled business risk; that is, where the line of sight between effort and reward is obscured and unclear. In such situations, risk-averse CEOs can be expected to respond by demanding a greater pro-portion of fixed remuneration and/or higher levels of potential incentive pay to compensate for the additional risk. It follows that riskier firms that have less pay-performance sensitivity can be expected to outperform high-risk firms that have high pay-performance sensitivity, a proposition borne out by a study of 150,000 executives in 700 US firms by Bloom and Milkovich (1998). Such findings suggest that having less pay-performance sensitivity may be an optimal approach to CEO reward management in riskier firms. As such, while simple agency theory prescriptions regarding the superiority of performance-contingent pay may be invalid in high-risk contexts, the basic assumptions of the principal–agent model appear to hold. The key message here is that risk must be recognised as a crucial mediating variable in the relationship between CEO remuneration and firm performance.

## Managerial power

Despite its growing sophistication, the empirical and normative literature supportive of agency theory still has some significant shortcomings. One of these is the under-recognition of the ambiguous position occupied by the company board itself in relation to the principal–agent problem. A second and related weakness is inadequate consideration of organisational power, especially the balance of power between the board and company executives. The latter is the central concern of managerial power theory.

The most forceful articulation of the managerial power interpretation to date is that offered by US law academics Lucien Bebchuk and Jesse Fried (Bebchuk, Fried & Walker 2002; Bebchuk & Fried 2004, 2005b, 2006; Bebchuk & Jackson 2005). Bebchuk and Fried provide a detailed account of how executive influence can undermine arm's-length negotiation and optimal contracting, weaken pay-performance sensitivity and even produce perverse incentives. They argue that compliant boards and compensation committees agree to pay suboptimal or excessive rewards that are not in shareholders' interests and which amount to 'rent extraction'. CEOs are said to command such power that they are able to pressure boards to approve pay that is not coupled to genuine performance and which commonly involves 'camouflaged' remuneration that circumvents mandatory reporting requirements. They are able to influence the appointment and reappointment of directors both to the board and to its remuneration committee. The claim, in essence, is that CEOs exercise undue influence over how their pay is set, constrained only by the possibility of shareholder 'outrage' if they are caught extracting rents.

Bebchuk and Fried argue that, despite closer scrutiny and tighter reporting requirements, US CEOs continue to extract rents, first, by persuading or forcing boards to decouple pay from performance and, second, by pressuring boards to offer greater amounts of disguised remuneration that largely goes unreported in annual remuneration statements. In support of their case, Bebchuk and Fried point to the continued prevalence of unhurdled or non-indexed option plans in US companies (which deliver undeserved windfall gains to option-holders in rising markets), option exercise prices set at grant date market prices, options without non-exercise periods (which encourage speculative behaviour by allowing executives to unwind holdings at will) and plans that allow for the repricing of 'out-of-the-money' options. Further, they contend that even where hurdles are applied, these tend to favour absolute over relative targets and are frequently softened to ensure payout despite declining performance by their firm. They also highlight the use of automatic 'reloading' of options following exercise of an existing option holding.

Bebchuk and Fried also identify a range of 'stealth compensation' arrangements by which CEOs are able to extract disguised and deferred income in the form of generous sign-on payments (or 'golden hellos'), special retirement benefits, retention and long-service bonuses, no-interest company loans, post-termination consulting fees, special payments for termination following takeover or merger (or 'golden parachutes') and the like. Bebchuk and Fried reserve particular criticism for retirement benefits that are not performance-linked, are excluded from the annual remuneration reports and, hence, from pay-performance sensitivity estimates, and thus create false readings of both annual reward level and incentive sensitivity. They estimate that, on average, pension payments increase the total earnings of top US CEOs over their term of service by more than a third. Including these pension payments in total remuneration reduces the proportion of equity-based reward from 55 to 41 per cent, while the proportion of fixed 'salary-like' reward increases from 17 to 39 per cent (Bebchuk & Jackson 2005: 848, 851–2). As such, according to Bebchuk and Fried, executive incentive plans that purport to advance shareholders' interests may be little more than devices to camouflage economically unwarranted levels of income and wealth appropriation.

The solutions recommended by Bebchuk and Fried include:

- increasing shareholder power over directors
- exclusion of all but independent directors from board compensation committees
- mandatory shareholder ratification of all components of top executives' remuneration
- use of indexed options
- compulsory share ownership, and
- full disclosure of all post-employment benefits.

However, the managerial power account has itself come under challenge. Gumbel (2006: 230) notes that relative performance hurdles may do more harm than good to shareholder interests. Gordon (2005) observes that the increased rate of CEO turnover and the shortening of average CEO tenure since the mid-1990s are at odds with the managerial power thesis. Murphy (2002) and Conyon (2006) note that the escalation in executive pay during the 1990s coincided with increasing rather than decreasing board independence, that the proportion of externally hired CEOs increased during the 1990s and that external hires actually receive a pay premium over internal hires. They also furnish evidence that boards and remuneration committees with more 'interlocked' or 'affiliated' directors – that is, non-independent directors who share one or more external board positions with the CEO – do not set more generous total pay levels, provide greater fixed pay or impose fewer performance-contingent rewards and that externally hired CEOs with no ties to the existing board enjoy higher rather than lower remuneration levels. Invoking tournament theory, Conyon (2006: 40) contends that high CEO pay cannot be taken as signifying inefficient contracting; rather, it 'may simply reflect the market for CEOs and the pay necessary to attract, retain and motivate talented individuals'.

To Murphy (2002), who is a prominent agency theorist, the underlying cause of the rise of option-based remuneration is not board weakness and executive powerfulness *per se* but rather the mistaken belief on the part of company boards that options are a low-cost form of remuneration. The solution, according to Murphy, lies not in tighter corporate governance regulation or greater board independence but rather in educating directors as to the true economic costs of granting options and in changing accounting and tax rules so as to recognise such costs in full.

Despite these interpretative differences, however, the agency theory and managerial power perspectives actually have much in common. Both share the view that executives are risk-averse agents. Both favour the use of share ownership over option plans. Both also recognise that the prospects for greater 'optimal contracting' and stronger bi-directional associations between executive reward and firm performance lie with the outlook and behaviour of those stakeholders most directly responsible and accountable for executive performance and reward management, namely the members of the board.

Whatever its empirical limitations, the chief value of the managerial power model, both descriptively and prescriptively, lies in extending analysis of the principal–agent problem to the relationship between external shareholders and the board itself: ' . . . there is one agency problem between shareholders and the board directors and a further agency problem between the board and the CEO.' (Gumbel 2006: 225.) Responsibility for achieving more effective executive reward management practices rests ultimately with those who accept the legal responsibility for administering the company in the interests both of its immediate owners and of other internal and external stakeholders.

## Implications for effective executive reward practice

Effective management of senior executive performance and reward, and CEO reward in particular, involves striking a positive balance between the potentially competing expectations of five key stakeholder groupings:

(1) shareholders, (2) the board, (3) executives themselves, (4) the firm's employees and (5) external stakeholders, including corporate regulators, the media, customers, suppliers and the general community.

## Shareholders

Shareholders will clearly be concerned, above all else, with shareholder returns on the firm's investment in executive 'talent'. As such, they will expect reward practices that are competitive but not excessive; that is, a level of reward adequate to attract and retain appropriate talent within the relevant local market, and a reward mix that motivates high shareholder returns.

STIs should not encourage short-termism and manipulation of annual accounting results at the expense of long-term shareholder value creation. Equity-based rewards should be linked closely to shareholder value, with equity plans aligned as closely as possible with the risk-and-return conditions faced by ordinary shareholders. As such, it is desirable that LTIs in particular should incorporate relative performance measures and hurdles. There should also be minimal opportunity for executives to hedge against market risk, which means avoidance of option repricing and hurdle softening, as well as prohibition of option conversion practices such as 'cap-and-collar' schemes. Straight option plans do impose direct and indirect costs on shareholders, while the research evidence indicates that the most transparent and effective devices for aligning shareholder and executive interest are restricted plans and mandatory shareholding plans.

At the same time, it is vital to recognise and reward not just share market results but also the controllable internal processes and results that also contribute to overall corporate performance. As we have seen (chapter 5), within the balanced scorecard method, these performance drivers include not just financial results but also human resource engagement, growth and creativity, internal process efficiency, customer satisfaction and market share and image. A rounded executive LTI plan should thus include targets related to these non-financial criteria since it is these that ultimately determine the firm's sustainability.

## The board

As well as being interested in setting rewards that are externally competitive, company directors must now take seriously their legal and ethical obligation to act without fear or favour, to engage in arm's-length pay bargaining, to specify and justify STI and LTI policies and practices, including performance payments, payout targets, hurdles, actual payout levels, equity type and vesting periods. Boards must also be prepared to explain and substantiate all termination and post-employment rights and entitlements. Close attention is now being paid to levels of post-employment benefit. In most regulatory jurisdictions, new grants of options and other equity instruments must be valued and expensed against annual profit. In short, it is now incumbent on all board members to be accountable both to shareholders and to regulatory authorities for the level and mix of top executives' reward.

Equally, beyond enhancing shareholder value *per se*, it is incumbent on the board to choose performance measures that truly reflect the firm's competitive strategy and success factors. For both cost and quality defenders, the accent should be on short-term profitability and long-term market stability, while a quality defender should also emphasise continuous process and quality improvement and customer satisfaction. An analyser firm will want to recognise and reward steady growth, perhaps involving diversification by acquisition, while a prospector will emphasise both fast financial returns and sustained organisational creativity and innovation. In short, to be strategically appropriate, the performance measures applied to executive incentives must pass the test of construct, content and criterion-related validity (see chapter 1 for a discussion of these concepts).

## Executives

Given the global trend towards shorter CEO tenure and greater emphasis on performance-contingent rewards, the key requirement in terms of executive expectations is the maintenance of a positive transactional psychological contract, although, as Kidder and Buchholtz (2002) contend, care should also be taken not to breach reasonable relational expectations, especially in high-risk contexts. This means that reward should reflect the executive's human capital; expected tenure; location (local, national, global region, fully global); level of risk involved, including the prospect of failure and sector volatility; and personal contribution to short-term and long-term value creation. In these respects, careful attention must be paid to appropriate reward benchmarking for both fixed and variable reward. Should the benchmarks be the sector, peer groups, firm size, geographical location, past firm performance or perhaps a combination of all of these?

The balance between fixed reward, STI and LTI should depend chiefly on the firm's size and strategic time frame. An emphasis on STIs will be more appropriate in a prospector organisation, since such firms will have short product cycles and require rapid turnaround. Conversely, LTIs should be contingent on sustained performance over a longer time frame, as is typical of firms with defender or analyser business strategies. The research evidence indicates that in high-risk contexts (such as start-up firms and firms in highly volatile market contexts) less rather than more emphasis should be placed on 'at risk' reward.

## Non-executive employees

The expectations of the firm's non-executive employees, including line managers, are likely to be informed chiefly by perceptions of internal equity or inequity; that is, by distributive justice perceptions. Greater public disclosure of executive rewards means that ordinary employees are more inclined than previously to draw what distributive justice theorists refer to as 'upward dissimilar comparisons' (Martin 1982: 112). Cowherd and Levine (1992) have found that the wider the pay differential between lower-level employees and senior managers, the greater the degree of lower-level dissonance and the lower the level of lower-level commitment, cooperation, effort and attention to quality. Byrne and Bongiorno (1997) report similar findings.

As such, company boards need to take account of employee perceptions of the total reward of executives relative to that of other employees in the organisation. Should the organisation's pay level structure be steep or flat? Wide internal pay inequality may be appropriate for a firm with a mechanistic structure and traditional culture, but a flatter structure would be more appropriate for an organic high-involvement firm.

Equally, the assumption that firm performance is attributable largely or entirely to the top management echelon is open to question. Leadership counts, but it is not all that matters. Accordingly, a reward system that allocates the lion's share of incentive payments to senior executives while providing only token recognition to non-executive employees is almost certain to impair perceptions of distributive justice. It is also worth recalling that the escalation in executive reward levels during the 1990s coincided with a protracted round of 'down-sizing' and 'delayering' that saw the elimination of many line employee and middle manager positions. As many commentators have argued, perceptions of inequitable sacrifice have just as much potential to breach the employee psychological contract as do perceptions of inequitable reward (Cropanzano & Prehar 2001).

## External stakeholders

Now, more than ever before, executive reward setting must take heed of the expectations of external stakeholders, including legislators, listing bodies, suppliers, customers, the media and the wider community. Above and beyond compliance with mandatory disclosure requirements, there is now a need for boards to anticipate community perceptions of executive reward practices. Whether rightly or wrongly, negative public reactions to levels of executive reward can damage a firm's 'brand image' and affect its market fate. As enlightened boards know, practising 'corporate social responsibility' in relation to determination of executive reward can return a healthy dividend both to the firm and to its shareholders.

# Chapter summary

This chapter traverses the most complex and controversial topic in the field of performance and reward management, namely management of performance and reward for top executives, and especially CEOs. We began by considering the place and role of hired executives in corporate governance as well as introducing the reader to three distinct descriptive or prescriptive theories of executive motivation and behaviour: tournament theory, agency theory and managerial power theory. We then reviewed the main components of executive reward, as well as trends in the level and composition of CEOs' reward in a number of developed countries in recent years, noting in particular the rising importance of equity-based incentives. Next we examined the various short-term and long-term incentive plans and associated techniques, including the types of performance targets or 'hurdles' incorporated into such plans. Attention then turned to recent developments in the mandatory public reporting of remuneration packages for senior executives. Next, we examined evidence and arguments regarding the effectiveness of executive reward practices, particularly the extent of the association between company performance and executive pay outcomes, paying particular attention to recent debates between agency theorists and advocates of the managerial power model. Here, we argued that the value of the managerial power approach lies chiefly in extending agency theory assumptions to the company board itself as the entity responsible and accountable for determination of executives' reward.

## Discussion questions

1 What are the strengths and weaknesses of agency theory as a means of understanding executives' motivation and behaviour?
2 What are the arguments for and against public disclosure of top executives' remuneration in public companies?
3 How should CEOs' performance be measured?
4 Should executives' LTI plans reward absolute or relative returns to shareholders?
5 How much truth is there in the managerial power account of recent executive reward practice?

Part 4 Case study

# BEYOND THE HARD SELL
## Performance incentives at Southbank

Three weeks into her new job as director of human resources at Southbank and things have yet to start looking up for 30-something high-flyer Alison Lee. The enormity of the challenge she faces in redesigning performance-related rewards for the 8,000 staff and 400 remaining branches in South-bank's nation-wide retail division seems to loom larger by the day. Since her appointment, Alison has held daily crisis talks with her new boss – and the bank's new CEO – James Allright, about the public relations and reward management shambles in the retail division and how it can be addressed.

The challenge they face is enormous. Staff morale has plummeted, reward satisfaction is at an all-time low, the Financial Services Union is planning to make performance pay a key issue in the next round of enterprise agreement negotiations, ten employees have been charged with fraud, customers are deserting in droves, investors have dumped Southbank shares, and the National Consumer Affairs Commission has launched an investigation into allegations of unethical sales practices in the bank's branches. At the heart of these problems lies the Sales Incentive Scheme (SIS) introduced two and a half years ago amid much fanfare by Alison's predecessor, Graham Starbuck.

## The culture of selling

Under its previous CEO Jonathan Rockwell, Southbank pursued aggressive market expansion in the highly competitive field of retail banking, especially in personal loans, housing loans, credit card business and business loans. Rockwell's strategy centred on a program of thoroughgoing corporate transformation involving the closure of low-profit branches, the adoption of e-commerce technology (including internet banking and EFTPOS) and, most importantly, the conversion of remaining branches from a service culture to a sales culture based on individual 'entrepreneurship'. Rockwell was certain that such an approach would increase both market share and shareholder value. The SIS was the reward keystone of this ambitious strategy of corporate transformation. Rockwell had recruited Starbuck two and a half years earlier from his position as global marketing manager for a major international fast-moving consumer goods supplier specifically to oversee the scheme's introduction. Under the 'sales culture' championed by Rockwell and Starbuck, every visit by a customer to a branch is seen as an opportunity to generate additional business: a new personal, housing or business loan, an extension on a credit card limit, a transfer of funds to a more lucrative account, opening a personal superannuation account, referral to one of the bank's specialist financial advisers, and the like.

Under the SIS, branch employees are eligible for individual bonuses tied to the volume of new credit business they generate each month. Each 'customer sales officer' is assigned monthly sales targets by the HR division. Sales staff targets are set for each of three key result areas: new accounts opened; value of extended credit card limits; and number of referrals to loans advisers. All criteria are weighted equally. The monthly targets in each of the three result areas are set at 110 per cent of average monthly nationwide results achieved per staff member over the preceding twelve months. A similar 'moving average' formula is used to set monthly targets for loans advisers and branch managers themselves. For these more senior employees, however, just one key result area measure is applied, namely the total value of new loan business generated. For sales advisers, the monthly target is set at 110 per cent of the national average per adviser over the previous twelve months; for branch managers, it is set at 110 per cent of the national average per branch over the preceding twelve months. To contain overall payroll costs, only the top 40 per cent of staff meeting or exceeding the targets in each position category (sales officer, loans adviser, branch manager) qualify for a monthly bonus.

In a bid to deliver immediate results, the scheme was rolled out quickly and with minimal change to other HR functions, such as work organisation, staff selection, training and performance management. To reinforce the culture of individualism, pre-existing work teams set up in several branches to focus on the needs of particular client groups (such as high-value business customers and ethnic Chinese account-holders) were dismantled.

At first, the SIS appeared to deliver the desired results. Both new loan business and product cross-selling to existing customers rose appreciably. Many employees evidently unsuited to the new sales culture resigned voluntarily, and many others from branches in poorer suburbs were 'managed out' for consistently failing to meet their targets. On the other hand, the scheme also allowed top performers to significantly increase their total remuneration – by as much as $1000 per month in the case of some of the more successful loans advisers.

## The crisis and the coup

However, after two years of operation, neither Rockwell nor Starbuck were convinced that the scheme had reached its full potential. Accordingly, six months ago, under pressure from Rockwell, Starbuck released a strongly worded internal staff memo accusing employees in some branches of being 'risk-averse' and of failing to embrace the 'culture of entrepreneurship' that he and Rockwell had championed. For both men, the move proved to be a fatal career miscalculation.

A disgruntled branch manager leaked the Starbuck memo to the business press. The leak triggered a flood of damaging public revelations about the SIS: from impossible sales targets and employee stress, breakdown and suicide, to high-pressure selling and fraudulent behaviour. One well-placed informant – one of the few remaining 'old-style' managers in the bank's HR division – alleged that the SIS had indeed affected a change in workplace culture – it had, he said, become 'dishonest and shonky'. Union representatives claimed that the SIS placed at risk not only their members' pay but also the industry's 'core values of trust and integrity'. The union also drew a contrast between the unrealistic targets imposed on ordinary branch employees and the 'extremely generous' share option entitlements extended to the bank's senior executives.

Other leaked internal documents revealed the full extent of scheme dysfunction. One manager was dismissed after it was discovered accidentally that he had increased the size of his own home loan, then claimed this as additional business. At least ten other staff members had been disciplined for various acts of 'fraudulent behaviour' under the scheme, including the generation of fake sales revenue. One had attempted to claim a bonus for opening new accounts that were never authorised by customers; others had sought to claim credit for sales revenue that they had played no part in generating; a few had persuaded customers to close one account and open another, claiming the latter as new business. Poaching clients and business from fellow employees had also become a daily occurrence in some branches. In theory, individual and branch sales levels were to be checked on a monthly basis by the HR division, with the sales activity of top performers being subject to weekly audits. However, these checks were not always properly executed, and one internal source suggested that 'monitoring and compliance had been practically non-existent'. More damaging still were the revelations in relation to the treatment of customers under the scheme. Many had been subjected to aggressive 'push-selling' tactics; others had been offered increased overdraft and credit limits that were well beyond their debt-servicing capacity. Customers who complained about the 'hard sell' either had a red sticker attached to their passbook or a coded warning inserted in their electronic account records. Pressure to meet sales targets and daily abuse from irate customers has caused a dramatic increase in staff stress levels, illness and absenteeism. The manager of one suburban branch left a suicide note indicating that he could no longer cope with the pressure from head office and from his subordinates to 'push more business through the branch door'.

The financial press and the radio 'shock-jocks' have had a field day with these revelations, forcing senior management into damage control mode. Starbuck's initial response was to claim that the cases of abuse involved only a 'few rotten apples'. However, a month after the original memo leak, and with the bank's share price in free fall, a nervous Rockwell reluctantly moved to shore up his own position by dismissing the hapless Starbuck. Two days later, however, the bank's board of directors decided to sacrifice Rockwell himself.

## The context

Although the crisis in the retail division is not yet life-threatening for Southbank, competitors are monitoring the situation – and the share price – closely, and there is talk around the market of a takeover bid by one of Southbank's larger domestic competitors. The smallest of the 'big five' in the Southland banking sector, Southbank now appears all the more vulnerable to takeover. It is a distant fourth in terms of market capitalisation and has far less funds under management than its four larger competitors and less than half of their average customer base. Its share of business and investment banking – the key 'high value-adding' activities of its larger rivals – is lower still. At the same time, a new generation of smaller financial institutions have been pursuing market share aggressively in retail banking. So far, Southbank has managed to retain market share in retail banking, which has always been its core business. It currently controls 10 per cent of the total housing loan market, 12 per cent of current personal loans and 13 per cent of all domestically issued credit cards. Its retail division handles five million sales transactions per year. However, in the wake of the SIS revelations, the loyalty of customers and shareholders alike has begun to wear thin.

In the retail division itself, 60 per cent of the customer sales positions are of a permanent part-time nature, 80 per cent of the workforce is female, and the average length of staff tenure is just four years. By contrast, the loans adviser and branch manager positions are full time and male-dominated. As a result of organisational delayering, internal promotion opportunities are virtually non-existent. While most tasks involve one-on-one relations with customers, much of the work is interdependent and requires considerable cooperation, information-sharing and informal mentoring. In addition, the more senior advisory jobs involve considerable discretion and a wide knowledge of bank products and processes.

## The challenge

Now, with Rockwell about to launch civil action over his own dismissal, his successor James Allright and Southbank's new human resources director Alison Lee face the daunting task of repairing the damage caused by the SIS. At the board's request, Allright and Lee have been asked to give top priority to reviewing the shortcomings of the SIS and to developing and implementing a new, more effective performance-related reward system for the bank's retail division. Alison's first move is to turn to you for expert advice. In doing so, she asks you to respond to three key questions:

1. What are the main design and administrative shortcomings of the existing SIS?
2. What performance criteria should Southbank be seeking to recognise and reward?
3. What method(s) of performance-related reward should the bank apply?

   *Source*: adapted from Shields 2002a. Reproduced with permission.

   Model responses to this case study are in the book's appendix.

# Part 5

# FITTING IT ALL TOGETHER

Having now laid out all of the pieces of the performance and reward puzzle, it is time for us to consider how to go about assembling these elements into a coherent whole. In this concluding chapter, we detail a 'best fit' approach to assembling the various concepts, evaluation techniques and practices explored in parts 1–4 into an integrated and strategically aligned whole. Specifically, we examine the requirements for and challenges associated with performance and reward system review and the steps involved in system change and development. Although our approach here is primarily prescriptive in nature, our prescriptions also draw on a range of insights available in the empirical or descriptive and critical literatures that have been referred to at various points throughout the text.

## Chapter Twenty-one

# SYSTEM REVIEW, CHANGE AND DEVELOPMENT

In the past, managing employee performance and reward was a relatively uncomplicated affair. On the performance management side, it was a matter of requiring supervisors to assess each of their subordinates once a year using a simple rating scale instrument, perhaps with a few management-imposed objectives included for good measure. On the remuneration side, the focus was on developing and maintaining a job-based base pay and benefits structure that tempered external competitiveness with a degree of attention to internal equity. In the more complex traditional pay systems, there may also have been an element of individual performance-related reward, perhaps in the form of assessment-based merit increments or one or other of the traditional forms of payment by results, possibly coupled with a modest level of collective STI in the form of profitsharing. Underlying all was an accent on the maintenance of a traditional top-down management culture, a mechanistic organisational structure and a stable relational psychological contract.

How things have changed! Today, performance and reward practitioners find themselves confronted by myriad alternative design options: everything from competency-based assessment and performance coaching, with broad-graded and broad-banded base pay structures, to goal-based STIs for individuals, teams and business units, and an ever-growing range of sophisticated equity plans for employees at all levels – from those on the production line to the habitués of the executive suite. The world of the management practitioner is positively awash with competing performance and reward theories, fads and fashions, with specialist consultants ever keen to push their products, and this has made the task of managing employee performance and reward far more challenging than ever before. And today's employees also have different expectations from those of twenty years ago. In many organisations, the very basis of the employment deal has shifted from long-term engagement to short-term transaction; and there is evidence that in many developed countries younger employees have embraced this 'new deal' and adjusted their expectations and reward valences accordingly.

In the face of the bewildering array of possibilities, there is a great temptation to join in the 'best practice' bandwagon; to take up the latest fashion simply because that is what other organisations 'around here' seem to be doing. The danger here is that the organisation ends up with a bundle of performance and reward practices that amount to little more than a fashion-driven pastiche of initiatives bearing little relationship to the real needs of the organisation, its customers and its employees. As noted in chapter 4, the problem with off-the-shelf approaches of this sort is that they are incapable of addressing organisational specifics in a comprehensive and integrated way. Fashion-driven approaches often bear little or no relationship to the strategic goals and objectives of the organisation concerned, are only loosely aligned with the organisation's actual or preferred structure and culture and, most importantly, often bear little or no relationship to the needs, expectations or aspirations of the organisation's present or prospective employees.

The most appropriate approach, we have argued, is that of integrated internal and external 'best fit'. As noted in chapter 4, the best fit formula has two main elements:

1 the 'bundle' of human resource practices should support the organisation's strategic aims in its chosen product or service market(s) (i.e. provide 'external fit'), and
2 the practices should both be integrated and cohesive and synergistic with the organisation's preferred structure and culture (i.e. provide 'internal fit').

The critical message here is that one size does not fit all. Human resource practices should be tailored specifically to the particular context, strategy, structure and culture of each organisation. The point is to develop a performance and reward system that matches organisational success factors and delivers the attitudes, behaviour, competencies and results that the organisation requires from its employees. This means that, in developing an integrated performance and reward system, the organisation should select the combination of practices that is best suited to helping it achieve its goals within its chosen operating environment and with the human resources it has available. Note, however, that this does not preclude organisations from benchmarking their practices against similarly situated or competitor organisations.

At the same time, 'best fit' requires that performance and reward practices should be chosen in a holistic and integrated manner. In essence, this means selecting practices that, in terms of desired results, behaviour and competencies, are synergistic (i.e. complementary and/or supplementary) rather than pulling in different directions. For instance, implementing an individual incentive plan in a team environment may well impair cooperation between team members and undermine any team incentive plan, or implementing broad-banding without a carefully thought-out system of person-based base pay progression could have disastrous consequences. A holistic reward approach also means choosing financial rewards compatible with the various non-financial rewards that the organisation may offer its employees. In the literature, this is referred to as a 'total reward' approach (Fuehrer 1994; Kao & Kantor 2004; O'Neal 1998; Zingheim & Schuster 2000a: 1–65).

With a best fit approach, then, performance and reward practices should be simultaneously *strategic, integrated* and *total*. In this chapter, we consider the steps that an organisation should follow in designing or redesigning its performance and reward system. We begin by outlining a general framework for developing or revising performance and reward practice in line with the tenets of the best fit model. Attention then turns to the processes and methods associated with reviewing or evaluating current practices in terms of their strengths and weaknesses in supporting strategic objectives, especially in eliciting desired attitudes, competencies, behaviour and results. Revisiting the model of strategic alignment presented in chapter 4, we next examine the key issues and considerations involved in developing a new, strategically aligned and integrated system of performance and reward management. Finally, we consider the importance of rehearsing and piloting the proposed changes before full roll-out, as well as the basic requirements for effective implementation.

## A framework for system development

In this section, we present a general framework for reviewing and transforming current performance and reward strategy, policy and practices in

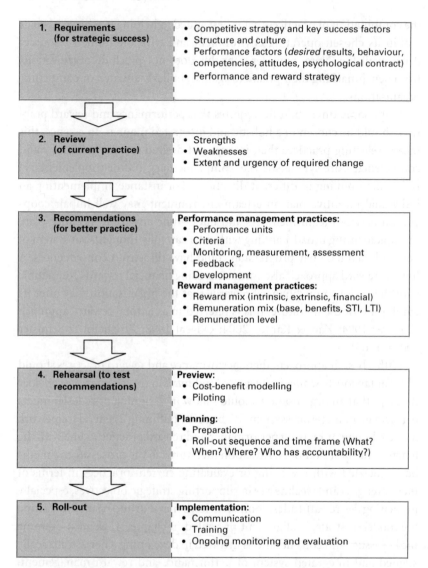

**Figure 21.1** Framework for performance and reward system development

line with the tenets of the best fit model. As indicated in figure 21.1, the framework involves five main steps:

1 establishing the basic strategic *requirements*
2 *reviewing* current practice against these strategic requirements to identify specific areas for improvement

3 *recommending* an altered or new configuration of performance and reward practices

4 *rehearsing* the proposed changes and planning their implementation

5 *rolling-out* the changes.

In essence, the framework follows the prescriptions offered in the mainstream strategic management and best fit literature, including the need for SWOT analysis and integrated internal or external fit (see chapter 4). As such, it is also predicated on the rationalistic and instrumental assumptions that characterise this literature, including, most importantly, the belief that the strategic choice and changes to human resource policies are primarily 'intended' (i.e. premeditated, preplanned) management processes and that neither internal nor external constraints pose an insuperable barrier to management-initiated change. As we shall see, however, it would be wrong to infer from this that management of the change process itself is uncomplicated or free from uncertainty and risk.

## Basic strategic requirements

In chapter 4, we outlined a basic model for strategic performance and reward management practice. It will be helpful to recap the details of this model briefly since it provides the basis for much of the ensuing discussion. The model proposes that taking a strategic approach to performance and reward management requires careful analysis of and alignment between four key sets of factors: (1) competitive strategy, (2) organisational structure, (3) management culture and (4) performance and reward principles and practices. To optimise their effectiveness, performance and reward policies and practices should be compatible with, and aligned with, strategy, structure and culture – or, more precisely, with *intended* strategy, *desired* structure and *espoused* culture. Misalignment between any of the four factors is likely to produce suboptimal outcomes.

Throughout this text, with a view to reducing the complexities of strategic fit to manageable proportions, we have drawn on the following basic typologies of each of the above three key organisational factors:

1 competitive strategy:
   – cost defender
   – quality defender

   – analyser
   – prospector
2  organisational structure:
   – mechanistic
   – organic
3  management culture:
   – traditional
   – high involvement.

Adopting the insights offered the behavioural contingency model of strategic human resource management (see chapter 4) our argument throughout this text has been that employees' attitudes and behaviour are the critical bridge between human resource practices, each of the above organisational factors and an organisation's effectiveness.

In chapter 2, we identified the following chief attitudinal states and behavioural dimensions over which performance and reward practices have some influence, as well as exploring the possible causal associations between these cognitive variables themselves, as well as between them and the above behavioural categories:

1  behavioural dimensions:
   – membership behaviour
   – task behaviour
   – organisational citizenship behaviour
2  attitudinal dimensions:
   – job and reward satisfaction
   – task motivation
   – organisational commitment.

Chapter 2 also examined the nature of the overarching cognitive and emotional variable, namely the employee psychological contract, which, we have suggested, offers a valid and practical means of understanding and managing the complex associations between employees' experience, expectations, perceptions, emotions, attitudes and behaviour. Following Guest, we have suggested that the employee psychological contact comprises three main cognitions: organisational trust, perception of 'deal' fulfilment and perception of organisational justice or 'felt-fairness'. As we have argued, the degree to which an organisation will require its employees to demonstrate each of the above attitudinal and behavioural categories, and to embrace one form of psychological contract rather than another, will vary greatly according to the organisation's characteristics. For instance, in relation to commitment and membership behaviour, does the organisation require long-term engagement or merely day-to-day compliance? Are the costs of low membership behaviour and high labour turnover likely to have a significant effect on organisational success? Regarding task motivation and task behaviour, are tasks simple or complex? Is task execution individualised or interdependent? Are employees closely supervised or self-managing? Do employees have to excel at what they do or merely work to a prescribed standard? Regarding organisational citizenship behaviour, is personal initiative and discretionary effort important to organisational success? Are employees expected to be 'team players' or to pursue individual excellence? Equally, one organisation may be looking to maintain a long-term relational understanding with some or all of its employees whereas another may be more interested in fostering relationships of a more short-term, transactional nature. Clearly, the nature of the espoused 'deal', of desired attitudes and of desired behaviour carries profound implications for the types of performance and reward practices required.

In chapter 5, building on the discussion of major behavioural and attitudinal dimensions in earlier chapters, it was suggested that certain combinations of organisational factors are viable and sustainable whereas others are not. Overall, we identified six sustainable strategic configurations. At this stage, you may wish to revisit figure 4.4 (in chapter 4), which summarises these configurations and the key performance factors associated with each. It is the identification, application, measurement and reward of these factors that holds the key to achieving fit or alignment between the three chief organisational variables (i.e. strategy, structure, culture) on the one hand and performance and reward practice on the other. Above all else, this means, first, identifying which attitudes, behaviour, competencies and results the organisation requires its employees to demonstrate in order to maximise their contribution to strategic success and, second, configuring performance and reward practices so as to elicit the strongest possible demonstration of these performance requirements.

Once the main performance requirements have been identified, it is advisable to incorporate them into a brief statement of performance and reward 'philosophy' and strategy. This may also form part of a wider human resource strategy statement. Either way, the aim is to define succinctly the broad role that performance and reward practices should play in assisting the organisation to be successful and sustainable and the values or 'philosophy' that will inform the approach taken. A performance and reward strategy statement is basically a normative blueprint, or set of guiding principles, as to how associated practices will be applied to support the organisation's aims. It should set down the general principles that will guide the design of specific performance and reward practices. This also presents the opportunity to define in broad terms the desired relationship between these and other human resource functions (Armstrong & Murlis 2004: 533–5; Dolmat-Connell 1999b; Long 2006: 187–213; Wilson 1998).

Most importantly, the strategy statement should indicate the primary purposes to which performance and reward management will be directed. For instance, will performance management be directed chiefly to a developmental or an evaluative purpose, or to balancing the two? With reward management, will the focus be on staffing (i.e. attraction and retention), on motivation, or on cost-effectiveness, or on a three-way balance? A reward strategy that has a cost focus would be concerned, first and foremost, with controlling labour costs and keeping labour costs in line with industry levels and external labour market practices. A strategy that focuses on a staffing role would highlight the role of remuneration in attracting and retaining staff of the right type. A strategy that has a motivational focus would emphasise the role of financial and non-financial rewards in eliciting desired performance factors.

Figure 21.2 illustrates the form that a performance and reward strategy statement may take. In this example, the strategic requirements and performance factors are those of a high-involvement organic prospector ('HIOP') firm (see figure 4.4, chapter 4).

As noted in chapter 4, although the best fit model posits that misalignment is not sustainable in the longer term, an organisation (or one or more of its constituent business units) may well be in a state of misalignment at any given point in time. Yet it is precisely for this reason that regular strategic analysis and systematic pursuit of better alignment or fit are imperative to long-term effectiveness and sustainability. Moreover, while the above prescriptive model of strategic alignment is an abstraction, its does provide a convenient and, we suggest, helpful means of categorising and comparing actual organisations. It also provides us with a useful template for analysing organisations in terms of performance and reward practice possibilities and needs.

At Globalco, competitive success flows from our agility, adaptability, creativity and innovation – from our ability to anticipate market trends and to be the global leader in new product and service innovation. At Globalco, we celebrate diversity both in our human capabilities and in the products and services that we deliver to our customers and clients in all parts of the world. We see the capabilities and contributions of our people as holding the key to success in our ever-changing competitive environment.

We offer our people work that is exciting, diverse and challenging, with a high degree of accountability and autonomy. To us, the essence of high contribution and performance is:
- ☑ self-management and growth of personal knowledge, abilities and talent
- ☑ championing our core competencies: citizenship, flexibility, creativity, market-focus, and ethics
- ☑ individual creativity and innovation
- ☑ strategic decisiveness and risk-taking
- ☑ timeliness and effectiveness in meeting challenging goals
- ☑ maintaining a positive balance between individual and team commitments
- ☑ demonstrating excellence, leadership and citizenship in every assignment.

To these ends, our approach to performance management will ensure that:
- ☑ individual assessment is valid, reliable and fair, and based on multistakeholder input
- ☑ individuals receive timely feedback, coaching and development assistance
- ☑ individual and group goals are challenging but realistic
- ☑ individuals and teams have a voice in determining their performance standards, and
- ☑ assessment is linked to reward in a transparent and accepted manner.

At Globalco, we offer work that is intrinsically exciting and rewards that recognise and celebrate individual and team excellence and that share the fruits of our competitive success. Above all else, our approach to employee reward will acknowledge:
- ☑ our strategic goals and priorities
- ☑ the worth of attracting the best available talent for as long as is mutually acceptable
- ☑ the importance of career self-management and portability
- ☑ individual creativity and contribution
- ☑ team working and citizenship
- ☑ the principle of reward for individual contribution and effectiveness rather than for seniority or position
- ☑ the importance of seeing our people as stakeholders and shareholders in our competitive success
- ☑ the importance of flexibility in reward choice
- ☑ the need to maintain fairness, transparency and consistency in reward administration
- ☑ the value of involving staff in system development and administration.

**Figure 21.2** Example of a performance and reward strategy statement

We shall return to the matter of translating broad strategy into best fit practice shortly. First, however, we need to consider the second step in our framework for system development: that of reviewing current practice.

## Practice review

Once the basic performance requirements have been translated into a general statement of performance and reward strategy, the way is clear to review current practices to assess their strengths and weaknesses, particularly in relation to how effectively they support the organisation's strategic objectives by promoting desired attitudes, behaviour, competencies and results.

The overall aim is to establish the nature and extent of any 'gap' between actual and desired practice outcomes so as to determine the extent, nature and degree of urgency of required change (Manas & Graham 2003: 162–6). Essentially, this involves a process of functionally specific human resource evaluation that requires the gathering of quantitative and qualitative data on outcomes from current practice. While such reviews have traditionally been undertaken on an *ad hoc* basis, for organisations operating in rapidly changing environments – and this would certainly include those with prospector strategies – adherence to a process of formal annual review would certainly be advisable.

Quantitative data of a hard or financial nature is particularly useful in pinpointing areas of weakness. For instance, data on rates of voluntary staff turnover and on recruitment levels and applicant quality may signal general shortcomings in reward effectiveness in attracting and retaining appropriately qualified staff. Data on productivity can also indicate general problems in performance and/or reward practice, while financial data on unit labour costs, returns per payroll dollar spent and associated Return on Investment (ROI) measures may signal problems with remuneration level, mix and/or administration. Quantitative data-gathering techniques can also be used to ascertain the financial returns per dollar outlaid on specific incentive pay plans and the relative contribution of each component of total reward to existing payroll costs.

Adapting the balanced scorecard model (see chapter 5), Fitz-enz (2000: 111) proposes a 'human capital scorecard' that lists the following as quantitative measures for evaluating practice effects in four core areas: 'acquisition', 'retention', 'maintenance' and 'development'. Figure 21.3 replicates his suggested impact metrics in each area. Note, too, that Fitz-enz also suggests measurement of job satisfaction and employee morale. The latter would also encompass measurement of the cognitions that are most revealing of the state of the employee psychological contract, including organisational trust and felt-fairness.

While hard measures can highlight problem areas, they are generally not so helpful in diagnosing underlying causes. Proper diagnosis is likely to require the gathering of detailed attitudinal data, and here there are a range of techniques available to the reviewer. Focus group techniques can be used to assess the degree of employee satisfaction and dissatisfaction with specific practices. Exit interviews may be even more revealing of staff

| Acquisition | Maintenance |
|---|---|
| • Cost per hire<br>• Time to fill jobs<br>• Number of new hires<br>• Number of replacements<br>• Quality of new hires | • Total labour cost as percentage of operating expense<br>• Average pay per employee<br>• Benefits costs as a percentage of payroll<br>• Average performance score compared to revenue per full-time employee |
| Retention | Development |
| • Total separation rate<br>• Percentage of voluntary separations<br>• Separations by service length<br>• Percentage of separations among top-level performers<br>• Cost of turnover | • Training cost as percentage of payroll<br>• Total training hours provided<br>• Average number of hours of training per employee<br>• Training hours by function<br>• Training hours by job group<br>• Training ROI |
| Job satisfaction | Employee morale |

**Figure 21.3** The 'human capital management scorecard'
*Source:* Fitz-enz 2000: 111.

attitudes, including areas of perceived contractual breach or violation. Regular staff attitude surveys are another means of gauging employee views about particular practices as well as the overall state of the psychological contract.

Figure 21.4 illustrates some of the factors that may be measured by means of a simple diagnostic staff attitude survey. In this case, the degree of feeling about each of the performance and reward statements included in the survey instrument is ascertained by means of five-point Likert scales. Individual responses can then be averaged to provide summative data on each dimension, although care must be taken to ensure that the responses constitute a representative sample of the workforce. Note, too, that when aggregating Likert scale data, the scoring associated with negative statements should be reversed to make the scales compatible with those attached to positive statements. It is advisable to maintain the anonymity of respondents, but requiring respondents to provide relevant occupational and demographic information will permit the identification of potentially illuminating correlations between staff perceptions and employee type.

While diagnostic surveys can assist in identifying the causes of dissatisfaction, they may not shed much light on how employees would prefer to be treated practice-wise. This is where prescriptive questionnaires of the type illustrated in figure 21.5 may be especially helpful. In this example,

*Circle the number that best describes your response to each of the following statements:*

|  | Disagree strongly | Disagree somewhat | Neither agree nor disagree | Agree somewhat | Agree strongly |
|---|---|---|---|---|---|
| We need to make changes to our current pay policies | 1 | 2 | 3 | 4 | 5 |
| I am motivated to help this firm be successful | 1 | 2 | 3 | 4 | 5 |
| The criteria by which my performance is assessed are appropriate to my work | 1 | 2 | 3 | 4 | 5 |
| My performance is fairly assessed | 1 | 2 | 3 | 4 | 5 |
| The overall package of pay and conditions here is a good one | 1 | 2 | 3 | 4 | 5 |
| There is a strong link between my earnings and my individual performance | 1 | 2 | 3 | 4 | 5 |
| There is a strong link between my earnings and the firm's performance | 1 | 2 | 3 | 4 | 5 |
| I am clear about the performance goals of the business | 1 | 2 | 3 | 4 | 5 |
| We are paid competitively compared to similar jobs in other firms | 1 | 2 | 3 | 4 | 5 |
| My pay is fair compared to other jobs inside this firm | 1 | 2 | 3 | 4 | 5 |
| Outstanding performance is appropriately recognised and rewarded here | 1 | 2 | 3 | 4 | 5 |
| The bonus scheme uses appropriate performance measures | 1 | 2 | 3 | 4 | 5 |
| The bonus scheme motivates me to perform highly | 1 | 2 | 3 | 4 | 5 |
| The bonus scheme is realistic and achievable | 1 | 2 | 3 | 4 | 5 |

**Figure 21.4** Example of a diagnostic employee attitude survey

each respondent is asked to choose between practices arranged as paired opposites. Instruments of this type can be used to ascertain which practices employees most prefer and which are regarded as least valuable and meaningful by specific groups of employees. As such, they may be particularly helpful in recommending practices that are a better fit for the needs and expectations of particular types of employee.

By combining hard and soft data, it is possible to construct a profile of the effectiveness of the existing pay system and to identify causes of weakness.

*For each pair of statements, tick the response that best describes your preference. Tick only one box per pair.*

*I would like the performance and reward management system to have the following characteristics:*

| Option A | Prefer A over B | No preference either way | Prefer B over A | Option B |
|---|---|---|---|---|
| Performance measurement based on results | | | | Performance measurement based on behaviour |
| Performance appraisal by fellow employees | | | | Performance appraisal by the supervisor |
| Performance management linked mainly to pay | | | | Performance management for development purposes |
| Pay according to job importance | | | | Pay for what each person contributes in the job |
| Pay progression based on seniority | | | | Pay progression based on personal competencies |
| Pay based on equal pay for jobs of the same size within this organisation | | | | Pay based on rates in outside organisations |
| Variable pay linked mainly to individual performance | | | | Variable pay linked to the performance of my work group |
| Performance rewards through pay | | | | Performance rewards of a non-financial nature |

**Figure 21.5** Prescriptive questionnaire

The review of existing practices should also clarify the urgency of required change. Where the review indicates a need for selective, incremental change, the change recommendations should address identified weaknesses within the scope of the existing system. Since the problems are limited, the change itself could move at a moderate pace. Perhaps the organisation is finding it difficult to attract qualified staff. The problem here might simply be that existing base pay levels are too low relative to market and need recalibrating. However, where the review indicates widespread and entrenched shortcomings, change of a more wide-ranging and urgent nature may be required, perhaps going as far as a complete overhaul of current practice. For instance, if pay dissatisfaction is rife among the staff, turnover is sky-high, product quality at rock-bottom, and market share is collapsing, current practice may require radical change. It may be necessary to completely rethink performance criteria, base pay structure and progression, performance incentives and total remuneration levels. To illustrate some of the possibilities here, table 21.1 lists a select number of human resource problems that may be symptomatic of shortcomings in performance and reward practice, along with possible specific causes. Note that the possible causes mentioned are suggestive rather than exhaustive.

**Table 21.1** Illustrative review findings and diagnoses

| Identified weakness | Possible causes |
|---|---|
| General dissatisfaction with individual performance assessment | • Invalid performance criteria<br>• Unrealistic goals<br>• Poorly communicated criteria<br>• Unreliable assessment<br>• Inadequate assessor training<br>• Inadequate assessee 'voice'<br>• Inadequate or inappropriate feedback<br>• Inadequate resourcing for performance improvement<br>• Confusion between evaluative and developmental purposes |
| Desired behaviour not adequately demonstrated | • Excessive focus on results<br>• Poorly communicated performance criteria<br>• Behaviour not reward-linked |
| Difficulty in attracting and retaining high-quality staff | • Uncompetitive base pay level<br>• Slow response to movements in market rates<br>• Perceived inequity in reward system administration<br>• Wrong reward mix<br>• Low reward valence<br>• Inadequate benefits |
| Reward dissatisfaction among high performers | • Performance assessment central tendency error<br>• Individual incentives do not adequately recognise or reward high performance<br>• Collective incentives encourage free-riding |
| Widespread dissatisfaction with internal pay relativities | • Job descriptions and job evaluation scores are out of date<br>• Job evaluation is discriminatory<br>• Poor communication of job pricing criteria |

**Table 21.1** (*cont.*)

| Identified weakness | Possible causes |
|---|---|
| High payroll costs relative to return | • Base pay progression inadequately linked to contribution or insufficiently rigorous<br>• Leniency error in individual performance assessment<br>• Excessively high pay level relative to market |
| Low level of organisational engagement | • Performance criteria do not adequately communicate organisational values and goals<br>• Rewards not linked adequately to organisational success |

*Source:* adapted from Armstrong & Murlis 2004: 528–30.

Obviously, a review of existing pay practices is relevant only to established organisations. Where the organisation is wholly new, the initial practice mix will need to be derived directly from the anticipated success factors, the preferred employment 'deal' and desired attitudes, competencies, behaviour and results. Where possible, a prudent designer may also wish to review existing practices in comparable or competitor organisations to ascertain challenges and issues that will need to be addressed and to identify specific initiatives that might be adopted in the new organisation's start-up approach to managing employee performance and reward. Where resources permit, it may be appropriate to hire the services of a consulting firm to furnish 'benchmarking' advice along these lines.

## Recommending best fit practices

Having identified the general strengths and weaknesses of existing practices, and having sketched out the magnitude and possible direction of required change, the organisation can now begin to fill in the details of a new approach. The review may simply have indicated administrative shortcomings in one or two practices that are otherwise well suited to the organisation's purpose. Conversely, the review may have highlighted a fundamental misalignment between strategy and practice; a gap that may well necessitate the development of detailed policies on the full range of performance and reward practices: from individual performance assessment and feedback, through fixed and variable cash remuneration, to non-financial benefits and non-cash recognition, and collective equity-based LTIs. The challenge here is to identify those practices best suited to the task. Thankfully, this does not have to be a matter of educated guesswork. A cautious application of the best fit model shows us the way forward.

Note the emphasis on the need for caution. As you may have ascertained from the discussions in earlier chapters, 'fit' is a multidimensional and multiscalar phenomenon. On the widest scale, practices should fit organisation-wide strategy, structure, culture and life stage. At the same time, however, taken to its logical conclusion, the best fit model also requires that the practices applied should match the strategic and technical requirements of particular business units within the organisation, the configuration of particular work groups or teams within each business unit, the particular roles and occupations within the organisation and, as far as possible, the particular needs and expectations of individual employees. Clearly, this is a tall order – and something that can only be aspired to, or approximated. Further, in the face of this complexity, it may be tempting to resort to a 'one-size-fits-all' approach to practice configuration. Yet, as we have argued throughout this book, the pursuit of best fit, however demanding it may be, offers the best means of harnessing human resource capabilities to an organisation's strategic purpose.

Drawing on the main suggestions made in the practice-specific chapters in parts 2, 3 and 4 of this text, we can now turn to consider the issues and options for determining best fit performance and reward practice. By way of illustration, we shall focus on three areas of practice choice: (1) performance management method(s), (2) reward mix and (3) remuneration level.

## Determining a performance management method

As indicated in part 2, the three main approaches to performance management are the results-based, behaviourally based and competency-based approaches. A focus on results, we have proposed, may be most appropriate where the ends can be more accurately specified and measured than the means, as in work of a highly discretionary nature, such as management work and many areas of professional knowledge work, and in work of a highly interdependent nature, such as teamwork. A focus on membership and task behaviour would be appropriate in routine, closely supervised service and administrative work, whereas an approach that targeted citizenship behaviour would be compatible with service work of a more discretionary nature, as well as with most professional and managerial roles. An accent on competencies would be appropriate where work has high knowledge content, as with, say, research and development roles. It would also be suitable where underlying traits and other personal attributes are seen as being just as important to high performance as are technical skills and knowledge, routine behaviour or measurable results *per se*, as is the case with much professional service work, emotional labour, such as teaching and health care work, and management work, all of which require strong interpersonal abilities. Competencies may also be an appropriate choice where results are difficult to quantify but where the work itself is not closely supervised, as with teachers and other knowledge workers. A focus on role competencies may also be appropriate where the narrow, closely supervised jobs have been replaced by more broadly defined work roles and where the organisation wishes to recognise and reward personal abilities rather than job content.

In many cases, however, the best fit is likely to lie with a composite approach, involving a combination of results and behavioural and competency criteria. A composite approach will allow the organisation to manage all three aspects of the performance process: input, work actions and work outcomes. This would be most appropriate where inputs, means and ends can all be specified and measured to some degree and where all are considered important to overall individual and collective performance. In such cases, the main design challenge is to determine the relative weightings to be attached to each of the three performance components, and this, in turn, will be primarily a matter of relative importance in relation to the organisation's strategic and cultural priorities.

## Determining reward mix

As noted in chapter 1, rewards are of two main types: extrinsic and intrinsic. Extrinsic rewards are rewards that flow from the work context. They take three main forms: financial rewards or remuneration (i.e. pay and benefits), social rewards and developmental rewards. Developmental rewards chiefly cover training and development opportunities (organisational learning), in-house mentoring and coaching, and in-house career development. Social rewards cover such aspects of the job context as a high-trust work environment, friendly and cooperative work relations, supportive supervision and opportunities for improved work–life balance. Intrinsic rewards are those psychological rewards that arise from the content of the work itself, such as task achievement, self-esteem, a sense of responsibility, job autonomy and involvement in decision-making. According to exponents of intrinsic motivational strategies, for work to be intrinsically rewarding, it must be meaningful, challenging and varied.

The first design challenge here is to determine an appropriate balance between these four generic reward types. Developmental and social rewards may be particularly effective in enhancing organisational commitment and citizenship behaviour since they address the so-called middle- and higher-order needs: the needs for social affiliation, esteem and 'self-actualisation' or personal growth (see chapter 3). As such, developmental and social rewards can play a vital part in reinforcing the effects of remuneration. Financial rewards alone might not be enough to bind employees to the organisation or to elicit affective commitment to the organisation's success. O'Neal (1998) also makes the point that non-monetary rewards may well hold the key to competitive advantage. Pay systems can be easily copied by competitors, but it will be far harder for them to emulate an effective system of developmental and social rewards.

Equally, an emphasis on non-financial rewards will be better suited to some organisations than others. In traditional mechanistic organisations, where tasks are narrow, individualised and closely supervised, the emphasis will fall squarely on financial rewards. Intrinsic rewards will play little real part, although firms adopting a paternalistic management style may apply social rewards whereas those with a quality defender strategy are likely to emphasise developmental rewards in the form of free in-house training. Conversely, in firms with a high-involvement culture, intrinsic rewards will have an important role to play in promoting all types of desired behaviour since the work itself will be varied, skilled, challenging, partly self-directed and interdependent.

Overall, however, with the exception of non-profit organisations relying largely on volunteer labour, the emphasis will almost certainly fall primarily on financial rewards, and this brings us to our second major design challenge relating to reward mix, namely the mix of remuneration plans. There are many questions that need to be considered here:

- How much importance should be placed on base pay?
- How should base pay be structured?
- Does the nature of the work lend itself to skill- or competency-based base pay?
- What role should benefits play?
- How much emphasis should be placed on performance pay?
- Can the organisation afford cash incentives?
- Should incentives be individual or collective?
- Should incentives be cash- or equity-based?
- How should incentives be tailored to meet employee needs and expectations?
- What proportion of employees' total pay should be performance-linked and 'at risk'?
- What use should be made of non-cash incentives?

There will always be a need to make choices about the basis of base pay and performance pay, the mix between the two and the mix of pay-for-performance methods. This latter choice requires careful thought since, as we have seen, there is considerable potential for conflict between the various pay delivery methods, particularly between individual and collective incentives. As noted in parts 3 and 4, different pay methods will have different behavioural outcomes. The challenge is to select those methods that are likely to work best together to maximise the desired behavioural impact. To generalise: base pay and benefits will have most impact on membership behaviour, individual incentives on task behaviour and collective incentives on organisational citizenship behaviour. An equally important concern here is the need to maximise employee feelings of fairness about the pay mix. What combination of pay methods and procedures are employees most likely to see as being distributively fair and equitable? Remember, the mix of pay methods used will have a major influence on the degree of pay inequality within the organisation.

Again, the choice of pay mix should depend very much on the type of organisation concerned. Even within the one organisation, a 'one size fits all' approach may be singularly inappropriate, especially where business units are autonomous and diversified. In such cases, it would be best to formulate a multitiered strategy sensitive to the needs of specific units. Moreover, in all but the flattest of organisations, the pay mix will differ according to organisational level, with distinct combinations for senior managers, middle managers, lower-level managers, knowledge workers, administrators and line employees. The main challenge here is to identify, for each business unit and employee group, that mix of pay methods (base pay, individual incentives, collective incentives and benefits) that best promotes the range of membership, task and citizenship behaviour required for organisational success (Heneman, Fisher & Dixon 2001).

Drawing on insights offered in the chapters in part 3, let us summarise some of the chief best fit recommendations for base pay for non-managerial employees. Pay scales and narrow job grades, with progression based on seniority or merit increments and job promotion, are well suited to mechanistic organisational structures. Base pay built around broad grades and skill-based progression would be best adapted to high-involvement analysers and quality defenders with looser, more organic structures. A broad-banded base pay structure, with competency- and/or performance-related pay progression, would be a better match for an organically structured, high-involvement prospector, since these practices facilitate devolution, responsible autonomy and flexibility, and encourage informed risk-taking.

Turning now to the observations on incentive plan best fit offered in part 4, we can say that merit increments and results-based individual incentives will be a strong match for traditional mechanistic firms, with a limited amount of profitsharing perhaps thrown in for good measure. These practices also align with the relational psychological contract preferred by traditionally managed firms. Re-earnable merit bonuses based on multisource assessment offer a better means of rewarding individual excellence in high-involvement organic organisations. Goal-based individual incentives offer an ideal means of recognising and rewarding individual contribution in prospector firms, particularly given the preference for transactional psychological contracting. Collective incentives in the form of gainsharing, goalsharing, team incentives and group non-cash recognition will be a good match for high-involvement analysers and quality defenders, especially given that work in such organisations will be interdependent and typically team-based, while such firms will espouse a balanced (i.e. hybrid relational–transactional) psychological contract. Broadly based equity plans are also well suited to all high-involvement organisations, particularly as a means of eliciting employee engagement and citizenship behaviour. For prospectors, where the emphasis is on innovation, agility and a transactional contract, goal-sharing and share options would be a strong fit.

A further consideration here is whether performance pay plans serve as substitutes for or complements to one another. The substitution explanation posits, for example, that if employees receive collective performance pay, use of individual incentives would be both an unnecessary duplication and counter-productive in terms of teamwork and cooperative work relations. Similarly, if an organisation does wish to recognise and reward individual performance, it should choose between, say, an output-based method, such as piece rates or commissions, and an appraisal-based method, such as merit pay. Conversely, the complementarity explanation proposes that a mix of methods may allow the organisation to capitalise on the advantages of each while minimising any deficiencies. For example, a combination of collective and individual plans may counter the tendency to self-interest possible in individual plans while at the same time reducing the possibility of free riding within work units. Adding an organisation-wide incentive plan to the mix would then serve to counter the tendency of group incentives to discourage cooperation between work units, while the presence of individual incentives would counter the still greater potential for free riding in stand-alone organisational plans.

Therefore, in choosing between the different plans, it may be best not to think of substitution and complementarity as being mutually exclusive possibilities at all. Complementarity is perhaps best suited to choices made *between* the broad performance pay categories whereas substitution is more appropriate to plan choice *within* each category, especially given that the plans in any one category are, by definition, directed to eliciting similar dimensions of performance.

Before leaving the matter of reward mix, we have one final matter to consider. Within each organisation, reward and remuneration mix will need to be configured to the needs and desired behavioural outcomes of each distinct employee group. This means drawing up a pay component matrix that specifies the mix of pay methods for each group and the target contribution of each component to the total pay of a typical employee in each group. There are two widely followed 'rules' here:

1 The higher up the organisational hierarchy, the greater the proportion of total pay that can be performance-variable.
2 The higher up the hierarchy, the greater the proportion of total pay that can be linked to organisational performance.

Table 21.2 provides an example of remuneration target matrix for a traditional mechanistic organisation; that is, one with a steep internal hierarchy. Note the inverse relationship between proportional targets for fixed remuneration (base pay and benefits), on the one hand, and individual STIs and

**Table 21.2** Setting targets for total pre-tax remuneration mix

| Group | Base pay and benefits | Individual and collective STIs | Organisational LTIs |
|---|---|---|---|
| Process worker | 90% | 7% | 3% |
| Administrative | 90% | 7% | 3% |
| Professional or technical | 85% | 9% | 6% |
| Supervisor | 80% | 10% | 10% |
| Senior manager | 60% | 20% | 20% |
| Executive | 40% | 30% | 30% |

LTIs on the other, as we ascend the hierarchy. In high-involvement organic firms, in particular, the STI and LTI incentive components should be higher for all groups.

## Determining remuneration level

Having determined the proposed pay mix and target proportionalities for each employee group, the next step is to set appropriate levels of base pay and total pay for particular jobs and employees. Whether the base pay structure consists of narrow grades, broad grades or broad bands, market-relative pay ranges must be established for each designated position. What will be the target amount and range of total pay and base pay for each position? What range of pay does the organisation wish to attach to each job or role, and what degree of range overlap will apply between adjacent jobs or roles? Essentially, this involves a choice about whether the organisation is going to pay at, above or below prevailing median market rates for comparable positions. This will depend largely on whether the reward strategy emphasises attraction and retention or payroll cost containment. A firm might choose to pay below market if it wishes to gain a cost edge over competitors in the product market. Alternatively, it may choose to pay above market if it wants to attract and retain employees capable of making a high contribution.

Some organisations may have no choice but to pay under market. For instance, many start-up firms are cash poor, and pay levels are likely to be determined mainly by reference to market rates rather than internal equity, with the organisation typically paying less than its larger competitors to establish a market foothold. However, some firms may choose a low pay setting voluntarily, especially if employees are offered a significant trade-off in the form, say, of rewards of a non-financial type, such as developmental opportunities. For instance, many accounting and legal firms that offer in-house support for professional development and accreditation set pay rates for new graduate hires below the relevant market median. Start-up firms and firms in rapidly emerging industries, or in resurgent industries, may also choose to pay below market base pay but offer company equity as a trade-off.

However, a low total pay strategy may also have major costs. It may mean that the firm is unable to attract qualified or high-performing staff. Paying low can cause considerable reward dissatisfaction. It can also mean that the firm is saddled with high turnover, particularly if intrinsic, developmental or social rewards are few. For these reasons, low-paying firms tend to have lower productivity than high payers, and this can and often does prove fatal to new firms. One way around the cash flow problem would be to offer prospective employees share options in the company as a means of promoting membership behaviour. So where might a low-pay approach work best? Where recruitment and labour turnover costs are low, where work is labour intensive and where dysfunctional consequences of pay dissatisfaction can be controlled, for instance by means of close supervision or technical control; in other words, in a traditional mechanistic cost defender firm.

There are many reasons why an organisation may choose (or be compelled) to pay above the market median. It may wish to be a pay leader if it needs to recruit highly capable and high-quality employees who are in short supply or where employees require special compensation because the work is dangerous or isolated. The corollary, of course, is that they will also be under greater pressure to extract higher performance for the money paid and will therefore be more inclined to link more of total pay to individual or collective performance. Many firms achieve this by gearing base pay and benefits to the market median but top up total pay with STIs and LTIs. For instance, a high-involvement prospector is likely to be a high payer because of the need to attract mobile high-flyers and to reward excellence. The emphasis here would be on high variable rewards for successful risk-taking, innovation and timeliness. Of course, some organisations may have no choice but to pay over market, particularly if there is a strong union presence. Moreover, given that they offer few rewards of a non-financial nature, in times of general labour shortage, even cost defenders may actually find that they have to pay above market simply to attract sufficient recruits.

The option of paying at the market median is often chosen as a way of minimising risk associated with the above two alternatives. On the one hand, it may avoid the possible demotivational effects of paying under market; on the other, it lessens the high-pay strategy risk of compromising cost competitiveness. Quality defenders and analyser firms may well be able to get away with matching the market median for the required skill labour simply because of the high level of intrinsic reward associated with work undertaken.

## Best fit practices for sustainability and success

Drawing together the insights offered above, it is now possible for us to sketch in the broad contours of best fit performance and reward practice choice for the sustainable configurations of strategy, structure and culture identified earlier in this chapter. Table 21.3 (pp. 534–5) summarises the key performance factors for three out of six sustainable organisational types, as well as identifying a range of best fit practices for each.

Notice that there are substantial differences between the three cases in relation to each main area of practice, from appropriate performance units and criteria, through accent on non-financial rewards, base pay configuration and choice of STIs and LTIs, to the total pay level relative to market. Take base pay and pay level, for instance. Here, the logical choice for a 'TMCD' firm is a structure based on pay scales or narrow grades, with progression based on seniority, individual merit and grade promotion, an emphasis on internal equity, and low positioning relative to market rates. For an 'HIOQD', the best fit base-pay-wise would be broad grades with skill-based progression, an emphasis on internal equity, and pay level positioned around the market median. The appropriate base pay configuration for an 'HIOP' would be different again: broad bands, with competency- and/or performance-based progression, and a high market relativity that maximises competitiveness in attracting and retaining scarce talent.

## Rehearsal

As with any blueprint for change, before being implemented, the recommended practices should be carefully evaluated for their likely impact:

- Will they address current weaknesses?
- Will they support the organisation's success factors?
- Will they elicit the desired behaviour and results?

- Will they address employees' needs and expectations?
- Are they timely?
- Are they realistic and manageable?
- Are they going to be affordable?
- Are the proposals well integrated?

## Forecasting costs and benefits

Most importantly, the organisation has to decide whether the benefits of making the proposed changes are likely to outweigh the costs of doing so. Obviously, if a proposed change fails the test of projected net benefit, then it should be taken no further. To estimate the likely impact of each recommendation, it will be necessary to produce cost projections and compare them with the expected benefits of making the proposed change. Future costs and benefits can never be ascertained with total certainty precisely because so many relevant cost and market variables will be difficult to quantify in advance. Moreover, the effect on employee attitudes, behaviour and performance can only be approximated. However, forecasting is still essential to reducing the risk of inappropriate change.

In large organisations, forecasting may require detailed financial modelling of projected costs and benefits using best-case and worst-case scenarios. Cost estimates may include projected payroll cost increases or reductions, training costs, administrative overheads, staff turnover and recruitment costs and the like. Estimates of financial benefits could include increases in sales volume, production cost savings, increases in net profit, reduced supervision costs and other savings. Where the human resource information system permits, forecasting could also seek to estimate the financial impact of projected changes in key employee attitudes. For instance, using existing time series data, it may be possible to predict with some confidence the impact of each 1 per cent improvement in employee reward satisfaction on 'hard' outcomes, such as productivity, profitability and turnover.

Careful forecasting is especially important where a change in overall market pay relativity is proposed. Changing the pay level settings will have an impact on three key factors: (1) the total cost of remunerating the current workforce, (2) total labour turnover costs and (3) overall workforce quality and performance. Say an organisation is currently paying at the market median (i.e. at the 50th percentile of the market range) and wants to know the

**Table 21.3** Aligning strategy, structure, culture and practice

| | Traditional mechanistic cost defender (case 1: TMCD) | High involvement organic quality defender (case 4: HIOQD) | High involvement organic prospector (case 6: HIOP) |
|---|---|---|---|
| Espoused psychological contract | Relational | Balanced; semi-relational or semi-transactional | Transactional |
| Desired attitudes | Motivation; commitment | Motivation; commitment | Motivation, short-term commitment |
| Desired behaviour | Membership; task | Membership; task; citizenship | Task, citizenship |
| Results | Individual quantity or productivity; cost; long-term market share | Collective quality; long-term market share | Individual and collective short-term contribution, timeliness, creativity, risk-taking. |
| Performance unit | Individuals; business units; whole organisation | Work teams; parallel teams; business units | Individuals, project teams, business units, whole organisation |
| Performance criteria and measurement | Individual behaviour; results | Hard competencies; behaviour; results | Soft competencies, results |
| Performance monitoring | Supervisor | Self, peers and customers (180°) | 360° |
| Feedback and development | Tell and sell; counselling | Tell and listen; mentoring | Problem-solving, coaching |

| | | | |
|---|---|---|---|
| Non-financial rewards | Few | Intrinsic; developmental; social | Intrinsic |
| Base pay structure | Pay scales; narrow job grades | Broad grades | Broadbands |
| Pay progression | Annual seniority or merit increments; scale or grade promotion | Skill-based pay | Competency-based pay |
| Benefits | Fixed; minimal | Mix of fixed plus flexible | Flexible; extensive |
| Individual incentives | Piece-rates; commissions; merit raises; non-cash recognition | Commissions; merit bonuses; recognition awards | Commissions; discretionary bonuses |
| Collective STIs | Cost-based gain-sharing; selective profit-sharing | Multifactor goalsharing | Team and/or business unit goalsharing |
| Collective LTIs | Executive share bonuses | Share bonus or purchase plans | Share options, profit-sharing |
| Pay level | Below market median (with high attention to internal equity) | Around market median (with moderate attention to internal equity) | Above market median (with low attention to internal equity) |

likely costs and benefits of moving downmarket, say to the 40th percentile, as well as the costs and benefits that may arise from moving upmarket, to say the 60th percentile. If it moves downmarket, turnover rates and hence total turnover costs will increase and the quality and performance of employees hired is likely to fall. It will already know turnover cost per employee, and it will also be able to gauge the likely increase in turnover volume by examining turnover rates in organisations with pay set at the lower level, so the total turnover cost effect can be gauged quite accurately. To this will have to be added an estimate of the cost impact of a likely fall in workforce quality and performance. If average employee performance falls (as it almost certainly will), and if the organisation wishes to maintain current production levels, it will have to hire additional employees to cover the productivity shortfall. All of these factors will add to total payroll costs. Thus, to gauge whether a move downmarket is cost-effective, the organisation will need to balance these additional costs against the cost savings associated with cutting pay rates.

Conversely, a move up-market to the 60th percentile is likely to decrease the volume and total cost of labour turnover while increasing employee performance and, hence, reducing the number of employees required to maintain current output levels. However, against these cost savings must be set the additional costs associated with the general increase in pay level. If the estimated net benefit is negligible, the organisation may well be better off staying where it is, or perhaps opting for a more modest increase, say to the 55th percentile. The decision will hinge largely on the estimated shifts in employee contribution. However, other variables will also need to be factored in. For instance, what are conditions like in the relevant external labour market(s)? Will the required labour be readily available or in short supply? Will the median market rate rise or fall, and by how much? The decision on pay level will need to be based on some careful and well-informed forward projections as to likely conditions in the relevant product or service and labour markets.

A check should also be made to ensure that the recommendations meet all prevailing legal requirements. Do the proposed changes to pay practice comply with legal minimum pay requirements? Do employees receive all of the benefits to which they are legally entitled? Are the proposed changes to individual performance assessment non-discriminatory and compliant with equal opportunity requirements? Does the proposed share plan qualify for tax-exempt status?

## Piloting and preparatory planning

Even after all of these paper checks have been run, the organisation may still prefer to proceed with caution. One way to 'test the water', so to speak, with any proposed initiative is to pilot it among selected sections of the workforce. Obviously, how this is done will depend on the nature of the initiative under consideration. For instance, where the organisation is contemplating a change from narrow grades to broad grades and skill-based pay for production line employees, a trial roll-out to relevant employees in one plant may reveal design flaws that can be remedied ahead of full implementation.

Once the preview and piloting process is complete, the organisation can proceed to draw up an implementation plan. This entails production of a roll-out agenda that details the initiatives to be taken, which parts of the organisation they will be applied to, when and in what sequence they will be applied, over what time frame they will be applied, and how they will be resourced. The organisation will need to have a clear idea of the likely time requirements for implementing each initiative and the sequence in which they should be introduced. Should base pay be changed before or after the new performance incentives are in place, or should the changes be simultaneous? Obviously, implementation of a new performance pay plan should follow rather than precede associated changes in performance assessment or measurement. The time frame for change will depend on both the urgency of the required change and the nature of the practices to be applied. Minor modifications to existing incentive systems could be introduced quite quickly and with little prior preparation. However, more substantial changes will need to be phased in gradually. For instance, a proposal to convert a job-graded structure into competency-based broad-banding will require many months – and possibly several years – and would need to be implemented in stages and with careful attention to supporting changes, such as the way work tasks are organised and programs for competency assessment and staff development. A related issue is whether the strategy should be applied simultaneously across the board or to certain work units or levels first up, then subsequently to others.

Decisions should also be made in advance as to who will have accountability for each initiative. Will accountability for particular initiatives rest mainly with human resource professionals or with line managers and team leaders? If the latter, it may be necessary to plan for cost control safeguards to maintain cost-effectiveness. There may also be a need to predetermine the extent to which union representatives will be involved in the change process.

## Roll-out

For the change initiatives to succeed, it is crucial that the people most affected, namely employees and line managers, are fully informed as to both the rationale for change and the details of what is planned. Whether the management culture is traditional or high involvement, a proper communication program is an essential feature of any comprehensive change process. With a view to maintaining a positive psychological contract, management should openly and comprehensively explain and justify all changes to current practice, especially those initiatives likely to affect employee reward outcomes. This is especially so of high-involvement organisations, where there will be a strong expectation of employee participation in all aspects of the implementation process. All shareholders involved in and affected by the change process should also receive appropriate prior training in the nature of the new practices and processes.

Implementation really marks both a culmination and a new beginning. Once the roll-out is underway, the new practices should be subject to continuous review to ascertain how effective they are in delivering desired performance outcomes and whether and where further adjustment may be required. It is most unlikely that even the most carefully rehearsed, planned and implemented change agendas will be problem-free. In this sense, it would be wise to anticipate problems, expect resistance and be prepared to modify, revise and adapt. Every new performance and reward system is likely to need modification or refurbishment to accommodate subsequent change in the organisation's internal and external environment. After all, this is the core tenet of the best fit model.

## Chapter summary

Revisiting key points from earlier chapters, and in prescriptive mode, this final chapter has proposed a model for practical application of the best fit model to performance and reward system modification and improvement. After recapping the basic aims of performance and reward management practice discussed in chapter 1, and the model of strategic alignment presented in chapter 4, we have outlined a general five-step framework for developing or redeveloping performance and reward practice in line with the best fit model. In discussing best fit options for three pivotal aspects of practice choice, namely performance management approach, reward mix and remuneration level, we made use of the typology of sustainable (i.e. aligned) configurations of strategy, structure, culture and associated success and performance factors presented in chapter 4 to illustrate the importance and worth of matching practice choice to the performance factors particular to each sustainable organisational type, including desired attitudes, behaviour, competencies, results and the espoused 'deal'. Although misalignment is more likely to be the natural state in the short term, it is precisely for this reason that regular strategic analysis and systematic pursuit of better alignment or fit are imperative to long-term effectiveness and sustainability. This approach, we suggest, offers the best means of maximising positive outcomes from performance and reward practice for all organisational stakeholders.

## Discussion questions

1 What are the tell-tale signs of performance and reward system failure?
2 '"Best fit" looks good on paper but is impossible to achieve in practice.' Discuss.
3 'Total reward management' requires a balanced mix of reward types, but how can we know what mix to aim for?
4 'A good strategy well applied will always outdo a brilliant strategy badly applied.' Discuss.
5 What performance and reward practices best fit or match the performance requirements of a firm with a traditional management culture, a mechanistic structure and a quality defender competitive strategy?

# APPENDIX
# MODEL RESPONSES
# TO CASE STUDIES

This appendix provides model responses to the challenges posed in each of the major case studies at the end of parts 2, 3 and 4. Once you have formulated your own responses, you may find it helpful to compare these with those offered here. Pay particular attention to points that you may have misunderstood or overlooked.

## Part 2 Case study

## Delivering fairness: Performance assessment at Mercury Couriers

The instrument is a generic assessment tool applied to all non-managerial positions in the firm and uses single-source (supervisory) assessment as well as ranking technique for an evaluative purpose. It does so in a low-involvement context where there is little employee 'voice'.

The performance criteria used are best described as a combination of results (criteria 1 and 2: 'quantity' and 'accuracy'), trait-related competencies (criteria 3, 5 and 6: 'alertness', 'dependability' and 'mental flexibility') and directly observable behaviour (criteria 4, 7 and 9: 'respect and courtesy' and 'doing that which is apart from his/her own job' – or organisational citizenship behaviour – and 'attendance' – or membership behaviour). There is also a summative assessment criterion ('overall performance').

The main measuring techniques used are Behaviourally Anchored Rating Scales (BARS) with a combination of positive and negative anchors (criteria 1–4 and 6). However, three of the criteria (5, 7 and 8) are measured by means of the Mixed Standards Scales (MSS) variant of the Graphic Rating Scale (GRS) technique. Elements of a frequency-focused Behavioural Observation Scale (BOS) measurement technique are also present in some of the behavioural scales (for criteria 2, 3 and 6). Narrative technique is present in relation to criterion 9. Straight ranking method is also applied to employees within each unit or department, although there is no indication as to the criteria on which this should be based.

## Instrument strengths

The instrument does have a number of strengths. It has involved minimal development costs. Since it applies a common set of performance standards to all employees, it has the appearance of consistency. It also has the virtue of simplicity, which means that assessors with heavy work commitments may be inclined to take the process more seriously. The use of mixed criteria (i.e. results, behaviour and competencies) could be said to be a plus in that it strikes a balance of sorts and may thus have higher construct and content validity. In most cases, the instrument does provide grade descriptors or anchors, which may strengthen assessor consistency and reliability. The use of straight ranking may serve to moderate the potential for leniency, harshness and central tendency error in the rating scale components.

However, both the instrument and the system of which it is the centrepiece have some major shortcomings in the areas of validity, reliability and procedural justice, which are discussed below.

## Instrument weaknesses

### Validity

The instrument falls well short of the requirements for construct, content and criterion-related validity.

The use of uniform criteria for all non-managerial roles tends to compromise job-specific construct and content validity. Since all non-managerial job-holders are assessed using just eight specific criteria, it is highly unlikely that this will adequately cover all relevant facets of job performance. Some criteria and measures may be relevant to certain jobs but not to others. For instance, while 'respect and courtesy' may be valid for call centre work, it is of doubtful validity in relation to vehicle maintenance work, since there is little or no customer interface here. Likewise, 'mental flexibility' (criterion 5) would be construct invalid for many employees in a firm structured on mechanistic lines, as is currently the case with Mercury Couriers, since the work is by definition routine, non-discretionary and closely supervised. Thus, 'mental flexibility' may be less relevant to some jobs, such as parcel despatch, drivers or administration than to others such as marketing, legal or human resources. Likewise, 'dependability' (criterion 6) may be most relevant to those positions where reliable task completion is critical, such as despatch driving.

Content validity also seems to have been compromised by the omission of several performance criteria of obvious relevance to a number of work roles covered. For instance, although an attempt is made to measure quantity and accuracy, there is no recognition of another critical results-related criterion: that of timeliness. This would certainly be relevant to several of Mercury Couriers' line roles, including vehicle maintenance, despatch and call centre work. There is also inadequate recognition of the importance of effective communication and customer focus, criteria of vital importance in marketing and call centre work, for instance. It may be that 'respect and courtesy' (criterion 4) covers some aspects of customer relations, but it is not clear from the definition or the behavioural anchors included whether this criterion relates to work relations, customer relations or both. So content validity is also impaired by sins of omission and definition. However, adding additional generic criteria will not eliminate invalidity problems. Given that the instrument is currently applied to all non-managerial roles, the underlying problem remains that of construct invalidity. For instance, adding a 'customer focus' criterion may increase validity for those roles that do have high customer contact, especially call centre staff, marketing staff and despatch drivers, but would be construct invalid for roles with minimal direct customer contact, such as those in vehicle maintenance and office administration.

The conflation of different behaviour and competencies within the one criterion is also problematic in terms of construct validity (and reliability). A good example is criterion 3: 'Alertness is the ability to grasp instructions, to meet changing conditions and to resolve unexpected problems', which seeks to cover three different competencies: ability to understand, adaptability to change and problem-solving, none of which is really a valid signifier of 'alertness' at all. This means that construct validity is fundamentally compromised. Criterion definitions should be unidimensional and unambiguous. Moreover, the rating scale for criterion 3 is a clear example of criterion-related invalidity, since the scale anchors do not measure what the criterion description purports to be concerned with. Grade anchors 1–4 relate only to 'ability to grasp instructions' while anchor 5 ('Exceptionally keen and alert') conflates alertness and conscientiousness. Further, none of the grade anchors for criterion 3 relate explicitly to 'ability . . . to resolve unexpected problems'. Indeed, this subcriterion appears to be addressed more validly by criterion 5: 'mental flexibility', which in turn indicates an unacceptable degree of criterion transposition and duplication that may impair content validity, at least for some roles. The same applies to the duplication of anchors relating to required level of supervision in the grade anchors for criteria 2 ('accuracy') and 6 ('dependability'). By skewing both measures and measurement, duplication of this type stands to undermine both validity and reliability.

With the two purportedly results-based criteria (criteria 1 and 2), behavioural anchors are applied as the means of determining performance grade, which stands to compromise criterion-related validity. While behavioural measures may be an appropriate means of measuring desired outcomes in customer service jobs, a preferable approach, certainly in production and distribution jobs, would be to apply straight results measures in the form of key performance indicators (KPIs) and/or goal-setting.

Criterion-related invalidity is also evident in the rating scales for other criteria, with some scale anchors being partly or fully invalid for the criterion concerned. For example, in criterion 2 ('accuracy') the inclusion of the statements 'Requires little supervision' and 'Requires absolute minimum of supervision' (partial anchors for grades 4 and 5) is clearly invalid for the stated criterion. Likewise, in criterion 4 ('respect and courtesy'), the part of grade anchor 4 referring to 'willingness to help' is not a valid measure for this criterion, and clearly relates more to criterion 7.

### Reliability

The reliance on single-source (supervisory) assessment may well compromise assessment reliability, especially in those roles that are not closely supervised and observed, such as parcel delivery. The use of trait-like criteria (criteria 3, 5 and 6) may encourage judgement of the person rather than their performance. The use of five-grade scales may encourage central tendency error. In some scales, the lack of clear differentiation – that is, the degree of overlap between adjacent grade anchors – means that assessors will have great difficulty differentiating reliably and consistently between them. For instance, compare the anchors for grades 3 and 4 in criterion 4 ('respect and courtesy'). The difference between the two is far from clear. Excessive grade overlap is also evident in grade anchors 1 and 2 of criterion 2 ('accuracy') and in grade anchors 3 and 4 of criterion 6 ('dependability').

As noted above, anchor subcriteria relating to degree of supervision required are duplicated in grade anchors for several different criteria (grades 4 and 5 for criterion 2, grade 2 for criterion 3, and all grades for criterion 6). The privileging of particular anchors in this manner not only gives rise to the possibility that assessors will double-count or over-weight such behaviour but also to the likelihood of an unwitting halo or horns error.

The inconsistent application of behavioural frequency measures in the grade anchors for some criteria also stands to compromise assessment reliability. For example, while the anchors for criterion 2 ('accuracy') are consistently frequency-related, those for criterion 3 ('alertness') are a mixture of frequency-related and non-frequency-related anchors. Although the term 'usually' appears in the anchor for grade 4, frequency is not signalled in any of the other four grade descriptors for this criterion. Similarly, in criterion 4, only grade anchor 2 ('sometimes tactless') is explicitly frequency-related. Conversely, in criterion 6, frequency-related anchors are applied to grades 2 and 3 ('sometimes' and 'usually'), but not explicitly to grades 1, 4 and 5.

The absence of some anchors in two of the mixed standards rating scales (criteria 5 and 7) also increases the likelihood of inter-rater inconsistency, since assessors receive no guidance about when to choose a '2' or a '4' rather than an adjacent grade. The anchors that are applied in the mixed standards scales also invite idiosyncratic interpretation. For instance, what is 'average' when it comes to 'mental flexibility', how rigid is 'rigid', and how flexible is 'flexible' (criterion 5)? What is 'normal' readiness to help others (criterion 7)? One problem here is the absence of any indication of behavioural frequency. Some anchors specify frequency of observation, others do not. This leaves the assessor unsure as to how much overall importance to attach to behavioural frequency.

There are no guidelines as to how assessment of the specific criteria should be summed to obtain a judgement of 'overall performance'. The assessors have no guidance as to whether or not all seven criteria should be weighted equally. It is also unclear how or where assessors are to take attendance (criterion 9) into account in arriving at an overall assessment. The possibility of unintentional error is also increased by the fact that assessors are not required to maintain critical incident records.

### Procedural justice

There is nothing to indicate that either assessors or assessees have received prior training in system content, nor that system purpose has been communicated to stakeholders in advance. As such, none have received adequate notice of assessment procedures.

Given the system's evaluative intent, the application of a single ranking system to individuals performing in different job categories is unfair as well as invalid. Uniform ranking of this type also assumes reliable assessment across different assessors and job categories yet, as we have seen, this instrument is riddled with potential for inter-rater inconsistency and hence for unreliability and felt-unfairness. For those liable to be retrenched, the absence of adequate notice and opportunity to improve is a violation of due process.

Employee 'voice' is also minimal, even for a traditionally managed organisation. There has been no employee input to system development. The instrument provides no space in which to provide concrete examples (critical incident evidence) to support judgements. There is no provision for employee input to the assessment process itself, such as self-assessment. The system makes no provision for formal feedback, counselling, development or action planning. There is no evidence of any appeal mechanism, meaning that procedural fairness is likely to be compromised. As such, the approach falls short of commonly accepted requirements for procedural fairness. Provision of a formal appeal procedure is especially important in organisations with traditional, low-trust management cultures since they serve as a critical 'safety-valve' for inevitable discontent.

## Possible improvements

### Validity

The above problems highlight a number of areas in which assessment validity may be enhanced. The firm should consider developing distinct job-specific assessment instruments to better address construct and content validity requirements. In doing so, it should distinguish more clearly between generic performance criteria (such as core competencies) and those that are job specific (such as task behaviour and result areas).

Given that Mercury Couriers has a cost-focused competitive strategy, increasing the importance of results-based criteria would also serve the ends of construct validity, since cost efficiency is clearly a key desired outcome. In particular, it would be desirable to include KPIs or goals relating to cost-effectiveness, resource efficiency, timeliness and productivity, moderated by criteria and measures for quality, safety and customer satisfaction, where these are role valid.

Further, in a mechanistically structured firm, where jobs are narrowly defined, there is a clear need to ensure that there are criteria for each key result area (KRA), even if this means using modified instruments for different roles or at least allowing for additional job-specific KRAs to be recognised and assessed. Results-based and behaviourally based criteria should also be separated and measured by criterion-valid means, with strategically informed weightings being attached to each set of criteria. Results should be measured by means of key performance indicators (KPIs) and/or goal-setting rather than by means of behavioural anchors. Equally, all behavioural anchors must be criterion valid, with adjacent behavioural anchors being clearly differentiated.

## Reliability

Reliability of behavioural assessment could be improved by standardising reference to behavioural frequency in all behavioural rating scales; that is, by moving from GRS/MSS and BARS to BOS. Alternatively, behavioural anchors should be more comprehensive, perhaps including three to five specific anchors for each rating grade. Assessors should be required to maintain a performance diary or to complete critical incident forms, and should be required to provide specific behavioural examples to justify each behavioural judgement. Assessors should also be given guidelines as to how the overall assessment is to be determined, including criterion-specific weightings.

A reduction in the number of trait-related criteria would also reduce the possibility of person-based as opposed to performance-based judgements. It may also be advisable to switch to a six-point scale to minimise the possibility of central tendency error. Assessors should also receive training in the main forms of unintentional error, and they should be made more accountable for intentional error by having their assessments made subject to a formal arm's-length verification process.

## Procedural justice

Given the firm's traditional culture and the system's evaluative purpose, the absence of self-assessment might not be a problem. A switch to 360-degree assessment would also be incompatible with a top-down structure and culture. However, it may be appropriate to use peer and customer assessment, albeit anonymously. If the firm is willing to move from a traditional to a high-involvement culture, it should consider allowing a multisource assessment, including peer and self-assessment, and possibly even assessment of supervisors by subordinates. Even if the firm retains its emphasis on an evaluative purpose, it would still be advisable to institute formal feedback reviews, perhaps incorporating a 'tell and listen' feedback style.

Since the culture is traditional in nature, it is all the more important that the system should include a formal 'arm's-length' appeal mechanism. Felt-fairness could also be enhanced by providing training for assessors and assessees, as well as by clarifying the system's purpose.

It may also be advisable to rethink the use of forced distribution for retrenchment purposes and to increase the scope for developmental feedback and planning, albeit as a second-order purpose. To increase reward equity, it would be appropriate to move from a flat bonus system to a system that rewards individuals differentially according to their overall performance grade, so that there is a clearer line of sight between measured differences in performance and differences in performance payments.

# Part 3 Case study

## Just rewards: Rethinking base pay and benefits at Court, Case & McGowan, Commercial Law Partners

First up, the firm needs a systematic HR audit involving the gathering of both quantitative and qualitative information. Required quantitative information includes salary survey data on pay levels and pay composition in organisations of similar size operating in the same labour markets in Sydney and other capital cities. Pay composition data must include both fixed and variable elements. Qualitative information includes data generated by employee attitude surveys and exit interviews. Here it is necessary to identify employees' perceptions of both current reward practice and expected or desired rewards in relation to self-defined needs. Fiona should not assume that she knows what the firm's employees want or need; she must set about asking them, albeit in a timely fashion.

## Base pay

### Position-based pay

Notwithstanding its well-documented drawbacks, position-based pay has a number of potential advantages that cannot be overlooked. It gives employees a guaranteed minimum level of pay, which may encourage higher commitment to the organisation. When geared to job size (as it usually is) it legitimates organisational hierarchy. A single rate for the job stands to minimise interpersonal conflict over individual pay differences for people in the same job. For the same reason, ensuring the same rate of pay for the same job may also encourage teamworking, and it also encourages inter-employee cooperation. It facilitates ease of pay administration, particularly where there are large numbers of employees in any given job, position or grade. In this sense, it also enables greater certainty in payroll budgeting.

With Court, Case & McGowan, however, there is an obvious need to recalibrate position-base pay levels, since it is now paying significantly below its competitors and hence is experiencing major problems in staff attraction, retention and motivation. As a first step, the firm needs to undertake a survey of salary levels among organisations competing in the same labour market, then to make an informed strategic choice about where it positions itself in relation to the market median for comparable jobs or positions. It may also want to introduce a wider pay range for each of its position grades, to allow greater scope for the recognition of differences in individual knowledge, competencies and performance within each job or position grade.

Note, however, that there is nothing to indicate the existence of an internal equity problem that may require the application of job evaluation. The apparent gender inequities relate chiefly to promotion decision-making and opportunity to perform rather than to gender-based inequality in base pay levels. Of course, in undertaking its market survey, the firm may wish to conduct a job *analysis* so that it can be sure that it is benchmarking against jobs elsewhere of comparable content and 'size'.

### Person-based pay

Person-based pay opens up a wide range of possibilities. In terms of a new base pay structure, the firm could combine the existing grades into broad grades involving wider pay ranges within position descriptions. For instance, the law graduate and one- to three-year solicitor grades could be combined to allow a greater spread of pay irrespective of period of service. The grades senior solicitor and senior associate could be combined with the same objective in mind. This would give the firm more scope to recognise and reward individual differences in performance capacity and contribution.

Alternatively, the firm might opt to broad band its base pay structure and give far more scope for recognising individual contribution. For instance it might decide to collapse all four solicitor grades into one broad band with a pay range of perhaps 200 to 300 per cent. The firm would then have to determine how individuals would progress their base pay within this broad band. For instance, positions within the band could be based on demonstrated knowledge and skills, assessed competencies and/or measured individual performance.

This presents its own problems, of course. The adoption of competency-based assessment would inevitably involve high administrative costs. Moreover, since it seeks to de-emphasise seniority-based hierarchy and promotion, broad-banding will necessarily require a major change in organisational culture and structure, something that the firm would have to support and lead. Moving to broad-banding necessarily involves the removal of promotion opportunities, and this must be fully explained to the employees affected; otherwise employees will be demotivated by the change. Employees should be fully informed as to the pay-progression criteria applied and how these translate into specific pay outcomes. Finally, broad-banding is not a 'quick-fix' solution. It should be rolled out carefully and fully communicated to those affected, and it may take three to five years to implement successfully. Knowledge workers like solicitors will not take kindly to not being kept fully informed about the changes affecting them. Given the time lag involved, it may be desirable to begin the process by recalibrating the existing position grades using market survey data, then commencing the more fundamental change to broadbanding only after the firm has established market-competitive base pay levels.

## Benefits

Given that the regimen of billable hours places pressure on solicitors to work long hours, rewards links to work–life quality may be especially apposite here. Such initiatives might include time-in-lieu arrangements, staff massages, meditation classes, life coaching, staff sabbaticals, gym and sports club membership, subsidised holiday travel and accommodation, and the like. Given that the firm is failing to capitalise fully on the talent and expertise of its female solicitors, it may also wish to consider offering more generous leave arrangements, more flexible billable hours provisions, paid maternity leave, in-house childcare, subsidised further study, courses in time management and career management, and so on. While such initiatives would undoubtedly add to staffing costs, they may well deliver a net return in terms of reduced turnover, higher retention and improved satisfaction and commitment among the firm's female solicitors.

# Performance assessment and reward

## Individual performance assessment

A system of formal individual performance assessment that incorporates competency, behavioural and results criteria may allow the firm to better communicate strategic priorities to staff and to provide staff with more meaningful feedback on their performance levels and how performance can be enhanced. However, to be effective, performance appraisal needs to be taken seriously by all parties and to deliver assessments that are valid, reliable and perceived to be fair. Reliability and fairness problems are particularly pronounced where behavioural judgments are made but, where knowledge work involving direct interaction with clients is concerned, simply relying on easily measured results (such as billable hours) can also be quite dysfunctional. The firm must also consider how the assessment process itself is to be undertaken. For instance, if it wishes to reinforce organisational hierarchy it may choose to use assessment by partners only. Alternatively, if it wishes to accentuate a more egalitarian culture, it may choose to introduce an element of peer or even subordinate appraisal. A further design issue has to do with whether appraisal scores will be used only for staff development purposes or whether they will be linked to pay via, say, merit increments or merit bonuses.

## Individual incentives

Although the focal issues of this case study are those of base pay and employee benefits, it is also appropriate for us to consider in general terms whether Court, Case & McGowan should incorporate performance-contingent pay into its reward mix. Organisations have a tendency to opt for individual performance incentives as the perceived instant solution to most labour management problems, but the consequences are often quite disastrous. On the one hand, the use of individual incentives may allow the firm to recognise and reward individual excellence and, thus, to retain valued high performers. On the other hand, individual cash incentives may be inimical to the very nature of legal work, especially given that much legal work is team-based, that solicitors expect to be well paid irrespective of whether they win or lose the case at hand, that some cases are inherently more difficult than others, that some clients and cases are more lucrative than others, and that individual incentives may encourage unscrupulous behaviour inimical to the profession's reputation.

There is also the question of how individual cash incentives should be determined. Should they be linked just to billable hours or should a wider set of performance measures be applied? Should individual incentives be based on results-based performance measures or on behavioural criteria, as in behaviourally based performance appraisal? Should they take the form of permanent increments to base pay ('merit raises') or stand-alone payments ('merit bonuses' or 'discretionary bonuses')? The firm may even wish to implement one or more incentive plans of a non-cash nature, perhaps a 'solicitor of the month' award.

### Collective incentives

Given the importance of teamworking at Court, Case & McGowan, the firm may also wish to consider introducing rewards geared to collective performance. It may be that a group incentive plan, such as goalsharing, profitsharing or team incentives, would be more appropriate in legal work where much of the work is necessarily interdependent rather than individualised. As such, it may also be appropriate to consider including legal support staff in group incentive plans. It would also be possible to combine group and individual approaches but using group-based performance measures to determine the magnitude of an incentive payment pool, then using individual performance measures to allocate the pool to individuals. This, however, would require a careful balance to ensure that the group and individual components work in harmony rather than pulling in opposite directions.

You may wish to revisit these performance pay possibilities once you have read the chapters on performance-related rewards.

## Part 4 Case study

## Beyond the hard sell: Redesigning performance-related rewards at Southbank

### SIS strengths and weaknesses

The SIS is an individual short-term incentive plan based on management by objectives. As such, it exhibits many of the generic strengths and weaknesses of results-based incentives. Note, however, that the SIS cannot be said to meet the requirements for an incentive plan based on formal goal-setting since the targets are centrally imposed rather than being negotiated and agreed at individual level. Moreover, although it resembles a commission-based approach, the SIS departs from a straight commission plan in that incentive payments do not follow a simple rate-per-unit formula but rather are issued only to the top-ranked 40 per cent of employees.

On the positive side, it makes use of 'objective' and clearly defined performance criteria that are seemingly construct valid (in that they are based on job-specific KRAs) and criterion valid (in that the KPIs used to measure results are relevant to the KRAs targeted). The use of performance targets also focuses employee attention on exactly what needs to be achieved in the way of performance improvement, as well as allowing employees discretion as to how to achieve the specified results. The use of monthly targets also means that feedback on performance outcomes is virtually instantaneous. Since the SIS uses criterion-valid data (that is, degree of target achievement in construct valid KRAs) the scheme also appears to support performance assessment reliability.

On the negative side, the scheme is proof positive of two key tenets of reward management: first, that 'rewards motivate people to get the rewards'; and second, at least in low-trust work cultures of the type prevailing in Southbank, that 'it is only what gets measured and rewarded that gets done'. Equally, it is clear that the emphasis on individual rewards has disrupted cooperative work relationships. The singular focus on sales results has also encouraged an aggressive and deceptive approach to customer relations by some employees, caused dysfunctional competitive relations between employees themselves, including customer poaching, and precipitated systematic fraud by some staff members. The approach has privileged 'how much' (i.e. results) over 'how' (i.e. work behaviour).

The SIS also fails the expectancy theory test of instrumentality (i.e. reward for performance delivered) since 60 per cent of employees who do meet the monthly targets do not receive any bonus. This also contradicts distributive justice expectations. As such, the plan has a fundamental design flaw in respect of motivation. The expectancy cognition itself (i.e. employee perception of target achievability) is also compromised by the manner in which monthly targets are determined. The setting of targets according to nationwide performance data fails to take adequate account of situational factors, particularly the greater challenge faced by staff and branches in poorer areas in meeting nationwide standards. The automatic ratcheting effect on target difficulty arising from the use of a moving average base line must also erode expectancy and self-efficacy cognitions and hence motivation. The target-setting mechanism also fails to take adequate account of variance in demand for credit arising from the influence of factors beyond employees' control, such as an upward movement in interest rates. Likewise, the fact that targets are imposed rather than agreed stands to undermine both goal commitment and procedural justice perceptions.

Finally, the case highlights the dangers of using stand-alone incentive plans to drive organisational change. In seeking to impose a transactional psychological contract using extrinsic incentives, Southbank's previous leadership has overlooked the need to 'manage' the cultural transition away from the values and expectations associated with the pre-existing service culture and relational psychological contract. Incentive plans can support broader initiatives and interventions designed to effect organisational change, but only in extreme cases should they be used as the change driver.

## Appropriate performance criteria

The results-based standards currently used may be construct valid, but in a service sector organisation such as this, the requirement for content validity (i.e. for a range of criteria fully representative of job content) is not met. In particular, the exclusive focus on 'hard' results overlooks 'soft' results, as well as essential behavioural requirements. Unless an individual incentive plan signals the importance of 'how' and 'how good' as well as 'how much', there is a strong likelihood that it will encourage short-termism and self-interest at the expense of behaviour and results that are in the firm's long-term interest.

Most obviously, while the SIS has certainly encouraged a perverted form of employee creativity and timeliness (i.e. fraud, deception and corner-cutting), it also ignores service quality, customer focus, ethical behaviour, due diligence in investigating loan applicants, organisational citizenship behaviour, information-sharing, teamworking and other forms of behaviour that are essential to a financial institution's long-term sustainability. In short, in addition to applying hard quantity-based performance criteria and measures, Southbank should also be recognising and rewarding behaviour that moderates a single-minded focus on individual financial results over the short term.

## A new approach to performance-related reward

With the above points in mind, it is possible to identify a number of alternative reward strategies that may well allow Southbank to enhance its staff performance and increase its market share in retail banking.

At the very least, if it wishes to retain the focus on individual short-term results-based incentives, it should substitute proper goal-setting for the top-down 'MBO' approach. Goals should be set by participative means. This would enhance organisational communication and trust. Goals should also be set at branch level, so that interbranch differences in situational factors and 'opportunity to perform' are adequately recognised, albeit within general guidelines set down by the bank's HR department. To maximise content validity, goals should include 'soft' as well as 'hard' criteria. For example, it would be most appropriate to include one or more goals for service quality (such as reduction in customer complaints).

This, however, would still leave desired work behaviour largely unrecognised. To remedy this, Alison may wish to recommend the introduction of a system of formal behavioural assessment to accompany goal-setting. Incentive payments would then be geared to a combination of goal achievement and behavioural assessment, perhaps over a quarterly, six-monthly or annual time frame, rather than on a monthly basis. Behavioural criteria should cover membership behaviour, task behaviour and organisational citizenship behaviour. To enhance reliability and felt-fairness, behavioural assessment could also be multisource, ideally including peer input. Given the link to pay, self-assessment may not be appropriate in this case. In addition to cash STI payments, Alison might also recommend the introduction of a system of special non-cash recognition awards for individual sales and service excellence.

Yet this still fails to recognise the fact that work (and hence performance) in Southbank is still substantially interdependent, particularly at branch level. As such, in addition to individual incentives, Alison may decide to recommend the introduction of a collective STI plan, perhaps based on branch-level KPIs or goalsharing. Again, the approach should combine 'hard' and 'soft' results criteria. Such an approach would reinforce teamworking and cooperative work relations, as well as reducing destructive competition between individual employees. She might also consider introducing group non-cash recognition awards at branch level.

But even this may not deliver the organisation-wide strategic alignment necessary for competitive success. To this end, Alison may decide to recommend the introduction of a profitshare plan, an employee share plan or, perhaps, a fully integrated balanced scorecard approach for the bank's retail division. A balanced scorecard approach would allow the bank to align short- and long-term goals for staff development, business process improvement, customer service and financial or shareholder outcomes. Of course, to be effective the balanced scorecard option would require across-the-board cultural change supported by a wide range of human resource enablers, not the least being the adoption of systematic employee involvement. Arguably, it is only by genuinely empowering employees that Southbank will be able to realise the previous leadership's aspiration to instil a culture of entrepreneurial high performance.

# REFERENCES

Aboody, D. & Kasznik, R. (1998), 'CEO stock options and corporate voluntary disclosures', Stanford Graduate School of Business Research Paper Series, No. 1535, November.

Abosch, K. (1995), 'The promise of broadbanding', *Compensation and Benefits Review*, January–February: 54–8.

— (1998a), 'Confronting six myths of broadbanding', *WorldatWork Journal*, 7(3): 28–36.

— (1998b), 'Variable pay: Do we have the basics in place?', *Compensation and Benefits Review*, 30(4): 12–22.

Abosch, K. & Hand, J. (1994a), *Broadbanding Design, Approaches and Practices*, American Compensation Association, Scottsdale, AZ.

— (1994b), 'Characteristics and practices of organizations with broadbanding: A study of alternative approaches', *WorldatWork Journal*, 3(3): 6–17.

— (1998), *Life with Broadbands*, American Compensation Association, Scottsdale, AZ.

Abosch, K. & Hmurovic, B. (1998), 'A traveler's guide to global broadbanding', *WorldatWork Journal*, 7(2): 38–47.

ABS (2004), ABS Cat. 6310.0, *Employee Earnings, Benefits and Trade Union Membership – Australia*, Australian Bureau of Statistics, August.

Ackroyd, S. & Thompson, P. (1999), *Organizational Misbehaviour*, Sage, London.

Adams, J. S. (1963), 'Towards an understanding of inequity', *Journal of Abnormal and Social Psychology*, 67: 422–36.

— (1965), 'Inequity in social exchange', in Berkowitz, L. (ed.), *Advances in Experimental Social Psychology*, Academic Press, New York, vol. 2, pp. 267–99.

Aggrawal, R., & Samwick, A. A. (1999), 'The other side of the tradeoff: The impact of risk on executive compensation', *Journal of Political Economy*, 107(1): 65–105.

Aitken, M. & Wood, R. (1989), 'Employee stock ownership plans: Issues and evidence', *Journal of Industrial Relations*, 31(2): 147–68.

Alderfer, C. P. (1972), *Existence, Relatedness, and Growth*, Free Press, New York.

Altmansberger, H. & Wallace, M. (1995), 'Strategic use of goalsharing at Corning: Taking incentives beyond gainsharing', *WorldatWork Journal*, 4(4): 64–73.

Ambrose, M. L. & Arnaud, A. (2005), 'Are procedural justice and distributive justice conceptually distinct?', in J. Greenberg & J. A. Colquitt (eds), *Handbook of Organizational Justice*, Lawrence Erlbaum & Associates, Mahwah, NJ, pp. 59–84.

American Compensation Association Competencies Research Team (1996), 'The role of competencies in an integrated HR strategy', *WorldatWork Journal*, 5(2): 6–21.

Anderson, N. & Schalk, R. (1998), 'The psychological contract in retrospect and prospect', *Journal of Organizational Behavior*, 19(Special issue): 637–47.

Andon, P., Baxter, J. & Mahana, H. (2005), 'The balanced scorecard: Slogans, seduction and state of play', *Australian Accounting Review*, 15(1): 29–38.

Antonioni, D. (1994), 'The effects of feedback accountability on upward appraisal ratings', *Personnel Psychology*, 47: 349–56.

— (1996), 'Designing an effective 360 degree appraisal feedback process', *Organizational Dynamics*, 24(3): 24–38.

Applebaum, E., Bailey, T., Berg, P. & Kallenberg, A. (2000), *Manufacturing Competitive Advantage: The Effects of High Performance Work Systems on Plant Performance and Company Outcomes*, Cornell University Press, Ithaca, NY.

Applebaum, E. & Batt, R. (1994), *The New American Workplace*, Cornell University Press, Ithaca, NY.

Applebaum, S. H. & Kamal, R. (2000), 'An analysis of the utilization and effectiveness of non-financial incentives in small business', *Journal of Management Development*, 19(9): 733–63.

Argyris, C. (1960), *Understanding Organizational Behaviour*, Dorsey Press, Homewood, IL.

Armitage, K. (1997), 'The wages of fear', *British Journal of Administrative Management*, May–June: 25.

Armstrong, M. (1996), *Employee Reward*, Chartered Institute of Personnel and Development, London.

— (2000), *Performance Management*, 2nd edn, Kogan Page, London.

Armstrong, M. & Baron, A. (1998), *Performance Management: The New Realities*, Chartered Institute for Personnel and Development, London.

Armstrong, M. & Brown, D. (1998), 'Relating competencies to pay: The UK experience', *Compensation and Benefits Review*, May–June, 28–39.

— (2005), 'Reward strategies and trends in the United Kingdom: The land of diverse and pragmatic dreams', *Compensation and Benefits Review*, 37(4): 41–53.

— (2006), *Strategic Reward: Making It Happen*, Kogan Page, London.

Armstrong, M. & Murlis, H. (1994), *Reward Management: A Handbook of Remuneration Strategy and Practice*, 3rd edn, Kogan Page, London.

— (1998), *Reward Management: A Handbook of Remuneration Strategy and Practice*, 4th edn, Kogan Page, London.

— (2004), *Reward Management: A Handbook of Remuneration Strategy and Practice*, 5th edn, Kogan Page, London.

Arthur, J. B. (1992), 'The link between business strategy and industrial relations systems in American steel minimills', *Industrial and Labor Relations Review*, 45(3): 488–506.

— (1994), 'Effects of human resource systems on manufacturing performance and turnover', *Academy of Management Journal*, 37(3): 670–87.

Arthur, J. B. & Jelf, G. S. (1999), 'The effects of gainsharing on grievance rates and absenteeism over time', *Journal of Labor Research*, 20: 133–45.

Arthur, J. B. & Kim, D.-O. (2005), 'Gainsharing and knowledge-sharing: The effects of labour-management co-operation', *International Journal of Human Resource Management*, 16(9): 1564–82.

Arthurs, A. (1996), 'Job evaluation', in Warner, M. (ed.), *International Encyclopaedia of Business and Management*, Routledge, London, vol. 3, pp. 2430–8.

Ashton, C. (1996), 'How competencies boost performance', *Management Development Review*, 9(3): 14–19.

Atkinson, A. A., Waterhouse, J. H. & Well, R. B. (1997), 'A stakeholder approach to strategic performance measurement', *Sloan Management Review*, Spring: 25–37.

Atwater, L. E. (1998), 'The advantages and pitfalls of self-assessment in organizations', in Smither, J. W. (ed.), *Performance Appraisal: State of the Art in Practice*, Jossey-Bass, San Francisco, pp. 331–69.

Audia, P. G. & Locke, E. A. (2003), 'Benefiting from negative feedback', *Human Resource Management Review*, 13: 631–46.

References 557

Australian Public Service Commission (2005), *State of the Service Report 2004-05*, Australian Public Service Commission, Canberra.

Australian Stock Exchange (2005), *Australia's Share Owners: An ASX Study of Share Investors in 2004*, ASX, Sydney.

Australian Stock Exchange Corporate Governance Council (2003), *Principles of Good Corporate Governance and Best Practice Recommendations*, ASX, Sydney.

Bacal, R. (1998), *Performance Management*, McGraw-Hill, New York.

Bach, S. (1999), 'From performance appraisal to performance management', in Bach, S. & Sisson, K. (eds), *Personnel Management: A Comprehensive Guide to Theory and Practice*, 3rd edn, Blackwell, Oxford, pp. 111–36.

Bacharach, S. B. & Bamberger, P. (1995), 'Beyond situational constraints: Job resource inadequacy and individual performance at work', *Human Resource Management Review*, 5(2): 79–102.

Baird, M. (2006), 'The gender agenda: Women, work and maternity leave', in M. Hearn & G. Michelson (eds), *Rethinking Work: Time, Space, Discourse*, Cambridge University Press, Melbourne, pp. 39–59.

Baker, R. (1997), 'A slice of the action', *Weekend Australian*, 18–19 October: 35.

Balkin, D. B. & Montemayor, E. F. (2000), 'Explaining team-based pay: A contingency perspective based on the organizational life cycle, team design, and organisational learning literatures', *Human Resource Management Review*, 10(3): 249–69.

Bandura, A. (1986), *Social Foundations of Thought and Action: A Social Cognitive Theory*, Prentice Hall, Englewood Cliffs, NJ.

Barber, A., Dunham, R. & Formisano, R. (1992), 'The impact of flexible benefits on employee satisfaction: A field study', *Personnel Psychology*, 45: 55–75.

Barkema, H. & Gomez-Mejia, L. R. 1998, 'Managerial compensation and firm performance: A general research framework', *Academy of Management Journal*, 42(2): 131–46.

Barnes, A., Josev, T., Lenne, J., Marshall, S., Mitchell, R., Ramsay, I. & Rider, C. (2006), 'Employee share ownership schemes: Two case studies', Research Report, Centre for Corporate Law and Securities Regulation & Centre for Employment and Labour Relations Law, University of Melbourne, Melbourne.

Barney, J. B. (1991) 'Firm resources and sustained competitive advantage', *Journal of Management*, 17: 99–120.

— (1995), 'Looking inside for competitive advantage', *Academy of Management Executive*, 9(4): 49–61.

Barney, J. B. & Wright, P. M (1998), 'On becoming a strategic partner: The role of human resources in gaining competitive advantage', *Human Resource Management*, 37(1): 31–46.

Barrick, M. R. & Mount, M. K. (1991), 'The big five personality dimensions and job performance: A meta-analysis', *Personnel Psychology*, 44: 1–26.

Bartol, K. M. & Locke, E. A. (2000), 'Incentives and motivation', in Rynes, S. L. & Gerhart, B. (eds), *Compensation in Organizations: Current Research and Practice*, Jossey-Bass, San Francisco, pp. 104–50.

Bassett, G. (1994), 'Merit pay increases are a mistake', & Gilbert, D. (1994), 'Response', *Compensation and Benefits Review*, 26(2): 20–5.

Bateman, T. S. & Organ, D. W. (1983), 'Job satisfaction and the good soldier: The relationship between affect and employee "citizenship" ', *Academy of Management Journal*, 26: 587–95.

Bebchuk, L. & Fried, J. (2004), *Pay Without Performance: The Unfulfilled Promise of Executive Compensation*, Harvard University Press, Cambridge, MA.

— (2005a), 'Executive compensation at Fannie Mae: A case study of perverse incentives, nonperformance pay, and camouflage', *Journal of Corporation Law*, 30(4): 807–22.

— (2005b), 'Pay without performance: Overview of the issues', *Journal of Corporation Law*, 30(4): 647–74.

— (2006), 'Pay without performance: Overview of the issues', *Academy of Management Perspectives*, 20(1): 5–24.

Bebchuk, L., Fried, J. & Walker, D. (2002), 'Managerial power and executive compensation', *University of Chicago Law Review*, 69: 751–85.

Bebchuk, L. & Jackson, R. (2005), 'Executive pensions', *Journal of Corporation Law*, 30(4): 823–55.

Becker, B. & Gerhart, B. (1996), 'The impact of human resource management on organizational performance: Progress and prospects', *Academy of Management Journal*, 39(4): 779–801.

Becker, B. E. & Huselid, M. A. (1998), 'High performance work systems and firm performance: A synthesis of research and managerial implications', in Ferris, G. (ed.), *Research in Personnel and Human Resource Management*, vol. 16, JAI Press, Greenwich, CT, pp. 53–101.

Becker, B. E., Huselid, M., Pickus, P. & Spratt, M. (1997), 'HR as a source of shareholder value: Research and recommendations', *Human Resource Management*, 36(1): 39–47.

Bedaux, C. E. (1921), 'The Bedaux-Unit principle of industrial management', *Journal of Applied Psychology*, 5: 119–26.

Beer, M. (1981), 'Performance appraisal: Dilemmas and possibilities', *Organizational Dynamics*, 9(3): 24–36.

Beer, M. & Cannon, M. D. (2004), 'Promise and peril in implementing pay-for-performance', *Human Resource Management*, 43(1): 3–48.

Beer, M. & Katz, N. (2003), 'Do incentives work? The perceptions of a worldwide sample of senior executives', *Human Resource Planning*, 26(3): 30–44.

Beer, M., Spector, B., Lawrence, P., Quinn Mills, D. & Walton, R. (1984), *Managing Human Assets: The Ground Breaking Harvard Business School Program*, Free Press, NY.

Behrend, H. (1957), 'The effort bargain', *Industrial and Labor Relations Review*, 10: 503–15.

— (1961), 'A fair day's work', *Scottish Journal of Political Economy*, 8: 102–18.

Belcher, J. (1995), 'Group incentives: Improving performance through shared goals and rewards' in Risher, H. & Fay, C. (eds), *The Performance Imperative: Strategies for Enhancing Workforce Effectiveness*, Jossey-Bass, San Francisco, pp. 343–60.

Ben-Ner, A. & Jones, D. (1995), 'Employee Participation, ownership, and productivity: A theoretical framework', *Industrial Relations*, 34(4): 532–54.

Bennett Stewart, G. et al. (1993), 'Rethinking rewards', *Harvard Business Review*, 71(6): 37–49.

Bergel, G. (1994), 'Choosing the right pay system to fit banding', *Compensation and Benefits Review*, 26(4): 34–8.

Berglas, S. (2002), 'The very real dangers of executive coaching', *Harvard Business Review*, 80(6) 86–93.

Berle, A. A. & Means, G. C. (1932), *The Modern Corporation and Private Property*, Commerce Clearing House, New York.

Bernardin, H. J. (1986), 'Subordinate appraisal: A valuable source of information about managers', *Human Resource Management*, 25: 421–39.

Bettenhausen, K. L. & Fedor, D. B. (1997), 'Peer and upward appraisals: A comparison of their benefits and problems', *Group and Organization Management*, 22(2): 236–63.

Beugre, C. (1998), *Managing Fairness in Organizations*, Quorum Books, Westport, CT.

Bies, R. J. (2005), 'Are procedural justice and interactional justice conceptually distinct?', in Greenberg, J. & Colquitt, J. A. (eds), *Handbook of Organizational Justice*, Lawrence Erlbaum & Associates, Mahwah, NJ, pp. 85–112.

Bies, R. J. & Mogg, J. S. (1986), 'Interactional justice: Communication criteria of fairness', in Lewicki, R., Sheppard, B. & Bazerman, M. (eds), *Research on Negotiations in Organizations*, vol. 1, JAI Press, Greenwich, CT, pp. 43–55.

Blake Dawson Waldron Lawyers (2004), *The BDW Guide to CLERP 9*, Blake Dawson Waldron Lawyers, Sydney, www.bdw.com.au/publications/clerp9/clerp9guide.pdf.

Blasi, J., Conte, M. & Kruse, D. (1996), 'Employee stock ownership and corporate performance among public companies', *Industrial and Labor Relations Review*, 50(1): 60–79.

Blinder, A. S. (ed.) (1990), *Paying for Productivity: A Look at the Evidence*, Brookings Institution, Washington DC.

Bloom, M. & Milkovich, G. T. (1998), 'Relationships among risk, incentive pay, and organisational performance', *Academy of Management Journal*, 41(3): 283–97.

Bodie, Z., Kaplan, R. S. & Merton, R. C. (2003), 'For the last time: Stock options are an expense', *Harvard Business Review*, 81(3): 63–71.

Borman, W. C., & Motowidlo, S. J. (1993), 'Expanding the criterion domain to include elements of contextual performance', in Schmitt. N. & Borman, W. C. (eds), *Personnel Selecton in Organizations*, Jossey-Bass, San Francisco, pp. 71–98.

— (1997), 'Organizational citizenship behavior and contextual performance', *Human Performance*, 10(2): 67–70.

Boudreau, J. W. & Berman, R. (1991), 'Using performance measurement to evaluate strategic human resource management decisions: Kodak's experience with profit sharing', *Human Resource Management*, 30(3): 393–409.

Bowers, J. (2003), 'Valuing work: An integrated approach', *WorldatWork Journal*, 12(2): 28–39.

Boxall, P. & Purcell, J. (2003), 'Strategic HRM: "Best fit" or "best practice"?', in Boxall, P. & Purcell, J., *Strategy and Human Resource Management*, Palgrave Macmillan, Basingstoke, pp. 47–70.

Boyatzis, R. (1982), *The Competent Manager: A Model for Effective Performance*, John Wiley & Sons, New York.

Brender-Ilan, Y. & Shultz, T. (2005), 'Perceived fairness of the mystery customer method: Comparing two employee evaluation practices', *Employee Responsibilities and Rights Journal*, 17(4): 231–43.

Bretz, R. D., Milkovich, G. T. & Read, W. (1992), 'The current state of performance appraisal research and practice', *Journal of Management*, 18: 321–52.

Brooks, S. (1994), 'Noncash ways to compensate employees', *HR Magazine*, April, 38–43.

Brough, I. (1994), 'PRP for manual workers: Issues and experience', *Employee Relations*, 16(7): 18–32.

Brown, D. (1996), 'Broadbanding: A study of company practices in the United Kingdom', *Compensation and Benefits Review*, 28(6): 41–9.

Brown, D. & Armstrong, M. (1999), *Paying for Contribution: Real Performance-Related Pay Strategies*, Kogan Page, London.

Brown, K. 2005, 'Putting the life back into work', *Human Resources Magazine*, 13 July, n.p.

Brown, M. & Heywood, J. (eds) (2002), *Paying for Performance: An International Comparison*, M. E. Sharpe, Armonk, NY.

Buck, T., Brice, A., Main, G. & Udueni, H. (2003), 'Long term incentive plans, executive pay and UK company performance', *Journal of Management Studies*, 40(7): 1709–27.

Budman, M. (1997), 'Is there merit in merit pay?', *Across the Board*, 34, June: 33–6.

— (1998), 'Mixed results', *Across the Board*, 35(6), June: 23–8.

Bullock, R. & Lawler, E. E. (1984), 'Gainsharing, a few questions and fewer answers', *Human Resource Management*, 23(1): 23–40.

Burns, T. & Stalker, G. M. (1961), *The Management of Innovation*, Tavistock Publications, London.

Business Council of Australia (2004), *CEO Turnover 2003*, BCA, Melbourne.

Byrne, J. A & Bongiorno, L. (1997), 'How ordinary workers feel when fat cats get the cream', *Management Development Review*, 10(4/5): 164–5.

Callus, R. (2005), 'ANZ', in Callus, R. (ed), *Performance Management: HiP HR in Practice*, ACIRRT, University of Sydney, Sydney, pp. 19–22.

Cameron, J. & Pierce, D. (1997), 'Rewards, interest and performance: An evaluation of experimental findings', *WorldatWork Journal*, 6(4): 6–15.

Carson, K., Cardy, R. & Dobbins, G. (1991), 'Performance appraisal as effective management or deadly management disease: Two empirical investigations', *Group and Organisational Studies*, 16(2): 143–59.

Chandler, S. (1996), 'United we own', *Business Week*, 3467, 18 March: 40–4.

Chartered Institute of Personnel and Development (2005a), *Annual Survey Report 2005: Performance Management*, CIPD, London.

— (2005b), *Annual Survey Report 2005: Reward Management*, CIPD, London.

Chen, C., Steiner, T. & Whyte, A. (2006), 'Does stock option-based executive compensation induce risk-taking? An analysis of the banking industry', *Journal of Banking and Finance*, 30: 915–45.

Cherrington, D. J. (1991), 'Need theories of motivation', in Steers, R. M. & Porter, L. W. (eds), *Motivation and Work Behavior*, 5th edn, McGraw-Hill, New York, pp. 31–43.

Chilton, K. W. (1993), 'Lincoln Electric's incentive system: Can it be transferred overseas?', *Compensation and Benefits Review*, 25(6): 21–30.

— (1994), 'Lincoln Electric's incentive system: A reservoir of trust', *Compensation and Benefits Review*, 26(6): 29–34.

Church, R. A. (1971), 'Profit-sharing and labour relations in England in the nineteenth century', *International Review of Social History*, 16(1): 2–16.

Cin, B., Han, T. & Smith, S. C. (2003) 'A tale of two tigers: Employee financial participation in Korea and Taiwan', *International Journal of Human Resource Management*, 14(6): 920–41.

Cira, D. J. & Benjamin, E. R. (1998), 'Competency-based pay: A concept in evolution', *Compensation and Benefits Review*, 30(5): 21–8.

Clark, R. (1992), *Australian Human Resources Management: Framework and Practice*, 2nd edn, McGraw-Hill, Sydney.

Cole, G. D. H. (1918), *The Payment of Wages: A Study in Payment by Results Under the Wage-System*, Fabian Research Department and George Allen & Unwin, London.

Coleman, V. & Borman, W., 'Investigating the underlying structure of the citizenship performance domain', *Human Resource Management Review*, 10(1): 25–44.

Collins, D. (1996), '15 lessons learned from the death of a gainsharing plan', *Compensation and Benefits Review*, 28(2): 31–40.

Collins, D., Hatcher, L. & Ross, T. (1993), 'The decision to implement gainsharing: The role of work climate, expected outcomes, and union status', *Personnel Psychology*, 46: 77–104.

Colquitt, J. A., Greenberg, J. & Zapata-Phelan, C. P. (2005), 'What is organizational justice? A historical overview', in J. A. Colquitt & J. Greenberg (eds), *Handbook of Organizational Justice*, Lawrence Erlbaum & Associates, Mahwah, NJ, pp. 3–56.

Contu, A. & Willmott, H. (2005), 'You spin me round: The realist turn in organization and management studies', *Journal of Management Studies*, 42(8): 1645–62.

Conway, N. & Briner, R. B. (2005), *Understanding Psychological Contracts at Work: A Critical Evaluation of Theory and Research*, Oxford University Press.

Conyon, M. (2006), 'Executive compensation and incentives', *Academy of Management Perspectives*, 20(1): 25–44.

Conyon, M. & Sadler, G. (2001), 'Executive pay, tournaments and corporate performance in UK firms', *International Journal of Management Reviews*, 3(2): 141–68.

Cook, F. (1994), 'Compensation surveys are biased', *Compensation and Benefits Review*, 26(5): 19–22.

Cooke, W. N. (1994), 'Employee participation programs, group-based incentives and company performance: A union–nonunion comparison', *Industrial and Labor Relations Review*, 47: 594–609.

Cooper, C., Dyck, B. & Frohlich, N. (1992), 'Improving the effectiveness of gainsharing: The role of fairness and participation', *Administrative Science Quarterly*, 37(3): 471–90.

Costello, C. (1996), 'ESOPs: No fable', *Australian Accountant*, 66(4): 70–2.

Cowherd, D. M. & Levine, D. I. (1992), 'Product quality and pay equity between lower-level employees and top management: An investigation of distributive justice theory', *Administrative Science Quarterly*, 37: 302–20.

Coyle-Shapiro, J. (2002), 'A psychological contract perspective on organizational citizenship behavior', *Journal of Organizational Behavior*, 23(8): 927–46.

Creelman, J. (1995), 'Pay and performance drive human resource agendas', *Management Development Review*, 8(3): 6–9.

Cropanzano, R. & Folger, R. (1991), 'Procedural justice and worker motivation', in Steers, R. M. & Porter, L. W. (eds), *Motivation and Work Behavior*, 5th edn, McGraw-Hill, New York, pp. 131–43.

Cropanzano, R. & Prehar, C. (2001), 'Emerging justice concerns in an era of changing psychological contracts', in Cropanzano, R. (ed.), *Justice in the Workplace: From Theory to Practice*, 2nd edn, Lawrence Erlbaum, Mahwah, NJ, pp. 245–70.

Crotty, M. (1998), *The Foundations of Social Research: Meaning and Perspective in the Research Process*, Allen & Unwin, Sydney.

Crystal, G. (1988), 'The wacky, wacky world of CEO pay', *Fortune*, 6 June: 34–40.

— (1991a), *In Search of Excess: The Overcompensation of American Executives*, Norton.

— (1991b), 'Why CEO compensation is so high', *California Management Review*, 34: 9–29.

Cullinane, N. & Dundon, T. (2006), 'The psychological contract: A critical review', *International Journal of Management Reviews*, 8(2): 113–29.

Cumming, C. (1994), 'Incentives that really do motivate', *Compensation and Benefits Review*, 26(3), 38–40.

Cutcher-Gerchenfeld, J. (1991), 'The impact on economic performance of a transformation in labor relations', *Industrial and Labor Relations Review*, 44: 241–60.

Dalton, G. (1998), 'The glass wall: Shattering the myth that alternative rewards won't work with unions', *Compensation and Benefits Review*, 30(6): 38–45.

Davis, J. H. (1995), 'Why rewards undermine performance: An exclusive interview with Alfie Kohn', *WorldatWork Journal*, 4(2): 6–19.

Deci, E. L. (1992), 'The effects of contingent and non-contingent rewards and controls on intrinsic motivation', *Organizational Behavior and Human Performance*, 8: 217–29.

Deci, E. L., Koestner, R. & Ryan, R. M. (1999), 'A meta-analytic review of experiments examining the effects of extrinsic rewards on intrinsic motivation', *Psychological Bulletin*, 125(6): 627–68.

Deci, E. L. & Ryan, R. M. (1985), *Intrinsic Motivation and Self-Determination in Human Behavior*, Plenum Press, New York.

Deckop, J. R., Mangel, R. & Cirka, C. C. (1999), 'Getting more than you pay for: organizational citizenship behavior and pay-for-performance plans', *Academy of Management Journal*, 42(4): 420–9.

Deery, S., Iverson, R. D. & Walsh, J. (2006), 'Toward a better understanding of psychological contract breach: A study of customer service employees', *Journal of Applied Psychology*, 91(1): 166–75.

Delery, J. E. (1998), 'Issues of fit in strategic human resource management: Implications for research', *Human Resource Management Review*, 8: 289–309.

Delery, J. E. & Doty, H. (1996), 'Modes of theorizing in strategic human resource management: Tests of universalistic, contingency, and configurational performance predictions', *Academy of Management Journal*, 39(4): 802–35.

Deming, W. E. (1986), *Out of the Crisis*, Massachusetts Institute of Technology Centre for Advanced Engineering, Cambridge, MA.

DeNisi, A. S. & Peters, L. H. (1996), 'Organization of information in memory and the performance appraisal process: Evidence from the field', *Journal of Applied Psychology*, 81(6): 717–37.

DeNisi, A. S. & Williams, K. J. (1988), 'Cognitive research in performance appraisal', in Rowland, K. & Ferris, G. S. (eds), *Research in Personnel and Human Resource Management*, vol. 6, JAI Press, Greenwich, CT, pp. 109–56.

Dessler, G., Griffiths, J. & Lloyd-Walker, B. (2004), *Human Resource Management*, 2nd edn, Prentice Hall, Sydney.

Devanna, M. A., Fombrun, C. & Tichy, N. (1981), 'Human resource management: A strategic perspective', *Organizational Dynamics*, 9(3): 51–67.

Dewey, B. (1994), 'Changing to skill-based pay: Disarming the transition landmines', *Compensation and Benefits Review*, 26(1): 38–43.

Dickinson, T. L. & Zellinger, P. M. (1980), 'A comparison of the behaviorally anchored rating and mixed standard scale formats', *Journal of Applied Psychology*, 65: 147–54.

Dobbins, G., Cardy, R., Facteau, J. & Miller, J. (1993), 'Implications of situational constraints on performance evaluation and performance management', *Human Resource Management Review*, 3(2): 105–25.

Dolmat-Connell, J. (1999a), 'Changing measures for changing times', in Berger, L. A. & Berger, D. R. (eds), *The Compensation Handbook: A State-of-the-Art Guide to Compensation Strategy and Design*, 4th edn, McGraw-Hill, New York, pp. 467–80.

— (1999b), 'Developing a reward strategy that delivers shareholder and employee value', *Compensation and Benefits Review*, 31(2): 46–53.

Dornstein, M. (1991), *Conceptions of Fair Pay: Theoretical Perspectives and Empirical Research*, Praeger, New York.

Dowling, B. & Richardson, R. (1997), 'Evaluating performance-related pay for managers in the National Health Service', *International Journal of Human Resource Management*, 8(3): 348–66.

Drago, R. & Heywood, J. S. (1995), 'The choice of payment schemes: Australian establishment data', *Industrial Relations*, 34(4): 507–31.

Drenth, P. J. D. (1998), 'Personnel appraisal', in Drenth, P. J. D., Thierry, H. & de Wolff, C. J. (eds), *Handbook of Work and Organizational Psychology*, vol. 2, 'Personnel Psychology', Psychology Press, Hove, East Sussex, pp. 59–87.

Dubois, D. D. & Rothwell, W. J. (2004), *Competency-based Human Resource Management*, Davies-Black Publishing, Palo Alto, CA.

Dunphy, D. & Hackman, B. K. (1988), 'Performance appraisal as a strategic intervention', *Human Resource Management Australia*, 26(2): 23–34.

Edwards, M. & Ewen, A. (1996a), *Providing 360-Degree Feedback: An Approach to Enhancing Individual and Organizational Performance*, American Compensation Association, Scottsdale, AZ.

— (1996b), 'How to manage performance and pay with 360-degree feedback', *Compensation and Benefits Review*, 28(3): 41–6.

Egan, J. (2004), 'Equity incentive plans', unpublished lecture presentation on behalf of Egan Associates, University of Sydney, May 2004.

Ehrich, L. C. & Hansford, B. (1999), 'Mentoring: Pros and cons for HRM', *Asia Pacific Journal of Human Resources*, 37(3): 92–107.

Eisenhardt, K. M. (1989), 'Agency theory: An assessment and review', *Academy of Management Review*, 14(1): 57–74.

Ellig, B. R. (2002), *The Complete Guide to Executive Compensation*, McGraw-Hill, New York.

Emerson, S. M. (1991), 'Job evaluation: A barrier to excellence?', *Compensation and Benefits Review*, 23(1): 38–51.

England, P. & Kilbourne, B. (1991), 'Using job evaluation to achieve pay equity', *International Journal of Public Administration*, 14(5): 823–43.

Enos, M. & Limoges, G. (2000), 'Broadbanding: Is that your company's final answer?', *WorldatWork*, 9(3): 61–8.

EOWA (2006), *Equal Opportunity for Women in the Workplace Survey 2005: Paid Parental Leave*, Equal Opportunity for Women in the Workplace Agency, Australian Government, Canberra.

Erdogan, B. (2002), 'Antecedents and consequences of justice perceptions in performance appraisals', *Human Resource Management Review*, 12(4): 555–76.

Evans, E. et al. (1995), 'A series of essays about how rewards can succeed', *WorldatWork Journal*, 4(2): 20–35.

Fakhfakh, F. & Perotin, V. (2002), 'France: Weitzman under state paternalism', in Brown, M. & Heywood, J. (eds), *Paying for Performance. An International Comparison*, M. E. Sharpe, Armonk, NY, pp. 90–114.

Fein, M. (1999), 'Improshare: Sharing productivity gains with employees', in Berger, L. A. & Berger, D. R., *The Compensation Handbook: A State-of-the-Art Guide to Compensation Strategy and Design*, 4th edn, McGraw-Hill, New York, pp. 158–75.

Fenwick, M. & De Cieri, H. (1995), 'Building an integrated approach to performance management using critical incident technique', *Asia-Pacific Journal of Human Resources*, 33(3): 76–91.

Finkelstein, S. (1992), 'Power in top management teams: Dimensions, measurement, and validation', *Academy of Management Journal*, 35: 505–38.

Finkelstein, S. & Hambrick, D. (1989), 'Chief executive compensation: A study of the intersection of markets and political processes', *Strategic Management Journal*, 10: 121–34.

Fitz-enz, J. (2000), *The ROI of Human Capital: Measuring the Economic Value of Employee Performance*, AMACOM, New York.

Flanagan, J. C. (1954), 'The critical incident technique', *Psychological Bulletin*, 51: 327–58.

Flannery, T., Hofrichter, D. & Platten, P. (1996), *People, Performance and Pay*, Free Press, New York.

Folger, R. & Bies, R. J. (1989), 'Managerial responsibilities and procedural justice', *Employee Responsibilities and Rights Journal*, 2: 79–90.

Folger, R. & Cropanzano, R. (1998), *Organizational Justice and Human Resource Management*, Sage Publications, Thousand Oaks, CA.

Folger, R. & Konovsky, M. A. (1989), 'Effects of procedural and distributive justice in reactions to pay raise decisions', *Academy of Management Journal*, 32: 115–30.

Folger, R., Konovsky, M. A. & Cropanzano, R. (1992), 'A due process metaphor for performance appraisal', in Cummings, L. L. & Staw, B. (eds), *Research in Organizational Behavior*, vol. 14, JAI Press, Greenwich, CT, pp. 129–77.

Fombrun, C., Tichy, N. & Devanna, M. (1984), *Strategic Human Resource Management*, John Wiley & Sons, New York.

Forkosch, M. D. (1958), 'American democracy and procedural due process', *Brooklyn Law Review*, 24: 173–253.

Fox, A. (1974), *Beyond Contract*, Faber & Faber, London.

Fox, S., Ben-Nahum, Z. & Yinon, Y. (1989), 'Perceived similarity and accuracy of peer ratings', *Journal of Applied Psychology*, 73: 239–44.

Freeman, J. (1996), 'Rewarding workers: Why it pays to nurture staff', *The Australian*, 14 September.

Freeman, R. B., Kleiner, M., & Ostroff, C. (2000), *The Anatomy of Employee Involvement and Its Effects on Firms and Workers*, National Bureau of Economic Research, Cambridge, MA.

Fuehrer, V. (1994), 'Total reward strategy: A prescription for organizational survival', *Compensation and Benefits Review*, 26(1): 44–53.

Gaertner, K. N. & Gaertner, G. H. (1985), 'Performance-contingent pay for federal managers', *Administration and Society*, 17 (May), 7–20.

Gantt, H. L. (1913), *Work, Wages and Profits*, Engineering Magazine Co.

Garavan, T. N., Morley, M. & Flynn, M. (1997), '360 degree feedback: Its role in employee development', *Journal of Management Development*, 16(2): 134–47.

Gerhart, B. (2000), 'Compensation strategy and organizational performance', in Rynes, S. L. & Gerhart, B. (eds), *Compensation in Organizations: Current Research and Practice*, Jossey-Bass, San Francisco, pp. 151–94.

Gerhart, B. & Milkovich, G. (1990), 'Organizational differences in managerial compensation and financial performance', *Academy of Management Journal*, 33: 663–90.

— (1992), 'Employee compensation: Research and practice', in Dunnette, M. D. & Hough, L. M. (eds), *Handbook of Industrial and Organizational Psychology*, vol. 3, Consulting Psychologists Press, Palo Alto, CA, pp. 1009–55.

Gerhart, B. & Rynes, S. (2003), *Compensation: Theory, Evidence, and Strategic Implications*, Sage Publications, Thousand Oaks, CA.

Gilbert, D. (1994), 'Broadbands and winning in today's marketplace', *WorldatWork Journal*, 3(1): 48–50.

Gilbert, D. & Abosch, K. (1996), *Improving Organizational Effectiveness Through Broadbanding*, American Compensation Association, Scottsdale, AZ.

Gilliland, S. W. & Langdon, J. C. (1998), 'Creating performance management systems that promote perceptions of fairness', in Smither, J. W. (ed.), *Performance Appraisal: State of the Art in Practice*, Jossey-Bass, San Francisco, pp. 209–43.

Golden, H. J. (2004), 'Corporate governance issues affecting executive compensation', in Chingos, P. T. (ed.), *Responsible Executive Compensation for a New Era of Accountability*, John Wiley & Sons, Hoboken, NJ, pp. 76–96.

Goleman, D. (1995), *Emotional Intelligence*, Bantam Books, New York.

Gomez-Mejia, L. & Wiseman, R. M. (1997), 'Reframing executive compensation: An assessment and outlook', *Journal of Management*, 23: 291–374.

Gordon, J. N. (2005), 'Executive compensation: If there's a problem, what's the remedy? The case for compensation discussion and analysis', *Journal of Corporation Law*, 30(4): 675–702.

Grant, D., O'Donnell, M. & Shields, J. (2003), 'The new performance management paradigm in the Australian Public Service: Discourse, practice, impact', in Duvillier, T., Genard, J.-L & Priaux, A. (ed.), *La Motivation au Travail dans les Services Publics*, L'Marmattan, Paris, pp. 247–59.

Grant, D. & Shields, J. (2006), 'Identifying the subject: Worker identity as discursively contested terrain', in Hearn, M. & Michelson. G. (eds), *Rethinking Work: Time, Space and Discourse*, Cambridge University Press, Melbourne, pp. 285–307.

Greenberg, J. (1986), 'Organizational performance appraisal procedures: What makes them fair?', in Lewicki, R. J., Sheppard, B. H. & Bazerman, M. H. (eds), *Research on Negotiation in Organizations*, vol. 1, JAI Press, Greenwich, CT, pp. 25–41.

— (1987), 'Using diaries to promote procedural justice in performance appraisals', *Social Justice Research*, 1(2): 219–34.

— (1990), 'Organizational justice: Yesterday, today and tomorrow', *Journal of Management*, 16(2): 399–432.

— (1993), 'Justice and organizational citizenship: A commentary on the state of the science', *Employee Responsibilities and Rights Journal*, 6(3): 222–37.

— (1995), *The Quest for Justice on the Job: Essays and Experiments*, Sage Publications, Thousand Oaks, CA.

Greene, R. J. (1993), 'Person-focused pay: Should it replace job-based pay?', *Compensation and Benefits Management*, 9(4): 46–54.

Grint, K. (1995), *Management: A Sociological Introduction*, Polity Press, Cambridge.

Grote, D. (2005), *Forced Ranking: Making Performance Management Work*, Harvard Business School Press, Boston.

Guest, D. (1997), 'Human resource management and performance: A review and research agenda', *International Journal of Human Resource Management*, 8(3): 263–76.

— (1998), 'Is the psychological contract worth taking seriously?', *Journal of Organizational Behavior*, 19(Special issue): 649–64.

— (1999), 'Human resource management – the workers' verdict', *Human Resource Management Journal*, 9(3): 5–25.

— (2001), 'Human resource management: When research confronts theory', *International Journal of Human Resource Management*, 12(7): 1092–106.

— (2002), 'Human resource management, corporate performance and employee wellbeing: Building the worker into HRM', *Journal of Industrial Relations*, 44(3): 335–58.

Guest, D. & Conway, N. (1998), *Fairness at Work and the Psychological Contract*, Institute of Personnel and Development, London.

— (2002), 'Communicating the psychological contract: An employer perspective', *Human Resource Management Journal*, 12(2): 22–38.

Guest, D. E. & Peccei, R. (2001), 'Partnership at work: Mutuality and the balance of advantage', *British Journal of Human Resource Management*, 39(2): 207–36.

Gumbel, A. (2006), 'Managerial power and executive pay', *Oxford Journal of Legal Studies*, 26(1): 219–33.

Gupta, N. (1997), 'Rewarding skills in the public sector', in Risher, H. & Fay, C. (eds), *New Strategies for Public Pay*, Jossey-Bass, San Francisco, pp. 125–44.

Gupta, N. & Jenkins, G. D. (1991), 'Practical problems in using job evaluation systems to determine compensation', *Human Resource Management Review*, 1(2): 133–44.

Gupta, N., Ledford, G., Jenkins, D. & Doty, D. (1992), 'Survey-based prescriptions for skill-based pay', *WorldatWork Journal*, 1(1): 48–59.

Gupta, N. & Mitra, A. (1998), 'The value of financial incentives: Myths and empirical realities', *WorldatWork Journal*, 7(3): 58–66.

Gupta, N. & Shaw, J. (1998), 'Let the evidence speak: Financial incentives are effective!!', *Compensation and Benefits Review*, 30(2): 26, 28–32.

Hackman, J. R. & Oldham, G. R. (1976), 'Motivation through the design of work: Test of a theory', *Organizational Behavior and Human Performance*, 16: 250–79.

Hall, B. J. & Liebman, J. B. (1998), 'Are CEOs really paid like bureaucrats?', *Quarterly Journal of Economics*, 111(3): 653–91.

Halsey, F. A. (1896), 'The premium plan for paying for labour', *Economic Studies*, 1(2): 51–73.

Hammer, M. & Champy, J. (1993), *Reengineering the Corporation: A Manifesto for Business Revolution*, Harper Business Books, New York.

Hammer, T. (1991), 'Gainsharing', in Steers, R. M. & Porter, L. W. (eds), *Motivation and Work Behavior*, 5th edn, McGraw-Hill, New York, pp. 531–43.

Handlin, H. C. (1992), 'The company built upon the golden rule: Lincoln Electric', in Hopkins, B. & Mawhinney, T. (eds), *Pay for Performance: History, Controversy, and*

*Evidence*, Hawthorne Press, New York, pp. 151–64 (special issue of the *Journal of Organizational Behaviour Management*, 12(1)).

Harley, B. & Hardy, C. (2004), 'Firing blanks? An analysis of discursive struggle in HRM', *Journal of Management Studies*, 41(3): 377–400.

Harris, M. M. & Schaubroeck, J. (1988), 'A meta-analysis of self-supervisor, self-peer, and peer-supervisor ratings', *Personnel Psychology*, 41(1): 43–62.

Haslett, S. (1995), 'Broadbanding: A strategic tool for organisational change', *Compensation and Benefits Review*, 27(6): 40–6.

Hastings, D. F. (1999), 'Lincoln Electric's harsh lessons from international expansion', *Harvard Business Review*, 77(3): 162–80.

Hastings, S. (2000), 'Grading systems and estimating value', in White, G. & Drucker, J. (eds) (2000), *Reward Management: A Critical Text*, Routledge, London, pp. 84–105.

Hatcher, L. & Ross, T. L. (1991), 'From individual incentives to organization-wide gainsharing plan: Effects on teamwork and product quality', *Journal of Organizational Behavior*, 12(3): 169–83.

Hattrup, K., O'Connell, M. S. & Wingate, P. H. (1998), 'Prediction of multidimensional criteria: Distinguishing task and contextual performance', *Human Performance*, 11(4): 305–19.

Hay, D. (1998), *Maximising the Impact of Recognition: An Approach to Rewarding Employee Contributions*, American Compensation Association, Scottsdale, AZ.

Heery, E. (1996), 'Risk, representation and the "new pay" ', *Personnel Review*, 25(6): 54–65.

— (1997a), 'Performance-related pay and trade union de-recognition', *Employee Relations*, 19(3): 208–21.

— (1997b), 'Performance-related pay and trade union membership', *Employee Relations*, 19(5): 430–42.

Heider, F. (1958), *The Psychology of Interpersonal Relations*, John Wiley & Sons, New York.

Heneman, H. G. & Judge, T. A. (2000), 'Compensation attitudes', in Rynes, S. L. & Gerhart, B. (eds), *Compensation in Organizations: Current Research and Practice*, Jossey-Bass, San Francisco, pp. 61–103.

Heneman, R. (1990), 'Merit pay research', *Research in Personnel and Human Resources Management*, 8: 203–63.

— (1992), *Merit Pay: Linking Pay Increases to Performance Ratings*, Addison Wesley, Reading, MA.

Heneman, R. L., Fisher, M. M. & Dixon, K. E. (2001), 'Reward and organizational systems alignment: An expert system', *Compensation and Benefits Review*, 33(6): 18–29.

Heneman, R. L. & LeBlanc, P. (2002), 'Developing a more relevant and competitive approach for valuing knowledge work', *Compensation and Benefits Review*, 34(4): 43–7.

— (2003), 'Work valuation addresses shortcomings of both job evaluation and market pricing', *Compensation and Benefits Review*, 35(1): 7–11.

Heneman, R. L., Ledford, G. E. & Gresham, M. T. (2000), 'The changing nature of work and its effects on compensation design and delivery', in Rynes, S. L. & Gerhart, B. (eds), *Compensation in Organizations: Current Research and Practice*, Jossey-Bass, San Francisco, pp. 195–240.

Heneman, R. L. & Von Hipple, C. (1995), 'Balancing group and individual rewards: Rewarding individual contributions to the team', *Compensation and Benefits Review*, 27(4): 63–8.

Herriot, P., Manning, W. E. G. & Kidd, J. M. (1997), 'The content of the psychological contract', *British Journal of Management*, 8: 151–62.

Herzberg, F. (1966), *Work and the Nature of Man*, Staples Press, New York.

— (1987), 'One more time: How do you motivate employees?', *Harvard Business Review*, 65(5): 109–20 (first published 1967).

Heywood, J. S., Hubler, O. & Jirjahn, U. (1998), 'Variable payment schemes and industrial relations: Evidence from Germany', *Kyklos* 51: 237–57.

Hilling, F. (2003), 'Job evaluation is here to stay', *WorldatWork Journal*, 12(3): 14–21.

Hiltrop, J. M. (1996), 'The impact of human resource management on organisational performance: Theory and research', *European Management Journal*, 14(6): 628–37.

Ho, V. T. (2005), 'Social influence on evaluations of psychological contract fulfillment', *Academy of Management Review*, 30(1): 113–29.

Hodgetts, R. M. (1997), 'Discussing incentive compensation with Donald Hastings of Lincoln Electric', *Compensation and Benefits Review*, 29(5): 60–6.

Hofrichter, D. (1993), 'Broadbanding: A second generation approach', *Compensation and Benefits Review*, 25(5): 53–8.

Hofrichter, D. & McGovern, T. (2001), 'People, competencies and performance: Clarifying means and ends', *Compensation and Benefits Review*, 33(4): 34–8.

Hofrichter, D. & Spencer, L. (1996), 'Competencies: The right foundation for effective human resources management', *Compensation and Benefits Review*, 28(6): 21–6.

Hofstede, G. (1984), *Culture's Consequences*, Sage, London.

Hogan, J., Rybicki, S. L., Motowidlo, S. J. & Borman, W. (1998), 'Relations between contextual performance, personality, and occupational advancement', *Human Performance*, 11(2/3): 189–207.

Holmes, R. W. (1980–81), 'Job evaluation: Theory and practice', Parts 1 & 2, *Human Resource Management Australia*, 18(4): 42–9 & 19(1): 45–52.

Homans, G. C. (1961), *Social Behavior: Its Elementary Forms*, Harcourt, Brace & World, New York.

Houldsworth, E. & Jirasinghe, D. 2006, *Managing and Measuring Employee Performance*, Kogan Page, London.

House of Representatives Standing Committee on Employment, Education and Workplace Relations (2000), *Shared Endeavours: Inquiry into Employee Share Ownership in Australian Enterprises*, Parliament of the Commonwealth of Australia, Canberra.

Hurtz, G. M. & Donovan, J. J. (2000), 'Personality and job performance: The big five revisited', *Journal of Applied Psychology*, 85: 869–79.

Huselid, M. A. (1995), 'The impact of human resource management practices on turnover, productivity, and corporate financial performance', *Academy of Management Journal*, 38: 635–72.

Huselid, M. A. & Becker, B. (1995), *The Strategic Impact of High Performance Work Systems*, Working Paper, School of Management and Labor Relations, Rutgers University, NJ.

— (1996), 'Methodological issues in cross-sectional and panel estimates of the human resource-performance link', *Industrial Relations*, 35: 400–22.

Huselid, M. A., Becker, B. & Ulrich, D. (2001), *The HR Scorecard: Linking People, Strategy and Performance*, Harvard Business School Press, Boston.

Hyman, R. & Brough, T., 1975, *Values and Industrial Relations: A Study in Fairness and Equity*, Blackwell, Oxford.

Ichniowski, C., Shaw, K. & Prennushi, G. (1997), 'The effects of human resource management practices on productivity: A study of steel finishing lines', *American Economic Review*, 87(3): 291–313.

Iverson, R. D. & Buttigieg, D. (1999), 'Affective, normative and continuance commitment: Can the "right kind" of commitment be managed?', *Journal of Management Studies*, 36(3): 307–33.

Jackson, S. E. & Schuler, R. S. (1995), 'Understanding human resource management in the context of organizations and their environments', *Annual Review of Psychology*, 46: 237–64.

568    References

Jackson, S. E., Schuler, R. S. & Rivero, J. C. (1989), 'Organization characteristics as predictors of personnel practices', *Personnel Psychology*, 42: 727–86.
Janssens, M. & Steyaert, C. (1999), 'The inhuman space of HRM', *Organization*, 6(2): 371–83.
Jenkins, G. D., Ledford, G. E., Gupta, N. & Doty, H. (1992), *Skill-Based Pay: Practices, Payoffs, Pitfalls and Prescriptions*, American Compensation Association, Scottsdale, AZ.
Jensen, M. & Meckling, W. H. (1976), 'Theory of the firm: Managerial behavior, agency costs, and ownership structures', *Journal of Financial Economics*, 3: 305–60.
Jensen, M. & Murphy, K. (1990), 'Performance pay and top-management incentives', *Journal of Political Economy*, 98(2): 225–64.
Jensen, M., Murphy, K. J. & Wruck, E. (2004), 'Remuneration: Where we've been, how we got here, what are the problems, and how to fix them', European Corporate Governance Institute, Finance Working Paper No. 44/2004, www.ecgi.org/wp.
Johnson, A. (1999), 'Should options reward absolute or relative shareholder returns?', *Compensation and Benefits Review*, 31(1): 38–43.
Jones, E. E. & Harris, V. A. (1967), 'The attribution of attitudes', *Journal of Experimental Social Psychology*, 3: 1–24.
Kahn, L. M. & Sherer, P. D. (1990), 'Contingent pay and managerial performance', *Industrial and Labor Relations Review*, 43: 107S–20S.
Kampa-Kokesch, S. & Anderson, M. Z. (2001), 'Executive coaching: A comprehensive review of the literature', *Consulting Psychology Journal: Practice and Research*, 53(4): 205–28.
Kanfer, R. (1998), 'Motivation', in Nicholson, N. (ed.), *Blackwell Encyclopaedic Dictionary of Organizational Behavior*, Blackwell, Oxford, pp. 330–6.
Kao, T. & Kantor, R. (2004), 'Total rewards: From clarity to action', *WorldatWork Journal*, 13(4): 32–40.
Kaplan, R. S. & Norton, D. P. (1992), 'The balanced scorecard – measures that drive performance', *Harvard Business Review*, 69(1): 71–9.
— (1996a), *The Balanced Scorecard: Translating Strategy into Action*, Harvard Business School Press, Boston.
— (1996b), 'Using the balanced scorecard as a strategic management system', *Harvard Business Review*, 73(1), 75–85.
Kates, C. & Tuttle, T. J. (1996), 'A labor perspective on fair pay: High performance work at Corning Inc.', *Employee Responsibilities and Rights Journal*, 9(1): 73–83.
Kaufman, R. T. (1992), 'The effects of improshare on productivity', *Industrial and Labor Relations Review*, 45: 311–22.
Kay, I. (1999), 'Growing shareholder value: Why executive stock ownership works', *Compensation and Benefits Review*, 31(1): 32–7.
Keenoy, T. (1990a), 'HRM: A case of the wolf in sheep's clothing?', *Personnel Review*, 19(2): 3–9.
— (1990b), 'HRM: Rhetoric, reality and contradiction', *International Journal of Human Resource Management*, 1(3): 363–84.
Keenoy, T. & Anthony, P. (1992), 'HRM: Metaphor, meaning and morality', in Blyton, P. & Turnbull, P. (eds), *Reassessing Human Resource Management*, Sage Publications, London, pp. 233–52.
Kessler, I. (1994), 'Performance pay', in Sisson, K. (ed.), *Personnel Management*, 2nd edn, Blackwell, Oxford, pp. 465–94.
Kessler, I. & Purcell, J. (1995), 'Individualism and collectivism in theory and practice: Management style and the design of pay systems', in Edwards, P. (ed.), *Industrial Relations*, Blackwell, Oxford, pp. 337–67.
Kidder, D. L. & Buchholtz, A. K. (2002), 'Can excess bring success? CEO compensation and the psychological contract', *Human Resource Management Review*, 12: 599–617.
Kilburg, R. R. (1996), 'Toward a conceptual understanding and definition of executive coaching', *Consulting Psychology Journal: Practice and Research*, 48(2): 134–44.

Kim, D.-O. & Voos, P. (1997), 'Unionization, union involvement, and the performance of gainsharing programs', *Industrial Relations(Relations Industrielles)*, 52(2): 304–32.

Kim, S. (1998), 'Does profit sharing increase firms' profits?', *Journal of Labor Research*, 19: 351–70.

Klaas, B. (2002), 'Compensation in the jobless organisation', *Human Resource Management Review*, 12: 43–61.

Klein, A. L. (1996), 'Validity and reliability for competency-based systems', *Compensation and Benefits Review*, 28(4): 31–7.

Klein, K. (1987), 'Employee stock ownership and employee attitudes: A test of three models', *Journal of Applied Psychology*, 72(2): 319–32.

Klinger, S., Hartman, C., Anderson, S., Cavanagh, J. & Sklar, H. (2002), 'Executive excess 2002: Ninth annual CEO compensation survey', Institute for Policy Studies and United for a Fair Economy, Boston, www.faireconomy.org.

Kochan, T., McKersie, R., & Cappelli, P. (1984), 'Strategic choice and industrial relations theory', *Industrial Relations*, 23(1): 16–39.

Kochan, T. & Osterman, P. (1995), *The Mutual Gains Enterprise*, Harvard University Press, Cambridge, MA.

Kochanski, J. & Risher, H. (1999), 'Paying for competencies: Rewarding knowledge, skills and behaviors', in Risher, H. (ed.), *Aligning Pay and Results: Compensation Strategies that Work from the Boardroom to the Shop Floor*, AMACOM, New York, pp. 145–71.

Kohn, A. (1993a), *Punished by Rewards*, Houghton Mifflin, Boston.

— (1993b), 'Why incentive plans cannot work', *Harvard Business Review*, 71(5): 54–63.

— (1998), 'Challenging behaviorist dogma: Myths about money and motivation', *Compensation and Benefits Review*, 30(2): 27 & 33–7.

Konovsky, M. A. (2000), 'Understanding procedural justice and its impact on business organisations', *Journal of Management*, 26(3): 489–511.

Konovsky, M. A. & Organ, D. W. (1996), 'Dispositional and contextual determinants of organizational citizenship behavior', *Journal of Organizational Behavior*, 17(3): 253–66.

Kozlowski, S. W. J., Chao, G. T. & Morrison, R. F. (1998), 'Games raters play: Politics, strategies, and impression management in performance appraisal', in Smither, J. W. (ed.), *Performance Appraisal: State of the Art in Practice*, Jossey-Bass, San Francisco, pp. 163–208.

Kramer, R. M. (1999), 'Trust and distrust in organisations: Emerging perspectives, enduring questions', *Annual Review of Psychology*, 50: 569–98.

Kruse, D. (1991), 'Profit sharing and employment variability: Microeconomic evidence on the Weitzman theory', *Industrial and Labor Relations Review*, 44: 437–53.

— (1993), *Profit Sharing: Does it Make a Difference?*, Upjohn Institute, Kalamazoo, MI.

Lander, D. & O'Neill, G. (1991), 'Pay equity: Apples, oranges and a can of worms', *Asia Pacific Human Resource Management*, Autumn: 16–28.

Landy, F. S. & Farr, J. L. (1983), *The Measurement of Work Performance: Methods, Theory, and Applications*, Academic Press, Orlando, FL.

Lansbury, R., Braithwaite, J. & Westbrook, J. (1995), 'Goal-directed approaches to performance appraisal', in O'Neill, G. & Kramar, R. (eds), *Australian Human Resource Management*, Pitman Publishers, Melbourne, Vic, pp. 145–54.

Latham, G. P. & Locke, E. A. (2006), 'Enhancing the benefits and overcoming the pitfalls of goal setting', *Organizational Dynamics*, 35(4): 332–40.

Latham, G. P. & Pinder, C. C. (2005), 'Work motivation theory and research at the dawn of the twenty-first century', *Annual Review of Psychology*, 56: 485–516.

Latham, G. P. & Wexley, K. N. (1977), 'Behavioral observation scales', *Personnel Psychology*, 30: 255–68.

— (1994), *Increasing Productivity Through Performance Appraisal*, 2nd edn, Addison-Wesley, Reading, MA.

Lawler, E. E. (1971), *Pay and Organizational Effectiveness*, McGraw-Hill, New York.
— (1986), *High Involvement Management*, Jossey-Bass, San Francisco.
— (1988), 'What's wrong with point-factor job evaluation', *Compensation and Benefits Review*, 18(2): 20–8.
— (1990), *Strategic Pay: Aligning Organizational Strategies and Pay Systems*, Jossey-Bass, San Francisco.
— (1991), 'Paying the person: A better approach to management?', *Human Resource Management Review*, 1(2): 145–54.
— (1992), *The Ultimate Advantage: Creating the High Involvement Organization*, Jossey-Bass, San Francisco.
— (1994a), 'From job-based to competency-based organisations', *Journal of Organizational Behaviour*, 15: 3–15.
— (1994b; first published 1973), *Motivation in Work Organizations*, Jossey-Bass, San Francisco.
— (1994c), 'Performance management: The next generation', *Compensation and Benefits Review*, 26(3): 16–28.
— (1996), 'Competencies: A poor foundation for the new pay', *Compensation and Benefits Review*, 28(6): 20–6.
— (2000), *Rewarding Excellence: Pay Strategies for the New Economy*, Jossey-Bass, San Francisco.
— (2002), 'The folly of forced ranking', *Strategy and Business*, 28: 28–33.
— (2003), 'Reward practices and performance management system effectiveness', *Organizational Dynamics*, 32(4): 396–404.
— (2005), 'Creating high performance organizations', *Asia Pacific Journal of Human Resources*, 43(1): 10–17.
Lawler, E. E. & Cohen, S. G. (1992), 'Designing pay systems for teams', *WorldatWork Journal*, 1(1): 6–19.
Lawler, E. E. & Ledford, G. E. (1985), 'Skill-based pay: A concept that's catching on', *Personnel* 62(9): 30–7.
Lawler, E. E., Ledford, G. E. & Chang, L. (1993), 'Who uses skill-based pay, and why?', *Compensation and Benefits Review*, 25(2): 22–6.
Lawler, E. E. & Mohrman, S. A. (1989), 'High-involvement management', *Personnel*, 66(4): 27–31.
Lawler, E. E., Mohrman, S. A. & Ledford, G. E. (1992), *Employee Involvement and Total Quality Management: Practices and Results in Fortune 1000 Companies*, Jossey-Bass, San Francisco.
Lazear, E., & Rosen, S. (1981), 'Rank order tournaments as optimum labour contracts', *Journal of Political Economy*, 89: 841–64.
LeBlanc, P. V. (1991), 'Skill-based pay case study number 2: Northern Telecom', *Compensation and Benefits Review*, 23(2): 39–56.
LeBlanc, P. V. & Ellis, C. (1995), 'A testimonial from eight organizations: The many faces of banding', *WorldatWork Journal*, 4(4): 52–63.
LeBlanc, P. V. & Mulvey, P. W. (1998), 'How American workers see the rewards of work', *Compensation and Benefits Review*, 30(1): 24–8.
Ledford, G. E. (1991a), 'Three case studies on skill-based pay: An overview', *Compensation and Benefits Review*, 23(2): 11–23.
— (1991b), 'The design of skill-based pay plans', in Rock, M. & Berger, L. (eds), *The Compensation Handbook: A State of the Art Guide to Compensation Strategy and Design*, 3rd edn, McGraw-Hill, New York, pp. 199–217.
Ledford, G. E. & Bergel, G. (1991), 'Skill-based pay case number 1: General Mills', *Compensation and Benefits Review*, 23(2): 24–38.

Ledford, G. E., Tyler, W. R. & Dixey, W. B. (1991), 'Skill-based pay case number 3: Honeywell Ammunition Assembly Plant', *Compensation and Benefits Review*, 23(2): 57–77.

Lee, J., Havighurst, L. & Rassel, G. (2004), 'Factors related to court references to performance appraisal fairness and validity', *Public Personnel Management*, 33(1): 61–77.

Legge, K. (1995a), *Human Resource Management: Rhetorics and Realities*, Macmillan, London.

— (1995b), 'HRM: Rhetoric, reality and hidden agendas', in Storey, J. (ed.), *Human Resource Management: A Critical Text*, Routledge, London, pp. 33–59.

Lengnick-Hall, M. L. & Bereman, N. A. (1994), 'A conceptual framework for the study of employee benefits', *Human Resource Management Review*, 4(2): 101–15.

Lenne, J., Mitchell, R. & Ramsay, I. (2005), 'Employee share ownership schemes in Australia: A survey of key issues and themes', Centre for Corporate Law and Securities Regulation & Centre for Employment and Labour Relations Law, University of Melbourne.

Lesieur, F. G. (ed.) (1958), *The Scanlon Plan: A Frontier in Labor–Management Cooperation*, Technology Press of Massachusetts Institute of Technology, Cambridge, MA.

Levenson, R. A., Van der Stede, A. W. & Cohen, G. S. (2006), 'Measuring the relationship between managerial competencies and performance', *Journal of Management*, 32(3): 360–80.

Leventhal, G. S., Karuza, J. & Fry, W. R. (1980), 'Beyond fairness: A theory of allocation preferences', in G. Mikula (ed.), *Justice and Social Interaction*, Springer-Verlag, New York, pp. 167–218.

Levinson, H. (1970), 'Management by whose objectives?', *Harvard Business Review*, July–August: 125–34.

Levinthal, D. 1988, 'A survey of agency models of organizations', *Journal of Economic Behavior and Organizations*, 9: 153–85.

Lichty, D. T. (1999), 'Compensation surveys', in Berger, L. A. & Berger, D. R., *The Compensation Handbook: A State-of-the-Art Guide to Compensation Strategy and Design*, 4th edn, McGraw-Hill, New York, pp. 87–103.

Lilling, M. S. (2006), 'The link between CEO compensation and firm performance: Does simultaneity matter?', *Atlantic Economic Journal*, 34: 101–14.

Littler, C. (1982), *The Development of the Labour Process in Capitalist Societies*, Heinemann, London.

Locke, E. A. & Henne, D. (1986), 'Work motivation theories', in Cooper, C. L. & Robertson, I. T. (eds), *International Review of Industrial and Organizational Psychology: 1986*, John Wiley & Sons, New York, pp. 1–35.

Locke, E. A. & Latham, G. P. (1984), *Goal Setting: A Motivational Technique That Works!* Prentice Hall, Englewood Cliffs, NJ.

— (1990), *A Theory of Goal-Setting and Task Performance*, Prentice Hall, Englewood Cliffs, NJ.

— (2002), 'Building a practically useful theory of goal setting and task motivation: A 35-year odyssey', *American Psychologist*, 57: 705–17.

Long, J. (1997), 'The dark side of mentoring', *Australian Educational Research*, 24(2): 115–83.

Long, R. (1978), 'The effects of employee ownership on organisational identification, employee job attitudes, and organisational performance: A tentative framework and empirical findings', *Human Relations*, 31(1): 29–48.

— (1981), 'The effects of formal employee participation in ownership and decision making on perceived and desired patterns of organizational influence: A longitudinal study', *Human Relations*, 34(10): 847–76.

— (1982), 'Worker ownership and job attitudes: A field study', *Industrial Relations*, 21(2): 196–215.

— (1989), 'Patterns of workplace innovation in Canada', *Relations Industrielles* (*Industrial Relations*), 44: 805–26.

— (1994), 'Gain sharing, hierarchy, and managers: Are they substitutes?', *Proceeding of the Administrative Sciences Association of Canada (Organization Theory Division)*, 15: 51–60.

— (1997), 'Motives for profit sharing: Study of Canadian chief executive officers', *Relations Industrielles*, 52(4): 712–33.

— (2006), *Strategic Compensation in Canada*, 3rd edn, Thomson Nelson, Scarborough, Ont.

Long, R. & Shields, J. (2005a), 'Best practice or best fit? High involvement management and base pay practices in Canadian and Australian firms', *Asia Pacific Journal of Human Resources*, 43(1): 52–75.

— (2005b), 'High involvement management and performance pay in Canadian and Australian firms', *International Journal of Human Resource Management*, 16(1): 1783–811.

Longenecker, C., Sims, H, & Gioia, D. (1987), 'Behind the mask: The politics of employee appraisal', *Academy of Management Executive*, 1(3): 183–93.

Lowe, K. B., Milliman, J., De Cieri, H., & Dowling, P. J. (2002), 'International compensation practices: A ten-country comparative analysis', *Asia Pacific Journal of Human Resources*, 40(1): 55–80.

Lowery, C., Beadles, N. A., Petty, M. M., Amsler, G. M. & Thompson, J. W. (2002), 'An empirical examination of a merit bonus plan', *Journal of Management Issues*, 14(1): 100–17.

Lowry, J. & Dignam, A. (2006), *Company Law*, 3rd edn, Oxford University Press, Oxford.

Lucia, A. D. & Lepsinger. R. (1999), *The Art and Science of Competency Models: Pinpointing the Critical Success Factors in Organizations*, Jossey-Bass/Pfeiffer, San Francisco.

McAdams, J. L. (1991), 'Nonmonetary awards', in Rock, M. & Berger, L. (eds), *The Compensation Handbook: A State of the Art Guide to Compensation Strategy and Design*, 3rd edn, McGraw-Hill, New York, pp. 218–35.

— (1995), 'Rewarding special performance: Low-cost, high-impact awards', in Risher, H. & Fay, C. (eds), *The Performance Imperative: Strategies for Enhancing Workforce Effectiveness*, Jossey-Bass, San Francisco, pp. 361–88.

— (1996), *The Reward Plan Advantage: A Manager's Guide to Improving Business Performance Through People*, Jossey-Bass, San Francisco.

— (1999), 'Nonmonetary rewards: Cash equivalents and tangible awards', in Berger, L. A. & Berger, D. R. *The Compensation Handbook: A State-of-the-Art Guide to Compensation Strategy and Design*, 4th edn, McGraw-Hill, New York, pp. 241–60.

— (2000), 'The essential role of rewarding teams and teamwork', *Compensation and Benefits Management*, 16(4): 15–27.

McClelland, D. C. (1961), *The Achieving Society*, Van Nostrand, Princeton, NJ.

— (1973), 'Testing for competence rather than for "intelligence" ', *American Psychologist*, 28(1): 1–14.

McClelland, D. C. & Burnham, D. H. (1976), 'Power is the great motivator', *Harvard Business Review*, 54(2): 100–10.

MacDuffie, J. P. (1995), 'Human resource bundles and manufacturing performance: Organizational logic and flexible production systems in the world auto industry', *Industrial and Labor Relations Review*, 48(2): 197–221.

McGregor, D. (1960), *The Human Side of the Enterprise*, McGraw-Hill, New York.

Manas, T. (1999), 'Making the balanced scorecard approach pay off', *WorldatWork Journal*, 8(2): 12–21.

Manas, T. M. & Graham, M. D. (2003), *Creating a Total Rewards Strategy: A Toolkit for Designing Business-Based Plans*, AMACOM, New York.

Marchington, M. & Grugulis, I. (2000), ' "Best practice" human resource management: Perfect opportunity or dangerous illusion?', *International Journal of Human Resource Management*, 11(6): 1104–124.

Marquardt, E. (1997), 'Aligning strategy and performance with the balanced scorecard: An interview with David P. Norton', *WorldatWork Journal*, 6(3): 18–27.

Marriott, R. (1957), *Incentive Payment Systems*, Staples Press, London.

Marsden, D. (2004), 'The role of performance-related pay in renegotiating the "effort bargain": The case of the British Public Service', *Industrial and Labor Relations Review*, 57(3): 350–70.

Marsden, D. & Richardson, R. (1994), 'Performing for pay? The effects of "merit pay" on motivation in a public service', *British Journal of Industrial Relations*, 32(2): 243–61.

Marshall, V. & Wood, R. E. (2000), 'The dynamics of effective performance appraisal: An integrated model', *Asia-Pacific Journal of Human Resources*, 38(3): 62–90.

Martin, J. (1981), 'Relative deprivation: A theory of distributive injustice for an era of shrinking resources', in L. L. Cummins & B. M. Staw (eds), *Research in Organizational Behavior*, JAI Press, Greenwich, CT, pp. 53–107.

— (1982), 'The fairness of earning differentials: An experimental study of the perceptions of blue-collar workers', *Journal of Human Resources*, 17: 110–22.

Martocchio, J. J. (2006), *Strategic Compensation: A Human Resource Management Approach*, 3rd edn, Prentice Hall, Upper Saddle River, NJ.

Maslow, A. H. (1943), 'A theory of human motivation', *Psychological Review*, July: 370–96.

Mercer Human Resource Consulting (2004), *Australian Benefits Review*, Mercer, Sydney.

Merhebi, R., Swan, P. L. & Zhou, X. (2006), 'Australian CEO remuneration: Pay and performance', *Journal of Accounting and Economics*, 46(3): 481–97.

Meyer, H. H. (1980), 'Self-appraisal of job performance', *Personnel Psychology*, 33: 291–5.

Meyer, J. & Allen, N. J. (1991), 'A three-component conceptualization of organizational commitment', *Human Resource Management Review*, (1)1: 61–89.

Meyer, J. & Herscovitch, L. (2001), 'Commitment in the workplace: Towards a general model', *Human Resource Management Review*, 11(3): 299–326.

Meyer, J., Stanley, D., Herscovich, L. & Topolnytsky, L. (2002), 'Affective, continuance, and normative commitment to the organization: A meta-analysis of antecedents, correlates, and consequences', *Journal of Vocational Behavior*, 61: 20–52.

Meyer, J. & Topolnytsky, L. (2000), 'Building and maintaining employee commitment: Implications for HRM policy and practice', in Travaglione, A. & Marshall, V. (eds), *Human Resource Strategies: An Applied Approach*, Irwin/McGraw-Hill, Sydney, pp. 335–73.

Miles, R. E. & Snow, C. C. (1978), *Organizational Strategy, Structure, and Process*, McGraw-Hill, New York.

— (1984), 'Designing strategic human resource systems', *Organizational Dynamics*, 13(1): 36–52.

Mishra, C. S., McConaughy, D. L. & Gobeli, D. H. (2000), 'Effectiveness of CEO pay-for-performance', *Review of Financial Economics*, 9(1): 1–13.

Mitchell, D. J. B., Lewin, D. & Lawler, E. E. (1990), 'Alternative pay systems, firm performance and productivity', in Blinder, A. S. (ed.), *Paying for Productivity: A Look at the Evidence*, Brookings Institution, Washington DC, pp. 15–95.

Mitra, A., Gupta, N. & Jenkins, G. (1995), 'The case of the invisible merit rise: How people see their pay rises', *Compensation and Benefits Review*, 27(3): 71–6.

— (1997), 'A drop in the bucket: When is a pay raise a pay raise?', *Journal of Organizational Behavior*, 18(2): 117–37.

Mohrman, A. M. & Mohrman, S. A. (1995), 'Performance management is "running the business"', *Compensation and Benefits Review*, 27(3): 69–75.

Mone, E. M. & London, M. (2002), *Fundamentals of Performance Management*, Spiro Press, London.

Montemayor, E. (1994), 'A model for aligning teamwork and pay', *WorldatWork Journal*, 3(2): 18–25.

Mooraj, S., Oyon, D. & Hostettler, D. (1999), 'The balanced scorecard: A necessary good or an unnecessary evil?', *European Management Journal*, 17(5): 481–91.

Moorman, R. H., Niehoff, B. P. & Organ, D. W. (1993), 'Treating employees fairly and organizational citizenship behavior: Sorting the effects of job satisfaction, organizational commitment, and procedural justice', *Employee Responsibilities and Rights Journal*, 6(3): 209–25.

Morehead, A., Steele, M., Alexander, M., Stephen, K. & Duffin, L. (1997), *Changes at Work: The 1995 Australian Workplace Industrial Relations Survey*, Longman, Melbourne.

Morrison, E. W. & Robinson, S. L. (1997), 'When employees feel betrayed: A model of how psychological contract violation develops', *Academy of Management Review*, 22(1): 226–56.

Mount, M. K. & Barrick, M. R. (1998), 'Five reasons why the "big five" article has been frequently cited', *Personnel Psychology*, 51: 849–57.

Mowday, R. T. (1991), 'Equity theory predictions of behavior in organizations', in Steers R. M. & Porter, L. W. (eds), *Motivation and Work Behavior*, 5th edn, McGraw-Hill, New York, pp. 111–30.

Murphy, K. J. (2002), 'Explaining executive compensation: Managerial power versus the perceived cost of stock options', *University of Chicago Law Review*, 69: 847–69.

Murphy, K. R. & Cleveland, J. N. (1995), *Understanding Performance Appraisal: Social, Organizational and Goal-Based Perspectives*, Sage Publications, Thousand Oaks, CA.

Murphy, K. R. & Constans, J. I. (1987), 'Behavioral anchors as a source of bias in rating', *Journal of Applied Psychology*, 72(4): 573–7.

Murphy, K. R., Jako, R. A., & Anhalt, R. L. (1993), 'The nature and consequences of halo error: A critical analysis', *Journal of Applied Psychology*, 78(2): 218–25.

Murphy, K. R., Martin, C. & Garcia, M. (1982), 'Do behavioral observation scales measure observation?', *Journal of Applied Psychology*, 67(5): 562–7.

Murray, B. & Gerhart, B. (2000), 'Skill-based pay and skill seeking', *Human Resource Management Review*, 10(3): 271–87.

Murray, M. & Owen, M. A. (1991), *Beyond the Myths and Magic of Mentoring: How to Facilitate an Effective Mentoring Programme*, Jossey-Bass, San Francisco.

Nankervis, A. & Compton, R. (2006), 'Performance management: Theory in practice?', *Asia Pacific Journal of Human Resources*, 44(1): 83–101.

Nankervis, A. & Leece, P. (1997), 'Performance appraisal: Two steps forward, one step back?', *Asia Pacific Journal of Human Resources*, 35(2): 80–92.

Neal, A., & Griffin, M. A. (1999), 'Developing a model of individual performance for human resource management', *Asia Pacific Journal of Human Resources*, 37(3): 44–59.

Nelson, B. (1994), *1001 Ways to Reward Employees*, Workman Publishing, New York.

—— (1996), 'Dump the cash, load on the praise', *Personnel Journal*, July: 65–70.

—— (1997), 'Does one reward fit all?', *Workforce*, 76(2): 67–70.

Neubauer, R. (1995), 'Broadbanding: Management fad or savior?', *Compensation and Benefits Management*, 11(4): 50–4.

Neuhold, K. & Hay Group (2005), 'Trends in executive remuneration', paper presented at Informa Conference on Executive Remuneration, Sydney, 15 March.

Noon, M. (1992), 'HRM: A map, model or theory?', in Blyton, P. & Turnbull, P. (eds), *Reassessing Human Resource Management*, Sage Publications, London, pp. 16–32.

Norreklit, H. (2000), 'The balance on the balanced scorecard: A critical analysis of some of its assumptions', *Management Accounting Research*, 11: 65–88.

O'Byrne, S. E. & Young, S. D. (2006), 'Why executive pay is failing', *Harvard Business Review*, 84(6): 28.

O'Donnell, M. (1998), 'Creating a performance culture? Performance-based pay in the Australian Public Service', *Australian Journal of Public Administration*, 57(3): 28–40.

O'Donnell, M. & O'Brien, J. (2000), 'Performance-based pay in the Australian Public Service: Employee perspectives', *Review of Public Personnel Administration*, 20(2): 20–34.

O'Donnell, M. & Shields, J. (2002a), 'The new pay: Performance-related pay in Australia', in Teicher, J., Holland, P. & Gough, R. (eds), *Employee Relations Management: Australia in a Global Context*, Prentice Hall, Sydney, pp. 406–34.

— (2002b), 'Performance management and the psychological contract in the Australian federal public sector', *Journal of Industrial Relations*, 44(3): 435–57.

Oliver, N. (1990), 'Work rewards, work values, and organisational commitment in an employee-owned firm: Evidence from the UK', *Human Relations*, 43(6): 513–26.

O'Neal, S. (1993), 'Competencies: The DNA of the Corporation', *WorldatWork Journal*, 2(3): 6–13.

— (1995), 'Competencies and pay in the evolving world of work', *WorldatWork Journal*, 4(3): 72–9.

— (1996), 'Reengineering and compensation: An interview with Michael Hammer', *WorldatWork Journal*, 5(1): 6–11.

— (1998), 'The phenomenon of total rewards', *WorldatWork Journal*, 7(3): 6–18.

O'Neill, G. (1995), 'Linking pay to performance: Conflicting views and conflicting evidence', *Asia Pacific Journal of Human Resource Management*, 33(2): 20–35.

O'Neill, G. & Berry, A. (2002), 'Remuneration of Australian executives: A practitioner view', *Asia Pacific Journal of Human Resources*, 40(2): 228–45.

O'Neill, G. & Doig, D. (1997), 'Definition and use of competencies by Australian organizations: A survey of HR practitioners', *WorldatWork Journal*, 6(4): 45–56.

O'Neill, G. & Iob, M. (1999), 'Determinants of executive remuneration in Australian organisations: An exploratory study', *Asia Pacific Journal of Human Resources*, 37(1): 65–75.

O'Neill, G. & Lander, D. (1993–94), 'Linking employee skills to pay: A framework for skill-based pay plans', *WorldatWork Journal*, 2(3): 14–27.

O'Reilly, C., Main, B. & Crystal, G. (1988), 'CEO compensation as tournament and social comparison: A tale of two theories', *Administrative Science Quarterly*, 33(2): 257–74.

Organ, D. W. (1988a), 'A restatement of the satisfaction-performance hypothesis', *Journal of Management*, 14(4): 547–57.

— (1988b), *Organizational Citizenship Behavior: The Good Soldier Syndrome*, Lexington Books, Lexington, MA.

— (1994), 'Personality and organizational citizenship behavior', *Journal of Management*, 20(2): 465–78.

— (1997), 'Organizational citizenship behavior: It's construct clean-up time', *Human Performance*, 10(2): 85–97.

Organ, D. W. & Ryan, K. (1995), 'A meta-analytic review of attitudinal and dispositional predictors of organizational citizenship behavior', *Personnel Psychology*, 48(4): 775–802.

Osterman, P. (1994), 'How common is workplace transformation and who adopts it?', *Industrial and Labor Relations Review*, 47(2): 173(2)–88.

Pass, C. (2003), 'Long-term incentive schemes, executive remuneration and corporate performance: An empirical study', *Corporate Governance*, 3(4): 18–27.

Pate, J., Martin, G. & McGoldrick, J. (2003), 'The impact of psychological contract violation on employee attitudes and behaviour', *Employee Relations*, 25(6): 557–73.

Patmore, G. (1988), 'Systematic management and bureaucracy: The NSW Railways prior to 1932', *Labour and Industry*, 1(2): 306–21.

Patrickson, M. (2001), 'Stimulating high-performance outcomes through non-financial incentives', in Weiser, R. & Millett, B. (eds), *Management and Organisational Behaviour*, John Wiley & Sons, Brisbane, pp. 25–34.

Patten, T. (1988), *Fair Pay: The Managerial Challenge of Comparable Worth and Job Evaluation*, Jossey-Bass, San Francisco.

Peach, E. & Wren, D. (1992), 'Pay for performance from antiquity to the 1950s', in Hopkins, B. & Mawhinney, T. (eds), *Pay for Performance: History, Controversy, and Evidence*, Hawthorne Press, New York, pp. 5–26 (special issue of the *Journal of Organizational Behaviour Management*, 12(1)).

Pearce, J. L. (1991), 'Why merit pay doesn't work: Implications from organization theory', in Steers, R. M. & Porter, L. W. (eds), *Motivation and Work Behavior*, 5th edn, McGraw-Hill, New York, pp. 498–506.

Peiperl, M. A. (2001), 'Getting 360° feedback right', *Harvard Business Review*, 79(1): 142–7.

Pendleton, A., Poutsma, E., Brewster, C. & Van Ommeren, J. (2001), *Employee Share Ownership and Profit-Sharing in the European Union*, European Foundation for the Improvement of Living and Working Conditions, Dublin.

Pendleton, A., Wilson, N. & Wright, M. (1998), 'The perception and effects of share ownership: Empirical evidence from employee buy-outs', *British Journal of Industrial Relations*, 36(3): 99–123.

Peters, L. H., O'Connor, E. J. & Eulberg, J. R. (1985), 'Situational constraints: Sources, consequences, and considerations', in Rowland, K. M. & Ferris, G. R. (eds), *Research in Personnel and Human Resource Management*, JAI Press, Greenwich, CT, pp. 79–113.

Peterson, S. J. & Luthans, F. (2006), 'The impact of financial and non-financial incentives on business-unit outcomes over time', *Journal of Applied Psychology*, 91(1): 156–65.

Pfeffer, J. (1994), *Competitive Advantage Through People: Unleashing the Power of the Workforce*, Harvard Business School Press, Boston.

— (1996), 'When it comes to "best practices", why do smart organizations occasionally do dumb things?', *Organizational Dynamics*, 25(1): 33–44.

— (1998a), *The Human Equation*, Harvard Business School Press. Boston.

— (1998b), 'Six dangerous myths about pay', *Harvard Business Review*, 76(3): 108–20.

Pfeffer, J. & Veiga, J. F. (1999), 'Putting people first for organisational success', *Academy of Management Executive*, 13(2): 37–48.

Pierce, J. L., Rubenfeld, S. A. & Morgan, S. (1991), 'Employee ownership: A conceptual model of process and effects', *Academy of Management Review*, 16(1): 121–44.

Pil, F. K. & MacDuffie, J. P. (1996), 'The adoption of high-involvement work practices', *Industrial Relations*, 33(3): 423–55.

Pinder, C. C. (1991), 'Valence-instrumentality-expectancy theory', in Steers, R. M. & Porter, L. W. (eds) (1991), *Motivation and Work Behavior*, 5th edn, McGraw-Hill, New York, pp. 144–63.

— (1998), *Work Motivation in Organizational Behavior*, Prentice Hall, Upper Saddle River, NJ.

Pollock, T. G., Fischer, H. M & Wade, J. B. (2002), 'The role of power and politics in the repricing of executive options', *Academy of Management Journal*, 45(6): 1172–82.

Porter, L. W. & Lawler, E. E. (1967), *Managerial Attitudes and Performance*, Irwin-Dorsey, Homewood, IL.

Porter, M. E. (1980), *Competitive Strategy*, Free Press, New York.

Poutsma, E. & de Nijs, W. (2003), 'Broad-based employee financial participation in the European Union', *International Journal of Human Resource Management*, 14(6): 863–92.

Poutsma, E., de Nijs, W. & Poole, M. (2003), 'The global phenomenon of employee financial participation', *International Journal of Human Resource Management*, 14(6): 855–62.

Prahalad, C. K. & Hamel, G. (1990), 'The core competences of the organization', *Harvard Business Review*, 68(3): 79–93.

Prince, J. B., & Lawler, E. E. (1986), 'Does salary discussion hurt the developmental appraisal?', *Organizational Behavior and Human Decision Processes*, 37: 357–75.

Probert, B. (1992), 'Award restructuring and clerical work: Skills, training and careers in a feminized occupation', *Journal of Industrial Relations*, 34(3): 436–54.

Purcell, J. (1999), 'Best practice and best fit: Chimera or cul-de-sac?', *Human Resource Management Journal*, 9(3): 26–41.

Quaid, M. (1993), 'Job evaluation as institutional myth', *Journal of Management Studies*, 30(2): 239–60.

Rabin, B. (1994), 'Assessing employee benefit satisfaction under flexible benefit', *Compensation and Benefits Management*, 10(3): 33–44.

Rahbar-Daniels, D. (2002), 'Competency-based reward design approaches', in Chingos, P. T. (ed.), *Paying for Performance: A Guide to Compensation Management*, John Wiley & Sons, New York, pp. 63–85.

Rahbar-Daniels, D., Erickson, M. L. & Dalik, A. (2001), 'Here to stay: Taking competencies to the next level', *WorldatWork Journal*, 10(1): 70–9.

Redman, T. & Mathews, B. P. (1995), 'Do corporate turkeys vote for Christmas? Managers' attitudes towards upward appraisal', *Personnel Review*, 24(7): 13–24.

Redman, T., Snape, E., Thompson, D. & Yan, F. (2000), 'Performance appraisal in an NHS hospital', *Human Resource Management Journal*, 10(1): 48–62.

Reed, M. (2005a), 'Reflections on the "realist turn" in organization and management studies', *Journal of Management Studies*, 42(8): 1621–44.

— (2005b), 'Doing the loco-motion: Response to Contu and Willmott's commentary on "The realist turn in organization and management studies"', *Journal of Management Studies*, 42(8): 1663–73.

Reissman, L. (1995), 'Nine common myths about broadbands', *HR Magazine*, August, 79–86.

Risher, H. (1995), 'Base pay: Rethinking the basic framework', in Risher, H. & Fay, C. (eds), *The Performance Imperative: Strategies for Enhancing Workforce Effectiveness*, Jossey-Bass, San Francisco, pp. 299–322.

— (1997a), 'Competency-based pay: The next model of salary management', in Risher, H. & Fay, C. (eds), *New Strategies for Public Pay*, Jossey-Bass, San Francisco, pp. 145–58.

— (1997b), 'The end of jobs: Planning and managing rewards in the New Work paradigm', *Compensation and Benefits Review*, 29(1): 13–17.

— (1997c), 'Salary structures: The framework for salary management', in Risher, H. & Fay, C. (eds), *New Strategies for Public Pay*, Jossey-Bass, San Francisco, pp. 40–56.

— (1999a), 'Aligning pay and results', in Risher, H. (ed.), *Aligning Pay and Results: Compensation Strategies that Work from the Boardroom to the Shop Floor*, AMACOM, New York, pp. 1–20.

— (1999b), 'Are public employers ready for a "new pay" programme?', *Public Personnel Management*, 28(3): 323–44.

— (ed.) (1999c), *Aligning Pay and Results: Compensation Strategies that Work from the Boardroom to the Shop Floor*, AMACOM, New York.

— (2002) 'Planning the "next generation" salary system', *Compensation and Benefits Review*, 34(6): 15–25.

— (2003), 'Round two: A response to Heneman and LeBlanc', *Compensation and Benefits Review*, 35(1): 12–17.

— (2005), 'Getting serious about performance management', *Compensation and Benefits Review*, 37(6): 18–26.

Risher, H. & Butler, R. (1993), 'Salary banding: An alternative salary-management concept', *WorldatWork Journal*, 2(3): 48–57.

Risher, H., Fay, C. & Perry, J. (1997), 'Merit pay: Motivating and rewarding individual performance', in Risher, H. & Fay, C. (eds), *New Strategies for Public Pay*, Jossey-Bass, San Francisco, pp. 207–30.

Robinson, S. L. (1996), 'Trust and breach of the psychological contract', *Administrative Science Quarterly*, 41(4): 574–99.

Robinson, S. L. & Rousseau, D. M. (1994), 'Violating the psychological contract: Not the exception but the norm', *Journal of Organizational Behaviour*, 15(3): 245–59.

Rose, M. (1978), *Industrial Behaviour: Theoretical Developments Since Taylor*, 2nd edn, Penguin, Harmondsworth, UK.

Rosen, A. S. & Turetsky, D. (2002), 'Broadbanding: The construction of a career management framework', *WorldatWork Journal*, 11(4): 45–55.

Rosen, C. & Quarrey, M. (1997), 'How well is employee ownership working?', in Kerr, S. (ed.), *Ultimate Rewards*, Harvard Business School Press, Boston, pp. 45–50.

Rosen, C. & Young, K. (eds) (1991), *Understanding Employee Ownership*, ILR Press, Ithaca, NY.

Ross, T. L. & Ross, R. A. (1999), 'Gain sharing: Shared improved performance', in Berger, L. A. & Berger, D. R., *The Compensation Handbook: A State-of-the-Art Guide to Compensation Strategy and Design*, 4th edn, McGraw-Hill, New York, pp. 227–40.

Rousseau, D. M. (1989), 'Psychological and implied contracts in organizations', *Employee Responsibilities and Rights Journal*, 2(2): 121–39.

— (1990), 'New hire perceptions of their own and their employer's obligations: A study of psychological contracts', *Journal of Organizational Behavior*, 11(5): 389–400.

Rousseau, D. M. & Ho, V. T. (2000), 'Psychological contract issues in compensation', in Rynes, S. L. & Gerhart, B. (eds), *Compensation in Organizations: Current Research and Practice*, Jossey-Bass, San Francisco, pp. 273–310.

Rubery, J. (1995), 'Performance-related pay and the prospects for gender pay equity', *Journal of Management Studies*, 32(5): 637–53.

Rudman, R. (1995), *Performance Planning and Review: Making Employee Appraisals Work*, Pitman Publishers, Melbourne, Vic.

Runciman, W. G. (1966), *Relative Deprivation and Social Justice*, Routledge, London.

Russell, T. (2003), 'Evolution – not revolution: Employee assistance programs', *Human Resources Magazine*, 3 December, n.p.

— (2004a), 'Financial benefits that make staff stick', *Human Resources Magazine*, 19 October, n.p.

— (2004b), 'The money or the box? Cash vs non-cash incentives', *Human Resources Magazine*, 7 September, n.p.

— (2004c), 'Finetuning finances through employee benefits', *Human Resources Magazine*, 5 February, n.p.

— (2006), 'Firing up workforce health and fitness', *Human Resources Magazine*, 20 February, n.p.

Rynes, S. L. & Gerhart, B. (eds) (2000), *Compensation in Organizations: Current Research and Practice*, Jossey-Bass, San Francisco.

Rynes, S. L., Gerhart, B. & Parks, L. (2005), 'Personnel psychology: Performance evaluation and pay for performance', *Annual Review of Psychology*, 56: 571–600.

Rynes, S. L. & Milkovich, G. T. (1986), 'Wage surveys: Dispelling some of the myths about the "market wage"', *Personnel Psychology*, 39: 571–95.

Saal, F. E. & Landy, F. J. (1977), 'The mixed standard rating scale: An evaluation', *Organizational Behavior and Human Performance*, 18: 19–35.

Saul, P. (1992), 'Rethinking performance appraisal', *Asia-Pacific Journal of Human Resources*, 30(3): 25–40.

Schappe, S. P. (1998), 'The influence of job satisfaction, organizational commitment, and fairness perceptions on organizational citizenship behavior', *Journal of Psychology*, 132(3): 277–90.

Schay, B. (1996), 'Broadbanding in the federal government: A 16-year experiment', *WorldatWork Journal*, 5(3): 32–43.

Schein, E. (2004), *Organizational Culture and Leadership*, 3rd edn, Jossey-Bass, San Francisco.

Schloss, D. F. (1898), *Methods of Industrial Remuneration*, 3rd edn, Williams & Norgate, London.

Schuler, R. S. (1987), 'Human resource management practice choices', *Human Resource Planning*, 10(1): 1–19.

— (1989), 'Strategic human resource management and industrial relations', *Human Relations*, 42(2): 157–84.

— (1992), 'Strategic human resource management: Linking people with the needs of the business', *Organizational Dynamics*, 21(1): 18–32.

Schuler, R. S., Dowling, P. J. & De Cieri, H. (1993), 'An integrative framework of strategic international human resource management', *International Journal of Human Resource Management*, 4(4): 717–64.

Schuler, R. S. & Jackson, S. (1987), 'Linking competitive strategies with human resource management practices', *Academy of Management Executive*, 1(3): 209–13.

— (2005), 'A quarter-century review of human resource management in the US: The growth in importance of the international perspective', *Management Review*, 16(1): 11–35.

Schuler, R. S. & MacMillan, I. C. (1984), 'Gaining competitive advantage through human resource management practices', *Human Resource Management*, 23(2): 241–55.

Schuster, J. & Zingheim, P. (1996), *The New Pay: Linking Employee and Organizational Performance*, Jossey-Bass, San Francisco.

Schuster, M. H. (1984), 'The Scanlon plan: A longitudinal analysis', *Journal of Applied Behavioral Science*, 20(1): 23–8.

Scott, K., Markham, S. & Vest, M. (1996), 'The influence of a merit pay guide chart on employee attitudes towards pay at a transit authority', *Public Personnel Management*, 25(1): 103–17.

Scullen, S. E., Bergey, P. K. & Aiman-Smith, L. (2005), 'Forced distribution rating systems and the improvement of workforce potential: A base line simulation', *Personnel Psychology*, 58(1): 1–32.

Seaman, D. A. (2004), 'Microsoft case study: A lesson in stock awards', *WorldatWork Journal*, 13(4): 56–63.

Seltz, S. P. & Heneman, R. L. (1993), *Linking Pay to Performance: An Approach to Designing a Merit Pay Plan*, American Compensation Association, Scottsdale, AZ.

Serino, B. (2002), 'Noncash awards boost sales compensation plans', *Workspan*, 45(8): 24–7.

Sherman, S. & Freas, A. (2004), 'The Wild West of executive coaching', *Harvard Business Review*, 82(11): 82–90.

Shields, J. (2002a), 'Beyond the hard sell: Redesigning performance-related rewards at Bidgee Bank', in Stone, R. *Human Resource Management*, 4th edn, John Wiley & Sons Australia, Brisbane, pp. 522–4.

— (2002b), 'Performance related pay in Australia', in Brown, M. & Heywood, J. (eds), *Paying for Performance: An International Comparison*, M. E. Sharpe, Armonk, NY, pp. 179–213.

— (2005), 'Soliciting excellence: Strategic reward management at Winton Wynne Moore & Associates, commercial law partners', in Stone, R. (ed.), *Human Resource Management*, 5th edn, John Wiley & Sons Australia, Brisbane, pp. 540–3.

Sibbald, A. (1993), 'Closing some gaps in our understanding of wage surveys and job evaluation: Implications for pay determination', *International Journal of Employment Studies*, 1(2): 236–52.

Sibson & Company (1997), 'Six companies share their insights: The challenges in applying competencies', *Compensation and Benefits Review*, 29(2): 64–75.

Simpson, N. (2005), 'Incentive programs are cash in the bank', *National Accountant Magazine*, 23 May: 1–3.

Skenes, C. & Kleiner, B. H. (2003), 'The Hay system of compensation', *Management Research News*, 26: 109–15.

Skiffington, S. & Zeus, P. (2003), *Behavioral Coaching: Building Sustainable Personal and Organizational Strengths*, McGraw-Hill, Sydney.

Skinner, B. F. (1969), *Contingencies of Reinforcement: A Theoretical Analysis*, Prentice Hall, Englewood Cliffs, NJ.

Smith, F. (2006), 'No worries about performance, mate', *Australian Financial Review*, 11 July: 59.

Souter, F. (2005), 'Behind every great boss ...', *Good Weekend Magazine, Sydney Morning Herald*, 29 January: 31–6.

Sparrow, P. (1996), 'Too good to be true?', *People Management*, 2(24): 22–7.

Spencer, L. M. & Spencer, S. M. (1993), *Competence at Work: Models for Superior Performance*, John Wiley & Sons, New York.

Spillane, R. & Martin, J. (2005), *Personality and Performance*, University of New South Wales Press, Sydney.

Stapledon, G. (2006), 'CEO compensation in Australia's largest companies', in Ali, P. & Gregoriou, G. (eds), *International Corporate Governance After Sarbanes-Oxley*, John Wiley & Sons, Hoboken, NJ, pp. 319–36.

Steers, R. M. & Porter, L. W. (1991), 'The role of motivation in organizations', in Steers, R. M. & Porter, L. W. (eds), *Motivation and Work Behaviour*, 5th edn, McGraw-Hill, New York, pp. 3–26.

Stiles, P., Gratton, L., Truss, C., Hope-Haily, V. & McGovern, P. (1997), 'Performance management and the psychological contract', *Human Resource Management Journal*, 7(1): 57–66.

Stone, R. (2005), *Human Resource Management*, 5th edn, John Wiley & Sons Australia, Brisbane.

Storey, J. (1995), 'Human resource management: Still marching on, or marching out?', in Storey, J. (ed.), *Human Resource Management: A Critical Text*, Routledge, London, pp. 3–32.

— (2001), 'Human resource management today: An assessment', in Storey, J. (ed.), *Human Resource Management: A Critical Text*, 2nd edn, Thomson Learning, London, pp. 3–20.

Stoskopf, G. A. (2002), 'Choosing the best salary structure for your organization', *WorldatWork Journal*, 11(4): 28–36.

Strauss, G. (2001), 'HRM in the USA: Correcting some British impressions', *International Journal of Human Resource Management*, 12(6): 873–97.

Stredwick, J. (1997), *Cases in Reward Management*, Kogan Page, London.

Stuart, D. (2006), 'Trading away disclosure responsibilities', *Company Director*, 5 August, 24–6.

Sue-Chan, C. & Ong, M. (2002), 'Goal assignment and performance: Assessing the mediating roles of goal commitment and self-efficacy and the moderating role of power distance', *Organizational Behavior and Human Decision Processes*, 89: 1140–61.

Sweeny, P. D. & McFarlin, D. B. (1993), 'Workers' evaluations of the "ends" and the "means": An examination of four models of distributive and procedural justice', *Organizational Behavior and Human Decision Processes*, 55: 23–40.

Taylor, F. W. (1895), 'A piece-rate system', *Transactions, American Society of Mechanical Engineers*, 16: 856–903.

Taylor, M. S., Tracy, K. B., Renard, M. K., Harrison, J. K. & Carroll, S. J. (1995), 'Due process in performance appraisal: A quasi-experiment in procedural justice', *Administrative Science Quarterly*, 40: 495–523.

Teel, K. S. (1986), 'Are merit raises really based on merit?', *Personnel Journal*, 65(3): 88–95.

Terpstra, D. & Honoree, A. L. (2003), 'The relative importance of external, internal, individual and procedural equity to pay satisfaction', *Compensation and Benefits Review*, 35(6): 67–74.

— (2005), 'Employees' responses to merit pay inequity', *Compensation and Benefits Review*, 37(1): 51–8.

Tett, R. P. & Burnett, D. D. (2003), 'A personality trait-based interactionist model of job performance', *Journal of Applied Psychology*, 88(3): 500–17.

Thompson, P. & McHugh, D. (1995), *Work Organisations: A Critical Introduction*, 2nd edn, Macmillan, London.

Tichy, N. M., Fombrun, C. J. & Devanna, M. A. (1982), 'Strategic human resources management', *Sloan Management Review*, 23(2): 47–61.

Tinker, T. (2002), 'Spectres of Marx and Braverman in the twilight of post-structuralist labour process research', *Work, Employment and Society*, 16(2): 251–81.

TNS Social Research (2005), *Employee Share Ownership in Australia: Aligning Interests*, TNS Social Research & Department of Employment and Workplace Relations, Canberra.

Tosi, H. L., Werner, S., Kats, J. P., & Gomez-Mejia, L. R. (2000), 'How much does performance matter? A meta-analysis of CEO pay studies', *Journal of Management*, 26: 301–39.

Towers Perrin (2003), *Managing Performance and Rewards in a Challenging Business Environment*, Towers Perrin, New York.

Townley, B. (1993a), 'Foucault, power/knowledge, and its relevance for human resource management', *Academy of Management Review*, 18(3): 518–45.

— (1993b), 'Performance appraisal and the emergence of management', *Journal of Management Studies*, 31(2): 221–38.

— (1994), *Reframing Human Resource Management: Power, Ethics and the Subject at Work*, Sage Publications, London.

Tremblay, M. & Chenevert, D. (2004), 'The effectiveness of compensation strategies in international technology intensive firms', *International Journal of Technology Management*, 10(10): 1–17.

Tremblay, M., Sire, B. & Pelchat, A. (1998), 'A study of the determinants and of the impact of flexibility on employee benefits satisfaction', *Human Relations*, 51(5): 677–88.

Trunko, M. (1993), 'Open to suggestions', *HR Magazine*, 38(2): 85–9.

Tucker, S. (1995), 'The role of pay in the boundaryless organization', *WorldatWork Journal*, 4(3): 48–59.

Tucker, S. A. & Cofsky, K. M. (1994), 'Competency-based pay on a banding platform', *WorldatWork Journal*, 3(1): 30–45.

Tulgan, B. & Greene, R. J. (1999), 'Generation X compatible reward strategies', *WorldatWork Journal*, 8(1): 20–7.

Ulrich, D. (1998), 'A new mandate for human resources', *Harvard Business Review*, 76(1): 124–34.

Ulrich, D. & Beatty, D. (2001), 'From partners to players: Extending the HR playing field', *Human Resource Management*, 40(4): 293–307.

Varma, A., Beatty, R., Schneier, C. & Ulrich, D. (1999), 'High performance work systems: Exciting discovery or passing fad?', *Human Resource Planning*, 22(1): 26–37.

Vroom, V. H. (1964), *Work and Motivation*, John Wiley & Sons, New York.

Wagar, T. H., & Long, R. J. (1995), 'Profit sharing in Canada: Incidence and predictors', *Proceedings of the Administrative Sciences Association of Canada (Human Resources Division)*, 16: 97–105.

Walker, P. & Bowey, A. M. (1989), 'Sex discrimination and job evaluation', in Bowey, A. M. & Lupton, T. (eds), *Managing Salary and Wage Systems*, 3rd edn, Gower, Aldershot, pp. 91–108.

Walters, M. (ed.) (1995), *The Performance Management Handbook*, Institute of Personnel and Development, London.

Walton, R. (1985), 'From control to commitment in the workplace', *Harvard Business Review*, 63(2): 77–84.

Walton, R. E. & Lawrence, P. R. (eds) (1985), *Human Resource Management: Trends and Challenges*, Harvard Business School Press, Boston.

Watson, T. J. (2004), 'HRM and critical social science analysis', *Journal of Management Studies*, 41(3): 447–67.

Weiner, N. J. (1991), 'Job evaluation systems: A critique', *Human Resource Management Review*, 1(2): 119–32.

Weiss, T. B. & Hartle, F. (1997), *Reengineering Performance Management: Breakthroughs in Achieving Strategy Through People*, St Lucie Press, Boca Raton, FL.

Weitzman, M. L. & Kruse, D. L. (1990), 'Profit sharing and productivity', in Blinder, A. (ed.), *Paying for Productivity: A Look at the Evidence*, Brookings Institution, Washington DC, pp. 95–142.

Welbourne, T. & Gomez-Mejia, L. (1995), 'Gainsharing: A critical review and a future research agenda', *Journal of Management*, 21(3): 559–609.

— (1999), 'Optimizing team-based incentives', in Berger, L. A. & Berger, D. R. *The Compensation Handbook: A State-of-the-Art Guide to Compensation Strategy and Design*, 4th edn, McGraw-Hill, New York, pp. 275–90.

Wells, J. (2004), 'Fit for work: Healthy workers are better business', *HR Monthly*, June: 36–42.

Werner, J. M., & Bolino, M. C. 1997, 'Explaining US Courts of Appeals decisions involving performance appraisal: Accuracy, fairness, and validation', *Personnel Psychology*, 50(1): 1–24.

West, M. (2006), 'Execs hedge incentives to protect pay', *The Australian*, 4 March.

White, R. (1959), 'Motivation reconsidered: The concept of competence', *Psychological Review*, 66: 279–333.

Williams, M. C. (1995), 'Antecedents of employee benefit level satisfaction', *Journal of Management*, 21(6): 1097–128.

Williams, M. L. & MacDermid, S. M. (1994), 'Linkages between employee benefits and attitudinal and behavioral outcomes: A research review and agenda', *Human Resource Management Review*, 4(2): 101–15.

Williams, R. S. (2002), *Managing Employee Performance: Design and Implementation in Organisations*, International Thomson Business Press, London.

Wilson, F. & Bowey, A. M. (1989), 'Profit- and performance-based systems', in Bowey, A. M. & Lupton, T. (eds), *Managing Salary and Wage Systems*, 3rd edn, Gower, Aldershot, pp. 339–73.

Wilson, T. B. (1994), *Innovative Reward Systems for the Changing Workplace*, McGraw-Hill, New York.

— (1998), 'Reward strategy: Time to rethink the methods and the messages', *WorldatWork Journal*, 7(2): 62–70.

— (1999), *Rewards That Drive High Performance: Success Stories from Leading Organizations*, AMACOM, New York.

Wilson, T. B. & Phelan, C. C. (1996), *Rewarding Group Performance*, American Compensation Association, Scottsdale, AZ.

Wood, R., Allen, J., Pillinger, T. & Kohn, N. (2000), '360 degree feedback: Theory, research and practice', in Travaglione, A. & Marshall, V. (eds), *Human Resource Strategies: An Applied Approach*, Irwin/McGraw-Hill, pp. 209–30.

Wood, S. (1996), 'High commitment management and payment systems', *Journal of Management Studies*, 33(1): 53–77.

Wren, D. A. (2005), *The History of Management Thought*, 5th edn, John Wiley & Sons, New York.

Wright, P. M., Dunford, B. B. & Snell, S. A. (2001), 'Human resources and the resource-based view of the firm', *Journal of Management*, 27: 701–21.

Wright, P. M. & McMahan, G. C. (1992), 'Alternative theoretical perspectives for strategic human resource management', *Journal of Management*, 18: 295–320.

Wright, P. M., McMahan, G. C. & McWilliams, A. (1994), 'Human resources and sustained competitive advantage: A resource-based perspective', *International Journal of Human Resource Management*, 5(2): 301–26.

Wright, P. M. & Snell, S. (1991), 'Towards an integrative view of strategic human resource management', *Human Resource Management Review*, 1(3): 203–25.

— (1998), 'Towards a unifying framework for exploring fit and flexibility in strategic human resource management', *Academy of Management Review*, 23(4): 756–72.

Yermack, D. (1997), 'Good timing: CEO stock option awards and company news announcements', *Journal of Finance*, 52: 449–76.

Yeung, A. K. & Berman, B. (1997), 'Adding value through human resources: Reorienting human resource measurement to drive business performance', *Human Resource Management*, 36(3): 321–35.

Youndt, M., Snell, S., Dean, J. & Lepak, D. (1996), 'Human resource management, manufacturing strategy, and firm performance', *Academy of Management Journal*, 39(4): 836–66.

Zeus, P. & Skiffington, S. (2000), *The Complete Guide Coaching at Work*, London,

— (2002), *The Coaching at Work Toolkit*, McGraw-Hill, New York.

Zhou, X. (2000), 'CEO pay, firm size, and corporate performance: Evidence from Canada', *Canadian Journal of Economics*, 33(1): 213–51.

Zingheim, P. & Schuster, J. (2000a), *Pay People Right! Breakthrough Reward Strategies to Create Great Companies*, Jossey-Bass, San Francisco.

— (2000b), 'Total rewards for new and old economy companies', *Compensation and Benefits Review*, 32(6): 20–3.

— (2002), 'Pay changes going forward', *Compensation and Benefits Review*, 34(4): 48–53.

— (2003), 'Competence and rewards: Substance or just style', *Compensation and Benefits Review*, 35(5): 40–4.

— (2005), 'Revisiting effective incentive design', *WorldatWork Journal*, 14(1): 50–8.

Zuckerman, L. (2001), 'Management: Employee-ownership experiment unravels at United', *New York Times*, 14 March.

Zylberstajn, H. (2002), 'The Brazilian case: Performance pay as workers' rights', in Brown, M. & Heywood, J. (eds), *Paying for Performance: An International Comparison*, M. E. Sharpe, Armonk, NY, pp. 236–60.

# INDEX